Wissenschaftliche Untersuchungen
zum Neuen Testament

Herausgeber/Editor

Jörg Frey (Zürich)

Mitherausgeber/Associate Editors

Markus Bockmuehl (Oxford) · James A. Kelhoffer (Uppsala)
Tobias Nicklas (Regensburg) · Janet Spittler (Charlottesville, VA)
J. Ross Wagner (Durham, NC)

425

Prayer in the Sayings Gospel Q

Edited by
Daniel A. Smith and Christoph Heil

Mohr Siebeck

Daniel A. Smith, born 1963; 2001 Ph.D. from the University of St. Michael's College, University of Toronto; 2004 Assistant Professor of New Testament Language and Literature, Huron University College; since 2018 Clark and Mary Wright Professor of New Testament Theology, Faculty of Theology, Huron University College, London, Canada.

Christoph Heil, born 1965; 1994 Dr. theol. from the University of Bonn; 2000 Habilitation from the University of Bamberg; since 2004 Professor for New Testament; since 2017 Dean of the Catholic Theological Faculty of the Karl-Franzens-University Graz.
orcid.org/0000-0002-3434-0674

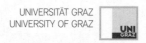

The authors acknowledge the financial support of the University of Graz.

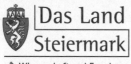

Published with the support of the Austrian Science Fund (FWF): P 26844-G19, and Land Steiermark: Abteilung Wissenschaft und Forschung.

ISBN 978-3-16-156660-8 / eISBN 978-3-16-156661-5
DOI 10.1628/978-3-16-156661-5

ISSN 0512-1604 / eISSN 2568-7476
(Wissenschaftliche Untersuchungen zum Neuen Testament)

The Deutsche Nationalbibliothek lists this publication in the Deutsche Nationalbibliographie; detailed bibliographic data are available at http://dnb.dnb.de.

© 2019 Mohr Siebeck Tübingen, Germany. www.mohrsiebeck.com

This book may not be reproduced, in whole or in part, in any form (beyond that permitted by copyright law) without the publisher's written permission. This applies particularly to reproductions, translations and storage and processing in electronic systems.

The book was typeset by epline in Böblingen using Minion typeface, printed on non-aging paper by Gulde Druck in Tübingen, and bound by Großbuchbinderei Spinner in Ottersweier.

Printed in Germany.

Table of Contents

Daniel A. Smith and Christoph Heil
Introduction 1

Irmtraud Fischer
Mehr reden über das Gebet als Beten:
Eine Alttestamentlerin liest Gebetstexte in Q 11

Ursula Schattner-Rieser
The Lord's Prayer in the Context of Jewish-Aramaic Prayer Traditions
in the Time of Jesus 23

Simon J. Joseph
The Promise of Providence and the Problem of the *Parables*:
Revisiting Prayer in the Sayings Gospel Q 57

Karl-Heinrich Ostmeyer
Beten für und gegen Feinde 89

Catherine Hezser
Prayer in the Sayings Source Q and in Early Rabbinic Texts 103

Hildegard Scherer
Gott und die Feinde: Traditionen und neutestamentliche Vernetzung
von Q 6,28 123

Markus Tiwald
Gebet und Gottesreich: Gebetstexte aus Q im Vergleich mit den
qumranischen Sabbatopferliedern 141

Michael Labahn
Identitätsstiftung durch Jesu Gebet: Q 10,21–24, Jesus
und die Offenbarung an die Unmündigen 157

Giovanni B. Bazzana
Praying to God and the Kingdom: Q's Lord's Prayer in Its Rhetorical
and Literary Context 185

John S. Kloppenborg
The Lord's Prayer and Debt Recovery:
Insights from Graeco-Egyptian Papyri 201

Thomas Klampfl
Lukas 11,5–8: Freundschaft, Gastfreundschaft und ἀναίδεια 219

Niclas Förster
Die lukanische Rezeption der Gebetstexte in Q im Kontext des
frühen Judentums und Christentums 243

Daniel A. Smith
The Influence of Q's Prayer Texts in Matthew 261

List of Contributors 283

Index of Ancient Sources 285
Index of Authors 305
Index of Subjects 313

Introduction

Daniel A. Smith and Christoph Heil

This volume publishes revised versions of papers originally presented at an international conference entitled "Gebet im Spruchevangelium Q / Prayer in the Sayings Gospel Q," held March 23–25, 2017 at the Institut für Neutestamentliche Bibelwissenschaft, Karl-Franzens-Universität Graz, Austria. The conference, organized by Christoph Heil (Graz) and Daniel Smith (London, Canada), was the culmination of a three-year major research project on the topic "Gottes Liebe und Gericht im Spruchevangelium Q – Rekonstruktion und Interpretation," funded by the Fonds zur Förderung der wissenschaftlichen Forschung/Austrian Science Foundation (FWF project no. P 26844-G19). It brought together scholars from Germany and Austria, Belgium, Britain, Canada, and the United States, with a wide variety of specialties and methodological approaches within biblical and Jewish studies represented. Some essays by contributors who were not able to attend the conference in person are also included in this volume. One central issue addressed at the conference was whether, and to what extent, prayer receives a distinctive profile in Q, when compared with contemporary Jewish materials; some presenters also addressed questions of the historical, social and rhetorical meaning of Q texts related to prayer, or their early reception in Christian literature.

One might think, as many of the presenters observed, that there is not much related to prayer in the Sayings Gospel Q. Indeed, the list of relevant passages can be quickly summarized: foremost of all is, of course, the Lord's Prayer (Q 11:2b–4), and the following commentary on the reliability of the Father to whom one prays (11:9–13); but there are also commands to pray, for one's enemies (6:28) or for labourers to help with the harvest (10:2), Jesus' own prayer of thanksgiving for the giving and restricting of revelation (10:21), and the devil's offer of all the kingdoms of the world in exchange for Jesus' worship (4:5–8).[1] This, how-

---

[1] Conventionally, materials from the Sayings Gospel Q are cited in this volume according to their Lukan versification, without any assumption that Luke necessarily preserves the wording or order of Q more faithfully than Matthew in any given instance. Thus, "Q 10:21" refers to the original saying in Q behind Luke 10:21 and Matt 11:25–26. Although the reconstruction of Q is still a much-debated topic, many of the authors in the present volume will refer to the standard reconstruction: James M. Robinson, Paul Hoffmann, and John S. Kloppenborg, eds., *The Critical Edition of Q*, Hermeneia Supplements (Minneapolis: Fortress; Leuven: Peeters, 2000).

ever, does not mean there is not much to say about prayer in Q. Although these texts are addressed by the contributors to this volume multiple times, they are examined from widely varying viewpoints, specialties, and methodological approaches; many of the contributors, after all, are not specifically "Q Scholars," but bring their own expertise to bear on these texts. In addition, the careful reader will notice diverging perspectives on issues of central importance to the study of Q and the Synoptic Gospels, for example the place of composition and authorship of Q. This collection is especially rich for its strong emphasis on early Jewish texts and traditions related to prayer, as can be seen in the many references to the Qumran materials, early Jewish pseudepigrapha, and rabbinic texts. Three of the authors also examine papyrological materials from Judea and Egypt in order to illuminate their studies of long-standing questions, such as the nature of the "testing" (πειρασμός) mentioned in the Lord's Prayer (Q 11:4), or the meaning of "shamelessness" (ἀναίδεια) in the Parable of the Friend at Midnight (Luke 11:5–8). Others use insights from the latest developments in narratology and reception history, for example. Thus, this collection represents an important contribution to the study of Q and also to the study of prayer in early Judaism and Christianity.

In the opening essay of the collection, "Mehr reden über das Gebet als Beten," Old Testament Scholar Irmtraud Fischer (Institut für Alttestamentliche Bibelwissenschaft, Karl-Franzens-Universität Graz) reads the prayer texts in Q from the perspective of reception history. Following a survey of different patterns of scriptural reception in the Hebrew Bible and early Jewish and Christian literature, Fischer observes that the New Testament writings receive and interpret scriptural traditions according to contemporary Jewish conventions of literary and theological reception. Fischer then turns to Q and its reception of biblical texts and themes related to prayer. She finds that certain approaches to prayer typical in the Hebrew Bible are found also in Q and in Matthean and Lukan uses of Q. For example, just as certain psalms and prayers in the Hebrew Bible are contextualized narratively, so too is Q's Lord's Prayer (Q 11:2b–4): although Matthew and Luke give the Prayer more specific narrative contexts, Q situates it in relation to Jesus' wise instruction, not a specific occasion in Jesus' life. The only direct-address prayers in Q are formulated in ways typical of the Hebrew Bible (Q 10:21–22; 10:2), with well-attested forms of address to God (as will also be seen in the following essay). In addition, certain prayers from the Hebrew Bible are found in the Temptation Story (Q 4:1–13), where they are no longer prayers per se, but instead serve an instructional purpose as "scripture." Fischer argues that prayer is practically non-existent in Q, because the spirituality endorsed by the Sayings Gospel is less about the practices of piety and more about the praxis of everyday life.

Ursula Schattner-Rieser (Martin-Buber-Institut für Judaistik, Universität zu Köln) investigates the Aramaic foundations of the Lord's Prayer (Q 11:2b–4;

Matt 6:9–13; Luke 11:2b–4) in her contribution, "The Lord's Prayer in the Context of Jewish-Aramaic Prayer Traditions in the Time of Jesus." Schattner-Rieser begins by assessing the relevance of the Aramaic Qumran materials for our understanding of prayer in early Judaism, and of the linguistic situation in Palestine at the time of Jesus. The Qumran materials provide evidence that prayer in Aramaic was acceptable, and also that there was a developing trend towards fixed formulae in prayers. Next, Schattner-Rieser presents an Aramaic retroversion of the Lord's Prayer in its Matthean and Lukan forms, and gives a detailed petition-by-petition commentary on ancient Aramaic parallels. Even though our only certain texts are in Greek, translation (back) into Aramaic is made possible by the numerous formulaic and morphological correspondences to ancient Aramaic materials. Such a (re-)translation does not afford access to "the original Lord's Prayer," but to a possible primitive Aramaic *Urform*, illustrating how consistent the Prayer was to its Palestinian Jewish milieu. "For every [Greek] petition there is a clear underlying Jewish-Semitic background, one that could display both cross-linguistic influences (with Hebrew or Aramaic in the background), as well as cross-cultural influences in relation to the Jewish milieu, the biblical history, and the expectations of that time" (p. 46). This Semitic background is reflected in Septuagintal parallels as well. Schattner-Rieser finds the strongest correspondences to the individual petitions of the Lord's Prayer in Aramaic materials that tell, re-tell, or evoke aspects of the Exodus story (especially Exod 16:4–5).

In his essay "The Promise of Providence and the Problem of the *Parables*: Revisiting Prayer in the Sayings Gospel Q," Simon J. Joseph (University of California at Los Angeles) begins by exploring how Q recommends prayerful reliance on a providential and impartial Father-figure, who can address real-life needs such as lack of food and surplus of debt (e. g., Q 11:2b–4). Though Joseph agrees with other Q scholars that this seems to be "the earliest recoverable … conceptualization of deity" in Q, he also observes that it stands juxtaposed with another, one focused on separation and judgment (p. 63). Since the writing known as the Parables (or Similitudes) of Enoch (1 Enoch 37–71) represents a close and roughly contemporary approach to a divine mediator figure, called "the/that Son of Man," under whose aegis judgment is executed on behalf of the oppressed, Joseph next examines the evidence for linkages between Q and this Enochic text. Scholarly consensus, which now dates the Parables of Enoch to around the turn of the era, holds that at several points this text has influenced the Synoptic Gospels. Joseph finds several interesting conceptual parallels between Q and the Parables, especially in the apocalyptic frameworks of the two documents, concluding that the Parables – though not slavishly copied by the author of Q – exerted a significant conceptual and narrative influence on Q in its secondary redaction. Finally, Joseph returns to the tension in Q between the providential view of an impartial God and the recurrent theme of judgment, investigating this tension in microcosm in the Q Beatitudes (Q 6:20–23). Q's "promise of providence," Joseph concludes, came to be "narratively reset in the past and simultaneously postponed [apocalyptically]" until the coming of Jesus the Son of Man (p. 87).

Karl-Heinrich Ostmeyer (Institut für Evangelische Theologie, Technische Universität Dortmund) investigates the theme of "Beten für und gegen Feinde" in early Jewish texts, especially the Qumran Genesis Apocryphon (1Q20 = 1QapGen ar), as a way to contextualize Jesus' commands to love and pray for one's enemies (Q 6:27–28). Ostmeyer notes that the significance of the prayer command is often overlooked, or diminished in relation to the command to love one's enemies, but prayer was thought to involve a kind of eternal connection before God of the one who prays with the one on whose behalf they pray. One instance of prayer for an enemy is found in Genesis 20, when Abraham petitions God on behalf of Abimilech, whom he had deceived regarding Sarah (Gen 20:17). Although prayer is not mentioned in the parallel story involving the Pharaoh of Egypt (Gen 12:10–20), prayers both against Pharaoh and on his behalf are found in the version of the story told in the Genesis Apocryphon (1QapGen ar XX, 12–16, 28–29), which Ostmeyer examines in detail. Like later rabbinic writings, the Genesis Apocryphon emphasizes the salvation-historical importance of this episode by heightening parallels to the Exodus story; it also includes an early instance of someone laying hands on the head of the one for whom prayer is being offered. Prayers against enemies, including pronouncements of woe, are common in the Hebrew Bible, early Jewish literature, and early Jesus traditions, but love of enemies – including prayer on their behalf – is not as unique to the instruction of Jesus as the author of Matthew indicates (Matt 5:43–44).

Next, Catherine Hezser (SOAS University of London) examines "Prayer in the Sayings Source Q and in Early Rabbinic Texts." Hezser observes that Q, which depicts prayer as an integral part of Jesus' teaching in relation to God and others, represents an "early branch of Jewish-Christianity"; therefore, a comparative analysis of prayer in Q and in early rabbinic writings will help us to refine our understanding of the group or groups originally connected with Q. The later interest in more formalized or ritualized aspects of prayer (for instance, prescribed timing and frequency) is noticeably absent from Q. Meanwhile, Hezser shows that there are some important similarities in how the Jesus of Q and the early Jewish charismatics described in the rabbinic writings (for example, Honi the Circle-Drawer) approach prayer as an individualized and direct appeal to God; the rabbinic authorities could appreciate Honi's directness and success in prayer, even if they could not commend his "impertinence" (e. g. m. Ta'an. 3:8). Q and the rabbinic writings also share common motifs related to prayer: bowing or prostration (Q 4:8); praying for one's enemies or persecutors (Q 6:28); prayer in relation to workers in a "harvest" (Q 10:2); prayer for release from debt (or sin) (Q 11:4); prayer for food (Q 11:3, 11–12). While rabbinic sources may not have advocated Q's directness in prayer, based on the idea of God as Father and adherents as children, both the similarities and differences to which Hezser draws our attention reveal that "we are dealing here with variant forms of ancient Jewish religiosity that could coexist and be practiced by some of the same people" (p. 122).

Hildegard Scherer (Theologische Hochschule Chur) also takes up the topic of prayer on behalf of one's enemy in her contribution, entitled "Gott und die Feinde: Traditionen und neutestamentliche Vernetzung von Q 6,28." Scherer begins by discussing questions of reconstruction of Q 6:27–28, noting that both the Matthean and Lukan forms of the saying preserve both horizontal ("love your enemies") and vertical ("pray for those [persecuting] you") dimensions. Although similar commands are found in Rom 12:9–21 and 1 Pet 3:8–19, neither of these passages support their paraenesis with reference to the teachings of Jesus and neither speaks of "loving" one's enemy; Scherer, however, sees the influence of Jesus' command to love the enemy in the paradoxical (even provoking) commands to bless and do good, and not only to avoid retaliation. Next, Scherer surveys the Hebrew Bible and early Jewish texts for the idea of praying for enemies, finding particularly close parallels to Q 6:28 in the Testaments of the Twelve Patriarchs (e. g. T. Jos. 18:2; T. Benj. 3:6). In order to give a broader picture of the literary contexts, Scherer also surveys the Synoptic Gospels for narrative or paraenetic material related to prayer or to the active engagement with enemies. In the end, the command to pray for one's enemies – especially in connection with the command to show love to them (cf. Q 6:27, 29–30) – seems unique in the Synoptic tradition: although it is characteristic of Q in that it reflects attacks on the group and advises a paradoxical reaction to them, it probably was not a creation of the authors or tradents of Q.

Like other contributors to this volume, Markus Tiwald (Institut für Katholische Theologie, Universität Duisburg-Essen) also finds rich comparative material in the Qumran writings for the study of prayer in Q, in his essay "Gebet und Gottesreich: Gebetstexte aus Q im Vergleich mit den qumranischen Sabbatopferliedern." Tiwald first observes that the expectation of the coming βασιλεία is Q's "Motivationshorizont": recent narratological studies of Q (by Michael Labahn and Arne Bork) show that the coming kingdom represents a kind of alternate reality, both in the present and the eschatological future, that determines how the reader is to act in light of it. Q's concept of prayer cannot be understood apart from this. Tiwald next surveys the Q-passages that deal with prayer, and identifies the primary motifs which determine how prayer is conceived and approached in Q, namely the kingdom of God and the concept of God as a loving father. Probably composed in the first century BCE, the Qumran Songs of the Sabbath Sacrifices are an important set of comparative texts for the study of prayer in Q, because they also show evidence of an imminent expectation of the divine realm, a view of God as caring father, and an intense interest in the holiness of God (also obvious in the Lord's Prayer). However, there are also significant differences from Q – for example, the emphasis on purity, the focus on formalized participation in the heavenly liturgy rather than on immediacy and "unverschämte Freiheit" (p. 146) in prayer, and a certain exclusivity in contrast with Q's approach to "sinners" and outcasts. An appreciation of the similarities and differences helps us to situate Q within the pluriform Judaism of its time, but also to understand its distinctive aspects in relation to prayer.

In his essay entitled "Identitätsstiftung durch Jesu Gebet: Q 10,21–24, Jesus und die Offenbarung an die Unmündigen," Michael Labahn (Theologische Fakultät, Martin-Luther-Universität Halle-Wittenberg) addresses the identity-forming narrative function of Jesus' thanksgiving for revelation to children (Q 10:21, with vv. 22, 23–24). Labahn begins by discussing the reconstruction of Q 10:21–24, its place within the central section of Q (9:57–11:51), and redactional, compositional, and thematic issues. The opening verse (v. 21), which corresponds structurally to other Jewish prayers of thanksgiving, addresses God in relation to a third party – the "infants" (νήπιοι) – whose identity is thereby defined as those who have received divine revelation. Labahn understands these "infants" as the "non-elite," whose access to the tradition was limited by their intellectual capacity, economic means, or social status; this subverts the traditional view, which restricted revelation to the wise, in that the wise and understanding are now denied access to "these things." This prayer, with the following self-reflection (v. 22) and beatitude (vv. 23–24), is a significant component of Q's narrative construction of meaning ("narrative Sinnbildung," p. 174). Both the direct contrast with the elite and the diminutive description of the non-elite contribute to the identity-defining rhetoric of the passage. The affirmation of exclusive revelation of the Father by the Son (Q 10:22) validates both the message of Jesus and that of the Q people, both rejected by the wise and understanding. This makes the "infants" the "true elite" in Israel, as the closing beatitude affirms (vv. 23–24), while at the same time they participate in the relationship of Father and Son.

Giovanni B. Bazzana (Harvard Divinity School) also investigates the rhetorical function of Q's prayer material in his essay, "Praying to God and the Kingdom: Q's Lord's Prayer in Its Rhetorical and Literary Context." Bazzana takes the perspective, first advanced by John Kloppenborg and William Arnal, that Q was composed by sub-elite village scribes in Galilee. Useful comparative material for understanding Q's compositional and ideological interests with respect to prayer may be found in Egyptian documentary papyri, from which Bazzana offers several examples to illustrate the composition of hymns and prayers by such sub-elite scribes; he also suggests that their capacity to write hymns – which probably should not be distinguished too carefully from prayers, neither as literary genres nor as religious practices – would have been due to their rhetorical training. Bazzana suggests that those who composed Q would also have possessed this competency, but he is also careful to insist that this result of his comparative exercise does not exclude the obvious influence of Jewish texts and traditions on the prayers of Q. Bazzana next analyzes the Lord's Prayer in Q, with reference to other ancient hymnic materials, as part of a larger hymnic section (Q 10:21–11:13) that follows the threefold structure prescribed for hymns in the rhetorical handbooks: invocation (Q 10:21a); argument (10:21b–24, which includes an authorization of the speaker's inspired status); prayer (11:2b–4, with requests paralleled in many other ancient materials), with a brief closing argumentative elaboration on appropriate patterns of prayer (11:9–13). Bazzana thus demonstrates that whatever traditional resources were drawn upon in the Q material on prayer (e. g. Jewish texts and traditions, or memories of Jesus' teaching), the village scribes proposed as the composers of the Sayings Gospel would have had the rhetorical skill and scribal competency to compose, shape and elaborate prayers.

Papyrological study also informs the contribution of John S. Kloppenborg (University of Toronto), "The Lord's Prayer and Debt Recovery: Insights from Graeco-Egyptian Papyri." Kloppenborg observes first of all that although πειρασμός in the Lord's Prayer is often interpreted as eschatological testing or tribulation (as for example in Rev 3:10), especially in the Matthean version (Matt 6:13) where it is followed by a petition for rescue from "evil" (v. 13b), this reading has little to commend it in Luke or Q 11:4b. The word, which can be used for adverse circumstances related to war, disease, natural disaster, or aggression from others, typically derives its meaning from its context. Looking therefore to the preceding petition on debt relief (Q 11:4a), Kloppenborg examines papyrological material related to debt and debt release. Ancient Egyptian and Judean loan documents tend to share many similarities, which permits the use of relevant Egyptian papyri as comparative material for studying Q. These documents show many adverse circumstances related to debt for both lenders and borrowers, owing as much to the debt instruments themselves as to systemic inequity in the courts. Repayment was not always documented, which could lead to problems; debtors could be subject to arrest and all their possessions forfeit if they failed to repay the debt on time; extra-judicial responses were also common. Borrowing therefore put a person at risk of physical violence or financial ruin, and lending could be equally fraught. Kloppenborg concludes that "a petition not to be led into such a πειρασμός makes perfect sense in the context of a prayer that petitions the deity for subsistence and freedom from debt" (p. 218).

In the next essay, Thomas Klampfl (Rohrbach a. d. Lafnitz) examines "Lukas 11,5–8: Freundschaft, Gastfreundschaft und ἀναίδεια." The Parable of the Friends at Midnight has sometimes been assigned to Q, located as it is by Luke between the Lord's Prayer (Q 11:2b–4) and the sayings on asking, seeking, and knocking (Q 11:9–13). Klampfl begins with a historical survey of scholarship on the meaning of ἀναίδεια in Luke 11:8, finding that scholars take the word to denote ideas from persistence to invasiveness to impertinence to shamelessness, depending to a large degree on how they assess the dynamics (especially the social dynamics) in the parable. Very rich surveys of ancient materials useful for understanding both the root αἰδώς ("shame," etc.) and ἀναίδεια follow next. Again, both terms have a variety of possible translations into German (or English), but a significant factor is the ancient cultural sense of "honour" (τιμή), whether of gods or human persons, and the cooperative and competitive ways that honour is enacted. Klampfl also refers to four documentary papyri, in which ἀναίδεια describes behaviour that is violent or aggressive. These surveys reveal that ἀναίδεια must be understood as a relational term: it is used to indicate an action that either disregards the honour of another, or the honour of oneself (that is, not giving due regard to one's own honour in the view of others). In Luke 11:8 it could either refer to the friend being asked for bread, who might be disregarding his obligation to his fellow, or to the friend who asks, who might be bringing shame on himself with his continuing appeal. In the end, Klampfl leaves open the question whether Luke 11:5-8 was originally in Q.

The final two essays of the collection deal with the reception of Q passages on prayer in Luke and Matthew, respectively. Niclas Förster (Evangelisch-Theologische Fakultät, Universität Münster) offers a study of "Die lukanische Rezeption der Gebetstexte in Q im Kontext des frühen Judentums und Christentums." Förster is aware that "identity formation" is a major interest in current studies on prayer (see also Michael Labahn's essay in this volume), but a major result of his investigation relates to the way Luke adapts the Q prayer texts with respect to self-assurance ("Selbstvergewisserung"). Förster examines closely how Luke has altered the context and/or wording of the following prayer texts in Q: the devil's request for Jesus' προσκύνησις (Q/Luke 4:5-7) in the Temptation Story; the command to pray for those who mistreat and abuse (Q/Luke 6:28); the request for labourers for the harvest (Q/Luke 10:2); Jesus' cry of praise and thanksgiving for revelation (Q/Luke 10:21); the Lord's Prayer (Q/Luke 11:2-4); the instruction on asking, searching and knocking (Q/Luke 11:9-13). Förster concludes that a few general tendencies can be noticed: first, Jesus' refusal of the devil's offer shows that the overthrow of earthly powers remains in God's hands alone; second, the disciples' joy at the end of their missionary excursion shows that for Luke prayer is not magic but in fact subjects the demons to divine control; and third, a dominant theme in multiple passages asserts that those who pray to God may be certain that their requests are heard.

Finally, Daniel A. Smith (Huron University College) offers a contribution that analyzes "The Influence of Q's Prayer Texts in Matthew." Smith makes a case for the view that the Q material, including the material on prayer, is not simply received (i. e. incorporated with interpretive revisions) as inert content, but in fact exercises an influence on the concepts and composition of the author. After illustrating how Matthew sometimes uses Q as a source not only to copy and rearrange, but also to emulate, that is, to produce new, Q-inspired compositions, Smith tackles the influence on Matthew of two major Q sections on prayer (Q 10:21-22 in Matthew 11; Q 11:2b-4, 9-13 in Matthew 6-7). As Smith explains, Matthew disconnected Q 10:21-22 (with Q 10:13-15) from the Q Mission Speech and used this material because of its thematic relevance to his Chapter 11; the identification of Jesus with Wisdom in Q 10:21–22 seems also to have inspired the creation of two new logia, namely Matt 11:28–30 and 28:18–20. Smith also analyzes Matthew's use of Q 11:2b–4, 9–13: the author of Matthew also disconnects these for use separately in the Sermon on the Mount. These sayings may have inspired others elsewhere in Matthew (Matt 6:8; 18:19–20) and influenced the narration of the Gethsemane episode (Matt 26:39–42). Smith's analysis confirms Alan Kirk's view that the author of Matthew valued Q not only as a source of material but also as an authoritative text whose narrative and rhetorical shape was as influential to the new composition as was the Gospel of Mark.

The editors would like to thank the following people, whose help and cooperation ensured that the March 2017 conference "Gebet im Spruchevangelium Q / Prayer in the Sayings Gospel Q" ran smoothly: Thomas Klampfl and Elke Handl-Prutsch, and student assistants Franziska Almer, Raphael Bergmann, Johannes Neubauer, Theresa Ofner, Clemens-Karl Peyrer, Robert J. Thaler, Johanna Walcher, and Lukas Weissensteiner. As already noted, the conference was financed mainly by a substantial grant from the Fonds zur Förderung der wissenschaftlichen Forschung (FWF), which has generously supported research on the Sayings Gospel Q at the University of Graz. Further essential support for the conference was also provided by the following organizations: Land Steiermark; Karl-Franzens-Universität Graz; Katholisch-Theologische Fakultät der Karl-Franzens-Universität Graz; Verein zur Förderung der Theologie der Karl-Franzens-Universität Graz an der Katholisch-Theologischen Fakultät; Diözese Graz-Seckau; Österreichische Humanistische Gesellschaft für die Steiermark; and Stadt Graz. We are very grateful to these organizations for their generous sponsorship.

Many thanks are also due to Elke Handl-Prutsch for her efficient and capable assistance in helping to prepare the manuscripts for publication, and also to Ida Maria Jaritz, who provided valuable help with one of the essays. The editors would also like to thank Katharina Gutekunst of Mohr Siebeck and the editorial board of the series *Wissenschaftliche Untersuchungen zum Neuen Testament* for accepting this volume in the series and for their support in bringing it to publication. The indexes were prepared by Rita Corstjens and we are also grateful for her work in preparing the volume for publication.

One final note: the abbreviations used in this volume follow *The SBL Handbook of Style*, 2nd ed. (Atlanta: Society of Biblical Literature, 2014), or, where no abbreviation exists in *The SBL Handbook*, we follow Siegfried M. Schwertner, ed., *IATG³ – Internationales Abkürzungsverzeichnis für Theologie und Grenzgebiete*, 3rd ed. (Berlin: de Gruyter, 2014).

Mehr reden über das Gebet als Beten

Eine Alttestamentlerin liest Gebetstexte in Q

Irmtraud Fischer

Die Frage, welche Psalmen oder Gebetstexte das Vater Unser einspielt, füllt Bibliotheken.[1] Für eine Alttestamentlerin kommt es also einem Himmelfahrtskommando gleich, sich hier bei einer Tagung von Q-Spezialisten und Q-Spezialistinnen auch noch dazwischenzudrängen.

Wenn so ein Beitrag[2] Sinn machen soll, muss er der neutestamentlichen *community* etwas anderes als die üblichen Aspekte aufzeigen und nicht den Aufguss vom Aufguss vom Aufguss darstellen. Mein Beitrag wird mit dem Konzept der Rezeption an die Q-Texte, die mit Gebet zusammenhängen, herangehen.

A. Vielfältige Formen der Schriftrezeption zwischen Exegese, „Fehlrezeption" und „Wildern in Texten"[3]

Wer heute eine wissenschaftliche Qualifizierungsarbeit verfasst, wird darum bemüht sein, den Forschungsgegenstand unter möglichst breiter Bezugnahme auf die Forschungsgeschichte darzustellen. Für die eigenen Thesen wird man möglichst viele Argumente aus bereits Publiziertem zusammentragen, um sodann das Neue darauf aufzubauen und gleichzeitig vom bereits Dagewesenen abzuheben. Wer in antiken Texten mit diesen Standards nach Zitaten sucht, wird einerseits unter der heute so bezeichneten Rubrik „Plagiat" fündig werden, da viele Texteinspielungen gar nicht gekennzeichnet werden, andererseits aber auch ganz wenige Hinweise finden, da man in einer Kultur, in der der Zugang zu Schriften

---

[1] Siehe dazu exemplarisch Florian Wilk (Hg.), *Das Vaterunser in seinen antiken Kontexten: Zum Gedenken an Eduard Lohse*, FRLANT 266 (Göttingen: Vandenhoeck & Ruprecht, 2016), hier insbesonders den Artikel von Jörg Frey, „Das Vaterunser im Horizont anti-jüdischen Betens unter besonderer Berücksichtigung der Textfunde vom Toten Meer," 1–24.

[2] Es ist der guten und kontinuierlichen Zusammenarbeit in der Lehre mit Christoph Heil und dem guten menschlichen Verhältnis zwischen uns zu verdanken, dass ich diesen Beitrag angenommen habe, was ich in der Vorbereitung denn dann auch bald bereut habe.

[3] Der Ausdruck stammt von Michel de Certeau, *Kunst des Handelns*, Internationaler Merve-Diskurs 140 (Berlin: Merve, 1988), 12.

unvergleichlich schwieriger war als heute, auch aus dem Gedächtnis zitiert und dabei – je nach Intention der Verwendung – durchaus bewusst Abweichungen vom Wortlaut des Referenztextes gesetzt werden, um ihn besser in den neuen Argumentationszusammenhang einzubetten.[4]

Große Teile des NTs verwenden *Schriftzitate* mit der rhetorischen Strategie, die Taten Jesu und das in ihm personalisierte Heilsgeschehen als das Gegebene zu präsentieren. Die Heilige Schrift wird (in welcher Form wir sie uns auch immer vorzustellen haben[5]) durch das Erzählte (abermals) aktualisiert und damit in ihrer Heilsrelevanz in die Gegenwart geholt. Ps 22,4–6 (der Passus wird weiter unten zitiert) beschreibt diesen bereits in der Hebräischen Bibel bezeugten Prozess[6] ganz treffend: Gott wird als über/auf dem Lobpreis Israels thronend dargestellt, der seit den Anfängen offenkundig durch die Generationen hindurch sich stetig mehrt, indem immer neue Erfahrungen immer neue Danksagungen und neues Lob provozieren.

In manchen Fällen stellen neutestamentliche Texte den sogenannten *Schriftbeweis* aber auch in einer Weise vor, als ob die Schrift ihren vollen Sinn erst durch die erzählten Ereignisse bekäme. Dass diese Art der Schriftverwendung in der Christentumsgeschichte häufig zu einer Enteignungstheologie in Bezug auf das Judentum und damit auch zu Antijudaismus führte, brauche ich nicht auszuführen. Klar ist aber auch, dass das Aufgreifen der Schriften in weiteren – später kanonisch gewordenen – Texten nicht neu, sondern bereits dem AT inhärent ist.[7]

---

[4] Zu den unterschiedlichen Arten des Schriftgebrauchs siehe Paul Foster, „Scriptural Authority in Q," in *Scriptural Authority in Early Judaism and Ancient Christianity*, hg. v. Géza Xeravits, Tobias Nicklas und Isaac Kalimi, DCLS 16 (Berlin: de Gruyter, 2013), 279–304, sowie Christopher Tuckett, „Scripture and Q," in idem, *From the Sayings to the Gospels*, WUNT 328 (Tübingen: Mohr Siebeck, 2014), 196–218.

[5] Die Diskussion, welche Gestalt die jüdische Heilige Schrift zur Zeit Jesu und der Entstehung der neutestamentlichen Texte hatte, ist nicht abgeschlossen. Tora, Prophetie und Psalmen sind ganz sicher darunter. Die Wendung „das Gesetz und die Propheten" (vgl. Mt 7,12; 11,13; Lk 16,16) verweist auf alle Fälle darauf, dass diese Schriften kanonischen Status genießen. Das sogenannte „Väterlob" in Sir 44–49, das um die Wende zum 2. Jh. v. Chr. entstanden ist, belegt jedenfalls bereits einen abgeschlossenen großen jüdischen Prophetiekanon (Jos–Mal). In Q 11,51 wird offenkundig durch den Verweis auf „das Blut Abels bis zum Blut des Zacharias, der zwischen dem Altar und dem Tempel umgekommen ist" auf 2 Chr 24,20–21, auf das letzte Buch im Jüdischen Kanon, angespielt. Ob das bedeuten muss, dass alle Schriften bereits vorhanden sind, ist fraglich, aber möglich. Siehe dazu ausführlicher Foster, „Authority," 298–99.

[6] Siehe zu den bereits innerbiblisch beginnenden Prozessen den erhellenden Artikel von Konrad Schmid, „Die Schrift als Text und Kommentar verstehen: Theologische Konsequenzen der neuesten literaturgeschichtlichen Forschung an der Hebräischen Bibel," *JBTh* 31 (2016): 47–63.

[7] Vgl. dazu etwa Konrad Schmid, *Schriftgelehrte Traditionsliteratur: Fallstudien zur innerbiblischen Schriftauslegung im Alten Testament*, FAT 77 (Tübingen: Mohr Siebeck, 2011), oder Bernard M. Levinson, *Der kreative Kanon: Innerbiblische Schriftauslegung und religionsgeschichtlicher Wandel im Alten Israel* (Tübingen: Mohr Siebeck, 2012). Vgl. ebenso Irmtraud Fischer, „Reception of Biblical Texts within the Bible: A Starting Point of Midrash?," in *Narrato-*

Schon innerhalb der Hebräischen Bibel wird, wenn man sie als Erzählzusammenhang liest, auf Ereignisse voraus- bzw. zurückverwiesen und dies nicht nur bei denselben Schichten (z. B. Priesterschrift Gen 1,28 in Ex 1,7) bzw. Redaktionen (wie etwa die Scharniertexte[8] von Gen 15 und Ex 3), die sich ja teils über viele Bücher ziehen, sondern auch in Texten, deren zeitlicher Abstand evident und eklatant ist. Als Beispiel sei hier das Aufgreifen der in 2 Kön 14,25 nicht weiter ausgeführten Handlungsfigur des Jona als Hauptfigur des gleichnamigen Prophetenbuches erwähnt. Q 11,16.29–35 rezipiert letzteres, wobei die Figur des Jona für das prophetische Buch, zumindest im Verweis auf die Kapitel 2 und 3 desselben, steht.

Aber es gibt in der Hebräischen Bibel auch bereits das, was im NT und später *typologische Bibelauslegung* genannt wird. So wird etwa Ester als neuer Josef konstruiert, beides Protagonisten am fremden Königshof, die zur Rettung des ganzen Volkes werden.[9] In der Griechischen Bibel ist das Buch Judit ein hervorragendes Zeugnis dafür: Sie enthauptet als neuer David (wie dieser als junger Knabe, ist sie als Frau für das Soldatenhandwerk ungeeignet) den fremden Feldherrn mit dem eigenen Schwert und beendet damit den Krieg (vgl. 1 Sam 17,47–51; Jdt 13,4–10).[10] In den Evangelien ist Elija eine solche typologische Figur, die aufgrund der Erzählung der Entrückung und Himmelfahrt des Propheten (2 Kön 2) bereits in Mal 3,23 als wiederkehrender Vorläufer des Messias gesehen wird und daher auch in der Deutung der prophetisch auftretenden Handlungsträger Johannes des Täufers und Jesus einen Antitypus bildet (vgl. Mt 11,14; 16,14; 17,10–12 parr.).

Als weitere Art der Schriftrezeption, die im NT wichtig ist und in der Auslegungsgeschichte teils jedoch zur üblen Enteignungstheologie geführt hat, ist die *Überbietung* zu nennen. Hierzu möchte ich als Beispiel aus der Hebräischen Bibel Jes 55,1–3[11] anführen:

---

logy, Hermeneutics, and Midrash: Jewish, Christian, and Muslims Narratives from the Late Antiquity through to Modern Times, hg. v. Constanza Cordoni und Gerhard Langer, Poetik, Exegese und Narrative 2 (Göttingen: Vandenhoeck & Ruprecht, 2014), 15–24.

[8] Konrad Schmid, *Erzväter und Exodus: Untersuchungen zur doppelten Begründung der Ursprünge Israels innerhalb der Geschichtsbücher des Alten Testaments*, WMANT 81 (Neukirchen-Vluyn: Neukirchener, 1999), insbes. 63–64, 73.

[9] Dies hat bereits Klara Butting, *Die Buchstaben werden sich noch wundern: Innerbiblische Kritik als Wegweisung feministischer Hermeneutik*, Alektor-Hochschulschriften (Berlin: Alektor, 1994), 67–77, aufgezeigt.

[10] Vgl. dazu ausführlich Claudia Rakel, *Judit – über Schönheit, Macht und Widerstand im Krieg: Eine feministisch-intertextuelle Lektüre*, BZAW 334 (Berlin: de Gruyter, 2003), 260–65.

[11] Einen rezenten Überblick über die Forschung zu diesem Text gibt Erasmus Gass, „‚Auf, all ihr Durstigen, kommt zum Wasser' (Jes 55,1): Zum Heil Gottes für alle zu jeder Zeit," *TThZ* 126 (2017): 1–30; zum Zusammenhang der Texte siehe bereits Irmtraud Fischer, „Der Schriftausleger als Marktschreier: Jes 55,1–3a und seine innerbiblischen Bezüge," in *Schriftauslegung in der Schrift: Festschrift für Odil Hannes Steck zu seinem 65. Geburtstag*, hg. v. Reinhard G. Kratz, Thomas Krüger und Konrad Schmid, BZAW 300 (Berlin: de Gruyter, 2000), 153–62.

Dtn 2,6	Dtn 2,28	Jes 55,1–2
אֹ֣כֶל תִּשְׁבְּר֧וּ מֵאִתָּ֛ם בַּכֶּ֖סֶף וַאֲכַלְתֶּ֑ם וְגַם־מַ֜יִם תִּכְר֧וּ מֵאִתָּ֛ם בַּכֶּ֖סֶף וּשְׁתִיתֶֽם׃	אֹ֣כֶל בַּכֶּ֤סֶף תַּשְׁבִּרֵ֙נִי֙ וְאָכַ֔לְתִּי וּמַ֛יִם בַּכֶּ֥סֶף תִּתֶּן־לִ֖י וְשָׁתִ֑יתִי	ה֤וֹי כָּל־צָמֵא֙ לְכ֣וּ לַמַּ֔יִם וַאֲשֶׁ֥ר אֵֽין־ל֖וֹ כָּ֑סֶף לְכ֤וּ שִׁבְרוּ֙ וֶֽאֱכֹ֔לוּ וּלְכ֣וּ שִׁבְר֗וּ בְּלוֹא־כֶ֛סֶף וּבְל֥וֹא מְחִ֖יר יַ֥יִן וְחָלָֽב׃ לָ֤מָּה תִשְׁקְלוּ־כֶ֙סֶף֙ בְּֽלוֹא־לֶ֔חֶם וִיגִיעֲכֶ֖ם בְּל֣וֹא לְשָׂבְעָ֑ה
Essen kauft ihr von ihnen für Silber und esst es. Und auch das Wasser handelt von ihnen für Silber und trinkt es.	Was ich an Getreide zum Essen brauche, wirst du mir für Silber verkaufen, auch das Trinkwasser wirst du mir gegen Silber geben.	Auf, ihr Durstigen, kommt zum Wasser! Die ihr kein Silber habt, kommt, kauft Getreide und esst! Kommt und kauft ohne Silber und ohne Bezahlung Wein und Milch! Warum bezahlt ihr mit Silber, was euch nicht nährt? Und mit dem Lohn eurer Mühen, was euch nicht satt macht?

Musste beim ersten Exodus für die Versorgung mit Brot und Wasser bezahlt werden, so stellt Gott beim zweiten Exodus aus dem Exil nun nicht nur diese gratis zur Verfügung, sondern auch Wein und Milch, die Lebensmittel des Wohlstands. Ohne Verweiszitat und ohne Einspielung des Kontexts von Dtn 2 ist durch die Häufung des verwendeten Vokabulars und des äquivalenten Kontexts des Auszugs klar, dass der eine Text den anderen auslegt.[12] Wir finden hier also bereits in der Hebräischen Bibel die im NT verwendete Überbietungsstrategie vor, die sagen will: Das Neue wird besser als das Alte war, und dennoch ist das Neue nicht ohne das Alte wirkmächtig und schon gar nicht verstehbar. Das Neue ersetzt auch das Alte nicht, sondern führt es in der Weise fort, dass damit die Heilserweise vermehrt werden.

Auch im NT gibt es Verweise auf die Schrift, um *Überbietung* darzustellen. Ein treffendes Beispiel bildet der Verweis auf Jona (vgl. Q 11,16.29–35): Einerseits wird auf das Zeichenhafte dieses Prophetenbuches verwiesen, das die drei Tage, die Jona im Bauch des Fisches zubringt (vgl. Mt 12,40), mit den drei Tagen, die Jesus im Grab verbringt, auslegt. Andererseits wird die Bekehrung der großen, bösen Stadt Ninive (vgl. Jon 1,2) als beispielhaft hervorgehoben, wenn den Bekehrten aus den Völkern Gerichtsfunktion über „dieses Geschlecht" zugesprochen wird. Diese Aktualisierung steht in der breiten prophetischen Tradition, die von langwierigen oder auch gar nicht geglückten Bekehrungsversuchen des Gottesvolkes zeugt, und hier selbst die Hauptstadt des imperialen Unterdrückers als Vorbild für Umkehr und Buße nehmen kann.

Q 11,31–32 spielt im Kontext zwei Beispielsgeschichten[13] für Vorbildhafte aus den Völkern, Jona und den Besuch der Königin von Saba (1 Kön 11), ein und beschließt sie mit dem expliziten Überbietungsverweis: „und siehe, mehr als Sa-

---

[12] Vermutlich sind die Texte auch zeitlich nicht allzu weit voneinander entfernt entstanden.
[13] Vgl. zum Verweis Foster, „Authority," 295–97.

lomo ist hier" (V. 31) „und siehe, mehr als Jona ist hier" (V. 32).¹⁴ Während die Lk-Version mitten in den Jonaverweis die Episode aus der Salomo-Erzählung einspielt, bleibt Mt 12,41–42 vorerst konsequent beim Deutungspotential Jonas (V. 41), um sodann noch den Verweis auf die Königin des Südens anzuhängen, die von weit her kam, um Salomos Weisheit zu hören (V. 42).

Was soll damit aufgezeigt werden? Es gibt Rezeptionen mit *Überbietungsstrategien, die jedoch das Rezipierte nicht abwerten*. Es gibt sie bereits im Judentum und auch im NT, in Q, ohne antijüdischen Beigeschmack, der freilich erst durch die endgültige Ablösung der christlichen Gemeinde von der jüdischen bedingt ist, die zur Entstehungszeit des NTs noch lange nicht in allen Bereichen und Gegenden erfolgt ist. Das NT kreiert damit nichts Neues, sondern steht in guter biblischer Tradition der Rezeption von biblischen Themen, Figuren und Paradigmen. Dabei muss klar sein, dass Rezeption nur dann stattfindet, wenn diese biblischen Elemente auch in anderen Zeiten und Kreisen resonant sind. Rezeption¹⁵ bedeutet allerdings nie eine quasi keimfreie Auslegung des Textes. Sie bedeutet immer auch Aktualisierung. Wäre nichts Neues zu sagen, würde man den Text nicht aufgreifen und mit ihm argumentieren.

Allerdings gibt es auch Beispiele für Schriftverwendung, die eklatant den Sinn des rezipierten Textes verfälschen oder sogar explizit das Gegenteil damit belegen wollen. Das beste Beispiel – zwar außerhalb von Q – ist hier wohl Gal 4,21–31, das Juden auf die unfreie Hagar und Christusgläubige auf die jüdische Ahnfrau und Herrin Sara zurückführt. Nach heutigen historisch-kritischen Maßstäben müsste man hier von einer *Fehlrezeption* sprechen, da die Auslegung dem Text Gewalt antut und gegen den Literalsinn erfolgt. Aber darum scheren sich bekanntlich das NT und die nachfolgende patristische Exegese nicht: Wir können nicht heutige Methoden und Standards auf beinah zweitausendjährige Texte anwenden; das wäre anachronistisch. Fehlrezeptionen als falsche Auslegung des ursprünglichen Sinnes gibt es nur im historisch-kritischen Paradigma, nicht im typologischen, nicht im allegorischen, nicht im moralischen und auch nicht im anagogischen.

Das bedeutet, dass Alttestamentlerinnen und Alttestamentler, wenn sie im historisch-kritischen Paradigma das NT lesen, zwar die Problematik aufzeigen müssen, eine derart heikle Auslegung jedoch nicht als „falsche Rezeption" abtun dürfen. Historisch gesehen gibt es viele Bibelauslegungen – als Hauptherausgeberin eines großen rezeptionsgeschichtlichen Projekts¹⁶ weiß ich das nur allzu

---

¹⁴ Die Zitate stammen aus: Paul Hoffmann und Christoph Heil (Hg.), *Die Spruchquelle Q: Studienausgabe, Griechisch und Deutsch*, 4. Aufl. (Darmstadt: Wissenschaftliche Buchgesellschaft, 2013).
¹⁵ Siehe dazu bereits ausführlicher Irmtraud Fischer, „Forschungsgeschichte als Rezeptionsgeschichte in nuce," in *Congress Volume Munich 2013*, hg. v. Christl M. Maier, VTSup 163 (Leiden: Brill, 2014), 182–216.
¹⁶ Siehe das rezeptionsgeschichtliche Großprojekt „Die Bibel und die Frauen," das in vier Sprachen und 22 Bänden erscheint: www.bibleandwomen.org.

gut –, die mehr als fraglich sind, und dennoch hatten sie oft eine größere Wirkungsgeschichte als saubere Textexegesen.[17] Problematisch wird es erst dann, wenn wir *heute* solche Rezeptionen ohne kritischen Blick als Deutung alttestamentlicher Texte rezipieren.

B. Gebet im AT und die Rezeption in Q

Worum geht es, wenn wir uns mit dem Gebet beschäftigen? Eine rezente *Definition* lautet wie folgt:

> Das Gebet, das den Vorgang des Betens zusammenfassend bezeichnet, ist die in den allermeisten und namentlich in sämtlichen altorientalischen Religionen geübte (einseitige) verbale Kommunikation („Gespräch") von Menschen mit Gottheiten bzw. himmlischen Wesen, die in aller Regel personal (und d. h. im Unterschied zu vielen neuzeitlichen Positionen grundsätzlich ansprechbar, beeinflussbar und handlungsfähig) vorgestellt werden …. Die Kommunikationssituation *coram deo* impliziert, dass es sich beim Gebet insgesamt um direkte Anrede, um Rede zu, mit oder auch gegen Gott handelt – im Unterschied zur Rede über Gott. Um Engführungen zu vermeiden, kann man explizit auch nonverbale Kommunikationsformen einbeziehen …, die jedoch zumeist die Gebetsrede begleiten und unabhängig davon nur ganz allgemeine Interpretationen zulassen.[18]

Leuenberger definiert Gebet also als einseitigen Kommunikationsprozess, von dem man natürlich im Vollzug bereits eine Zweiseitigkeit im Sinne des Erhörens erwartet. Wichtig erscheint mir auch seine Verwendung des Plurals: Im AT steht nicht der oder die Einzelne vor Gott, sondern die Volksdimension ist dem alttestamentlichen Gebet wohl insgesamt inhärent – zumindest, was den Endeffekt angeht, das rettende Eingreifen Gottes. So heißt es in Ps 22,4–6:

> Aber du bist heilig, du thronst über dem Lobpreis Israels.
> Dir haben unsere Eltern vertraut und du hast sie gerettet.
> Zu dir riefen sie und du hast sie befreit,
> dir vertrauten sie und wurden nicht zuschanden.

Selbst wenn der oder die Einzelne betet wie im Klagelied von Ps 22, ist dennoch sein/ihr Gebet aufgehoben in einer langen, heilvollen Tradition, die gleichsam Garant der Hoffnung darauf ist, dass ähnliches wieder geschieht. Diese Aktualisierung des heilvollen Eingreifens Gottes muss logischerweise immer eine andere sein, wenn es Rettung vor individuell sehr verschiedenen Bedrängnissen thematisieren soll.

---

[17] Siehe zu den alten „Übersetzungen" von Gen 3,16, die vielmehr Inkulturationen darstellen, Ciriaca Morano Rodriguez, „Soziale Veränderungen und Entwicklungen des Frauenbildes im frühen Christentum: Philologische Zugänge zu lateinischen Bibelübersetzungen und auslegungen," in *Christliche Autoren der Antike*, hg. v. Kari E. Børresen und Emanuela Prinzivalli, Die Bibel und die Frauen 5.1 (Stuttgart: Kohlhammer, 2016), 177–92.

[18] Martin Leuenberger, „Gebet/Beten (AT)," https://www.bibelwissenschaft.de/stichwort/19002/.

Ein weiterer Aspekt ist bei der Leuenbergerschen Definition noch hervorzuheben: Es gibt auch Hinweise auf *Gebetshaltungen*, die ohne direkte Zitate von Gebeten auskommen, wenngleich wir wohl auch da nicht von einem stummen Gebet ausgehen können. Aber die körperlichen Aktivitäten von Niederfallen, die Hände erheben, vor der Gottheit stehen, den Blick erheben, sind klare Hinweise auf Gottesverehrung und Kontaktaufnahme mit einer personal vorgestellten Gottheit.

Die narrativen Texte der Hebräischen Bibel sind in ihren älteren Versionen vor allem durch solche Verben der Gottesverehrung geprägt. Erst in nachexilischer Zeit beginnt man nach und nach *Gebete in Erzählungen* einzufügen und damit *kontextualisierte Gebete* zu verfassen: Abrahams Knecht betet ausführlich, bevor er unter den Frauen, die zum Brunnen kommen, eine um Wasser bittet (Gen 24,12–14). Jakob betet, nachdem man ihm mitgeteilt hat, dass sein Bruder Esau, den er vor mehr als zwanzig Jahren um den Erstgeburtssegen und damit um die Sippenlegitimität betrogen hat, ihm mit 400 Bewaffneten entgegenkommt (Gen 32,10–13). Auch im Jonabuch würde man ohne den Psalm in Jon 2 ebenso wissen, dass der Prophet im Bauch des Fisches seinen Gott angerufen hat (vgl. 2,2).

Dem nachexilischen Usus, den Verben der Gottesverehrung Worte in direkter Rede folgen zu lassen, entspricht umgekehrt die Besonderheit, dass den Psalmen narrative Einführungen hinzugefügt werden, um die Gebete zu kontextualisieren: „Ein Psalm Davids, als der Prophet Natan zu ihm kam, nachdem er zu Batseba gegangen war" (Ps 51,1–2).[19]

Diese Phänomene einer Explikation des Betens und der *narrativen Kontextualisierung* lassen sich auch für die beiden Kontexte des Vaterunsers nachweisen: Matthäus situiert sein Vaterunser in der Bergpredigt (Mt 6,9–13) im Kontext der Kritik an einer offen zur Schau getragenen Frömmigkeit (Almosen, Beten: Mt 6,1–5): Wer Almosen gibt und betet, um gesehen zu werden, habe den Lohn bereits erhalten und kann offenkundig weder eine Gegengabe Gottes noch die Erhörung des Gebetes mehr erwarten. Die Fortführung in Vers 6 sticht insofern hervor, als sie in 2.P. Sg. gehalten ist und dem Du beim Beten im Verborgenen Abgeltung versprochen, vorher und nachher jedoch ein Kollektiv angesprochen wird (2.P. Pl.). Vers 7 thematisiert offenkundig Häufigkeit, Ausführlichkeit und Oberflächlichkeit des Gebetes, das als „Plappern" gebrandmarkt und als typisch für die Völker angesehen wird. Der Lehrsatz in Vers 8 plädiert von seinem Kontext her selbstverständlich nicht für eine Unterlassung des Gebetes, da „der Vater" ja schon vor dem Gebet wisse, was nottut, sondern für Kürze und Konzentration,[20] die sodann im folgenden Vaterunser (V. 9–13) als gegeben erschei-

---

[19] Siehe dazu bereits Hans-Joachim Kraus, *Psalmen*, Teilband 1: *Psalmen 1–59*, 5. Aufl., BKAT 15/1 (Neukirchen-Vluyn: Neukirchener, 1978), 14–29.
[20] Ulrich Luz, *Das Evangelium nach Matthäus*, Band 1: *Matthäus 1–7*, 4. Aufl., EKKNT 1/1 (Zürich: Benziger; Neukirchen-Vluyn: Neukirchener, 1997), 330, übersetzt daher „quasselt nicht."

nen. Der anschließende Kontext legt Vers 12 näher aus, indem die Reziprozität der Vergebung betont wird. Ab Verse 16–18 widmet sich der Text in Aufnahme der Form von Verse 1–5 einer weiteren spirituellen Praxis, dem Fasten.

Eine völlig andere Einbettung bietet Lk 11,2–4. In Verse 1–2 wird erzählt, dass Jesus betet und die anwesenden Jüngerinnen und Jünger ihn während des Vorgangs nicht belästigen. Als er aber geendet hat, tritt einer aus dem Kreis hervor und bittet ihn – mit Verweis auf Johannes den Täufer und sein Gefolge – stellvertretend für die Gruppe, sie beten zu lehren, was Jesus dann mit dem zitierten Vaterunser auch tut. Dem einführenden Wunsch entsprechend stellt sich der Text nicht als Individualgebet dar, sondern ist als kollektives Bittgebet gestaltet. Der literarische Anschluss 11,5–13 ist eine Lehrrede über das richtige Beten, insbesondere über die Intensität des Bittgebetes. Zur Illustration werden zwei Beispiele herangezogen: der gastfreundliche Mann, der seinen Freund für seine überraschenden Gäste noch am späten Abend um Brot bittet, und der Vater, der seinem um Fisch bittenden Sohn sicher keine Schlange geben würde. Beide Situationen, die aus dem Alltag genommen die Selbstverständlichkeit der Gabe veranschaulichen, werden durch einen verallgemeinernden Lehrsatz, der auf Erhörungsgewissheit zielt, abgeschlossen (V. 8.13). In Vers 9 wird dabei das sowohl in prophetischem als auch in weisheitlichem Kontext verwendete Motiv des Suchens und Findens aufgegriffen (vgl. Jes 55,6; 65,1f.; Spr 1,24.28),[21] wodurch das Lehrhaft-Didaktische der Gottsuche durch und im Gebet betont wird.

In beiden Zusammenhängen findet sich das Vaterunser als Lehrrede Jesu an ein Kollektiv und unterscheidet sich insofern von den alttestamentlichen Kontexten von Gebeten, als es *nicht als das Gebet Jesu in einer konkreten Situation* gekennzeichnet wird, sondern *als prophetisch-weisheitliche Unterweisung*, durch die er sein Publikum das rechte Gebet lehren will.

Im Großkontext der Berg- bzw. Feldpredigt steht das Gebot zur Liebe der Feinde, das von der *Aufforderung zum Beten* für sie gefolgt wird (Q 6,28). Lk 6,27–28 fordert in einer Jesusrede dazu auf, Hass, Verfluchung und Verleumdung mit Gutem zu beantworten und für jene zu beten, die „euch" verfolgen. Matthäus setzt dieses Gebot in 5,44 in den Rahmen seiner Antithesen, in denen er halachisch und unter Verwendung von Theologumena des Heiligkeitsgesetzes (V. 48; vgl. z. B. Lev 19,2) die Auslegung der Tora diskutiert und dabei die Thesen seiner Gegner pointiert und überspitzt darstellt (z. B. ist nirgends im AT vom Gebot des Hassens die Rede). Dass diese Auseinandersetzung um die richtige Auslegung der Tradition nicht deren Verwerfung darstellt, sondern die durch alle Zeiten notwendige Diskussion um die Aktualisierung derselben, ist oft gezeigt worden. Sie findet sich nicht nur bei Matthäus, sondern durchaus auch in Q 6,49, wobei

---

[21] Zum Motiv des Suchens und Findens Gottes und der Gottesfurcht (vgl. Spr 1,7) siehe Susanne Gorges-Braunwarth, *„Frauenbilder – Weisheitsbilder – Gottesbilder" in Spr 1–9: Die personifizierte Weisheit im Gottesbild der nachexilischen Zeit*, Exegese in unserer Zeit 9 (Münster: LIT, 2002), 218–32.

Lukas die Befolgung bzw. Nichtbefolgung der gehörten Worte in 6,47.49 aufgreift und damit ganz in der dtn-dtr Tradition steht, dass die Tora und die sie aktualisierenden Anweisungen der Prophetie[22] zu befolgen, „zu tun," seien: An der Orthopraxie entscheidet sich, wer gerecht ist, nicht an der Orthodoxie.

Das einzige *in direkter Rede überlieferte Gebet Jesu* in Q hat die Form einer typisch jüdischen *Beracha*, die Gott vorerst mit mehreren Epitheta anredet:

In diesem Augenblick sagte er: Ich preise dich, Vater, Herr des Himmels und der Erde, denn du hast dies vor den Weisen und Gebildeten verborgen und es Unmündigen enthüllt. Ja, Vater, denn so war es wohlgefällig vor dir. (Q 10,21)

Die Titulierungen „Vater"[23] und „Herr des Himmels und der Erde"[24] stellen im Rahmen alttestamentlicher Gottesrede durchaus keine Besonderheit dar, ebenso ist es mit der Freiheit Gottes, sich zu verbergen oder sich zu offenbaren. Wenn hier gegen Weise und Gebildete polemisiert wird, ist damit wohl die schriftgelehrte Schicht angesprochen, die für sich die Interpretationshoheit in Anspruch nimmt. Sowohl Matthäus als auch Lukas setzen die Preisung, die Gott direkt anspricht, durch einen Spruch fort, der über Gott als Vater redet, Jesus sich als Sohn bezeichnet und betont, dass das gegenseitige Kennen nirgends so intensiv sei als in dieser Beziehung (Mt 11,25).

Die *Bitte als Form des Gebetes* ist zudem in Q 10,2 belegt. In einer Jesusrede werden die 72 Anwesenden, die er vor sich aussendet, aufgefordert, den „Herrn der Ernte" zu bitten, Arbeiter zu schicken, um eine derart große Ernte bewerkstelligen zu können.

Als weiteres Phänomen ist die *Rezeption von Gebeten außerhalb von Gebetskontexten*[25] zu beschreiben. Hier ist vor allem die zitatenreiche und sich deswegen vom üblichen Q-Stil absetzende[26] Perikope von der Versuchung Jesu zu nennen. Von alttestamentlicher Seite hat Thomas Hieke[27] die Versuchungs-

---

[22] Zu meinem Verständnis von Prophetie als Auslegung der Tora im kanonischen Endtext vgl. Irmtraud Fischer, *Gotteskünderinnen: Zu einer geschlechterfairen Deutung des Phänomens der Prophetie und der Prophetinnen in der Hebräischen Bibel* (Stuttgart: Kohlhammer, 2002), 32–62.

[23] Zu dieser bereits im AT bezeugten Metapher siehe Gottfried Vanoni, „*Du bist doch unser Vater" (Jes 63,16): Zur Gottesvorstellung des Ersten Testaments*, SBS 159 (Stuttgart: Katholisches Bibelwerk, 1995), sowie Angelika Strotmann, „*Mein Vater bist du!" (Sir 51,10): Zur Bedeutung der Vaterschaft Gottes in kanonischen und nichtkanonischen frühjüdischen Schriften*, FTS 39 (Frankfurt: Knecht, 1991).

[24] Vgl. dazu schon Herbert Niehr, *Der höchste Gott. Alttestamentlicher JHWH-Glaube im Kontext syrisch-kanaanäischer Religion des 1. Jahrtausends v. Chr.*, BZAW 190 (Berlin: de Gruyter, 1990).

[25] Unter Umständen könnte man in diese Kategorie auch den Spruch stellen: „Wir haben Abraham zum Vater" (Q 3,8), da er vom Kontext die Vaterschaft des Erzvaters ebenso negiert wie im Volksklagelied Jes 63,16, wo dies allerdings mit völlig anderer Argumentationsrichtung geschieht.

[26] Siehe zu diesem auffälligen Faktum bereits Foster, „Authority," 281–84.

[27] Vgl. Thomas Hieke, „Schriftgelehrsamkeit in der Logienquelle: Die alttestamentlichen

geschichte in Q 4,1–3 ausführlich untersucht; dem ist nicht viel hinzuzufügen, zumal ich seine Grundthese der alttestamentlichen Geistigkeit, die aus der Erzählung spricht, mit voller Überzeugung teile.

Für unsere Fragestellung sind einige wenige Beobachtungen relevant: Die Versuchungserzählung wird geprägt von einem Streitgespräch zwischen Jesus und dem Teufel[28], beide erweisen sich dabei als schriftgelehrt. Obwohl ein Psalmentext (Ps 91,11 f.) und ein Text aus dem Hauptgebet Israels, dem *Schema^c Israel*, mit Bezug auf das Hauptgebot des Dekalogs zitiert werden, betet in dieser Geschichte niemand, weder Jesus noch der Teufel. Beide erweisen sich jedoch als schriftgelehrt und beide zitieren aus Gebetstexten wie aus anderen Schrifttexten, ohne dem Gebetscharakter Aufmerksamkeit zu zollen. Das in der Rede des Teufels zitierte Psalmenwort wird als Vertrauensbekenntnis rezipiert. Durch die Zusage der Engelsfürsorge könne man sich an keinem Stein stoßen, nicht einmal, wenn man sich von der Zinne des Tempels stürzen sollte. Was der Teufel als Erprobung unbedingten Gottesvertrauens darstellt, deklassiert Jesus dagegen als Versuchung Gottes (Q 4,9–12): Mutwillige Selbstbeschädigung kann nicht auf göttliche Bewahrung hoffen. Gott zu versuchen läuft zudem einem Leben nach der Tora diametral zuwider.[29] Wenn Jesus hier in einem frühen Stadium seines Wirkens das Hauptgebot und das *Schema^c Israel* in den Mund gelegt werden, wirkt dieser Text freilich als hermeneutischer Schlüssel zum Folgenden. Mit den Zitaten aus Dtn 6,13.16[30] parr. 10,20; 8,3 wird der gesamte Kontext der das dtn Gesetz einleitenden Moserede und deren Theologie[31] eingespielt. Daher geht es um die Unterweisung und Befolgung der göttlichen Weisung sowie um die Kon-

---

Zitate in der Versuchungsgeschichte Q 4,1–13," in *From Quest to Q: Festschrift James M. Robinson*, hg. v. Jon M. Asgeirsson, Kristin De Troyer und Marvin W. Meyers, BETL 146 (Leuven: Peeters, 2000), 43–71.

[28] Die Darstellung des Teufels ist an den Satan im Ijobsprolog angelehnt, der sich als schriftgelehrt erweist, indem er Ijob ausgerechnet mit jenen Krankheitssymptomen schlägt, die auf Missachtung der Tora schließen lassen (Dtn 28,35; Ijob 2,7). Siehe dazu Irmtraud Fischer, *Gotteslehrerinnen: Weise Frauen und Frau Weisheit im Alten Testament* (Stuttgart: Kohlhammer, 2006), 100–101.

[29] Hieke, „Schriftgelehrsamkeit," 64, verweist in diesem Kontext auf Ps 78,56, wo die mangelnde Bewahrung der Satzungen mit Gott versuchen im Parallelismus stehen.

[30] Andreas Michel, „Die Versuchung bzw. Erprobung Jesu in Mt 4,1–11: Anmerkungen zum Thema Christologie und Deuteronomium," in *Erinnerung an Jesus: Kontinuität und Diskontinuität in der neutestamentlichen Überlieferung: Festschrift Rudolf Hoppe*, hg. v. Ulrich Busse, Michael Reichardt und Michael Theobald, BBB 166 (Göttingen: V&R Unipress; Bonn University Press, 2011), 73–85, hier 73, weist darauf hin, dass Dtn 6,16 in der LXX-Version zitiert wird, da bereits sie den MT-Plural in einen Singular verwandelt hat und diese Version wesentlich besser in den Q-Kontext passt.

[31] Zur berechtigten Annahme, dass nicht nur das direkt zitierte Wort präsent gesetzt wird, sondern auch dessen Kontext, siehe Hieke, „Schriftgelehrsamkeit," 50. Zur Rezeption der Tora in Q siehe Christoph Heil, „Nachfolge und Tora in Q 9,57–60," in idem, *Das Spruchevangelium Q und der historische Jesus*, SBAB 58 (Stuttgart: Katholisches Bibelwerk, 2014), 87–117, insbes. 87–93.

zentration auf das Wort (Q 4,4; Dtn 8,3), nicht aber um die spirituelle Übung des Gebetes.

Ein Schriftgebrauch eines Gebetstextes ist auch für Q 13,27 zu erheben. Ps 6,9a wird dort ohne jeglichen Gebetsbezug in einem Gerichtswort zitiert.[32]

Resümee: Zur Spiritualität von Q

Das Gebetbuch der Kirche war und ist – gerade durch die Tagzeitenliturgie noch immer – das jüdische Buch der *Psalmen*. Ein ganzes Buch der Hebräischen Bibel ist dem Gebet, und zwar in seinen unterschiedlichsten Formen, gewidmet. Verglichen mit dieser Breite ist das NT an Gebetsliteratur relativ arm und, wie mir bei Q erscheint, ziemlich eindimensional auf das Bittgebet hin ausgerichtet. Obwohl sich das Phänomen der kontextualisierten Gebete flächendeckend zeigt, finden sich – sieht man von der Beracha in Q ab – keine Gebete eines einzelnen oder einer Gemeinschaft. Q behandelt Psalmen vielmehr als Schriftzitate wie andere und legt seinen Schwerpunkt auf Anleitung und Anweisung zum Gebet. Die Spiritualität von Q zeigt sich vielmehr in der gelebten Praxis des Alltags als in Frömmigkeitsübungen. Insofern kann resümiert werden: Gebetet wird in Q fast gar nicht!

---

[32] Zur unterschiedlichen Akzentsetzung des rezipierten Psalmwortes bei Q, Matthäus und Lukas siehe ausführlich Christoph Heil, „‚πάντες ἐργάται ἀδικίας' Revisited: The Reception of Ps 6,9a LXX in Q and in Luke," in idem, *Das Spruchevangelium Q*, 159–75.

The Lord's Prayer in the Context of Jewish-Aramaic Prayer Traditions in the Time of Jesus

Ursula Schattner-Rieser

This paper discusses the Jewish formulae in the Lord's Prayer (Matt 6:9–13; Luke 11:2–4; cf. Did 8:2) and analyzes its terminology, language and structure from a philological point of view. This analysis is carried out from the perspective of a scholar in Jewish studies, and not that of a scholar of early Christianity. Our main sources for the reconstruction of the Lord's Prayer, roughly contemporary to the Q Source, are the Dead Sea Scrolls, chiefly their Aramaic witnesses. Following some more general observations about prayer in the Second Temple Jewish context and the linguistic milieu of Jesus, the essay examines the Lord's Prayer petition by petition in proposed Aramaic versions which parallel the Greek texts of Matthew and Luke, surveying the parallel materials found in the Aramaic texts from Qumran and in the Targumim, and discussing their implications for our understanding of Jesus' Prayer.[1]

A. Prayers as Substitutes for Offerings

The biblical texts of pre-exilic times ignore the worship of public communal prayers, as a liturgical institution, apart from the sacrificial cult. Priests and Levites served as officiants, while the ordinary laypeople listened to the reciter and

---

[1] I would like to express my sincere gratitude to the organizers of the conference, Christoph Heil and Daniel A. Smith, for inviting me to present my research on the Lord's Prayer, Jesus' Prayer to the Lord in Heaven, in Aramaic. This essay is based in part on two earlier studies on Jewish Aramaic Prayer formulas and the Lord's Prayer: Ursula Schattner-Rieser, "Das Aramäische zur Zeit Jesu, 'ABBA!' und das Vaterunser: Reflexionen zur Muttersprache Jesu anhand der Texte von Qumran und der frühen Targumim," in *Jesus, Paulus und die Texte von Qumran*, ed. Jörg Frey and Enno Edzard Popkes with Sophie Tätweiler, WUNT II 390 (Tübingen: Mohr Siebeck, 2015), 81–144; Ursula Schattner-Rieser, "Emotions and Expressions of Emotion as a Didactic Guide as to How to Pray: B^{e}rakhot in the Aramaic Prayers of Qumran," in *Ancient Jewish Prayers and Emotions: Emotions Associated with Jewish Prayer in and around the Second Temple Period*, ed. Stefan C. Reif and Renate Egger-Wenzel, DCLS 26 (Berlin: de Gruyter, 2015), 273–96. I would also like to thank Daniel Smith for his detailed comments and suggestions that improved the quality of the present essay, and for correcting the English of the manuscript. Without his help this essay would not have been completed.

answered: Amen, amen, "it is true." Individual prayers, by contrast, are widely reported in the biblical writings since pre-exilic times.[2] Only in the latter part of the Second Temple era do we find fully formed liturgy, both in the temple area of Jerusalem[3] and in the synagogues.

From the beginning of the Babylonian Exile in 587 BCE, during a time when the Israelites had no temple, communal and personal prayers replaced sacrifices and temple offerings. The post-exilic prophets Hosea and Third Isaiah, as well as some Psalms, testify to the transformation of the cult towards its "intellectualization" by means of substitution.[4] Under the leadership of Ezra at the end of the fifth century BCE, the returning Exiles together with the common Judeans who had not been deported gathered together at a certain place in Jerusalem for the public recitation of the Torah – but apparently not in the temple. It might appear striking that Ezra, the priestly scribe, did not gather the people in the newly reconstructed Second Temple. The French scholar Maurice Liber summarized the phenomenon of cult and worship without temple in this way: "Il faut laisser au Temple ce qui est au Temple, à savoir le sacrifice; la prière sans sacrifice n'a point de place dans l'enceinte du Temple."[5] The innovation ("on peut dire la révolution") instituted by Ezra after the Exile consisted of a religious ceremony detached from the cult of sacrifices: "Désormais le culte de la prière ne sera pas lié à un lieu consacré."[6] Communal and personal prayer became the pillars of Jewish religious life, ensuring the survival of Judaism in times without a temple and its sacrificial cult. The cult that is known as the "offering of the lips" enabled the survival of the Jewish cult in times of Exile and Diaspora, and communal prayer served as a substitute for sacrifice. One distinctive feature is that prayer, in contrast with temple worship, does not require the ministry of a priestly staff, dressed in consecrated vestments with ornamentation. Besides communal prayer, there also developed during this period an increasing interest in personal prayer. The example of Daniel's daily prayers, set during the Babylonian Exile, proves the need of the individual to communicate with God by prayer and to believe in God's help and support in time of distress.[7]

Thanks to these practices that developed during the Exile, the members of a conservative Jewish sect that withdrew and exiled themselves in the Judean desert during the Seleucid Era, namely, the Qumran community (Yahad), could live and survive far from the temple in Jerusalem. Prayer and liturgy fulfilled

---

[2] Maurice Liber, "Sur les origines de la prière publique dans le judaïsme," AEPHE.R 42 (1932): 3–17.

[3] But apparently not in the temple itself (!): in Nehemiah 8–9 the public reading and liturgical ceremony took place somewhere in Jerusalem.

[4] In the Psalms, words of thanksgiving serve as a replacement for offerings, for example: Ps 50:5, 13–14; 51:17–19; 69:30–31. See further Isa 1:11–13, 17; Hos 3:4; 14:3; Jer 7:22.

[5] Liber, "Sur les origines," 8.

[6] Ibid., 8.

[7] See Dan 6:11; 9:3–21.

daily life in Qumran, but "without the flesh of burnt offerings and without the fats of sacrifice" (4Q258 2 II, 5). This belief is common to both early Jewish and Christian traditions, despite some conceptual differences. In Jewish belief, the validity of this practice is limited to a period without a temple, but when the temple will be rebuilt again, the ancient cult with its bloody offerings on the temple mount will be reconstituted. In early Christianity, on the other hand, prayers and the offering of the lips (*Wortgottesdienst*) replace sacrifices definitively.

B. Individual Prayer: A Dialogue with God

From pre-exilic times, we are familiar with biblical reports of individual and spontaneous prayers. After the destruction of the temple, thus in a time where the Israelites had no temple, communal prayer and private prayer became the pillars of Jewish religious life, which ensured the survival of Judaism. Prayers, blessings and hymns became very important features of Second Temple literature. Within the Dead Sea Scrolls, there are many communal and individual prayers.[8] The community of pious Jews established in Qumran refused the legitimacy of the temple in Jerusalem, considering it an illegitimate cult of human origin. While the communal prayers in the Dead Sea Scrolls serve a cultic function as a substitute for sacrifices (1QS IX, 5),[9] personal prayers are an appeal to God for intercession and assistance and serve as a bridge between the individual and God through direct contact. One innovation is that Qumran individual prayers developed and followed well-structured patterns for prayer and benediction formulae.[10]

C. The Importance of the Dead Sea Scrolls as Evidence for the Linguistic Situation at the Time of Jesus

The discovery of the Dead Sea Scrolls between 1947 and 1956 provided us with a spectacular literary treasure and one of the most important sources for biblical studies; they provide a wealth of information about the linguistic situation in the Roman period and the turn of the era.

---

[8] Judith H. Newman, *Praying by the Book: The Scripturalization of Prayer in Second Temple Judaism*, EJL 14 (Atlanta: Scholars Press, 1999), 5.

[9] Richard S. Sarason, "Communal Prayer at Qumran and among the Rabbis: Certainties and Uncertainties," in *Liturgical Perspectives: Prayer and Poetry in Light of the Dead Sea Scrolls*, ed. Esther G. Chazon with Ruth Clements and Avital Pinnik, STDJ 48 (Leiden: Brill, 2003), 151–72, here 154.

[10] Schattner-Rieser, "Emotions," 277, 290–91.

Of the roughly 900 texts found at Qumran, about 750 are in Hebrew, 120 in Aramaic and 27 in Greek. The great number of Hebrew texts can be explained by the fact that the majority are biblical and sacred texts, as well as liturgical and mystical writings. The Aramaic texts, on the other hand, are generally not biblical texts, with the exception of fragments of the Book of Daniel. They are literary productions of parabiblical, apocryphal, and pseudepigraphical content.

The sectarian Hebrew texts of the Qumran group are written in a dialect quite different from classical biblical Hebrew. Whether the daily language of the community was Hebrew or Aramaic, which was the vernacular at Jesus' time, cannot be determined with any certainty. In any case, the everyday language of the community was certainly not Greek, as can be deduced from the small number of Greek texts, although some members obviously must have been skilled in Greek. The Qumran community itself was at least bilingual – Hebrew and Aramaic. There are more personal and individual prayers within the Dead Sea Scrolls than in the Bible. The various prayer formulae and genres, such as complaints, prayers of thanksgiving, blessings and praises, contemporaneous with Jesus' lifetime, can serve as an important connecting link between early Jewish personal prayer and what became the most important Christian Prayer, namely, the Lord's Prayer.

D. Aramaic Prayers from Qumran

In the 120 Aramaic texts from Qumran, we count about twenty personal prayers and benedictions[11] written in Imperial and Middle Aramaic.[12] No Aramaic text contains examples of communal prayers, and none of the prayers in the Aramaic Qumran texts contains sectarian elements.[13]

Emplotted in narrative contexts and embodied in family scenes, the prayers are presented as spontaneous expressions of individuals that open a dialogue with God.[14] This impression, however, is misleading. A closer look at the prayers

---

[11] See Schattner-Rieser, "Emotions," 278–279. Several prayers are only mentioned, but not given in full, such as the thanksgiving of Noah in 1QapGen ar XI, 12–14 and Abram's exorcism prayer on Pharoah's behalf in 1QapGen ar XI, 28–29.

[12] Ursula Schattner-Rieser, "L'apport de la philologie araméenne et l'interprétation des archaïsmes linguistiques pour la datation des textes araméens de Qumrân," in *Aramaica Qumranica: Proceedings of the Conference on the Aramaic Texts from Qumran at Aix-en-Provence*, ed. Katell Berthelot and Daniel Stökl Ben Ezra, STDJ 94 (Leiden: Brill, 2010), 101–23.

[13] Three Aramaic texts (4QTobit, 4QTestament of Qahat and 4QVisions of Amram) contain dualistic elements that can easily be explained by Persian influence. See Schattner-Rieser, "Emotions," 277 n. 15.

[14] Such personal experiences are presented in the books of Tobit, the Genesis Apocryphon (1QapGen ar) and the Enoch cycle. These prayers are similar to the Mesopotamian shu-ila prayers; see Annette Zgoll, "Der betende Mensch: Zur Anthropologie in Mesopotamien," in *Der Mensch im Alten Israel: Neue Forschungen zur alttestamentlichen Anthropologie*, ed. Bernd Janowski and Kathrin Liess, HBS 59 (Freiburg i. B.: Herder, 2009), 121–40.

shows that there is a fixed prayer tradition underlying them. They confirm the trend towards standardization of private Aramaic prayer and its formulae.

The Aramaic prayers of Qumran are therefore extremely important for understanding Jesus' personal prayer, that is, the Lord's Prayer. It should also be emphasized that the Aramaic prayers from Qumran also confirm the value and justification of the Aramaic language as an authorized language of prayer.

1. Aramaic as a Language for Prayer

Around the turn of the Common Era, the practice of personal prayer was not widespread and established. The temple was still in operation, and so cultic worship and liturgy still concentrated on sacrifices and burnt offerings, which were performed by Priests and Levites. In combination with the physical offerings, the priests also recited hymns, psalms and liturgical texts in Hebrew. In Qumran, however, the cult concentrated *only* on the word. Communal prayers and hymns were written in Hebrew, while personal prayers were given in Aramaic.

The rabbinic texts are ambiguous concerning the authorized language(s) for prayer. On the one hand, the sages forbid praying in Aramaic. The Gemara of Tractate Shabbat 12b states that one who is praying by himself should not pray in Aramaic, because it is borne up by angels *(melakhim)* who only understand Hebrew. However, the Gemara says that if a lone supplicant is praying beside or for weak and sick persons, he may pray in Aramaic, because the Divine Presence hovers above their head.[15] Others interpret this passage to mean that any language other than Hebrew can be used for prayer.[16] According to Mishna Berurah, "the angels know every language, but they are not bound to Aramaic, which is anathema to them." Furthermore, "women are permitted to pray in other languages," and it continues that "in the multitude even the Aramaic language is permitted."[17] The Tractate Soṭah also confirms the validity of the Aramaic language for prayer, because "the ministering angels are familiar with the Aramaic language" and that even "the Divine Voice was speaking in the Aramaic language" from heaven at the most important moments.[18] So, despite the fact that the rabbis preferred Hebrew, the holy tongue *(lāšôn haq-qōdeš)*, as the principal language for public worship, the use of Aramaic for personal petitionary prayer was accepted and practiced (b. Soṭah 32b–33a).

---

[15] b. Šabb. 12b: "One should never petition for his needs in Aramaic; and R. Johanan said: When one petitions for his needs in Aramaic, the Ministering Angels do not heed him, for they do not understand Aramaic? An invalid is different, because the Divine Presence is with him." See also b. Soṭah 33a; Schattner-Rieser, "Emotions," 292.

[16] Mishna Berurah 101, subparagraphs 13–16.

[17] Mishna Berurah 101, subparagraphs 18–19.

[18] b. Soṭah 33a; m. Soṭah 7:1.

2. Towards Fixed Formulae for Prayers

The Aramaic prayers in general follow a common pattern in their structure from beginning to end. This is important to emphasize, when we examine Jesus' personal prayer before it became the official prayer of his disciples. The common structure is as follows:

- blessing *(B^{e}rikh)*[19] formula and address to God
- epithetical divine names instead of the Tetragrammaton
- God named Creator of all
- mention of God's Kingship
- second person-address
- *Q^{e}dushat ha-Shem* (optional)

According to the rabbinic halakah, it is said in the Talmudic tractate Berakhot (Blessings): a *b^{e}rakha* (blessing) that does not contain God's name or title, nor mention his kingship as a ruler of the universe, is not a valid one (b. Ber. 12a).[20]

The address in the second person is also characteristic for the *B^{e}rakhot* (blessings) of the late biblical and intertestamental literature.[21] The liturgical *b^{e}rakhah* is often expanded by words such as "according to your will," as in Tob 3:6 and in the Testament of Qahat. The Blessing is very similar to the Blessing of the Kedusha (sanctification of the name of God), which is the high point of the Amidah (Shemoneh Esreh[22]) that is itself the central prayer of the Jewish daily service.

Although the Lord's Prayer does not open with an explicit blessing formula, the first part of the prayer has almost all elements that a full *b^{e}rakha* must contain, from the invocation Abba to the second-person petitions: 1) the name of God, here Abba; 2) the sanctification of God's holy name; 3) the mention of God's kingship;[23] and 4) the petition for fulfillment of his will.[24]

---

[19] Hereafter, *B^{e}rîkh*-formula: "Blessed are you."

[20] b. Ber. 12a: "This works out well according to Rav, who said: Any blessing that does not include mention of God's name is not considered a blessing, and since: Who creates light, includes God's name, it constitutes a complete, independent blessing. However, according to Rabbi Yoḥanan, who said: Any blessing that does not include mention of God's sovereignty, i. e., our God, King of the universe, is not considered a blessing ...." See also b. Ber. 40b and 49a, which add the sanctification and grace after meals formulae.

[21] Esther Chazon, "Looking Back: What the Dead Sea Scrolls Teach Us About Biblical Blessings," in *The Hebrew Bible in Light of the Dead Sea Scrolls*, ed. Nora David, Kristin De Troyer, and Shani Tzoref, FRLANT 239 (Göttingen: Vandenhoeck & Ruprecht, 2011), 155–71, esp. 162 and 166.

[22] Also called Tefillah.

[23] See b. Ber. 12a and 46a; see further Joseph Heinemann, "Once again Melekh ha 'Olam," *JJS* 15 (1964): 149–54.

[24] Cf. b. Ber. 40b: "Regarding blessings that do not conform to the formula instituted by the Sages, the Gemara relates that Binyamin the shepherd ate bread and afterward recited in Aramaic: Blessed is the Master of this bread. Rav said, He thereby fulfilled his obligation to recite a blessing. The Gemara objects: But didn't Rav himself say, Any blessing that does not con-

Moreover, thanks to the Matthean expansions, "your will be done" as well as the addition "in heaven and on earth" (Matt 6:10bc) – which encloses the whole universe – the Lord's Prayer includes all the elements that a full B^erakha (praise and blessing formula) must include.

3. The Name(s) of God in Aramaic Personal Prayers[25]

In the Qumran Aramaic prayers and b^erikh formulae we find many substitutes for God's name as King of the Worlds or Eternal King *(melek š^emayya)*, as ruler *(šalliṭ)*, and sometimes as king, which is the standard form that the rabbis required for a liturgical blessing *(b^erakhah)* and statutory prayers (b. Ber. 40b).

A common feature in the Aramaic prayers from the Dead Sea Scrolls is that there is never any mention of the holy name of God, the Tetragrammaton (YHWH), due to the high respect in which it was held. Instead, the Tetragrammaton is replaced by dots or other titles, such as: Great Name *(šēm rabbâ)*, Almighty God *(ʾEl ʿElyon)*, Lord of Heaven *(mārēʾ š^emayya)*, Eternal Lord *(mārēʾ ʿālmâ* and *mārēʾ ʿālmayyâ)*; Celestial King *(melek š^emayyâ)*; and Great Holy One *(qaddîša rabbâ)*.

E. The Lord's Prayer

The linguistic situation of Judaea during the time of Jesus was complex. Three languages were spoken: Hebrew, Aramaic and Greek.[26] Hebrew was the language of the Scriptures and of liturgy; a later dialect of Hebrew was spoken by some people; Aramaic was the everyday language of most of the Jewish inhabitants; and Greek was the language of administration and communication with Gentiles, used by foreigners, merchants and the upper class of Jews. Although Greek was widespread among the Jews of the Judean society, the language of the synagogue was Hebrew and the Semitic idiom (Hebrew and Aramaic) influenced

---

tain mention of God's name is not considered a blessing? The Gemara emends the formula of his blessing. He said: Blessed is the All-Merciful, Master of this bread." See Joseph Heinemann, *Prayer in the Talmud: Forms and Patterns*, SJ 9 (Berlin: de Gruyter, 1977), 157, 161, 180.

[25] Schattner-Rieser, "Das Aramäische zur Zeit Jesu," 98–100, 108–9.

[26] For a detailed discussion of the linguistic situation and the emergence of Greek, see Schattner-Rieser, "Das Aramäische zur Zeit Jesu," 83–87. See further Joseph A. Fitzmyer, "The Languages of Palestine in the First Century AD," *CBQ* 32 (1970): 501–31; J. N. Sevenster, *Do You Know Greek? How Much Greek Could the First Jewish Christians Have Known?*, NovTSup 19 (Leiden: Brill, 1968); Martin Hengel, *Judentum und Hellenismus: Studien zu ihrer Begegnung unter besonderer Berücksichtigung Palästinas bis zur Mitte des 2 Jh.s v. Chr.*, 3rd ed., WUNT 10 (Tübingen: Mohr, 1988 [1969]); Martin Hengel with Christoph Markschies, "Zum Problem der 'Hellenisierung' Judäas im 1. Jahrhundert nach Christus," in Hengel, *Judaica et Hellenistica: Kleine Schriften I*, WUNT 90 (Tübingen: Mohr Siebeck, 1996), 1–90; for the literary material, Pierre Grelot, "Sémitismes dans le Nouveau Testament," *DBSup* 12 (1991), col. 333–424, here 359.

the Greek used in Judaea and, consequently, Judean literary productions as well.[27] That means that the oral memorization is reflected in the Greek written tradition.[28] In an earlier study, I demonstrated that Jesus himself surely spoke and prayed in Aramaic.[29]

The prayer begins with the address: Father, or our Father who is in heaven, which is then followed by five petitions in the Lukan version, or seven petitions in the Matthean.

Luke 11:2-4	Matthew 6:9-13
Father	Our Father, who is in the heavens,
may your name be made holy;	may your name be made holy;
may your kingdom come;	may your kingdom come;
	may your will come to pass,
	as in heaven, also on earth.
Give us our bread that we need on that day;	Give us our bread that we need today;
and forgive us our sins,	and forgive us our debts,
for we also forgive everyone indebted to us;	as we also have forgiven those indebted to us;
and do not put us to the test.	and do not put us to the test,
	but deliver us from evil.

1. Introductory Remarks

The Lord's Prayer belongs to the literary genre of supplication. Except for the prayer's opening address (to God as Father), it consists exclusively of requests

---

[27] Grelot, "Sémitismes dans le Nouveau Testament," 359; Mireille Hadas-Lebel, "La connaissance du grec en milieu juif (IIIe s. av.–VIe s. ap. n. è.)," in *La Méditerranée d'une rive à l'autre: Culture classique et cultures périphériques*, ed. André Laronde and Jean Leclan (Paris: Académie des Inscriptions et Belles-Lettres, 2007), 231–42.

[28] The French anthropologist and linguist Marcel Jousse studied the linguistic situation in Palestine using his excellent Greco-Latin and Hebrew-Aramaic knowledge as an instrument of discovery and understanding of the mechanisms of oral-style milieus in the time of Jesus. Jousse's study focussed on the oral period of the Gospels and the culture into which they were born. He demonstrates that the Gospels written in Greek are Hellenistic encodings of the Aramaic and Hebrew scriptures, which were memorised and orally transmitted up to Jesus' time. See Marcel Jousse, "Les outils gestuels de la mémoire dans le milieu ethnique palestinien: Le Formulisme araméen des récits évangéliques," *L'Ethnographie* 30 (1935): 1–20; "Le mimisme humain et l'anthropologie du langage," *RAnth* 46 (1936): 201–15; "Le bilatéralisme humain et l'anthropologie du langage," *RAnth* 50 (1940): 2–30; "Judâhen, Judéen, Judaïste dans le milieu ethnique palestinien," *L'Ethnographie* 38 (1940), 320; "Père, Fils et Paraclet dans le milieu ethnique palestinien," *L'Ethnographie* 39 (1941): 3–58; "Les formules targoumiques du Pater dans le milieu éthnique palestinien,", *L'éthnographie* 42 (1944): 1–52. Some of these essays are now collected in English translation: Marcel Jousse, *Memory, Memorization, and Memorizers: The Galilean Oral-Style Tradition and Its Traditionists*, ed., trans. Edgard Sienaert, Biblical Performance Criticism 15 (Eugene, OR: Cascade Books, 2018).

[29] Schattner-Rieser, "Das Aramäische zur Zeit Jesu," 48–49.

or petitions in the imperative mood. The final doxology enriches the Matthean version of the prayer with elements of praise, although it is not found in the earliest witnesses to Matthew. The introductory formula is followed by two theocentric You-petitions and three anthropocentric We-petitions in the shorter Lukan version. Luke' version consists of five petitions in total, compared with seven in the longer version of Matthew. The first three are imperative-jussive forms in the third person (may be hallowed, may come, may be done), three imperatives (give, forgive, deliver) and a prohibition (do not introduce/bring). The three jussives are to be understood in a volitional or optative sense, expressing desire.

It is generally accepted that the shorter version of Luke represents the more original form of the Lord's Prayer. This corresponds to the usual opinion of the development of the Synoptic material, according to the Two Source Theory, or Two Document Hypothesis (2DH). Many proponents of the 2DH believe that Luke generally has followed the wording and order of the *Logienquelle* (Sayings Source Q) more closely than Matthew. In the specific case of the Lord's Prayer, however, this might not necessarily be the case, because the additional elements of Matthew take up formulations that are well documented in the papyri of the Jewish community of Elephantine (fifth century BCE), the Hebrew and Aramaic Dead Sea Scrolls from Qumran, the biblical writings, the Targumim, and other early Jewish literature.[30] Addressing God as the Father in heaven also corresponds to a well-known epithetical designation from the turn of the era; furthermore, as for the request for the coming of the Kingdom, this expectation – whether it refers to an eschatological kingdom or a spiritual kingdom – corresponds to early Jewish expectations in Palestine.

It seems almost certain that Jesus would have taught the Prayer to his earliest followers in Aramaic for several reasons. Aramaic, of course, was the common language of the non-elite people, like Jesus himself, among whom he travelled and taught. The thought and speech of Jesus himself would have been permeated by this living Hebrew-Aramaic Jewish tradition. Moreover, as we shall see, the Lord's Prayer itself in Aramaic would probably have been very easy to retain and repeat, thanks to its alliterations and final rhymes, which are genuine Aramaic linguistic features. Although there is no evidence of a written document in Aramaic of the "original Prayer," it is not only the linguistic assessment of the Greek versions of Matthew, Luke, and Q that leads me to this conclusion, but also the underlying Semitic textual evidence when one looks at the possible retroversion of the Greek segments of the prayer, compared with the parallels in the Septua-

---

[30] The addition "in heaven" or "of heaven" in association with the name of God is found since ancient times and also in pagan Aramaic inscriptions, becoming increasingly frequent in the Hellenistic-Roman period, as the Biblical-Aramaic and Qumranic Aramaic texts show. For a more detailed discussion, see Schattner-Rieser, "Das Aramäische zur Zeit Jesu," 110, and see also the epigraphic examples in Dirk Schwiderski, ed., *Die alt- und reichsaramäischen Inschriften*, 2 vols., FSBP 2, 4 (Berlin: de Gruyter, 2008), 1:797.

gint.³¹ By checking the address and the petition one by one, we can rediscover the underlying biblical Hebrew-Aramaic thought and expressions.

What I mean is that *the underlying biblical-Semitic formulations will remain even if one writes directly in Greek*.³² Any native bilingual speaker can confirm that one can think in one language and transmit it in the syntax or linguistic character of another language. Although the Greek version of Jesus' prayer would have been intended to teach the prayer to a Greek audience, Aramaic speakers with minimal knowledge of Greek could also understand the Greek version because they would recognize the underlying expressions. Therefore, both Greek and Aramaic speakers could profit from the Lord's Prayer in Greek.

The consonantal text can be reconstructed from the Greek thanks to our knowledge of Qumran Aramaic. However, the pronunciation is not certain where the vowels of the pretonic syllables are concerned. The Aramaic words of the New Testament written in Greek confirm that those vowels were still pronounced in the time of Jesus and that they generally were not shortened to *sheva*, but the comparative corpus is small and we lack other Greek transcriptions in order to be sure of the exact pronunciation.

2. Aramaic Retroversions

Luke 11:2–4	Luke (Aramaic)	Matt (Aramaic)	Matt 6:9–13
Πάτερ	אבא	אבונא די בשמיא	Πάτερ ἡμῶν ὁ ἐν τοῖς οὐρανοῖς·
ἁγιασθήτω τὸ ὄνομά σου·	יתקדש שמך	יתקדש שמך	ἁγιασθήτω τὸ ὄνομά σου·
ἐλθέτω ἡ βασιλεία σου	תאתי מלכותך	תאתי מלכותך	ἐλθέτω ἡ βασιλεία σου
		תתעבד רעותך כבשמיא אף בארעא	γενηθήτω τὸ θέλημά σου, ὡς ἐν οὐρανῷ καὶ ἐπὶ γῆς·
τὸν ἄρτον ἡμῶν τὸν ἐπιούσιον δίδου ἡμῖν τὸ καθ' ἡμέραν·	לחמנא פתגם יום הב לנא יום ביומא³³	לחמנא פתגם יום הב לנא יומא דנה	τὸν ἄρτον ἡμῶν τὸν ἐπιούσιον δὸς ἡμῖν σήμερον·

---

³¹ Parallels from the Septuagint are noted at the beginning of the discussion of each petition.

³² See also Jan Joosten, "*Aramaic or Hebrew* behind the Greek Gospels?," *Analecta Bruxellensia* 9 (2004): 88–101.

³³ In my opinion the underlying oral Aramaic formulation is: הב לנא יום לחמנא פתגם יום ביומא "Give us our bread! The matter of a day for the day," which means the "daily portion for each day." This is for two reasons: first, the structure of the Prayer always starts with imperative/ jussive forms and second, if we consider the underlying Hebrew/Aramaic biblical allusions,

Luke 11:2–4	Luke (Aramaic)	Matt (Aramaic)	Matt 6:9–13
καὶ ἄφες ἡμῖν τὰς ἁμαρτίας ἡμῶν, καὶ γὰρ αὐτοὶ ἀφίομεν παντὶ ὀφείλοντι ἡμῖν·	ושבק לנא חובינא כמא די אף אנחנא שבקין לכל חייבינא	ושבק לנא חובינא כמא די שבקנא לחייבינא	καὶ ἄφες ἡμῖν τὰ ὀφειλήματα ἡμῶν, ὡς καὶ ἡμεῖς ἀφήκαμεν τοῖς ὀφειλέταις ἡμῶν·
καὶ μὴ εἰσενέγκῃς ἡμᾶς εἰς πειρασμόν.	ואל תנסינא בנסיונא	ואל תנסינא בנסיונא	καὶ μὴ εἰσενέγκῃς ἡμᾶς εἰς πειρασμόν,
		אלא פצינא מן באישא	ἀλλὰ ῥῦσαι ἡμᾶς ἀπὸ τοῦ πονηροῦ.

3. The Petitions with Commentary

There are then seven petitions. The first three requests are connected with the worship of God (for example, "Your name be made holy") and God's ways. The next four concern the needs of humankind – and gather together both physical and spiritual needs. In the discussions that follow, the Greek is given with an English translation, followed by a suggested Palestinian Aramaic (hereafter, PA) translation of Matthew and/or Luke, and then Aramaic and Septuagintal parallels respectively. The final set of parallels is included because the expressions of the Greek petitions in Matthew and Luke have important parallels in the Septuagint, which can be useful when considering the Aramaic renderings of those passages.

3.1. The Address to God as Father:[34] אבא and אבונא די בשמיא

Luke 11:2: Father
Gr.: Πάτερ
PA: ʾabbâ[35]
Parallels: Tg. Ps 89:27; Tg. Job 34:36; Tg. Sir 23:1, 4
LXX: Wisd 14:3; Sir 23:3; 23:4; Ps 113:11; Isa 64:7; 3 Macc 6:3, 8

Matt 6:9: Our Father who is in the heavens
Gr.: Πάτερ ἡμῶν ὁ ἐν τοῖς οὐρανοῖς

---

the petition is composed of two parts, excerpts of two biblical verses, both in connection with Egypt, famine and God's donation of heavenly bread, namely Gen 47:15 (Give us bread!) and Exod 16:4 (the matter of a day for its day). As for the difference between Luke and Matthew, the Aramaic behind the Greek words τὸ καθ᾽ ἡμέραν and σήμερον in the LXX *yom beyoma* or *yom beyome* and *yoma dena*. The corresponding Hebrew is *devar yom beyom(o)* and *ha-yom*. In any case, the expression "the matter of day on its day" is a fixed expression in Aramaic and/or Hebrew *(devar yom bᵉyomo)* and is built with the word *yom* "day."

[34] For a more detailed overview of Jewish traditions concerning appellations of God, God as Father in prayers, Father as academic title, as well as the word "Abba" and the christological problem, see Schattner-Rieser, "Das Aramäische zur Zeit Jesu," 97–106.

[35] The doubling of the /b/-sound in ʾabba is analoguous to ʾimma, "Mother."

PA: *ʾabûnâ dî bišmayyâ*
Parallels: QA Tob 13:4; Tg. Isa 63:16; 64:7; Tg. Esth. II 3:3; etc.
LXX: Isa 63:16; Ps 88:27; 113:11(115:3); 1 Kgs 8:23; Eccl 5:1; Tob 5:17

The designation "Father" for God is rare in the Hebrew Bible, occurring only 17 times, with seven times as an address to "my/our God-Father."[36] It is a substitute for the Tetragrammaton, which was avoided out of respect, but it accumulated the sense of a paternalistic father, and also became a title for a "master" or "teacher."

In the Elephantine and Samaritan papyri of the fifth and fourth centuries BCE, the Tetragrammaton and its derivatives are still written. However, it is replaced in later literature the third or second century BCE.[37] The Septuagint consequently uses various substitutes such as κύριος and θεός ("Lord" and "God"). We do not know precisely when and for what reason the Tetragrammaton was avoided and no longer pronounced.[38] The non-pronunciation of the holy name led to its replacement by substitutes and alternative titles, such as "the Name" *(ha-Shem)* and "my Lord/My lord" *(Adonai)*. The divine name became so sacred that it required special treatment and respect. In many biblical and non-biblical Hebrew manuscripts from Qumran, the Tetragrammaton is written in paleo-Hebrew script. This usage is also found in Old Greek Manuscripts. Thus it is not surprising that the holy name of God, YHWH, the Tetragrammaton, does not occur in any Aramaic manuscript of Qumran nor in the New Testament. Instead, many surrogates and substitutes replace it.

In the Persian period, from the fifth century BCE, titles such as "God of heaven" and "Lord of heaven" are frequent and common: they are found, for example, in the Elephantine Papyri as well as in the Aramaic sections of Daniel and Ezra and the Aramaic Dead Sea Scrolls, where we find *mrh šmyʾ* "Lord of heaven" (1QapGen ar II, 14), *šlṭn šmyʾ* "Ruler of Heaven" (4QEnGiants[b] ar 2 II + 6–12(?), 16), and *mlk šmyʾ* "King of heaven" (1QapGen ar VII, 7; XII, 17).[39] In the apocryphal Book of Tobit, which is found in Qumran in four Aramaic and one Hebrew manuscripts, God is also referred to by epithetic circumlocutions such as "Great King," and in the Greek versions of the same book as the "King of Heaven" just as in biblical Aramaic (Tob 13:9, 13). In the Dead Sea Scrolls and intertestamental literature, God is pictured as surrounded by angels in his celestial kingdom,

---

[36] Schattner-Rieser, "Das Aramäische zur Zeit Jesu," 100–106, 108–11.

[37] Kristin De Troyer, "The Names of God, Their Pronunciation and Their Translation: A Digital Tour of Some of the Main Witnesses," *Lectio Difficilior* 2005/2, http://www.lectio.unibe.ch/05_2/troyer_names_of_god.htm; see further Martin Rösel, "The Reading and Translation of the Divine Name in the Masoretic Tradition and the Greek Pentateuch," *JSOT* 31 (2007): 411–28.

[38] An exception is the papyrus 4QpapLXXLev[b] (4Q120), a manuscript of Leviticus in Greek in which God's name is written IAW, thus in its pronunciation IAO.

[39] See Schattner-Rieser, "Das Aramäische zur Zeit Jesu," 110; see also the epigraphic examples in Schwiderski, *Die alt- und reichsaramäischen Inschriften*, 1:797.

where he is sometimes also addressed as "Father." The expression "Father who is in heaven" became more and more frequent in the Targumim and Rabbinic literature.⁴⁰ The Matthean address "Our Father in Heaven," literally "in the heavens" (ἐν τοῖς οὐρανοῖς), is considered by some Q-exegetes to be a secondary addition. But this addition is characteristic of the literature of post-exilic Judaism since the Persian period and is also well attested in the Aramaic epigraphical texts from Elephantine, in biblical and Qumran Aramaic.⁴¹

The Aramaic documents from Qumran prove that the pronouns "my" and "our" (e. g. אנובא "our father" in 4QTobitᵇ ar 4 I, 17) were still added to the nouns around Jesus' lifetime and not expressed by the status emphaticus. In the Genesis Apocryphon from Qumran (1QapGen ar II, 24), Methuselah addresses his father Enoch as "Oh my father, O my Lord/Master!" (yāʾ ʾabī, yāʾ mārī).⁴² These examples contradict the thesis of Joachim Jeremias that "Abba" means "my (dear) father" or "daddy," and that the title connotes not only the relational aspects of caring, faithfulness and mercy, but also aspects of respect and instruction, which of course do not exclude connotations of love. As a matter of fact, the address "Abba" in the time of Jesus was still a pure vocative and a respectful form for "oh father!"⁴³

Only the Middle Aramaic examples from inscriptions of the second century, for example the Bar Kochba letters, testify to the change in the linguistic usage of אבא / Abba and the loss of the emphatic meaning which tends toward the sense "my father." Only in the Targumim, of which Onkelos can be dated to the second or third century, אבא stands for the Hebrew-Masoretic אבי "my father."⁴⁴

Jeremias's assertion that the title "father" does not appear before Jesus in Jewish prayer formulations⁴⁵ is clearly refuted by the studies of Angelika Strotmann, Christiane Zimmermann, and Georg Schelbert.⁴⁶

---

⁴⁰ Schattner-Rieser, "Das Aramäische zur Zeit Jesu," 109, based mainly on Georg Schelbert, *Abba Vater: Der literarische Befund vom Altaramäischen bis zu den späten Midrasch- und Haggada-Werken in Auseinandersetzung mit den Thesen von Joachim Jeremias*, SUNT 81 (Göttingen: Vandenhoeck & Ruprecht, 2011), 118–21.

⁴¹ Already in the Aramaic papyri of the Jewish colony of Elephantine (5th century BCE), JHW (Jaho) is generally referred to as "JHW, God of Heaven" (אלה שמיא) and "Lord of Heaven" (מרא שמיא).

⁴² See also Lutz Doering, "God as Father in the Dead Sea Scrolls," in *The Divine Father: Religious and Philosophical Concepts of Divine Parenthood in Antiquity*, ed. Felix Albrecht and Reinhard Feldmeier, TBN 18 (Leiden: Brill, 2014), 107–35.

⁴³ In Mk 5:41 *talitha* (*qum/qumi*) "girl (stand up)!" is a vocative, and no one would render this command as "my dear little girl, please get up."

⁴⁴ See Schelbert, *Abba Vater*, 96, and Ursula Schattner-Rieser, review of *Abba Vater*, by Georg Schelbert, *EC* 4 (2013): 141–47, here 144.

⁴⁵ Joachim Jeremias, *Abba: Studien zur neutestamentlichen Theologie und Zeitgeschichte* (Göttingen: Vandenhoeck & Ruprecht, 1966), 63.

⁴⁶ Angelika Strotmann, *Mein Vater bist du! (Sir 51,10): Zur Bedeutung der Vaterschaft Gottes in kanonischen und nichtkanonischen frühjüdischen Schriften*, FTS 39 (Frankfurt a. M.: Knecht, 1991); Georg Schelbert, "ABBA, Vater! Stand der Frage," *FZPhT* 40 (1993): 359–81; Christiane Zimmermann, *Die Namen des Vaters: Studien zu ausgewählten neutestamentlichen Gottesbezeichnungen vor ihrem frühjüdischen und paganen Sprachhorizont*, AGJU 69 (Leiden: Brill, 2007), 52–64.

Despite the abundance of the father-language in the New Testament writings, the Aramaic transliteration "Abba" as a form of address is only documented three times (Mark 14:36; Gal 4:6; Rom 8:15), where the Greek translation ὁ πατήρ confirms that here there is a vocative *status emphaticus* for "Father" and not a child's "Papa," for which the Greek would be πάππας. In my opinion, both the Lukan and the Matthean forms of the Middle Ages are historically imaginable in this horizon: the earthly Jesus could have addressed his individual prayer to God with "Father," but the address of the disciples or the early Jesus-adherents could have been "Our Father." As God was often named with the addition "in heaven" at the time of Jesus, the Matthean address could well be traced back to a parallel original interpretation. In conclusion, it should also be noted that the Old Testament address of God mentioned in Isaiah 63:11–15 connects the Exodus motif with God-Father's salvation and forms therein a bridge to the Lord's Prayer. Moreover, in this prayer context God is not only addressed two times as "our Father" (and a third time in Isa 64:7), but the passage also contains a connection to the Exodus Redeemer typology, which itself is preceded by a reminder of salvation from bondage, a motif that runs like a red thread through the Lord's Prayer and which is also present in the request for bread and the petition against temptation.

The expression "Our Father in Heaven" became more and more common in the Targumim of the second century CE as well as in later rabbinic literature and prayers.

3.2. Hallowing God's Name

Luke 11:2; Matt 6:9: May your name be made holy.
Gr: ἁγιασθήτω τὸ ὄνομά σου
PA: *yitkaddaš šᵉmāḵ*
Parallels: Tg. Lev 20:7; 29:23; Tg. Ezek 36:23; Tg. 2 Chron 6:26; 4Q196 [papTobᵃ ar] 6, 7; 18, 11 = QA Tob 3:11; 13:3; Tg. Ps 110:9; etc.
LXX: Dan 3:26, 52; Pr Azar 1:29; Ezek 36:23; Ps 144(145):1; 1 Chron 16:35; Tob 3:11

The Greek word in this petition can be translated as "sanctified" or "make holy" your name. The translation into Aramaic is not difficult. There are examples of it in the Hebrew Bible and its Aramaic Versions, the Targumim. In the Septuagint, ἁγιασθήτω is rendered by *yitqaddash* (יתקדש) in the Targums. In the Lord's Prayer, we have an Aorist passive third person singular imperative. The difficulty is in the meaning of the verb in Aramaic. In an earlier study, I offered a long and detailed analysis of the jussive *yitqaddash* which can be understood as a reflexive form or as the passive voice.[47] The problem with the Aramaic language is that it does not distinguish between the passive voice and the reflexive mood. It is the same form, with infixed /t/: יתקדש. Now the question is, what does it mean? What is the sense of that? Does the expression indicate that human persons can

---

[47] Schattner-Rieser, "Das Aramäische zur Zeit Jesu," 112–15.

add anything to the holiness of God's name? Or does it mean that God shows or demonstrates himself as holy? The mediopassive can indeed be used in a reflexive sense. Therefore, it might be that the petition can mean either "hallowed be thy name by us the people" or "set yourself apart and show yourself as to be the holy one."

In the Aramaic Prayers from the Dead Sea Scrolls, there is no evidence of Verbs in the Hithpael conjugation; instead, the internal passive *qetîl* from the root *brk* is used in combination with the adjective *qaddish*, for example: בריך שמיה קדישא "Blessed is his Name." The association of the adjective from *qdš* (קדש) with the noun "name" (God) is also well documented in the Targumim: *qaddish shemâ* or *qaddish shemeh/shemakh* "holy is the name" or "holy is his/your name." The form *yitqaddash* exists, but it is rare in the Targums. As far as I know, even in the Hebrew Qumran texts there are only two examples of *yitqaddesh* (plus one more instance reconstructed).[48] In the early prayers and passages, the name of God is not "hallowed" but is already holy, as in: "Blessed be your holy name," in Greek εὐλογητὸν τὸ ὄνομά σου τὸ ἅγιον (Tob 3:11).[49]

3.3. The Kingship of God: תאתי מלכותך

Matt 6:10: May your kingdom come.
Gr: ἐλθέτω ἡ βασιλεία σου
PA: *tēʾtē malkûtāk*
Parallels: 4Q246; Dan 3:33; 4:34; 7:27; Tg. Onq. Gen 49:10
LXX: Ps 144(145):13; 1 Sam 13:14; 20:31; Dan 5:26

The request is composed of the third person feminine singular jussive (imperative) from the root *ʾth* (אתה), "come," and the feminine noun *malkû* "kingdom" augmented with the second person masculine singular suffix pronoun "your." The imperfect *Peʿal* second person feminine singular *tʾth*, "she shall come," is attested in the Aramaic manuscript of Tobit from Qumran (4QTobit[b] ar 5, 10). The termination of the imperative and jussive forms of the lamed-he verbs in the Qumran documents ends with yod. Therefore previous retroversions must be corrected.

A parallel passage to the New Testament conception of the heavenly kingdom of God and the request of the Lord's Prayer is found in the Aramaic text of the Son of God from Qumran (4Q246), where it says that a Savior, the "Son of God" (*brh dy ʾl*) and "Son of the Most High" (*br ʿlywn*) (Luke 1:33), whose kingdom will last forever, (*malkutēh malkût ʿālam*) and whose ways are truth and whose dominion is an eternal/everlasting reign (*šoltānēh šoltān ʿālam*) (cf. Exod 15:18). This passage seems to be inspired by Psalm 145, where it is quoted according to the Targum: *mlkwtk mlkwtʾ dkl ʿlmyʾ wšltnwtk bkl dr wdr*, "Your kingdom is

---

[48] ולוא יתקדש בימים ונהרות (1QS III, 4); יתקדש בכבוד (4Q504 3 II, 6).
[49] Septuaginta Text Family BA.

an everlasting kingdom, and your reign is from generation to generation" (Tg. Ps 145:13). This psalm also contains the praise of his name (Ps 145:1–2). In addition, we should also mention the Targum of Micah 4:8 which identifies the place where the kingdom of God will be established with the city of Jerusalem. The God-King motif (and the associated motif of the kingdom of God) is old and not specifically Jewish. It is common to the literature of the Ancient Near East and the Hebrew Bible, and was probably used in its anthemic form, in the royal psalms, in the temple liturgy. However, the abstractions associated with the idea of the kingdom of God (1 Chron 17:14; Ps 103:19; etc.), *mamlāḵâ* (1 Chron 29:11) and *memšālâ* (Ps 103:22; 145:13; etc.) are first encountered in recent texts. In Qumran, this idea is well documented, especially in the Sabbath Songs. The kingdom of God appears several times in the apocalyptic passages of the Aramaic portions of the Book of Daniel (Dan 3:33; 4:34; 7:27). And in the Targumim of Gen 49:10, Ruth 1:1, and Qoh 7:24, the Messiah is called King and is interpreted in an eschatological manner. The place of the testamentary decree of Jacob to his son Judah is similar to the request of the Lord's Prayer: "until he comes, the king Messiah (of the house of Judah) to whom the Kingdom of kingdoms belongs *(dy yty mlkʾ mšyḥʾ ddydyh hyʾ mlkwtʾ)* and before whom all kingdoms of the nations will be placed" (Tg. Neof. Gen 49:10).

3.4. *The will of God:* תתעבד רעותך בשמיא ובארעא *(or* תתעבד רעותך כבשמיא אף בארעא*)*

Matt 6:10b: May your will be done, as in heaven, also on earth.
Gr: γενηθήτω τὸ θέλημά σου, ὡς ἐν οὐρανῷ καὶ ἐπὶ γῆς
PA: *titʿaḇēd rᵉʿûtāḵ kᵉḇišmayyāʾ ʾaf bᵉʾarʿā*
Parallels: Ezra 7:18: "do it according to the will of your God *(krʿwt ʾlhkwm tʿbdwn)*"; 4Q198 (Tobᶜ ar) I, 5: "everything happens in its time" *(klʾ ytʿbd lzmnyhwn)*; Tg. Ps 135:6 *(kl dy ytrʿy ʿbd bšmyʾ wbʾrʿʾ)*; Tg. Isa 48:14; Tg. Ps 40:9; Tg. Ps 143:10
LXX: Ps 39(40):9; 134(135):6; 142(143):10; Isa 48:14; Odes 14:43; for "in heaven, also on earth," see: Deut 4:39; Dan 4:17; 6:28

The third request is common to Matthew and the Didache but is not found in the Lukan version. It is quite possible that it is original but had not been taken up in Luke for metrical reasons, as Philonenko suggests.[50] This liturgical formula is also found in the Jewish prayer Qaddish. It is worth mentioning that this petition in Matthew is built with the verb γενηθήτω from γίγνομαι/γίνομαι, "come to exist, to be, to become." More typically, similar ideas are expressed in the Septuagint with constructions from the verb ποιέω, "to cause to be, to make to be, to make," which in Aramaic is always rendered with the root ʿ*bd* (עבד), "to make (to be)."

---

[50] Marc Philonenko, *Le Notre Père: De la prière de Jésus à la prière des disciples*, Bibliothèque des histoires (Paris: Gallimard, 2001), 104.

The entire vocabulary of this request is attested in Biblical and Qumran Aramaic. The feminine noun רעו, "will" is found in 1Q20 XX, 23, 4Q545 4, 18, and in the Testament of Qahat (4Q542 1 I, 3): "because he is the eternal God, the master of all works, and the ruler of all things, to act on them according to his will *(lmʿbd bhwn lrʿwth)*." The corresponding Aramaic form of γενηθήτω is the feminine singular jussive Hithpael *ttʿbd*, "(it) is made to happen," which is attested in Aramaic Tobit (4Q198 [Tob^c ar] 1, 5): "everything happens in its time *(klʾ ytʿbd lzmnyhwn)*."[51] The Targums offer also exact parallels, built with *rʿw* "will," and *ʿbd*, "to do, make" (as in 1 Sam 13:14; 2 Kings 18:12; Isa 48:14), but never in the passive voice Hithpael. The expression "to act according to one's (God's) will" is well documented, as in Ps 143:10 ("teach me to do your will," *ʾlp yty lmyʿbd rʿwtk*), and Ps 40:9 ("to do your will *(lmʿbd rʿwtk)*, my God, I feel like it, and I carry your law in my heart" (Heb., *lʿśwt rṣwnk*). An especially close parallel to this request in Matthew's version of the prayer is a sentence in rabbinic Hebrew attributed to R. Eliezer: "When the Israelites do God's will, his name is great in the world, and if they do not, his name is desecrated in the world, as it were."[52] The additional idea of fulfillment occurring "in heaven as on earth" is well documented in the Targums. The comparative ὡς, "as well as" can be formulated in first century Aramaic on the basis of particles *k-, kmh d-* or *kdy* in connection with the affirmative particles *ʾaf* or *kēn*, which are well documented in Qumranic Aramaic. With respect to the phrase "as on earth," it may be noted that the Greek has never ἐν τῆς γῆς, but always ἐπὶ τῆς γῆς (Lev 22:24 LXX), which corresponds to Aramaic בארעא *(bʾrʿʾ)* and is parallel to בשמיא *(bšmyʾ)*. The Matthean petition, then, brings the heavenly world "down" to earth, and agrees in its wording with the Targum to Ps 135:6: "all that the Lord willed, he did in in heaven, and on earth" *(kl dy ytrʿh YHWH ʿbd bsmyʾ wbʾrʿʾ)*.

3.5. *The Bread Request:* לחמנא פתגם יום הב לנא יומא דנה or perhaps originally:
הב לנא לחמנא פתגם יום ביומא

Luke 11:3: Give us the bread we need on that day.
Gr: τὸν ἄρτον ἡμῶν τὸν ἐπιούσιον δίδου ἡμῖν τὸ καθ' ἡμέραν
PA: *laḥmānā pitgām (sᵉḳôm) yôm/hab lánā yôm bᵉyômā* (or: *yômā denā*)
Parallels: Tg. Gen 47:15 *(hb lnʾ lḥmʾ)*; Tg. Exod 16:4, 15, 25 *(ptgm ywm bywmh)*; Tg. Esth. II 3:8 *(ʾlhʾ dšmyʾ ... dyhb lnʾ lḥmʾ)*
LXX: Gen 47:15; Exod 16:4, 15; Isa 4:1

---

[51] The differences of the retranslations concern the particles of the phrase "as in heaven, so on earth," with the Greek element ὡς – καί (as in the request for debt forgiveness). The comparative particle "as" in Aramaic is *k-, kmh*, or *kwt* (similar to, for example, Tob or 1QapGen). In Targum Onqelos and Qumran one finds *kmh d (y) – kyn* for "as well as"; in Targum Neofiti one finds *hyk mh d- ... kdn* (attested in the Targumim to Lev 8:34; 24:19–20).
[52] Mekhilta to Exod 15:2, quoted in Gustaf Dalman, *Die Worte Jesu: mit Berücksichtigung des nachkanonischen jüdischen Schrifttums und der aramäischen Sprache*, 2. Aufl. (Leipzig: Hinrichs, 1930), 318.

Matt 6:11: Give us the bread we need today.
Gr: τὸν ἄρτον ἡμῶν τὸν ἐπιούσιον δὸς ἡμῖν σήμερον
PA: *laḥmánā pitgām (s^eḵôm) yômlhaḇ lánā yômā d^enā*
Parallels: Tg. Neof. Exod 16:4; Tg. Ps.-J. Exod 16:13; 1Q20 XX, 30
LXX: in addition to those listed above, see also Exod 15:25 (σήμερον)

The first part, "Give us (our) bread that we need," is identical in Matthew and Luke, while the second part differs; but it might be that the two variants stem from a common Aramaic source which was more simply phrased, as for example: הב לנא לחמנא פתגם יום ביומא, "Give us our bread/food, according to its day by day necessity." The given word order in the Gospels is perhaps the result of a "(theological) reflection" with the aim that the bread petition, which connects the heavenly and earthly realms – because it comes from heaven down to earth – introduce the We-petitions, which concern humans and earthly things. All the requests begin with a verb, which is the general word order in Hebrew and Aramaic, but the request for bread starts with a noun. This is acceptable in both Semitic languages, but it adds emphasis to accentuate what is being requested (bread!): לחמנא פתגם יום הב לנא יומא דנה "Our bread – the matter of a day – give us for the/each day!" Compared with the word-order of the other petitions, one would expect the imperative before the rest: Give us bread!

The individual vocabulary items "bread," "give," "daily," "according to …" are completely documented in Qumran Aramaic as well *(lḥm', yhb, ywm bywm', ywm' dnh/dn, ptgm)*, and parallel phrases are found in the Targumim and in Qumran Hebrew. The root *yhb* "give" is well documented in Qumran Aramaic, including the imperative *hb* "give!" (1QapGen ar XXII, 19). The adverb "today" is in Qumran Aramaic *yômâ d^enâ* (ב[יומ]א דנא in 1QapGen ar XX, 30) or *yômâ dēn* (יומא דן in 1QapGen ar XX, 5) and has *b^eyômâ hādēn* (see Tg. Neof. Gen 30:33) as a targumic equivalent.

Remarkable, and perhaps not accidental, is the fact that the search for the common vocabulary and expressions in the Hebrew Bible and the Septuagint leads to episodes associated with the Exodus, where the Hebrews demanded bread from the Lord in times of famine and where it rained heavenly bread that saved the people.[53] A corresponding imperative for the request of the bread is found in Targums to Gen 47:15 where the hungry Egyptians turn to Joseph with the request, *hb ln' lḥm'* (Tg. Onq.): "Give us bread!"

The idea of the daily bread-ration is expressed in the *manna* episode from Exodus 16:

And the Lord said to Moses, Behold, I will cause bread to come down to you from heaven (Tg. Onq.: *lḥm' mn šmy'*), and the people shall go out and collect their daily portion for

---

[53] Similarly: "This is the bread which the LORD has given you for food (Tg. Onq.: *hw' lḥm' dyhb lkwn YWY lmykl*)" (Ex 16:29). A similar wording is found in the Targum Sheni to Esth 3:18: "We bless the God of heaven, who gives us bread and water" (לאלהא דשמיא מברכין דיהב לנא לחמא ומיא).

the day (LXX: τὸ τῆς ἡμέρας εἰς ἡμέραν; Tg. Onq.: *pitgām yôm bᵉyômēh*; Tg. Neof.: *sᵉkôm yôm bᵉyômēh*; Syriac: *sûnkon … ma'akûlto dᵉyaumo bᵉyaumo*) that I may put it to the test (Tg. Onq.: *bᵉdîl da'anasenûn*; LXX: ὅπως πειράσω αὐτοὺς) whether they will walk in my law, or not. But if they prepare what they bring in on the sixth day, it will be twice as much as they would otherwise have collected day after day (LXX: τὸ καθ᾽ ἡμέραν εἰς ἡμέραν; Tg. Onq.: *yôm yôm*; Tg. Ps.-J.: *yômâ wᵉyômâ*; Syr: *dᵉyaumo bᵉyaumo*). (Exod 16:4–5)

The syntactic construction *pitgām*[54] + *yôm bᵉyômēh*, found in almost all the Targums, is rendered by *sᵉkôm yôm bᵉyômēh/bᵉyômâ* in Targum Neofiti and the Cairo Targum Fragments to Exod 5:13, 19; 16:4, 5, and Lev 23:37. It means literally, "the matter of each day on its day," that is, "the daily rate/total" or "the assigned part." The noun *sᵉkom*,[55] which means "fixed number, amount, sum total, daily rate, one's assigned part/substance," corresponds to the Syriac *sunkono*, "the necessary, need" of the *Peshitta*.[56]

Only the word ἐπιούσιος seems at the first glance problematic. The etymology of the word is obscure. It occurs only in Luke 11:3 and Matt 6:11, and is composed either from ἐπ' + ἰέναι (as participle adjective: coming) or ἐπί + οὐσιος, ἐπὶ τὴν οὐσίαν, or ἐπὶ τὴν οὐσίαν οὐσία (being, substance, essence). In my opinion, ἐπιούσιος … τὸ καθ᾽ ἡμέραν represents the Hebrew Bible expression *pitgam ywm bywm'*, "(according to) the day by day necessary," where the meaning of the necessary thing/matter (Aram. *pitgam*) has merged with the meaning of "day by day, coming" (ἐπί + εἶναι, Aram. *ywm bywm'*) in one word.

This particular word order, which places the noun at the beginning, puts an emphasis on "our bread/food" and appears like a bridge between the celestial sphere and the earthly life, above all with the obvious association with the Exodus material in which the heavenly bread comes down to earth. By the way, *laḥmā* in Aramaic has a broader meaning than in Hebrew, and means not only "bread" but also "meal" and "food." The allusion to the heavenly bread of the Exodus story seems obvious and, in my opinion, it cannot be ignored for the reconstruction of the Lord's Prayer and should be taken into consideration philologically.

Oral tradition, linguistic reality, historical facts, and political expectations must also be taken in account. The interpretation of the miracle of the manna, which was expected again for the Messianic era and was believed to procure eternal life to the righteous in the world to come, is well represented in Jewish

---

[54] *Pitgam* covers a large semantic field and means "word, matter, thing, copy."

[55] See Marcus Jastrow, *A Dictionary of the Targumim, the Talmud Babli and Yerushalmi, and the Midrashic Literature* (London: Luzac & Co., 1903), 989; Michael Sokoloff, *A Dictionary of Jewish Palestinian Aramaic of the Byzantine Period*, 1st ed. (Ramat Gan: Bar Ilan University Press, 1990), at http://cal.huc.edu/djpa.php?lemma=skwm+N. The feminine abstract noun of the same root, *skmw(t')*, means "destiny"; see Jacob Levy, *Chaldäisches Wörterbuch über die Targumim und einen grossen Theil der rabbinischen Schrifttums*, 2 vols. (Leipzig: Baumgärtner, 1867–68), 2:164, at http://cal.huc.edu/showlevy.php?page=2:164.

[56] See Matt 6:11 and 1 Cor 12:22.

rabbinic and apocryphal literature (e. g. Wisd 16:20–28; 2 Bar 29:3–8). As early as Deut 8:3, the heavenly bread "manna"[57] symbolizes the word of God, a word that awaited fulfillment.[58] On a purely textual and grammatical basis, the request for bread in Luke and Matthew combines elements from Gen 47:15 and Exod 16:4–5.[59]

To conclude, I offer one final linguistic observation about the Bread Petition. The Hebrew expression דבר יום ביומו "the matter of a day for its day; daily rate" (and its corresponding Aramaic expression פתגם יום ביומה/א or סכום יום ביומה/א) is, in the Septuagint as well as Luke 11:3, rendered by different constructions but always with ἡμέρα, thus: καθ' ἡμέραν (Exod 5:13; Num 4:16; Lev 23:37; etc.); ἐξ ἡμέρας εἰς ἡμέραν (Jer 52:34); τὸ τῆς ἡμέρας εἰς ἡμέραν (Exod 16:4); ἡμέρας ἐν ἡμέρᾳ (Neh 12:47); but never with the adverb σήμερον, "today." This word translates the Hebrew *ha-yôm* and the Aramaic *yôm' d^enâ* יומא דנה/יומא דין)) (Gen 19:38), "this very day > to-day." The construction καθ' ἡμέραν, "daily," is common in Luke (5x: 9:23; 11:3; 16:19; 19:47; 22:53) and Acts (6x: 2:46, 47; 3:2; 16:5; 17:11; 19:9), while it only appears once in Matthew (26:55) and Mark (14:49). The expression is Lukan, but it is also quite common in the Septuagint (e. g. Exod 16:5; Lev 23:37).

In good Aramaic and in conformity with the construction of the other petitions, one expects the imperative at the beginning of the sentence: *hb ln' lhm' ptgm ywm bywm'*. And this is indeed the case in Luke 11:3 in the Syriac versions: ܗܒ ܠܝ ܠܣܘܟ ܕܗܘܡܢܝ ܚܠܡܐ (Peshitta); ܗܒ ܠܝ ܠܣܘܟ ܠܚܡܐ ܐܡܝܢܐ ܕܚܠܡܢ (Old Syriac Sinaiticus and Curetonianus). The Syriac versions render ἐπιούσιος either with *sunkono* or *amino* "constant, constantly."[60] Luke 11:3: τὸν ἄρτον ἡμῶν *(lhmn')* τὸν ἐπιούσιον *(ptgm/skwm)* δίδου ἡμῖν *(hb ln')* τὸ καθ' ἡμέραν *(ywmh dnh/ywmh dn)*.

3.6. *Forgiveness of debts/sins:* ושבק לנא חובינא כמא די אף אנחנא שבקנא לחיבינא

Luke 11:4: and forgive us our sins, for we also forgive everyone indebted to us
Gr: καὶ ἄφες ἡμῖν τὰς ἁμαρτίας ἡμῶν, καὶ γὰρ αὐτοὶ ἀφίομεν παντὶ ὀφείλοντι ἡμῖν·
PA: *ûš^ebuq lánâ hôbênâ k^emâ dî 'af 'anahnâ šab^eqîn l^ekol hayyābânâ*

Matt 6:12: and forgive us our debts, as we also have forgiven those indebted to us
Gr: καὶ ἄφες ἡμῖν τὰ ὀφειλήματα ἡμῶν, ὡς καὶ ἡμεῖς ἀφήκαμεν τοῖς ὀφειλέταις ἡμῶν

---

[57] *Manna* can be translated as "portion, rate" from the root m-n-h "to count."

[58] Although I cannot agree with Carmignac that Hebrew was the language that Jesus spoke, his analysis and commentary on the Lord's Prayer, especially the Exodus manna-episode, contains very valuable material: see Jean Carmignac, *Recherches sur le "Notre Père"* (Paris: Letouzey & Ané, 1969), 196–200.

[59] In Greek thus: Δὸς ἡμῖν ἄρτους! (Gen 47:15) + ἄρτους (ἐκ τοῦ οὐρανοῦ) ... τὸ τῆς ἡμέρας εἰς ἡμέραν/τὸ καθ' ἡμέραν (Exod 16:4–5).

[60] The Syriac *'amîn* translates Hebrew *tamîd* (תמיד) "constant, daily practice," esp. (sub. קרבן) the daily burnt-offering (Num 28:3), and Aramiac *tadîr* (תדיר) "constant, regular; steadily," also for the "daily offering."

PA: *ûš*ᵉ*buq lánâ ḥôbênâ kᵉmâ dî [ʾaf ʾanaḥnâ]*⁶¹ *šᵉbaqnâ lᵉḥayyābânâ*
Parallels: Tg. Num 14:19 (*šboq kᵃʿan lᵃhobê...kᵃmâ dišᵃbaqtâ*); Tg. Exod 34:9 (*wtšbwq lḥwbyn*ʾ); Tg. Isa 53:5 (*ḥwbn*ʾ *yštbwq ln*ʾ); Tg. Isa 53:12; Tg. Ps 95:9; Tg. 2 Chron 6:26; Tg. Lev 5:26; Tg. Exod 32:32; 34:7, 9
LXX: for τὰς ἁμαρτίας etc.: Exod 34:9; Num 14:19; Ps 25(24):18; 3 Macc 2:19; for ἀφήκαμεν etc.: Exod 34:7

The vocabulary for the Aramaic retroversion of the fifth petition is completely attested in the Dead Sea Scrolls and early Targums: to forgive (*šbq*),⁶² debt (*ḥwb*)⁶³ and the debtor or guilty one (*ḥyyb*).⁶⁴ The verb *šbq* "leave, forgive," is well documented in the Targums and the Aramaic texts of Qumran and corresponds to Greek ἀφίημι. The root *šbq* in the sense of "leave (alone), abandon" also occurs in the transliterated form of ηλι ηλι λεμα σαβαχθανι (Matt 27:46; Ps 22[21]:2),⁶⁵ which is the Aramaic rendering of the psalm. The Greek variants ὀφειλήματα "debts" and ἁμαρτίαι "sins" can be represented by one and the same Aramaic word, namely *ḥôb* (חוב) or *ḥôbah*, which means both "guilt" and "sin," and more generally any fault, but might stand also for a monetary debt.⁶⁶ The noun "guilt, fault" appears five times in the Aramaic texts of Qumran, of which three times it is in the masculine, *ḥôb* (חוב), and twice in the feminine, *ḥôbah* (חובה).

The first part is identical in Matthew and Luke, and the corresponding Aramaic would be *ûšᵉbuq lánâ ḥôbênâ*. The construction with the dativus ethicus *lánâ* is not necessary, as the Targumic parallels confirm, but is well documented in Qumran Aramaic: for example, *wḥṭʾy šbq lh gzr*, "my sins exorcised an exorcist" (4Q242 1 III, 4); and *wšbq lhwn ḥṭʾhwn*, "and he released them their sin(s)" in the Qumran Targum to Job (11QTgJob XXXVIII, 3). Here, as in the Lord's Prayer, the subject is emphasized by the particle *l-* (*lhwn*) and repeated in the personal suffix-pronoun *ḥṭʾhwn*. Such a construction uses the preposition *l-* only once, which introduces the accusative addition of the verb *šbq*, although there are numerous reference points in the Targumim and all have the same structure. In Targum Onqelos to Exod 34:9, there is the perfect corresponding to the Lord's Prayer with the difference that instead of the imperative, there is an imperfect Qal second person masculine, and the subject is appended to the noun only as a suffix pronoun: *wtšbwq lḥwbn*ʾ (וְתִשְׁבּוֹק לְחוֹבָנָא) *wlḥṭʾn*ʾ, "and release our guilt and our sins." The imperative is also well documented: *šbwq lḥwby* (ושבוק לחובי), "release my guilt" (Exod 10:17; Gen 50:17). Once again, there is a reference to the Exodus from Egypt in connection with the sin of the people and the golden calf:

---

⁶¹ The addition *ʾaf ʾanaḥnâ* is not necessary with the Perfect and adds mainly an emphatic nuance.
⁶² The root means also means "abandon, leave, leave alone, release, permit."
⁶³ Also "obligation, duty, sin."
⁶⁴ Also "sinner."
⁶⁵ Matthew translates this into Greek as follows: Θεέ μου Θεέ μου, ἱνατί με ἐγκατέλιπες, "My God, my God, why have you abandoned me?" Mark 15:34 has ελωι ελωι λεμα σαβαχθανι.
⁶⁶ Contra Jeremias, *Abba*, 159.

"And now if you will forgive their sin *(šbqt lḥwbyhwn)*! If not, then blot me out of the book that you have written" (Tg. Onq. Exod 32:32).

The second part of the request is presented differently in Matthew and Luke, with regard to the morphology. Instead of the perfect ἀφήκαμεν (Aram. *šbqnʾ*) "we have forgiven" in Matt 6:12, Luke has the present form ἀφίομεν (Aram. *šbqyn*) "we forgive." In light of the formulation of Targum Onqelos Num 14:19, the Matthean version *(kᵉmā dī šᵉbaqnā lᵉḥayyābânā)* has strong support in the parallel materials and might represent a primitive wording in Aramaic. Luke's version might represent a different understanding of the verb which explains the rendering by the perfect *šbqnʾ*. At the same time, this explanation is not very satisfactory, not even the explanation that it is a small spelling mistake for *šbqyn*, or a present with enclitic personal pronoun *šābᵉqīn-nan*. This form is a late phenomenon, common in Syriac but not documented in Palestinian Aramaic before 130 CE and first in a letter of the Jewish rebel Bar Kokhba.[67] The most appropriate parallel, which also serves as a template for our retranslation, can be found in Targum Onqelos Num 14:19: "Now, forgive the guilt *(šᵉboq kᵉʿan lᵉḥobê)* of this people according to your great goodness and as you have forgiven this people *(kᵉmā dišᵉbaqtā lᵉʿammā)* from Egypt to here!"

3.7. *And do not put us to the test:* ואל תנסינא בנסיונא

Luke 11:4 and Matt 6:13: And do not put us to the test
Gr: καὶ μὴ εἰσενέγκῃς ἡμᾶς εἰς πειρασμόν
PA: *weʾal tᵉnassînâ bᵉnisyônâ*
Parallels: Tg. Onq. Exod 17:7; Tg. Ps 66:10; Tg. Neof. Gen 22:1 *(nsy ... bnsywnyh)*; Tg. Sir 2:1
LXX: Exod 17:7; Deut 6:16

The expression "to trying/tempt someone" has the connotation of "to put someone to the test" (Hebrew/Aramaic, *nsy*; Greek. πειράζω, ἐκπειράζω), as can be seen in Deut 6:16 and Isa 7:12. To the Greek noun πειρασμός corresponds the Aramaic *nissayôn/nissyona* or *niseta*. It appears in the "temptation episode" of Massa and Meriba in Exod 17:7 and also in Sir 2:1 (εἰς πειρασμόν). The root *nsh*, "put to the test, try" is documented in various verb forms of Qumran texts, but perhaps by chance there is no instance of *nsywn* or *nsytʾ*, which are however common in the Targumim.

---

[67] For the use of the particles: in the LXX, Hebrew *kʾšr* is usually translated as καὶ γάρ, and in the Targumim again as *ʾarûm (ʾrw* in QA) or *ʾûf*; ὡς καί or καὶ ὡς in the Septuagint translates the Hebrew particles *k-* and *kʾšr*, which the Targumim translate with *k-* or *kmh / ʾd-* or *hykmh*, the latter variant sometimes passing the comparative "as-well as"; καί alone also renders the Hebrew *gam* and *ʾaf*. Since *dy* can in and of itself already have causal meaning, the following particles could be used in the Lord's Prayer *kmʾ/h dy* or *kdy*. The Lukan variant also requires the particle *ʾaf*, which is well documented in Qumran Aramaic, to achieve the comparative significance of the Greek with the past participle. See further Schattner-Rieser, "Das Aramäische zur Zeit Jesu," 127.

Influenced by the Greek εἰσενέγκῃς (from εἰσφέρω, "to bring into, to lead to"), various retroversions of the Lord's Prayer into Aramaic reconstructed the petition with the verb *'ll* "enter, to bring in, to lead" (Jeremias, Kuhn, Grelot). Since Dalman, the petition has been rendered by *lâ* or *'al taʿelna(n)*.[68] But in the Hebrew Bible and the Targumim the verb *nsh/y* is constructed with an internal object *nisyônâ*, "to introduce into the sin."[69] The pair of words "in temptation" *(nsy bnsyn')* on which I base my retranslation, and which is formed with the preposition *b-* but is incorrectly translated as *l-* in other retroversions, is found in the Targumim to Gen 22:1 (except Tg. Neof.), in Targum Neofiti to Deut 33:8 *(dnsyth ... bnsywnh)*, in the fragmentary tale of Exod 15:25, and in the Targum of Song 7:19. In the latter passage, the Genesis is referenced: "and I tempted Daniel *(w'nsh)* to see whether he could withstand the temptation *(lmqm bnsywn')*, as Abraham withstood the ten temptations."

One could emphasize "us" and insert the dativus ethicus *lánâ*: *wᵉ'al tᵉnassī lánā* (ואל תנסי (נא) לנה), "and us, do not tempt us." But this is not a must. This wording is found in Tg. Esth. II 5:1 in connection with the temptation of Abraham, who offers his son Isaac. Again, in the Exodus narrative, we find "tempting" in a few matching passages associated with the verb נסי/נסה "try," for example in Targum Onqelos to Exod 20:20, where God "tests/tries" the people by the waters of Mara: "there he (the Lord) tried *(ns'h)* it (the people of Israel)." Another passage in connection with the "waters of Massa and Meribah" is Exod 17:7: "because the Israelites had hassled there and had tried the LORD." Also in the Targums to Exod 16:4, the single verse that seems to have inspired Jesus' prayer in multiple ways, God tempted the people, putting them to the test: "Then said the LORD to Moses, Behold, I will cause bread to descend (LXX: "rain") to you from heaven, and the people shall go out and they shall gather what it takes for the day, that I may test them, whether they will walk according to my Torah (instruction) or not."

3.8. *Request for salvation:* אלא פצינא מן באישא

Matt 6:13: but deliver us from evil.
Gr: ἀλλὰ ῥῦσαι ἡμᾶς ἀπὸ τοῦ πονηροῦ
PA: *'ellâ pᵉṣînâ min bᵉ'îšâ*
Parallels: 11QTgJob XIV, 6; 11QapGen ar XII, 11; Tg. Ps 119:153
LXX: Judg 10:15; Isa 25:4; Jer 15:21; 1 Macc 14:14

---

[68] Although for this variant one relies only on a (not appropriate) reference in b. Ber. 60b, namely, *tby'ny l' lydy ht'*, "and do not bring me in the vicinity (literally in the hands) of sin."

[69] In the Bible, it is usually God who "tests" and tempts his people, such as in the account of the binding of Isaac and the testing of Abraham, concerning which Targum Neofiti to Gen 22:1 reads, "and the Lord put *(nsy)* Abraham to the test *(bnsywnh)*"; so also in the Targum to Ps 66:10, "You have tried our fathers." But it also happens that the people of God challenge and try their Lord.

The final sentence occurs only in Matt 6:13, and the retranslation itself is not difficult. The adversative particle ἀλλά has the similar sounding ʾellâ as an Aramaic equivalent. Which Aramaic verb may have been behind the Greek ῥύομαι "redeem, save" is not to be determined with certainty. In the Targumim there are three possible correspondences for ῥύομαι: *pṣy*, *prq* and *šyzb*. I found in the Aramaic of Qumran texts only *pṣy* and once the verb *šyzb* with the meaning "save, redeem," for example in the Qumran Targum to Job: "Behold, I have redeemed (*šzybt*) the wretched one" (11QTgJob XIV, 6). With the root *pṣy*, however, there are more pertinent parallels: *pṣyhy*, "he redeemed him" in 11QTgJob XVI, 1; XXIII 1; and *pṣʾhy mn ḥblʾ*, "he delivered him from evil" in 11QTgJob XVI, 1; *pṣʾ*, "he saved" in 1QapGen ar XXII, 11. Taking into account the frequency, as well as the probably intentional alliteration (labials *b/f*; sibilants *š/z*; *î*-sound/vowels), I prefer the root *pṣy* in the Lord's Prayer and would render the sentence with: *ʾellâ pᵉṣînâ min bᵉʾîšâ*.

F. Concluding Remarks

The Aramaic retroversion of the Lord's Prayer proposed here is based on the vocabulary and morphology of the Aramaic materials from Qumran and the formulations in the Palestinian Targumim that correspond to the Lord's Prayer. One might argue, in opposition to this proposal, that the Qumran texts do not constitute a homogeneous corpus and that literary Aramaic differs significantly from everyday language use; but one should not stress the difference too strongly, for written texts are always literary to a certain extent. The consonantal text offered in this essay (see also the Appendices) largely corresponds to the Aramaic *Urform*, which itself was based on the biblical text and Jewish thought of its time. Even in the case that the Lord's Prayer had been composed first in Greek, it is obvious from this study that for every petition there is a clear underlying Jewish-Semitic background, one that could display both cross-linguistic influences (with Hebrew or Aramaic in the background), as well as cross-cultural influences in relation to the Jewish milieu, the biblical history, and the expectations of that time.

As an Aramaist and Jewish Studies scholar, I discern in Jesus' prayer a skilled combination of Jewish formulae from the Bible and the apocalyptic thought of his period. I therefore agree with Matthew Black, who concluded from his study that "an Aramaic sayings-source or tradition lies behind the Synoptic Gospels," while conceding that "whether that source was written or oral it is not possible from the evidence to decide."[70] There is in my opinion much evidence in favour

---

[70] Matthew Black, *An Aramaic Approach to the Gospels and Acts*, 3rd ed. (Oxford: Clarendon, 1967), 271; see further ibid., 271–75.

of orally-transmitted sayings, originally of Aramaic provenance, which would conform with the Jewish tradition of learning and reciting by heart without the need of a written Aramaic text. And Simon Joseph is right when he says, "if there was once an Aramaic source, it is now, like Q itself, submerged in the Gospels"[71] – and they are in Greek.

There might have been numerous Greek-speaking foreigners, but the Jewish community and the milieu of Jesus and his peers were embedded in the Jewish traditions in Hebrew and Aramaic. Neither the epigraphic texts nor the Dead Sea Scrolls confirm the image of a Jewish Greek-speaking community in the land of Israel. For me, the question is not if the first written version of the Lord's Prayer was in Aramaic/Hebrew or in Greek. The issue is that each segment of the Prayer corresponds to well-known Jewish texts and formulae. The Prayer might have been written in Greek first – which was surely the case, for the written version was destined to reach a wide-spread public, Gentiles and not only Jews, who tended to stick closely to their ancestral languages: Hebrew and Aramaic. In my opinion, the written text was directly formulated in Greek and is not necessarily a translation of a written Aramaic original, but this is not to deny the Prayer's obvious Aramaic or Semitic origin. We can rightly assume that Jesus himself recited his personal prayer in Aramaic and that this Jewish-Aramaic background underlies the Greek-edited prayer of the Gospels.

Perhaps Jesus was one of the first "Rabbis" to promote the Aramaic vernacular language as an official language for prayer, which would have been in contrast with Pharisaic practice and the views of rabbinic Judaism. It seems that the Rabbis later tolerated the use of Aramaic for some "popular prayers," including the Qaddish (which is not is documented before the fourth century CE), when Aramaic transitioned from a popular language to a respected literary language. This is in conformity with the Mishna (m. Soṭah 7:1), which permitted any (vernacular) language for prayer. It is not impossible that the acceptance of Aramaic by the Rabbis had been influenced by the use of the early Jesus-followers.

The trilingual situation of Palestine in the time of Jesus is also reflected in the New Testament, quite vividly in Luke's account of Paul's appearance in Jerusalem (Acts 21–22). Paul speaks Greek with the Roman commander who arrests him in the temple (Acts 21:37), but he addresses himself in Aramaic to the people (Acts 21:40; 22:2; see also Acts 26:14), and the fact that he was a practicing Jew of Hebrew speech, managing Hebrew for cultic reasons, is self-evident to Luke and presumably also to be presupposed historically (see also Phil 3:5). Even for Jesus himself, at least some knowledge of Greek may probably be assumed, so that even a conversation in Greek with Pontius Pilate is not historically unthinkable. In the synagogue, Jesus probably read and prayed in Hebrew, but in everyday

---

[71] Simon J. Joseph, *Jesus, Q, and the Dead Sea Scrolls: A Judaic Approach to Q*, WUNT II 333 (Tubingen: Mohr Siebeck, 2012), 57.

life and in his proclamation, he must have spoken Aramaic. In this respect, his teaching in Galilee and the Aramaisms preserved in the Synoptic Gospels in his sayings fit into the image of an Aramaic-speaking Galilee. Several studies have been devoted to this Aramaic background of the Greek writings of the New Testament, concerning linguistic phenomena ranging from lexical Aramaisms, to the transition from Aramaic to Greek, to Semitic syntax and traces of Aramaic (or even Semitic) language and expression underlying the Greek phrasings of the New Testament. Even if no New Testament texts are preserved in Aramaic and even if no such records existed at first, it is in my opinion quite clear that the Lord's Prayer in Greek was based on an Aramaic *Urform* – written or oral. This should be enough to explain some of the linguistic features paralleled in Qumran and Targumic Aramaic.

I cannot agree with those who claim that earliest post-Easter Christians lived and thought mainly in Greek, the common tongue of all Mediterranean cities, including Jerusalem.[72] How can one claim this? Pierre Grelot presented a different picture in his study of the Semitic background of the New Testament.[73] As an Aramaist, I would ask such scholars, when did Christianity then start for them? The earthly Jesus was a Jew who grew up in a Jewish context, knowing Hebrew and Aramaic. He and his followers were taught the holy texts in Hebrew and spoke in Aramaic. Greek was the language to communicate with foreigners for diplomatic and other purposes, thus it was the common language with non-indigenous persons. Although Jesus' sayings and teachings only survive in Greek, it should also come as no surprise that those sayings and teachings – including the Lord's Prayer – bear the indelible stamp of the language, thought patterns, and scriptural traditions of his Hebrew- and Aramaic-speaking milieu. With respect to the Lord's Prayer, I have shown in this essay the biblically rich traditions and expressions that lie behind the individual petitions. In what follows, a brief summary of these results and their implications is presented.[74]

---

[72] Hengel, *Judentum und Hellenismus*, 111, 120–152; idem, "Der vorchristliche Paulus," in *Paulus und das antike Judentum: Tübingen-Durham-Symposium im Gedenken an den 50. Todestag Adolf Schlatters (19. Mai 1938)*, ed. Martin Hengel and Ulrich Heckel, WUNT 58 (Tübingen: Mohr Siebeck, 1991), 177–293, here 257–58; idem, *Jews, Greeks, and Barbarians: Aspects of the Hellenization of Judaism in the Pre-Christian Period* (Philadephia: Fortress, 1980), 75; Heinz O. Guenther, "The Sayings Gospel Q and the Quest for Aramaic Sources: Rethinking Christian Origins," in *Early Christianity, Q and Jesus*, ed. John S. Kloppenborg with Leif E. Vaage, Semeia 55 (Atlanta: Scholars Press, 1991), 41–76.

[73] Pierre Grelot, "Sémitismes dans la Bible grecque," *DBSup* 12 (1991), col. 333–424; idem, "L'arrière-plan araméen"; idem, "La quatrième demande du 'Pater' et son arrière-plan sémitique," *NTS* 25 (1978/79): 299–314. See also here the work of Marcel Jousse (for literature, see above, n. 28), and Hans Peter Rüger, "Die lexikalischen Aramaismen im Markusevangelium," in *Markus-Philologie: Historische, literargeschichtliche und stilistische Untersuchungen zum zweiten Evangelium*, ed. Hubert Cancik, WUNT 33 (Tübingen: Mohr Siebeck, 1984), 73–84.

[74] For a more detailed presentation of these results, see Schattner-Rieser, "Das Aramäische zur Zeit Jesu," 131–37. Recently, Jörg Frey based a study of the Lord's Prayer on my analysis and

a) Linguistically, it is worth pointing out that the vocabulary of the Lord's Prayer – with the exception of the root *nsy* ("tempt, test, examine")[75] – is thoroughly documented in the Palestinian Aramaic of the Qumran texts of Jesus' time (first century BCE – first century CE),[76] which clearly differs from the later Galilean dialect which Joachim Jeremias and Gustaf Dalman before him relied upon for their reconstructions of the Lord's Prayer in Aramaic. This assessment of the appropriate linguistic background of the Lord's prayer allows us to exclude once and for all the "daddy" interpretation of "Abba." It also allows us to confirm Karl Georg Kuhn's observations concerning the final rhyme and vowel assonance featured in the Lord's Prayer.[77] I would also add here that a retroversion based on Qumran and Targumic Aramaic shows a conspicuous consonantal alliteration in the We-requests.[78]

b) Despite its brevity, the Lord's Prayer is a highly structured and poetic masterpiece, distinct from other Jewish prayers because of its conciseness and expressiveness. It does not open with the *Berîkh*-formula "blessed are you," but the first section contains everything that a proper *Berakha* should contain: the divine name (here, Abba); the sanctification of the name; the mention of the divine reign;[79] and a petition for the completion of the divine will.[80] The second person address is characteristic of the late biblical and apocryphal *Berakhot* of early Jewish literature.[81] The first section therefore serves as an opening *Berakha* which leads to the actual topics, in the We-petitions. Uniquely, the Lord's Prayer combines both divine and human dimensions in a matter-of-fact way: God and human person, heaven and earth, promise and fulfilment, testing, debt, and remission of debt. A concluding formula is lacking in the Lukan version, in contrast with which the doxology of the Matthean version (not found in the earliest

---

results: see "Das Vaterunser im Horizont antik-jüdischen Betens unter besonderer Berücksichtigung der Textfunde vom Toten Meer," in *Das Vaterunser in seinen antiken Kontexten: Zum Gedenken an Eduard Lohse*, ed. Florian Wilk, FRLANT 266 (Göttingen: Vandenhoeck & Ruprecht, 2016), 1–24.

[75] The root *nsy* ("tempt, test, put to the text, examine") is well documented in the Hebrew texts from Qumran, and its absence from the Aramaic Qumran materials is simply accidental.

[76] These texts were not composed in a homogeneous Aramaic and are, in part, copies of much older texts in Imperial Aramaic; nonetheless they show common characteristics and are representative of the later stages of the Imperial Aramaic phase. Developments in dialectic are initially found in later texts, such as 11QTgJob (1st c. BCE) und 1QapGen ar (1st c. BCE). Additionally, the consonantal text of Targum Onqelos belongs to this stratum, as well as the core elements of the Palestinian Targumim.

[77] Karl Georg Kuhn, *Achtzehngebet und Vaterunser und der Reim*, WUNT 1 (Tübingen: Mohr, 1950), 80.

[78] For specific details, see Schattner-Rieser, "Das Aramäische zur Zeit Jesu," 132.

[79] See b. Ber. 12a and 46a; see also Heinemann, "Once again Melekh ha 'Olam."

[80] See b. Ber. 40b. The Matthean expansions, "Your will be done" and "as in heaven, so on earth," align the Lord's Prayer with a virtually standardized model for private prayers in rabbinic Judaism. See Heinemann, *Prayer in the Talmud*, 157, 161, 180.

[81] Chazon, "Looking Back," 162, 166.

witnesses to Matthew) presents a closing framework that corresponds to rabbinic liturgical practice.[82] That the prayer does not conclude with a doxology may be explained by its early non-liturgical use. The doxology could only be added after the personal prayer of Jesus had come to be used in a liturgical setting.

c) In terms of content, there is a remarkably strong affinity between the formulae of the Lord's Prayer and the Targumic formulae that reference the story of the Exodus (Exodus 15–17, especially Exod 16:4–5) as well as other passages that look back on the Exodus (e. g. Isaiah 63; Psalm 89; 1 Chronicles 29). References to the Exodus in the Lord's Prayer are strikingly obvious from the middle part on, especially in the petition for bread, as well as in the petition concerning testing.

d) Concerning the original form of the Lord's Prayer, one should probably differentiate between two versions, first, the personal prayer which Jesus himself recited, and second, the one which he taught his followers. This might explain why there are two forms of address in the Matthean and Lukan versions of the Prayer: Jesus himself would have addressed God as his Father, "Abba," while his followers would have addressed God as "our Father," while describing God as being "in heaven" was a very common, and ancient, addition to Semitic epithets. The expression "Father in heaven" is also a common phrase in rabbinic literature after 70 CE. It is worth noting, therefore, that there is nothing specifically Christian or Messianic in the wording of the Lord's Prayer: all the expressions and phrases which characterize the prayer can all be individually found verbatim in the Targumic texts. This indicates that the Prayer corresponds to a larger Jewish tradition in which the biblical materials were known (and recited) by heart. Every formulaic expression has significant connections to contemporary interpretations and ideas, such as the messianic expectation of salvation and hope of divine assistance during a time in which the Jewish population lived under Roman oppression. One difference from the Targumic prayer formulations consists in the use of emphatic personal pronouns, which are not required here but which are quite pronounced (as in "give us *our* bread," "deliver us from *our* sin").

e) The various retroversions into Aramaic are identical in the You-petitions, except for the feminine jussive form *tᵓty* ("it [shall] come!"). My own retranslation differs from the older suggestions in the We-petitions, and resembles that of Pierre Grelot.[83] Like Grelot, I am convinced that the enigmatic ἐπιούσιος echoes the idiom *ptgm*[84] or *skwm ywm bywmh*[85] from Exodus 16:4. While he trans-

---

[82] This observation concerns a matter for further investigation. In the personal and daily Hebrew prayers from Qumran, both types of prayers can be observed (with an introductory or concluding formula) and anticipates the standardised Rabbinic traditional model: see Chazon, "Looking Back," 170–71.

[83] Grelot, "L'arrière-plan araméen," 546; idem, "La quatrième demande," 306.

[84] In this well-documented figure of speech, *ptgm* traditionally stands for the Hebrew *dbr*. Other than its basic meaning "word," it also describes the semantic Hebrew scope, namely:

lated ἐπιούσιος with *sᵉkôm* (amount, ratio), following the Neofiti variant (Tg. Neof. Exod 16:4), without excluding *pitgām*, I prefer *pitgām* (found in Targum Onqelos), because *skwm*, in contrast to *ptgm*, is not attested in Qumran, and is found only in the later Aramaic of Targum Neofiti. The translation of the sins-forgiveness petition in the retroversions is identical, except for the particle "as." My choice for *kmh dy* is first based on the comparative usage in the Aramaic of Qumran, and the identical structure in Tg. Onq. Num 14:19 *(kmh dšbqtʾ lʿmʾ)*.[86] Finally, following parallel Targumic usage, I formulate the sixth petition differently, because there is no evidence in the Jewish Rabbinic literature or the texts found in Qumran of the idea of being "led into temptation" expressed using a verb of action (like *ʿll*). Instead, one uses a common Semitic construction in which the verb and its internal object are formed from the same root.

The retroversion undertaken here and in my earlier study is a Palestinian-Aramaic version which can possibly be said to be close to the original oral form (*Urform*), but which we obviously cannot claim to be a precise representation of the original itself. Each and every such retroversion must remain hypothetical, and as long as we do not have the Aramaic original text, the Greek forms of the Prayer must remain essential. However, the retranslation is able to explain somewhat the differences between the Matthean and Lukan versions, without resolving every issue. The influence of the Old Testament on the New Testament is mediated mainly through its Greek version, the Septuagint. The Septuagint, with its Semitic substratum, whether it was Hebrew or Aramaic, "a fourni aux chrétiens des citations, prises en association avec celles du Nouveau Testament, comme fondement de leurs doctrines, pour l'expression de leur piété, pour les formes de leur piété." And we should not ignore, that "la Septante doit-elle être considérée comme une préparation à l'évangile."[87] The Septuagint is at the foundation of the "religious and cultural milieu" in which the New Testament and Early Church took shape and prospered; therefore, "New Testament Greek can be best analysed, interpreted, and understood when one is intimately familiar with [Septuagint Greek]."[88] One final remark: one should bear in mind that the biblical books were translated into Greek in Egypt to meet the needs of the Jewish community, which had adopted Aramaic as a spoken language from the fifth century BCE, before it began speaking Greek.[89]

"matter/thing, issue/affair/concern, ratio" and *ywm-bywmh* or *ywm bywmʾ* describes something which repeats itself, something mundane, meaning: "a thing, each on its said day/appointed day."

[85] Literally: "each thing/substance, on its (given) day (or daily)."

[86] Targum Neofiti and Targum Pseudo-Jonathan have, instead of *kmh d-*, the composite particle *hykmh d-*. In Qumranic Aramaic, *ʾyk*, "as," is found a few times, but not in the comparative construction *ʾyk kmhdy*, which corresponds to the targumic *hykmh d-*.

[87] Marguerite Harl, *La langue de Japhet: Qunize études sur la Septante et le grec des chrétiens* (Paris: Cerf, 1994), 268–69.

[88] Takamitsu Muraoka, *A Syntax of Septuagint Greek* (Leuven: Peeters, 2016), xli.

[89] Jan Joosten, "On Aramaising Renderings in the Septuagint," in *Hamlet on a Hill: Semitic*

I cannot make any statement on the question of the Q Source as a whole, but where Jesus' Prayer is concerned, the differences between the two versions can be resolved with reference to a common origin, in the oral phase of the tradition, with the additions in Matthew being representative of Jewish thought in Jesus' time.

The result of the philological examination presented in this paper provides at least an idea of a possible original form of the Lord's Prayer and, as Pierre Grelot put it, "une idée rapprochante vaut mieux que rien."[90]

Appendices

1. The Disciples' Proto-Prayer[91]

אבא/אבונה [די בשמיא]	Father/Our Father [who is in the heavens]
יתקדש שמך	your name be made holy/holy is your name
תאתי מלכותך	your kingdom come;
[תתעבד רעותך בשמיא ובארעא]	[your will be done, on earth as in heaven.]
הב לנא לחמנא פתגם יום ביומא	Give us our daily bread;
ושבוק לחובינא	and forgive us our debts,
כמא די שבקנא לחיבינא	as we also have forgiven those indebted to us;
ואל תנסינא בנסיונא	do not test us with testing,
[אלא פצינא מן באישא]	[but deliver us from evil].

2. The Lord's Prayer Reconstructed according to Parallels from the Aramaic Texts of Qumran and from the Targumim[92]

	Aramaic Text	Aramaic Parallel	Parallel in Context
3.1	אַבָּא/ אֲבוּנָא	Father! (Tg. Ps 89:27); Our Father![93] (Tg. Ps.-J. Jer 2:27);	You are my Father (ʾabbâ ʾat), my God and the rock of my salvation! (Tg. Ps 89:27); Our Father! (ʾaḇûnâ!) (Tg. Ps.-J. Jer 2:27)

---

and Greek Studies Presented to Professor T. Muraoka on the Occasion of his Sixty-Fifth Birthday, ed. M. F. J. Baasten and W. Th. van Peursen, OLA 118 (Leuven: Peeters, 2003), 587–600; idem, "The Septuagint as a Source of Information on Egyptian Aramaic in the Hellenistic Period," in Aramaic in its Historical and Linguistic Setting, ed. Holger Gzella and Margaretha L. Folmer, VOK 50 (Wiesbaden: Harrassowitz, 2008), 93–105; idem, "The Aramaic Background of the Seventy: Language, Culture and History," BIOSCS 43 (2010): 53–72; idem, "Des Targoumismes dans la Septante?," in The Targums in the Light of Traditions of the Second Temple Period, ed. Jan Joosten and Thierry Legrand, JSJ.S 167, (Leiden: Brill, 2014), 54–71.

[90] Grelot, "L'arrière-plan araméen," 554.

[91] Elements unique to Matthew are placed in square brackets.

[92] Note: this table does not represent a retroversion from the Greek text of the Gospels, but only collects together parallels mentioned earlier in this essay. The numbers in the first column indicate the section in which the petition is discussed, in Part E of the essay above.

[93] The threefold address "our Father" is from Isa 63:16; 64:7 MT.

	Aramaic Text	Aramaic Parallel	Parallel in Context
	אֲבוּנָא דִּי בִשְׁמַיָּא	Our Father in heaven (Tg. Esth. II 1:2); Lord of heaven[94] (1QapGen ar XI, 12–13; XII, 17)	We praise the God of heaven, who gives us bread and water[95] (Tg. Esth. II 3:8); And I praised the Lord of heaven (1QapGen ar XI, 12–13)[96]
3.2	יִתְקַדַּשׁ שְׁמִי	May my name be hallowed / Prove my name holy / My name will be holy[97] (Tg. Lev 22:32)	And he sanctified his name (wqdš šmh) (Tg. Neof. Num 20:13); Do not defile my holy name (šᵉmî qaddîšâ), that I may prove myself holy [or: that I may be sanctified] (ויתקדש שמי = wᵉyitqaddaš šᵉmî) among the Israelites; I the Lord am he who sanctifies you! (Tg. Lev 22:32)
	בְּרִיךְ שְׁמָךְ קַדִּישָׁא	Praised be your holy name! (Tob 3:11)	Your holy name be praised! (bᵉrîk šᵉmāk qaddîšâ) (4Q196 [papTobᵃ ar] 6, 7 = Tob 3:11); One praises your holy name (4Q196 [papTobᵃ ar] 18, 11 = Tob 13:3)
3.3	עַד דְּיֵיתֵי מְשִׁיחָא דְדִילֵיהּ[98] הִיא מַלְכוּתָא	Until the King Messiah comes, and his kingdom! (Tg. Onq. Gen 49:10)	The scepter will not pass away from Judah, nor the ruler's staff from between his feet, until the King Messiah comes, to whom belongs the kingdom, and whom the peoples will obey (Tg. Onq., Neof. Gen 49:10)
3.4	דִּי יִתְרְעֵי יי עָבֵד בִּשְׁמַיָּא וּבְאַרְעָא	What corresponds to his will happens in heaven as on earth (Tg. Ps 135:6)	Tg. Ps 135:6: Everything that corresponds to the will of the Lord happens in heaven as on earth (kol dî yitrᵉʿê ʿābed bišᵉmayyâ ûbᵉʔarʿâ); We have not fulfilled (lit. done) the will of our Father in heaven (Tg. Esth. II 1:2); see also Tg. Isa. 48:14; Tg. Ps 40:9
	אַלֵּף יָתִי לְמֶעְבַּד רְעוּתָךְ	Teach me to do your will (Tg. Ps 143:10)	Tg. Ps 143:10: Teach me to do your will (ʔallêf yātî lᵉmeʿbad rᵉʿûtāk), for you are my God! Your good spirit leads me to flat land.

---

[94] The expression "Lord of heaven" is common in biblical and epigraphic Jewish texts from the Persian Period. In the Aramaic papyri of the Jewish colony of Elephantine (5th c. BCE), JHW (Jaho) is generally referred to as "JHW, God of Heaven" (אלה שמיא) and "Lord of Heaven" (מרא שמיא).

[95] The passage refers to the Exodus from Egypt, in which God supplied his people with food and drink during the crossing of the desert, thus saving them from hunger and thirst.

[96] The expression "Lord of heaven" is common in biblical and epigraphic Jewish texts from the Persian Period. In the Aramaic papyri of the Jewish colony of Elephantine (5th c. BCE), JHW (Jaho) is generally referred to as "JHW, God of Heaven" (אלה שמיא) and "Lord of Heaven" (מרא שמיא).

[97] In Targum Neofiti one also finds yhwwy qdyš, [he] is holy.

[98] Targum Neofiti has the late form of the possessive particle dyd-: דידיה

	Aramaic Text	Aramaic Parallel	Parallel in Context
3.5	הַב לָנָא לַחְמָא!	Give us bread! (Tg. Onq. Gen 47:15)	And all the Egyptians came to Joseph, saying, Give us bread! *(haḇ lanâ laḥmâ)*, for why should he die before you? For our money is all gone (Tg. Onq. and Tg. Neof. Gen 47:15); We pray to the God of heaven, who gives us bread and water[99] (Tg. Esth. II 3:8)
	לַחְמָא מִן שְׁמַיָּא פִּתְגַם יוֹם בְּיוֹמֵיהּ	(The bread of heaven), the daily necessities (Tg. Exod 16:4)	Thus said the LORD to Moses, Behold I will make it rain for you bread from heaven *(laḥmâ min šᵉmayyâ)*; then the people should go out and gather the daily necessities, every day *(pitgām*[100] *yôm bᵉyômēh)*, so that I can examine [or: test] them, whether they want to live by my law, or not (Tg. Onq., Neof. Exod 16:4, 15, 25)
3.6	וְתִשְׁבּוֹק לְחוֹבֶנָא שְׁבוֹק כְּעַן לְחוֹבֵי עַמָּא הָדֵין	And forgive our sin (Tg. Exod 34:9) Just as you have forgiven this people (Tg. Onq. Num 14:19)	And he said: If I have found favour in your eyes, Lord, so let the Lord go in the midst of us. Although they are a stubborn people, yet forgive our guilt *(wᵉtišbôq lᵉḥôbênâ)* and take possession of us (Tg. Onq. Exod 34:9); (And)[101] forgive now the guilt of this people *(ûšᵉboq lᵉḥôbê ʿammâ hādên)*, in keeping with your great goodness, and as you have forgiven this people from Egypt to here *(kᵉmâ dišᵉbaqtâ lᵉʿammâ hādên mimmiṣrayîm wᵉʿad kᵉʿan)* (Tg. Onq. and Tg. Neof. Num 14:19;[102]); see further Tg. Isa 53:5; Tg. 1 Kings 8:34; Tg. 2 Chron 6:26; Tg. Lev 5:26
3.7	לָא תְנַסּוּן קֳדָם יְיָ כְּמָא־דִי נַסֵּיתוּן בְּנִסֵּיתָא	Do not test the LORD ... as you have (already) put him to the test (Tg. Onq. Deut 6:16)	You shall not put the LORD your God to the test [or: test, examine] *(lâ tᵉnassû)*, as you put him (in Massah) to the test [or in testing] *(kᵉmâ dinᵉsatûn bᵉnisitâ)* (Tg. Deut 6:16); So he called that place, "Testing" [MT: Massah and Meribah], because the Israelites quarreled there, and tested the LORD, and said: Is the Shekinah [presence] of God among us or not? (Tg. Exod 17:7); see also Tg. Ps 66:10

---

[99] See footnote 2 and the memory of the escape from Egypt and the Exodus.
[100] Instead of *pitgām*, which here is equivalent to "need, matter, thing," Tg. Neof. has *sᵉkôm*, "ration, lot" + *yôm bᵉyômēh*, everyday > literally "each to its day."
[101] The conjunction "and" is found in Targum Neofiti, but not in Targum Onqelos.
[102] Moses intervened on behalf of the rebellious, lamenting people at Kadesh.

	Aramaic Text	Aramaic Parallel	Parallel in Context
3.8	פְּצִי יָתִי	Rescue me! (Tg. Ps 119[118]:153)	See my misery and rescue (*pᵉṣî yātî*), for I have not forgotten your instruction! (Tg. Ps 119:153); In distress you called, and I rescued you (*pᵉṣît yātāk*)! (Tg. Ps 81:8)
	שֵׁיזִיבְנָא מִיַד בַעֲלֵי דְבָבְנָא	Deliver us out of the hand of our enemies! (Tg. 1 Sam 12:10)	And I rescue/deliver you from the hand of the wicked (*waʾašêzḇinnāḵ miy-yad maḇʾašîn*), and rescue you from the clutches of those who do violence (Tg. Jer 15:21); Deliver me now from the hand of my brother! (Tg. Gen 32:12). We have sinned .... Only, deliver us this day! (Tg. Judg 10:15)

The Promise of Providence and the Problem of the *Parables*

Revisiting Prayer in the Sayings Gospel Q[1]

Simon J. Joseph

A. The Promise of Providence: Prayer in Q

Since the 1960s, the composition of Q has widely been identified with instructional wisdom.[2] The author of Q drew from the literary conventions, style, rhetoric, and content of Jewish wisdom literature.[3] In this paper, I wish to re-examine Q's prayer-texts within the context of early Jewish texts, particularly the Enochic *Book of Parables*. I presuppose here that Q is a "textual" product of Palestinian Judaism,[4]

---

[1] I would like to thank Christoph Heil and Daniel A. Smith for the invitation to present this paper at the Q-Conference 2017 on "Prayer in the Sayings Gospel Q" in Graz, Austria on March 23, 2017. I would also like to thank John S. Kloppenborg, Joseph Verheyden, Ursula Schattner-Rieser, and Giovanni Bazzana for their helpful comments and suggestions on this paper.

[2] James M. Robinson, "ΛΟΓΟΙ ΣΟΦΩΝ: Zur Gattung der Spruchquelle Q," in *Zeit und Geschichte: Dankesgabe an Rudolf Bultmann zum 80. Geburtstag*, ed. Erich Dinkler (Tübingen: Mohr Siebeck, 1964), 77–96; ET: "ΛΟΓΟΙ ΣΟΦΩΝ: On the *Gattung* of Q," in idem, *The Sayings Gospel Q: Collected Essays*, ed. Christoph Heil and Joseph Verheyden, BETL 189 (Leuven: Peeters, 2005), 37–74; cf. John S. Kloppenborg, *The Formation of Q: Trajectories in Ancient Christian Wisdom Collections* (Philadelphia: Fortress, 1987).

[3] Dieter Zeller, *Die weisheitlichen Mahnsprüche bei den Synoptikern*, FB 17 (Würzburg: Echter, 1977), 191; Ronald A. Piper, *Wisdom in the Q-Tradition: The Aphoristic Teaching of Jesus*, SNTSMS 61 (Cambridge: Cambridge University Press, 1989); Patrick J. Hartin, "The Wisdom and Apocalyptic Layers of the Sayings Gospel Q: What is their Significance?," *HvTSt* 50 (1994): 556–82. Cf. William E. Arnal, "The Trouble with Q," *Foundations and Facets Forum*, 3rd series 2.1 (2013): 7–77, here 24.

[4] John S. Kloppenborg, *Excavating Q: The History and Setting of the Sayings Gospel* (Minneapolis: Fortress, 2000), 256; William E. Arnal, "The Q Document," in *Jewish Christianity Reconsidered: Rethinking Ancient Groups and Texts*, ed. Matt Jackson-McCabe (Minneapolis: Fortress, 2007), 119–54, here 129; Markus Cromhout, *Jesus and Identity: Reconstructing Judean Ethnicity in Q*, Matrix: The Bible in Mediterranean Context (Eugene, OR: Cascade, 2007), 260; Christopher M. Tuckett, "Q and the 'Church': The Role of the Christian Community within Judaism according to Q," in idem, *From the Sayings to the Gospels*, WUNT 328 (Tübingen: Mohr Siebeck, 2014), 219–31; Markus Tiwald, ed., *Q in Context I: The Separation between the Just and the Unjust in Early Judaism and in the Sayings Source*, BBB 172 (Göttingen: V&R Unipress; Bonn University Press, 2015).

a literary work centered on the figure of "Jesus," who came to be featured in prayer-practices as both exemplar for and as recipient of prayer.[5]

In the Hebrew Bible, "prayer" (תפילה) includes a variety of forms such as petition, praise, confession, and thanksgiving.[6] Prayers are typically spontaneous, circumstantial, and occasional,[7] reflecting what seems to be pre-"scripturalized" or pre-"institutionalized" modes of prayer.[8] In Early Judaism, prayer can be defined as "any form of human communication directed at God."[9]

There are only two *explicit* uses of the word "pray" (προσεύχομαι) in Q – Q 6:28 and Q 11:2b–4. Yet Q contains a number of petitionary prayers, exhortations, and other forms of address that reflect Q's understanding and instructions on how to live in relationship to others and God.[10] These texts include Q 11:2b–4,[11]

---

[5] Reidar Hvalvik and Karl Olav Sandnes, eds., *Early Christian Prayer and Identity Formation*, WUNT 336 (Tübingen: Mohr Siebeck, 2014); Albert Gerhards, Andrea Doeker, and Peter Ebenbauer, eds., *Identität durch Gebet: Zur gemeinschaftsbildenden Funktion institutionalisierten Betens in Judentum und Christentum*, Studien zu Judentum und Christentum (Paderborn: Ferdinand Schöningh, 2003).

[6] Emmanuel O. Tukasi, *Determinism and Petitionary Prayer in John and the Dead Sea Scrolls: An Ideological Reading of John and the Rule of the Community (1QS)*, LSTS 66 (London: T & T Clark International, 2008), 19.

[7] Tukasi, *Determinism and Petitionary Prayer*, 23.

[8] Judith H. Newman, *Praying by the Book: The Scripturalization of Prayer in Second Temple Judaism*, EJL 14 (Atlanta: Scholars, 1999); Shemaryahu Talmon, "The Emergence of Institutionalized Prayer in Israel in Light of Qumran Literature," in idem, *The World of Qumran from Within* (Jerusalem: Magnes; Leiden: Brill, 1989), 200–43, here 201, refers to this as progressive "institutionalization."

[9] Esther Chazon, "Prayers from Qumran and Their Historical Implications," *DSD* 1 (1994): 265–84, here 266. See also Newman, *Praying by the Book*, 6–7: "address to God that is initiated by humans."

[10] Arland D. Jacobson, *The First Gospel: An Introduction to Q* (Sonoma, CA: Polebridge, 1992), 257.

[11] On the Lord's Prayer (Matt 6:9b–13 // Luke 11:2b–4) as focusing on daily existence in the present world, see David R. Catchpole, *The Quest for Q* (Edinburgh: T & T Clark, 1993), 224; John S. Kloppenborg, "Discursive Practices in the Sayings Gospel Q and the Historical Jesus," in *The Sayings Source Q and the Historical Jesus*, ed. Andreas Lindemann, BETL 158 (Leuven: Peeters, 2001), 149–90, here 176; Piper, *Wisdom in the Q-Tradition*, 20, 23–24; Dale C. Allison Jr., *The Jesus Tradition in Q* (Valley Forge, PA: Trinity Press International, 1997), 13–15; Alan Kirk, *The Composition of the Sayings Source: Genre, Synchrony, and Wisdom Redaction in Q*, NovTSup 91 (Leiden: Brill, 1998), 177–80. See also Olli Hallikainen, "The Lord's Prayer in the Sayings Gospel Q," (PhD diss., University of Helsinki, 2005). On the Lord's Prayer as *futuristic*, see Johannes Weiss, *Die Predigt Jesu vom Reiche Gottes* (Göttingen: Vandenhoeck & Ruprecht, 1892); Ernst Lohmeyer, *The Lord's Prayer* (London: Collins, 1965); Joachim Jeremias, *The Lord's Prayer* (Philadelphia: Fortress, 1964); Raymond E. Brown, "The Pater Noster as an Eschatological Prayer," in idem, *New Testament Essays* (Garden City: Doubleday, 1968), 275–320; John P. Meier, *A Marginal Jew: Rethinking the Historical Jesus*, vol. 2: *Mentor, Message, and Miracles*, ABRL (New York: Doubleday, 1994), 291–302; W. D. Davies and Dale C. Allison, *Matthew 1–7*, ICC (Edinburgh: T & T Clark, 1998), 594–95.

Q 11:9–13,[12] Q 12:22b–31,[13] and Q 6:27–35.[14] These four passages share distinctive features and a common theme, argumentation, tone, and audience: they are addressed to disciples; they are instructional; they appeal to natural observations and a metaphorical Father/Son relationship.

Here God is envisioned as a caring Father who can be appealed to for worldly needs.[15] A petitionary supplication envisions God as the Sovereign who truly takes care of the hungry, the poor, and the oppressed, unlike the Herodian and Roman overlords who starve, enslave, tax, and oppress.[16] Q's kingdom discourse is thus semantically related to the reigns of Hellenistic rulers as a political statement and reflects material interests in bread and debt.[17] The promise of prov-

---

[12] Q 11:9–13 also refers to daily existence. See Piper, *Wisdom in the Q-Tradition*, 20, 23–4; Allison, *The Jesus Tradition in Q*, 13–15; Catchpole, *The Quest for Q*, 201–23; Kirk, *The Composition of the Sayings Source*, 177–80; Kloppenborg, "Discursive Practices," 177–78. Piper, *Wisdom in the Q-Tradition*, 19, refers to Q 11:13 as "the first direct reference in the compilation to God and therefore also the first clear reference to 'asking' in terms of petitionary prayer." See also Paul Sevier Minear, "'Ask, Seek, Knock'," in idem, *Commands of Christ: Authority and Implications* (Nashville: Abingdon, 1972), 113–31; Dale Goldsmith, "'Ask, and It Will Be Given …': Toward Writing the History of a Logion," *NTS* 35 (1989): 254–65.

[13] Cf. Simon J. Joseph, "'Seek His Kingdom': Q 12,22b–31, God's Providence, and Adamic Wisdom," *Biblica* 92 (2011): 392–410.

[14] Q 10:21–22 is distinctive in so far as it is *Jesus*' Thanksgiving prayer to the Father (ὁ Πατήρ). Q 10:21 has been likened to a *Hodayot* (הודיות) "formula" as found in the Qumran writings. See James M. Robinson, "The *Hodayot* Formula in Prayers and Hymns of Early Christianity," in idem, *The Sayings Gospel Q*, 75–118. Olegs Andrejevs, "Q 10:21–22 and Formative Christology," (Ph.D. diss., Loyola University Chicago, 2013), locates Q 10:21–22 in the third "edition" of Q (Q³).

[15] On God as "our Father" (Πάτερ ἡμῶν), see also Isa 63:16; 64:8; Tob 13:4; cf. the Eighteen Benedictions; m. Soṭah 9:15; m. Yoma 8:9. Kloppenborg, "Discursive Practices," 177, draws attention to the second "we petition" (Q 11:4), which seems "to reflect the view, attested at Qumran, that a sabbatical or jubilee debt release, leads to a release from sins" (cf. 11Q13 II, 1–6 [11QMelch]). Both Q and Qumran "presuppose a sense of eschatological expectation, [but] the point of both is to promote a social practice in the present, which is buttressed by the assurance of sin forgiveness" (ibid.).

[16] Giovanni Bazzana, *Kingdom of Bureaucracy: The Political Theology of Village Scribes in the Sayings Gospel Q*, BETL 274 (Leuven: Peeters, 2015), 317, suggests that the Galilean Jesus movement was an intellectual-ideological response to the political and economic pressures of Roman/Herodian rule.

[17] Marco Frenschkowski, "Welche Biographischen Kenntnisse von Jesus setzt die Logienquelle voraus? Beobachtungen zur Gattung von Q in Kontext Antiker Spruchsammlungen," in *From Quest to Q: Festschrift James M. Robinson*, ed. Jon Ma Asgeirsson, Kristin De Troyer and Marvin W. Meyer, BETL 146 (Leuven: Peeters, 2000), 3–42, here 34 n. 90, suggests that the Lord's Prayer "ist nicht einfach ein austauschbares exemplarisches Gebet, sondern gehört zu einen spezifischen sozialgeschichtlichen Prozess." Markus Tiwald, "The Brazen Freedom of God's Children: 'Insolent Ravens' (Q 12:24) and 'Carefree Lilies' (Q 12:27) as Response to Mass-Poverty and Social Disruption," in *Q in Context II: Social Setting and Archeological Background of the Sayings Source*, ed. Markus Tiwald, BBB 173 (Göttingen: V&R Unipress; Bonn University Press, 2015), 111–32, here 130: "The forthcoming reign of God … will create a counter-reality by restoring the prelapsarian world that God created in the beginning."

idence seems to be a central theme in this instructional material. The optimism of these maxims is indeed "remarkable."[18]

These prayers directed to the Father are concerned with physical, everyday needs like bread and debt, but it is the affirmation that these prayers are effective that is truly remarkable.[19] In everyday experience, worldly wisdom tells us that everything we ask for is not given; our needs are not always met; and God does not always seem to care for us.[20] God's providence is a theme present in the biblical tradition (Gen 3:29; Ps 104:14, 145:15–19, Ps Sol 5:10), but what seems distinctive about Q is its confidence in assuring that God *will* answer prayer.[21]

In Q 12:22–31, Jesus' assurance that God will provide seems to contradict worldly experience where human beings generally earn a living by the "sweat of their brow."[22] Nonetheless, Jesus promises that "All these things will be given to you" (ταῦτα προστεθήσεται ὑμῖν). The message seems to be that "'God will provide' without human labor."[23] Q contrasts trust in God with the ways of the "nations," which worry about their needs, and insists that the necessities of life "come to us as God's gift" when the kingdom is a "constant consideration."[24] God loves his sons and daughters and will provide for them, provided that they *seek* – that is, actively strive[25] – to have God "reign" over their lives, and have total trust he will do so. The present imperative ζητεῖτε ("seek") further indicates that the "kingdom" is accessible in the present (otherwise we could not *seek* it).[26] This seems to be an eschatological reversal of worldly fortunes. After all, one of the consequences of sin in Genesis is that humanity must *earn* its daily food through labor. Q's vision of God's providence stands in tension with such ideas, not to mention more "worldly" advice about the necessities of earning a living.[27]

---

[18] Piper, *Wisdom in the Q-Tradition*, 17, referring to Q 11:10. Arnal, "The Trouble with Q," 42, refers to the "serene confidence" of Q 11:9–10 and 12:22–31, and "the self-assured petition for daily bread in 11:3."

[19] Cf. Kloppenborg, *Formation of Q*, 241, who recognizes that a different situation is presumed in a saying like Q 11:10 that takes it beyond "worldly wisdom."

[20] Christopher M. Tuckett, *Q and the History of Early Christianity: Studies on Q* (Edinburgh: T&T Clark, 1996), 154–55, for example, posits a *futuristic* fulfillment being envisioned: "their prayer will be answered. ... Such vocabulary can be understood eschatologically .... The 'good things' ... are the gifts of the Eschaton."

[21] The same is also the case with Matthew's community. See John Riches, "Matthew's World," in *The Synoptic Gospels*, ed. John Riches, William R. Telford, and Christopher M. Tuckett, NTG (Sheffield: Sheffield Academic Press, 2001), 74–108, here 94.

[22] Piper, *Wisdom in the Q-Tradition*, 35.

[23] Claude G. Montefiore, *The Synoptic Gospels: Edited with an Introduction and a Commentary*, 2 vols. (London: Macmillan, 1927), 111–12.

[24] John Nolland, *Luke 9:21–18:34*, WBC 35B (Dallas: Word, 1993), 695–96.

[25] Heinrich Greeven, "ζητέω," *TDNT* 2:892–94, here 893 n. 5.

[26] Kloppenborg, "Discursive Practices," 178.

[27] David L. Mealand, "'Paradisial' Elements in the Teaching of Jesus," in *Studia Biblica II*, ed. Elizabeth A. Livingstone, JSNTSup 2 (Sheffield: JSOT Press, 1980), 179–84, suggests that there are "Paradisial" elements in Q 12:22b–31, noting that it is "not unreasonable to see a con-

The second appearance of the word "pray" (προσεύχομαι) occurs in Q 6:27–28. Disciples are to "love" their enemies and "pray" for those persecuting them. Both Q 11:2a and Q 6:27–28, 35b contain an admonition to pray (προσεύχομαι); both refer to the "Father" (Πατήρ) (6:35b; 11:2b); and both contain references to "son" (υἱός) (6:35b; 11:11). In Q 6:28, 35b, the argument – that God is impartially loving, as observable in Nature – is similar to that in Q 11:2–4, 9–13.

Jesus' instruction to "love enemies" is based on God's unconditional love.[28] The Inaugural Sermon contains a number of sayings indicating that God is non-judgmental, merciful, unconditionally loving, and forgiving.[29] I am not aware of any extant parallel within pre-Christian Judaism that advocates *love* of enemies (*Feindesliebe*) based on the imitation of God *(imitatio dei)*.[30] There are examples of first-century Jewish nonviolent resistance to systemic violence mentioned by Josephus (*B. J.* 2.174; 2.197), but strategic defiance of the threat of imminent violence is still quite capable of harboring resentment and hatred. Philo refers to *helping* the enemy (*QE* 2.11), but Philo often Platonizes his subjects.

The *War Scroll* (1QM) and the *Rule of the Community* (1/4QS) combine hatred of enemies with the expectation of judgment and seem to be plotting a kind of strategic temporary nonviolence.[31] The *Yahad* could affirm the idea of not exacting vengeance on the enemy for now, but only because God would do so in the future (1QS X, 17–21).[32] The Book of Proverbs advises feeding the enemy if he is hungry or giving him a drink of water if he is thirsty, but the *motivation* – "for so

---

nection between the expectation of the Reign of God and that of a return to the condition of Paradise." Since "the need to worry about clothing, and the need to work for food came after the Fall" in Genesis, Jesus "seems to disregard the emphasis on the fall," and demonstrates "a simple dependence on God characteristic of Paradisial conditions" (ibid., 179, 182).

[28] Q 6:27–28, 35c–d.

[29] Q 6:20; 6:27, 28, 35c–d; Q 6:31; Q 6:32–34; Q 6:36; Q 6:37–39; Q 7:22; Q 14:16–18, 21, 23; Q 15:4–5a, 7; Q 15:8–10; Q 17:3–4.

[30] Martin Ebner, "Feindeslieb – ein Ratschlag zum Überleben? Sozial- und religionsgeschichtliche Überlegungen zu Mt 5,38–47/Lk 6,27–35," in Asgeirsson, De Troyer, and Meyer, *From Quest to Q*, 119–42, sees the tradition as responses to "Gewaltsame Übergriffe auf menschliches Leben" ("violent attacks on human life"), "Machtdemonstration" ("demonstration of power"), and "öffentliche *Beleidigung*," ("public insults") (here, 141; emphasis original) located in Jesus' ministry and his follower's subsequent efforts, which were perceived as rejection. Cf. Paul Hoffmann, "Tradition und Situation: Zur 'Verbindlichkeit' des Gebots der Feindesliebe in der synoptischen Überlieferung und in der gegenwärtigen Friedensdiskussion," in idem, *Tradition und Situation: Studien zur Jesusüberlieferung in der Logienquelle und den synoptischen Evangelien*, NTAbh 28 (Münster: Aschendorff, 1995), 3–61. Hoffmann proposes that Q 6:27–28 began locally and subsequently developed into an anti-imperial political orientation.

[31] Alex P. Jassen, "The Dead Sea Scrolls and Violence: Sectarian Formation and Eschatological Imagination," *BibInt* 17 (2009): 12–44; Raija Sollama, "War and Violence in the Ideology of the Qumran Community," in *Verbum et Calamus: Semitic and Related Studies in Honour of the Sixtieth Birthday of Professor Tapani Harviainen*, ed. Hannu Juusola, Juha Laulainen, and Heikki Palva, StOr 99 (Helsinki: Finnish Oriental Society, 2004), 341–52.

[32] 1QS X, 17–21; 1QS I, 10. Cf. Josephus, *B. J.* 2.135; 2.139–140. On the Essenes during the Jewish Revolt, see *B. J.* 2.152–153; *B. J.* 2.567.

you will heap live coals on his head and the Lord will reward you" – simply seems to be another way of saying "'Vengeance is mine,' saith the Lord," and does not resemble the *ethical* imperative based on imitating God's unconditional love that we find in Q 6:27–35.³³

B. Does Prayer Make A Difference?

The Jesus of Q seems to represent a distinctive voice within early Judaism by instructing enemy-love as *imitatio dei*. This imperative seems to have had pride of place in the early composition of Q.³⁴ It also seems to have had quite a successful after-life in early Christian writings (if not practice).³⁵ It is reasonable to posit the historical Jesus as the expositor of this instruction. Not only is the general *ethos* of the Inaugural Sermon "characterized by nonviolence,"³⁶ but Jesus'

---

³³ Prov 25:21–22; cf. Rom 12:20.

³⁴ Walter Bauer, "Das Gebot der Feindesliebe und die alten Christen," ZTK 27 (1917): 37–54, here 39: "Da war sie nicht als eine Tugend neben anderen erschienen, sondern als das Höchste, was man überhaupt von einem Menschen erwarten kann, als etwas, was die Jünger Jesu hoch hinaushebt über die Sphäre des allgemein Menschlichen und sie Gott selber gleich macht (Mt. 5:45–48 = Luk. 6:32–36). Demgemäß hatte in der Urgestalt der Bergpredigt die Forderung der Feindesliebe die beherrschende Stellung eingenommen und war nach dem Auftakt der Seligpreisungen an die Spitze der ganzen Ermahnungsreihe getreten."

³⁵ See, in the present volume, Karl-Heinrich Ostmeyer, "Beten für und gegen Feinde," 89–101, here 89: "Jesu Aufforderung zur Feindesliebe (Q 6,27) ist Kernthema seiner Ethik und gilt nicht selten als das Spezifikum der christlichen Botschaft." Ostmeyer identifies several instances of *prayer for* (but not *love of*) enemies in Early Judaism (e. g., 2 Kgs 6:18; 2 Macc 3:18–22; 1Q20 XX, 12–16). For Ostmeyer, Q 6:28 represents *"einen* wichtigen und wirkmächtigen Abschnitt dieses Traditionsstroms" (ibid., 101). For studies, see John Piper, *"Love Your Enemies": Jesus' Love Command in the Synoptic Gospels and in the Early Paraenesis. A History of the Tradition and Interpretation of Its Uses*, SNTSMS 38 (Cambridge: Cambridge University Press, 1979); William Klassen, "'Love Your Enemies': Some Reflections on the Current Status of Research," in *The Love of Enemy and Nonretaliation*, ed. Willard M. Swartley, Studies in Peace and Scripture (Louisville, KY: Westminster John Knox, 1992), 1–31; idem, "Love Your Enemy: A Study of New Testament Teaching on Coping with an Enemy," *MQR* 37 (1963): 147–71; idem, "Coals of Fire: Sign of Repentance or Revenge?" *NTS* 9 (1963): 337–50; idem, *Love of Enemies: The Way to Peace*, OBT 15 (Philadelphia: Fortress, 1984); R. Conrad Douglas, "'Love Your Enemies': Rhetoric, Tradents, and Ethos," in *Conflict and Invention: Literary, Rhetorical and Social Studies on the Sayings Gospel Q*, ed. John S. Kloppenborg (Valley Forge: Trinity, 2004), 116–31; Ronald A. Piper, "The Language of Violence and the Aphoristic Sayings in Q," in Kloppenborg, *Conflict and Invention*, 53–72. As authentic, see Jürgen Becker, "Feindesliebe-Nächstenliebe-Bruderliebe: Exegetische Beobachtungen als Anfrage an ein ethisches Problemfeld," *ZEE* 25 (1981): 5–18; Heinz-Wolfgang Kuhn, "Das Liebesgebot Jesus als Tora und als Evangelium: Zur Feindesliebe und zur christlichen und jüdischen Auslegung der Bergpredigt," in *Vom Urchristentum zu Jesus: Für Joachim Gnilka*, ed. Hubert Frankemölle and Karl Kertelge (Freiburg: Herder, 1989), 194–230; Otto J. F. Seitz, "Love Your Enemies: The Historical Setting of Matthew V. 43 f.; Luke VI. 27 f.," *NTS* 16 (1970): 39–54; W. C. van Unnik, "Die Motivierung der Feindesliebe in Lukas 6:32–35," *NovT* 8 (1966): 284–300; Dieter Lührmann, "Liebet eure Feinde (Lk 6,27–36/Mt 5,39–48)," *ZTK* 69 (1972): 412–38.

³⁶ John S. Kloppenborg, "The Function of Apocalyptic Language in Q," in *Society of Biblical*

biographers "remembered" and re-interpreted him as a Teacher who eschewed violence.[37] The Matthean Jesus, for example, calls his disciples to be "peacemakers" (εἰρηνοποιοί) (Matt 5:9; cf. Matt 5:38–48 par. Luke 6:27–32).[38] To be sure, the Jesus of Q is not to be confused with the historical Jesus.[39] Q is a distinctive literary composition in its own right. Yet the composition of Q also represents a nexus within which pre-Christian Judaism, the historical Jesus, and early literary conceptualization(s) of "Jesus" intersect.[40] Some continuities between Q and Jesus, therefore, can indeed be affirmed,[41] even if these may only be vestiges of Jesus. In any case, the Jesus of Q advocates the performance of prayer, instructs disciples on properly addressing the Father, provides instruction on the proper attitude to adopt, and assures them that their prayers will be answered.[42] Q's prayer texts appeal to a loving Father of impartial benevolence.

It is noteworthy that so much of Q's instructional material is oriented towards prayer and expresses such confidence in prayers being answered by a loving Father. This would seem to be the earliest recoverable theology or conceptualization of deity in Q. Yet this conceptualization of deity is not the only way that deity is conceived of in Q. After all, Q begins with sayings describing how the chaff will be thrown into the fire.[43] This apparent conceptual and thematic

---

Literature 1986 Seminar Papers (Atlanta: Scholars, 1986), 224–35, here 235; cf. idem, "Symbolic Eschatology and the Apocalypticism of Q," *HTR* 80 (1987): 287–306.

[37] John S. Kloppenborg, "Sources, Methods, and Discursive Locations in the Quest of the Historical Jesus," in *Handbook for the Study of the Historical Jesus*, ed. Tom Holmén and Stanley E. Porter, 4 vols. (Leiden: Brill, 2011), 1:241–90, here 1:259. Kloppenborg also suggests attending to "the rhetorical inscriptions of sayings and stories in later documents ... and which uses these inscriptions as an index of earlier, perhaps dominical usage" (ibid., 262).

[38] Lührmann, "Liebet eure Feinde."

[39] John S. Kloppenborg, "The Sayings Gospel Q and the Quest of the Historical Jesus," *HTR* 89 (1996): 307–44.

[40] Per Bilde, *The Originality of Jesus: A Critical Discussion and a Comparative Attempt*, Studia Aarhusiana Neotestamentica 1 (Göttingen: Vandenhoeck & Ruprecht, 2013), 104, denies that Jesus' teaching is "unique" or "original" in "an absolute sense" (105), but admits that the Gospels present this imperative as "close to unique" (107). See also Andreas Nissen, *Gott und der Nächste im antiken Judentum: Untersuchungen zum Doppelgebot der Liebe*, WUNT 15 (Tübingen: Mohr Siebeck, 1974), 304–39. Gerd Theissen and Annette Merz, "Der umstrittene historische Jesus, oder: Wie historisch ist der historische Jesus?," in *Jesus als historische Gestalt: Beiträge zur Jesusforschung*, ed. Annette Merz, FRLANT 202 (Göttingen: Vandenhoeck & Ruprecht, 2003), 3–32, here 15–17, refer to this as a "radicalization" of the imperative to love one's neighbor.

[41] Kloppenborg, "Discursive Practices," 158, suggests that Q's "depiction of Jesus is unlikely to have represented a substantial deformation of earlier depictions, either in its scope or its presentation." Moreover, "The ways in which early followers of Jesus actually inscribed and employed the canon is the first, and perhaps best, guide to the rhetorical and social practice of the historical Jesus" (ibid., 190).

[42] Hallikainen, "The Lord's Prayer," 63.

[43] Q 3:9; Q 3:17; Q 6:49; Q 10:10–12; Q 11:23; Q 11:51; Q 13:24; Q 17:34–35. Q 3:9 and Q 3:17 represent *John's* pronouncement of Judgment. On "John's" preaching as redactional, see William Arnal, "Redactional Fabrication and Group Legitimation: The Baptist's Preaching in Q 3:7–9, 16–17," in Kloppenborg, *Conflict and Invention*, 165–80.

inconsistency between an *impartial* God who rains on the just and unjust and a *judgmental* God who casts the chaff into an eternal fire seems to call out for what Rudolf Bultmann labeled *Sachkritik*.[44] James M. Robinson identified this "tension" as a key to understanding the "Q trajectory" as well as how the historical Jesus was mis-remembered.[45] According to Robinson, the instructional material in Q represented a "sapiential deviation" from the apocalyptic "trajectory" running from John the Baptist to Matthew,[46] now framed within the eschatological narrative of a coming Judgment.[47] It has been suggested that the Q group ultimately "succeeded in *attracting scholars*, perhaps only a handful, for whom the institutions of Torah and Temple had essential and positive meaning."[48] One example of such scholarly erudition and exegetical ingenuity might be found in Q 7:22, which combines several scriptural passages to defend Jesus' identification as the fulfillment of John's expectations. Here I would like to revisit another possibility: that the conceptual and narrative framework of Q – that is, its vision of a coming judgment and the Son of Man associated with the rejected figure of Wisdom – can be understood as indirectly reflecting, and

---

[44] Rudolf Bultmann, "The Problem of a Theological Exegesis of the New Testament," in *The Beginnings of Dialectical Theology: Volume 1*, ed. James M. Robinson (Richmond, VA: John Knox, 1968 [original German 1925]), 236–56. This is the classic essay in which Bultmann refers to *Sachkritik*, or "material criticism," by which he indicated a critical exegesis concerned with evaluating internal inconsistencies within a document and interpreting its meaning for today. See also idem, "Karl Barth, 'Die Auferstehung der Toten'," in idem, *Glauben und Verstehen: Gesammelte Aufsätze* (Tübingen: Mohr Siebeck, 1933 [original German 1926]), 38–64. Regarding Bultmann's *Sachkritik*, see James M. Robinson, "The Critical Edition of Q and the Historical Jesus," in Lindemann, *The Sayings Source Q and the Historical Jesus*, 27–52, here 41–42 and n. 26. Robinson, "Basic Shifts in German Theology," *Int* 16 (1962): 76–97, likens *Sachkritik* to "theological reflection" (ibid., 86).

[45] Llewellyn Howes, *Judging Q and Saving Jesus: Q's Contribution to the Wisdom-Apocalypticism Debate in Historical Jesus Studies* (Durbanville, South Africa: AOSIS, 2015), notes Robinson's "resolute" effort to spell out this "contradiction" and concedes that "one can quite clearly notice a shift in focus from the loving, merciful and non-judgmental content of Q^1 to the hypercritical, condemnatory and judgmental attitude of Q^2," but claims that finding "two opposing theologies and moralities" to be "unwarranted" because this is only "a shift in group boundaries" (ibid., 254).

[46] James M. Robinson, "The Q Trajectory: Between John and Matthew via Jesus," in *The Future of Early Christianity: Essays in Honor of Helmut Koester*, ed. Birger A. Pearson et al. (Minneapolis: Fortress, 1991), 173–94, here 190.

[47] On Q as a "sapiential text with an apocalyptic worldview," see Matthew Goff, "Discerning Trajectories: 4QInstruction and the Sapiential Background of the Sayings Source Q," *JBL* 124 (2005): 657–73, here 658. For a more semantically-anchored definition of "apocalypticism" as "revelation," see Christopher Rowland, "Apocalypticism: The Disclosure of Heavenly Knowledge," in *The Mystery of God: Early Jewish Mysticism and the New Testament*, ed. Christopher Rowland and Christopher R. A. Morray-Jones, CRINT 12 (Leiden: Brill, 2009), 13–31.

[48] John S. Kloppenborg, "Literary Convention, Self-Evidence, and the Social History of the Q People," in *Early Christianity, Q and Jesus*, ed. John S. Kloppenborg with Leif E. Vaage, Semeia 55 (Atlanta: Scholars Press, 1991), 77–102, here 100 (emphasis added).

so betraying knowledge of, the conceptual world of the Enochic *Book of Parables*.[49]

The *Book of Parables*, a text extant only in Ethiopic *Ge'ez*, describes a time of coming apocalyptic judgment and salvation. The *Book of Parables* combines the myths of Wisdom/Sophia and the Son of Man, associating the latter with the arrival of the day of judgment,[50] providing (at the very least) analogical comparanda that may illuminate how Jesus' rejection, suffering, vindication, and return was associated with the eschatological figure of the Son of Man.[51] There are, of course, different ways to formulate or conceptualize the possibilities of knowledge transference. George Nickelsburg, for example, has suggested that an "Enochic Community" lies behind the composition of the *Book of Parables and* represents a "common milieu" shared with the early Jesus movement.[52]

Perhaps most significantly, it is the "assumption" *(Entrückung)* model implicit in the Enochic writings, in particular, that warrants critical comparison with Q, in so far as Q represents a *different* interpretation of Jesus' post-mortem vindication, that is, one possibly modeled on the concept of assumption rather than resurrection.[53] As is well known, the biblical figure of Enoch ap-

---

[49] John J. Collins, *The Apocalyptic Imagination: An Introduction to Jewish Apocalyptic Literature*, 3rd ed. (Grand Rapids: Eerdmans, 2016), 329 n. 37, notes that I am "unusual in arguing for broad influence of the Similitudes of Enoch on the Jesus tradition." Cf. George W. E. Nickelsburg, *Jewish Literature between the Bible and the Mishnah: A Historical and Literary Introduction* (Philadelphia: Fortress, 1981), 222: "Mark, the Q source, and the apostle Paul knew a form of the son of man tradition that we find in the Parables but not in [Daniel] 7." Cf. also Helge S. Kvanvig, "The Son of Man in the Parables of Enoch," in *Enoch and the Messiah Son of Man: Revisiting the Book of Parables*, ed. Gabriele Boccaccini (Grand Rapids: Eerdmans, 2007), 179–215, here 213: "If there has been any kind of diffusion, the direction from the Parables to the Gospels seems most likely. ... No other texts from the Hebrew Bible or Second Temple Judaism come closer to the Gospels in these eschatological sayings than the Parables." Cf. also Andrejevs, "Q 10:21–22 and Formative Christology," 152, 156: "Many aspects of the Son of Man mythology occurring in *Similitudes* are found also in Q. ... The similarities between the eschatological Son of Man personage in Q² and *Similitudes* are sufficiently numerous to suggest at the very least a shared tradition."

[50] 1 En. 45:3–4; 61:5; 62:3, 13; 48:8; 51:1, 5a, 3–4; 52:7; 63:1.

[51] Gabriele Boccaccini, "Forgiveness of Sins: An Enochic Problem, A Synoptic Answer," in *Enoch and the Synoptic Gospels: Reminiscences, Allusions, Intertextuality*, ed. Loren T. Stuckenbruck and Gabriele Boccaccini, EJL 44 (Atlanta: SBL Press, 2016), 153–67, here 154–55, suggests that the "Enoch movements" represent "the kind of Judaism from which the early followers of Jesus developed their own interpretation of Judaism." Cf. Christopher Rowland, "Enoch in Jewish and Early Christian Tradition," in Rowland and Morray-Jones, *The Mystery of God*, 33–61, here 61: "The ideas connected with Enoch seem to form part of the *structure* of early Christian theological reflection, and not so much motivated by polemic to counteract Enochic speculation" (emphasis added).

[52] George W. E. Nickelsburg, *1 Enoch 1: A Commentary on the Book of 1 Enoch, Chapters 1–36, 81–108*, Hermeneia (Minneapolis: Fortress, 2001), 66; George W. E. Nickelsburg and James C. VanderKam, *1 Enoch: A New Translation* (Minneapolis: Fortress, 2004), 6.

[53] Daniel A. Smith, *The Post-Mortem Vindication of Jesus in the Sayings Gospel Q*, LNTS 338 (London and New York: T & T Clark, 2006), 2, suggests that Q 13:34–35 contains "the character-

pears in Gen 5:24 as Noah's grandfather, but does not die because he was "taken" by God:

Enoch walked with God; then he was no more, because God took him.

ויתהלך חנוך את האלהים ואיננו כי לקח אתו אלהים

The word used to describe Enoch being "taken" (לקח) was also used to describe Elijah's disappearance from the earth (2 Kgs 2:9), and suggested heavenly ascent. If, then, the *Parables* were composed by the middle of the first century CE,[54] it would not only provide "the most striking example in early Jewish literature of the connection between assumption and exaltation or eschatological function,"[55] and the closest "analogy" to Q's assumption-language, it would also strengthen the case for assumption being "a more appropriate theological category from which to consider the development of Q's Son of man christology than resurrection."[56] Since the "Christian" concept of the son of man first appears in Q, it would seem that Q Studies must shoulder much of this interpretive burden, especially since the Gospel of Matthew seems to have known the work.[57]

C. Jesus, Q, and the Son of Man: The *Parables* in Q Studies

For over a century, many New Testament scholars presupposed the existence of an apocalyptic "Son of Man concept" (*Menschensohnbegriff*) in Early Judaism. Rudolf Bultmann held that Jesus did not use the apocalyptic title to refer to himself, but did refer to a coming apocalyptic figure, although the early Church

---

istic language and associations of 'assumption' – the bodily removal of a human being from earth to heaven at (or as) the end of their life." See further ibid., 52: "Assumption involves the disappearance of the body. ... Resurrection involves an appearance of the resurrected person ... whether or not the body is thought of as being reconstituted or revived." Cf. Dieter Zeller, "Entrückung zur Ankunft als Menschensohn (Lk 13,34 f.; 11,29 f.)," in *À Cause de l'Évangile: Études sur les Synoptiques et les Actes. Festschrift J. Dupont*, LD 123 (Paris: Cerf, 1985), 513–30.

[54] Smith, *Post-Mortem Vindication*, 72: "probably composed in the first century CE (or somewhat earlier)." Smith concludes that the identification of Enoch as the Son of Man is secondary: "it seems unlikely that this was intended elsewhere in the work, nor is there a hint that Enoch is some kind of earthly manifestation of the (probably pre-existent) Son of man."

[55] Ibid., 73–74.

[56] Ibid., 119.

[57] Loren T. Stuckenbruck and Gabriele Boccaccini, "1 Enoch and the Synoptic Gospels: The Method and Benefits of a Conversation," in Stuckenbruck and Boccaccini, *Enoch and the Synoptic Gospels*, 1–17 state that a "connection" is "certain" between Matthew and the *Parables* (ibid., 6). Cf. Johannes Theisohn, *Der auserwählte Richter: Untersuchungen zum traditiongeschichtlichen Ort der Menschensohngestalt der Bilderreden des Äthiopischen Henoch*, SUNT 12 (Göttingen: Vandenhoeck & Ruprecht, 1975); Leslie W. Walck, "The Son of Man in the Parables of Enoch and the Gospels," in Boccaccini, *Enoch and the Messiah Son of Man*, 299–337, here 336. See also Leslie W. Walck, *The Son of Man in the Parables of Enoch and in Matthew*, Jewish and Christian Texts in Contexts 9 (London: T&T Clark, 2011).

applied that title to Jesus.⁵⁸ Heinz Eduard Tödt's 1956 Heidelberg dissertation, which developed Bultmann's inference that the "sayings source" (*Spruchquelle*) implied a "primitive community," posited that there were "two spheres of tradition" (*zwei Traditionskreise*), with the passion kerygma remaining outside the "sphere" represented by Q.⁵⁹ While "Christological cognition" (*christologische Erkenntnis*) occurred in the earliest period in response to Jesus' own words,⁶⁰ the Q material represents a "second sphere" (*zweiten Kreis*) of the Jesus movement which took up Jesus' initial "proclamation" (*Verkündigung*).⁶¹ While Jesus spoke of the *coming* Son of Man – presupposing an apocalyptic Son of Man concept accessible to the Jesus movement⁶² – "the primitive community" (*der Urgemeinde gehörige*) created the "earthly" Son of Man sayings.⁶³

Tödt accepted the authenticity of the apocalyptic Son of Man sayings because Jesus could have derived their core ideas from his Jewish context, and identified the Son of Man as the eschatological guarantor of his own ministry.⁶⁴ Moreover, the Gospel of Matthew knew the Enochic tradition.⁶⁵ Yet Jesus did not identify himself with that figure.⁶⁶ Tödt rejected the authenticity of the Son of Man sayings referring to the public ministry of Jesus because the Easter experience imposed the identification of the Son of Man onto Jesus. Like Tödt, Philipp Vielhauer also appealed to the *Parables* as precedent for the exaltation of a human being, noting that the *Parables*' Son of Man is "an individual figure" ("eine individuelle Gestalt") and "a pre-existent heavenly being" ("ein präexistentes Himmelswesen").⁶⁷ Since the "concept" (*Vorstellung*) of the Son of Man was useful in

---

⁵⁸ Rudolf Bultmann, *The Theology of the New Testament*, trans. K. Grobel, 2 vols. (New York: Scribner's, 1951–55), 29–31, 49; cf. *The History of the Synoptic Tradition*, trans. J. Marsh; rev. ed. (New York: Harper and Row, 1968 [1921]), 112, 122, 128, 151–52.

⁵⁹ Heinz Eduard Tödt, *Der Menschensohn in der synoptischen Überlieferung* (Gütersloh: Gerd Mohn, 1959); ET: *The Son of Man in the Synoptic Tradition*, trans. D. M. Barton, NTL (Philadelphia: Westminster, 1965), 268–69. See also Dieter Lührmann, *Die Redaktion der Logienquelle*, WMANT 33 (Neukirchener-Vluyn: Neukirchener, 1969), 94–96; John S. Kloppenborg, "'Easter Faith' and the Sayings Gospel Q," in *The Apocryphal Jesus and Christian Origins*, ed. Ron Cameron, Semeia 49 (Atlanta: Scholars Press, 1990), 71–99.

⁶⁰ Tödt, *Menschensohn*, 211; *Son of Man*, 230.

⁶¹ Tödt, *Menschensohn*, 244; *Son of Man*, 268.

⁶² Tödt, *Menschensohn*, 204: "Bevor die Menschensohnvorstellung in der synoptische Tradition auftaucht, hat sie bereits in der spätjüdischen Apokalyptik ihren Platz gehalten. … An einem Zusammenhang der apokalyptischen Menschensohnvorstellungen mit den synoptischen Sprüchen ist nicht zu zweifeln."

⁶³ Ibid., 26–27.

⁶⁴ Tödt, *Menschensohn*, 266; *Son of Man*, 294.

⁶⁵ Tödt, *Menschensohn*, 205: "Matthäus dagegen auf breitere Traditionsbereiche. Etliche seiner Formulierungen sind mit Aussagen aus dem Henochbuche eng verwandt." Cf. Matt 25:31 and 1 En. 61:8, 62:2, 69:27; Matt 19:28 and 1 En. 108:12, 96:1, 50:22; and Matt 16:27 and 1 En. 45:3.

⁶⁶ Ibid., 61.

⁶⁷ Philipp Vielhauer, "Gottesreich und Menschensohn in der Verkündigung Jesu," in *Festschrift für Günther Dehn, zum 75. Geburtstag am 18. April 1957*, ed. Wilhelm Schneemelcher (Neukirchen: Kreis Moers, 1957), 51–79, here 74.

identifying an earthly Son of Man with an exalted Son of Man – an identification which had already been formulated in the *Parables*[68] – Vielhauer concluded that *none* of the coming Son of Man sayings could be attributed to the historical Jesus.[69] The "traditionelle Erwartung der Ankunft des Menschensohns wurde nun zur Erwartung der Wiederkunft *Jesu*."[70] The expectation of Jesus' return effectively replaced Jesus' proclamation of the kingdom of God.

Subsequent studies have suggested that many Son of Man sayings are redactional,[71] illustrating a growing tendency to regard them as secondary creations.[72] Paul Hoffmann, for example,[73] took "final leave from the often too 'self-evident' assumption that in the SM sayings we are dealing with the oldest Christian or even dominical tradition."[74] Hoffmann suggested that "the SM concept gained special significance for Christian circles during this late phase in the transmission of Q, i. e. in the period around 70 CE, and that it was then that there took place its reception and theological integration into the traditional Q material *that was not previously characterized by it*."[75] This late dating connected the re-

---

[68] Ibid., 79: "Die Vorstellung vom Menschensohn war am besten geeignet, die Identität des Irdischen mit dem Erhöhten und seine eschatologische Bedeutsamkeit klarzumachen, zumal die Erhöhung eines Menschen zum Menschensohn schon im Henochbuch (c. 71) präformiert war."

[69] Ibid., 71: "Alle Worte vom kommenden Menschensohn stammen mit einer an Sicherheit grenzenden Wahrscheinlichkeit nicht vom historischen Jesus."

[70] Ibid., 79 (emphasis added).

[71] Cf. Paul Hoffmann, "The Redaction of Q and the Son of Man: A Preliminary Sketch," in *The Gospel behind the Gospels*, ed. Ronald A. Piper, NovTSup 75 (Leiden: Brill, 1994), 159–198; "QR und der Menschensohn: Eine vorläufige Skizze," in *The Four Gospels 1992: Festschrift Frans Neirynck*, ed. Frans Van Segbroeck et al., 3 vols., BETL 100 (Leuven: Peeters, 1992), 1:421–6. Heinz Schürmann, "Beobachtungen zum Menschensohn-Titel in der Redequelle," in *Jesus und der Menschensohn: für Anton Vögtle*, ed. Rudolf Pesch and Rudolf Schnackenburg (Freiburg: Herder, 1975), 124–47, suggests that the Son of Man sayings are redactional ("Kommentarworte").

[72] Cf. Kloppenborg, "The Sayings Gospel Q and the Quest of the Historical Jesus," 319: "[It is] likely that the coming Son of Man sayings are not the earliest sayings in Q from a compositional point of view and probably not from a tradition-historical perspective either." Cf. Kloppenborg, "'Easter Faith'," 84 n. 60: "We urgently need a re-examination of the Son of Man problem from the standpoint of the results of recent redaction-critical work on Q."

[73] Paul Hoffmann, *Studien zur Theologie der Logienquelle*, NTAbh 8 (Münster: Aschendorff, 1972), initially endorsed Tödt's view of an early apocalyptic Son of Man tradition.

[74] Hoffmann, "Redaction of Q," 193 n. 56.

[75] Hoffmann, "Redaction of Q," 193 (emphasis added). Cf. "QR und der Menschensohn," 452: "Dennoch könnte das parallele Auftreten dieser Erwartung in Mk 13 und in QR darauf hinweisen, daß in dieser Spätphase der Q-Überlieferung, also in der Zeit vor 70 n. Chr., die MS-Vorstellung für christliche Kreise besondere Bedeutung gewann und es zu ihrer Rezeption und theologischen Integration in das von ihr nicht geprägte Überlieferungsgut von Q kam." So too Matti Myllykoski, "The Social History of Q and the Jewish War," in *Symbols and Strata: Essays on the Sayings Gospel Q*, ed. Risto Uro, Publications of the Finnish Exegetical Society 65 (Helsinki: Finnish Exegetical Society; Göttingen: Vandenhoeck and Ruprecht, 1996), 143–99, here 183: "It is possible that the idea of Jesus as the Son of Man originates only in the late apocalyptic imagination of the Jesus movement."

The Promise of Providence and the Problem of the Parables 69

daction of Q to the composition of Matthew, which "clearly displays influence from the Similitudes."[76] Hoffmann left the date of the *Parables*, and its relationship to Q – as well as the *dominical* authenticity of the Son of Man tradition – an open question.[77] Nonetheless, the *Parables* not only provide "a contemporary Jewish context" ("einen aktuellen jüdischen Kontext") and "correspondence to the secondary connection" of Deuteronomistic tradition with the son of man concept in Q; it also represents the "nearest analogy" ("die nächste Analogie") to the Christian identification of Jesus as the Son of Man in its elevation of Enoch. At the very least, the *Parables* illustrate "the currency ('die Aktualität') of the concept in the milieu of Palestinian Jewish Christianity."[78]

The *Parables* also seem to have played a not insignificant role in James M. Robinson's identification of Q as a Wisdom text.[79] While 1 Enoch is introduced as "the word[s] of the blessing of Enoch" (1 En. 1:1), it was the *Parables*' appeal to the rejected figure of Wisdom (1 Enoch 42),[80] that led Robinson to identify the *Parables* within his "trajectories" model of Q's *Gattung* (λόγοι σοφῶν).[81] Helmut Koester subsequently accepted Robinson's model, as well as Vielhauer's conclusions about the Son of Man sayings, noting that the apocalyptic Son of Man sayings do not fit a sapiential profile.[82] Coupled with the absence of such sayings in the Gospel of Thomas (cf. logion 86), Koester conjectured that Son of Man Christology was a redactional addition and posited an early sapiential

---

[76] Hoffmann, "Redaction of Q," 195; cf. "QR und der Menschensohn," 453–54: "die zudem deutlich den Einfluß der Bilderreden erkennen läßt."

[77] Hoffmann, "Redaction of Q," 193–94.

[78] Hoffmann, "QR und der Menschensohn," 453.

[79] Robinson suggested that a *Gattung* of "words of the wise" could be identified in sapiential collections like Prov. 22:17–24:22, the *Gospel of Thomas*, Q, and Near Eastern instructions. 1 Enoch, including the *Parables*, is usually identified as "apocalyptic" literature that *includes* and incorporates sapiential-wisdom literary forms.

[80] Ulrich Wilckens, *Weisheit und Torheit: Eine exegetisch-religionsgeschichtliche Untersuchung zu 1. Kor. 1 und 2*, BHT 26 (Tübingen: Mohr Siebeck, 1959), 163–64: "Here an echo of the myth 1 Enoch 42 becomes clear: In resignation, Wisdom withdraws herself back into heaven."

[81] James M. Robinson, "Introduction," *The Sayings Gospel Q in Greek and English*, ed. J. M. Robinson, P. Hoffmann, and J. S. Kloppenborg (Minneapolis: Fortress, 2002), 49, notes that it was this distinctive aspect of the (rejected) figure of Wisdom in Q that led him to conclude, "while on sabbatical leave in Heidelberg 1959–60," that the literary *genre* of Q was sapiential. Robinson, "ΛΟΓΟΙ ΣΟΦΩΝ," 70, identifies the *Parables* as "a step further back, into the wisdom literature in the narrower sense" of the *Gattung*: "Here the work is introduced as 'Words of Wisdom' … since the Lord of spirits has never before granted such 'wisdom.' Here it is not surprising to find in chap. 42 the locus classicus for the Sophia myth."

[82] Helmut Koester, "GNOMAI DIAPHOROI: The Origin and Nature of Diversification in the History of Early Christianity," in James M. Robinson and Helmut Koester, *Trajectories through Early Christianity* (Philadelphia: Fortress, 1971), 114–57, here 138; see also "One Jesus and Four Primitive Gospels," *HTR* 61 (1968): 203–47. Cf. Christopher M. Tuckett, "Q and Thomas: Evidence of a Primitive 'Wisdom Gospel?' A Response to H. Koester," *ETL* 67 (1991): 346–60.

"formation" of Q, a thesis further developed and refined by John S. Kloppenborg.[83]

By the late 1960s, New Testament studies on the Son of Man problem had begun to reflect a shift in focus. Carsten Colpe concluded "daß das jüdisch-apokalyptische Material" did *not* provide a definitive answer to the New Testament's development *(Präformation)* of the term.[84] The absence of the *Book of Parables* at Qumran led to the conclusion that "Son of Man" was not a "title" at the time of Jesus.[85] Some scholars proposed that the origin of the Son of Man sayings could be understood as an Aramaic idiom.[86] By 1994, James Robinson came to conclude that the *Parables* were not "pre-Christian" and that "the usual appeal to the Similitudes of Enoch has gradually had to give ground."[87] For Robinson, the term originated as an "unimpressive Aramaic idiom" that was subsequently developed into an apocalyptic title,[88] and so the so-called earthly sayings of Jesus were not apocalyptic. Robinson could now argue for the authenticity of

---

[83] Helmut Koester, "Apocryphal and Canonical Gospels," *HTR* 73 (1980): 105–30, here 113: "a secondary redaction of an older wisdom book"; cf. Kloppenborg, *Formation of Q*.

[84] Carsten Colpe, "ὁ υἱὸς τοῦ ἀνθρώπου," *TDNT* 8:400–77, here 431. Colpe proposed that the apocalyptic Son of Man sayings were, rather, "esoterically" transmitted by Jesus and his followers.

[85] Cf. Kloppenborg, "The Sayings Gospel Q and the Quest of the Historical Jesus," 318: "the general acknowledgement that there was no Son of Man title in Second Temple Judaism."

[86] Geza Vermes, "Appendix E: The Use of בר נש/בר נשא in Jewish Aramaic," in Matthew Black, *An Aramaic Approach to the Gospels and Acts*, 3rd ed. (Oxford: Clarendon, 1967), 310–30; P. Maurice Casey, *The Solution to the 'Son of Man' Problem* (London: T&T Clark, 2007); Barnabas Lindars, *Jesus Son of Man: A Fresh Examination of the Son of Man Sayings in the Gospels in the Light of Recent Research* (Grand Rapids: Eerdmans, 1984); Richard Bauckham, "The Son of Man: 'A Man in My Position' or 'Someone'?" *JSNT* 23 (1985): 23–33; Reginald Fuller, "The Son of Man: A Reconsideration," in *The Living Text: Essays in Honor of Ernest W. Saunders*, ed. Dennis E. Groh and Robert Jewett (Lanham, MD: University Press of America, 1985), 207–17; Christopher L. Mearns, "The Son of Man Trajectory and Eschatological Development," *ExpT* 97 (1985/86): 8–12; Donald J. Goergen, *The Mission and Ministry of Jesus* (Wilmington, DE: Michael Glazier, 1986), 180–202; Rollin Kearns, *Die Entchristologisierung des Menschensohnes: Die Übertragung des Traditionsgefüges um den Menschensohn auf Jesus* (Tübingen: Mohr Siebeck, 1988).

[87] Robinson, "The Son of Man in the Sayings Gospel Q," in idem, *The Sayings Gospel Q*, 405–25, here 420–21. Cf. Matthew Black, "The Son of Man Problem in Recent Research and Debate," *BJRL* 45 (1963), 305–18, here 312: "it seems to me that the *Similitudes* (with the exception of chapters 70–71) cannot be cited as first-class evidence for pre-Christian Judaism. ... They must be used with caution. The view of Bultmann, Vielhauer, Conzelmann, etc., that the early church took over its Son of Man conception from a form of apocalyptic Judaism which held a belief in a 'pre-existent heavenly being' receives therefore only a very qualified support from the Ethiopic *Similitudes* – and that would seem hitherto to have been the main prop of the theory."

[88] Robinson, "The Son of Man in the Sayings Gospel Q," 415: "the ability to use the term to refer to Jesus during his public ministry would seem [to be due] ... to the term's use as an unimpressive Aramaic idiom. ... [Such instances] could well be the origin of the early Christian reminiscence that the idiom was distinctive of Jesus' language." See also ibid., 425: "Q tends to indicate the initial stages of the christological development from a non-titular, non-apocalyptic idiom of a generic meaning. ... When the Q community then ascribed to him a decisive role at

the earthly Son of Man sayings.⁸⁹ So, whereas Bultmann and Tödt argued for the authenticity of the apocalyptic Son of Man sayings but denied the authenticity of the earthly Son of Man sayings,⁹⁰ Robinson now argued for the authenticity of the (idiomatic) earthly sayings and attributed the apocalyptic Son of Man sayings to the creative efforts of the "Q Community."

The problem, however, is that *all* of the Son of Man sayings may re-present scribal reflections on Jesus after Easter,⁹¹ using the expression as a title.⁹² We proceed, then, from the observation that Q *casts* Jesus in the role of the Son of Man and presupposes a preconceived interpretation of "Jesus'" role. This identification functions as a unifying theme and characterization around which the sayings make narrative sense, not least because the expression "Son of Man" resonates with "roughly contemporary texts" like the *Parables*.⁹³

Christopher M. Tuckett has also explored Q's Son of Man sayings in light of early Jewish texts, and first states that he is not "necessarily seeking to determine the ultimate origin of [a given] saying."⁹⁴ Second, Tuckett surveys a number of Son of Man sayings in Q (Q 6:22; Q 9:58; Q 12:8, 10; 40; Q 17:23) and finds them all to be remarkably coherent, "embedded in Q at all stages of the tradition."⁹⁵ Third, Tuckett finds the "present SM sayings" – once thought to be the invention of the Q "community" – to cohere with the "apocalyptic" Son of Man sayings.⁹⁶ Fourth, Tuckett appeals to *analogical* parallels in non-Christian Judaism – particularly the *Parables* – to buttress these claims.⁹⁷ Tuckett does not argue that the *Parables* are a pre-Christian text; the *Parables* only provide "parallels in roughly

---

the judgment, the idiom characteristic of his speech was put on his tongue in apocalyptic sayings."

⁸⁹ Ibid., 406: "The layers of Q may be quite useful as archaic documentation making it possible to trace the emergence of christological titles" in the New Testament.

⁹⁰ Tödt, *Menschensohn*, 116.

⁹¹ Cf. Philip Vielhauer, "Gottesreich und Menschensohn," 90–91; idem, "Jesus und der Menschensohn: Zur Diskussion mit Heinz Eduard Tödt und Eduard Schweizer," ZTK 60 (1963): 133–77; Norman Perrin, *Rediscovering the Teachings of Jesus* (New York: Harper and Row, 1967), 154–206, esp. 197–98; Koester, "One Jesus and Four Primitive Gospels," 203–47; idem, *Ancient Christian Gospels: Their History and Development* (Philadelphia: Trinity Press International, 1990), 149–62; Hans Conzelmann, "Present and Future in the Synoptic Tradition," JTC 5 (1968): 26–44.

⁹² Kloppenborg, *Formation of Q*, 192: "in Q … Son of Man has come to be used as a christological *title*" (emphasis added). See further ibid., 213: "Q uses Son of Man as a *title* of dignity" (emphasis added). See also Kirk, *The Composition of the Sayings Source*, 341, 380; Piper, *Wisdom in the Q-Tradition*, 126.

⁹³ Tuckett, Q, 267.

⁹⁴ Ibid., 244, suggesting an "editor" could have "positioned" sayings from "elsewhere."

⁹⁵ Ibid., 252, concluding that they *cannot* be ascribed "to a later strand within Q."

⁹⁶ Ibid., 266, displaying "a remarkable homogeneity" as "crypto-suffering SM sayings."

⁹⁷ Ibid., 267, 269, noting that any "exclusive concentration on Dan 7 alone is misleading and unhelpful" since the figure in Daniel 7 does not "dispense" judgment, but "receives" it.

contemporary texts which are indebted or related in some way to Daniel 7."[98] Finally, Tuckett suggests that this tradition "might be traceable" to Jesus.[99]

Tuckett's exploration of the Son of Man problem is exemplary insofar as it takes seriously the coherence of the Son of Man concept in Q as well as extant "parallels" in non-Christian Judaism. Yet Tuckett's analogical methodology equivocates: he does not posit a pre-Christian Jewish origin of the *text* of the *Parables*, but nonetheless affirms the possibility of "earlier traditions."[100] He holds that both *4 Ezra* and *1 Enoch* are post-70 CE compositions with (possibly) "earlier traditions," but his Q is chronologically *prior* to the *Parables*. Moreover, Tuckett's claim that he is not "necessarily seeking to determine the ultimate origin of the saying" stands in some tension with his conclusion that the expression "might be traceable" to Jesus. It must be said, however, that even if a Son of Man concept was present in pre-Christian Judaism, and did play a role in the redaction of Q, this does not mean that it can be "traced" back to the historical Jesus or to the earliest literary conceptualization of Jesus in Q.[101]

It has been suggested that the expression "Son of Man" represents Jesus' sense that he had "a particular, even unique, vocation in God's redemptive purposes,"[102] and that Jesus used the expression as a (non-titular) self-reference.[103]

---

[98] Ibid., 274, cf. 276.

[99] Christopher M. Tuckett, "On the Stratification of Q: A Response," in Kloppenborg and Vaage, *Early Christianity, Q and Jesus*, 213–22, here 221: "It may also be dangerous to drive a wedge between Q and Jesus at this point. ... The terminology is not identical, but there is an underlying agreement here which makes it at least plausible that some such idea might be traceable back to Jesus." Cf. Tuckett, "The Son of Man and Daniel 7: Q and Jesus," in Lindemann, *The Sayings Source Q and the Historical Jesus*, 371–94, here 390.

[100] Christopher M. Tuckett, *Christology and the New Testament: Jesus and His Earliest Followers* (Louisville, KY: Westminster John Knox Press, 2001), 26: "*1 Enoch* and *4 Ezra* are both probably to be dated after the time of the New Testament. ... But even if the two books in question are to be dated later rather than earlier, they may still preserve earlier traditions. This evidence may then show the existence of a developing exegetical tradition whereby the figure of the vision of Daniel 7 was interpreted in individualistic terms as a figure who would play an active role in the final judgment." See also ibid., 36 n. 59: "the final version of [1 Enoch] may well be relatively late. At the same time, it may well preserve earlier traditions." Tuckett, *Q*, 268 n. 99 refers to Knibb's late dating (c. 100 CE), which is predominantly based on the *Parables*' absence at Qumran, an argument from silence which Tuckett notes is not "compelling" in this context. Cf. Howes, *Judging Q and Saving Jesus*, 274 (emphasis added): "the Similitudes *should* be dated to a period after 70 CE." Elsewhere, Howes concludes that the absence of the *Parables* at Qumran meant that "the Similitudes *had* to be dated to a period no earlier than 70 CE" (ibid., 27).

[101] Kloppenborg, *Excavating Q*, 390 n. 53, suggests that Tuckett "overinterprets" the reading of Daniel 7 in the present son of man sayings.

[102] Larry W. Hurtado, "Summary and Concluding Observations," in *Who is This Son of Man? The Latest Scholarship on a Puzzling Expression of the Historical Jesus*, ed. Larry W. Hurtado and Paul L. Owen, LNTS 390 (London: T & T Clark, 2011), 159–77, here 174.

[103] D. R. A. Hare, *The Son of Man Tradition* (Minneapolis: Fortress, 1990); Mogens Müller, *Der Ausdruck 'Menschensohn' in den Evangelien: Voraussetzungen und Bedeutung*, ATDan 17 (Leiden: Brill, 1984); Günther Schwarz, *Jesus der 'Menschensohn': Aramaistische Untersuchun-*

That is, the expression drew attention to his distinctiveness.[104] While it is theoretically possible that the historical Jesus invented the term as a name for himself,[105] either because it was mysterious, deflective, and could esoterically refer to his eschatological self-understanding as "the prototypical renewer of the human race,"[106] and many scholars have thought that Jesus used the expression,[107] largely based on its multiple attestation,[108] we cannot simply assume that "Son of Man" was Jesus' characteristic pattern of speech simply because it is so well attested on Jesus' lips in the Synoptic tradition.[109] If the historical Jesus characteristically used the expression "Son of Man" to refer to himself, we might expect Paul to know something about it. But Paul doesn't use the expression, despite the fact that his Christology is reminiscent of the *Parables'* "Son of Man."[110] Yet Paul *does* identify Jesus as "the last Adam" (ὁ ἔσχατος Ἀδάμ), echoing early Jewish apocalyptic Adam and *Urzeit/Endzeit* traditions.[111] The Aramaic expression

---

gen zu den synoptischen Menschensohnworten Jesu, BWANT 19 (Stuttgart: Kohlhammer, 1986); Mahlon H. Smith, "To Judge the Son of Man: The Synoptic Sayings," *Forum* 7 (1991): 207–42.

[104] Cf. Jens Schröter, *Jesus von Nazaret: Jude aus Galiläa – Retter der Welt*, 4th ed., Biblische Gestalten 15 (Leipzig: Evangelische Verlagsanstalt, 2006), 254–55: "Man kann die Verwendung durch Jesus also als ein Aufmerksamkeitssignal verstehen, mit dem er auf die Besonderheit seiner Person hinwies."

[105] Mathias Kreplin, "The Self-Understanding of Jesus," in Holmén and Porter, *Handbook for the Study of the Historical Jesus*, 3:2473–2515, here 3:2487, proposes that "the best solution to the question of the Son of Man begins with the *assumption* that Jesus himself coined this expression as a name which he habitually employed to speak (indirectly) about himself" (emphasis added).

[106] So Kreplin, "The Self-Understanding of Jesus," 3:2492–93.

[107] Jürgen Becker, *Jesus von Nazaret* (Berlin: de Gruyter, 1996), 249–67; David R. Catchpole, "The Angelic Son of Man in Luke 12:8," *NovT* 24 (1982): 255–65; John J. Collins, "The Second Coming," *Chicago Studies* 34 (1995): 262–74; Adela Yarbro Collins, "Apocalyptic Son of Man Sayings," in *The Future of Early Christianity*, ed. Birger A. Pearson (Minneapolis: Fortress, 1991), 220–28; Volker Hampel, *Menschensohn und historischer Jesus* (Neukirchen-Vluyn: Neukirchener, 1990).

[108] James D. G. Dunn, "Remembering Jesus: How the Quest of the Historical Jesus Lost Its Way," in *The Historical Jesus: Five Views*, ed. James K. Beilby and Paul R. Eddy (Downers Grove, IL: InterVarsity, 2009), 221, states that it "beggars belief" to think he did *not* do so.

[109] Dale C. Allison, *Constructing Jesus: Memory, Imagination, and History* (Grand Rapids: Baker Academic, 2010), 293–303, appealing to the *Parables'* identification of Enoch as son of man, suggests that Jesus referred to himself as the Son of Man, his heavenly *Doppelgänger*. Drawing on the Son of Man sayings as a "family of traditions," Allison mounts a cumulative case based on "recurrent attestation," rejecting the idea that Jesus used "a mundane idiom," but used the Aramaic idiom *both* to refer to Daniel's "Son of Man" *and* to "his heavenly twin or counterpart" (294, 300).

[110] James A. Waddell, *The Messiah: A Comparative Study of the Enochic Son of Man and the Pauline Kyrios*, Jewish and Christian Texts in Contexts 10 (London: T&T Clark, 2011), 8.

[111] On the *Urzeit/Endzeit* Adamic Christology apparently "current" in the 40s and 50s CE, see James D. G. Dunn, *Christology in the Making: An Inquiry into the Origins of the Doctrine of the Incarnation* (London: SCM, 1980), 114. Cf. 4Q504 VII, 4–5; 1QS IV, 22–23, CD III, 20, and 1QH IV, 15; 4Q171; 4Q174. See Bertil Gärtner, *The Temple and the Community in Qumran and the New Testament: A Comparative Study in the Temple Symbolism of the Qumran Texts and the*

"Son of *Man*" may have been useful to the author of Q, then, because it signified Jesus's humanity in a way parallel to and yet reminiscent of Paul's identification of Jesus as the "last Adam," the eschatological-Adam figure of 1 Enoch 90, and the human-like figure in Daniel 7:13. Yet all of this is only to say that Jesus's first Aramaic-speaking Judean followers were convinced that Jesus was the eschatological agent *par excellence*.

In short, whether Q is read as a unified composition that "remembers" Jesus as the Son of Man whose earthly life and teachings were and are integral to his present reality or as a redacted document that "remembers" Jesus as the "Son of Man" because the theme provided a useful narrative device to frame (earlier) collections of sayings originating within a different narrative and/or generic orientation, we may still ask the question: Does Q contain narrative concepts shared with its contemporaneous Palestinian cousin, the *Book of Parables*?

D. "In Those Days ... the Prayer of the Righteous" (1 En. 47:1): Jesus, Q, and the *Parables*

In 2005, the Third Enoch Seminar met in Camaldoli (Italy) to discuss the significance of the *Parables*, with most specialists present "passionately" arguing for "a composition of the Parables at the turn of the era."[112] In 2013, James Charlesworth proposed that there was now a "consensus" that the *Parables* is a pre-Christian Jewish text that can be dated earlier than the ministry of Jesus and influenced some of the writings in the New Testament.[113] That same year, the Seventh Enoch Seminar explored the relationship between the Enoch tradition and the Synoptic Gospels, focusing on angelology, demonology, cosmology,

---

New Testament, SNTSMS 1 (Cambridge: Cambridge University Press, 1965), 30–42; Devorah Dimant, "4QFlorilegium and the Idea of Community as Temple," in *Hellenica et Judaica: Hommage à Valentin Nikiprowetzky*, ed. André Caquot, Mireille Hadas-Lebel, and Jean Riaud, CREJ 3 (Leuven: Peeters, 1986), 165–89. On "Temple of Adam," see Michael O. Wise, "4QFlorilegium and the Temple of Adam," *RevQ* 15 (1991): 103–32; George J. Brooke, *The Dead Sea Scrolls and the New Testament* (Minneapolis: Fortress, 2005), 242–43.

[112] Gabriele Boccaccini, "The Enoch Seminar at Camaldoli: Re-entering the Parables of Enoch in the Study of Second Temple Judaism and Christian Origins," in idem, *Enoch and the Messiah Son of Man*, 3–16, here 16. In fact, the proposed dates actually range from 20 BCE to 100 CE. For the latter, see Michael A. Knibb, "The Date of the Parables of Enoch: A Critical Review," *NTS* 25 (1979): 345–59. A *possible*, albeit ambiguous, allusion to the Parthians (1 En. 56:5–7) suggests a date after their invasion into Roman territory in 40 BCE. A passing reference to hot springs that "serve the kings" also seems to refer to Herod the Great at Callirhoe (1 En. 67:4–13; Josephus, *Ant*. 17.6.5 §§ 171–73; *B. J.* 1.33. 5. 657–58), which suggests a date around the turn of the era or the early to mid-first century CE. The *Parables* do not refer to or suggest knowledge of the Revolt or the destruction of the Temple, so it would seem that a date before 70 CE is likely.

[113] James H. Charlesworth and Darrell L. Bock, eds., *Parables of Enoch – A Paradigm Shift* (New York/London: T & T Clark, 2013). See also Boccaccini, *Enoch and the Messiah Son of Man*.

soteriology, and different portrayals of God.[114] The most common point of comparison, of course, was the Son of Man figure in the *Book of Parables*.

The scribe(s) responsible for the *Parables* seems to have been "familiar with the environs of Jerusalem and the Dead Sea." The text betrays a "thorough grasp of Scripture," a focused interest in Wisdom, and familiarity with "the political, legal, and military arenas of the social system." Insofar as the author represents the "righteous" and the "elect," he/they are "not in power at present," but "look forward to a reversal of status" and "await their transformation."[115] Now they are oppressed (1 En. 53:7; 62:11), but in the future they will have peace (58:4). They will be vindicated by the arrival and judgment of the/that Son of Man (1 Enoch 62), envisioned as the divine response to the "*prayer* of the righteous":

> In those days, there had arisen the *prayer* of the righteous ... In these days the holy ones who dwell in the heights of heaven were uniting with one voice, and they were glorifying and praising and blessing the name of the Lord of Spirits, and they were interceding and *praying* in behalf of the blood of the righteous that had been shed, and the *prayer* of the righteous, that it might not be in vain in the presence of the Lord of Spirits. (1 En. 47:1–2)[116]

The Ethiopic text contains three different expressions of the term: *(zeku) walda sab'* ([that] "son of humankind" or "(that) son of man") (1 En. 46:2–4; 48:2),[117] or *walda be'si* ("son of a man") (62:5; 69:29; 71:14), and *walda 'eg^{w}āla 'emma-heyāw* ("son of the offspring of the mother of the living") (62:7, 9, 14; 63:11; 69:26–27; 70:1; 71:17),[118] which has led some scholars to question whether the expression should even be considered a title. The text's use of the demonstrative ("*that* son of man") suggests that the expression is not a title *per se*, but rather a literarily allusive reference to the Danielic figure.

The *Parables* represent the (re-)interpretation of the book of Daniel and the Enochic literature in Early Judaism.[119] The "pseudo-Danielic" literature of

---

[114] See Stuckenbruck and Boccaccini, *Enoch and the Synoptic Gospels*. Daniel Boyarin, "How Enoch Can Teach Us about Jesus," *Early Christianity* 2 (2011): 51–76, here 57, suggests that "Son of Man as a divine human redeemer figure was current in the Judaism into which Jesus was born."

[115] Walck, *Son of Man*, 30–49, 49. Walck suggests that the (implied) author "was quite well versed in Scripture, and quite well-trained as a 'scribe.' He was interested in scribal, sapiential matters as well ... clearly of the scribal, retainer class."

[116] Translation from George W. E. Nickelsburg and James C. VanderKam, *1 Enoch: The Hermeneia Translation* (Minneapolis: Fortress, 2012), 61.

[117] 1 En. 46:4 uses the demonstrative *zentu* ("this"); 1 En. 69:26, 29; 70:1; 71:17 use *we'etu* ("that"); and sometimes there is no demonstrative at all (46:3; 60:10; 62:7; 69:27; 71:14).

[118] George W. E. Nickelsburg and James C. VanderKam, *1 Enoch 2: A Commentary on the Book of 1 Enoch, Chapters 37–82* (Minneapolis: Fortress, 2012), 115; Michael A. Knibb, *Essays on the Book of Enoch and Other Early Jewish Texts and Traditions*, SVTP 22 (Leiden: Brill, 2009), 173.

[119] Cf. Simon J. Joseph, "'His Wisdom Will Reach All Peoples': 4Q534–536, Q 17:26–27, 30, and 1 En. 65:1–67:3, 90," *DSD* 19 (2012): 71–105.

4Q243-245, for example, seems to have read Daniel in light of 1 Enoch 83-90.[120] The *Book of Giants* (4Q530) also illustrates how "Danielic and Enochic apocalyptic traditions overlap."[121] There seems to have been "a cross-fertilization" of Danielic and Enochic traditions taking place in these texts.[122] Like the author of the *Parables*, the author of Daniel also knew the *Book of the Watchers*.[123]

In Daniel 7:13, "one like a son of man" (כבר אנש/ὡς υἱὸς ἀνθρώπου) appears before the "Ancient of Days" in heaven and is given "dominion, glory and a kingdom," ushering in the end of wicked empires and the victory of the righteous. The Qumran community regarded the book of Daniel as authoritative prophecy. 4Q246, for example, describes a figure based on Daniel 7:13 who is given the title "Son of God" (ברה די אל) and may be the earliest extant interpretation of Daniel's "Son of Man" as a messianic title.[124] Identified as a "pseudo-Danielic" text and paleographically dated to the late first century BCE, 4Q246 contains a number of structural similarities with the "one like a son of man" in Daniel 7:13.[125] 4Q246 can thus be seen as a textual bridge connecting Daniel's "one like a son of man" tradition with royal messianism.[126] Scholarly opinion is, of course, notoriously divided on the identification of the "Son of God,"[127] but there is little question

---

[120] Gabriele Boccaccini, *Beyond the Essene Hypothesis: The Parting of the Ways between Qumran and Enochic Judaism* (Grand Rapids: Eerdmans, 1998), 81-86; John J. Collins and Peter W. Flint, eds., *The Book of Daniel: Composition and Reception*, 2 vols., VTSup 83 (Leiden: Brill, 2002).

[121] Loren T. Stuckenbruck, "Daniel and Early Enoch Traditions in the Dead Sea Scrolls," in Collins and Flint, *The Book of Daniel*, 2: 368-86, here 371; idem, *The Book of Giants from Qumran: Text, Translation, and Commentary*, TSAJ 63 (Tübingen: Mohr Siebeck, 1997).

[122] Stuckenbruck, "Daniel and Early Enoch Traditions," 376.

[123] Cf. the term "Watcher" (עיר) in 1 En. 10:7, 9; 12:2-3; 13:10; 14:1; Dan 4:13, 17, 23.

[124] I. Howard Marshall, "The Synoptic Son of Man Sayings in Recent Discussion," *NTS* 12 (1966): 327-51, here 350; idem, "The Synoptic Son of Man Sayings in the Light of Linguistic Study," in *To Tell the Mystery: Essays on New Testament Eschatology in Honor of Robert H. Gundry*, ed. Thomas E. Schmidt and Moises Silva, JSNTSup 100 (Sheffield: JSOT Press, 1994), 72-94, here 73; Seyoon Kim, '*The Son of Man' as the Son of God*, WUNT 30 (Tübingen: Mohr Siebeck, 1983), 26.

[125] John J. Collins, "The Son of God Text from Qumran," in *From Jesus to John: Essays on Jesus and New Testament Christology*, ed. Martinus C. de Boer, JSNTSup 84 (Sheffield: JSOT Press, 1993), 65-82; Antti Laato, *A Star is Rising: The Historical Development of the Old Testament Royal Ideology and the Rise of the Jewish Messianic Expectations* (Atlanta: Scholars Press, 1997), 314.

[126] Lawrence H. Schiffman, *Reclaiming the Dead Sea Scrolls: The History of Judaism, the Background of Christianity, the Lost Library at Qumran* (Philadelphia: Jewish Publication Society, 1994), 344; Craig A. Evans, "Jesus and the Messianic Texts from Qumran: A Preliminary Assessment of the Recently Published Materials," in idem, *Jesus and His Contemporaries: Comparative Studies*, AGJU 25 (Leiden: Brill, 1995), 83-154, here 107-110; James D. G. Dunn, "'Son of God' as 'Son of Man' in the Dead Sea Scrolls? A Response to John Collins on 4Q246," in *The Scrolls and the Scriptures: Qumran Fifty Years After*, ed. Stanley E. Porter and Craig A. Evans, JSPSup 26 (Sheffield: JSOT Press, 1997), 198-210, here 209.

[127] As Alexander Balas, see Józef T. Milik, *The Books of Enoch: Aramaic Fragments of Qumran Cave 4* (Oxford: Clarendon, 1976), 60, 213, 261; idem, "Les modèles araméens du Livre d'Esther dans la grotte 4 de Qumrân," *RevQ* 59 (1992): 321-406, esp. 383-84. As an anti-Christ,

that an "anointed/messianic" figure could be identified as "Son of God" in Early Judaism.[128] It is also well known that 4Q246 contains a number of terminological similarities to Luke 1:32–35 (υἱὸς ὑψίστου/υἱὸς θεοῦ).[129]

4Q534–36, another Qumran Aramaic text, describes the birth, physical features, and divine wisdom of a figure identified as the "*Elect* of God" (בחיר אלהא).[130] This Aramaic fragment, presumably a copy of an earlier composition, has been dated between 30 BCE and 20 CE.[131] 4Q534 has the features of an astrological physiognomy,[132] that is, a prophetic horoscope of a child's future and character based on his appearance at birth: his "hair will be red" (ישמק שערה); there will be "lentil-like marks" (וטלופחין) on his thigh; he will learn about the "three books" (תלתת ספריא) and gain "counsel and prudence" (מלכה וערמומה).[133] 4Q534, although originally titled 4QMess Ar, is now called 4QNoah, and the dominant consensus is that the text describes the "birth of Noah."[134] This proposal has not gone unchallenged.[135] Indeed, the case for the Noachic identification is "not very

---

see David Flusser, "The Hubris of the Antichrist in a Fragment from Qumran," *Immanuel* 10 (1980): 31–37. As an angelic figure, see Florentino García Martínez, "The Eschatological Figure of 4Q246," in idem, *Qumran and Apocalyptic: Studies on the Aramaic Texts from Qumran*, STDJ 9 (Leiden: Brill, 1992), 162–79. As a messianic figure, see Émile Puech, "Le fils de Dieu, le fils du Très-Haut, messie roi en 4Q246," in *Le jugement dans l'un et l'autre testament: Mélanges offerts à Raymond Kuntzmann*, ed. Eberhard Bons, LD 197 (Paris: Cerf, 2004), 271–86. As a royal figure, see Joseph A. Fitzmyer, "4Q246: The 'Son of God' Document from Qumran," *Bib* 74 (1993): 153–74; cf. Collins, "The Son of God Text from Qumran," 65–82; Andrew Chester, *Messiah and Exaltation: Jewish Messianic and Visionary Traditions and New Testament Christology*, WUNT 207 (Tübingen: Mohr, 2007), 232; Årstein Justnes, *The Time of Salvation: An Analysis of 4QApocryphon of Daniel ar (4Q246), 4QMessianic Apocalypse (4Q521 2), and 4QTime of Righteousness (4Q215a)*, EHS.T 893 (Frankfurt: Peter Lang, 2009); Daniel Stökl Ben Ezra, "Messianic Figures in the Aramaic Texts from Qumran," in *Aramaica Qumranica: Proceedings of the Conference on the Aramaic Texts from Qumran at Aix-en-Provence*, ed. Katell Berthelot and Daniel Stökl Ben Ezra, STDJ 94 (Leiden: Brill, 2010), 515–40, here 524.

[128] Schiffman, *Reclaiming the Dead Sea Scrolls*, 342.

[129] John J. Collins, *The Scepter and the Star: The Messiahs of the Dead Sea Scrolls and Other Ancient Literature*, ABRL (New York: Doubleday, 1995), 155.

[130] Jean Starcky, "Les quatre étapes du messianisme à Qumran," *RB* 70 (1963): 481–505, here 502–4; idem, "Un texte messianique araméen de la grotte 4 de Qumrân," *École des langues orientales anciennes de l'Institut Catholique de Paris: Mémorial du cinquantenaire 1914–1964*, TICP 10 (Paris: Bloud et Gay, 1964), 51–66.

[131] Émile Puech, "4Q534–536. 4QNaissance de Noé$^{B-C}$," *Qumrân Grotte 4, XXII: Textes Araméens Premiére Partie 4Q529–549*, DJD 31 (Oxford: Clarendon, 2001), 117–70.

[132] Joseph A. Fitzmyer, "The Aramaic 'Elect of God' Text from Qumran Cave 4," *CBQ* 27 (1965): 348–72, here 357–58.

[133] Evans, *Jesus and His Contemporaries*, 111.

[134] Fitzmyer, "Aramaic 'Elect of God' Text"; idem, *Essays on the Semitic Background of the New Testament* (Missoula, MT: Scholars Press, 1974), 127–60; Jean Carmignac, "Les Horoscopes de Qumran," *RevQ* 5 (1965): 199–217; Pierre Grelot, "Hénoch et ses écritures," *RB* 82 (1975): 481–50, esp. 488–99; Jean Starcky, "Le Maître de Justice et Jésus," *MdB* 4 (1978): 53–55; Florentino García Martínez, "4QMess Ar and the Book of Noah," in idem, *Qumran Apocalyptic: Studies on the Aramaic Texts from Qumran*, STDJ 9 (Leiden: Brill, 1992), 1–44.

[135] André Dupont-Sommer, "Deux documents horoscopiques esséniens découverts à

compelling."[136] Doubts have also been raised regarding the existence of a "Book of Noah."[137] Since 4Q534 appears to be a prediction of an "Elect of God" figure who will receive wisdom, experience visions, and know the "secrets of humankind," these motifs are not easily reconciled with Noah.[138] 1 Enoch 68:1 describes Noah as receiving "secrets" from his great-grandfather Enoch, but the physical features of the figure described in 4Q534 *contradict* how Noah is described in 1 Enoch. In 1 Enoch 106:2, 10, Noah's hair at the time of his birth is like "white wool" and "whiter than the snow."[139] The figure in 4Q534 has *red* hair. Moreover, Noah is never described as having eternal "designs," being opposed, or as knowing the "secrets of humankind" or the "secrets of all the living." Noah is never described as having *wisdom* that will reach "all peoples."

The title "Elect of God" is only found in 1 Enoch 37–71, where it has "a clear messianic meaning."[140] Noah is never called the "Elect of God" (בחיר אלהא). Noah is not referred to as the Elect of God anywhere else.[141] The title never refers to Noah in Second Temple literature.[142] In the New Testament, a "voice" at the Transfiguration explicitly identifies Jesus as "my Son, the Elect/Chosen One" (ὁ ἐκλελεγμένος, Luke 9:35). In the crucifixion scene (Luke 23:35), the soldiers mock Jesus as the "anointed of God, the Elect/Chosen One" (ὁ Χριστὸς τοῦ θεοῦ ὁ ἐκλεκτός). The appearance of a figure known as the "Elect of God" provides a striking parallel to 1 Enoch 37–71, where this phrase refers to a messiah and son of man.[143] The wisdom of the "Elect of God" (בחיר אלהא) will reach "all peoples." The Elect of God possesses counsel and prudence (4Q534 I, 7); he will come to know the mysteries of humanity and all living things (I, 8); and he will have plans that will last forever (I, 9).

Qoomrân, près de la mer morte," in *Comptes rendus de l'Académie des Inscriptions et Belles-Lettres, 1965* (Paris, 1966), 239–53, suggested that this figure be seen as either the Enoch of 1 Enoch or a Enoch redivivus. Cf. Evans, *Jesus and His Contemporaries*, 111–13; Michael O. Wise, Martin Abegg and Edward Cook, *The Dead Sea Scrolls: A New Translation* (San Francisco: Harper Collins, 1996), 427–29; Stuckenbruck, *Book of Giants*, 214–18, esp. 215, n. 8; Martin Hengel, *Studies in Early Christology* (Edinburgh: T & T Clark, 1995), 100–101. For a more detailed analysis of the problem, see Joseph, "'His Wisdom Will Reach All Peoples,'" 71–105.

[136] James C. VanderKam, "Mantic Wisdom in the Dead Sea Scrolls," *DSD* 4 (1997): 336–53, here 345.

[137] Cana Werman, "Qumran and the Book of Noah," in *Pseudepigraphic Perspectives: The Apocrypha and Pseudepigrapha in Light of the Dead Sea Scrolls*, ed. Esther G. Chazon and Michael Stone, STDJ 31 (Leiden: Brill, 1999), 171–81.

[138] García Martínez, "4QMess Ar and the Book of Noah," 19, admits that "the identification ... rests on a series of indications. None of them is conclusive as such."

[139] Matthew Black, *The Book of Enoch, or 1 Enoch: A New English Edition*, SVTP 7 (Leiden: Brill, 1985), 99.

[140] García Martínez, "4QMess Ar and the Book of Noah," 22.

[141] Fitzmyer, "Aramaic 'Elect of God' Text," 159.

[142] 1 Enoch 37–71, John 1:34, and Luke 23:35.

[143] In the *Parables*, the "Elect One" has insight into all the hidden mysteries of creation, authority over the powers of creation and understands the secrets of humanity (1 Enoch 49).

The *Book of Parables*, in short, represents a relatively late stage in the Palestinian Jewish Aramaic apocalyptic tradition, preceded by Daniel 7:13, the *Book of the Watchers*, the *Book of Dream Visions*, 4Q246, and 4Q534.[144] The *Parables* conflate multiple titles – the "Anointed (One)" (1 En. 48:10; 52:4; 53:2), the "Elect (One)," the "Righteous (One)," and the "Servant."[145] The/that "Son of Man" appears to be a heavenly figure with "the appearance of a man" (1 En. 46:1). He is seated on a "throne of glory" as a "heavenly judge" (1 En. 45:3; 51:3; 55:4; 61:8; 62:2, 3, 5; 69:27, 29). He is (possibly) "preexistent," "chosen and hidden,"[146] but will be revealed to "the holy and righteous" (1 En. 48:3, 6; 62:7; 48:7). It is widely accepted that the *Parables* betray secondary redaction, particularly in its identification of Enoch as "Son of Man."[147]

The relationship between Q and the *Parables* is more complex than the insoluble "Son of Man" problem and involves identifying distinctive narrative themes and motifs within a common, yet multifaceted worldview. A number of conceptual parallels between the *Parables* and Q have been identified.[148] Here I will review the most prominent: (1) the eschatological judgment associated with the Son of Man; (2) the rejection of Wisdom; (3) the oppression of the righteous;

---

[144] Stökl Ben Ezra, "Messianic Figures," 526, 530, n. 73, suggests that 4Q534 "may have influenced messianic conceptions as expressed in the Similitudes" and that it "should be explored further to possibly shed light on the background of the Similitudes."

[145] 1 En. 48:2–6, 49:1–4; for the title, see 1 En. 46:2, 3, 4; 48:2; 62:5, 7, 9, 14; 63:11; 69:26, 27, 29; 70:1; 71:14; 71:17.

[146] In "pre-existence," the figure resembles Wisdom (Prov. 8:22–26; 1 En. 49:1–4; 51:1–3).

[147] In 1 Enoch 71:14, Enoch is told "You are that son of man" (*'anta wĕ'ĕtu walda bĕ'si*). On the identification as a secondary addition, see Stefan Schreiber, "Henoch als Menschensohn: Zur problematischen Schlußidentifikation in den Bilderreden des äthiopischen Henochbuches (äthHen 71,14)," *ZNW* 91 (2000): 1–17; Darrell D. Hannah, "The Elect Son of Man of the *Parables of Enoch*," in Hurtado and Owen, *Who is This Son of Man?*, 130–58, here 154–55; Delbert Burkett, *The Son of Man Debate: A History and Evaluation*, SNTSMS 107 (Cambridge: Cambridge University Press, 1999), 101; Colpe, "ὁ υἱὸς τοῦ ἀνθρώπου," 426–27; Ulrich Müller, *Messias und Menschensohn in jüdischen Apokalypsen und in der Offenbarung des Johannes*, SNT 6 (Gütersloh: Mohn, 1972), 54–59; Theisohn, *Der auserwählte Richter*, 216 n. 4. See also John J. Collins, "The Interpretation of Psalm 2 in 4QFlorilegium and in the New Testament," in *Echoes from the Caves: Qumran and the New Testament*, ed. Florentino García Martínez, STDJ 85 (Leiden: Brill, 2009), 49–66, here 59: "this passage … is almost certainly a secondary addition." See further Michael A. Knibb, "The Structure and Composition of the Parables of Enoch," in Boccaccini, *Enoch and the Messiah Son of Man*, 48–64, here 63: "chs. 70–71 are a secondary addition to the Book of Parables." Collins, "Enoch and the Son of Man: A Response to Sabino Chialà and Helge Kvanvig," in Boccaccini, *Enoch and the Messiah Son of Man*, 216–27, here 222, notes that "it is possible to construe the Ethiopic text of 1 En 71:14 so that it does not require that the two figures be identified. One can translate 'you are a son of man,' taking the Ethiopic word *we'etu* as a copula rather than as a demonstrative adjective." Collins cautions that "[there] is no consensus, however, on whether this identification is implied throughout the Parables." Nonetheless, Collins concludes that "the passage that contains the apparent identification of Enoch and the Son of Man is a secondary addition" (ibid., 221).

[148] Nickelsburg and VanderKam, *1 Enoch 2*, 71; cf. Q 12:8–9; 12:39–40; 17:22–30.

(4) eschatological feasting with the Son of Man; and (5) the possibility of repentance for the "others" with the salvation of Gentiles.

1. The Eschatological Judgment of the Son of Man

Q and the *Parables* both envision the Son of Man as a figure of apocalyptic judgment. The *Parables* envision "a deep valley with burning fire," with the "kings and mighty" being "cast into this deep valley" (1 En. 54:1-2). Q opens with John the Baptist's announcement of judgment (Q 3:7-8). Both presuppose a cosmological dualism dividing the kingdoms of God and Satan; and both presuppose the view that diseases can be caused by evil spirits requiring exorcism. Both presuppose the coming "day" of the "Son of Man." In the *Parables*, the "Son of Man" will bring about an unexpected judgment which "produces the surprise on the faces of the kings and mighty ones when they recognize their judge" (1 En. 62:5).[149] Similarly, according to Q 12:40, the "Son of Man" will come like a thief at an unexpected hour. In the *Parables*, Noah and the Flood are described after the revelation of the "Elect One" is introduced (1 En. 62; 65:1-67:3). Similarly, in Q 17:26-27, 30, the "day" of the "Son of Man" will be like "the days of Noah." That both texts envision a "judicial function" for the "Son of Man" seems to reflect "the *interpretation* of Daniel 7 in the Parables of Enoch rather than simple dependence on Daniel 7."[150] The Jesus tradition seems to have been familiar with the conceptual world of the *Parables*.[151]

2. The Rejection of Wisdom/Sophia

The *Parables* provide insight into the different ways Jewish scribes reconfigured wisdom and apocalypticism. The *Book of Parables* is presented as Enoch's "vision of *wisdom*" (*rā'ya tĕbab*) and "speech of *wisdom*" (*nagara tĕbab*):[152]

The vision of *Wisdom* that Enoch saw ....
This is the beginning of the words of *Wisdom*,
   which I took up to recount to those who dwell on the earth.
Listen, O ancients, and look, you who come after –
   the words of the Holy One [alt. "the holy words"] .... (1 En. 37:2)[153]

---

[149] Walck, "The Son of Man," 321.

[150] Nickelsburg, *1 Enoch*, 83, referring to Q 12:8-9; cf. Nickelsburg and VanderKam, *1 Enoch: The Hermeneia Translation*, 6: "the description of the Chosen One/son of man (if not the entire book) is presumed in the gospel traditions about Jesus, the Son of Man."

[151] Nickelsburg and VanderKam, *1 Enoch: A New Translation*, 6. Cf. Nickelsburg, *Jewish Literature*, 222: "Mark, the Q source, and the apostle Paul knew a form of the son of man tradition that we find in the Parables but not in Dan 7."

[152] Kvanvig, "The Son of Man in the Parables of Enoch," 179.

[153] Trans. Nickelsburg and VanderKam, *1 Enoch: The Hermeneia Translation*, 50 (emphases added).

The narrative is immediately described as the time of coming judgment:

When the congregation of the righteous appears,
 the sinners are judged for their sins …
And when the Righteous One appears in the presence of the righteous,
 whose chosen works depend on the Lord of Spirits,
 and light appears to the righteous and chosen who dwell on the earth …. (1 En. 38:1–2)
When his hidden things are revealed to the righteous …. (1 En. 38:3)[154]

Moreover, the Son of Man is described as being "revealed" to the "holy and the righteous" (1 En. 48:7). The spirit of Wisdom dwells within the "Chosen One" (1 En. 49:3) and the "righteous" will drink from the fountains of Wisdom (48:1). The Son of Man appears to be a *messenger* of Wisdom. While there is no explicit identification of the Son of Man *as* Wisdom, both Q and the *Parables* associate the "Son of Man" with the rejected figure of Wisdom (cf. Q 7:35).[155] According to 1 En. 42:1–2, "Wisdom found no place where she could dwell." Similarly, according to Q, Jesus as the son of man has "nowhere to lay his head" (Q 9:58; cf. Gos. Thom. 86).[156] Both figures have been relocated to a heavenly dwelling (1 En. 42:1–2; 48:6).[157] Despite the fact that Q 9:58 does not say that the Son of Man has left the earth and taken a place among the angels, the Son of Man *is* homeless and has been rejected by "this generation" as "a glutton and a drunkard" (Q 7:34). Insofar as Jesus is identified as the Son of Man in Q, the Son of Man has indeed been relocated, especially if we interpret Q 13:34–35 as being a saying of Jesus spoken on behalf of Wisdom. In both Q and the *Parables*, we find the following combination: (1) an eschatological judgment heralded by the appearance of the Son of Man; with (2) the/that Son of Man described as an agent, representative, or messenger of Wisdom. This seems like more than coincidence.

---

[154] Ibid., 51 (emphasis added).

[155] 1 En. 41:1; 48:7; 49:3; 51:3; Q 9:58; cf. Sirach 24. Cf. Hoffmann, *Studien*, 181; Piper, *Wisdom in the Q-Tradition*, 167; Jacobson, *First Gospel*, 136: "it is entirely possible Wisdom's futile search for rest may stand in the background (cf. 1 Enoch 42) [of Q 9:58]." Kloppenborg, *Formation*, 192, sees the comparison as "far-fetched" since the saying "says nothing of rejection and it does not state that the Son of Man could not find a place of rest or that he subsequently found one among the angels (as in 1 Enoch 42). Instead the saying describes the vagrant existence of the Son of Man." Cf. Tuckett, *Q*, 182: "the idea of rejected Wisdom, who also can find no home in texts such as *1 Enoch* 42, is quite in line with the Q saying here." Nickelsburg and VanderKam, *1 Enoch 2*, 138, note that 1 Enoch 42:1–3 "reads very much like a negative counterpart of Sir 24:7–11. [...] For Ben Sira, she becomes embodied in the Mosaic Torah …. In 1 Enoch 42, Wisdom finds no home among humans."

[156] Walck, "The Son of Man," 313 sees this as "conceptual and general rather than precise and direct."

[157] Andrejevs, "Q 10:21–22 and Formative Christology," 161–75 suggests that Q 9:57–58 identifies Jesus as the incarnation of (rejected) Sophia and locates the saying in Q² as the original conclusion of Q 7:18–38.

3. The Oppression of the Righteous

Q and the *Parables* both presuppose that the righteous and the elect will be oppressed and/or persecuted.[158] Similarly, Q 6:22 refers to the persecuted, which recalls the persecution of the "righteous" and the "elect" in the *Parables* (1 En. 46:8; 47:2, 4; 62:15). Moreover, both Q and the *Parables* link the "Son of Man" figure with the oppressed and persecuted "righteous."[159]

4. Feasting with the Son of Man

Q 7:34 refers to the Son of Man as a "glutton and a drunkard," but "no such accusation is leveled against the Son of Man" in the *Parables*.[160] On the other hand, "the blessedness of the reversal of fortunes to be brought about by the Son of Man is described in terms of eternal feasting in the presence of the Son of Man (1 En. 62:13–15). ... Feasting in the presence of the Son of Man, then, is a quality of the reversal of fortunes shared by both Q and the Parables."[161]

5. The Repentance of the "Others"?

Both Q and the *Parables* envision "the presence of the Son of Man as a revelation of judgment on behalf of an omnipotent God" against the unrepentant.[162] It has even been suggested that 1 Enoch 50:1–5 refers to a third group (in addition to the oppressed/righteous and the "sinners") of repentant sinners ("the others") who will be "saved" at the judgment. In the *Parables*, these are "those who repent and abandon the works of their hands."[163] It is also worth noting that 1 Enoch 48:4 refers to the Son of Man (not "Israel") being a/the "light to the Gentiles/nations," which could, in part, explain Q's relatively few, but positive references to Gentiles may have provided an exegetical warrant for missionary activity and the eschatological inclusion of Gentiles.[164]

---

[158] 1 En. 46:8; 47:2, 4; 48:7; 62:15; cf. Q 6:22–23; Q 7:35; Q 9:58; Q 4:1–13; Q 14:27; Q 6:40.

[159] Walck, "The Son of Man," 312, attributes this to "the general, apocalyptic attributes of the oppressed that were current at the time."

[160] Ibid.

[161] Ibid., 313, concluding that "The similarities in feasting for the righteous are general, however, and too minimal to suggest direct influence."

[162] Ibid., 314, concluding that "The Book of Parables does not include the possibility of repentance," whereas "in Q repentance and forgiveness are possible."

[163] Boccaccini, "Forgiveness of Sins," 161, insists that these "others" represent "the relation between the justice and mercy of God, a theme that we would find at the center of the Jesus movement." The "others" "who repent will be saved by God's mercy, even though they should not be saved according to God's justice. Repentance makes God's mercy prevail on God's justice .... The Book of Parables refers to the time of the manifestation of God and the Messiah as a (short) time in which a last opportunity of repentance will be offered to the sinners."

[164] Smith, *Post-Mortem Vindication*, 147–48: "Q 11:31–32 draws attention to the fact that Gentiles responded favourably to God. ... Q 13:28–29 foresees the inclusion of Gentiles."

Q does not betray direct literary knowledge of the *Parables*.[165] Nonetheless, Q's narrative characterization of a Son of Man figure certainly seems to betray indirect knowledge of and allusion to such a tradition. The Son of Man sayings in Q "do not seem to reflect any *direct verbal influence* from the Parables," but they do seem to betray *conceptual* influence.[166] The constellation of correspondences between Q and the *Parables* require more complex theories than "general conceptions of an eschatological judge and deliverer" to explain and account for them.[167]

The author of Q does not need to have slavishly "copied" the "text" of the *Parables* to have been influenced by its conceptual universe. On the contrary, it is the creative adaptation of its themes – reworked to fit the context and needs of Jesus' actual life, ministry, suffering, and vindication – that seems to make the best sense of these correspondences. In short, the *Parables* seem to have entered the textual streams of the Q tradition at a secondary stage of conceptualization, providing new exegetical tools and rhetorical weapons, as well as a symbolic social identity and an eschatological schematic that answered the "prayers of the righteous" and vindicated their Teacher now exalted in heaven, remembered now as the agent and mediator of the "revelation" of Wisdom.[168]

E. The Beatitude of the Son of Man (Q 6:22–23)

The Son of Man first appears in Q 6:22–23, widely regarded as the beginning of the Inaugural Sermon. Form-critically sapiential,[169] the beatitudes function as "proclamations of eschatological salvation."[170] They presuppose a group experiencing oppression and poverty.[171] They represent reversals of poverty, hunger, and mourning.[172] This reversal of expectations is characteristic of Q's "language

---

[165] Cf. Walck, *Son of Man*, 249–50: "it is very possible that Matthew allowed the Parables to shape his portrayal of the Son of Man."

[166] Walck, "The Son of Man," 315, emphasis added.

[167] Ibid., 331: "Shared characteristics do exist. They could be explained as deriving from Dan 7, or from the general conceptions of an eschatological judge and deliverer current in the milieu of the first century C. E. as well as in the Parables."

[168] On the Son of Man as a symbol of social identity, see Simon J. Joseph, "A Social Identity Approach to the Rhetoric of Apocalyptic Violence in the Sayings Source Q," *HR* 57 (2017): 28–49.

[169] For beatitudes occurring in series, see Tob 13:14; Ps 32:1–2; 119:1–2; 128:1–2; 137:8–9; Sir 14:1–2; 25:8–9; 2 En. 52:1–5; 42:6–14; Ps 1:1; 41:1; 112:1; 1 En. 10:6–7.

[170] Kloppenborg, *Formation of Q*, 188; James M. Robinson, "The Formal Structure of Jesus' Message," in *Current Issues in New Testament Interpretation: Essays in Honor of Otto A. Piper*, ed. William Klassen and Graydon F. Snyder (New York: Harper & Row, 1962), 91–110, 273–84, esp. 98, 278 n. 25.

[171] Kloppenborg, *Formation of Q*, 188.

[172] Tuckett, *Q*, 141.

of reversal," its "inversionary ethical injunctions and encomia on detachment from cultural norms."[173] Q envisions a world where "conventional values are inverted and turned on their heads."[174] Numerous "reversal sayings" are found in Q.[175] They represent Q's promise of providence.

Q's first three beatitudes follow a similar structural pattern. Each beatitude contains a formulaic μακάριοι οἱ plus a substantive. They are bipartite, consisting of a beatitude and an ὅτι-clause. They pronounce blessings by using the ὅτι-clause in giving the reason for the reversal of conditions. They illustrate the eschatological reversal on earth, referring to general conditions of poverty.

The fourth is markedly different. It does not use the formulaic μακάριοι οἱ plus substantive, but rather μακάριοί ἐστε ὅταν. It is not bipartite, but contains a beatitude and an imperative with a motive clause. It uses the postpositive γάρ, not ὅτι, to give the reason for the blessing. It also uses the verb ἐστε, does not refer to the reversal of values on earth, but to a reward in heaven. In short, the fourth beatitude diverges from the first three in length, form, vocabulary, and content. The first three beatitudes conclude with an ὅτι-clause. In the fourth, there is a change in wording (γάρ) and an additional γάρ-clause (Q 6:23c) which diverges from the theme of reversal towards an analogy with the prophets: "for this is how they persecuted the prophets who were before you."[176] This *second* γάρ-clause seems to be a relatively straightforward instance of secondary editing.[177] The persecution of the prophets is thematically linked to Q 11:49–51 and Q 13:34–35 and seems to belong to the redactional interests of these passages.

Q 6:23c may be a redactional addition, but the fourth beatitude seems to have been added early on to the Inaugural Sermon.[178] There are, of course, precedents

---

[173] William E. Arnal, *Jesus and the Village Scribes: Galilean Conflicts and the Setting of Q* (Minneapolis: Fortress, 2001), 160.

[174] Arnal, *Jesus and the Village Scribes*, 2.

[175] Q 3:8; Q 4:5–8; Q 6:20–23; Q 6:27–28; Q 6:32–34; Q 7:9; Q 7:22; Q 12:2–3; Q 13:30; Q 13:18–19; Q 13:20–21; Q 14:11; Q 14:16–18; Q 14:26; Q 16:18; Q 17:33.

[176] οὕτως γὰρ ⟦ἐδίωξαν⟧ τοὺς προφήτας τοὺς πρὸ ὑμῶν.

[177] Odil Hannes Steck, *Israel und das gewaltsame Geschick der Propheten: Untersuchungen zur Überlieferung des deuteronomistischen Geschichtsbildes im Alten Testament, Spätjudentum und Urchristentum*, WMANT 23 (Neukirchen-Vluyn: Neukirchener, 1967), 259; Kloppenborg, *Excavating Q*, 149–50; Migaku Sato, *Q und Prophetie: Studien zur Gattungs- und Traditionsgeschichte der Quelle Q*, WUNT II 29 (Tübingen: Mohr Siebeck, 1988), 259; Tuckett, *Q*, 180; Catchpole, *The Quest for Q*, 91. Kloppenborg (*Excavating Q*, 149) sees this as "intrusive on literary grounds" because it is "redundant" after 6:23b. and expresses the Deuteronomistic view of killing the prophets. This phrase is absent from the parallel versions in Thomas (Gos. Thom. 68, 69a; cf. 1 Pet 3:14; 4:13–14). Q 6:23c is linked thematically to 11:49–51 and 13:34–35 and "this phrase is most plausibly associated with the redactional stratum in which those pericopae appear" (ibid.).

[178] Cf. the catchwords διώκειν and μισθός. See Allison, *The Jesus Tradition in Q*, 102; Harry T. Fleddermann, *Q: A Reconstruction and Commentary*, BTS 1 (Leuven: Peeters, 2005), 176–77; see also James M. Robinson, "The Sayings Gospel Q," in idem, *The Sayings Gospel Q*, 319–48, here 327: "The fourth Beatitude (Q 6,22–23) was secondarily appended (as is evident also from

for extended beatitudes in early Jewish literature,[179] yet the more pressing question here is not whether some editorial activity has been conducted, but whether the appearance of the "Son of Man" itself (in Q 6:22) is part of the earlier composition or, like Q 6:23c, part of the redaction.[180] Considering that Q 6:22–23 is secondary to the first three beatitudes and that Q 6:23 is secondary to the fourth beatitude, it is clear that Q's Sermon represents at least three distinct stages of editorial activity: (1) the first three beatitudes; (2) the fourth beatitude; and (3) redactional addition(s) to the fourth beatitude. Consequently, both the beatitude and the reference to the "Son of Man" seem to be Q redaction.[181] This may have occurred at a relatively early stage in the formation of the "final" Q Sermon.[182] Q 6:22 does use the catchword διώκω (διώξωσιν) ("to persecute"), found also in Q 6:28 (διωκόντων), and Q 6:23 does use μισθός ("reward"), as does Q 6:32 (μισθόν), but the reconstruction of the fourth beatitude with these catchwords does not require the inclusion of either Q 6:22b or Q 6:23c, and may have first been composed in more conformity to the first three beatitudes:

μακάριοί ἐστε ὅταν ὀνειδίσωσιν ὑμᾶς καὶ διώξωσιν
χαίρετε καὶ ἀγαλλιᾶσθε, ὅτι ὁ μισθὸς ὑμῶν πολὺς ἐν τῷ οὐρανῷ

Blessed are you when they insult and persecute you.
Be glad and exult, for vast is your reward in heaven.

---

its divergent formulation)." Cf. Jacobson, *The First Gospel*, 99–100: "The small collection of beatitudes, whatever their origin, had therefore already been supplemented in Q by the addition of one more. This added beatitude (Q 6:22) .... [is] clearly the results of later editorial activity in Q." Jacobson suggests, however, that perhaps "the Q community did not understand the title 'son of man' as a reference to an apocalyptic figure of judgment," but cautiously "assumes" it to be "a later addition."

[179] 4Q525 contains three short beatitudes followed by a longer and different, fourth beatitude.

[180] Thomas 68:1 contains neither Q's reference to the "Son of Man" nor Q 6:23c's γάρ-clause: "Jesus said, 'Blessed are you when they hate you and persecute you.'"

[181] John S. Kloppenborg, "Blessing and Marginality: The 'Persecution Beatitude' in Q, Thomas and Early Christianity," *Foundations and Facets Forum* (1986): 36–56, 37: "the original independence of 6:22–23 from 6:20b–21." Cf. David Seeley, "Blessings and Boundaries: Interpretations of Jesus' Death in Q," in Kloppenborg and Vaage, *Early Christianity, Q and Jesus*, 131–146, here 134. Cf. Schürmann, "Beobachtungen zum Menschensohn-Titel," 130, as a secondary *Kommentarwort*. Cf. Hoffmann, *Studien*, 73, 148; Catchpole, *Quest*, 91. On the other hand, Arnal, "The Trouble with Q," 50 n. 164, suggests, citing Kloppenborg, *Formation of Q*, 178, that it is "literarily necessary that this text have been in Q¹" and states that "resistance to finding titular references to the 'son of man' in Q¹ has led some ... to ignore this literary data and attribute the whole last beatitude to Q² on essentially thematic grounds. This is a methodological step backwards." Arnal suggests that "one *could* make a case" Q 9:58 is "generic, signifying 'humanity,' rather than titular," seemingly open to the possibility that the expression did not "originate" as a title in Q.

[182] Arland D. Jacobson, review of *The Formation of Q*, by John S. Kloppenborg, *JBL* 108 (1989): 150–52, here 152, notes that "arguably prophetic sayings occur in the sapiential layer (e. g., Q 6:23–23b)."

The Son of Man (first) appears in Q 6:22 without explanation, presumably because the figure is already *known*. It is not clear from the immediate context whether Jesus should be identified as the Son of Man, but the Son of Man is clearly the reason (ἕνεκεν) why Jesus' followers are being persecuted.[183] If Luke preserves the original reference to the "Son of Man" as opposed to Matthew's "me" (ἐμοῦ),[184] then the "Son of Man" is not an "unimpressive idiom" subsequently apocalypticized, but the name or title of a divinely authorized guarantor of eschatological blessing.[185] That is, the Son of Man is the cause of both persecution and blessing. Here the boundary between present and future is also blurred, with the promise of providence being projected into the future. This first reference to the Son of Man in Q frames the instructional wisdom of the Inaugural Sermon, but is nowhere mentioned within the Sermon itself (Q 6:27–49).[186] This seems to be a significant datum indicating that the Son of Man figure referred to in Q 6:22 was not originally integral to what follows but then came to determine how the text – and subsequently "Jesus" – was to be interpreted.[187]

F. Conclusion

The thematic juxtaposition of salvation and judgment is not unusual in early Judaism.[188] Q clearly accommodates the twin themes of salvation and judgment. Nor was it apparently difficult to conceptualize a deity capable of reconciling opposites. Yet Q's conceptualization and characterization of the Father as un-

---

[183] Piper, *Wisdom in the Q-Tradition*, 61; Catchpole, *The Quest for Q*, 94; Kirk, *The Composition of the Sayings Source*, 391–92.

[184] Tuckett, *Q*, 247: "the 'I' form is more naturally explained as MattR and there is no other example of a 'for the sake of the SM' being added to a tradition secondarily." Cf. Matt 10:32; 16:21. Cf. Lührmann, *Die Redaktion der Logienquelle*, 55.

[185] Tödt, *Son of Man*, 271–72: "In Luke 6.22 the name Son of Man is mentioned for the first time in order to emphasize the significance of Jesus on earth. ... By the insertion the name Son of Man the present situation of those who receive the promise was interpreted anew. Now the promise of salvation was understood as given to him who suffers for Jesus' sake."

[186] Schürmann, "Beobachtungen zum Menschensohn-Titel," 130. Cf. Tuckett, *Q*, 245: "The lack of any explicit reference to 'SM' later in the Sermon is not decisive."

[187] Cf. Kloppenborg, "The Sayings Gospel Q and the Quest of the Historical Jesus," 319: "if the coming Son of Man sayings are neither authentic nor part of the formative stratum of the Q tradition, but belong to the redactional theme of the announcement of judgment (as I think more probable), important parts of Q remain discontinuous in some measure with the preaching of the historical Jesus."

[188] Gerd Theissen and Annette Merz, *The Historical Jesus: A Comprehensive Guide* (London: SCM; Minneapolis Fortress, 1998), 264: "God's eschatological action always has an aspect of judgment and an aspect of salvation." For Theissen and Merz, the eschatological Judgment is "self-chosen or deserved" (ibid., 265). So also Marius Reiser, *Jesus and Judgment: The Eschatological Proclamation in Its Jewish Context*, trans. Linda M. Maloney (Minneapolis: Fortress, 1997), 20, where the promise of providence has *already* been *postponed* to the Eschaton: "followed by an enduring time of salvation in which the righteous need no longer suffer."

conditionally providential remained distinctive in relation to the eschatological framework of Q, where salvation is contingent on one's response to Jesus.[189]

In the *Parables*, salvation is contingent on the "day" of the Son of Man, portrayed as the divine response to the "prayer of the righteous." The righteous are saved and the wicked damned, but there is still hope for repentant sinners (the "others"). The *Parables* thus provide us with a comparative narrative framework, allowing us to see Q's distinctiveness in envisioning a scenario – evidently based on the life, teachings, death, and postmortem vindication of Jesus – in which the Son of Man had, in part, *already* arrived.

The identification of Jesus as the Son of Man in Q juxtaposes Q's instructional collections within a new conceptual narrative framework of apocalyptic judgment. Now the present-day promise of providence, once inscribed in Q as the ostensible purpose, goal, and experiential result of prayer,[190] has been narratively reset in the past and simultaneously postponed as Q looks both back to the ministry of Jesus and forward to his return as the apocalyptic Son of Man.[191]

---

[189] Cf. Smith, *Post-Mortem Vindication*, 142, who refers to correspondences between how Q and the *Parables* envision the relationship between Jesus and the community in terms of "a shared mission (Q 10:16), a shared experience of persecution and rejection (Q 6:22–23; 10:10–11; 10:16; 11:49–51; 12:2–3; 12:11–12; 13:34–35) and also revelation (10:21–22; 10:23–24), and a shared heavenly or eschatological vindication (6:22; 12:8–9; 22:28–30)."

[190] Arnal, "The Trouble with Q," 35, refers to "the assumption that God is *immediately* present" in the earliest stratum of Q, and describes "a program of transparency and immediacy in social relations, predicated on the theological notion of the immediacy of God .... [One] should live as though God is immediately present in everyday (village) life" (ibid., 36). Arnal insists that Q's theology is "a socio-rhetorical intervention," but one is still struck by its rhetorical assertion that "God is present here and now in ordinary life, and in its insistence on the social enactment of that premise" (ibid., 37).

[191] The Aramaic מרנא תא (μαράνα θά), "Our Lord, come!," points to *re-appearance* (1 Cor 16:22; cf. *Did.* 10:6). Martin Hengel, "Abba, Maranatha, Hosanna und die Anfänge der Christologie," in idem, *Studien zur Christologie: Kleine Schriften IV*, ed. Claus-Jürgen Thornton, WUNT 201 (Tübingen: Mohr Siebeck, 2006), 496–534, here 521, refers to this as *"das früheste Gebet zu Jesu ... das wir kennen."*

Beten für und gegen Feinde

Karl-Heinrich Ostmeyer

A. Feindesliebe: Q 6,27 als Ausgangspunkt

Jesu Aufforderung zur Feindesliebe (Q 6,27) ist Kernthema seiner Ethik und gilt nicht selten als *das* Spezifikum der christlichen Botschaft.[1] Das scheint insbesondere dann zuzutreffen, wenn der Anfang der sechsten Antithese bei Matthäus hinzugezogen wird: „Ihr habt gehört, dass gesagt ist: Du sollst deinen Nächsten lieben und deinen Feind hassen" (Mt 5,43).[2]

Zwar weisen die meisten Kommentare darauf hin, dass die Aussage so weder im Alten Testament noch in der rabbinischen Tradition zu finden ist, doch prägend bleibt das Votum Billerbecks, es handele sich dabei um eine „populäre Maxime, … der der Durchschnittsisraelit in Jesu Tagen" gefolgt sei.[3] Die Aufforderung, den Feind zu hassen, findet sich z. B. in der Gemeinderegel aus Qumran: 1QS I, 9–10 gemahnt u. a., die Licht-Söhne zu lieben und die Finsternis-Söhne zu hassen.[4] An persönliche Feinde ist dabei weniger gedacht, vielmehr handelt es sich bei der Wendung um apokalyptische Redeweise. In diesem Zusammenhang sei daran erinnert, dass die Evangelien auch Jesus drastische Weherufe[5] und Drohworte[6] in den Mund legen.[7]

---

[1] Wolfgang Wiefel, *Das Evangelium nach Matthäus*, THKNT 1 (Leipzig: Evangelische Verlagsanstalt, 1998), 122: Die Form der Antithesen „erweist sich als besonders adäquat, wenn man den urchristlichen Tradenten die Ansicht zutraut, Jesus habe mit dem Gebot der Feindesliebe etwas radikal Neues in die Welt gebracht." Vgl. Rudolf Bultmann, *Die Geschichte der synoptischen Tradition*, 7. Aufl., FRLANT 12 (Göttingen: Vandenhoeck & Ruprecht, 1967), 110: Hier muss „das Charakteristische der Verkündigung Jesu zu finden sein."

[2] Deutsch wiedergegebene Bibeltexte richten sich in der Regel nach *Die Bibel, nach Martin Luthers Übersetzung*, revidierten Fassung (Stuttgart: Deutsche Bibelgesellschaft, 2017); andere Übersetzungen sind, soweit nicht anders angegeben, vom Verfasser.

[3] Str-B 1:353; vgl. Walter Grundmann, *Das Evangelium nach Matthäus*, 6. Aufl., THKNT 1 (Berlin: Evangelische Verlagsanstalt, 1986), 176; Hans Dieter Betz, *The Sermon on the Mount, including the Sermon on the Plain (Matthew 5:3–7:27 and Luke 6:20–49)*, Hermeneia (Minneapolis: Fortress, 1995), 302.

[4] Zitiert u. a. bei Walter Klaiber, *Das Matthäusevangelium*, Teilband 1: *Matthäus 1,1–16,20*, BNT (Neukirchen-Vluyn: Vandenhoeck & Ruprecht, 2015), 114; Matthias Konradt, *Das Evangelium nach Matthäus*, NTD 1 (Göttingen: Vandenhoeck & Ruprecht, 2015), 97.

[5] Q 10,13–15 (Verfluchung der galiläischen Städte; vgl. Mt 11,20–24); Mt 23,13–36 (Weherufe über die Pharisäer); Lk 6,24–26 (Weherufe über die Reichen und die, die jetzt lachen).

Der Aufruf zum Hass den Feinden gegenüber ist nicht typisch für das gesamte von der Qumrangemeinde bewahrte Schrifttum: U. a. im Genesis-Apokryphon begegnet eine differenzierte Haltung. Auch wenn zu unterscheiden ist zwischen programmatisch essenischen Texten und sonstigen Manuskripten, so sind doch immerhin Texte, wie das Genesis-Apokryphon von der Qumrangemeinde in ihre Bibliothek aufgenommen und unmittelbar vor der Auslöschung der Gemeinde durch die Römer in Höhlen versteckt und so vor der Vernichtung gerettet worden.

B. Konkretisierung des Gebotes der Feindesliebe in Q 6,28

Die Aufforderung zur Feindesliebe in Q 6,27 bliebe blass, wenn sie nicht in Q 6,28 unmittelbar unterfüttert würde. In einem psalmenartigen Parallelismus membrorum ergeht die Aufforderung: „Liebet eure Feinde, betet für die, die euch verfolgen!"; d. h. die Fürbitte ist Ausdruck der Feindesliebe.

Das Lukasevangelium scheint in Lk 6,27b gegenüber Q 6,28 das Schwerere zu fordern, indem es erst an zweiter Stelle zum Gebet aufruft und zunächst mahnt, den Hassenden Gutes zu tun. Doch die Bewertung, das Tun des Guten[8] sei gegenüber dem Fürbitten der anspruchsvollere Part, ist modernes Denken. Die Fürbitte, an die in neutestamentlicher Zeit gedacht ist, hat eine andere Dimension: Der Betende stellt sich gleichsam mit dem, für den er betet, vor Gott.[9] Wer zu Gott betet, der befindet sich im Bereich des ewigen Gottes. Das heißt, im Gebet taucht der Betende ein in die Ewigkeit.

Fürbitte heißt mehr, als dem Objekt der Fürbitte „nur" einen Liebesdienst zu erweisen. Fürbitte bedeutet, dem anderen den Zugang zu Gottes Reich zu eröffnen. Das gilt nicht nur punktuell für die Dauer des Betens, sondern für ewig. Vor diesem Hintergrund erhält das Gebet für die Feinde seinen besonderen Rang. Gemeinsam mit dem Feind stehen bildlich gesprochen die Betenden im Gebet vor Gottes Angesicht – auf ewig. *Das* ist gemeint mit Feindesliebe, denn die Alternative einer zeitlichen Begrenzung, etwa durch ein zweites Gebet, mit dem

---

[6] Mk 9,42: „Und wer einen dieser Kleinen, die an mich glauben, zum Abfall verführt, für den wäre es besser, dass ihm ein Mühlstein an den Hals gehängt und er ins Meer geworfen würde" (vgl. Q 17,2 [umstritten]; Mt 18,6); Lk 21,22–23 parr.: „Denn das sind die Tage der Vergeltung...."

[7] Vgl. Peter Fiedler, *Das Matthäusevangelium*, Theologischer Kommentar zum Neuen Testament 1 (Stuttgart: Kohlhammer, 2006), 150. Q 12,10 betont, dass ein Wort wider den Heiligen Geist *nicht* vergeben wird.

[8] In TestXII.Jos 18,2; Jürgen Becker, *Die Testamente der zwölf Patriarchen*, 2. Aufl., JSHRZ 3.1 (Gütersloh: Gütersloher Verlagshaus, 1980), 128, erscheinen Gutestun und Fürbitte synonym: „Und wenn euch jemand Böses zufügen will, so betet ihr durch Gutestun für ihn, und ihr werdet von allem Bösen vom Herrn befreit werden"; Entstehung nach 198 v. Chr. und vor 200 n. Chr.

[9] Vgl. Ernst Lohmeyer, *Das Evangelium des Matthäus*, 3. Aufl., hg. v. Werner Schmauch, KEK Sonderband (Göttingen: Vandenhoeck & Ruprecht, 1962), 145.

der Feind wieder aus dem ewigen Reich Gottes „rausgebetet" würde, wäre absurd.

Die Botschaft aus Q 6,27–28 ist eine Zumutung. Dass ein Gebet für die Feinde Konsequenzen für den Alltag hat, versteht sich: Für einen Feind zu beten und gleichzeitig im täglichen Leben feindlich mit ihm umzugehen, lässt sich nicht in Einklang bringen. D. h., das Gebet für die Feinde ist das Innigste und Schwierigste, was für einen gläubigen Menschen vorstellbar ist. Dem Feind Gutes zu tun, ist eine zeitlich begrenzte Handlung – für den Feind zu beten, ist eine auf Ewigkeit angelegte Haltung.

Wird ein solches Verständnis von Gebet und Feindesliebe vorausgesetzt, dann ist verständlich, dass Matthäus beides in seiner sechsten und letzten Antithese (Mt 5,43–44) zu einem Spezifikum der Botschaft Jesu machen wollte. Die Frage, wo das Motiv des Betens für Feinde erstmalig begegnet, ist Gegenstand der nachstehenden Abschnitte. Die Auswahl der vorgestellten Texte beschränkt sich auf ältere oder zeitlich parallel zu Q entstandene Texte. Spätere Texte finden zum Vergleich in den Anmerkungen Erwähnung.

Gebete *für* Feinde begegnen selten in *ausformulierten* Fassungen, denn es ist etwas Anderes, zum Beten aufzufordern oder ein Gebet zu konstatieren, als konkret und expressis verbis ein Gebet zugunsten von Feinden zu artikulieren. Im zweiten Makkabäerbuch[10] ist das Scheitern des Tempelschänders Heliodor das Ergebnis des Betens der Jerusalemer Bevölkerung (2 Makk 3,18–22): Der Priester Onias wird von Begleitern des niedergestreckten Heliodors gebeten, vor Gott für ihren Herrn einzutreten (V. 31). Es wird berichtet, dass Onias *für* Heliodor opfert (V. 32) und der Feind sich daraufhin erholt. Ein eventuell gesprochenes Gebet wird im Wortlaut nicht zitiert.

Anders als von nicht wenigen Exegeten behauptet,[11] begegnet bereits im Alten Testament in 2 Kön 6,18–23 neben einem Gebet des Propheten Elisa *gegen* seine Feinde (2 Kön 6,18) auch ein ausformuliertes Kurzgebet *für die* Feinde

---

[10] Vgl. Jan Willem van Henten, „Makkabäerbücher," *RGG* 5:702–5, hier 704; er nennt als Entstehungszeitraum der Schrift die Jahre zwischen 124 v. und 63 v. Chr.

[11] Eduard Schweizer, *Das Evangelium nach Matthäus*, NTD 2 (Göttingen: Vandenhoeck & Ruprecht, 1976), 81, zur Aufforderung Jesu, für die Feinde zu beten in Mt 5,44: „Das geht über das Alte Testament hinaus, wo kein Gebet für Menschen, die nicht von Natur oder durch gemeinsame Geschichte mit dem Beter verbunden sind, etwa gar für Feinde, findet." Damit knüpft Schweizer an Ernst Lohmeyer an, bei dem es heißt: „Es ist Fürbitte, die geboten wird – und auch darin wird der Unterschied zum AT deutlich. Denn wo wir im AT ein Beten über die Feinde finden, da ist es ein Beten gegen Feinde … niemals für die Feinde" (Schweizer, *Evangelium nach Matthäus*, 145–46). Weiter zum matthäischen Gebot, für die Feinde zu beten: „Hier zum ersten Male in der Geschichte des Gebetes wird eine Fürbitte gefordert für Menschen, die den Beter deshalb angehen, weil auch sie Menschen, von Gott geschaffen sind, über die nicht eine menschliche Not oder Feindschaft, sondern das Wissen, daß auch sie vor Gott stehen, entscheidet" (ebd., 146); vgl. Grundmann, *Evangelium nach Matthäus*, 175. Dem oben Zitierten gegenüber kritisch z. B.: Fiedler, *Matthäusevangelium*, 152–53; vgl. Konradt, *Evangelium nach Matthäus*, 97.

(2 Kön 6,20): Elisa bittet zunächst darum, der Herr möge die ins Land eingefallenen feindlichen syrischen Soldaten, die ihm nach dem Leben trachten, mit Blindheit schlagen (V. 18). Als sich die Verblendeten in der Gewalt des Königs von Israel befinden, bittet Elisa Gott um ihre Heilung (V. 20). Statt sich an den Feinden zu rächen, setzt der Beter beim König die Bereitung eines Festmahls für seine Todfeinde durch und lässt sie unbehelligt abziehen (V. 23).[12]

In den biblischen Schriften Alten und Neuen Testamentes begegnet der expressis verbis überlieferte Text eines (Kurz-)Gebetes *für Feinde* außer in 2 Kön 6,20 noch im Todesgebet des Stephanus in Apg 7,60b.[13]

Als Beispiele biblisch-jüdischer Ethik der Feindesliebe wird auf der Basis der bei Paul Billerbeck genannten Parallelen[14] bis heute ein fester Kanon an Stellen angeführt.[15] Die hier und im nachstehenden Abschnitt erwähnten Gebete für die Verfolger bleiben in der Regel unerwähnt.

C. Abrams bzw. Abrahams Gebete für und gegen seine Feinde

Die erste innerbiblische Erwähnung einer Fürbitte zugunsten eines Feindes begegnet in Gen 20,7. Abraham hat sich in das Gebiet des Königs Abimelech begeben. Dort gibt er trotz der in Gen 12,10–20 berichteten schlechten Erfahrungen in Ägypten seine Frau Sara abermals als seine Schwester aus (V. 13), was Abimelech den Vorwand liefert, sie in seinen Harem aufzunehmen.

Die alttestamentliche Exegese diskutiert die Frage, ob es sich bei den Preisgabegeschichten der Ahnfrau Sara(i)[16] um Dubletten handelt.[17] Der Text und die Anlage der Perikope erlauben die Vermutung, dass hier bewusst mit Paral-

---

[12] 2 Kön 6,18–23: 18 Und als die Aramäer zu ihm herabkamen, betete Elisa und sprach: HERR, schlage dies Volk mit Blindheit! Und er schlug sie mit Blindheit nach dem Wort Elisas. 19 Und Elisa sprach zu ihnen: Dies ist nicht der Weg und nicht die Stadt. Folgt mir nach! Ich will euch führen zu dem Mann, den ihr sucht. Und er führte sie nach Samaria. 20 Und als sie nach Samaria kamen, sprach Elisa: HERR, öffne diesen die Augen, dass sie sehen! Und der HERR öffnete ihnen die Augen, und sie sahen, und siehe, da waren sie mitten in Samaria. 21 Und als der König von Israel sah, sprach er zu Elisa: Mein Vater, soll ich sie erschlagen? 22 Er sprach: Du sollst sie nicht erschlagen. Erschlägst du denn die, die du mit Schwert und Bogen gefangen hast? Setze ihnen Brot und Wasser vor, dass sie essen und trinken, und lass sie zu ihrem Herrn ziehen! 23 Da wurde ein großes Mahl bereitet. Und als sie gegessen und getrunken hatten, ließ er sie gehen, dass sie zu ihrem Herrn zogen. Seitdem kamen streifende Rotten der Aramäer nicht mehr ins Land Israel.

[13] Apg 7,60b: „Herr, rechne ihnen diese Sünde nicht an!"; das Todesgebet Jesu in Lk 23,34a: „Vater, vergib ihnen, denn sie wissen nicht, was sie tun!" fehlt in wichtigen Handschriften.

[14] Str-B 1:368–71.

[15] Z. B. Klaiber, *Matthäusevangelium*, 1:115; Grundmann, *Evangelium nach Matthäus*, 177: Ex 23,4–5; Spr 25,21–22.

[16] Vgl. Isaak und Rebekka bei Abimelech (Gen 26,6–11).

[17] Claus Westermann, *Genesis*, Teilband 2: *Genesis 12–36*, BKAT 1/2 (Neukirchen-Vluyn: Neukirchener Verlag, 1978), 185–96, 386–403; vgl. Irmtraud Fischer, *Die Erzeltern Israels:*

lelen und Unterschieden gearbeitet wird und die Perikopen von Sarai bei Pharao (Gen 12,10–20) und Sara bei Abimelech (Gen 20) komplementär zu verstehen sind.[18] Während des Aufenthalts Sarais in Ägypten werden Pharao und sein Haus, d. h. *die Männer*, geschlagen (Gen 12,17). Als die Ahnfrau am Hofe Abimelechs weilt, trifft die Strafe Gottes neben dem König *die Frauen* seines Landes (Gen 20,17–18). Pharao fordert Abram auf, das Land zu verlassen (Gen 12,19); Abimelech lädt Abraham ein, in seinem Lande zu wohnen (Gen 20,15); das Erzelternpaar verlässt das Land jeweils reich beschenkt (Gen 12,16.20; 20,14.16).

In der Genesis wird für Abrams Ägyptenaufenthalt keinerlei Gebet erwähnt. Anders verhält es sich bei Abimelech. Gott selbst erscheint dem Abimelech im Traum, fordert die Rückgabe Saras und verheißt ihm, dass Abraham *für ihn* bitten wird (Gen 20,7). In 20,17 heißt es ausdrücklich, dass Abraham zugunsten Abimelechs betet, und dass Gott daraufhin ihn und die Frauen seines Hofes heilt. Josephus erwähnt das Gebet Abrahams für Abimelech (*Ant.* 1.210). In BerR 52 zu Gen 20,17 heißt es, dass hier zum ersten Mal in der Genesis expressis verbis gefordert sei, dass jemand für einen anderen betet.[19]

1. Wurzeln des Betens Abrams gegen und für Pharao

Das von Gott persönlich zugesagte Gebet Abrahams für Abimelech in Gen 20,7[20] dürfte die Motivation für den Verfasser des Genesis-Apokryphons gewesen sein, bereits in seiner Schilderung der parallelen Erzählung in Gen 12,10–20 Gebete einzufügen.[21]

In Gen 20,6.17–18 straft Gott Abimelech, um ihn zu retten. Dasselbe bewirkt Abrams Gebet im Genesis-Apokryphon (1Q20 [1QapGen ar] XX, 12–16) mit Blick auf Pharao. Da es sich um Korrespondenzerzählungen handelt und Pharao deutlich schlechter als Abimelech bewertet wird, wäre die alleinige Einfügung einer *Fürbitte* dem Duktus der Geschichte kaum gerecht geworden. Es entspricht

---

Feministisch-theologische Studien zu Genesis 12–36, BZAW 222 (Berlin: de Gruyter, 1994), 190–92.

[18] So z. B. Yehuda T. Radday (Hg.), *Auf den Spuren der Parascha: Ein Stück Tora*, Band 6: *Welterziehung, Ssaraj im Serail, Die Nicht-Opferung Jizchaks, Kein gleiches Recht für alle?, Umkehr und Rückkehr* (Berlin: IKJ, 1997), 37–39.

[19] „R. Chama bar R. Chanina sagte: Vom Anfange des Buches [Genesis] bis zu dieser Stelle finden wir diese Redensart (für einen andern beten) nicht" (BerR 52 zu Gen 20,17). Übersetzung nach August Wünsche, *Der Midrasch Bereschit Rabba*, Bibliotheca Rabbinica 1 (Leipzig: Otto Schulze, 1881; Neudr. Hildesheim: Olms, 1993), 250.

[20] Gen 20,6–7: 6 Und Gott sprach zu ihm [Abimelech] im Traum: Ich weiß auch, dass du das mit einfältigem Herzen getan hast. Darum habe ich dich auch behütet, dass du nicht wider mich sündigtest, und habe es nicht zugelassen, dass du sie berührtest. 7 So gib nun dem Mann seine Frau wieder, denn er ist ein Prophet, und lass ihn für dich bitten, so wirst du am Leben bleiben. Wenn du sie aber nicht wiedergibst, so wisse, dass du des Todes sterben musst und alles, was dein ist.

[21] 1QapGen ar XX, 12–29.

der Gesamtanlage der Erzählung, dass Abram nach der Verschleppung Sarais zunächst ein Bittgebet *gegen* den ihm zum Feind gewordenen Pharao an Gott richtet.

Folgendes ist zu vergegenwärtigen: Abram erhält den Auftrag, Heimat und Vaterhaus zu verlassen und in ein ihm noch unbekanntes Land zu ziehen (Gen 12,1). In Gen 12,2 wird ihm verheißen, Gott werde ihn zu einer großen Nation machen und ihn segnen. Der 75-Jährige tut, wie ihm geheißen (Gen 12,4). Kaum im Land angekommen, nötigt eine Hungersnot Abram mit Sarai aus ebendiesem Land nach Ägypten auszuwandern (Gen 12,10).

Wenn die nachstehende Perikope als „Gefährdung" oder „Preisgabe" der Ahnfrau tituliert wird, handelt es sich um eine Verharmlosung. Mit der Eingliederung in den Harem Pharaos steht die Verheißung an Abram als solche und damit die Macht Gottes auf dem Spiel. Entscheidend ist, literarisch abzusichern, dass Sarai von niemand anderem als von Abram berührt wird. Das Genesis-Apokryphon sichert die Vollgültigkeit der Verheißung und die bleibende „Reinheit" der Ahnfrau ab, indem es die in Gen 12,17 geschilderten Plagen für Pharao und sein Haus als Impotenz infolge des Betens Abrams deutet.

2. Das Beten Abrams im Genesis-Apokryphon (1QapGen ar XX, 12–16)

Bei dem Genesis-Apokryphon (1Q20 oder 1QapGen ar)[22] handelt es sich um ein aramäisch verfasstes und nicht originär essenisches Werk.[23] Der Text ist auf Leder geschrieben; die eisenhaltige Tinte hat das Material stark geschädigt;[24] vergleichsweise gut erhalten sind die Kolumnen II und XIX–XXII.

Während Armin Lange mit anderen in 1QapGen ar XXI, 23–24[25] eine historische Anspielung erkennt und die Entstehung des Textes im ersten vor- oder nachchristlichen Jahrhundert ansetzt,[26] hält Hartmut Stegemann das dritte vorchristliche Jahrhundert für wahrscheinlich.[27]

---

[22] Johann Maier, *Die Qumran-Essener: Die Texte vom Toten Meer*, 3 Bde., UTB 1862–1863, 1916 (München: Ernst Reinhardt, 1995–1996), 1:212, kritisiert die Bezeichnung als unzutreffend und biblizistisch. Maier wählt als Abkürzung, ebd., 1:211: „1QGenAp."

[23] Armin Lange, „Qumran: Die Textfunde von Qumran," *TRE* 28:45–65, 75–79, hier 47; Hartmut Stegemann, *Die Essener, Qumran, Johannes der Täufer, Jesus: Ein Sachbuch*, 9. Aufl., HS 4128 (Freiburg: Herder, 1999), 139–40.

[24] Stegemann, *Essener*, 140.

[25] 1QapGen ar XXI, 23–24: 23 Vor diesen Tagen war(en) Kedorlaomer, König von Elam, Amrafel, König von Babel, Arjoch, König von Kaftok, (und) Tid'al, König von Gojim, 24 das liegt im Zweistromland, herbeigekommen und hatten Krieg geführt gegen Bera, den König von Sodom, mit Birscha, König von Gomorrah, mit Shinab, König von Admah (Übersetzung nach Maier, *Qumran-Essener*, 1:223).

[26] Lange, „Qumran," 47, versteht 1QapGen ar XXI, 23–24 als einen Hinweis auf die Teilung des Partherreiches im Jahre 91 v. Chr.

[27] Stegemann, *Essener*, 140.

Inhaltlich handelt es sich bei dem Genesis-Apokryphon ähnlich wie bei dem Jubiläenbuch um eine ausschmückende Nacherzählung von Teilen der Noah- und der Vätergeschichte. Sie setzt ein mit dem Bericht Lamechs über die Geburt Noahs (II–V). Laut Stegemann umfasste das Apokryphon den Textbestand der Genesis bis mindestens Genesis 25.[28] Nachweisbar sind Bezüge auf Gen 5,28–15,4. Der Beginn und das Ende der Rolle sind nicht erhalten.

Das Genesis-Apokryphon nimmt Anleihen beim Äthiopischen Henoch und beim Jubiläenbuch. Armin Lange klassifiziert 1QapGen ar XIX, 10–XX, 32 als „eine Gen 12,10 ff. entfaltende weisheitliche Lehrerzählung …, um eben diese Erzählung von der Gefährdung der Ahnfrau auszulegen."[29] Den weiteren Kontext, 1QapGen ar XIX, 7–10; XX, 33–XXI, 4, sieht Lange als „ein Itinerar, das die Reisen Abrahams im Land und nach Ägypten schildert."[30]

Die Erweiterungen des Genesis-Apokryphons füllen häufig „Leerstellen" des biblischen Originals. So geht aus Gen 12,10–20 nicht hervor, wie lange sich Sarai bei Pharao aufhielt. Auch spricht die Genesiserzählung nicht ausdrücklich über das Ergehen Sarais im Hause Pharaos. Das Apokryphon bietet für beides Erklärungen: Laut 1QapGen ar XIX, 23 erfolgt Sarais Entführung, nachdem sich Abram bereits fünf Jahre im Land aufgehalten hatte. Die in Gen 12,17 erwähnten Plagen an Pharao und seinem Haus deutet das Apokryphon als Impotenz und Folge des Gebetes Abrams (1QapGen ar XX, 16–17).[31]

Das Bittgebet Abrams in 1QapGen ar XX, 12–16 erscheint in der Form eines Gerichtsplädoyers. Gerahmt ist die Klage durch den Hinweis des Klägers auf seine Tränen (Z. 12.16). Es folgt die Anrufung des Richters unter ausführlichem Verweis auf dessen Zuständigkeit. Leitworte der Anrufung sind כול (alles; Z. 12c.13a.b.c.15a.c) und שליט (herrschen; Z. 13a.b.15b): Gott herrscht über alles. Ein zweiter, innerer Rahmen benennt wortgleich Gott als den Herrn über *alle* Könige der Erde (כול מלכי ארעא; Z. 13b.15e–16a). Er hat die allgemeine Gerichtsgewalt und ist folglich derjenige, der in dieser Sache gegen einen irdischen Herrscher Recht zu schaffen vermag.

Der Beter arbeitet mit dem Gegensatz von Preisung der *Allmacht* Gottes (שליט, Z. 13a.b) und Bitte um *Ohnmacht* Pharaos (לא שליט, Z. 15b). Der Mittelteil der Bitte formuliert die eigentliche Anklage. Der Beklagte wird benannt als Pharao Zoan (Z. 14b). Durch die Entführung der Frau Abrams hat Pharao eingegriffen in Gottes Erwählung und damit in den Herrschaftsbereich Gottes. Abram

---

[28] Ebd., 140.
[29] Lange, „Qumran," 47.
[30] Ebd. Klaus Berger, *Das Buch der Jubiläen*, JSHRZ 2.3 (Gütersloh: Gütersloher Verlagshaus, 1991), 398 Anm. 11e, macht aufmerksam auf Parallelen in der Chronologie in Jub 13,11 und 1QapGen ar XIX, 23.
[31] Auch Philo, *Abr.* 96–98, spricht von der Bewahrung der Keuschheit Sarais und benennt in *Abr.* 95 ein Gebet Abrams und Sarais. Vgl. das Gebet Sarais in BerR 41 zu Gen 12,17; vgl. unten, Anm. 38.

fordert, Gott möge seine Macht erweisen und ihm zu seinem Recht verhelfen. Durch die Ausweitung der Strafbitte auf das ganze Haus Pharaos greift der Beter eine biblische Notiz auf. Die in Gen 12,17 genannten großen Plagen an Pharao und seinem ganzen Haus erscheinen als Folge der konkreten Bitte Abrams. Sie werden von den Rezipienten des Gebetes verstanden als ein Vorspiel der in Ex 7–12 beschriebenen Plagen über die Ägypter vor dem Auszug des Volkes Israel.

Es entstehen Spannungen dadurch, dass sich Abrams Gebet konkret auf *eine* Nacht bezieht, dass aber laut 1QapGen ar XX, 18 der Aufenthalt Sarais bei Pharao zwei Jahre dauerte. Darüber hinaus werden die Plagen und Schläge, die das ganze Haus Pharaos treffen, am Ende der zwei Jahre schlimmer. Das deutet darauf hin, dass die Unfähigkeit zum Beischlaf als Erklärung dessen, was Pharao plagt, allein nicht ausreicht. Im Anschluss an die konkrete Strafbitte formuliert der Beter ein weiteres Ziel der göttlichen Intervention: Alle sollen Gott als den Herrn Abrams erkennen.

An derselben Stelle wie 1QapGen ar XX, 12–16 setzt das rabbinische Gebet aus Tanchuma an.[32] Eingeleitet wird das Gebet ebenfalls mit dem Weinen des Stammvaters. Duktus und Argumentation beider Gebete sind jedoch unterschiedlich. Während das Apokryphon Pharao anklagt und dessen Impotenz fordert, ist das rabbinische Gebet als *gegen Gott* gerichtete Klage Abrams formuliert: Er sieht sein Vertrauen auf Gott enttäuscht, bittet um Erbarmen und darum, dass seine Hoffnung nicht zuschanden werde.[33]

3. Text und Übersetzung des Gebetes Abrams zum Schutz der Sarai[34] (1QapGen ar XX, 12–16)[35]

בליליא דן צלית ובעית ואתחננת 12
In dieser Nacht betete ich und bat und flehte

---

[32] Günter Stemberger, *Einleitung in Talmud und Midrasch*, 8. Aufl. (München: C. H. Beck, 1992), 301, verortet mit anderen die materielle Basis der Schrift im vierten nachchristlichen Jahrhundert.

[33] Midrasch Tanchuma, Lekh 5 (פרשת לך לך ה'):
אברהם כך התחיל בוכה ומתפלל לפני הקב״ה
„so begann Abraham zu weinen und betete vor dem Heiligen, gesegnet sei er.
ואומר רבש״ע זו הוא בטחוני שבטחתי בך
Er sprach: ‚Herr der Welt, ist das mein Vertrauen, mit dem ich vertraut habe auf dich?
ועכשיו עשה למען רחמיך וחסדיך
Und jetzt handle um deines Erbarmens und deiner Gnade willen,
ואל תביישני מסברי
und nicht lass mich zuschanden werden in meiner Hoffnung.'" Text aus *Midrasch Tanchuma* (Hebr.), 2 Bde. (Jerusalem: Tifʿeret ha-Sefer, 1992–93), 1:44.

[34] Aramäischer Text nach Klaus Beyer, *Die aramäischen Texte vom Toten Meer, samt den Inschriften aus Palästina, dem Testament Levis aus der Kairoer Genisa, der Fastenrolle und den alten talmudischen Zitaten: Aramaistische Einleitung, Text, Übersetzung, Deutung, Grammatik*, 2 Bde. (Göttingen: Vandenhoeck & Ruprecht, 1984), 1:175.

[35] Der punktierte aramäische Text samt einer Übersetzung ins Französische findet sich bei

ואמרת באתעצבא ודמעי נחתן
und sprach in Not und meine Tränen strömten:
בריך אנתה אל עליון מרי לכול
Gesegnet bist du, höchster Gott, mein Herr, für alle
עלמים די אנתה מרה ושליט על כולא 13
Zeitalter. Denn du bist der Herr und Herrscher über alles
ובכול מלכי ארעא אנתה שליט
und über alle Könige der Erde herrschst du,
למעבד בכולהון דין וכען
um über sie alle zu richten. Und jetzt
קבלתך מרי 14
meine Anklage vor dich, mein Herr,
על פרעו צען מלך מצרין
über Pharao Zoan, den König Ägyptens.
די דברת אנתתי מני בתוקף
Denn weggeführt ist meine Frau von mir mit Gewalt.
עבד לי דין מנה ואחזי ידך רבתא
Schaffe mir Recht gegen ihn und lasse erscheinen deine mächtige Hand
בה ובכול ביתה 15
gegen ihn und gegen sein ganzes Haus.
ואל ישלט בליליא
Und nicht vermöge er es in dieser Nacht
דן לטמיא אנתתי[36]מני
zu verunreinigen meine Frau (getrennt) von mir.
וינדעוך מרי
Und sie sollen dich erkennen, mein Herr,
די אנתה מרה לכול מלכי
denn du bist der Herr für alle Könige
ארעא ובכית וחשית 16
der Erde. Und ich weinte und verstummte.

Die in Gen 12 geschilderte Gefährdung Abrams und Sarais unmittelbar nach ihrem Gehorsam Gott gegenüber und im Anschluss an ihren Auszug aus ihrer Heimat, hat schon früh die Frage nach dem Leiden des Gerechten aufgeworfen. Die Frage wird im spätantiken Tanchuma-Gebet explizit, steht jedoch bereits hinter dem Genesis-Apokryphon. Mit Blick auf Ps 92,13: „Der Gerechte wird grünen wie ein Palmbaum, er wird wachsen wie eine Zeder auf dem Libanon" wird in 1QapGen ar XIX, 14–23 begründet, warum Abrams Sorge berechtigt ist, dass Pharao ihn als Sarais Ehemann umbringen will, um sie selbst zu sich nehmen zu können: In der Nacht nach seinem Betreten Ägyptens träumt Abram mit eindeutigem Bezug auf Ps 92,13 von einer Palme und einer Zeder, die aus *einer* Wurzel wachsen. Als man die Zeder fällen und entwurzeln und die Palme stehen

---

Ursula Schattner-Rieser, *Textes Araméens de la Mer Morte: Édition bilingue, vocalisée et commentée*, Langues et cultures anciennes 5 (Brüssel: Safran, 2005), 74–75.

[36] Beyer, *Die aramaïschen Texte*, 175 Anm. 1, vermutet, מני (weg von mir) sei aufgrund einer Unaufmerksamkeit des Schreibers „versehentlich aus Zeile 14 eingedrungen."

lassen will, ruft die Palme, sie hätten eine gemeinsame Wurzel. Daraufhin lässt man die Zeder um der Palme willen stehen. Abram erwacht, erzählt Sarai seinen Traum und veranlasst sie so, ihn als ihren Bruder auszugeben, damit er nicht um ihretwillen getötet, sondern mit ihr gerettet werde. Zu beachten ist auch das *Traum*motiv in Gen 20,6. Gott erscheint dem Abimelech und verheißt ihm im Traum die Fürbitte Abrahams.

Die Verbindung des Motivs des Gerechten, der wie Palme und Zeder gedeihen wird (Ps 92,13), mit dem Ägyptenaufenthalt zieht sich durch die jüdische Kommentarliteratur: Bevor in Bereschit Rabba 41[37] zu Gen 12,17 Sarais Gebet um Beistand in der Nacht bei Pharao beschrieben wird,[38] behandelt Genesis (Bereschit) Rabba ausführlich die Zusammengehörigkeit von Palme und Zeder in Ps 92,13.

Das Gebet Abrams ist nicht nur in einer Hinsicht bemerkenswert. Abram bittet nicht um Strafen für Pharao, er wünscht ihm nicht den Tod. In dem Gebet ist auch nicht von den Plagen die Rede, mit denen Gott laut Gen 12,17 Pharao und sein Haus schlug.

Der gesegnete Abram ruft im Genesis-Apokryphon Gott an. Er segnet und rühmt ihn darin als Herrn und Mächtigen, der über alle Könige mächtig ist. Er erbittet konkret, der König Ägyptens sei in der Nacht der Entführung nicht mächtig, seine Frau zu verunreinigen (Schlüsselwort: שליט; mächtig sein, herrschen). Die Macht Gottes wird der Macht Pharaos entgegengestellt.

Da in jener Nacht tatsächlich die Verheißung an Abram und damit die gesamte Heilsgeschichte Gottes mit Israel auf dem Spiel steht, terminieren z. B. die Pirke de Rabbi Eliezer (Pirqe R. El. 26)[39] die Entführungsnacht mit innerer Logik auf den 15. Nisan. Es ist die Nacht, in der laut Ex 12,29 die Erstgeburt in Ägypten, einschließlich dem Haus Pharaos, geschlagen wird. Weitere Parallelen zwischen Abrams Aufenthalt in Ägypten und dem Auszug des Volkes Israel sind

---

[37] Stemberger, *Einleitung*, 275, setzt den Midrasch zur Genesis in der ersten Hälfte des fünften Jahrhunderts an.

[38] Bereschit Rabba 41 zu Gen 12,17:

וכל אותו הלילה היתה שרה שטוחה על פניה

Und die ganze Nacht war Sara ausgestreckt auf ihrem Gesicht

ואומרת רבון העולמים

und sprach: „Herr der Welten!

אברהם יצא בהבטחה ואני יצאתי באמונה

Abraham zog aus mit einer Verheißung und ich zog aus mit Vertrauen;

אברהם יצא חוץ לסירה ואני בתוך הסירה

Abraham zog heraus aus der Not, aber ich mitten in die Not."

אמר לה הקב"ה כל מה שאני עושה בשבילך אני עושה

Es sprach zu ihr der Heilige, gesegnet sei er: „Alles, was ich tue, tue ich deinetwegen,

והכל אומרים על דבר שרי אשת אברם

darum sagen auch alle: ‚Wegen Sarai, der Frau Abrams'." Text aus *Midrasch Rabba* (Hebr.), 2 Bde. (Wilna: Romm, 1878; Nachdr. Jerusalem, o. J.), 1:83; vgl. Wünsche, *Midrasch Bereschit Rabba*, 186.

[39] Nach Stemberger, *Einleitung*, 322, im achten oder neunten Jahrhundert redigiert.

neben den Plagen für Pharao und sein ganzes Haus noch die Geschenke für die Ausziehenden (Gen 12,16; Ex 12,35). Das Genesis-Apokryphon konkretisiert die Geschenke und berichtet in 1QapGen ar XX, 32 u. a., dass Pharao dem Abraham Hagar als Geschenk überlässt. Bereshit Rabba 45 zu 16,1 erklärt, Hagar sei die Tochter Pharaos gewesen.

Wurde Pharao laut dem Genesis-Apokryphon aufgrund des Gebetes Abrams impotent, dann legt es sich nahe, dass die Plage auch erst durch ein Gebet Abrams wieder von ihm genommen wird. Dieses Beten Abrams um Heilung für Pharao erwähnt 1QapGen ar XX, 28–29:

וצלית על[וה]י [על] רפאוהי וסמכת ידי על ראישה.
Und ich betete für ihn für seine Heilung, und ich legte meine Hände auf sein Haupt.

Laut Gen 20,6 straft Gott Abimelech, um ihn zu retten – letztlich tut Abram dasselbe für Pharao mit *seinem* ersten Gebet (1QapGen ar XX, 12–16). Bemerkenswert bei der Heilung Pharaos durch Abram im Genesis-Apokryphon ist, dass er dabei seinem ehemaligen Feind die Hand auflegt (1QapGen ar XX, 29). Heilung durch Gebet in Kombination mit Handauflegung wird eher selten ausdrücklich benannt.[40] Das Genesis-Apokryphon gibt das Gebet Abrams bei der Heilung des Pharaos anders als sein Gebet in der Nacht der Entführung Sarais nicht wörtlich wieder.

Bei einer neutestamentlichen Heilung eines Feindes wird ebenfalls eine Handauflegung des Heilenden erwähnt: Der Feind und Verfolger der jungen christlichen Gemeinde, der spätere Apostel Paulus, wird von Hananias im Gebet angetroffen (Apg 9,11) und durch Handauflegung (V. 17) von seiner Blindheit geheilt. Paulus lässt sich daraufhin taufen (V. 18). Paulus selbst heilt einen Fieberkranken in Apg 28,8 durch seine Fürbitte verbunden mit Handauflegung.

4. Das Motiv des Verstummens

Pointiert schließt das Gebet Abrams in der Nacht der Entführung Sarais mit seinem Schweigen. Sein Schweigen tritt an die Stelle des Amens in Lobgebeten. Es erscheint als Motiv auch im Kontext anderer Gebete, etwa dem Gebet Levis in den Testamenten der Zwölf Patriarchen (TestXII.Lev 2.3; vgl. 4Q213a)[41] oder dem Verstummen des Tempelschänders Heliodor in 2 Makk 3,29. Das Verstummen am Ende eines Bitt- oder Klagegebetes verdeutlicht sinnfällig das Ende aller menschlichen Handlungsoptionen (vgl. Ps 39,3.10). Der alleinigen Macht Got-

---

[40] Beyer, *Die aramaïschen Texte*, 176 Anm. 1.
[41] Der Schlussvers des griechisch überlieferten Gebetes Levis aus der Handschrift „e" der Testamente der zwölf Patriarchen lautet: „Und nicht verstoße den Sohn deines Knechts von deinem Angesicht alle Tage der Ewigkeit. Und ich verstummte noch betend" (TestXII.Lev 2.3 [19]); Marinus de Jonge, *The Testaments of the Twelve Patriarchs: A Critical Edition of the Greek Text*, PVTG 1.2 (Leiden: Brill, 1978).

tes stehen auf seiten des Beters Ohnmacht und Schweigen gegenüber.[42] In der apokryphen Tradition wird das Motiv z. B. in Bar 6,40–41 karikiert, indem dort ein Stummer erwähnt wird, vor den man zwecks Gebets ein Bild des Gottes Bel stellt.[43]

D. Fazit

Gebete um Vernichtung der Gegner begegnen u. a. in einzelnen Psalmenpassagen (Ps 58,7–11; 83,10–18; 109,6–20 etc.), im Gebet Moses gegen Datham und Abiram bei Josephus (*Ant.* 4.40–50; vgl. Num 16,28–35), in den Rachegebeten für Martine und Heraklea[44] auf den Grabstelen von Rheneia[45] oder in den Drohworten[46] und Weherufen[47] Jesu im Neuen Testament. Der Anteil solcher Gebete fällt im Vergleich zu Klagen *ohne* eine gleichzeitige Bitte um Schädigung der Gegner gering aus.

Jüdisches Beten *zugunsten* von Feinden ist zwar nicht dominierend, es begegnet aber durchgängig und in unterschiedlichen jüdischen Textgruppen: im Alten Testament (Gen 20,7.17; 2 Kön 6,18–20);[48] in den Apokryphen (2 Makk 3,29); den Pseudepigraphen (TestXII.Jos 18,2);[49] in Qumran (1QapGen ar XX, 21–22.28–

---

[42] Zur Zusammengehörigkeit von Beten und menschlichem Verstummen vgl. auch Zacharias in Lk 1,20–22: Er hatte viele Jahre unerhört gebetet, und er verstummte im Tempel, nachdem Gott ihm einen Sohn verheißen hatte.

[43] Bar 6,40–41: 40 Wie soll man sie denn für Götter halten oder so nennen? Ja, selbst die Chaldäer halten nichts von ihnen. 41 Wenn sie einen Stummen sehen, der nicht reden kann, bringen sie den Bel herbei und fordern vom Stummen, er sollte zu ihm schreien, als ob Bel das vernehmen könnte.

[44] Marmorstele aus Rheneia mit dem Rachegebet für die Jüdin Heraklea von Delos, ca. 100 v. Chr. (Vorder- u. Rückseite, Bukarest); Abbildung bei Adolf Deißmann, *Licht vom Osten: Das Neue Testament und die neuentdeckten Texte der hellenistisch-römischen Welt*, 4. Aufl. (Tübingen: J. C. B. Mohr, 1923), 352. Der geläufige Titel des Gebets lautet: „Ein Gebet um Rache für die Jüdin Heraklea" – die Klassifizierung als „jüdisch" ist weniger eindeutig, als die Titulatur vermuten lässt. Bei den Namen der beiden unverheirateten Mädchen oder Frauen handelt es sich um weibliche Formen griechischer Götternamen (Herakles und Mars). „Heraklea" ist für Jüdinnen sonst nicht belegt; für einen jüdischen Hintergrund spricht die Wortwahl, die sich an den Sprachgebrauch der Septuaginta anlehnt.

[45] Pieter Willem van der Horst, „A Prayer for Vengeance from Rheneia," in *Early Jewish Prayers in Greek: A Commentary*, hg. v. Pieter Willem van der Horst und Judith H. Newman, CEJL (Berlin: de Gruyter, 2008), 137–43, hier 137. Die beiden Grabsteine lassen sich vergleichsweise genau auf die Wende vom zweiten zum ersten Jahrhundert datieren. Die Entstehungszeit ist damit vergleichbar mit der des Genesis-Apokryphons und dem besprochenen Gebet Abrams.

[46] Mk 9,42 (vgl. Q 17,2 [umstritten]; Mt 18,6); Lk 21,22–23 parr.

[47] Q 10,13–15, vgl. Mt 11,20–24; 23,13–36; Lk 6,24–26.

[48] Vgl. Spr 25,11.

[49] Vgl. Anm. 8.

29); bei Josephus (*Ant.* 1.210; 9.56–57);[50] im Neuen Testament (Apg 9,17; vgl. Lk 23,34; Q 6,28); in den Rabbinica (b. Ber. 10a).[51]

Es fällt auf, dass einige Gebete *gegen* die Feinde letztlich zu deren Rettung und Gunsten ausgehen und allen Rachegedanken fernstehen. Modern gesprochen atmen sie einen Geist von Humanität: Elisas Gebet um Verblendung feindlicher Soldaten (2 Kön 6,18), die Klage des Volkes angesichts der drohenden Tempelschändung durch Heliodor (2 Makk 3,18–22) und das in Qumran überlieferte Gebet Abrams gegen Pharao (1QapGen ar XX, 12–16). Jeweils im Anschluss an die hier genannten Gebete *gegen* die Feinde folgt ein Gebet *für* sie, das ihre Heilung bewirkt.

Gebete für die Feinde als innigster Ausdruck der Feindesliebe (z. B. Q 6,27–28; vgl. Mt 5,44) sind weder eine Erfindung Jesu noch des Autors von Q. Das Neue Testament und Q sind nicht die Quelle, sondern sie stehen mit Josephus und den Rabbinica in einem breiten Traditionsstrom. Das Gebet für die Feinde ist im Judentum unterschiedlichster Prägung und Epochen verschriftlicht. Einen wichtigen und wirkmächtigen Abschnitt dieses Traditionsstroms bietet Q 6,28.

Gebete für die Feinde und das Gebot der Feindesliebe korrelieren (z. B. Q 6,27–28). Dort jedoch, wo die „Erfindung" der Feindesliebe oder des Gebetes für die Feinde *exklusiv* für die eigene Gruppe reklamiert wird, wird das lange Band der gemeinsamen Tradition gekappt. Anspruch auf Originalität des Konzeptes der Feindesliebe und des Betens für Feinde geht notwendig damit einher, anderen beides abzusprechen. Das wiederum impliziert, dass man bei dem Anderen Feindschaft sucht (und findet) und so letztlich den eigenen Anspruch eines liebenden Umgangs mit dem Anderen konterkariert.

---

[50] Vgl. das bei Josephus überlieferte Gebet des Onias zu Gott. Er bittet, Gott möge keiner der beiden feindlichen Parteien beistehen und bezahlt das Gebet mit seinem Leben (*Ant.* 14.24).

[51] Auf der Basis von Ps 104,35 wird im babylonischen Talmud, Traktat Berakhoth 10a (ca. 5. Jh.), argumentiert, es sei gefordert, gegen die Sünden, nicht aber gegen die Sünder zu beten. Hört ersteres auf, dann sind auch die Menschen, die einem begegnen, keine Sünder mehr; vgl. b. ʿArak. 10b; b. Sanh. 39b.

Prayer in the Sayings Source Q and in Early Rabbinic Texts

Catherine Hezser

The Sayings Source Q in its critical reconstruction from the gospels of Matthew and Luke is believed to represent (one of) the earliest collection(s) of traditional material associated with Jesus, going back to the very end of the Second Temple period and the First Jewish Revolt against Rome.[1] It is considered to have been created by Jewish Christians at a time when another Jewish Christian group was stationed in Jerusalem and Paul and Stephanus had begun their mission among gentiles.[2] Prayer appears in the collection only incidentally: Jesus is only once presented as praying (Q 10:21). More often, he gives instructions concerning prayer (Q 4:8; 6:28; 10:2; 11:2b–4; 11:9–13). The references to prayer are interwoven in story traditions (Q 4:4–8: Jesus' encounter with the devil) and appear

---

[1] A critical reconstruction of the text began with the International Q Project (IQP) of the Society for Biblical Literature (SBL) in the 1990s and was continued by colleagues in Bamberg, Claremont, and Toronto. The results are published in James M. Robinson, Paul Hoffmann, and John S. Kloppenborg, eds., *The Critical Edition of Q*, Hermeneia Supplements (Minneapolis: Fortress; Leuven: Peeters, 2000). Reconstructions and translations of Q in this essay are taken from the *Critical Edition of Q*. See also James M. Robinson, Paul Hoffmann, and John S. Kloppenborg, eds., *The Sayings Gospel Q in Greek and English* (Leuven: Peeters, 2001; Minneapolis: Fortress, 2002); James M. Robinson, ed., *The Sayings of Jesus: The Sayings Gospel Q* (Minneapolis: Fortress, 2002). For questions concerning its possible date and relationship to Mark, Matthew, and Luke, see John S. Kloppenborg, *Q, The Earliest Gospel: An Introduction to the Original Stories and Sayings of Jesus* (Louisville, KY: Westminster John Knox, 2008), 1–40. On Q's significance for the study of Jesus see James M. Robinson, "The Critical Edition of Q and the Study of Jesus," in *The Sayings Source Q and the Historical Jesus*, ed. Andreas Lindemann, BETL 158 (Leuven: Peeters, 2001), 27–52.

[2] On the Jewish-Christian context of Q see Robinson, "Critical Edition of Q," 47–48. See also Petri Luomanen, *Recovering Jewish-Christian Sects and Gospels*, SVigChr 110 (Leiden: Brill, 2012), 140–41. The common assumption among scholars is that Q was created in Galilee. Simon J. Joseph, *Jesus, Q, and the Dead Sea Scrolls: A Judaic Approach to Q*, WUNT II 333 (Tübingen: Mohr Siebeck, 2012), 74–87 and 187, has convincingly argued against this approach and the creation of a dichotomy between rural Galilee and Jerusalem/Judaea. He has shown that "Q contains polemic *against* Galilean villages" and that "the narrative world of Q begins and ends in Judea. Q is better understood as an ethnically and perhaps geographically Judean text" (ibid., 187). Giovanni B. Bazzana, *Kingdom and Bureaucracy: The Political Theology of Village Scribes in the Sayings Gospel Q*, BETL 274 (Leuven: Peeters, 2015), 54–81, perpetuates the "Galilean village scribe" model, which lacks a convincing socio-economic basis. There is no reason to assume that scribes who wrote in Greek would have been able to make a living in Galilean villages. On scribes, who are customarily associated with Jerusalem and the temple in Second Temple times, see also Catherine Hezser, *Jewish Literacy in Roman Palestine*, TSAJ 81 (Tübingen: Mohr Siebeck, 2001), 118–26.

in Jesus' moral and theological instructions to his followers (Q 6:27–28: love your enemies; Q 10:2: send workers into the harvest). Only one text, the so-called "Lord's Prayer," provides more detailed instructions for prayer (Q 11:2b–4) and the belief in its efficacy (11:9–13). Q presents prayer as an integral part of Jesus' teaching that exemplifies his and his followers' relationship to God and to other human beings.[3]

Previous studies of prayer in Q have focused on the "Lord's Prayer" and the question whether and to what extent it was part of the Sayings Source.[4] I shall look at all references to prayer in Q instead and discuss them in the context of early rabbinic literary sources and other sources on prayer in first- and second-century Judaism. If Q represents an early branch of Jewish-Christianity, a look at other Jewish sources may tell us more about the profile of this group. Two warnings are necessary at the outset, though. Firstly, the assumption that a somehow circumscribed local "community" stands behind a text seems problematic.[5] The Sayings Source may be the product of one or a few Greek-speaking or bilingual compilers only, who were committed to transmit some (mostly oral and Aramaic?) Jesus-traditions that had come down to them in written (Greek) form.[6] Secondly, the earliest rabbinic document, the Mishnah, was composed after 200 CE and the Tosefta and Tannaitic Midrashim may have been composed even later. These documents may contain traditions which, in some form or other, originated in earlier times, but there is no guarantee that their literary forms do not reflect later concerns and circumstances.[7]

---

[3] According to Florian Wilk, "'So sollt ihr beten...': Das Vaterunser als Element der frühen Jesusüberlieferung," in *Das Vaterunser in seinen antiken Kontexten: Zum Gedenken an Eduard Lohse*, ed. Florian Wilk, FRLANT 266 (Göttingen: Vandenhoeck & Ruprecht, 2016), 83–102, here 90, Q preserves memories of various prayer practices of Jesus.

[4] See, e. g., John S. Kloppenborg, "Discursive Practices in the Sayings Gospel Q and the Quest of the Historical Jesus," in Lindemann, *Sayings Source Q*, 149–90, here 178. See also Douglas E. Oakman, *Jesus, Debt, and the Lord's Prayer: First-Century Debt and Jesus' Intentions* (Eugene, OR: Cascade, 2014); Stephen C. Carlson, "Problems With the Non-Aversion Principle for Reconstructing Q," in *Marcan Priority Without Q: Explorations in the Farrer Hypothesis*, ed. John C. Poirier and Jeffrey Peterson, LNTS 455 (London: Bloomsbury T & T Clark, 2015), 44–57.

[5] On the problematic term "community" see also Brian C. Dennert, *John the Baptist and the Jewish Setting of Matthew*, WUNT II 403 (Tübingen: Mohr Siebeck, 2015), 22.

[6] There is a huge discussion on Q and orality, in regard to Q's sources and its own transmission; see, e. g., Delbert Burkett, *Rethinking the Gospel Sources*, vol. 2: *The Unity or Plurality of Q*, ECL 1 (Atlanta: Society of Biblical Literature, 2009), 46–47; Terence C. Mournet, *Oral Tradition and Literary Dependency: Variability and Stability in the Synoptic Tradition and Q*, WUNT II 195 (Tübingen: Mohr Siebeck, 2005), 43–45; and Jonathan A. Draper, "Jesus' 'Covenantal Discourse' on the Plain (Luke 6:12–7:17) as Oral Performance: Pointers to 'Q' as Multiple Oral Performance," in *Oral Performance, Popular Tradition, and Hidden Transcript in Q*, ed. Richard A. Horsley, SemeiaSt 60 (Atlanta: Society of Biblical Literature, 2006), 71–98, here 73–75, who argues that written transmission and oral tradition and performance could coexist. Most scholars believe that Q was composed in Greek, but it may be based on earlier Aramaic traditions; see, e. g., the discussion in Joseph, *Jesus, Q, and the Dead Sea Scrolls*, 51–62.

[7] The latest sages mentioned by name in the Mishnah (e. g., R. Yehudah ha-Nasi, the as-

In the following I shall argue that the prayer texts of the Sayings Source present Jesus in ways that are similar to the presentation of early Jewish charismatics in rabbinic sources. The descriptions of Jesus and other Jewish charismatics share the following motifs: prayer is presented as an always possible direct access to God that is believed to be effective and to receive an immediate response; the charismatic considers himself to be in an intimate relationship to God, compared to a child before his father. While some aspects, such as the monotheistic basis, are shared with rabbinic instructions on prayer, rabbinic texts differ from Q especially as far as their interest in formalization and ritualization is concerned. The Jesus represented in the Sayings Source explicitly distances himself from "sages and the learned" (Q 10:21). This leads me to the assumption that Q tries to portray Jesus as an early Jewish charismatic who stood in a particularly close relationship to God and gave instructions to other Jews who might be willing to follow him and "work in the harvest" he had sown.

A. Prayer as Individual Personal Expression
Versus Prayer as Shared Jewish Ritual Practice

Concerning prayer, the rabbis of the Mishnah were mainly interested in two aspects: in determining the "correct" prayer formulas and in discussing the proper times for prayers. Both concerns suggest an interest in standardization, although diversity in rabbinic opinions and historical uncertainty over rabbis' authority in liturgical matters suggest that prayers and the prayer service remained relatively unregulated until medieval times.[8] In the first centuries CE, the various local Jewish groups are likely to have followed their own customary practices, which the literary rabbinic opinions either reproduce or try to change and influence. The prayers that are repeatedly mentioned in rabbinic sources and that seem to have been the two most important prayers after 70 CE are the Shema Yisrael and the Amidah or Tefillah ("the Prayer"), also called Eighteen Benedictions (Shemoneh Esreh), prayers that were time-bound and supposed to be recited by all Jewish men two (Shema) or three times (Amidah) daily.[9]

---

sumed editor of the Mishnah) date to approximately 200 CE Tannaitic midrashim were "mostly redacted at the beginning of the amoraic period (mid-third century)": see Avigdor Shinan, "Midrashic, Paytanic, and Targumic Literature," in *The Cambridge History of Judaism*, vol. 4: *The Late Roman-Rabbinic Period*, ed. Steven T. Katz (Cambridge: Cambridge University Press, 2006), 678–98, here 687.

[8] See Lawrence A. Hoffman, *Beyond the Text: A Holistic Approach to Liturgy* (Bloomington, IN: Indiana University Press, 1989), 28, who points out that "as late as the geonic period (ca. 757–1038) disagreement continued, particularly in the Land of Israel, which continued to create new alternative texts and to insert them into the tefillah at different places."

[9] Note that Tannaitic documents do not provide the full text of the prayers; see also Reuven

Whether and to what extent these prayers were already customary in Second Temple times is disputed among scholars. Stefan Reif has argued that an early form of the Shema, that is, Deuteronomy 6:4, was already "a daily prayer in the temple and outside it" and "one of the earliest forerunners of synagogal liturgy."[10] The other parts of the Shema may have been added only later: "Whether the whole passage (6:4–9) and the second paragraph (Deut 11:13–21) were also recited is a more controversial point."[11] Although some of the benedictions that make up the Amidah may have emerged before 70 already, discussions about the proper number, formulation, and order of the *berakhot* appear in Tannaitic texts only.[12] A joined daily recitation of the Shema and Amidah also remains uncertain and, according to Reif, unlikely for temple times.[13]

One might argue that Jewish prayer was entirely unregulated in the first three quarters of the first century CE, both at the time of Jesus and when Q was created. Prayer may have been an individual and personal affair. Individuals may have formulated the texts themselves and recited them whenever they wished. Post-70 rabbinic attempts to regulate prayer and turn it into a more fixed religious ritual may have emerged as reactions to the vacuum left by the destruction of the temple and popular uncertainties as far as personal piety was concerned. Rabbinic insistence on a more formalized and regulated prayer practice may have been meant to unify Palestinian Jews in some shared rituals.[14]

Such a strict division between Jewish prayer before and after the destruction of the temple does not seem persuasive, however. Scholars no longer subscribe to the theory that so-called Yavnean rabbis fixed (the canon and) the liturgy.[15]

Kimelman, "The *Shema* and the *Amidah*: Rabbinic Prayer," in *Prayer from Alexander to Constantine: A Critical Anthology*, ed. Mark Kiley (London: Routledge, 1997), 108–20, here 108.

[10] Stefan C. Reif, *Judaism and Hebrew Prayer: New Perspectives on Jewish Liturgical History* (Cambridge: Cambridge University Press, 1993), 83.

[11] Ibid.

[12] For discussions of past scholarship on the question whether the Amidah originated before or after 70 CE, see Richard J. Bautsch, *Developments in Genre Between Post-Exilic Penitential Prayers and the Psalms*, AcBib 7 (Atlanta: Society of Biblical Literature, 2003), 170; Jeremy Penner, *Patterns of Daily Prayer in Second Temple Period Judaism*, STDJ 104 (Leiden: Brill, 2012), 20.

[13] Reif, *Judaism and Hebrew Prayer*, 84.

[14] Various scholars of the past considered rabbinic attempts to regulate prayer a post-70 innovation: see the discussion in Penner, *Patterns of Daily Prayer*, 19–21, with reference to Solomon Zeitlin, "The Tefillah, the Shemone Esreh: An Historical Study of the First Canonization of the Hebrew Liturgy," *JQR* 54 (1964): 208–49; Ezra Fleischer, "On the Beginnings of Obligatory Jewish Prayer [Hebr.]," *Tarbiz* 59 (1990): 397–441; Lee I. Levine, "The Development of Synagogue Liturgy in Late Antiquity," in *Galilee Through the Centuries: Confluence of Cultures*, ed. Eric M. Meyers, Duke Judaic Studies 1 (Winona Lake, IN: Eisenbrauns, 1999), 123–44.

[15] Against the old theory about a rabbinic "council" at Yavneh see, e. g., David E. Aune, "On the Origins of the 'Council of Javneh' Myth," *JBL* 110 (1991): 491–93. See also David M. Goodblatt, *The Monarchic Principle: Studies in Jewish Self-Government in Antiquity*, TSAJ 38 (Tübingen: Mohr Siebeck, 1994), 240.

Rabbinic discussions on the proper formulations and times of prayers seem to have been an ongoing process that was based on pre-70 precedents and continued into the Middle Ages. As far as pre-70 precedents to prayer times are concerned, Josephus already mentions some customary practices among his fellow Jews. He states that Moses called for a twice-daily prayer (*Ant.* 4.212), a rule that lacks a scriptural basis. According to Steve Mason, Josephus sees the "Law ... through the filter of ... current practices familiar to him."[16] Josephus may have known Jewish men of his time who prayed twice daily. Although this practice would have differed from the later rabbinic insistence on three daily prayer times (see m. Ber. 4:1), it indicates some Jews' adherence to a certain prayer pattern already in pre-rabbinic times. Penner has argued that in Second Temple times, "the custom of daily prayer was promoted as an important religious practice."[17] "Fixed daily prayer" could have been legitimized in a number of ways, for example, by recurrence to Deut 6:7 ("when you lie down and when you rise up"), connecting prayer "to sleeping and rising within one's daily routine in the household."[18] Another possibility was to link the twice daily prayers to the morning and afternoon sacrifice in the temple.[19] Although "prayer as a fixed daily practice was neither required nor encouraged formally by priests," some Jewish men may have adopted the practice.[20]

According to Mishnah Berakhot 4:1, "the morning Tefillah [can be recited] until midday, the afternoon Tefillah until evening, the evening Tefillah has no fixed [time]." The morning and afternoon recitation is probably modelled after the sacrificial services at the temple. Although the Shema is not mentioned here and the two prayers were originally separate, rabbis may have suggested a third evening recitation of the Tefillah to connect it with the recitation of the Shema that was scheduled to the mornings and evenings.[21] Mishnah Berakhot 1:1–2 discusses the times for the recitation of the Shema:

[1:1] From what time onwards do they recite the Shema in the evening? From the time when the priests enter [their houses] to eat their heave offering [*terumah*] until the end of the first night watch, the words of R. Eliezer. And sages say: Until midnight. R. Gamaliel

---

[16] Steve Mason, *Flavius Josephus on the Pharisees: A Composition-Critical Study*, StPB 39 (Leiden: Brill, 2001), 100.

[17] Penner, *Patterns of Daily Prayer*, 209.

[18] Ibid.

[19] According to the gospels and Acts, prayer was linked to the temple and the time of the sacrifices, even if it took place at home: the temple is called a "house of prayer" (Mark 11:17, Matt 21:13, Luke 19:46). See also Luke 1:10 (people were standing outside the temple, praying, at the time of the incense sacrifice); Luke 18:10 (a Pharisee and a tax-collector went to the temple to pray); Acts 3:1 (Peter and John went to the temple in the ninth hour, at the time of prayer); cf. Acts 10:30 (Cornelius says that he prayed at the ninth hour in his house).

[20] Penner, *Patterns of Daily Prayer*, 209.

[21] See also David Instone-Brewer, *Traditions of the Rabbis from the Era of the New Testament*, vol. 1: *Prayer and Agriculture* (Grand Rapids: Eerdmans, 2004), 53, commenting on this *mishnah*.

says: Until the pillar of dawn arises …. [1:2] From what time onwards do they recite the Shema in the morning? From when one can distinguish between blue and white. R. Eliezer says: Between blue and green. And one concludes it by sunrise ….

Rabbis take the twice daily recitation of the Shema as a given here. Its twice daily recitation was probably already practiced by some Jewish men in pre-70 times. What rabbis are concerned with in this passage is to specify the exact time slots for the twice daily recitation. This Mishnah shows that, except for the broad categories of morning and evening, the more specific times to fulfill the biblical commandment remained disputed among sages throughout Tannaitic times.

The twice daily prayer mentioned by Josephus was probably some form of the Shema. There seems to have been a convention among some Jewish men to declare their commitment to Jewish monotheism (Deut 6:4: "Hear, O Israel, the Lord is our God, the Lord is one …") when they got up in the mornings and when they went to sleep in the evenings. Whether an early form of the Amidah, or some of the blessings that eventually came to comprise it, was also recited by some Jewish men, perhaps already linked to the time of the (morning and) afternoon sacrifice at the temple, is also imaginable. Pieter van der Horst has recognized some elements that contributed to the Amidah in Philo's treatise *In Flaccum* (121–124).[22] The text states that, after Flaccus's arrest, the Jews of Alexandria spontaneously prayed outdoors, since their *proseuchai* (houses of prayer, i. e. synagogues) had been desecrated. The prayer consists of hymns in praise of God. Jutta Leonhardt believes that "*Flacc.* 121–123 actually refers to the regular practice of prayer and perhaps even song in the *proseuche*."[23] As the name *proseuche* already indicates, prayer seems to have been one of the activities that took place in Egyptian (and probably also Palestinian) institutions by that name in Hellenistic and early Roman times.[24]

According to Mark 12:40, scribes "devour widows' houses and, for a pretence, make long prayers."[25] It is uncertain whether the two allegations were associated with each other or should be understood separately. Are scribes accused of taking advantage of widows' houses, that is, using them for their own purposes, including prayer? This would be reminiscent of later rabbis' use of the "upper

---

[22] Pieter W. van der Horst, "Common Prayer in Philo's *In Flaccum* 121–124," *Kenishta* 2 (2003): 21–28, reprinted in idem, *Jews and Christians in Their Graeco-Roman Context*, WUNT 196 (Tübingen: Mohr Siebeck, 2006), 108–13.

[23] Jutta Leonhardt, *Jewish Worship in Philo of Alexandria*, TSAJ 84 (Tübingen: Mohr Siebeck, 2001), 80.

[24] See also Josephus, *Vita* 290–295, where Josephus states that he prayed in the *proseuche* in Tiberias: "We were proceeding with the ordinary service and engaged in prayer …." On this text see Daniel K. Falk, "Jewish Prayer Literature and the Jerusalem Church in Acts," in *The Book of Acts in its First Century Setting*, vol. 4: *Palestinian Setting*, ed. Richard Bauckham (Grand Rapids: Eerdmans, 1995), 261–301, here 278.

[25] The text has a parallel in some textual witnesses of Matt 23:14. In Matthew, scribes and Pharisees are mentioned together.

rooms" of wealthy hosts for Torah study.[26] Or are the "long prayers" an additional charge that is added to the alleged exploitation of widows? Clearly the tradents and editors of the text viewed the "long prayers" negatively. The claim that the length of the prayers was not due to devotion but to pretence amplifies the negative image of the scribes created here. If the "long prayers" have any historical basis, one could imagine that particularly devout Jews recited long versions of the Shema, including both Deut 6:4–9 and 11:13–21, or that they expressed long praises of God that preceded the later Amidah.

To summarize this discussion, it seems that already in pre-70 times some Jewish men prayed twice – and perhaps sometimes also three times – daily. What seems to have characterized this prayer practice was not only the adherence to a certain chronological schedule informed by the Torah (Deut 6:7) and/or the sacrificial service of the Jerusalem temple, but also, at least in some cases, the public, congregational nature of prayer, and the adherence to certain shared, biblically informed formulas. I am not claiming that prayer practice became fixed and institutionalized in pre-destruction times already. But there seem to have been some – probably pious and learned – Jewish men who based their private and public prayer practices on the accepted traditional institutions of the Torah and the temple, conventions that later post-70 rabbis picked up and developed further.

The prayers associated with Jesus in the Sayings Source are entirely different. There is no concern about the number or the times of daily prayers. Nor is there an indication of any adherence to traditional biblical formulas such as the Shema or to the times of temple sacrifices. Instead, it seems that Jesus encourages his followers to pray whenever they need to (Q 11:9: "I tell you, ask and it will be given to you …") and to use words that fit the occasion, expressing the particular concerns of the worshipers at a given time (Q 10:2: the need for Christian missionaries; Q 11:3: food, 11:4: cancellation of debts). Obviously, Q provides only scraps and pieces of the probably much larger tradition on Jesus and prayer that circulated in the first century CE. Nevertheless, the references point to an individual and personal prayer practice that does not follow traditional patterns. This type of personal and incidental prayer differs from the shared ritual practice advocated by rabbis that seems to have had precedents among some Jewish men before 70 already, as the above-mentioned references to Philo and Josephus suggest.

One might argue that the so-called "Lord's Prayer" (Q 11:2b–4) provided instructions for a new "communal" ritual among followers of Jesus, in the sense of a shared group practice among this set of Jewish Christians. Some scholars think that this portion did not belong to the Sayings Source or was added to it at a later

---

[26] On rabbis' acceptance of non-rabbis' hospitality, e. g., in "upper rooms," see Catherine Hezser, *The Social Structure of the Rabbinic Movement in Roman Palestine*, TSAJ 66 (Tübingen: Mohr Siebeck, 1997), 355–56.

stage.²⁷ The synoptic versions of the prayer, especially in Matthew (6:9-13) but also in Luke (11:2-4), are much more elaborate and formal. Matthew explicitly presents the prayer as a private Christian alternative to existing Jewish prayer practices in synagogues and public places (cf. Matt 6:5-6). He introduces the prayer as an obligation that all followers of Jesus are supposed to follow (Matt 6:9). In Q, on the other hand, followed by Luke (Luke 11:2), the prayer appears more like an occasional and voluntary practice: "When you pray, say: ...." The contents of the prayer, which will be discussed in more detail below, seem like a combination of a few traditional phrases (holy name, messianic kingdom) and the general needs of an impoverished (rural) population (daily bread, abolishment of debts). Whereas the Jesus of Q merely provides an example of how to formulate a short prayer when praying in private, Matthew has turned these suggestions into a formal (Jewish-?) Christian alternative to contemporary Jewish prayer practices.

Prayer is always a social act: "People are taught to pray, that is, they are socialized into prayer."²⁸ The Sayings Source seems to reflect an early stage of the process in which some Jewish Christians are taught to pray in a way that is partly based on but at the same time different from the prayer customs of other Jews. While traditional prayer patterns seem to be generally replaced by more personal and incidental addresses to God, the rudiments of the Lord's Prayer may reflect first steps toward early Jewish Christians' own more formalized prayer texts, later reflections of which can be found in Matthew and in the Didache.²⁹

B. The Prayer of a Jewish Charismatic: Jesus and Honi the Circle-Drawer

Several aspects of the way in which Jesus' (instructions on) prayer are represented in the Sayings Source are reminiscent of the rabbinic presentation of Honi the circle-drawer's prayer in a story tradition transmitted in Mishnah Ta'anit 3:8.³⁰

---

²⁷ See the discussion in Oakman, *Jesus, Debt, and the Lord's Prayer*, 50, with references.

²⁸ W. S. F. Pickering, "Introduction to an Unfinished Work," in Marcel Mauss, *On Prayer*, ed. W. S. F. Pickering (New York: Durkheim/Berghahn, 2003), 12.

²⁹ On the Lord's Prayer in Matthew and in the Didache, see Peter von der Osten-Sacken, "Das Vaterunser als Zugang zum Matthäusevangelium: Das Beispiel der Vergebungsbitte," in Wilk, *Das Vaterunser in seinen antiken Kontexten*, 103-24; Jürgen Wehnert, "*Ein* Gebet für alle christlichen Gemeinden: Zum Vaterunser in der Didache," in Wilk, *Das Vaterunser in seinen antiken Kontexten*, 143-62.

³⁰ For general comparisons between Jesus and Honi, see e. g. the discussion of Geza Vermes's approach in Mark Allan Powell, *Jesus As a Figure in History: How Modern Historians View the Man From Galilee* (Louisville, KY: Westminster John Knox Press, 1998), 54-56; Ekkehard W. Stegemann and Wolfgang Stegemann, *The Jesus Movement: A Social History of Its First Century* (Edinburgh: T & T Clark, 1999), 164; Alan J. Avery-Peck, "The Galilean Charismatic and Rabbinic Piety: The Holy Man in the Talmudic Literature," in *The Historical Jesus in Context*,

The story is set in the Second Temple period.[31] People are said to have asked Honi to pray for rain. When rain failed to materialize, "he drew a circle and stood within it, and said before him: 'Master of the Universe, your children turned to me, for I am like a child of the house [or: member of the household] before you [שאני כבן בית לפניך]. I swear by your great name that I shall not move from here until you have mercy on your children [בניך]'." His insistent prayer causes the rains to fall "as he ordered them." In reaction to Honi's behavior, Shimon b. Shetach criticizes him: "If you were not Honi, I would put you under a ban. But what can I do to you? For you are impertinent [מתחטא] before the Omnipresent and he grants you your wish [ועושה לך רצונך] like a child who is impertinent before his father and he grants him his wish. Scripture says of you: 'Your father and mother will rejoice; she who bore you will exult' [Prov 23:25]" (m. Ta'an. 3:8).

Rubenstein has already noticed that "the motif of parents and children runs throughout the story."[32] In his prayer Honi presents himself as a child in God's household. The validity of this self-presentation is confirmed by Shimon b. Shetach's eventual acknowledgment of his powers that are ascribed to his intimate relationship to God: he is like a naughty child before his father. The child-parent relationship reappears in the biblical proof text that is quoted at the end of the story. In Honi's direct address to God, those Jews who asked for his prayer for rain, that is, his local followers who believe in the efficacy of his intervention on their behalf, are also called "children" of God. The parent-child metaphor has precedents in biblical and especially prophetic texts.[33] While it appears in three passages of the Mishnah, "in later Judaism mention is made … rarely of God as Father of Israel. There seems to have been a tendency to avoid the designation."[34]

---

ed. Amy-Jill Levine, Dale C. Allison and John Dominic Crossan (Princeton, NJ: Princeton University Press, 2006), 149–65.

[31] Josephus mentions a certain Onias, at the time of Hyrcanus and Aristobulus, whose prayer for rain was successful (*Ant.* 14.22): "Now there was one, whose name was Onias, a righteous man he was, and beloved of God, who, in a certain drought, had prayed to God to put an end to the intense heat, and whose prayers God had heard, and had sent them rain …." Whether Onias was identical with Honi, or whether stories about several different rain makers circulated, remains uncertain.

[32] Jeffrey L. Rubenstein, trans., *Rabbinic Stories*, CWS (New York: Paulist, 2002), 129.

[33] For a survey see Brent A. Strawn, "'Israel, My Child': The Ethics of a Biblical Metaphor," in *The Child in the Bible*, ed. Marcia J. Bunge, Terence E. Fretheim, and Beverly Roberts Gaventa (Grand Rapids: Eerdmans, 2008), 103–40.

[34] Martin McNamara, "Targum and the New Testament: A Revisit," in *The New Testament and Rabbinic Literature*, ed. Reimund Bieringer et al., JSJ.S 136 (Leiden: Brill, 2010), 387–427, here 405. The formula אב שבשמים appears five times in the Mishnah, three times in m. Soṭah 9:15 ("our Father in heaven"), once in m. Yoma 8:9 ("your Father in heaven"), and once in m. Roš. Haš. 3:8 ("their Father in heaven"). McNamara wonders whether the terminology "was current in Palestinian Judaism at the time of Jesus, or whether its use in rabbinic Judaism is to be explained through influence from the Christian community" (ibid., 411). He assumes that early Christians used a Jewish expression that pre-dated Christianity. It should be noted that

The terms "Lord" (אדוני), "Master" (רבונו של עולם), and "King" (מלכינו), which stress the distance between God and humans, are used instead.

Interestingly, a tradition in the Babylonian Talmud states that R. Aqiva implored "Our Father, our King" for rain and his prayer was effective:

> Once R. Eliezer came before the Ark and recited the twenty-four blessings [said on fast days] but his prayer was not answered. R. Aqiva then came before the Ark and recited: "Our Father, Our King, we have no king but you. Our Father, Our King, have mercy upon us for your own sake!" whereupon the rain fell. (b. Ta'an. 25b)

The tradition, which lacks a Tannaitic parallel, seems to represent a late stage in the rabbinization of the charismatic tradition. Now a rabbi is presented as someone whose prayer causes rain to fall. The terminology, "Our Father, Our King," combines charismatic intimacy with the rabbinic insistence on God's sovereignty.[35] As Reuven Hammer has pointed out, "the formula is a unique one, combining what are usually seen as two contradictory features, that of a parent who is loving and accepting, and that of a sovereign who is usually seen as stern and demanding."[36]

Honi's emphasis on the intimate father-child relationship between the person who prays and the God he addresses is also evident in Jesus' prayer instructions in the Sayings Source. According to Q 10:21, Jesus said: "I thank you, Father, Lord of heaven and earth, for you hid these things from sages and the learned, and disclosed them to children. Yes, Father, for that is what it pleased you to do." Just as in the rabbinic story, where Shimon b. Shetach represents sages and Honi a popular charismatic, a distinction between Jesus, who identifies himself with "children" before God, and "sages and the learned" is drawn here. When viewed together with the rabbinic story in Mishnah Ta'anit 3:8, this Q text may preserve reminiscences of Jewish charismatics who distinguished themselves and their adherents from sages (scribes, Pharisees, rabbis) who claimed Torah knowledge and adherence to ancestral traditions for themselves. In contrast to these learned Jews, who emphasized the distance between humans and God and insisted that access to the divine is through intellectual knowledge and practice of his Torah only, the charismatics present a more simple, direct, and intimate way of communicating with God. For this intimate connection, the image of the child-parent relationship is used in both the Mishnah and the Sayings Source.

---

m. Soṭah 9:15, where the appellation appears three times and which also deals with messianic times, is sometimes seen as a later addition to the Mishnah.

[35] This tradition is often seen as the origin of the Avinu Malkeinu prayer that "has been included in an expanded version in the services during the period from Rosh Hashanah through Yom Kippur with the exception of the Sabbath, when such penitential prayers are never recited.... It is recited standing, before the open Ark, following the repetition of the Amidah." So Reuven Hammer, *Entering the High Holy Days: A Complete Guide to the History, Prayers, and Themes* (Philadelphia: Jewish Publication Society, 2005), 67.

[36] Ibid., 68.

Part of this analogy between Q and the Honi narrative is the presentation of prayer as efficacious, almost like a manipulation of God. In his prayer Honi threatens God to grant him his will: "I shall not move from here until you have mercy on your children." This behavior, which the sage Shimon b. Shetach calls "impertinent," is presented as effective in the story. It makes God react and rain fall, in accordance with Honi's (and the community's) wishes. Shimon acknowledges that Honi's relationship to God is so close that God allows him to act that way. References to the believed effectiveness of prayer also appear in the Sayings Source. In Q 11:9–10 Jesus tells his followers: "Ask and it will be given to you …. For everyone who asks receives."[37] In this same context the father-son relationship is brought up again: "What person of you, whose son asks for bread, will give him a stone? Or again, when he asks for a fish, will give him a snake? So if you, though evil, know how to give good gifts to your children, by how much more will the Father from heaven give good things to those who ask him!" (Q 11:11–13). Like Honi, the Jesus of the Sayings Source evokes the intimate household relationship between his followers and God. Because of this great intimacy, their prayers will be effective and almost self-fulfilling: who asks will receive. Underlying this approach to prayer is the belief in God's loving care for his children: if they need rain, he will cause rain to fall; if they desire bread or fish, he will not leave them hungry. This simple and direct approach to the divine stood in contrast to the more reverential approach of sages, as both the Sayings Source and the Mishnah point out.

The mishnaic story is usually seen as a first step in the so-called rabbinization of charismatics who existed outside of rabbinic circles and posed a threat to rabbis' attempts to gain popular adherents. As a representative of sages, Shimon b. Shetach eventually concedes to Honi's religious power. At the same time, "the rabbinic storytellers appear to be uncomfortable with charismatic holy men who present an alternative and challenge to their authority."[38] The Sayings Source does not present "learned" Jews' reactions to the prayer instructions associated with Jesus. Yet the explicit distinction from "sages and the learned," from whom God is said to have "hidden things" (Q 10:21)[39] may suggest that the tradents and

---

[37] Craig A. Evans, *Jesus and His Contemporaries: Comparative Studies*, AGJU 25 (Leiden: Brill, 2001), 230, points to parables in Luke that take up the persistence motif: the parables of the Persistent Friend (Luke 11:5–8) and the Importunate Widow (Luke 18:1–8).

[38] Rubenstein, *Rabbinic Stories*, 128. The rabbinization of Honi is carried further in the Babylonian Talmud: see b. Ta'an. 23a and Rubenstein, *Rabbinic Stories*, 130–35. On the analogous development of the Haninah b. Dosa tradition, see Baruch M. Bokser, "Wonder-Working and the Rabbinic Tradition: The Case of Haninah ben Dosa," *JSJ* 16 (1985): 42–92.

[39] The so-called secrecy motif is usually seen as a feature of the gospel of Mark, relating to Jesus' messianic self-consciousness: see Ben Witherington, *The Gospel of Mark: A Socio-Rhetorical Commentary* (Grand Rapids: Eerdmans, 2001), 41; Heikki Räisänen, *The Messianic Secret in Mark*, SNTW (London: T & T Clark, 1990). Q may represent an early, perhaps non-christological version of this motif.

editors of Q were aware of other, more traditional forms of prayer among their Jewish contemporaries.

When distinguishing between the intimate and efficacious prayers associated with Jesus and Honi and the more formal and traditional prayer customs of "the learned," Max Weber's distinction between charismatic and tradition-based authority comes to mind. Although "charisma" remains a somewhat residual category in Weber's thought and too strict distinctions between the two types of authority fit neither ancient Judaism nor emerging Christianity, charisma as "extremely personal," "highly irrational," and "unusual" would suit the representation of Jesus in Q and Honi in the Mishnah, if looked at from a detached sociological point of view.[40] Their intimate prayers to God as a father are "extremely personal," the belief in the prayers' efficacy is "highly irrational," and the religious practice they represent is more or less "unusual" in the Palestinian Jewish context in which they were active. A theological view of God as the "intimate immanent other" may lie at the roots of such prayer practices.[41] The sages or "learned," on the other hand, may have held a more transcendent, reverential view of God. To some extent, these perceptions would have competed in ancient Jewish society, but they were never entirely antithetical, either. In Q, Jesus also instructs his followers to "bow down to the Lord, your God" (Q 4:8) and hopes for the coming of God's "reign" (Q 11:2b). The rabbis of the Mishnah could refer to God as their "Father in heaven" (e. g., m. Soṭah 9:15).

C. Shared Motifs in Q and in Rabbinic Texts

In this final section I shall look at some motifs in Q that have analogies in rabbinic texts. Does the respective literary context suggest that they are used similarly or differently? The way in which motifs are combined, for example, in the "Lord's Prayer," is also relevant in this regard.

1. Prostration Before God

According to Q 4:5–8, the devil took Jesus on a high mountain and promised to give him "all the kingdoms of the world and their splendour," if he bowed down before him. Jesus refuses, since "it is written: Bow down to the Lord your God, and serve only him" (v. 8). In Roman society, prostration before emperors and idols was common and both may be alluded to here: the devil appears like a ruler

---

[40] For these characterizations of "charisma," see Christopher Adair-Toteff, *Max Weber's Sociology of Religion* (Tübingen: Mohr Siebeck, 2016), 31.

[41] Giuseppe Giordan, "Introduction: You Never Know. Prayer as Enchantment," in *A Sociology of Prayer*, ed. Giuseppe Giordan and Linda Woodhead (Farnham, UK: Ashgate, 2015), 1–8, here 5.

showing Jesus his kingdom; yet he is also a false deity in comparison with the Jewish God.[42] The story is also reminiscent of the Alexander legend: Alexander crossed high mountains, looked at the nations' wealth from above, and is criticized as greedy.[43] Unlike Alexander, Jesus does not give in to temptations here but declares his loyalty to the one Jewish God. Addressing God as "Lord" fits the gesture of prostration that is carried out in front of a superior only.

As Uri Ehrlich has shown, "during the biblical period [full-body] prostration constituted the preeminent, most ritualized physical gesture in the sacrificial and prayer services. Mentioned over a hundred times in the context of serving God, the biblical verb השתחויה came to denote divine worship in general."[44] Rabbis, on the other hand, reserved the more moderate form of bowing [שחייה] one's head or upper torso to certain benedictions of the Amidah.[45] Tosefta Berakhot 1:8 rules: "These are the benedictions during [the recitation of] which one bows: the first benediction [of the Amidah], at the beginning and the end, [and the penultimate benediction], 'We give thanks,' at the beginning and the end. One who bows through each and every benediction, they instruct him not to bow." Ehrlich stresses that "this is the sole halakhah relating to this subject found in Tannaitic literature."[46] Obviously, rabbis were not very fond of the gesture and tried to restrict it as much as possible. This was probably due to its association with pagan worship.[47] The formula, "the Lord your God," in front of whom Jesus suggests to bow down in the Sayings Source, is reminiscent of אדוני אלהינו in the Shema (Deut 6:4: "Hear, O Israel, the Lord is your God …"), but the recitation of the Shema does not require bowing. In any case, a prayer is not explicitly mentioned in Q 4:8, where the emphasis is on Jewish monotheism ("serve only him").

---

[42] C. E. V. Nixon and B. Saylor Rodgers, *In Praise of Later Roman Emperors: The Panegyrici Latini: Introduction, Translation, and Historical Commentary*, Transformation of the Classical Heritage 21 (Berkeley, CA: University of California Press, 1994), 52: "At Rome both gods and men were recipients of this form of supplication."

[43] See, e. g., Richard Stoneman, ed., *The Greek Alexander Romance* (London: Penguin, 1991), 147: "We left there and came to the harbor of Lyssos. Here there was a very high mountain which I climbed and saw beautiful houses full of gold and silver. I also saw a perimeter wall of sapphire …." Rabbis were critical of Alexander's hubris: see y. B. Mes. 2:5, 8c, where he is presented as greedy.

[44] Uri Ehrlich, *The Non-Verbal Language of Prayer: A New Approach of Jewish Liturgy* (Tübingen: Mohr Siebeck, 2004), 38.

[45] See ibid., 42.

[46] Ibid., 31.

[47] The governor of Africa allegedly asked a Christian woman on trial to "bow your head to the sacred rites of the Roman gods …. However devoted you are, we ask that you bow your head in the sacred temples and offer incense to the gods of the Romans" (*Acts of Crispina* 1.3–4, 2.1, 2.4), quoted in Mary Beard et al., *Religions of Rome*, vol. 1: *A History* (Cambridge: Cambridge University Press, 1998), 242. Although the text relates to late antiquity, there would have been a long tradition of bowing and prostration in Roman religion.

2. Praying for One's Persecutors

In Q 6:27–28 Jesus instructs his followers: "Love your enemies and pray for those persecuting you, so that you may become sons of your Father, for he raises his sun on bad and good and rains on the just and unjust." The notion not to delight in one's enemies' misfortune already appears in the Hebrew Bible, as John Piper has shown.[48] Especially noteworthy is Psalm 24:17: "Do not rejoice when your enemy falls and let not your heart be glad when he stumbles." The positive commands to "love" one's enemies and to pray for one's persecutors obviously goes a step further, though. In its connection with prayer, the Q text is reminiscent of Philo in *In Flaccum*. When the Roman governor Flaccus, who had persecuted Jews and brought various calamities over them, a situation which Pieter van der Horst calls "the first pogrom,"[49] was arrested, Alexandrian Jews are said to have raised their hands to heaven and sung a hymn in praise to God: "O Lord, we are not delighted at the punishment of our enemy, for we have learned from our holy laws that we should sympathize with our fellow men. But it is right to give thanks to you for having taken pity and compassion on us and for having relieved our constant and incessant oppression" (*Flacc.* 121).[50] The prayer almost sounds like an excuse for praising God for his protection. In the spirit of the mentioned biblical idea to "sympathize" with all human beings, even those who may persecute oneself, the Jews express their thanks to God for having saved them from the governor's harsh rule.

The Sayings Source goes on to present a reason for the instruction to love one's enemies and to pray for one's persecutors, referring to God himself as a model to emulate: "he raises his sun on bad and good and rains on the just and unjust" (Q 6:35c–d), that is, God's providence extends to all of humanity. He provides everyone with their basic needs. An analogy to this notion appears at the end of the Alexander story transmitted in the Talmud Yerushalmi and Amoraic Midrashim.[51] According to all versions of the story, Alexander of Macedon went to the king of Qasya (y. B. Meṣ. 2:5, 8c; Gen. Rab. 33:1; Lev. Rab. 27:1). The midrashic versions add "beyond the mountains of darkness."[52] The king "showed him a lot of gold and a lot of silver." Although Alexander maintains that he is not

---

[48] John Piper, *"Love Your Enemies": Jesus' Love Command in the Synoptic Gospels and in Early Christian Paraenesis*, SNTSMS 38 (Cambridge: Cambridge University Press, 1979), 28–35, with references.

[49] Pieter W. van der Horst, *Philo's Flaccus: The First Pogrom. Introduction, Translation, and Commentary*, PACS 2 (Leiden: Brill, 2003). On the historical background of the treatise see ibid., 18–34; on Flaccus see ibid., 34–37.

[50] Translation with van der Horst, *Jews and Christians*, 108.

[51] On this story see Catherine Hezser, *Form, Function, and Historical Significance of the Rabbinic Story in Yerushalmi Neziqin*, TSAJ 37 (Tübingen: Mohr Siebeck, 1993), 61–77.

[52] As already mentioned above, there is a certain analogy to Q 4:5–8, where the devil shows Jesus his kingdom from the top of a mountain, testing his greediness. Unlike Jesus, Alexander turns out to be a greedy and wicked person, not deserving God's mercy.

greedy, he turns out to be just that: "he loved gold and silver so much" (y. B. Meṣ. 2:5, 8c). At the end of the story, in reaction to Alexander's behavior,

> the king [of Qasya] said to him: Does the sun shine upon you? He said to him: Yes. Does the rain come down upon you? He said to him: Yes. He said to him: Perhaps there is small cattle with you [i. e., where you live]? He said to him: Yes. [He said to him:] May that man's breath expire![53] You live only through the merit of the small cattle, as it is written: 'Man and cattle do you save, God' [Ps. 36:7]. (y. B. Meṣ. 2:5, 8c)

Alexander is presented as so wicked here that God's providence, which was believed to cover both humans and animals, exempts him.[54] If he and his countrymen nevertheless enjoy sunshine and rain, which are necessary for agriculture to prosper, this must be due to God's concern for the well-being of the small cattle, whose merits preserve their human owners.

The notion that God protects all human beings, irrespective of their deeds, underlies both the Alexander story and the Q text. This notion seems to reflect ancient people's experience, for everyone is equally affected by the sun and rain. The comparison between the Saying Source and the rabbinic text shows that Q is more neutral in its views concerning "bad" and "unjust" people. In line with the suggestion to pray for one's persecutors, the model of God extending his sun and rain over all people, irrespective of their behavior, remains unqualified. The rabbis who formulated the Alexander story, on the other hand, use Psalm 36:7 to reinterpret the idea of a universal divine providence: the wicked are not worthy of it; it is the lowest of the low animals through whose merit they live.

3. The Workers in the Harvest Parable

In Q 10:2 Jesus tells his disciples "The harvest is plentiful, but the workers are few. So ask the Lord of the harvest to dispatch workers into his harvest."[55] First-century Jews would have been very familiar with the need for additional agricultural workers during harvest seasons, when crops had to be gathered in. The Mishnah deals with legal issues that might emerge in such a situation. For example, m. Ma'as. 2:7 rules: "If a man hired a worker to help him harvest figs," he may eat the figs and is exempt from tithe. The metaphorical use of the worker as

---

[53] The Escorial manuscript of the Talmud Yerushalmi adds here: "Through the merit of the small cattle does the sun shine upon you, and dew and rain come down only through the merit of the small cattle."

[54] For other critical presentations of Alexander that counter the idealized image of the Alexander Legend and present him as a pirate and brigand who looted the regions he conquered, see, e. g., Curtius Rufus, *Hist. Alex. Magn.* 9. 8. 12–30 and Augustine, *Civ.* 4.4, quoted in M. M. Austin, *The Hellenistic World From Alexander to the Roman Conquest: A Selection of Ancient Sources in Translation*, 2nd ed. (Cambridge: Cambridge University Press, 2006), 59. See also 1 Macc 1:1–9: "He marched to the end of the earth, and seized plunder from a mass of peoples ..." (quoted ibid., 60).

[55] See Matt 9:37–38 par. Luke 10:2.

an image of human beings before God appears several times in Mishnah Avot.[56] In analogy to the Q saying, a statement attributed to R. Tarfon is particularly relevant: "The day is short, the work is large, the workers are lazy, and the salary is much, and the householder urges [to get the work done]" (m. 'Abot 2:15). The Mishnah continues: "It is not up to you to finish the work, but you are also not free to stay away from it" (2:16). As in the Sayings Source, the image of a large amount of work is evoked here. Similarly, there is an urgency to get the work done. Whereas Q refers to a lack of workers, Mishnah Avot mentions their laziness. These different details may indicate the different meanings of the parables in the different contexts. Whereas R. Tarfon's saying tries to motivate Jews to be more efficient in their Torah observance (the "work"), Jesus' saying seems to encourage more Jews to become missionaries on behalf of Jewish Christianity (the "harvest").[57]

4. The Cancellation of Debts

In the so-called "Lord's Prayer" one of the requests is the cancellation of debts: "and cancel our debts for us, as we too have cancelled for those in debt to us" (Q 11:4). The image of debts would have had a strong impact on first-century Jews. Josephus associates the attempt to eliminate impoverished people's debts with Zealot leaders, as a means to gain adherents at the beginning of the First Revolt against Rome. In 66 CE the Sicarii allegedly burned down the public archives in Jerusalem, where the debt documents were kept. They were "eager to destroy the money-lenders' bonds and to prevent the recovery of debts, in order to win over a host of grateful debtors, and to cause a rising of the poor against the rich, sure of impunity" (*B. J.* 2.427).[58] Oakman views the request for the cancellation of debts in the "Lord's Prayer" against the social background of wide-spread debts among first-century Jews. He argues that the prayer "shows direct interest in the alleviation or mitigation of agrarian money debts."[59] Anyone who read or heard the formulation in Q must have considered Jesus an advocate for the release of debts, in analogy to the Zealot leaders described by Josephus.

---

[56] Some scholars consider m. 'Abot to be a creation of the third to fourth century. Amram Tropper, "Tractate *Avot* and Early Christian Succession Lists," in *The Ways that Never Parted: Jews and Christians in Late Antiquity and the Early Middle Ages*, ed. Adam H. Becker and Annette Yoshiko Reed, TSAJ 95 (Tübingen: Mohr Siebeck, 2003), 159–88, here 160, argues however that "the traditionalists were correct to regard *Avot* as a Mishnaic tractate" (see ibid., 160 n. 3 for a detailed discussion of the various opinions).

[57] Frederick Dale Bruner, *Matthew: A Commentary*, vol. 1: *The Christbook, Matthew 1–12* (Grand Rapids: Eerdmans, 2004), 450, interprets Matt 9:37–38 as a reference to the Christian mission.

[58] Translated with S. G. F. Brandon, *Jesus and the Zealots: A Study of the Political Factor in Primitive Christianity* (Manchester: Manchester University Press, 1967), 56.

[59] Oakman, *Jesus, Debt, and the Lord's Prayer*, xi.

The mutuality of the debt release envisioned in the Sayings Source may indicate that its meaning is theological and moral. Those whose debts are released by God are required to also release the debts of their fellow-human beings. Yet the debts of fellow-human beings may also be real material debts that the Jewish Christians who formulated the text confirm to have cancelled for their debtors (note that the formulation is in the past tense). If understood in this way, the release of debts by God, that is, the cancellation of sins (cf. Luke 11:4, who has replaced "debts" with "sins"),[60] may almost be considered a reward for the worldly moral action: we acted morally ourselves, so treat us leniently when it comes to our own failings. What is interesting here and reflective of biblical and rabbinic thinking is the importance of ethics, that is, the way one treats other human beings, in one's relationship with God. The way one acts towards others is closely related to the treatment one can expect of God. Humans are considered "capable of making moral choices and taking responsibility for those choices."[61] Therefore "the social legislation in the Bible, particularly laws concerning the care of the poor, the widow, the orphan, and the stranger, occupies a position of paramount importance."[62]

5. Prayer for Food and the Grace After Meals

The provision of food, especially bread as the basic staple of the ancient diet, seems to have been an important concern of the editors of the Sayings Source.[63] Bread is mentioned in the "Lord's Prayer" (Q 11:3) as well as in the following passage about the efficacy of prayer (Q 11:11), a text that also refers to fish as an important food (Q 11:12). Fish was probably part of Sabbath meals, especially among those who lived close to the Sea of Galilee.[64] Ze'ev Safrai assumes that it "was consumed in great amounts," but that probably depended on its avail-

---

[60] Nicholas Ayo, *The Lord's Prayer: A Survey Theological and Literary* (Notre Dame: University of Notre Dame Press, 1991), 72, points to the differences between Matthew and Luke: "Matthew writes of forgiving *debts*, and Luke of forgiving *sins* .... Matthew's 'debts' shows a more Semitic usage. The Aramaic word for sins was debts, with the primary analogue financial debts. To the Greek Gentile Christians of Luke's community, however, *sins* would be more understandable."

[61] Samuel Tobias Lachs, *Humanism in Talmud and Midrash* (Rutherford, NJ: Fairleigh Dickinson University Press, 1993), 37.

[62] Ibid., 57.

[63] On the centrality of bread in the ancient diet see Andrew Dalby, *Food in the Ancient World From A to Z* (London: Routledge, 2003), 59. Nathan MacDonald, *What Did the Ancient Israelites Eat? Diet in Biblical Times* (Grand Rapids: Eerdmans, 2008), 19, points to the triad of "bread, wine, and oil" as the basic food stuffs: "For the typical Israelite, bread or other grain-based foods such as porridge probably provided over half their caloric intake, with estimates varying between 53 and 75 percent."

[64] According to t. Pe'ah 4:8, the Sabbath foods of a poor person consisted of "oil, legumes, fish, and a vegetable." On fish as a Sabbath food see also Jordan D. Rosenblum, *Food and Identity in Early Rabbinic Judaism* (Cambridge: Cambridge University Press, 2010), 174.

ability.⁶⁵ In Q food is presented as a "gift" given to humans by God. The request for bread in the "Lord's Prayer" (Q 11:3) is followed by the firm belief that God will provide his "children" with bread and fish (Q 11:11–12). As such, the prayer is reminiscent of another text in Q that tries to alleviate anxiety about daily provisions: "Therefore I tell you, do not be anxious about your life, what you are to eat .... Consider the ravens: they neither sow nor reap nor gather into barns, and yet God feeds them" (Q 12:22b, 24).

The notion that it is ultimately God who provides food to humans also underlies the rabbinic blessing before eating food and the Grace After Meals. These blessings express thanks to God for the foods that form part of the meal. Mishnah Berakhot 6:1 lists the blessings that one is supposed to say over the different types of products: "over bread one says: [Blessed Are You, O Lord Our God, King of the Universe], who brings forth bread from the earth." The blessing holds God responsible for the agricultural harvest. Over food that does not come out of the earth one says the blessing, "For all came into being by his word" (m. Ber. 6:3). Although rabbis required the recitation of such a blessing before meals, the so-called Grace After Meals was considered more important, since it was based on a biblical commandment. According to Deut 8:10, "When you have eaten your fill, give thanks to the Lord your God for the good land which he has given you." Since the land is mentioned here, rabbis required the Grace After Meals for products that emerged from the earth only, the so-called seven kinds of produce, which were given precedence over other foods (cf. m. Ber. 6:4–5). Unlike the short blessing before meals, the Grace After Meals was "a full-blown liturgy consisting of four blessings."⁶⁶ Joseph Tabory summarizes as follows: "The motif of the first blessing is praise of God who sustains the world; the second, thanks God for the gift of the land of Israel; the third, a prayer for the rebuilding of Jerusalem; and the fourth is a general praise of God 'who is good and does good'."⁶⁷ The Grace After Meals thanks God in much more general terms, then, rather than focusing on specific foods.

Based on the shared assumption that it is God who ultimately provides food, the difference between the Q prayer and the mishnaic instructions becomes obvious. The Q prayer is a plea to God that lists various requests, the "daily bread" being one of them. The rabbinic prayers, on the other hand, are prayers of thanks for the food that God has provided and continues to provide daily. The different formulations point to different occasions. The rabbinic blessing of food and Grace After Meals are recited before and after an actual meal. Jesus' prayer in Q,

---

⁶⁵ Ze'ev Safrai, *The Economy of Roman Palestine* (London: Routledge, 2003), 92.

⁶⁶ Joseph Tabory, "Prayers and Berakhot," in *The Literature of the Sages*, part 2: *Midrash and Targum, Liturgy, Poetry, Mysticism, Contracts, Inscriptions, Ancient Science and the Languages of Rabbinic Literature*, ed. Shmuel Safrai et al., CRINT 2.3a (Assen: Royal Van Gorcum; Minneapolis: Fortress, 2006), 281–326, here 321.

⁶⁷ Ibid.

on the other hand, is a more general prayer that is not linked to a specific occasion.[68] It expresses the concerns of those who formulated it, concerns that are both pragmatic (bread; release of debts) and religious (hope for the beginning of the messianic kingdom; the forgiveness of sins; fear of being tested by the devil).

One might argue that the request for "daily bread" would have been most likely for someone who did not work in agriculture and food production (i. e., someone who did not live in rural Galilee and/or was itinerant?) and worried about where his or her daily provisions would come from. Prayer obtains an important role in Q. It serves to implore God to provide for his "children." As already mentioned above, this direct approach and the belief in the efficacy of prayer are reminiscent of Honi's prayer for rain, which can likewise be called an appeal or imploration, something rabbis, represented by Shimon b. Shetach, considered importunate. These requests, which were guided by the belief in their efficacy, were not supplications.[69] Rather than humbly approaching God to ask for his mercy, they formulate demands that God was supposed to fulfill, if he wanted to maintain the image of a loving father. The person formulating the prayer puts himself in the role of a naughty child who believes that his parents will fulfill his wishes, no matter what he does and how he behaves. Ulrich Luz has called this type of prayer a "conflict talk with God," "a dialogical wrestling with God" that views God as "a living dialogue-partner."[70] As such, it is more reminiscent of the biblical book of Job than of rabbinic prayer discourse.

D. Conclusions

The different ways in which prayer is represented in the Sayings Source and in early rabbinic texts point to different forms of Jewish religiosity and views of God in first and second century CE Palestinian Judaism. The Sayings Source presents Jesus and his followers in a close child-father relationship with God. The use of

---

[68] On the formal difference between prayers of request, "asking for something that you don't have at that moment," and prayers of thanksgiving see Carlo Genova, "Prayer as Practice: An Interpretative Proposal," in Giordan and Woodhead, *A Sociology of Prayer*, 9–23, here 13.

[69] Rabbis also knew of supplications (תחנונים) and welcomed them; see m. Ber. 4:4. They consisted of private petitions that are formulated in silence rather than being said aloud. They were probably formulated after the public recitation of the *Amidah* in rabbinic times. See Ismar Elbogen, *Der jüdische Gottesdienst in seiner geschichtlichen Entwicklung*, 3rd ed. (Frankfurt: J. Kauffmann, 1931), 73–75. Elbogen sees the origins of these supplicatory prayers in temple times and refers to Sir 50:16–21: when the priests sounded the silver trumpets, "all the people together ... fell down to the earth upon their faces to worship their Lord God Almighty .... And the people besought the Lord, the Most High, by prayer before him that is merciful ..." (vv. 17–19).

[70] Ulrich Luz, "Why Do Theologians Speak about God When They Speak about Humans?," in *Theologies of Creation in Early Judaism and Ancient Christianity: In Honour of Hans Klein*, ed. Tobias Nicklas and Korinna Zamfir, DCLS 6 (Berlin: de Gruyter, 2010), 1–16, here 11.

the parenthood metaphor suggests that God is regarded as a loving and forgiving father who tolerates his child's impertinent behavior and indulges him or her with gifts. This view also determines the prayer language: toward a father one can be direct, clear, and demanding, relinquishing any courtesies. The simple and direct prayer was believed to be more effective than any long-winded and carefully formulated prayer of the "learned" could ever be. This approach to the divine is reminiscent of Honi the circle-drawer in a Tannaitic story. By behaving like an insistent child, he could "force" God to make rain fall.

Rabbis underline the difference between Honi's approach and their own, which assumed a more distant, courteous attitude and behavior toward God. For rabbis, God was the Lord, king and master, whose instructions one had to carefully study and obey. They believed that daily prayer habits were part of these instructions that had to be followed and adapted to post-temple times. Accordingly, they discussed the proper times of prayers such as the Shema and Amidah and the Amidah's formulation. It is likely that this discourse continued discussions and practices that already emerged among some Jews in Second Temple times. For rabbis, just as for Philo and Josephus, prayer had traditional roots in the Hebrew Bible (the text of the Shema, formulations of the Amidah) and was linked to the temple and its sacrificial times. Although prayer formulas continued to be diverse throughout rabbinic times, rabbis viewed prayer as a shared ritual that all Jewish men should practice in approximately the same way.

Despite these differences, a certain overlap between prayer in Q and rabbinic prayer can be recognized. Both the Jesus of Q and rabbis were committed to biblical monotheism. They emphasized the importance of moral behavior in one's relationship with God. They knew that God's providence extended over all humans. While the tradents and editors of the Sayings Source were also familiar with God as the Lord, rabbis would occasionally use the Father metaphor.

The mentioned differences together with the shared concepts suggest that we are dealing here with variant forms of ancient Jewish religiosity that could coexist and be practiced by some of the same people. Just as Honi's closeness to God was appreciated by rabbis and eventually integrated into their own self-presentation, some pre-70 Pharisees and scribes may have been attracted to "charismatic" individuals and their more direct approach to God. Max Weber's categorical distinction between "charismatic" and "traditional" authority therefore seems to be too rigid. Ultimately, the representations of Jesus' prayer in Q and of Honi's and early rabbis' prayers in Tannaitic sources constitute religious varieties within Palestinian Judaism of the first centuries CE. Whether the so-called "Lord's Prayer" is indicative of the constitution of a specific Jewish Christian "community" of Jesus followers is possible but uncertain, since the Q version of the prayer remains rudimentary.

Gott und die Feinde

Traditionen und neutestamentliche Vernetzung von Q 6,28

Hildegard Scherer

Beim Thema „Gebet und Q" darf die Aufforderung zum Gebet für aktive Gegner in Q 6,28 nicht fehlen. In der Tat können ihre fünf griechischen Worte einen ganzen Beitrag füllen, denn sie provozieren Fragen. Zum einen: Welche Traditionen stehen hinter diesem nur bei Matthäus und Lukas auftretenden Appell? In welchem Verhältnis steht er zu den Feindparänesen des Römer und 1 Petrus; gibt es biblisch-jüdische Vorläufer? Und schließlich: Wie ist er innerhalb der synoptischen Tradition verankert? Diesen Fragen vorauszuschicken sind allerdings einige Bemerkungen zum Wortlaut des Appells, ist er doch bei Matthäus und Lukas in unterschiedlichen Fassungen überliefert.

A. Text: Lukas 6,28

Sowohl in Mt 5,44 als auch Lk 6,27–28 stehen parallele Mahnungen zur Feindesliebe und zum Gebet für die Gegner,[1] beides imperativische Mahnungen eines weisheitlichen Mahnspruchs.[2] Die Mahnung zur Feindesliebe stimmt in beiden Evangelien im Wortlaut überein, die Mahnung zum Gebet für Gegner enthält neben substanziellen Übereinstimmungen auch Abweichungen. Dies führt zur Frage nach dem Wortlaut einer möglichen gemeinsamen Vorlage.

---

[1] Ob in einer gemeinsamen Vorlage zwei oder vier Mahnungen enthalten waren, darüber lässt sich streiten. M. E. sind die überzähligen lukanischen Mahnungen Verdoppelungen, insbesondere die Mahnung zum Segen: Sie ist in klaren semantischen Oppositionen konstruiert, die der Mahnung zum Gebet fehlen. Zur Überlieferungsgeschichte der Segensmahnung, s. u. Abschnitt B.

[2] Zur Gattung vgl. Dieter Zeller, *Die weisheitlichen Mahnsprüche bei den Synoptikern*, FB 17 (Würzburg: Echter, 1977), 21–22, speziell zum Text ebd., 101–10. Den beiden Mahnungen folgt in der Q-Rekonstruktion eine Begründung, bei Matthäus sind es sogar zwei – diese werde ich im Folgenden weitgehend außer Acht lassen und mich auf die Mahnungen konzentrieren.

Mt 5,44	Lk 6,27-28
44 ἐγὼ δὲ λέγω ὑμῖν·	27 Ἀλλ᾽ ὑμῖν λέγω τοῖς ἀκούουσιν·
ἀγαπᾶτε τοὺς ἐχθροὺς ὑμῶν	ἀγαπᾶτε τοὺς ἐχθροὺς ὑμῶν,
	καλῶς ποιεῖτε τοῖς μισοῦσιν ὑμᾶς
	28 εὐλογεῖτε τοὺς καταρωμένους ὑμᾶς,
καὶ *προσεύχεσθε*	*προσεύχεσθε*
ὑπὲρ τῶν διωκόντων ὑμᾶς ...	περὶ τῶν ἐπηρεαζόντων ὑμᾶς.

1. προσεύχομαι *und die kommunikative Struktur der Appelle*

Der erste der hier zu besprechenden Imperative ruft zur Feindesliebe auf. Exegetische Erkenntnisse zum semantischen Gehalt von ἀγαπάω/lieben[3] haben zutage gefördert, dass damit ein praktisch-solidarisches Tun gemeint ist. Levitikus 19, an dessen Ende das Gebot der Nächstenliebe steht, mag dies illustrieren.[4] Die Mahnung fordert also zu einer zwischenmenschlichen Aktion auf und verbleibt damit auf horizontaler Ebene.

Anders der folgende Imperativ: προσεύχομαι ist intransitiv gebraucht, doch steht nicht in Frage, an wen sich das Bitten richtet. Das Verb ist der Kommunikation mit Gott vorbehalten; für menschliche Kommunikationspartner stünden z. B. αἰτέω oder δέομαι zur Verfügung.[5] Damit wird eine vertikale Dimension eröffnet. Die Aktion richtet sich an Gott, und nur über diesen werden die zwischenmenschlichen Gegenspieler erreicht.[6]

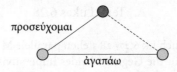

Die überzähligen lukanischen Imperative stützen exakt diese Struktur: „Tut gut den euch Hassenden" verbleibt auf der horizontalen Ebene, während „Segnet die euch Verfluchenden" wieder Gott einbezieht und sich damit im kommunikativen Dreieck bewegt.

---

[3] Prototypisch z. B. Ceslas Spicq, *Notes de lexicographie néo-testamentaire*, 3 Bde., OBO 22 (Freiburg, CH: Éditions universitaires; Göttingen: Vandenhoeck & Ruprecht, 1978), 1:19–20.

[4] Vgl. Martin Hochholzer, *Feindes- und Bruderliebe im Widerstreit? Eine vergleichende Studie zur synoptischen und johanneischen Ausprägung des Liebesgebots*, EHS.T 850 (Frankfurt: Peter Lang, 2007), 175.

[5] Horst Balz, „προσεύχομαι," *EWNT* 3:396–409, hier 398, 401.

[6] Vgl. Martin Ebner, „Feindesliebe – ein Ratschlag zum Überleben? Sozial- und religionsgeschichtliche Überlegungen zu Mt 5,38–47/Lk 6,27–35," in *From Quest to Q: Festschrift James M. Robinson*, hg. v. Jon Ma. Asgeirsson, Kristin De Troyer und Marvin W. Meyer, BETL 146 (Leuven: Peeters, 2000), 119–42, hier 140.

2. Das Thema des Gebets: Die Gegenspieler

Mit wem sich das Gebet beschäftigt, weicht bei Matthäus und Lukas ab. Das matthäische διώκω/verfolgen bleibt unbestimmt: Es bleibt offen, was geschehen wäre, wenn die Verfolger die Flüchtigen[7] tatsächlich eingeholt hätten. Speziell im Kontext des Matthäus ist das Wort jedoch besetzt: Die Verfolgung ist dort nicht durch persönliche Feindschaft, sondern durch Gruppenzugehörigkeit motiviert:[8] Diese Perspektive unterstützt die Pluralformulierung, die sich an eine Gruppe richtet.

Das seltene[9] ἐπηρεάζω wendet sich gegen die Ehre der Betroffenen, stigmatisiert sie negativ und demonstriert ihre Ohnmacht. Ob es sich dabei um eine Verbalattacke[10] handelt oder um tätliche Übergriffe,[11] lässt sich nur aus dem Kontext entscheiden: Der fehlt allerdings in diesem Fall.[12] Für eine Worthandlung spricht, dass diese mit der Worthandlung des Gebets beantwortet werden soll;[13] für den tätlichen Übergriff, dass Lukas im nächsten Atemzug einen Schlag ins Gesicht erwähnt.[14] Bei Philo und Josephus[15] erscheinen zudem symbolpolitische Konnotationen: Sie verwenden das Wort im Zusammenhang mit der Missachtung jüdischer Privilegien (*Ant.* 16,27.170) oder der Aufstellung von Kaiserbildern bzw. der Wegnahme von Synagogen (*Flacc.* 47.52; *Legat.* 213).

---

[7] Vgl. z. B. im kriegerischen Kontext Ex 15,9; Lev 26,7–8; 1 Makk 4,9.15; systematisches Aufspüren und Verfolgen: 1 Makk 3,5.

[8] Vgl. Mt 5,10–12; 10,23; 23,34. Zum Übersteigen der privaten Beziehungen vgl. Zeller, *Die weisheitlichen Mahnsprüche*, 107; Heinz-Wolfgang Kuhn, „Das Liebesgebot Jesu als Tora und als Evangelium: Zur Feindesliebe und zur christlichen und jüdischen Auslegung der Bergpredigt", in *Vom Urchristentum zu Jesus: Für Joachim Gnilka*, hg. v. Hubert Frankemölle und Karl Kertelge (Freiburg i. Br.: Herder, 1989), 194–230, hier 228; Matthias Konradt, *Das Evangelium nach Matthäus*, NTD 1 (Göttingen: Vandenhoeck & Ruprecht, 2015), 97.

[9] Im NT nur noch 1 Petr 3,16.

[10] So z. B. Philo, *Mos.* 2,199: Schädigung durch Sprache im Kontext von Fluch; in 1 Petr 3,16 ist aufgrund des Sinnzusammenhangs nur ein verbales Verständnis möglich.

[11] So z. B. Philo, *Ios.* 71: vom Körper.

[12] François Bovon, *Das Evangelium nach Lukas*, Band 1: *Lukas 1,1–9,50*, EKK 3/1 (Zürich: Benziger; Neukirchen-Vluyn: Neukirchener, 1989), 315 Anm. 28, erwähnt mit Rückgriff auf LSJ (ad loc.) Bedeutungsunterschiede je nach Kasus des Objekts, jedoch gebe es Ausnahmen; der lk Akkusativ weise mit 1 Petr 3,16 auf verbale Handlungen hin. Mir scheint (mit Bauer, ad loc.) diese Differenzierung nicht trennscharf zu sein; Plutarch konstruiert in *Alc.* 3,1; *Flam.* 18; *Quest. Conv.* 1,4 auch Worthandlungen mit Dativ; LSJ (ad loc.) führt gerade Lk 6,28 gemeinsam mit anderen Belegen von Dativobjekten unter der Bedeutung „deal despitefully with, act despitefully towards" an.

[13] Hans Klein, *Das Lukasevangelium*, 10. Aufl., KEK 1.3 (Göttingen: Vandenhoeck & Ruprecht, 2006), 256 Anm. 44, führt dafür noch die Parallele zum verbalen Segnen an.

[14] Vgl. Walter Radl, *Das Evangelium nach Lukas: Kommentar*, Band 1: *Lukas 1,1–9,50* (Freiburg i. Br.: Herder, 2003), 399, der ebenso die Ambivalenz im Kontext und (ebd. 398 mit Anm. 348) auch bei Philo, *Ios.* 71, gegenüber Philo, *Mos.* 2.199; Jos., *B. J.* 1.13 betont, doch im Kontext von Q die praktische Gewalt am Werk sieht.

[15] Philo, *Flacc.* 52; Josephus, *Ant.* 16.27 führt an Michael Wolter, *Das Lukasevangelium*, HNT 5 (Tübingen: Mohr Siebeck, 2008), 256.

Bei aller Unterschiedlichkeit teilen die beiden Begriffe semantische Merkmale: Sie bezeichnen Handlungen aus Sicht von Betroffenen, die diese als schädlich empfinden; beide Vorgänge bilden einen Konflikt ab; beide zielen darauf, das Gegenüber zu entmachten. Damit illustrieren beide auf ihre Weise ein Verhalten von Gegnern.

Fragt man nach einer gemeinsamen Vorlage für Matthäus und Lukas, so votiere ich für die ungewöhnlichere lukanische Fassung. Prinzipiell möglich ist an solchen Stellen auch eine dritte Form, die weder Matthäus noch Lukas aufgegriffen, sondern jeweils umformuliert haben.[16] Die Begründung für lukanische Ursprünglichkeit liefert m. E. der Abgleich mit den synoptischen Traditionen (s. u., D. 4), doch vorerst genügt zur Weiterarbeit die Grundstruktur: aktive Gegner.

3. Die Präposition

Das Profil der Präpositionen verschwimmt hier. Mit beiden kann ein Gebet zugunsten anderer bezeichnet sein,[17] was auch semantisch zur Forderung der Feindesliebe parallel liegt. Die Austauschbarkeit der Präposition demonstrieren z. B. die Einsetzungsworte: Mt 26,28 bezeichnet das Blut dort als τὸ περὶ πολλῶν ἐκχυννόμενον, Mk 14,24 und Lk 22,20 formulieren mit ὑπέρ. Im Fall von Q 6,28 legen beide Präpositionen also die Bitte nahe, Gott möge den Gegenspielern Gutes widerfahren lassen. Damit ist wiederum eine gemeinsame Grundstruktur erreicht, unabhängig davon, welche Präposition nun für Q veranschlagt wird.

B. Vernetzungen I: Überlieferungsgeschichte

Dass auch neutestamentliche Briefe Mahnungen zum Umgang mit Gegnern enthalten, ist immer wieder aufgefallen. Aktuell hat sich Christine Jacobi[18] mit ihnen auseinandergesetzt: Sie fragt, ob die Paränesen von Röm 12,9–21 und 1 Petr 3,8–19 Jesusüberlieferung verarbeiten. Die Frage drängt sich auf, denn die Mahnungen liegen auf der Linie des synoptischen Feindesliebegebots.

Sowohl Röm 12,17a als auch 1 Petr 3,9a[19] fordern Vergeltungsverzicht, Röm 12,17b darüber hinaus noch, Gutes zu wollen; Aktivität zum Wohl des Fein-

---

[16] Wie häufig in der Q-Forschung erwähnt, z. B. Michael Wolter, „Reconstructing Q?," *ExpTim* 115 (2003): 115–19, hier 118.

[17] περί zur Bezeichnung des Ziels von Fürsorge oder des Grundes von Sorge: LSJ ad loc. II.2: „with words which denote care or anxiety, about, on account of"; ὑπέρ: LSJ ad loc. II.1 „generally, for the prosperity or safety of"; II.2 „for, instead of, in the name of"; II.4 „of the cause or motive, for, because of, by reason of"; vgl. auch Balz, „προσεύχομαι," *EWNT* 3:399–400.

[18] Vgl. Christine Jacobi, *Jesusüberlieferung bei Paulus? Analogien zwischen den echten Paulusbriefen und den synoptischen Evangelien*, BZNW 213 (Berlin: de Gruyter, 2015), 48–122.

[19] Textvergleich Röm 12 – 1 Petr 3, der auch 1 Thess 5,12–22 einbezieht: ebd., 55–64; zum Vergeltungsverzicht, ebd., 59.

des ist nach Röm 12,20 angezeigt, eine Beschämung der Gegner findet sich wiederum in 1 Petr 3,16. Ebenso rufen beide Paränesen dazu auf, Gegner zu segnen (Röm 12,14; 1 Petr 3,9; vgl. 1 Kor 4,12). Neben der horizontalen Ausrichtung steht also auch hier eine vertikale, die Gott einbezieht. Zudem entsprechen sich in beiden Passagen Mahnungen für ein Verhalten innerhalb der Gruppe, nach außen die Mahnungen, Frieden zu halten und Böses zu lassen, Gutes zu tun, und schließlich der Verweis auf Gottes Gericht.

Keine dieser Paränesen, so beobachtet Jacobi, begründet dies jedoch mit Jesusworten, vielmehr stützt sich Paulus beim Verhalten gegenüber Feinden auf die Schrift.[20] Die synoptische Tradition biete nun, so Jacobi, ihrerseits in Jesusworten den Aufruf zum Vergeltungsverzicht und zu positivem Verhalten gegenüber Gegnern.[21]

Allerdings ortet Jacobi auch im Umfeld des NT solche Topoi, sogar zusammengestellt zu Clustern, so dass eine überlieferungsgeschichtliche Abhängigkeit nicht erwiesen sei.[22]

Jacobi zufolge kennzeichneten die christlichen Paränesen jedoch zwei Akzente:[23] (1) Sie formulieren „Kontrastparänesen": Beim Vergeltungsverzicht und auch beim Umgang mit dem Gegner steht neben dem zu vermeidenden Verhalten (Prohibitiv) auch immer eine positive Aufforderung zur Kontrasthandlung;[24] (2) Der Segensimperativ in Bezug auf Gegner steht in diesem Zusammenhang. In dieser Darstellung wäre also die Einschaltung Gottes angesichts der Gegner alte Tradition – wohingegen die Feindesliebe nicht in den Briefparänesen erscheint.

Jacobi bewertet einen jesuanischen Anfangsimpuls hinter den Paränesen agnostisch.[25] Mir erscheint dagegen plausibel, dass die Sprüche von Wangenschlag, Gewand und Meile (Q 6,29) einen solchen Impuls bieten. Sie sind nämlich nicht nur, wie längst erarbeitet, jesuanisch profiliert und milieutreu.[26] Sie tragen auch einen eigenen Akzent, der bisweilen in der wissenschaftlichen Klassifikation untergeht. Denn die Mahnungen rufen nicht, wie häufig zu le-

---

[20] Vgl. Jacobi, *Jesusüberlieferung bei Paulus*, 53, 64, 121.
[21] Vgl. ebd., 68.
[22] Vgl. ebd., 85.
[23] Vgl. ebd., 85–96.
[24] Hierbei kategorisiert Jacobi, *Jesusüberlieferung bei Paulus*, die Gegnerprovokation von Q 6,29 als positives Pendant zum Vergeltungsverzicht, so dass sie immer wieder in dieser Optik erscheinen, vgl. ebd., 65–69; ebd., 111–12 hebt sie auch die geforderte Aktivität hervor.
[25] Vgl. ebd., 65: Eine getrennte Entstehung von Q 6,28–29 sei nicht nachgewiesen; Röm 12 und 1 Petr 3 beinhalteten frühchristliche Traditionen (ebd., 115–16) mit unklärbarer Vorgeschichte, evtl. könnten sie auf einer Lehre Jesu beruhen (ebd., 118), doch stünden die Briefe gegen eine Autorisierung vom Herrenwort her (ebd., 120–21); Matthäus und Lukas hätten mit den Gegnerprovokationen eine Steigerung eingeführt (ebd., 118); der Wangenschlag könnte über die Passionsgeschichte aus der Gottesknechttradition stammen (ebd., 112); der Beginn von Mt 5,39 könne Redaktion sein, die von der Tradition gespeist sei (ebd., 66).
[26] Vgl. Ebner, „Feindesliebe," 121–30.

sen, zum „Vergeltungsverzicht" (wie Röm 12,17 oder 1 Petr 3,9) oder zur Gewaltlosigkeit[27] – dies träfe nur das jeweils unterlassene Verhalten. Vielmehr fordern die Mahnungen eine aktive Geste: paradoxes Handeln, welches das Unrecht verstärkt und damit provoziert.[28] Wer seinem Angreifer das viel wertlosere Hemd oder die zweite Wange bietet, erweist sich damit nicht als aktiv solidarisch (wie Röm 12,20 oder die Feindesliebe es fordern), sondern hält ihm die eigene Übergriffigkeit vor Augen. Zu diesen Gegnerprovokationen passt der Segensimperativ: Ein prägnanter Segen, gesprochen in der Situation des Angriffs, funktioniert unter Umständen ebenso provokativ – lässt sich aber auch außerhalb des Wanderradikalenmilieus bestens praktizieren.[29] Dass darüber hinaus Feindparänese abstrahiert, verallgemeinert und unter Beibehaltung der „Kontrastparänese" mit traditionellem Material formuliert würde, wäre durchaus folgerichtig.[30] Und dem könnte sich auch das allgemeine Feindesliebegebot verdanken.

---

[27] Vgl. neben Jacobi, *Jesusüberlieferung bei Paulus*, z. B. Ulrich Luz, *Das Evangelium nach Matthäus*, Band 1: *Matthäus 1–7*, 5. Aufl., EKK 1/1 (Düsseldorf: Benziger; Neukirchen-Vluyn: Neukirchener, 2002), 139: „Aufforderungen zur Gewaltlosigkeit." Der mt Rahmen um die Sprüche, „Widersteht nicht dem Bösen," führt auf diese Spur, der Luz (ebd., 140) folgt; er sieht das Problem, negiert, es gehe um „bloßen Verzicht auf Vergeltung" (ebd., 140), und findet darin „Protest" (ebd., 141). Vgl. Wilfried Eckey, *Das Lukasevangelium unter Berücksichtigung seiner Parallelen*, 2 Bde., 2. Aufl. (Neukirchen-Vluyn: Neukirchener, 2006), 1:306, zu V. 29–30: „Beispiele für Rechtsverzicht" – was für V. 30 zutrifft, die Andersartigkeit von V. 29 aber ausblendet; vgl. auch Bovon, *Das Evangelium nach Lukas*, 1:320: „Verzicht auf Widerstand" – aber ebd., 321: „provozierende Haltung" beim Wangenschlag; Zeller, *Die weisheitlichen Mahnsprüche*, 55–59, liest auch für Q mit dem Schwerpunkt des Verzichts. Weiterhin für Matthäus: Peter Fiedler, *Das Matthäusevangelium*, TKNT 1 (Stuttgart: Kohlhammer, 2006), 145–49; für Lukas und Matthäus: Matthias Konradt, „,… damit ihr Söhne eures Vaters im Himmel werdet': Erwägungen zur ‚Logik' von Gewaltverzicht und Feindesliebe in Matthäus 5,38–48," in idem, *Studien zum Matthäusevangelium*, hg. v. Alida Euler, WUNT 358 (Tübingen: Mohr Siebeck, 2016), 348–80, hier 349 und öfter; vgl. aber ebd., 362–66 zum provokativen Aspekt. Die Spannung thematisiert z. B. Ebner, „Feindesliebe," 129.

[28] Dies hebt hervor Ebner, „Feindesliebe," 130–31, der die Intention der „Selbsterhaltung" von der der „Feindesliebe" absetzt (ebd., 131), vgl. auch Hochholzer, *Feindes- und Bruderliebe*, 156, 205.

[29] Instruktiv die beiden Sitze im Leben, die Fritz Graf, „Fluch und Verwünschungen," in *Thesaurus Cultus et Rituum Antiquorum*, 9 Bde. (Los Angeles: J. Paul Getty Museum; Basel: Fondation pour le lexicon iconographicum mythologiae classicae, 2004–), 3:247–70, hier 247–48, für den Fluch – das Gegenstück zum Segen – benennt: Ein Fluch sei letzte Möglichkeit, Gerechtigkeit zu fordern; darüber hinaus könne ein Fluch aber als „besonders emphatische und besonders einschüchternde Geste" benutzt werden, „um eine Strafe noch schrecklicher und damit noch abschreckender zu machen" (ebd., 248). Der Segen wirkt entsprechend gegenläufig, passt also zum provokativen Rechtsverzicht der Jesustraditionen. Es ist plausibel anzunehmen, dass die konkret situierten Mahnungen vom Wangenschlag, dem Kleid und der Meile unter veränderten Lebensbedingungen den allgemeineren Formulierungen Platz machten und in sie aufgingen (vgl. z. B. Ebner, „Feindesliebe," 140, der eine spezifische Passung auf der Ebene von Q im Kontext abgelehnter Verkündigung sieht). Für ein differenziertes Wachstum spricht auch die Spannung gerade der Bitte zur Motivation mit der *imitatio Dei*: Die Bitte ist, anders als die Motivation, an einen kritischen Gott gerichtet, der den Feinden gerade nicht automatisch Wohlwollen entgegenbringt.

[30] Dass die paulinische, eventuell auch die vorpaulinische Paränese sich nicht auf Herren-

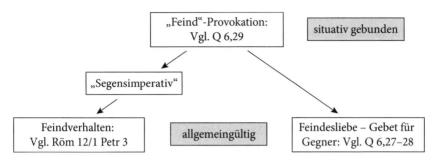

Die Feindparänese der Traditio duplex zeigt christliches Profil. In jedem Fall teilen hier Matthäus und Lukas eine eigenständige Formulierung der Feindparänese, sowohl was das horizontale als auch was das vertikale Element angeht. Insbesondere das Gebet für die Feinde trägt dabei einen eigenen Akzent: Während die Feindesliebe noch in direkter Face-to-Face-Begegnung mit den Gegnern zu praktizieren ist, lässt sich ein Gebet für die Feinde auch jenseits einer direkten Konfrontation sprechen.[31]

C. Gebet für die Gegner: Traditionen

Verglichen mit den Parallelen zur Wohltat an Feinden ist die Suche nach dem Topos des Gebets für die Gegner in der Umgebung des NT schwerer. Aus dem griechisch-römischen Umfeld – also dort, wo nicht der Gott Israels adressiert ist – ist mir kein Beleg bekannt.[32] Im biblisch-jüdischen Umfeld gibt es dagegen Hinweise, insbesondere in den Testamenten der zwölf Patriarchen.

---

worte gründet, muss nicht zwingend gegen Jesustradition sprechen: Dass Paulus sich nicht an sie bindet, lässt sich auch mit seiner späten Berufung begründen: Er selbst hat Jesus nicht erlebt, wäre also auf Autoritäten erster Hand angewiesen – und stützt sich deshalb auf seine eigenen Evidenzen, vgl. Hildegard Scherer, Rezension von *Jesusüberlieferungen bei Paulus? Analogien zwischen den echten Paulusbriefen und den synoptischen Evangelien*, von Christine Jacobi, BZ 61 (2017): 279–81, hier 280.

[31] Anders Bovon, *Das Evangelium nach Lukas*, 1:314: „letzte mögliche Geste der Verfolgten" gegenüber übermächtigen Feinden.

[32] Vgl. Udo Schnelle mit Manfred Lang und Michael Labahn (Hgg.), *Neuer Wettstein: Texte zum Neuen Testament aus Griechentum und Hellenismus*, Band I.1.2: *Texte zum Matthäusevangelium: Matthäus 1–10* (Berlin: de Gruyter, 2013), 522, der mit Josephus, *B. J.* 4.307, und Marc Aurel 8.51.2, Texte aufführt, die m. E. das Motiv nicht enthalten. In den zu Mt 5,44 aufgeführten Stellen (ebd., 484–522) ist vom Gebet nur in den beiden u. g. Stellen aus TestXII die Rede (ebd., 491). W. D. Davies und Dale C. Allison, Jr., *The Gospel according to Saint Matthew*, Band 1: *Matthew I–VII*, ICC (Edinburgh: T & T Clark, 1988), 553, verweisen auf Sent. Sextus 213: εὔχου τοὺς ἐχθροὺς δύνασθαι εὐεργετεῖν, „Bete darum, dass du deinen Feinden Gutes tun kannst"; Text und Übersetzung von Wilfried Eisele et al., *Die Sextussprüche und ihre Verwandten*, hg. v. Wilfried Eisele, SAPERE 26 (Tübingen: Mohr Siebeck, 2015); der Anmerkung in Eisele, *Sextussprüche*, 221, zufolge gehört der Spruch in die lukanische Nachgeschichte; das Gebet komme

Der Beitrag von Karl-Heinrich Ostmeyer in diesem Band widmet sich dem Thema ausführlich und diskutiert Parallelen.³³ An dieser Stelle nur einige Hinweise zu Möglichkeiten und Grenzen weiterer Stellen, auf die in der Literatur bisweilen verwiesen wird.

(1) Ps 108,4 LXX:³⁴ Hier klagt der Beter über Sünder bzw. Lügner, die gegen ihn agieren. Dabei hält er auch fest: ἀντὶ τοῦ ἀγαπᾶν με ἐνδιέβαλλόν με ἐγὼ δὲ προσευχόμην („Als Reaktion auf meine Liebe verleumdeten sie mich, ich aber betete"). Beide Handlungen stehen im Imperfekt, was auf Dauer oder Wiederholung hinweist. Es wird also keine spontane, situative Reaktion des Beters geschildert. Zudem bleibt offen, was und für wen der Psalmist betet. Im MT ist darüber hinaus die Konnotation des Gebets fraglich,³⁵ mit Franz-Lothar Hossfeld und Erich Zenger³⁶ ist vielmehr an eine Appellation an Gott zu denken, mit welcher der Beter sein Recht einfordert.

(2) Eine Verbindung von Gegnerschaft und Gebet schafft auch Ps 34,13 LXX: ἐγὼ δὲ ἐν τῷ αὐτοὺς παρενοχλεῖν μοι ἐνεδυόμην σάκκον καὶ ἐταπείνουν ἐν νηστείᾳ τὴν ψυχήν μου καὶ ἡ προσευχή μου εἰς κόλπον μου ἀποστραφήσεται („Ich aber, als sie [die ungerechten Zeugen] mir Probleme machten, umgab mich mit einem Sack und erniedrigte in Fasten meine Seele, und mein Gebet wird in meine Brust zurückkehren"). Auch hier ist der Inhalt des Gebets offen. Im Gesamtzusammenhang wünscht der Psalm den Feinden das Gericht; bereits Vers 1 ruft Gott zur Gegenwehr. Näher am Fürbittgebet wäre der MT: Anstelle des „als sie mir Probleme machten" hat er: „als sie krank waren." Hier hätte sich der Beter mit Fasten und Beten für die Gesundheit der falschen Zeugen eingesetzt.

„dem Feind jedoch indirekt zugute." Wilfried Eisele, „Papst oder Heide? Zum Charakter der Sextussprüche und ihres Verfassers," in idem, *Sextussprüche*, 3–53, hier 37, kommt in der Verfasserfrage zu dem Schluss: „Auf jeden Fall haben wir es beim Kompilator der Sextussprüche mit einem Christen zu tun," während der „um die Zeitenwende" agierende Philosoph Q. Sextus dafür „kaum ernsthaft in Betracht kommt" (ebd., 6). Dies macht für den Spruch christliche Wirkungsgeschichte, nicht vorchristliche Tradition wahrscheinlich. Der bei Davies und Allison, *Matthew*, 1:553; Kuhn, „Das Liebesgebot Jesu," 198, als Parallele angegebene P. Oxy. X 1224, 2.1 wird aufgrund des fragmentarischen Charakters und der möglichen Abhängigkeit nicht berücksichtigt, vgl. dazu Thomas J. Kraus, „Der Papyrus Oxyrhynchus X 1224 (P. Oxy. X 1224)," in *Antike christliche Apokryphen in deutscher Übersetzung*, hg. v. Christoph Markschies und Jens Schröter (Tübingen: Mohr Siebeck, 2012–), 1.1:370–72, hier 370.

³³ Karl-Heinrich Ostmeyer, „Beten für und gegen Feinde," infra 89–101.
³⁴ Ps 109,4–5; Ps 35,12–15, bzw. 14–15. MT: Kuhn, „Das Liebesgebot Jesu," 225; Radl, *Evangelium nach Lukas*, 402, allgemein im Kontext von Feindesliebetraditionen. Radl zitiert dort auch Arist 227 an – vollständig gelesen ist die Stelle aufschlussreich, auch wenn es hier noch nicht um aktive Gegnerschaft, sondern nur um Meinungsverschiedenheit geht: Dort wird die Meinung vertreten, man müsse den Andersdenkenden gegenüber (πρὸς τοὺς ἀντιδοξοῦντας) großzügig sein, um sie zu ihren Gunsten zu verändern. Dann soll aber Gott, der Macht über das Denken aller habe, angefleht werden (λιτανεύειν), dies zu vollenden.
³⁵ Vgl. auch Radl, *Evangelium nach Lukas*, 402 Anm. 368.
³⁶ Frank-Lothar Hossfeld und Erich Zenger, *Psalmen 101–150*, HThKAT (Freiburg i. Br.: Herder, 2008), 186.

(3) Jes 53,12:[37] Im MT heisst es vom Gottesknecht: „und für die Frevler bat er" (וְלַפֹּשְׁעִים יַפְגִּיעַ) wer dabei angesprochen wird, ist nicht gesagt; ebenso wenig ist klar, ob es sich um unmittelbare Feinde des Beters handelt; in der LXX ist der Satz darüber hinaus sinnverändernd ersetzt durch: καὶ διὰ τὰς ἁμαρτίας αὐτῶν παρεδόθη, „und für ihre Sünden wurde er hingegeben."

(4) Eine Fürbitte für Gegner berichtet die alttestamentliche Tradition von prominenten Gestalten:[38] In der Plagenerzählung appelliert der Pharao mehrmals an die Gebetsmacht des Mose, um aus den schlimmen Situationen befreit zu werden – Mose nutzt sie, und Gott lenkt ein (Ex 8,4–9.24–27; 9,27–33; 10,16–19). Hier liegt der Akzent auf der Macht des Mose, den wirksamen Kontakt zum wirkmächtigen Gott herzustellen. Es handelt sich um ein einmaliges Kräftemessen.

(5) Jer 29,7; 18,20: Jer 29,7 mahnt in einer Gottesrede die Verbannten in Babylon, für die Stadt zum Herrn zu beten: Hier ist ein längerer Zustand, eine gewohnheitsmässige Handlung im Blick; allerdings liegt die Unmittelbarkeit der Anfeindung zurück. Motiviert werden die Verbannten damit, dass sie letztlich für ihre eigenes Wohl beten: „denn in ihrem Frieden wird euer Friede sein." Näher an unseren Topos heran kommt Jer 18,20: „Soll Böses für Gutes vergolten werden? Denn sie haben meiner Seele eine Grube gegraben. Denke daran, dass ich vor dir gestanden habe, um Gutes über sie zu reden, um deinen Zorn von ihnen abzuwenden."[39] Doch nach Alexa Wilke schaut der Vers in die Vergangenheit, um das „Bild des Fürbitters zu zeichnen": Inzwischen ist er nämlich mit seiner Geduld am Ende und fordert das brutale Gericht über diejenigen, die ihm nachstellen (18,21–22).[40] Insgesamt kennt Jer (z. B. 14,11) ein Fürbittverbot für den Propheten.[41] Im Kontext von Jer 18,20 ist der persönliche Angriff auf den Propheten nicht Auslöser der Fürbitte, sondern letzte Spitze der Sünde des Volkes, eine ungerechte Reaktion auf die vorausgehende Fürbitte des Propheten – ob der Fürbitte schon persönliche Anfeindungen vorausgegangen waren, sagt der Text nicht direkt. Vielmehr erscheint die Feindseligkeit hier als paradoxe Folge des Guten.

---

[37] Vgl. im Zusammenhang mit Lk 23,34 Wolter, *Lukasevangelium*, 757–58, und Shelly Matthews, *Perfect Martyr: The Stoning of Stephen and the Construction of Christian Identity* (Oxford: Oxford University Press, 2010), 106, die auf die Diskrepanz MT-LXX hinweisen.

[38] Roland H. Worth, Jr., *The Sermon on the Mount: Its Old Testament Roots* (New York: Paulist, 1997), 125–26, nennt (unter Rückgriff auf eine Arbeit Pinchas Lapides) u. a. das Gebet des Mose für den Pharao, als Beispiel Ex 8,24–27, sowie das Gebet für Babylon Jer 29,7, die mir am aussagekräftigsten erscheinen. Zu Abrahams Fürbitte für Abimelech (Gen 20,17) und Elischas Fürbitte für seine Feinde (2 Kön 6,20) vgl. den Beitrag von Karl-Heinrich Ostmeyer in diesem Band; auf 1QapGen ar XX, 28–29 (Abraham) verweisen auch Davies und Allison, *Matthew*, 1:553.

[39] Analysiert bei Alexa F. Wilke, *Die Gebete der Propheten: Anrufungen Gottes im „corpus propheticum" der Hebräischen Bibel*, BZAW 451 (Berlin: de Gruyter, 2014), 304, die von einem späteren weisheitlichen Zusatz ähnlich Ps 35 ausgeht. Übersetzung des MT: Elberfelder Bibel.

[40] Wilke, *Gebete der Propheten*, 308.

[41] Vgl. Wilke, *Gebete der Propheten*, 307.

Am engsten scheint mir der Bezug zu den Testamenten der zwölf Patriarchen, in denen das Liebesgebot immer wieder thematisiert wird.[42] Im Testament des Joseph wird Joseph zum Beispiel der Bruderliebe – und damit auch zur Liebe an denen, die ihm Böses zugefügt hatten (TestXII.Jos 17).[43] Kurz darauf mahnt er (18,2): „Und wenn euch jemand Böses tun will, betet ihr durch Gutestun für ihn/ ὑμεῖς τῇ ἀγαθοποιΐᾳ εὔχεσθε ὑπὲρ αὐτοῦ; und von allem Bösen werdet ihr befreit werden durch den Herrn." Nochmals erscheint das Motiv in TestXII.Ben 3,6: „Auch Joseph bat nämlich unseren Vater, dass er für die Söhne bete, damit der Herr ihnen nicht anrechne, wenn sie etwas Böses gegen ihn erwogen"/ καὶ γὰρ ἐδεήθη τοῦ πατρὸς ἡμῶν Ἰωσὴφ ἵνα προσεύξηται περὶ τῶν υἱῶν ἵνα μὴ λογίσηται αὐτοῖς ὁ κύριος, εἴ τι ἐνεθυμήθησαν πονηρὸν περὶ αὐτοῦ.[44]

Besonders diese Parallelen sind bestechend – vorausgesetzt die Stellen stehen für eine eigenständige frühjüdische Tradition.[45] TestXII.Ben 3,6 steht in direk-

---

[42] Stellen bei Zeller, *Die weisheitlichen Mahnsprüche*, 106; Konradt, „Söhne eures Vaters," 351–54; Text von TestXII: Marinus de Jonge, *The Testaments of the Twelve Patriarchs: A Critical Edition of the Greek Text*, PVTG 1/2 (Leiden: Brill, 1978).

[43] Auf die Parallelen zum Gebet für die Gegner in TestXII.Jos 18,2 und TestXII.Ben 4,2–3 wird in der Literatur häufig verwiesen, vgl. Eckey, *Lukasevangelium*, 1:304; Bovon, *Das Evangelium nach Lukas*, 1:313 Anm. 19, allerdings ohne TestXII.Ben 3,6 zu nennen; vgl. dagegen Zeller, *Die weisheitlichen Mahnsprüche*, 106 Anm. 384, der die Stelle aufführt, ohne sie zu erläutern; Konradt, „Söhne eures Vaters," 353. Grund dafür, dass TestXII.Ben 3,6 aus dem Blick fällt, könnte sein, dass auch Neuer Wettstein den Text nicht aufführt, TestXII.Jos 18,2 und TestXII.Ben 4,2–3 dagegen schon.

[44] Eckey, *Lukasevangelium*, 1:304, nennt auch noch TestXII.Ben 5,5: „Und wenn jemand eine gerechte Seele verrät, betet der Gerechte"; Übersetzung Jürgen Becker, *Die Testamente der zwölf Patriarchen*, JSHRZ 3/1 (Gütersloh: Gütersloher Verlagshaus Mohn, 1974). Allerdings wird hier der Fürbittcharakter nicht deutlich, ebenso wenig der Inhalt. Zudem ist das Gebet des Gerechten in der Situation der Erniedrigung angesprochen, das – wie bei Joseph – zur Rechtfertigung führt. Eine Adressierung zugunsten der Gegner, wie Harm W. Hollander und Marinus de Jonge, *The Testaments of the Twelve Patriarchs: A Commentary*, SVTP 8 (Leiden: Brill, 1985), 425, sie für möglich halten, ist m. E. nicht zwingend.

[45] Das Verständnisproblem und die Möglichkeit der Interpolation notiert Radl, *Evangelium nach Lukas*, 402 Anm. 371; Kuhn, „Das Liebesgebot Jesu," 225, übergeht aufgrund des Interpolationsproblems die TestXII bewusst. In der Frage, ob es sich bei den TestXII um eine christlich konzipierte Schrift handelt oder ob ein frühjüdischer Grundbestand eruiert werden kann, hat David A. deSilva, „The Testaments of the Twelve Patriarchs as Witnesses to Pre-Christian Judaism: A Re-Assessment," *JSPE* 22 (2013): 21–68, zugunsten des Letzteren argumentiert; Konradt, „Söhne eures Vaters," 353 Anm. 10 schließt sich der Position an. Auch deSilva geht von einer fortschreitenden Christianisierung der Schrift aus (ebd., 29), die differenziert zu betrachtende, teils kürzende, teils aber auch erweiternde armenische Übersetzung stamme von einer früheren, weniger christlich interpolierten Textvorlage (ebd., 25–26); literarkritisch ließen sich christliche Interpolationen häufig gut erkennen (ebd., 31). TestXII.Ben 3,6 fiele nach deSilva dem jüdischen Kern zu, V. 8 dagegen sei christlich bearbeitet (ebd., 28–29) – m. E. leuchtet deSilvas Argumentation ein. Der Fall TestXII.Jos 18,2 liegt komplizierter: Die Passage fehlt in der armenischen Übersetzung (vgl. Michael E. Stone, *An Editio Minor of the Armenian Version of the Testaments of the Twelve Patriarchs*, HUAS 11 [Leuven: Peeters, 2012]), kann dort aber der häufiger zu beobachtenden Kürzung ethischer Passagen (vgl. deSilva, „The Testaments of the Twelve Patriarchs," 25) zum Opfer gefallen sein. Das TestXII.Jos integriert zwei Erzählblöcke, die mit Hollander und de Jonge, *Testaments*, 393, aus zwei verschiedenen

ter Linie zu den einzigen neutestamentlichen Realisierungen der Mahnung zum Gebet für die Gegner: zum Gebet des lukanischen Jesus[46] bei der Kreuzigung (Lk 23,24: Vater, erlass ihnen, sie wissen nämlich nicht, was sie tun/πάτερ, ἄφες αὐτοῖς, οὐ γὰρ οἴδασιν τί ποιοῦσιν) und zu den letzten Worten des Stephanus der Apg (Apg 7,60: Herr, rechne ihnen diese Sünde nicht an/κύριε, μὴ στήσῃς αὐτοῖς ταύτην τὴν ἁμαρτίαν).

Zudem wird die Fürbitte für die Feinde hier inhaltlich präzisiert. Vielerlei Bitten zum Wohl der Feinde sind vorstellbar – dass sie sich bessern und bereuen, dass es ihnen trotz allem wohlergehen möge. Doch sowohl das Testament des Benjamin als auch die lukanischen Belege bitten gleichermaßen darum, dass Gott die Feinde begnadigen möge.

Diese Entsprechung innerhalb des lukanischen Doppelwerks führt schließlich weiter zur Frage, wie sich diese außergewöhnliche Mahnung zum Gebet für die Feinde in die synoptischen Traditionen einordnen lässt.

D. Vernetzungen II: Synoptisches Material

Sucht man im synoptischen Material nach Bezugspunkten für den Fürbittappell, so ist einerseits zu überprüfen, wie dort das Thema „Gebet" behandelt wird,[47] andererseits, wie das Verhalten gegenüber aktiven Angreifern themati-

---

Quellen stammen: Die Kapitel 3–9 schildern, wie Joseph den Avancen der Ägypterin ausgesetzt ist; Kap. 11–16 sind eine Analepse in die Zeit, in der Joseph von den Ismaeliten zu verkaufen war, sich als Sklave ausgibt und damit seine Brüder schützt – dies kommentieren Kap. 17–18, die zudem Kap. 16 ausblenden und sich nur auf die Brüder konzentrieren. Die Aufforderung zum Gebet in 18,2 hat keinen Rückhalt in der Erzählung der Kap. 11–16: Hier betet Joseph nicht. Im ersten Erzählblock betet Joseph häufig (3,3.7; 4,8; 7,4; 8,1; vgl. 10,1) – wenn wir vom Inhalt erfahren, dann geht es um seine Rettung, wie dies 18,2 formuliert: Eine solche Rettung ist wiederum in Kap. 11–16 kein Thema. Damit eignet sich 18,2 zur Verzahnung der beiden Erzählblöcke und gehört damit m. E. auf die textliche Stufe, auf der die beiden Blöcke zusammenwuchsen. Hierfür lässt sich m. E. keine christliche Motivation erkennen. Dafür spricht weiterhin, dass sich in TestXII.Jos 18,2 die Bezüge zum NT nicht durch die Wortwahl aufdrängen (gilt auch für TestXII.Ben 3,6) und auch die Begründungsmotivation variiert: 18,2–4 hoffen auf Erlösung bzw. Belohnung und sprechen nicht wie der Q-Komplex von einer imitatio dei.

[46] Der Vers Lk 23,34 ist textkritisch zu problematisieren: NA28 markiert ihn als nicht ursprünglich. Doch mit guten inneren Gründen ist er m. E. als Ausgangstext anzunehmen, vor allem weil eine spätere Gestaltung nach dem Vorbild der Stephanusperikope weniger plausibel scheint als die umgekehrte Entstehungsreihenfolge, und weil sich eine spätere Auslassung aus antijudaistischen Gründen wahrscheinlich machen lässt. Zu ausführlichen Begründungen vgl. z. B. David M. Crump, *Jesus the Intercessor: Prayer and Christology in Luke-Acts*, WUNT II 49 (Tübingen: Mohr Siebeck, 1992), 79–85, oder Matthews, *Perfect Martyr*, 101–3; knapper Wolter, *Lukasevangelium*, 757–58; François Bovon, *Das Evangelium nach Lukas*, Band 4: *Lukas 19,28–24,53* EKK 3/4 (Zürich: Benziger; Neukirchen-Vluyn: Neukirchener, 2009), 461–62.

[47] Die Stellen aus Mk, Mt, Lk und Apg sind zusammengestellt bei Karl-Heinrich Ostmeyer, *Kommunikation mit Gott und Christus: Sprache und Theologie des Gebetes im Neuen Testament,*

siert ist.[48] Diese Themen können nun in Paränese besprochen werden – oder aber vom maßgeblichen Modell der synoptischen Traditionen, von der Erzählfigur Jesus, in Verhalten umgesetzt werden. Folgende Daten und Auswertungen ergeben sich:

1. Mk-Stoff

Mk	Gebet	Verhalten gg. aktiven Gegnern
Paränese	Beten für Dämonenaustreibung (9,29) Tempel als Haus des Gebets für Völker (11,17) Vertrauen beim Beten (11,24) Vergebung vor dem Beten (11,25) keine Scheingebete (12,40) Bitte: Katastrophe nicht im Winter (13,18) Bitte: nicht in Versuchung fallen (14,38)	Bedrängnis, Verfolgung > nicht skandalisiert werden (4,17) (?) > Leben verlieren (8,35) (Gegner) > vergeben (11,25) Verhöre > nicht um Rede sorgen (13,9.11) Auslieferung, Hass > aushalten (13,12–13)
Modell Jesu	Abgesondertes Beten (1,35; 6,46; 14,35.39) Dank/Lob beim Mahl (14,22.26; vgl. 6,41; 8,6) Bitte: Stunde/Kelch vorübergehen lassen (14,35–36) Verlassenheit > Anfrage an Gott (15,34)	Suche nach Anklagegrund > Zorn, Heilung (3,2.5) Apophthegmata: weish. Argumentation getötet werden > Vergeltung Gottes (12,1–9)

Soweit das Bittgebet in Markus thematisiert wird, sind keine Anknüpfungspunkte zur Bitte für die Feinde zu finden. Der Inhalt der Bitten konzentriert sich auf die Bedürfnisse der Betenden, sowohl in der Paränese (Mk 13,18; 14,38) als auch bei Jesu Beten (Mk 14,35–36), der im Angesicht seiner Feinde um Verschonung anfragt. Steht im Konfliktfall ein Gebet bevor, so ist laut der Paränese Mk 11,25 der Konflikt erst zu bereinigen; interessant dabei die Perspektive, der Beter habe sich selbst zum Feind gemacht.

Aktive Angriffe werden im Horizont des Markus thematisiert: Bei gegnerischen Attacken sind v. a. Aushalten (Mk 4,17; 13,12–13) und Vertrauen (Mk 8,35; 13,9.11) angeraten; das Weinbergsgleichnis rechnet fest mit der Vergeltung Gottes, die hier noch mahnend den Gegnern vor Augen gehalten wird. Während die Paränese rät, dem Gegner zu vergeben (Mk 11,25), zeigt die Jesusfigur in der Bedrängnis Zorn (Mk 3,2.5) und setzt sich aktiv gegen die Opponenten durch, mit einer Heilung (Mk 3,2.5) oder in den Apophthegmata mit weisheitlicher Argu-

---

WUNT 197 (Tübingen: Mohr Siebeck, 2006), 212–316, der die Stellen in der Regel jedoch nicht im Hinblick auf das Fürbittgebet auswertet.

[48] Hierbei liegt der Fokus auf dem aktiven Vorgehen der Angreifer. Texte, die von einer Nicht-Aufnahme oder reinen Ablehnung handeln, bleiben unberücksichtigt.

mentation. Es zeigen sich keine offensichtlichen Reflexe eines Einbezugs Gottes angesichts der Gegner oder allgemein eines aktiven Verhaltens zugunsten von Gegnern.

2. Traditio duplex

Q	Gebet	Verhalten gg. aktiven Gegnern
Paränese	Bitte: Name Gottes soll geheiligt werden, Basileia soll kommen, Brot geben, Schuld vergeben, nicht in Versuchung geführt werden (11,2–4) (Gutes bitten) > Vertrauen (11,9–12)	(verbale) Attacken > Freuen (6,22–23) Angriffe > provozieren (6,29) Feinde > lieben (6,27) Gegner > beten (6,27) Wölfe > Schafe sein (10,3) Schuldner > vergeben (11,4) Tötung > Vergeltung Gottes (11,47–51) Tötende > nicht fürchten (12,4) Synagogen > nicht um Rede sorgen (12,12) Prozessgegner > einigen (12,57–59) sündigender Bruder > vergeben (17,3–4) (?) > Leben verlieren (17,33)
Modell Jesu	Preisung (10,21)	Apophthegmata: weisheitliche Argumentation Tötung > Entzug (13,34–35)

Vergleicht man das Material der Traditio duplex mit Markus, so findet sich beim Bittgebet das neue Motiv, neben den eigenen Bedürfnissen auch um die Durchsetzung der Macht Gottes zu bitten (Q 11,2–4). Einen Anknüpfungspunkt zum Gebet für die Feinde zeigt die Gebetsthematik nicht.

Die Aufforderungen zum Vergeben bzw. Einlenken sind gegenüber Mk 11,25 ausgebaut: Sie finden sich im Vater unser (Q 11,4), in der Mahnung, sich mit dem Prozessgegner zu einigen (Q 12,57–59) und schließlich in der Aufforderung, dem sündigenden Bruder zu vergeben (Q 17,3–4).

Auch aktive Angriffe werden stärker thematisiert als bei Markus, nicht zuletzt aufgrund des Motivs von der Gewalt gegen Propheten Q 11,49–51; 13,34–35. Q 11,49–51 hält den den Gegnern das Gericht Gottes entgegen;[49] Q 13,34–35 sagt an, dass Jesus sich entziehen wird. Charakteristisch für das Material der Traditio duplex, bei Markus dagegen nicht vorhanden ist das Motiv der paradoxen Re-

---

[49] Gerade die Weherufe werden bisweilen in Kontrast zur Feindesliebe gebracht; vgl. für Mt 23 Ulrich Luz, *Das Evangelium nach Matthäus, Band 3: Matthäus 18–25*, EKK 1/3 (Zürich: Benziger; Neukirchen-Vluyn: Neukirchener, 1997), 145: „Diskrepanz zwischen dem Gebot der Feindesliebe … und den verbalen Aggressionen gegen die Führer der Jesus ablehnenden Mehrheit Israels …"; ebd. auch Hinweis auf weitere Reaktionen auf Ablehnung, u. a. Q 10,11–12 (Staub abschütteln, das „eher Gegenaggressionen" „weckt"), und ebd., 146–47 weitere Felder von Verbalaggressionen im NT: „Umgang mit Apostaten und Irrlehrern" und Umwelt.

aktion angesichts der Gegner. Neben Q 6,29, der provozierenden Geste bei Wangenschlag und Kleiderraub, und den besprochenen Q 6,27–28 erscheint es auch in der Seligpreisung der Verfolgten, die zur Freude aufgerufen werden (Q 6,22–23). Im herausgelösten Material der Traditio duplex bildet sich damit ein Cluster, das die letzte Seligpreisung mit zwei Paränesen zum Umgang mit Gegnern verknüpft. Doch beschränkt sich die paradoxe Reaktion nicht darauf, sie kommt vielmehr nochmals in Q 10,2 zu tragen, wo die Adressaten wie Schafe unter Wölfe gesandt werden.

3. Sondergut Mt/Redaktion

Sondergut Mt	Gebet	Verhalten gg. aktiven Gegnern
Paränese	Im Verborgenen beten (6,5–6) Nicht langatmig beten (6,7–8) Gottes Wille > geschehen (6,10) Böses > erlösen (6,13)	Verfolgung > (glücklich sein) (5,10) Böses > keinen Widerstand leisten (5,39) Beelzebul-Vorwurf > wie Jesus sein (10,25) Gefangennahme > kein Schwert (26,52)
Modell Jesu	Gefangennahme > Engelsheer erbitten (Möglichkeit; 23,53)	

In Sondergut und Redaktion des Matthäus ist kein positives Interesse an aktivem Verhalten zugunsten der Feinde nachweisbar, wenn auch auf Gewalt verzichtet wird.[50] Anders als bei Lukas wird zudem die Gegnerthematik in der Paränese der Bergpredigt ohne entsprechenden Anlass im erzählerischen Vorlauf eingeführt.

Der Akzent des Gebets für die eigenen Bedürfnisse wird noch verstärkt, wenn im Vater Unser die Erlösung vom Bösen erbeten und von Jesus bei der Gefangennahme die Möglichkeit der Bitte um ein Engelheer eingeräumt wird.

Wenn Matthäus die markinische Gefangennahme gestaltet, ist dagegen die Idee des matthäischen redaktionellen Rahmens um die Feindesliebemahnungen leitend: Jesus verbietet den Schwertgebrauch (Mt 26,52) – und damit den aktiven Widerstand, entsprechend der Vorgabe: „dem Bösen nicht widerstehen" (Mt 5,39); zur Gegnerprovokation im Sinne des Hinhaltens der anderen Wange kommt es nicht; was bei Matthäus als Illustration der Vorgabe in 5,39 erscheint, hat in der gesamten Erzählung des Matthäus kein Echo.[51] Dies bestärkt die

---

[50] Hochholzer, *Feindes- und Bruderliebe*, 166, führt noch die „Tempelaktion" (Mt 21,12–13) und die Verfluchung des Feigenbaums (21,19) als in Spannung zur fünften „Antithese" stehend an. Sie könnten jedoch auch auf die Feindesliebe bezogen werden; beide Texte sind aus Markus übernommen.

[51] Vgl. z. B. Luz, *Das Evangelium nach Matthäus*, Band 4: *Matthäus 26–28*, EKK 1/4 (Zürich: Benziger; Neukirchen-Vluyn: Neukirchener, 2002), 141–42, der allerdings rechtfertigt: „Das

schon vorgetragene These,[52] die sogenannten matthäischen „Antithesen," besser Stellungnahmen zur Halacha, seien mit älteren, weisheitlichen Jesus-Traditionen aufgefüllt, die in sich Wachstumsspuren zeigen. Matthäus scheint sich mit ihnen nicht voll identifiziert zu haben und hat sie nicht in Jesu Verhalten übersetzt.

4. Sondergut Lk/Redaktion

Sondergut Lk	Gebet	Verhalten gg. aktiven Gegnern
Paränese	immer beten (18,1–7) Haltung beim Gebet (Dank des Gerechten/Bitte des Sünders; 18,11–13)	Widerstand > Kräfte einschätzen (14,31) (?) > Schwert kaufen (22,36)
Modellbeter	Gebet im Tempel (1,10; 2,37; 18,10) Zacharias > Kind (1,13) Lobgebete: Maria (1,47–55); Zacharias (1,64.68–78); Simeon (2,28–32); Hannah (2,38)	Feinde > Rettung durch Gott (1,74)
Modell Jesu	Kontakt zu Gott (3,21; 6,12 und öfter) Geistübergabe (23,46) Segnen des Brotes (24,30)	Mordversuch > Entzug (4,29–30) Gefangennahme > Heilung des Geschädigten (22,51)
	23,33–34 Kreuzigende[53] > Gebet: Vergebung durch Gott	

Lukas geht in der Gebetsparänese gegenüber Matthäus eigene Wege, auch in seinen redaktionellen Akzenten: Er erzählt von Modellbetern, Gebet im Tempel, Gebet zur Kontaktaufnahme mit Gott, einem Gebet als letztem Wort Jesu.

Beim Umgang mit Angreifern verwirklicht der lukanische Jesus die Mahnung der Feindesliebe, anders als bei Matthäus: Bei der Gefangennahme kommt es zu einer Wunderheilung im Sinne von „Tut Gutes denen, die euch hassen." Eine

---

Moment des aktiven, die Gewalt verfremdenden Handelns, das für Mt 5,39b–41 so wichtig war, tritt in der Passionsgeschichte aus naheliegenden Gründen zurück," laut Luz bedingt durch die Vorstellung vom leidenden Gerechten. Konradt, „Söhne eures Vaters," 367, erwähnt den Zusammenhang zwischen Mt 5,39 und der Verspottungsszene Mt 26,67–68 - doch auch dort wird Jesus nicht aktiv und provokativ gezeigt.

[52] Vgl. Ebner, „Feindesliebe," 135 (mit älterer Literatur), zum Wachstumsprozess des Feindesliebekomplexes ebd., 133–42; Konradt, *Evangelium nach Matthäus*, 65, begründet die These, „dass das Unterweisungsgut erst bei Matthäus bzw. in seinem Umfeld ausdrücklich mit der Torathematik verbunden wurde," allerdings mit dem „Vergleich mit der lk Feldrede"; zum Überschuss von V. 39–41 gg. V. 39a, vgl. ebd., 95; zur Inkongruenz von V. 42, vgl. ebd., 96.

[53] Die Forschung diskutiert, für welchen Personenkreis das Personalpronomen steht, vgl. Crump, *Jesus the Intercessor*, 85–86 (römische Soldaten und jüdische Menge, alle Tätigkeiten); Eckey, *Lukasevangelium*, 2.945 (Vollstrecker, Anführer, Volk); Matthews, *Perfect Martyr*, 103–4 (bei Jesus ambivalent, bei Stephanus klar Juden); Wolter, *Lukasevangelium*, 757 (ambivalent): Dies ist relevant für Deutungen, die den Antijudaismus problematisieren, oder solche, die das lk Erzählkonzept offenlegen (s. u. Anm. 53) – für unsere Zwecke ist eine Entscheidung nicht von Gewicht.

Gegnerprovokation wie das Hinhalten der Wange oder die Übergabe des Untergewands findet aber auch bei ihm nicht statt.

Doch betet Jesus einzig bei Lukas für aktive Gegner und realisiert damit die entsprechende Mahnung. Gegenüber Lk 6,28 fällt auf, dass Jesus nicht bei den unzähligen kleinen Schmähungen im Lauf des Evangeliums betet – der Paulus der Apg übrigens auch nicht –, sondern nur in der Todesstunde; die Tötung ist aber mit ἐπηρεάζω nicht mehr treffend beschrieben: Was hier geschieht, ist mehr als Misshandlung. Dass Lukas die Mahnung und ihre Realisierung begrifflich nicht abgeglichen hat, spricht sogar dafür, dass hier Alternating primitivity vorliegt: Wenn Lukas seine Vorlage bewusst verändert hätte, dann hätte er wahrscheinlich abgeglichen; ein anderer plausibler Grund, weshalb Lukas gegebenenfalls zusammen mit der Segensbitte hier das Hapaxlegomenon aus 1 Petr als einzelnes Element eingefügt haben sollte, lässt sich schwer vorstellen – wäre eine Verallgemeinerung angezielt, so wäre ein Eingriff in eine matthäische Vorlage nicht nötig gewesen. Somit folgt wohl Lukas seiner Vorlage, Matthäus gestaltet redaktionell. Dass die Bitte für die Gegner sich auf die Todesstunde beschränkt, zeigt allerdings, dass auch Lukas sich damit nicht voll identifizieren konnte.[54]

Erstaunlicherweise hat das Gebet Jesu wie auch das des Stephanus in der Apostelgeschichte dieselbe Thematik wie das Gebet Jakobs im Testament des Benjamin: die stellvertretende Bitte um Vergebung, die mit dem strafenden, nicht bedingungslos verzeihenden Gott rechnet. Dies steht den letzten Worten und Gebeten der Märtyrer in 2 Makkabäer und 4 Makkabäer gegenüber, die allesamt dem König sein gerechtes Gericht ansagen.[55]

E. Fazit

Mit der Mahnung für die Feinde ist das zwischenmenschliche Liebesgebot um einen Gottesbezug erweitert worden. Dies stellt eine eigenständige Entwicklung innerhalb der uns zugänglichen christlichen Tradition dar. Hat man sich auch sonst mit dem christlichen Umgang mit Feinden beschäftigt – was durchaus in der jesuanischen Gegnerprovokation seine Wurzeln haben kann –, so geht die

---

[54] Allerdings stößt dieses Wort Jesu am Kreuz u. U. eine Dynamik an, die sich mit Stephanus verstärkt und antijudaistisch ausgespielt werden kann, wie Matthews, *Perfect Martyr*, 99–130, analysiert: Nach dieser Lesart werde die Vergebungsbitte für die Juden in der Apg nicht erzählerisch eingelöst; vielmehr entstehe „a radical discontinuity between Judaism and Christianity" und „ethical superiority of Christianity over Judaism" (100); die Gebete dienten einer Idealisierung der Beter (118) und seien auf dem Hintergrund der antiken *clementia*-Idee ein Machterweis gegenüber den Tätern (121). Anders Crump, *Jesus the Intercessor*, 91, für das Gebet Jesu: Es führe zum „Sehen" in der Dunkelheit und zur Reue.

[55] Vgl. dazu auch Matthews, *Perfect Martyr*, 107–9, die auch auf 2 Chr 24,22, den Racheruf des ermordeten Propheten Sacharja, und seinen Bezug zu Lk 11,50–51 verweist. Vgl. auch Eckey, *Lukasevangelium*, 2.944–45: „In jüdischen Märtyrerberichten gibt es dazu keine Parallele."

Fürbitte weiter als der Segen, dem noch eine gewisse situative Provokation anhaftet. Die Fürbitte eignet sich für Situationen, in der solidarische Hilfeleistung schwer fällt; sie wird komplementär an Gott delegiert, um dem Anspruch des Liebesgebots gerecht zu werden.

Die Fürbitte kann in biblisch-jüdischem Milieu anknüpfen. Innerhalb der synoptischen Tradition bleibt sie eigenwillig: Matthäus hat sie wohl vorgefunden und mittradiert; er lässt sich von der apotreptischen Mahnung seines Rahmens leiten, wenn er Jesus in der Passion agieren lässt; Lukas hat das Gebet für die Feinde in den dramatischen Todesberichten eventuell unter Aufnahme von Tradition (die Testamente der zwölf Patriarchen) inszeniert – aber beim Paulus der Apg bereits wieder aus dem Blick verloren.

Von einer Q-Redaktion scheint die Fürbitt-Mahnung auch nicht geschaffen worden zu sein – dazu sind die uns zugänglichen Vernetzungen zu gering. Allerdings spiegelt auch sie, wie weitere charakteristische Q-Traditionen, aggressive Übergriffe auf die Gruppe. Sie arbeitet mit dem Mittel der paradoxen Reaktion, die typisch für Q, nicht aber für markinische Tradition ist. Sie baut eine Brücke in eine Situation der alltäglichen Abweisung. Und damit fügt sich dieses neutestamentliche Detail hervorragend an seinen Platz in der rekonstruierten Programmatischen Rede von Q.

Gebet und Gottesreich

Gebetstexte aus Q im Vergleich mit den qumranischen Sabbatopferliedern

Markus Tiwald

Nirgendwo schlägt das Gottesbild der Menschen deutlicher zu Buche als in ihren Gebeten: Gott als Notnagel, der nur in Krisen angerufen wird; Gott als Freund, dem ich alles mitteile; Gott als Unbekannter, dem ich mich fragend nähere – im Gebet spiegelt sich unser Gottesbild am Existenziellsten. Wie aber hat Jesus gebetet – und wie seine frühen Nachfolger in der Logienquelle? Kann man auch hier deren ureigenstes Gottesbild erkennen?

Zunächst soll in Teil A grundsätzlich ein Blick auf den „Motivationshorizont" des Betens in Q geworfen werden, der in der eschatologischen Naherwartung erkannt wird. Dann erfolgt in Teil B ein Blick auf die in der Logienquelle erhalten gebliebene Gebetspraxis und die dafür in Frage kommenden Texte. Teil C versucht dann gemeinsame Motive der Gebetspraxis in Q zu erörtern, während Teil D dem frühjüdischen Kontext der Gebetstexte in Q und dabei besonders den Sabbatopferliedern von Qumran gewidmet ist. Teil E fasst die Resultate zusammen und stellt die Frage, wieweit sich anhand dieser Gebete bereits Ansätze einer rituellen Gebetspraxis ableiten lassen und/oder ob darin auch schon gemeinschaftliche Aspekte zum Tragen kommen.

A. Der Motivationshorizont der Logienquelle

Die gesamte Dynamik des Glaubens, Betens und Handelns Jesu findet seinen Brennpunkt in der Erwartung des unmittelbar bevorstehenden Anbruchs der βασιλεία τοῦ θεοῦ, der „Königsherrschaft Gottes." Seine Wunderhandlungen, seine Gleichnisse, seine Zuwendung zu Marginalisierten und Sündern wie auch seine zeichenhaften Mahl-Inszenierungen lassen sich nur im Motivationshorizont der nahegekommenen *basileia* verstehen.[1] Die Erwartung Jesu, dass in un-

---

[1] Vgl. dazu das noch immer fundamentale Werk von Helmut Merklein, *Jesu Botschaft von der Gottesherrschaft: Eine Skizze*, 3. Aufl., SBS 111 (Stuttgart: Katholisches Bibelwerk, 1989), pas-

mittelbar bevorstehender zeitlicher Nähe Gott mit dem Anbruch seiner Königsherrschaft zunächst Israel, doch von dort ausstrahlend die ganze Welt und Schöpfung einem sanften, doch umfassenden und alles durchdringenden Wandel (vgl. das Gleichnis vom Sauerteig, Q 13,21²) unterziehen wird, ist dabei *primum movens* und alles bestimmender Motivationshorizont.

Für die Gemeinden hinter der Logienquelle lässt sich mit gutem Grund vermuten, dass sie die imminente Naherwartung ihres Meisters teilten und ebenfalls mit dem baldigen Anbruch des Gottesreiches rechneten: Zwei umfangreiche narratologische Studien von Michael Labahn (2010) und Arne Bork (2015) haben *in extenso* herausgestellt, dass die „Figurenkonstellation [der Logienquelle] keinesfalls zufällig [konzipiert ist], sondern sie offenbart sich in einem Beziehungsgeflecht, welches sinnvoll auf das Zielobjekt der Narration – den Eintritt des Reiches Gottes – hingeordnet ist ...."[3] Denn, „... auf der Umkehr sowie der Ausrichtung des gegenwärtigen Lebens auf die eschatologische Präsenz des Gottesreiches liegt das Hauptaugenmerk der Verkündigung von Q."[4] Die *basileia*-Erwartung Jesu wird von den Q-Leuten dahingehend geweitet, dass jetzt nicht nur das anbrechende Gottesreich erwartet wird, sondern die Wiederkunft des Meisters Jesu: „Als *plot* der Q-Erzählung wurde die Erwartung, dass der *Gekommene* als *Wiederkommender* die Q-Missionare und ihre Gemeinden ins Recht setzt, festgestellt."[5] Demzufolge kann man schließen, dass Q „eine Erzählwelt inszeniert, die sich als alternative Realität für die Rezipienten offenbart ... sodass die Leser angesichts der dargestellten Realität von Q alternative Handlungsoptionen erkennen und ergreifen sollen."[6] Diese Funktion der *alternativen Realität* – die für die Q-Gruppe in der Erwartung der Wiederkunft Jesu und des Anbruchs des Gottesreiches auskristallisiert – findet sich nicht nur in den *narrativen Konzepten* (wie bei Labahn und Bork dargestellt), sondern besonders markant in der *Gebetspraxis* der Logienquelle.

---

sim, und Markus Tiwald, *Das Frühjudentum und die Anfänge des Christentums: Ein Studienbuch*, BWANT 208 (Stuttgart: Kohlhammer, 2016), 202–9.

[2] Die Logienquelle wird im Folgenden zitiert nach: Paul Hoffmann und Christoph Heil, *Die Spruchquelle Q: Studienausgabe Griechisch und Deutsch*, 4. Aufl. (Darmstadt: WBG, 2013). Dabei wurden sämtliche textkritische Zeichen zugunsten einer leichteren Lesbarkeit beiseitegelassen.

[3] Arne Bork, *Die Raumsemantik und Figurensemantik der Logienquelle*, WUNT II 404 (Tübingen: Mohr Siebeck, 2015), 314.

[4] Ebd., 314.

[5] Michael Labahn, *Der Gekommene als Wiederkommender: Die Logienquelle als erzählte Geschichte*, ABIG 32 (Leipzig: Evangelische Verlagsanstalt, 2010), 579 – daher auch der programmatische Titel von Labahns Monographie: *Der Gekommene als Wiederkommender: Die Logienquelle als erzählte Geschichte*. Auch bei der Logienquelle handelt es sich um „narrative Sinnbildung, auch wenn sie oftmals als Erzählung des Redens daherkommt ..." (ebd., 577).

[6] Bork, *Raumsemantik*, 315.

B. Gebetstexte und Gebetspraxis in Q

Erstaunlich häufig haben sich in Q Hinweise auf Gebete und Gebetspraxis erhalten. Dabei wären zu nennen:

1) Das „Colloquium Biblicum," das Jesus mit dem Satan in Q 4,4. 8. 11–12 im Rahmen der Versuchungsgeschichte führt. Die hier zur Anwendung kommenden Bibelzitate sind zwar vom narratologischen Kontext nicht als Gebetstexte, sondern als Streitgespräche funktionalisiert, doch ist ganz klar, dass Jesus mit seinen Antworten gängige biblische Gebetstraditionen des Judentums rezitiert. Der Wert dieser Texte liegt darin, dass ersichtlich wird, wie selbstverständlich der von der Logienquelle gezeichnete Jesus in den Frömmigkeitstraditionen seines Volkes verankert ist: Tempelfrömmigkeit und Rezitieren biblischer Gebete werden als natürlich vorausgesetzt – so selbstverständlich, dass selbst der Teufel das Psalmenwort 91,11–12 für seine Zwecke instrumentalisieren kann. In der unkommentierten und selbstverständlichen Verwendung dieser Texte durch Q wird klar, dass diese offensichtlich zum stehenden Repertoire der Q-Leserschaft gehörten und – da sie der Gebetspraxis des damaligen Judentums wie auch der Q Gemeinden entsprangen – keiner weiteren Erklärung bedurften.

2) Das Gebet für die Feinde (Q 6,27–28), ist zwar kein eigentlicher Gebets*text*, aber ein Gebets*auftrag*: „Betet für die, die euch verfolgen." Doch auch darin kommt die Gebetspraxis der Q-Gemeinde zum Tragen.

3) Ebenso ist das Gebet um Arbeiter für die Ernte (10,2: „Bittet daher den Herrn der Ernte, dass er Arbeiter zu seiner Ernte hinausschicke") ein Gebets*auftrag* und kein Gebets*text*. Nichtsdestotrotz lässt sich auch hier der Motivhorizont des „Betens in Q" gut verdeutlichen.

4) Ein genuiner Gebetstext hingegen ist der „Jubelruf Jesu" in Q 10,21:

Ich preise dich, Vater, Herr des Himmels und der Erde, denn du hast dies vor Weisen und Gebildeten verborgen und es Unmündigen enthüllt. Ja, Vater, denn so war es wohlgefällig vor dir. (Vgl. Sir 51,1–2.)

Der Text ist zwar kein Gebet der Q-Gemeinde, sondern Jesus in den Mund gelegt, doch erschließt sich auch hier besonders gut, mit welchem Selbstverständnis die Q-Gemeinde betete: Die Gemeinde identifiziert sich mit den hier genannten „Unmündigen": „Selig die Augen, die sehen, was ihr seht" (Q 10,23).

5) Das Vaterunser[7] (Q 11,2–4.9–13) ist der zentralste Gebetstext in Q. Gattungsmäßig handelt es sich hier zunächst eine Gebets*unterweisung* („Wenn ihr betet, sagt: ..."), doch darf man annehmen, dass die Q-Gemeinde dem Auftrag Jesu, in dieser Weise zu beten, real Folge geleistet hat. Die spätere Didache

---

[7] In Q ist allerdings noch nicht vom „Vater-*unser*" die Rede – gemäß der Fassung bei Lk 11,2 stand in Q wohl nur die Anrede Πάτερ ohne ἡμῶν. Da der Name aber zum Überbegriff für dieses Gebet geworden ist, soll der Ausdruck „Vaterunser" im Folgenden auch für die Logienquelle beibehalten werden.

schreibt jedenfalls schon vor, den Text des Vaterunsers dreimal täglich zu rezitieren (Did 8,3).

6) Im Anschluss an das Vaterunser erfolgt eine Unterweisung zum vertrauensvollen Beten: „Bittet, und euch wird gegeben werden, sucht, und ihr werdet finden, klopft an, und euch wird geöffnet werden" (Q 11,9). Dies ist zwar kein Gebetstext, beschreibt aber die innere Haltung, in der gebetet werden soll.

C. Gemeinsame Motive der Gebetspraxis in Q

1. Die basileia tou theou

Als durchgängiges Hauptmotiv der Gebetstexte in Q lässt sich die im Anbrechen befindliche Gottesherrschaft benennen. Unschwer kann dies an den soeben genannten Gebetstexten exemplifiziert werden:

In der Versuchungsgeschichte wird zwar nicht *expressis verbis* auf die *basileia* verwiesen, doch ist die Motivik der ganze Perikope vom endzeitlichen Ringen der Herrschaft Gottes gegen die Herrschaft des Satans gezeichnet (in Q 3,5 erscheint der Satan als „Herrscher dieser Welt" – vgl. Q 11,18; Joh 12,31; 16,11 – der seinem Vasallen Königreiche zuteilt) – einem Kampf, den Jesus als Protagonist der *basileia* schon bei der Versuchung in der Wüste und auch später klar für sich entscheidet (Q 11,14–20: Dämonenaustreibungen im Finger Gottes vernichten die *basileia* Satans; 11,21–22: Berauben des Starken). Allerdings sind die Dämonenaustreibungen Jesu erst Prolepsen der im Kommen begriffenen Gottesherrschaft, für deren endgültige Durchsetzung man noch beten muss, wie das Vaterunser belegt: „Deine Königsherrschaft komme." Als Grundhaltung des Betenden wird dann auch unerschütterliches Gottvertrauen gefordert (vgl. Q 17,6), der Glaube, dass das Reich Gottes tatsächlich schon mitten unter uns angebrochen ist (Q 17,20–21). Daraus resultiert die Urgenz, die hinter dem Gebet um „Arbeiter für die Ernte" steht. „Daß die Ernte das kommende Endgeschehen meint, ist aufgrund der alttestamentlichen und apokalyptischen Tradition des Bildes die nächstliegende Deutung ...."[8] Denn: „Vom Alten Testament und dem Judentum her ergibt sich für das Bild der Ernte das Gericht als fester Assoziationshorizont."[9] Traditionellerweise sind in LXX und Frühjudentum mit den Erntearbeitern sonst jedoch die zum eschatologischen Gericht sammelnden Engel gemeint.[10] Es spricht für das hohe Selbstbewusstsein der Q-Missionare, dass

---

[8] Paul Hoffmann, *Studien zur Theologie der Logienquelle*, 3. Aufl., NTAbh 8 (Münster: Aschendorff, 1983), 289.

[9] Ulrich Luz, *Das Evangelium nach Matthäus*, Band 2: *Matthäus 8–17*, 6. Aufl., EKK 1/2 (Neukirchen-Vluyn: Neukirchener Theologie, 2016), 81. Zu nennen wären: 4 Es 4,28–29; 9,17; 2 Bar 70,2.

[10] Belege bei Hoffmann, *Logienquelle*, 289, und Luz, *Evangelium nach Matthäus*, 2:81.

sie sich nicht nur an der Missionsarbeit, sondern auch am Gericht aktiv beteiligt wissen (Q 22,28–30: „die zwölf Stämme Israels richten"). Das große Selbstbewusstsein der Q-Gemeinde speist sich aus der eschatologischen Naherwartung – dem unmittelbar bevorstehenden Anbruch des Gottesreiches. Im Jubelruf Jesu (Q 10,21–24) kommt dies besonders deutlich zum Ausdruck: „Selig die Augen, die sehen, was ihr seht."

Somit verbleibt unter den oben angeführten Texten nur mehr das Gebet für die Feinde (Q 6,27–28), bei dem ein Konnex zur *basileia* festzustellen wäre. Nach frühjüdisch-apokalyptischen Erwartungen wurden für die Endzeit massive Spaltungen und Kriege (vgl. auch Mk 13,8 parr.) erwartet. So berichtet das Jub 23,19 über die Endzeit:

Und sie werden kämpfen, diese mit jenen, Jünglinge mit Greisen, und Greise mit Jünglingen, der Arme mit dem Reichen und der Niedrige mit dem Großen und der Arme mit dem Herrscher wegen des Gesetzes und wegen des Bundes, denn sie haben das Gebot und den Bund vergessen und Fest und Monat und Sabbat und Jubiläum und alles Recht.[11]

Ganz in dieser Tradition steht auch Q 12,51.53. Inmitten kataklystischer Aggressionen wird den Erwählten nun der eschatologische Friede des Gottesreiches zuteil. Den „Söhnen des Friedens" wird diese endzeitliche Gabe in Q 10,5–6 ausdrücklich zugesprochen – der Friede wird hier fast dinghaft-magisch verstanden, da er wie eine materielle Kraft in ein Haus herabkommt, bzw. zum Aussender zurückkehrt. Endzeitlicher Friede und die Feindesliebe werden dabei zum „Markenzeichen" der Q-Boten:

Q 6,27 Liebt eure Feinde, 28 und betet für die, die euch verfolgen, 35c damit ihr Söhne eures Vaters werdet, denn er lässt seine Sonne aufgehen über Schlechte und Gute, und er lässt regnen über Gerechte und Ungerechte. 29 Dem, der dich auf die Wange schlägt, dem halte auch die andere hin, und dem, der dich vor Gericht bringen und dir dein Untergewand wegnehmen will, dem lass auch das Obergewand.

2. Gott als liebender Vater – kindliches Gottvertrauen

Mit obigem Text ist auch schon das Stichwort zum zweiten durchgängigen Hauptmotiv der Gebetstexte in Q gefallen: die Anrede Gottes als „Vater" und die Haltung des kindlichen Vertrauens ihm gegenüber. In obigem Text sorgt Gott für seine Kinder (Sonne aufgehen und regnen lassen) und liebt auch die Sünder. Die unbedingt vertrauensvolle Grundhaltung dem himmlischen Vater gegenüber schlägt auch auf das tägliche Leben durch und kommt am deutlichsten in Q 12,29–31 zum Tragen:

Q 12,29 Sorgt euch also nicht, indem ihr sagt: Was sollen wir essen? Oder: Was sollen wir trinken? Oder: Was sollen wir anziehen? 30 Denn all dies suchen die Heidenvölker; denn

---

[11] Zitiert nach Klaus Berger, *Das Buch der Jubiläen*, JSHRZ III/3 (Gütersloh: Gütersloher Verlagshaus, 1981).

euer Vater weiß, dass ihr das alles braucht. 31 Sucht hingegen seine Königsherrschaft, und dies alles wird euch dazugegeben werden.

All diese Themen – Gebet, *basileia*, Vateranrede Gottes, Versorgung mit täglichem Brot durch Gott und Sündenvergebung – bündelt gerade das Vaterunser gleich einem Brennglas. Spätestens hier wird deutlich, dass dieses Gebet nicht eine nostalgische, längst veraltete und unverständliche „Nationalhymne" der ersten Jesusjünger darstellt, sondern den *Knotenpunkt des semantischen und theologischen Netzes des Betens in Q*.

Das kindliche Gottvertrauen kommt auch zum Tragen im „Jubelruf Jesu," in dem sich die Q-Boten als νήπιοι (Q 10,21), also als unmündige Kinder, bezeichnen. Doch gerade diesen offenbart Gott seine Geheimnisse. Kindliches Gottvertrauen steigert sich in den beiden Bildworten von den frechen Raben und den unbeschwerten Lilien (Q 22b–31) regelrecht zur „unverschämten Freiheit der Kinder Gottes,"[12] die für die Q-Jünger Jesu ebenso emblematisch wird wie der endzeitliche Friedenswunsch. Vollends deutlich wird diese Haltung dann in der unmittelbar an das Vaterunser anschließenden Gebetsanweisung Jesu:

Q 11,9 Ich sage euch: Bittet, und euch wird gegeben werden, sucht, und ihr werdet finden, klopft an, und euch wird geöffnet werden. 10 Denn jeder, der bittet, empfängt, und jeder, der sucht, findet, und jedem der anklopft, wird geöffnet werden. 11 Wer von euch ist ein Mensch, der, wenn sein Sohn ihn um ein Brot bittet, ihm einen Stein geben würde? 12 Oder der ihm, wenn er ihn um einen Fisch bittet, eine Schlange geben würde? 13 Wenn also ihr, die ihr schlecht seid, euren Kindern gute Gaben zu geben wisst, um wieviel mehr wird der Vater vom Himmel Gutes denen geben, die ihn bitten.

D. Der frühjüdische Kontext der Gebetstexte in Q

Als durchgängiges Hauptmotiv der Gebetstexte in Q haben wir die Erwartung der im Anbrechen befindlichen Gottesherrschaft benannt. Sucht man nach einer Vergleichsparallele zwischen „Königreich Gottes" und „Gebet" im Frühjudentum, dann drängen sich die qumranischen Sabbatopferlieder (4Q400–407[13]) förmlich auf: „Die Sabbatlieder aus Qumran sind nicht nur durch ihre auffallend häufige Verwendung von *mäläk* und *malkût* der wichtigste vorchristliche jüdische Text zum Thema ‚Gottes Königsherrschaft,' sondern werfen durch ihren theologisch tief reflektierten Sprachgebrauch ein deutliches Licht auf das ausgeprägt kultisch-präsentische Verständnis von *malkût* in einer Gruppierung

---

[12] Vgl. dazu Markus Tiwald, „The Brazen Freedom of God's Children: ‚Insolent Ravens' (Q 12:24) and ‚Carefree Lilies' (Q 12:27) as Response to Mass-Poverty and Social Disruption?" in *Q in Context II: Social Setting and Archeological Background of the Sayings Source*, hg. v. Markus Tiwald, BBB 173 (Göttingen: V&R Unipress; Bonn University Press, 2015), 111–31.

[13] Die Zitation der Qumrantexte erfolgt nach Johann Maier, *Die Qumran-Essener: Die Texte vom Toten Meer*, 3 Bde., UTB 1862–1863, 1916 (München: Ernst Reinhardt, 1995–1996).

des frühen Judentums."¹⁴ Die Handschriften der besterhaltenen Sabbatlieder (4Q400–405) datieren in die Zeit zwischen 75–25 v. Chr.¹⁵ und kommen dadurch als Vergleichsmaterial zur Logienquelle unmittelbar in Frage. Diese Texte „beschreiben den Gottesdienst der Engel im himmlischen Heiligtum, wobei jedoch die irdische Gemeinschaft daran teilnimmt. … In den Fragmenten des 1. und 2. Liedes wird zudem nicht nur indirekt von der Teilnahme der irdischen Gemeinde geredet, sondern auch die Auswirkungen des himmlischen Gottesdienstes auf die Frommen in Qumran beschrieben."¹⁶

Im Vergleich zwischen den qumranischen Sabbatliedern und den Gebetstexten in Q stechen signifikante Ähnlichkeiten, aber ebenso markante Unterschiede ins Auge. Diese sollen im Folgenden untersucht werden, um daran das Profil der Q-Gemeinde – gerade in ihrer Eingebundenheit in das Frühjudentum – zu schärfen.

1. Berührungspunkte zwischen qumranischen Sabbatliedern und Gebeten in Q

1) Imminente Naherwartung und Prolepse der Königsherrschaft Gottes

Ebenso wie die Q-Gemeinde lebte auch die Qumrangemeinde in der Erwartung, dass die Endzeit und damit der irdische Anbruch der Gottesherrschaft unmittelbar bevorstanden. Zusätzlich gab es allerdings auch die Vorstellung, dass dieses Gottesreich nicht nur *futurisch*, sondern auch *präsentisch* – als Prolepse – erfahrbar sei. Für die Sabbatlieder gilt: „Die eschatologische Erwartung der Gottesherrschaft auf Erden hat ihren Grund in der präsentischen kultischen Feier der Königsherrschaft Gottes im Himmel!"¹⁷ Dass in der Feier des Sabbats bereits die Königsherrschaft Gottes vorweggenommen wird, ergibt sich auch aus dem Jub 50,9:

---

¹⁴ Anna Maria Schwemer, „Gott als König und seine Königsherrschaft in den Sabbatliedern aus Qumran," in *Königsherrschaft Gottes und himmlischer Kult im Judentum, Urchristentum und in der hellenistischen Welt*, hg. v. Anna Maria Schwemer und Martin Hengel, WUNT 55 (Tübingen: Mohr Siebeck 1991), 45–118, hier 115. Vgl. zu dieser Thematik auch Odo Camponovo, *Königtum, Königsherrschaft und Reich Gottes in den frühjüdischen Schriften*, OBO 58 (Göttingen: Vandenhoeck & Ruprecht, 1984). Camponovo bringt geglückt zum Ausdruck, dass „die atl Theologie des Königtums Gottes … stark in der Tempeltheologie verwurzelt" war und – nach Ablehnung des Jerusalemer Tempels durch die Qumraniten – nun auf den himmlischen Tempel projiziert wurde (ebd., 306). Allerdings schätzt er die Rolle der Königtum Gottes Vorstellungen etwas zu gering ein, wenn er sagt, diese wäre „überhaupt nicht zentral in der qumranischen Spiritualität" (ebd., 307) gewesen. Zu nennen ist neben den Sabbatopferliedern auch noch die Kriegsrolle 1QM XII, 7–8.
¹⁵ Vgl. Maier, *Qumran-Essener*, 1:377–417; ebenso Schwemer, „Königsherrschaft," 60: „Die Sabbatlieder sind höchstwahrscheinlich in essenischen Kreisen zwischen 150–50 v. Chr. entstanden …." Ähnlich Daniel Stökl Ben Ezra, *Qumran: Die Texte vom Toten Meer und das antike Judentum*, UTB 4681 (Tübingen: Mohr Siebeck, 2016), 362 und 371–75.
¹⁶ Schwemer, „Königsherrschaft," 48.
¹⁷ Ebd., 117.

Und tut am Tage des Sabbats keinerlei Arbeit, die ihr nicht für euch vorbereitet habt am sechsten Tag, zu essen und zu trinken und zu ruhen und Sabbat zu halten von aller Arbeit an diesem Tag und zu segnen den Herrn euren Gott, der euch gegeben hat den Tag des Festes und einen heiligen Tag! Und ein Tag des heiligen Königreiches für ganz Israel ist dieser Tag unter euren Tagen unter allen Tagen.

In den qumranischen Sabbatliedern wird deutlich, dass die Qumraniten in der Vorstellung lebten, im Rahmen der Sabbatliturgie bereits mit den Engeln Gottes am himmlischen Sabbatgottesdienst zu partizipieren und damit auch am Königreich Gottes teilzuhaben:

4Q401 14 I,7 (ergänzt mit 4Q400 2,1–2): ... zu lobsingen Deiner Herrlichkeit wunderbar [unter Erkenntnis-Göttlichen, und Preisgesänge] Deiner Königsherrschaft unter Hochheiligen.

4Q403 1 I (ergänzt mit 4Q404 3+4+5): 30 Für den Maskîl: Lied des Brandopfers des siebten Sabbat am sechzehnten des Monats: Lobt den Gott (der) Erhabenheiten, ihr Hohen über alle 31 Göttlichen von Erkenntnis, beugt euch Ihm, Heilige Gottes, dem König der Herrlichkeit, der da heiligt die Einsicht Seiner Kenner für all Seine Heiligen! (Ihr) Häupter von Lobpreisungen 32 aller Gottesengel, preist den Gott[von Lob]preisungen von Prunk, und in der Pracht der Lobpreisungen der Herrlichkeit Seines Königtums. Dadurch (erfolgen) die Lobpreisungen aller 33 Göttlichen mit der Pracht all [Seines] König[tums.] ... 36 ... Jubelt, die ihr [Seine Erkenntnis] bejubelt [durch] Jubelgesang unter Gottesengeln auf wunderbare Weise, und sprecht aus Seine Herrlichkeit mit der Zunge aller, die Erkenntnis aussprechen, Jubelgesänge Seines Wunders 37 durch den Mund aller, die [...] aussprechen, [...] Gott(es) für alle Jubelnden der Erkenntnis, Zeuge und Richter in seiner Macht für alle Geister von Einsicht. 38 Bekennt, alle Göttlichen[18] von Majestät, den Kö[n]ig der Majestät, denn Seine Herrlichkeit bekennen alle Göttlichen von Erkenntnis, und alle Geister der Gerechtigkeit bekennen Seine Wahrheit 39 und machen wohlgefällig ihre Erkenntnis durch die Gesetze Seines Mundes, und ihre Loblieder beim Rückzug der Hand Seiner Macht bei Vergeltungs-Gerichtstaten. ...

Die Parallelen zum Vaterunser sind evident: In beiden Texten ist das Königreich Gottes schon im Himmel präsent. In beiden Fällen erwarten die Gläubigen den baldigen Anbruch von Gottes Königsherrschaft auch auf der Erde, so wie dies jetzt schon im Himmel der Fall ist. Dabei werden aber auch Unterschiede deutlich: In Qumran erfolgt die *Prolepse der Endzeit* durch die Feier des Sabbatgottesdienstes, also in der Liturgie, für die Q-Leute hingegen in den Wundern Jesu und im besonderen Wissen um Jesus:

Q 11,20 Wenn ich aber mit dem Finger Gottes die Dämonen austreibe, so ist die Königsherrschaft Gottes schon zu euch gekommen.

Q 10,21 In diesem Augenblick sagte er: Ich preise dich, Vater, Herr des Himmels und der Erde, denn du hast dies vor Weisen und Gebildeten verborgen und es Unmündigen enthüllt. Ja, Vater, denn so war es wohlgefällig vor dir. 22 Alles wurde mir von meinem Vater

---

[18] Mit den „Göttlichen" sind hier – ganz in archaischer Diktion – die Engel gemeint; vgl. Schwemer, „Königsherrschaft," 77.

übergeben, und keiner kennt den Sohn, nur der Vater, und keiner kennt den Vater, nur der Sohn und der, dem es der Sohn enthüllen will. 23 Selig die Augen, die sehen, was ihr seht. 24 Denn ich sage euch: Viele Propheten und Könige wünschten zu sehen, was ihr seht, und sahen es nicht, und zu hören, was ihr hört, und hörten es nicht.

2) Gotteslob, Heiligung des Gottesnamens und der Kult im Tempel

Die Qumraniten hatten mit dem Tempelkult in Jerusalem gebrochen, für sie war der aktuelle Tempel in Jerusalem entweiht. Bis zum Anbruch des Eschatons ersetzt die Gemeinde als Ganze gewisse Sühnefunktionen des Tempels durch einen „Tempel aus lebenden Menschen" (מקדש אדם), die statt Tieropfern מעשי תודה, „Werke des Lobpreises," darbringt (4Q174 III, 6–7).[19] Besonders deutlich wird dieser Aspekt in den Sabbatliedern, wenn dort in 4Q403 1 II, 26 vom „Hebopfer ih[rer] Zunge" (ותרומת לשוניהם) ebenso vom „Hebopfer der Zunge" (תרומת לשון) in 4Q400 2 VII oder in 4Q405 23 II, 12 vom „Hebopfer von Erkenntniszungen" (תרומות לשוני דעת) gesprochen wird.[20] Auch in der Logienquelle ist Tempelkritik spürbar – etwa die Androhung in Q 13,34–35, dass Gott „sein Haus," also den Tempel in Jerusalem, verlassen werde. Die Vorstellung, dass Gebete wie ein Opfer vor Gott gebracht werden, begegnet zwar in Offb 8,3 und Heb 13,15 („Opfer des Lobes," vgl. Ps 50,23), ist jedoch so explizit in der Logienquelle nicht greifbar.

Eine solche Metaphorisierung des Opferkultes ist in Q also noch nicht vorfindbar. Wohl aber kann man für Q die Heiligung des Gottesnamens mit dem Anbruch der *basileia* in Beziehung setzen: „Vater, dein Name werde geheiligt. Deine Königsherrschaft komme." Intensiv diskutiert wurde, ob diese Vaterunser-Bitte Gott ersucht, seinen Namen *selbst* zu heiligen, oder ob die *Menschen* dazu aufgefordert werden, den Namen Gottes zu heiligen. Beide Lesarten sind in AT und Frühjudentum gängig:[21] Nach Ez 36,22–23; 38,23; 39,7 heiligt Gott selbst seinen Namen, indem er seine Macht vor den Menschen erweist. Das Heiligen seines Namens wäre dann ein synonymer Begriff zum Durchsetzen seiner Königsherrschaft: Gott heiligt seinen Namen, indem er sein Reich anbrechen lässt! Möglich ist aber auch, dass die Menschen Gottes Namen heiligen sollen, so etwa in Jes 29,23: Dort heißt es im MT יַקְדִּישׁוּ שְׁמִי (also im Hiphil Imperfekt von קדש, „sie werden meinen Namen heilighalten"); doch noch deutlicher in der LXX: ἁγιάσουσιν τὸ ὄνομά μου („sie werden meinen Namen heiligen"). Weitere

---

[19] Vgl. dazu Jostein Ådna, *Jesu Stellung zum Tempel*, WUNT II 119 (Tübingen: Mohr, 2000), 104–5; Johann Maier, „Bausymbolik, Heiligtum und Gemeinde in den Qumrantexten," in *Volk Gottes als Tempel*, hg. v. Andreas Vonach und Reinhard Meßner, Synagoge und Kirchen 1 (Wien: LIT-Verlag, 2008), 49–106, hier 103–6; Lawrence H. Schiffman, „The Importance of the Temple for Ancient Jews," in *Jesus and Temple: Textual and Archaeological Explorations*, hg. v. James H. Charlesworth (Minneapolis: Fortress, 2014), 75–93.

[20] Der Begriff „Hebopfer" (תְּרוּמָה *tərûmāh*) drückt aus, dass das Opfer von den Israeliten erhoben wurde (z. B. Lev 7,34; Ez 44,30).

[21] Vgl. dazu Matthias Konradt, *Das Evangelium nach Matthäus*, NTD 1 (Göttingen: Vandenhoeck & Ruprecht, 2015), 105.

Stellen sind Dtn 32,51 (אוֹתִי קִדַּשְׁתֶּם לֹא־, Piel Perfekt, „Ihr habt mich nicht geheiligt!"; so auch LXX: οὐχ ἡγιάσατέ με); Ex 20,7; Lev 22,32; 1 Hen 61,12. Besonders 1 Hen 61,12 ist hier aufschlussreich, wie auch 1 Hen 39,12:[22]

1 Hen 61,12 Alle werden ihn preisen: die, die nicht schlafen in der Himmelshöhe, preisen werden ihn alle Heiligen, die im Himmel wohnen, und jeder Geist des Lichtes, der deinen gepriesenen Namen preisen, verherrlichen, erhöhen und heiligen kann, und alles Fleisch, das deinen Namen von Ewigkeit zu Ewigkeit gewaltig verherrlichen und preisen wird. 13 Denn die Barmherzigkeit des Herrn der Geister ist groß, und er ist langmütig ….

1 Hen 39,12: Dich preisen die, die nicht schlafen, und sie stehen vor deiner Herrlichkeit und preisen, verherrlichen und erheben (dich), indem sie sprechen: „Heilig, heilig, heilig ist der Herr der Geister – er füllt die Erde mit Geistern!" 13 Und hier sehen meine Augen all die, die nicht schlafen; sie standen vor ihm, priesen (ihn) und sprachen: „Gepriesen seist du, und gepriesen sei der Name des Herrn immer und ewig!"

Die Keduscha[23] (also die „Heiligung Gottes") wird hier zum Zentralstück der himmlischen Liturgie: In 1 Hen 61,12 wird der *Name Gottes geheiligt* durch die „Geister des Lichtes." Im Vergleichstext 39,12–13 ist zwar nicht von der Heiligung selbst die Rede, doch vom Preisen des Namens des Herrn, allerdings in Verbindung mit dem Trishagion (der dreimaligen „heilig"-Attribution Gottes, vgl. Jes 6,3). Die Keduscha ist auch in 11Q5 XXVI, 9–16 vorfindbar:

9 Groß und heilig ist JHWH, allerheiligst auf Geschlecht um Geschlecht, vor Ihm kommt 10 Herrlichkeit einher, hinter Ihm viel Wasser und Getose, Gnade und Wahrheit flankieren ihn vorn, Wahrheit, 11 Recht und Gerechtigkeit sind Seines Thrones Sockel. Da Er Licht und Dunkelheit scheidet, Morgenrot bereitet kundigen 12 Sinnes, sehen es Seine Engel und jubeln, denn Er zeigt ihnen, was sie nicht gewußt, 13 da mit Fruchterträgen Er Berge krönt [(leer)] als gute Speise für alles Lebendige: Gepriesen, der da gemacht hat 16 (die) Erde durch Seine Kraft, mit Seiner Weisheit den Weltkreis gesetzt, mit Seinem Verständnis die Himmel gespannt, und herausgeführt ….

---

[22] Zitiert nach Siegbert Uhlig, *Das äthiopische Henochbuch*, JSHRZ V. 6 (Gütersloh: Gütersloher Verlagshaus, 1984).

[23] Im Unterschied zur Keduscha ist allerdings das Kaddisch-Gebet nicht in die Zeit vor 70 n. Chr. zu datieren (gegen Konradt, *Matthäus*, 105). Vgl. Andreas Lehnardt, „Kaddisch-Gebet," *WiBiLex*, Jan. 2012, http://www.bibelwissenschaft.de/stichwort/22980/: „Trotz zahlreicher Versuche, das ‚aramäische' Kaddisch aufgrund einiger traditionsgeschichtlich zu erklärenden Übereinstimmungen (Königsreichs- und Friedensbitte) zu einem Vorläufer des in unterschiedlichen griechischen Fassungen überlieferten Vaterunser zu machen, dürfte das Kaddisch in seinen heute vorliegenden Versionen nicht früher als in der amoräischen Zeit (3.–5. Jh.) entstanden sein. In der frühen rabbinischen Literatur wird das Kaddisch nur in Midrasch Sifre Devarim 306 erwähnt. Sprachlich ist es in Hebräisch und in einem Aramäisch verfasst, welches sich am ehesten mit dem Aramäischen des Targum Onkelos bzw. des Targum Jonathan zu den Propheten und Schriften vergleichen lässt. Für diese Targumim nimmt man heute – trotz eines nicht näher zu bestimmenden Kerns aus Palästina – babylonische Herkunft an." Ebenso Andreas Lehnardt, „Die Geschichte des Kaddisch-Gebets," in *Liturgie als Theologie: Das Gebet als Zentrum im jüdischen Denken* hg. v. Walter Homolka (Berlin: Frank & Timme, 2005), 30–46, besonders 43–44.

Gebet und Gottesreich 151

Eine wichtige Verbindung ergibt sich hier zu Q 6,27–28.35c:

27 Liebt eure Feinde, 28 und betet für die, die euch verfolgen, 35c damit ihr Söhne eures Vaters werdet, denn er lässt seine Sonne aufgehen über Böse und Gute, und er lässt regnen über Gerechte und Ungerechte.

In 11Q5 XXVI, 9–16 und Q 6,27–28.35c werden die Schlüsselwörter *Gott als Schöpfer, der für seine Kreatur sorgt* und *Barmherzigkeit* miteinander verbunden. Dass Gott als liebender Vater und Schöpfer seine Kinder mit Speise versorgt, begegnet in 11Q5 XXVI, 13.16 wie auch in Q 11,3 (Brotbitte im Vaterunser), Q 10,7 („Der Arbeiter ist seines Lohnes wert!" – als Unterhaltsprivileg für Missionare) und Q 12,29–30 („Sorgt euch also nicht, indem ihr sagt: Was sollen wir essen? Oder: Was sollen wir trinken? Oder: Was sollen wir anziehen? 30 Denn all dies suchen die Heidenvölker; denn euer Vater weiß, dass ihr das alles braucht"). Nun tritt allerdings auch noch die *Barmherzigkeit* als Attribut des fürsorglichen Schöpfervaters hinzu. Barmherzigkeit ist präsent in 11Q5 XXVI, 10 im Ausdruck „Gnade," aber noch stärker in 11Q5 XXIV:

10 Denk an mich und vergiß mich nicht und bring mich nicht in allzu große Härten (ואל תביאני בקשות ממני), 11 laß meine Jugendsünde fern sein von mir und meiner Vergehen werde mir nicht gedacht.

Ein ähnliches semantisches Netz durchzieht auch das Vaterunser: *Heiligung des Gottesnamens, Gott als liebender Vater, der für die Seinen sorgt* (Brotbitte) und *Barmherzigkeit* (Sündenvergebung). Gottes Barmherzigkeit wird auch schon im Frühjudentum mit der Keduscha in Verbindung gebracht, etwa im oben zitierten Text 1 Hen 61,13: Die Sphäre der göttlichen Heiligkeit färbt auch auf den unheiligen Menschen ab und reinigt ihn von Sünde. Die Bitte aus 11Q5 XXIV, 10–11 „bring mich nicht in allzu große Härten, laß meine Jugendsünde fern sein von mir und meiner Vergehen werde mir nicht gedacht" erinnert stark an die Vaterunser-Bitte „erlass uns unsere Schulden ... und führe uns nicht in Versuchung" (Q 11,4).

Zusammenfassend könnte man sagen, dass 11Q5 wie auch das Vaterunser darin *konvergieren*, dass Heiligkeit eines der hervorragendsten Attribute Gottes ist – mit der Keduscha beginnen das Vaterunser („dein Name werde geheiligt") und der Hymnus in 11Q5 XXVI, 9 („Groß und heilig ist JHWH, allerheiligst auf Geschlecht um Geschlecht"). In dieser Sphäre der Heiligkeit ist Vergebung der Sünden möglich, aber auch das Hoffen, nicht in Versuchung geführt zu werden, wie Q 11,4 und 11Q5 XXIV, 10–11 belegen. Weiters ist die Vorstellung gegeben, dass diese Sphäre der Heiligkeit bereits im himmlischen Königreich Gottes verwirklicht ist, wie die Sabbatopferlieder verdeutlichen und ebenso das Vaterunser. Damit allerdings beginnen auch schon die Unterschiede, die wir gleich im nächsten Punkt beleuchten wollen.

2. *Unterschiede zwischen qumranischen Sabbatliedern und Gebeten in Q*

1) *Kultische Komponente/Heiligkeit und Reinheit*

Reinheit und Heiligkeit werden in Qumran streng kultisch-rituell definiert, wie die rigiden Reinheitsvorschriften der Qumraniten verdeutlichen.[24] Gerade für den Sabbat, an dem nach eigener Vorstellung die Qumraniten am himmlischen Kult partizipierten, waren diese Reinheitsnormen besonders krass. Josephus beschreibt in *B. J.* 2.147–149, dass die Essener am Sabbat nicht einmal wagten, Stuhlgang zu haben (οὐδὲ ἀποπατεῖν), „damit sie die Lichtstrahlen Gottes nicht beleidigen" (ὡς μὴ τὰς αὐγὰς ὑβρίζοιεν τοῦ θεοῦ): In der sabbatlichen Präsenz von Engeln und von Gottes Heiligkeit selbst wird dieses Verhalten besser verständlich. Tatsächlich befanden sich die Toiletten in Qumran so weit von der Niederlassung entfernt, dass dies einen Sabbatweg überstieg, das geht aus den archäologischen Befunden ebenso hervor, wie aus 11Q19 XLVI, 15 (dreitausend Ellen entfernt).[25] Obendrein „bleiben die Sabbatlieder bei ihrer Beschreibung des himmlischen Gottesdienstes in der jenseitigen Welt."[26] Die Qumraniten *verlassen die sündenverpestete Diesseitigkeit* und partizipieren an der jenseitigen Reinheit Gottes. Anders aber das Vaterunser: Hier ersucht der Beter, dass Gottes Reich und seine Heiligkeit *hier auf der Erde* zum Anbruch kommen mögen: „Dein Name werde geheiligt, deine Königsherrschaft komme." Ganz gleich, ob die Heiligung des Namens durch Gott oder den Beter erfolgt – Gott und Beter arbeiten zusammen, dass Gottes Königreich mit seiner Heiligkeit vom Himmel auf die Erde übergreift (die noch nicht in Q und Lk vorfindliche mt Erweiterung ὡς ἐν οὐρανῷ καὶ ἐπὶ γῆς, Mt 6,10, ist lediglich eine Verdeutlichung der auch *eo ipso* klaren Aussage). Das bedeutet allerdings einen gravierenden Unterschied: *Die Qumranleute steigen in den Himmel auf, um an der Heiligkeit Gottes zu partizipieren, für Q aber steigt der Himmel auf die Erde herab!* Die Vorstellung Jesu, dass die anbrechende Königsherrschaft Gottes die ganze Welt proaktiv mit ihrer Reinheit und Heiligkeit durchdringen wird, ist in der Wissenschaft bereits oft herausgestellt worden:[27] Nicht die Unreinheit steckt an, sondern die Rein-

---

[24] Vgl. dazu Tiwald, *Frühjudentum*, 141–42. Die zehn gefundenen Ritualbäder belegen, dass die Gemeinschaft die Regeln der kultischen Reinheit besonders genau nahm.

[25] Vgl. Jodi Magness, „A Reassessment of the Excavations of Qumran," in *The Dead Sea Scrolls: Fifty Years After Their Discovery*, hg. v. Lawrence H. Schiffman, Emanuel Tov und James C. VanderKam (Jerusalem: Israel Exploration Society, 2000), 708–19, hier 716–17.

[26] Schwemer, „Königsherrschaft," 93.

[27] Vgl. Gerd Theißen, „Das Reinheitslogion Mk 7,15 und die Trennung von Juden und Christen," in *Ja und Nein: Christliche Theologie im Angesicht Israels*, hg. v. Klaus Wengst und Gerhard Saß (Neukirchen-Vluyn: Neukirchener, 1998), 235–51, hier 242. Vgl. auch Gerd Theißen and Annette Merz, *Der historische Jesus* 2. Aufl., (Göttingen: Vandenhoeck & Ruprecht, 1997), 380: „,offensive Reinheit' und ,inklusive Heiligkeit', die den Kontakt mit dem Unheiligen nicht scheut ...." Ebenso Friedrich Avemarie, „Jesus and Purity," in *The New Testament and Rabbinic Literature*, hg. v. Reimund Bieringer et al., JSJ.S 136 (Leiden: Brill, 2010), 255–79, hier 276, 279, der von „dynamic purity" genau in diesem Sinne spricht. Zuletzt hat sich in ähnlicher Weise

heit der nun anbrechenden *basileia* macht alles rein. Die gleiche Vorstellung gerinnt auch in Bildern Jesu: Wie nach Q 13,21 ein kleines Stück Sauerteig das ganze Mehl durchsäuert, so wird auch die *basileia* alles mit ihrer heilmachenden Kraft durchdringen. Und wenn Jesus nach Q 11,14–20 Dämonen im Finger Gottes austreibt, dann besiegt er nach Q 11,21 in der Kraft der anbrechenden *basileia* den vormaligen Starken, den Satan als Herrscher der Erde (vgl. Q 4,5–6 und 11,18), und beraubt ihn seiner Macht. Der damit einhergehende Herrschaftswechsel führt zum Anbruch der Königsherrschaft Gottes auf Erden, wo nun Gottes Name geheiligt wird und seinerseits die Menschen heiligt! Jesu emblematische Gemeinschaft mit Sündern und Aussätzigen, also kultisch Unreinen, verdeutlicht, dass Jesus mit der Heiligkeit des Gottesreiches alle Menschen „anstecken" will. Hier wird „plastisch erkennbar, wie gerade die Verkündigung Jesu von der βασιλεία Gottes, des gütigen Vaters, als Gabe Gottes an die Sünder und Ausgestoßenen den kultischen Rahmen in seinem traditionellen Verständnis von Reinheit und Heiligkeit, wie er in Qumran rigoros verschärft wurde, in anstößiger Weise aufsprengt."[28] So auch Jodi Magness:

> Whereas Jesus' attitude towards the diseased and disabled can be characterized as inclusive and proactive, the Qumran sect was exclusive and reactive. During his Galilean ministry Jesus went out of his way to heal as many unfortunates as possible, even empowering his disciples to perform exorcisms and healings. In contrast, the Qumran sect established strict admission criteria which excluded the diseased and disabled from full membership. The Qumran sect attempted to create a demon-free congregation by banning the diseased and disabled .... In contrast, Jesus sought to overcome demons by casting them out. According to Q, Jesus' first act after his baptism by John was to overcome Satan's temptation (Mt 4:1–11; Mk 1:12–13; Lk 4:1–3), thereby establishing his ability to defeat demons.[29]

Betreffs des Tempels (siehe oben, D. 1.2) bedeutet das: Wenn die Sphäre der Heiligkeit Gottes die gesamte Erde umfasst, dann wird auch die ganze Welt in einen einzigen Tempel, ein einziges Heiligtum verwandelt. Das Tempellogion in Q 13,34–35 könnte dann ein Reflex auf Jesu Tempelkritik (vgl. Tempelaktion Mk 11,15–19 parr. und Tempellogion Mk 14,58; Joh 2,19) sein.[30] Ähnliche Konzeptionen haben sich ja in Offb 21,22 erhalten (wo die unmittelbare Gottesgegen-

---

Jodi Magness, „‚They Shall See the Glory of the Lord' (Isa 35:2): Eschatological Purity at Qumran and in Jesus' Movement," in Tiwald, *Q in Context II*, 179–93, hier 190, dazu geäußert, wenn sie Jesu Verständnis von ritueller Reinheit als „inclusive and proactive" bezeichnet. Jesu Wunderheilungen und seine Sündenvergebungen restituieren die für den Anbruch des Gottesreichs nötige rituelle und moralische Reinheit, doch lösen sie diese gewiss nicht auf. Vgl. Tiwald, *Frühjudentum*, 287, und Markus Tiwald, „ΑΠΟ ΔΕ ΑΡΧΗΣ ΚΤΙΣΕΩΣ (Mk 10,6): Die Entsprechung von Protologie und Eschatologie als Schlüssel für das Tora-Verständnis Jesu," in *Erinnerung an Jesus: Kontinuität und Diskontinuität in der neutestamentlichen Überlieferung. Festschrift Rudolf Hoppe*, hg. v. Ulrich Busse, Michael Reichardt und Michael Theobald, BBB 166 (Göttingen: V&R Unipress; Bonn University Press, 2011), 367–80, hier 375.

[28] Schwemer, „Königsherrschaft," 117.
[29] Magness, „Glory," 190–91.
[30] Vgl. Tiwald, *Frühjudentum*, 285–87.

wart im eschatologischen Jerusalem den Tempel ersetzt und die ganze Stadt damit in einen einzigen Tempel verwandelt) und in Joh 4,20–24, wo jeder Ort, wo Gottes Geist ist, ein Tempel sein kann.

2) Exklusivität versus Universalität

Die Sabbatopferlieder gehen von einer strengen Hierarchie aus: „Die besondere Feier der Sabbatlieder war vielleicht (ursprünglich?) nur der qumranitischen Priesterschaft vorbehalten. Auf der strengen Scheidung zwischen Priestern, Leviten und Laien beruhte die ganze Gemeindeordnung."[31] Allerdings nicht nur unter den Menschen, sondern auch unter den Engeln gibt es eine strikte Hierarchie: Angesichts der gestuften Zuständigkeit des Gotteslobes im sechsten Sabbatlied (4Q403, ergänzt mit 4Q404 und 4Q405) wird klar, „daß nicht nur die Engelfürsten, sondern auch die Engelscharen in den himmlischen Tempeln in hierarchisch aufsteigender Ordnung vorgestellt werden und diejenigen Engel, die vom 7. Hauptfürsten, d. h. dem obersten Hohepriester der Engel gesegnet werden, auch das höchste Amt des Lobes innehaben."[32]

Im Kontrast dazu weisen Jesus und die Logienquelle einen inklusiven und proaktiven Umgang mit Sündern und Ausgestoßenen auf, wie wir schon gesehen haben. Aber auch die Erkenntnis der göttlichen Mysterien ist in den qumranischen Sabbatliedern auf wenige Auserlesene beschränkt. 4Q403 1 II, 27 spricht von den „sieben Erkenntnis-Mysterien im Mysterium des Wunders" (שבע רזי דעת ברז הפלא); Wunder und Mysterien finden sich auch in 4Q405 XI, 9. Aus der Qumranschrift *Musar leMevin* (früher *4QInstruction*, doch umfasst das Corpus auch Textfragmente der ersten Höhle, insgesamt: 1Q26, 4Q415–418, 4Q423) ist uns der Ausdruck רז נהיה (*raṣ nihjeh*), das „Geheimnis des Werdens" („mystery of being") bekannt, eine stehende Wendung, „geradezu formelhaft verfestigt," die eine „offenbarungsvermittelnde Funktion"[33] trägt und „eine Welt- und Schöpfungsordnung, die ethische und historische Komponenten enthält und sich dereinst im Eschaton erfüllt,"[34] bezeichnet. Ähnliche Konzepte kommen im „Jubelruf Jesu" (Q 10,21) zum Tragen, wo allerdings das eigentliche Geheimnis (der Ausdruck μυστήριον kommt in Q nicht vor, allerdings in Röm 11,25; 1 Kor 2,7; 15,51) nun nicht einer elitären Gruppierung (wie sich die Qumraniten ja selber sahen), sondern den „Unmündigen" offenbart wird.

---

[31] Schwemer, „Königsherrschaft," 117.
[32] Ebd., 90.
[33] Armin Lange, *Weisheit und Prädestination: Weisheitliche Urordnung und Prädestination in den Textfunden von Qumran*, STDJ 18 (Leiden: Brill, 1995), 58.
[34] Lange, *Weisheit*, 60.

E. Schlussfolgerungen

Die von den Herausgebern dieses Bandes gestellten Fragen waren:
1. Wie lassen sich Gebetstexte der Logienquelle in den frühjüdischen Kontext einbetten?
2. Gibt es eine verbindende und durchgängige Gemeinsamkeit der Gebetstexte in Q?
3. Lassen sich anhand dieser Gebete bereits Ansätze zu einer rituellen Gebetspraxis ableiten und/oder kommen darin auch schon gemeinschaftliche Aspekte zum Tragen?

Die Gebetstexte in Q sind eindeutig ihrem frühjüdischen Kontext verpflichtet und zutiefst darin verhaftet. Allerdings positionieren sich diese Gebetstexte auch innerhalb des reichlich pluriformen frühjüdischen Kontextes eindeutig: Die Logienquelle erweist sich *qua* Gebetspraxis als eschatologisch motivierte Gruppe von jüdischen Jesusjüngern: Obwohl noch innerhalb des Verbandes des Judentums stehend, wird „eine *in- und out-group* in Q [gezeichnet], wobei es über den Grenzbereich zum Austausch und gegenseitigen Einwirken aufeinander kommt."[35] Die Ähnlichkeiten zu den qumranischen Sabbatliedern sind frappierend: Auch Qumran stellt eine eschatologisch motivierte Sondergruppe im Frühjudentum dar, die den Anbruch von Gottes Königsherrschaft als imminent erwartete und proleptisch antizipiert. *Heiligung des Gottesnamens, Erwartung der Königsherrschaft Gottes, Vateranrede Gottes und väterliche Fürsorge für seine Kinder* sowie *Anrufung der göttlichen Barmherzigkeit* sind dabei gemeinsame Motive in Qumran und Logienquelle.

Als trennend zwischen Qumran und Logienquelle muss herausgestellt werden, dass die kultisch-rituelle Komponente in Q ebenso wenig gegeben ist, wie die Vorstellung einer „Heiligung durch Abgrenzung." Die Logienquelle eröffnet ihren Anspruch – ganz in der Nachfolge Jesu – für die „Unmündigen" und nicht für Eliten. Damit allerdings wird sowohl für Qumran wie auch für die Logienquelle eine gewisse Gemeinschaftsbildung deutlich:

Jene Rezipienten von Q, die ihr Leben bereits gemäß der Botschaft Jesu ausgerichtet haben, erfahren sich somit als Gemeinschaft, welche ihren Zugehörigkeitsort im Königreich Gottes hat. Auf diese Weise wird in Q eine Gemeinschaft narrativ entfaltet. Freilich darf diese Gemeinschaft (noch) nicht im Sinn einer urchristlichen Kirche verstanden werden, sondern muss bei der Bestimmung als erzählte Gemeinschaft verbleiben, deren Konstitution über die Zugehörigkeit zum semiotischen Raum des Q-Dokuments, dem Königreich Gottes, literarisch inszeniert und definiert wird.[36]

---

[35] Bork, *Raumsemantik*, 315.
[36] Ebd., 315.

Spuren einer ritualisierten Gebetspraxis – wie wir sie aus Qumran kennen – finden sich allerdings in der Logienquelle noch nicht. Während die stark liturgisch durchkomponierte und streng hierarchisch konzeptionierte Gebetspraxis in den Sabbatliedern von Qumran eindeutig belegt ist, kennt die Logienquelle eher das Moment charismatischer Gebetsunmittelbarkeit, wie es in der „unverschämten Freiheit der Gotteskinder" gegeben ist: Wie sorglose Raben und unbeschwerte Lilien dürfen wir voll und ganz auf Gott vertrauen, wenn wir nur sein Reich suchen (vgl. Q 12,22b–31).

Identitätsstiftung durch Jesu Gebet

Q 10,21–24, Jesus und die Offenbarung an die Unmündigen

Michael Labahn

A. Vorbemerkungen

Gegenstand dieser Studie sind das Gebet aus Q 10,21 und seine identitätsstiftende Rhetorik, mit dem Jesus die geschehene Offenbarung Gottes an die Unmündigen feiert. Deutlich erkennbar ist, dass dies Gebet Jesu – jedenfalls, wenn wir der keineswegs unumstrittenen Zwei-Quellen-Theorie folgen können[1] – als Teil der Spruchfolge Q 10,21–24 in den literarischen Mikrokontext (Q 9,57–11,51) wie in den Makrokontext des Dokuments eingebettet und darin zu verstehen ist.[2] Daraus entwickelt sich für die Aufgabenstellung dieses Aufsatzes die Frage, ob das Gebet durchlässig ist für die liturgische und rituelle Praxis der Gemeinde oder Gruppe,[3] in der bzw. für die das Dokument Q verfasst wurde. Lässt sich

---

[1] Zur Zwei-Quellen-Theorie, ihrer Begründung und ihrer Kritik vgl. z. B. Michael Labahn, *Der Gekommene als Wiederkommender: Die Logienquelle als erzählte Geschichte*, ABG 32 (Leipzig: Evangelische Verlagsanstalt, 2010), 27–39; s. a. Udo Schnelle, *Einleitung in das Neue Testament*, 9. Aufl., UTB 1830 (Göttingen: Vandenhoeck & Ruprecht, 2017), 205–64, sowie John S. Kloppenborg, *Excavating Q: The History and Setting of the Sayings Gospel* (Minneapolis: Fortress, 2000); Markus Tiwald, *Die Logienquelle: Text, Kontext, Theologie* (Stuttgart: Kohlhammer, 2016), 15–21.

[2] Die Überlegung, dass Q „primär ein privates religiöses Sammelbewußtsein befriedigt" (Marco Frenschkowski, „Welche biographischen Kenntnisse von Jesus setzt die Logienquelle voraus? Beobachtungen zur Gattung von Q im Kontext antiker Spruchsammlungen," in *From Quest to Q. Festschrift James M. Robinson*, hg. v. Jon Ma. Asgeirsson, Kristin De Troyer und Marvin W. Meyer, BETL 146 [Leuven: Peeters, 2000], 3–42, hier 7) oder nach dem Modell eines Ringbuchs (Migaku Sato, *Q und Prophetie: Studien zur Gattungs- und Traditionsgeschichte der Quelle Q*, WUNT II 29 [Tübingen: Mohr Siebeck, 1988], 64–65) die Kontextorientierung der einzelnen Texte zu stellen; m. E. ist deutlich eine kompositorische Absicht in der Anordnung des Stoffes zu erkennen, die über das Modell einer bloßen Stoffsammlung weit hinausreicht. Gegen das Modell eines „Zettelkastens" votiert daher mit Recht Klaus-Stefan Krieger, *Was sagte Jesus wirklich? Die Botschaft der Spruchquelle Q*, 2. Aufl., MKS 141 (Münsterschwarzach: Vier Türme, 2004), 50.

[3] Zur Frage einer Gruppe/Gemeinde als soziologischem Kontext des Q-Dokuments vgl. jetzt z. B. Christoph Heil, „Die Q-Gruppe in Galiläa und Syrien," in *Spurensuche zur Einleitung in das Neue Testament: Eine Festschrift im Dialog mit Udo Schnelle*, hg. v. Michael Labahn, FRLANT 271 (Göttingen: Vandenhoeck & Ruprecht, 2017), 163–80, hier 163–66.

darüber hinaus erkennen, ob und welche Gebetspraxis Jesu die Überlieferung hinter Q 10,21 spiegelt? Dieser Klärungsbedarf gilt für alle Gebetstexte und Gebetsthemen in Q und wurde im Grazer Seminar „Gebet im Spruchevangelium Q – Prayer in Q" für weitere Texte bereits kritisch und kontrovers diskutiert.[4]

Neben diesen diachronen und eventuellen ritualgeschichtlichen Fragestellungen steht in diesem Beitrag ein zweiter Aspekt der antiken Gebetsliteratur im Fokus. Es geht um die Frage der Funktion und Aussageabsicht des Gebets in seinem literarischen Kontext. Dabei wird davon ausgegangen, dass die Analyse Rückschlüsse auf die soziologische Situation der Adressatengruppe des Dokuments zulässt bzw. nahelegt. Die These dieses Beitrages ist, dass das Dankgebet Jesu von Q 10,21 als Teil des konfliktreichen Mittelabschnitts des Q-Dokuments Klärung über die theologische und soteriologische Qualität der Adressatengruppe im Gegenüber zu ihren textexternen Gegnern gibt, die mit Hilfe narrativer Sinnbildung des Textes etabliert wird. Die Krisenerfahrung von Widerspruch und aktiver, teilweise wohl sogar existenzgefährdender Ablehnung führt zur Verschriftlichung der Jesuserinnerung als Krisenbewältigung.[5] Dieser Vorgang ist als eine Strategie narrativer Identitätsbildung[6] zu begreifen, mit der das Dokument die Adressatengruppe in ihrer gesellschaftlichen Stellung bestimmt und gegenüber anderen Gruppierungen abgrenzt. Der vorliegende Beitrag wird zeigen, dass die christologisch zugespitzte Sequenz um das Jesusgebet diese Pragmatik des Q-Dokuments vertieft und, obgleich das Gebet authentische Jesuserinnerung repräsentiert, nunmehr der literarischen Selbstvergewisserung der Adressaten dient, aber keine liturgische oder rituelle Praxis widerspiegelt.

---

[4] Ich danke den Herausgebern dieser Sammlung für die Einladung zur Mitwirkung in dieser Anthologie und besonders Herrn Prof. Dr. Christoph Heil für seinen ausführlichen Bericht über die Tagung bei meinem Aufenthalt in Graz im April 2017.

[5] Vgl. Michael Labahn, „Sinn im Sinnlosen: Hermeneutische und narratologische Überlegungen zu Q," in *Built on Rock or Sand? Q Studies – Retrospects, Introspects and Prospects*, hg. v. Christoph Heil, Gertraud Harb und Daniel A. Smith, BTS 34 (Leuven: Peeters, 2018), 131–73.

[6] Zum Zusammenhang zwischen Erzählen und Identitätsbildung vgl. Udo Schnelle, „Historische Anschlußfähigkeit: Zum hermeneutischen Horizont von Geschichts- und Traditionsbildung," in *Kontexte des Johannesevangeliums: Das vierte Evangelium in religions- und traditionsgeschichtlicher Perspektive*, hg. v. Jörg Frey und Udo Schnelle unter Mitarbeit von Julia Schlegel, WUNT 175 (Tübingen: Mohr Siebeck, 2004), 47–78, hier 53–55 (mit Lit.). Zum Konzept der „narrativen *Identität*" vgl. z. B. Paul Ricoeur, *Zeit und Erzählung*, Band III: *Die erzählte Zeit* (München: Wilhelm Fink, 1991); idem, „Narrative Identity," *Philosophy Today* 35 (1991): 73–81; Norbert Meuter, *Narrative Identität: Das Problem der personalen Identität im Anschluß an Ernst Tugendhat, Niklas Luhmann und Paul Ricoeur* (Stuttgart: J. B. Metzler, 1995); Wolfgang Kraus, „Falsche Freunde: Radikale Pluralisierung und der Ansatz einer narrativen Identität," in *Transitorische Identität: Der Prozeßcharakter des modernen Selbst*, hg. v. Jürgen Straub und Joachim Renn (Frankfurt a. M.: Campus, 2002), 157–86; Eckart Reinmuth, „Subjekt werden: Zur Konstruktion narrativer Identität bei Paulus, Johannes und Matthäus," in *Subjekt werden: Neutestamentliche Perspektiven und politische Theorie*, hg. v. Eckart Reinmuth, TBT 162 (Berlin: de Gruyter, 2013), 215–84. Zum Identitätsdiskurs vgl. z. B. Aleida Assmann und Heidrun Friese (Hg.), *Identitäten*, Erinnerung, Geschichte, Identität 3, Stw 1404 (Frankfurt a. M.: Suhrkamp, 1998).

B. Zum literarischen Kontext und zur Rekonstruktion von Q 10,21–24

1. Bemerkungen zur Rekonstruktion von Q 10,21–24

Der Abschnitt Q 10,21–24, dessen Pointe Paul Hoffmann und Christoph Heil durch die Überschrift „Das Geheimnis des Sohnes" christologisch bestimmen,[7] liest sich bei den synoptischen Seitenreferenten folgendermaßen:

Mt 11,25–27[.28–30]; 13,16–17	Lk 10,21–24
11,25 Ἐν ἐκείνῳ τῷ καιρῷ ἀποκριθεὶς ὁ Ἰησοῦς εἶπεν· ἐξομολογοῦμαί σοι, πάτερ, κύριε τοῦ οὐρανοῦ καὶ τῆς γῆς, ὅτι ἔκρυψας ταῦτα ἀπὸ σοφῶν καὶ συνετῶν καὶ ἀπεκάλυψας αὐτὰ νηπίοις· 26 ναὶ ὁ πατήρ, ὅτι οὕτως εὐδοκία ἐγένετο ἔμπροσθέν σου.	21 Ἐν αὐτῇ τῇ ὥρᾳ ἠγαλλιάσατο [ἐν] τῷ πνεύματι τῷ ἁγίῳ καὶ εἶπεν· ἐξομολογοῦμαί σοι, πάτερ, κύριε τοῦ οὐρανοῦ καὶ τῆς γῆς, ὅτι ἀπέκρυψας ταῦτα ἀπὸ σοφῶν καὶ συνετῶν καὶ ἀπεκάλυψας αὐτὰ νηπίοις· ναὶ ὁ πατήρ, ὅτι οὕτως εὐδοκία ἐγένετο ἔμπροσθέν σου.
27 Πάντα μοι παρεδόθη ὑπὸ τοῦ πατρός μου, καὶ οὐδεὶς ἐπιγινώσκει τὸν υἱὸν εἰ μὴ ὁ πατήρ, οὐδὲ τὸν πατέρα τις ἐπιγινώσκει εἰ μὴ ὁ υἱὸς καὶ ᾧ ἐὰν βούληται ὁ υἱὸς ἀποκαλύψαι.	22 πάντα μοι παρεδόθη ὑπὸ τοῦ πατρός μου, καὶ οὐδεὶς γινώσκει τίς ἐστιν ὁ υἱὸς εἰ μὴ ὁ πατήρ, καὶ τίς ἐστιν ὁ πατὴρ εἰ μὴ ὁ υἱὸς καὶ ᾧ ἐὰν βούληται ὁ υἱὸς ἀποκαλύψαι.
(28–30 Δεῦτε πρός με πάντες οἱ κοπιῶντες καὶ πεφορτισμένοι, κἀγὼ ἀναπαύσω ὑμᾶς. ἄρατε τὸν ζυγόν μου ἐφ᾽ ὑμᾶς καὶ μάθετε ἀπ᾽ ἐμοῦ, ὅτι πραΰς εἰμι καὶ ταπεινὸς τῇ καρδίᾳ, καὶ εὑρήσετε ἀνάπαυσιν ταῖς ψυχαῖς ὑμῶν· ὁ γὰρ ζυγός μου χρηστὸς καὶ τὸ φορτίον μου ἐλαφρόν ἐστιν.)	
13,16 ὑμῶν δὲ μακάριοι οἱ ὀφθαλμοὶ ὅτι βλέπουσιν καὶ τὰ ὦτα ὑμῶν ὅτι ἀκούουσιν.	23 Καὶ στραφεὶς πρὸς τοὺς μαθητὰς κατ᾽ ἰδίαν εἶπεν· μακάριοι οἱ ὀφθαλμοὶ οἱ βλέποντες ἃ βλέπετε.
17 ἀμὴν γὰρ λέγω ὑμῖν ὅτι πολλοὶ προφῆται καὶ δίκαιοι ἐπεθύμησαν ἰδεῖν ἃ βλέπετε καὶ οὐκ εἶδαν, καὶ ἀκοῦσαι ἃ ἀκούετε καὶ οὐκ ἤκουσαν.	24 λέγω γὰρ ὑμῖν ὅτι πολλοὶ προφῆται καὶ βασιλεῖς ἠθέλησαν ἰδεῖν ἃ ὑμεῖς βλέπετε καὶ οὐκ εἶδαν, καὶ ἀκοῦσαι ἃ ἀκούετε καὶ οὐκ ἤκουσαν.

Erkennbar ist ein beachtliches Maß sprachlicher Übereinstimmung bei Mt 11,25–27[.28–30]; 13,16–17 und Lk 10,21–24, das zwischen wortwörtlicher Übereinstimmung und leichter sprachlicher Modulation variiert. Demgegenüber fallen Differenzen in der Stellung und Anwendung von Q 10,21–22.23–24 auf. Das Gebetswort samt Charakterisierung des Sprechers in Mt 11,25–27 wird, die Wehe-

---

[7] Paul Hoffmann und Christoph Heil (Hg.), *Die Spruchquelle Q: Studienausgabe, Griechisch und Deutsch*, 3. Aufl. (Darmstadt: Wissenschaftliche Buchgesellschaft; Leuven: Peeters, 2009), 59.

rufe in Mt 11,20–24 konterkarierend, durch die Einladung an die Mühseligen und Beladenen fortgesetzt: Mt 11,28–30. Diese Einladung hat hingegen im Lukasevangelium keine Entsprechung. Eine überzeugende Begründung für die Auslassung durch „Lukas" ist nicht erkennbar,[8] so dass viel für eine Ergänzung von Mt 11,28–30 aus der matthäischen Tradition spricht, die durch den Erzähler hinzugefügt und in sein Evangelium eingearbeitet wurde.[9] „Matthäus" hat zugleich die ursprüngliche Einheit von Q 10,21–24 aufgesprengt und Q 11,23–24 sekundär an das Ende seiner Deutung der Gleichnisrede aus Mk 4,10–12 angehängt.[10] Im Gegensatz zum Verstockungsmotiv, das der matthäische Erzähler aus Jes 6,9–10 zitiert, wird die matthäische Gemeinde durch die Seligpreisung der Sehenden charakterisiert; diese Umstellung lässt noch den ursprünglichen Zusammenhang mit Q 10,21(–22) erkennen, wo es ebenfalls um Identität der Gemeinde geht. Im Lukasevangelium ist die ursprüngliche Textfolge des Dokuments Q bewahrt.[11]

Für die Rekonstruktion des Q-Textes von 10,21–24 besteht nur geringer Diskussionsbedarf, da der Sinn des Abschnitts auch bei Unsicherheiten der Rekonstruktion lediglich marginale Nuancierungen erfährt. Die angesprochenen sprachlichen Unterschiede finden sich vor allem in den Einleitungen und Übergängen der direkten Rede. Leichte Differenzen sind zudem durch stilistische Überarbeitungen verursacht.

Die Einleitung zu Jesu Gebet in Q 10,21a ist sprachlich nicht sicher zu rekonstruieren. Die inhaltlich sachentsprechenden Passagen – es geht um einen bestimmten und durch den Gebetsinhalt qualifizierten Zeitpunkt – sind im sprachlichen Duktus des jeweiligen

---

[8] S. a. die Argumentation bei Harry T. Fleddermann, *Q: A Reconstruction and Commentary*, BTS 1 (Leuven: Peeters, 2005), 441–42; Gerhard Schneider, *Das Evangelium nach Lukas*, Teilband 1: *Kapitel 1–10*, ÖTbK 3/1 (Gütersloh: Gütersloher Verlagshaus; Würzburg: Echter, 1977), 243.

[9] Z. B. Joachim Gnilka, *Das Matthäusevangelium*, 1. Teil: *Kommentar zu Kap. 1,1–13,58*, HThKNT 1/1 (Freiburg i. B.: Herder, 1986), 433; Ulrich Luz, *Das Evangelium nach Matthäus*, Band 2: *Matthäus 8–17*, 3. Aufl., EKK I/2 (Zürich: Benzinger; Neukirchen-Vluyn: Neukirchener, 1999), 198–99. Anders Eduard Norden, *Agnostos Theos: Untersuchungen zur Formengeschichte religiöser Rede*, 4. Aufl. (Darmstadt: Wissenschaftliche Buchgesellschaft, 1965), 277–308, bes. 280, 301, der in Mt 11,25–30 ein festes Kompositionsschema ausmacht, das bereits bei Sir 51,1–30 vorliegt; kritisch hierzu z. B. Felix Christ, *Jesus Sophia: Die Sophia-Christologie bei den Synoptikern*, ATANT 57 (Zürich: Zwingli, 1970), 96–97; Josef Ernst, *Das Evangelium nach Lukas*, RNT (Regensburg: Pustet, 1977), 339–40; Ferdinand Hahn, *Christologische Hoheitstitel: Ihre Geschichte im frühen Christentum*, 3. Aufl., FRLANT 83 (Göttingen: Vandenhoeck & Ruprecht, 1966), 322; auch Martin Dibelius, *Die Formgeschichte des Evangeliums*, 6. Aufl., hg. v. Günther Bornkamm (Tübingen: Mohr Siebeck, 1971), 280, reklamiert Mt 11,25–30 als ursprüngliche Einheit für Q.

[10] Anders z. B. Ernst, *Evangelium nach Lukas*, 343.

[11] S. a. z. B. Fleddermann, *Q*, 437; anders Dieter Lührmann, *Die Redaktion der Logienquelle*, WMANT 33 (Neukirchen-Vluyn: Neukirchener, 1969), 61, der beide Anschlusstexte im Matthäusevangelium wie im Lukasevangelium als nicht ursprünglich ansieht und die Fortsetzung des Gebetsrufs für nicht ermittelbar hält.

Seitenreferenten formuliert.¹² In der Studienausgabe von Paul Hoffmann und Christoph Heil wird daher „in ‚diesem Augenblick'" als „intendierte Aussage" vorgeschlagen.¹³ Der Hinweis auf das Wirken des Heiligen Geistes im Gebet Jesu ist eine lukanische Erweiterung. Das Gebet Jesu selbst wird bei beiden Seitenreferenten weitestgehend unverändert wiedergegeben, was wohl auch als Eigenart des Überlieferungsprozesses gewertet werden kann; ein Gebetstext scheint in der Überlieferung konservativer bewahrt zu werden.¹⁴ Auch wenn das lukanische ἀπέκρυψας entsprechend lukanischer Vorliebe für Komposita als Anpassung an den Kontext (ἀπεκάλυψας) angesehen werden kann,¹⁵ scheint es mir als ein lukanisches *hapax legomenon* dem matthäischen ἔκρυψας (vgl. Mt 5,14; 13,35; 13,44; 25,18.25) vorzuziehen zu sein. Die Fortsetzung des Gebets stimmt zwischen Mt 13,25-26 und Lk 10,21b wortwörtlich überein.

Die Selbstvorstellung Jesu in Q 10,22 ist in Mt 13,27 besser bewahrt als in der sprachlich nach griechischem Stilempfinden geglätteten Fassung von Lk 10,22. Lediglich die Rekonstruktion von Vers 22b gestaltet sich schwierig, da auch οὐδὲ τὸν πατέρα τις ἐπιγινώσκει nicht einfach den Q-Text, sondern eine mt. Übermalung darstellt.¹⁶ Harry Fleddermanns Vorschlag, 10,22b und 10,22c parallel zu rekonstruieren,¹⁷ ist keineswegs über jeden Zweifel erhaben, aber doch erwägenswert.

Ist der Q-Text der Seligpreisung Q 10,23-24 aus der Erzählung der beiden Seitenreferenten zu rekonstruieren oder ist die Seligpreisung in der Lukasfassung grundsätzlich sorgfältiger bewahrt als bei Matthäus?¹⁸ Wie üblich erweist sich eine von Fall zu Fall zu fällende Entscheidung für die Rekonstruktion als notwendig. Die Redeeinleitung Lk 10,23a ist dem lk. Erzähler zuzuschreiben.¹⁹ Die Wortfolge der Seligpreisung ist in Mt 13,16 dem literarischen Kontext angepasst, wo neben dem Sehen auch das Hören genannt ist (Mt 13,13-

---

¹² Die Wendung ἐν ἐκείνῳ τῷ καιρῷ fügt der matthäische Erzähler an zwei weiteren Stellen in seine Tradition ein: Mt 12,1; 14,1; vgl. z. B. Fleddermann, *Q*, 438; Gnilka, *Das Matthäusevangelium*, 1:433. Die Zeitangabe ἐν αὐτῇ τῇ ὥρᾳ ist eine lukanische Wendung, die sich im NT nur im Lukasevangelium findet: Lk 12,12 (s. a. Q 12,12); 13,21; 20,19; s. a. 2,38; Apg 16,18; 22,13, insofern lässt sich m. E. die „Stunde" nicht für Q wahrscheinlich machen (zu Fleddermann, *Q*, 438 bzw. zu Siegfried Schulz, *Q: Die Spruchquelle der Evangelisten* [Zürich: Theologischer Verlag, 1972], 213, der ἐν αὐτῇ τῇ ὥρᾳ insgesamt für Q erwägt). Auch ἠγαλλιάσατο [ἐν] τῷ πνεύματι τῷ ἁγίῳ entsprechen lukanischer Sprache: vgl. z. B. Michael Wolter, *Das Lukasevangelium*, HNT 5 (Tübingen: Mohr Siebeck, 2008), 387, mit entsprechenden Belegen. Zur lukanischen Gestaltung s. a. Fleddermann, *Q*, 438; Hans Klein, *Das Lukasevangelium*, KEK 1/3 (Göttingen: Vandenhoeck & Ruprecht, 2006), 382 Anm. 5, und François Bovon, *Das Evangelium nach Lukas*, 2. Teilband: *Lukas 9,51–14,35* (Zürich: Benziger; Neukirchen-Vluyn: Neukirchener, 1996), 67, der von einer mit Q verglichen „feierlicher" gestalteten Gebetseinleitung im Lukasevangelium spricht.
¹³ Heil und Hoffmann, *Die Spruchquelle Q*, 59, mit der Einleitung, ebd., 30.
¹⁴ S. a. Bovon, *Evangelium nach Lukas*, 2:67.
¹⁵ Z. B. Bovon, *Evangelium nach Lukas*, 2:67; Fleddermann, *Q*, 438; Schneider, *Evangelium nach Lukas*, 1:244.
¹⁶ Vgl. z. B. Norden, *Agnostos Theos*, 280 Anm. 1; Luz, *Evangelium nach Matthäus*, 2:198 Anm. 5, wonach allerdings ἐπιγινώσκω sowie οὐδέ matthäischen Ursprungs sind; s. a. Klein, *Lukasevangelium*, 382; Bovon, *Evangelium nach Lukas*, 2:67.
¹⁷ Fleddermann, *Q*, 439–40.
¹⁸ So Ulrich Wilckens, *Theologie des Neuen Testaments*, Band 1: *Geschichte der urchristlichen Theologie. Teilband 1: Geschichte des Wirkens Jesu in Galiläa* (Neukirchen-Vluyn: Neukirchener, 2002), 146 Anm. 39; s. a. Bovon, *Evangelium nach Lukas* 2, 68.
¹⁹ Vgl. z. B. Schneider, *Evangelium nach Lukas*, 1:245; s. a. Fleddermann, *Q*, 442–43, der allerdings einen narrativen Übergang mit der Redeeinleitung καὶ εἶπεν für Q reklamiert.

15.17),[20] so dass hier die lk. Version den Wortlaut von Q genauer wiedergeben dürfte. Das „Amen" von Mt 13,17 geht auf den mt. Erzähler zurück,[21] der vor dem Hintergrund seines Gerechtigkeitskonzepts auch die Könige durch die δίκαιοι ersetzt hat.[22] Unklar bleibt, welches Verb für die Sehnsucht der Honoratioren Israels, das aktuelle Geschehen zu sehen, in Q 10,24 verwendet wurde, das ἐπεθύμησαν aus Mt 13,17 oder das ἠθέλησαν aus Lk 10,24.[23] Es ist vielleicht die unproblematischere Annahme, „Lukas" habe den weiteren Text außer der Ergänzung des Pronomens ὑμεῖς vollständig übernommen.[24]

Damit ergibt sich folgender Text für Q 10,21–24:

Q 10,21–24

a 21	Ἐν ... εἶπεν· ἐξομολογοῦμαί σοι, πάτερ, κύριε τοῦ οὐρανοῦ καὶ τῆς γῆς, ὅτι ἀπέκρυψας ταῦτα ἀπὸ σοφῶν καὶ συνετῶν καὶ ἀπεκάλυψας αὐτὰ νηπίοις· ναὶ ὁ πατήρ, ὅτι οὕτως εὐδοκία ἐγένετο ἔμπροσθέν σου.
b 22	πάντα μοι παρεδόθη ὑπὸ τοῦ πατρός μου, καὶ οὐδεὶς γινώσκει τὸν υἱὸν εἰ μὴ ὁ πατήρ, καὶ οὐδεὶς τὸν πατέρα γινώσκει εἰ μὴ ὁ υἱὸς καὶ ᾧ ἐὰν βούληται ὁ υἱὸς ἀποκαλύψαι.
a' 23–24	μακάριοι οἱ ὀφθαλμοὶ οἱ βλέποντες ἃ βλέπετε. 24 λέγω γὰρ ὑμῖν ὅτι πολλοὶ προφῆται καὶ βασιλεῖς ἠθέλησαν ἰδεῖν ἃ βλέπετε καὶ οὐκ εἶδαν, καὶ ἀκοῦσαι ἃ ἀκούετε καὶ οὐκ ἤκουσαν.
a 21	In „diesem Augenblick" sagte er: Ich preise dich, Vater, Herr über den Himmel und die Erde, dass du dies verborgen hast vor den Weisen und Verständigen, aber es enthüllt hast den Unmündigen. Ja, Vater, denn so war es angemessen vor dir.
b 22	Alles ist mir von meinem Vater übergeben worden, und niemand erkennt den Sohn außer dem Vater und niemand erkennt den Vater außer der Sohn und wem es der Sohn enthüllen will.
a' 23–24	Selig die Augen, die sehen, was ihr seht. 24 Denn ich sage euch: Viele Propheten und Könige wollten sehen, was ihr seht, und haben es nicht gesehen und hören, was ihr hört, und haben es nicht gehört.

2. *Zur Stellung von Q 10,21–24 im Aufbau von Q*

Im Mittelabschnitt von Q (Q 9,57–11,51)[25] tut sich, ausgehend von Jesu Ruf in die bedingungslose Nachfolge (9,57–60[.61–62]), seiner Jüngeraussendung (Q 10,2–16) und der in den Weherufen gegen galiläische Städte (Q 10,13–15) geschilderten Verweigerung gegenüber Jesu Wirken und Selbstanspruch, ein fundamentaler

---

[20] Vgl. z. B. Gnilka, *Das Matthäusevangelium*, 1:481.
[21] Vgl. Schulz, *Q*, 420; anders z. B. Bovon, *Evangelium nach Lukas*, 2:68; Fleddermann, *Q*, 445.
[22] Vgl. z. B. Bovon, *Evangelium nach Lukas*, 2:68.
[23] S. a. Fleddermann, *Q*, 443. Pro ἐπεθύμησαν z. B. Bovon, *Evangelium nach Lukas*, 2:68.
[24] Anders Bovon, *Evangelium nach Lukas*, 2:68 Anm. 12.
[25] Zu Aufbau und Struktur von Q vgl. Labahn, *Der Gekommene*, 172–74; s. a. Detlev Dormeyer, „Q 7,1.3.6b–9.?10? Der Hauptmann von Kafarnaum: Narrative Strategie mit Chrie, Wundergeschichte und Gleichnis," in *Metaphor, Narrative and Parables in Q*, hg. v. Dieter T. Roth,

Konflikt mit den jüdischen Adressaten seiner Botschaft auf.[26] Der einleitende Hinweis auf die besondere Qualität der Zeit (10,21a)[27] und das unspezifische rückbezügliche ταῦτα (10,21b) verbinden Q 10,21–24 eng mit der Jüngeraussendung,[28] aber auch mit dem Hinweis auf das Wirken Jesu in seinen Machttaten (Q 10,13: αἱ δυνάμεις αἱ γενόμεναι ἐν ὑμῖν; sc. Chorazin und Bethsaida).[29] Die Kritik an Jesus wird in einem falschen Anspruch von religiösem Verstehen der Weisen und Verständigen gebündelt, indem die Missdeutung des Kommens und Wirkens Jesu sowie seiner Jünger[30] (vgl. die Weherufe über die religiösen Autoritäten der Pharisäer in 11,?39?–44 und der Gesetzeslehrer in 11,46–48) mit Gottes machtvollem Offenbaren bzw. Verhüllen verbunden wird.

Der grundlegende Konflikt mit Jesus (und seinen Nachfolgern) verknüpft die Einleitung (Q 3–7) und den Schluss des Dokuments (Q 12,2–22,30). Die Einleitung des Schlussabschnitts unterstreicht die Rolle von 10,21–24 für das Verständnis des Konflikts mit den religiösen Autoritäten in Q. In Q 12,2–3 geht es um die vollständige Enthüllung des Verborgenen als Offenbarung des Verborgenen; es bezieht sich damit auf das, was vor Weisen und Gebildeten verborgen bleibt (Q 10,21). Die Adressaten sind in der Rolle der Unmündigen, denen Jesus das vom Vater Übergebene offenbart (Q 10,22). In der Verkündigung Jesu wird etwas allgemein Unzugängliches, auch wenn es auf Öffentlichkeit hin drängt (12,2–3), enthüllt – dies umschreibt zugleich die Verkündigungspraxis der Q-Gemeinde.

3. Bemerkungen zur Redaktions-, Überlieferungs- und Kompositionsgeschichte von Q 10,21–24

Q 10,21–24 bildet eine kleine Spruchreihe aus drei Sprüchen, die formal und inhaltlich vom Kontext in Q unterschieden ist. Zunächst erfolgt mit kurzer Erzähleinleitung ein *Gebet* (a), als dessen Sprecher der Kontext Jesus bestimmt:

Ruben Zimmermann und Michael Labahn, WUNT 315 (Tübingen: Mohr Siebeck, 2014), 189–206, hier 194–95. Gerd Theißen, *Die Entstehung des Neuen Testaments als literaturgeschichtliches Problem*, SPHKAW 40 (Heidelberg: Winter, 2007), 61, beschränkt die Konfliktthematik auf den Kern des Abschnittes: Q 11,14–52.

[26] Der Konflikt ist nicht auf Q 9,57–11,51 beschränkt, sondern berücksichtigt zugleich die Abgrenzungen gegen „diese Generation," die noch in Q 7,31–35 der Präsentation und Vorstellung des Kommenden im Dialog mit seinem Wegbereiter, dem Täufer, dienten. Zugleich bereitet der Konflikt die Grenzziehungen im Blick auf die Jesusanhänger und ihre aktive Nachfolge in Q 12,2–22,30 vor.

[27] Ohne dass der Q-Text mit hinreichender Sicherheit rekonstruiert werden könnte; s. o. S. 160–61.

[28] Vgl. bes. Fleddermann, *Q*, 449; Hoffmann, *Studien*, 104, und öfter.

[29] So könnte man mit Markus Tiwald, *Wanderradikalismus: Jesu erste Jünger – ein Anfang und was davon bleibt*, ÖBS 20 (Frankfurt a. M.: Lang, 2002), 128, Q 10,13–24 als „verdeutlichender Nachspann zur Aussendungsrede" verstehen.

[30] Das Anbinden der Weherufe an die galiläischen Städte (10,13–15) bekräftigt die Interpretation des Konfliktszenarios als Problemstellung wie auch die Gleichstellung der Aufnahme von Jesusmissionaren mit Jesus selbst (10,16).

ἠγαλλιάσατο (V. 21). Das Gebet beginnt mit der Anrede Gottes als „Vater" und als „Herr über den Himmel und die Erde". Vor dem Hintergrund der sich anschließenden Einheit über das Gebet zum Vater, Q 11,2-13, hat die Vateranrede nicht allein die christologische Reflexion über den Sprecher des Gebets (V. 22) im Blick, sondern bereits die Leser/Leserinnen, deren Relation zum Tun des Vaters als Empfänger der Offenbarung durch die *Seligpreisung* (a'; Q 10,23-24) direkt angesprochen wird. Gott als Herrscher über Himmel und Erde entscheidet, wem er seine Botschaft enthüllt, und zwar nicht den „Weisen und Verständigen", sondern den unmündigen Kindern, die sich nach der Textfolge von Q an ihn wenden und sich auf verlassen dürfen.

Der Dank an Gott als Vater, dem sowohl apokalyptische als auch weisheitliche Motive und Sprache als Hintergrund dient, führt in direkter Rede zu einer *Selbstreflexion des Beters und seiner Rolle bei dem im Gebet dargestellten Offenbarungshandeln Gottes* (b; V. 22). So rückt sich der Beter Jesus als „Sohn" in die unmittelbare Nähe Gottes und kann in dessen Autorität auch über die Adressaten und ihre soteriologische Qualität ein gültiges Urteil sprechen.[31] Zugleich stellt sich der Jesus von Q damit an die Stelle, die ihm der Satan in der Versuchung auf der Grundlage der verweigerten Teufelsverehrung angetragen hat; die *Herr*schaft über die Reiche der Erde (Q 4,5: πάσας τὰς βασιλείας τοῦ κόσμου καὶ τὴν δόξαν αὐτῶν) und – darüber hinausgehend – über den Himmel.[32]

Jesus enthüllt seine eigene Autorität im Licht des Dankes an den aufklärenden Vater. Damit rückt die Relation des Sprechers zu Gott selbst an exponierter Stelle in den Blick neben der Bedeutung von Gottes Enthüllung zugunsten der Adressaten – m. E. ist hierbei, wie zu zeigen ist, die Identitätskonstruktion der Adressaten von zentraler Bedeutung.

Obgleich der Abschnitt 10,21-24 auf der Ebene von Q einen inhaltlich schlüssigen Aufbau und überzeugende Einbettung in den literarischen Kontext des Dokuments hat,[33] so verweisen unterschiedliche Akzente der Gedankenabfolge verbunden mit ihrer inhaltlichen und sprachlichen Varianz gleichzeitig deutlich auf ein überlieferungsgeschichtliches Wachstum des Abschnitts.[34]

---

[31] Nach Fleddermann, Q, 447, liegt ein Schema vor: „Typically for Q, the first question of the gospel genre, ‚Who is Jesus?,' arises out of the midst of the second question, ‚What does it mean to be Jesus' disciple?,' the question that dominates Part II."

[32] Für Q kann Satan Jesus nur das anbieten, was ihm als der sich bewährende Sohn bereits zueignet (vgl. Labahn, *Der Gekommene*, 263). Aus der Perspektive von Q 10,21 lässt sich sagen, sogar weniger als der Satan anzubieten vermag. Zum Zusammenhang von Q 10,22 mit der Versuchungsgeschichte s. a. Fleddermann, Q, 449.

[33] Heinz Schürmann, *Das Lukasevangelium*, 2. Teil, 1. Folge: *Kommentar zu Kapitel 9,51-11,54*, HThKNT 3/2.1 (Freiburg i. B.: Herder, 1993), 101, spricht davon, dass die Sprüche „irgendwie im Zusammenhang gelesen werden" wollen.
Der Spannungsbogen reicht von dem Enthüllen der gegenwärtigen Wirklichkeit durch Gott zugunsten der Unmündigen über den Anteil des Sprechers an dem Offenbarungsgeschehen in der Selbstreflektion bis hin zur Seligpreisung der Begünstigten (a-b-a').

[34] Schon der Erzähler des MtEvs hat diese Spannung wahrgenommen und sich durch die

Das Dankgebet Vers 21 lobpreist Gott, der als Vater und Herr über Himmel und Erde angesprochen wird. Der Kerngedanke spielt mit dem Gegensatz von Verhüllen und Enthüllen sowie den Weisen/Verständigen und Unmündigen. Ein Gegenstand des Verhüllens und Enthüllens wird nicht direkt benannt, sondern durch das ταῦτα offen und undefiniert gelassen,[35] was als Teil eines Gesamttextes nunmehr kontextorientiert zu lesen ist und vor allem auf das seit 9,57–60 geschilderte Geschehen zurückverweist.[36] Das Gebet hat seine Pointe in der erwartungswidrigen Enthüllung gegenüber den Unmündigen und damit in der Verhüllung gegenüber den Weisen. Es bildet eine in sich geschlossene Überlieferungseinheit, der möglicherweise der bestätigende Schluss des Gebets ὅτι οὕτως εὐδοκία ἐγένετο ἔμπροσθέν σου hinzugewachsen ist.[37]

Der folgende Spruch Vers 22 spricht im Überlieferungszusammenhang vom Beter selbst (μοι παρεδόθη, τοῦ πατρός μου), der im Enthüllungshandeln von Vers 21 noch keine Rolle spielte. Verwendet werden zudem als neue Schlüsselworte die Verben „übergeben" (παραδίδωμι) sowie „erkennen" (γινώσκω). Statt des offenen, erst durch den Kontext gefüllten ταῦτα spricht 10,22 an der rhetorisch betonten Eingangsposition des Spruchs vom πάντα. Es geht nicht mehr um die Enthüllung an die Unmündigen, sondern um die Übergabe von „Allem", was schlussendlich das gewährte Erkennen als Enthüllung (Offenbaren) einschließt; so kommt das Stichwort des Enthüllens (ἀποκαλύπτω) ins Spiel, das erst eine direkte Verbindung mit dem Gebet in Vers 21 herstellt. Bedenkt das Gebet das ‚Offenbarungshandeln' Gottes, der in beiden Versen als „Vater" bezeichnet ist, so blickt Vers 22 auf die umfassende Paradosis an den Sohn, dem ein „Erkennen des Sohnes" entspricht. Dadurch entsteht zwar eine inhaltliche Kohärenz, aber ein entstehungsgeschichtlicher Zusammenhang ist dennoch unwahrscheinlich.[38] Das substantivisch verwendete Adjektiv ταῦτα deutet an, dass als neuer Gedanke eine Reflektion über die Rolle Jesu vorliegt, die eine erhebliche christologische Tiefe aufweist und mit dem universalen Ansatz, den Schlüsselworten „übergeben" und „erkennen" sowie dem Nachdenken über die Vater-Sohn-Beziehung stark an johanneische Sprache erinnert. Dies keineswegs ad hoc geschaffene Überlieferungsstück unterbricht in 10,21–24 als kommentierende Bemerkung[39] die adressatenorientierten Sprüche in 10,21 und 10,23–24 Wegen seines Bezuges zu anderen Sohn-Worten, besonders in der Versuchungsgeschichte (4,1–13; s. a. ⟦3,17⟧) kann es als Er-

---

Textumstellung wenigstens partiell zunutze gemacht. Drei ursprüngliche Überlieferungseinheiten erkennt z. B. auch Klein, *Lukasevangelium*, 383–84.

[35] Ähnlich Wolter, *Lukasevangelium*, 389.

[36] Kompositionsgeschichtlich wird gerne ein ursprünglicher Zusammenhang mit der Jüngeraussendung bzw. ihrer Tradition hergestellt, die durch Q 10,21–24 abgeschlossen würde und in die Weherufe Q 10,13–15 sekundär eingefügt wären; vgl. z. B. Dieter Zeller, „Redaktionsprozesse und wechselnder ‚Sitz im Leben' beim Q-Material," in idem, *Jesus – Logienquelle – Evangelien*, SBAB 53 (Stuttgart: Katholisches Bibelwerk, 2012), 101–17, hier 111–112.

[37] S. a. Bovon, *Evangelium nach Lukas*, 2:68.

[38] Anders Wilckens, *Theologie*, 1/1:116: „Das lobpreisende Gebet Mt 11,25–26 und der Lehrsatz Vers 27 gehören trotz ihrer unterschiedlichen Redeform inhaltlich zusammen."

[39] Vgl. Gerhard Schneider, „Gott, der Vater Jesu Christi, in der Verkündigung Jesu und im urchristlichen Bekenntnis," in idem, *Jesusüberlieferung und Christologie. Neutestamentliche Aufsätze 1970–1990*, NTSup 67 (Leiden: Brill, 1992), 3–38, hier 11–12, mit Joachim Wanke, „*Bezugs- und Kommentarworte*" *in den synoptischen Evangelien: Beobachtungen zur Interpretationsgeschichte der Herrenworte in der vorevangelischen Überlieferung*, ETS 44 (Leipzig: St. Benno, 1981), 49; als ursprünglich unselbständiges, zur Interpretation geschaffenes Kommentarwort z. B. Paul Hoffmann, *Studien zur Theologie der Logienquelle*, NTAbh 8 (Münster: Aschendorff, 1972), 109.

gänzung bei der Eingliederung der Spruchfolge in das Dokument Q verstanden werden.[40] Für dieses Anhaften mag das besondere Interesse von Q an der Offenbarung Gottes durch Jesus mitverantwortlich sein.[41]

Die abschließende Seligpreisung, Verse 23–24, verwendet keinen der Kernbegriffe von Vers 21 bzw. Vers 22; auch die Gottesanrede „Vater" fehlt, was für ihre überlieferungsgeschichtliche Selbständigkeit spricht. Anstelle des Gegensatzes von Verhüllen / Enthüllen und dem semantischen Motivfeld Erkennen / Offenbaren wird von der sinnlichen Wahrnehmung des „Sehens" und „Nichtsehens" (V. 23.24) bzw. des „Hörens" und „Nicht-Hörens" (V. 24) gesprochen.[42] Diese sinnliche Wahrnehmung nimmt in der Spruchfolge Bezug auf das Enthüllen bzw. Verhüllen (V. 21) und entspricht der von Gott gewährten ‚Erkenntnis' (V. 22), entwickelt jedoch ein eigenständiges Bildprogramm. Seinen Adressaten wird eine Gunst gewährt, die den „Propheten und Königen", die als durch Gott besonders auszeichneter Personenkreis diese herbei sehnten, ihnen vor dem Kommen Jesu aber nicht gewährt wurde. Anders als in Vers 21 wird kein Gegensatz, sondern ein zeitliches Nacheinander aufgebaut, das die eschatologische Qualität der Gegenwart der Seliggepriesenen ausmacht. Daher ist vor vorschneller Vereinheitlichung der Gedanken und Motive zwischen Vers 21 und Versen 23–24 zu warnen. In der Spruchfolge variiert die eigentlich selbständige Seligpreisung den Gedanken der Enthüllung an die Unmündigen, in der nicht allein die Jetzt-Zeit als in der Geschichte Israels herbeigesehnte Zeit beschrieben ist, sondern die Unmündigen durch ihre besondere Erfahrung in der Gegenwart ausgezeichnet werden. Diese Erweiterung von 10,21 durch 10,23 f. kann bereits vor der Einfügung in das Dokument Q erfolgt sein, da die Kombination der „Propheten und Könige" in Q ungewöhnlich ist.

Die Veränderungen, die den jeweiligen Ausgangsgedanken ganz im Sinne einer „Relecture"[43] anerkennend aktualisierend und neu verantwortend weiterdenken, lassen sich als „Weiter-Erzählung" im Überlieferungsprozess (*re-narration*) be-

---

[40] Zu der vom Verfasser vorausgesetzten Entstehung von Q als einheitlichem schriftlichen Entwurf vgl. Labahn, *Der Gekommene*, 118–19. In kompositionsgeschichtlichen bzw. literarkritischen Modellen finden sich unterschiedliche Zuordnungen, die die Problematik einer entsprechenden Zuweisung der Spruchgruppe erkennen lassen; vgl. die folgenden Beispiele: John S. Kloppenborg, *The Formation of Q: Trajectories in Ancient Wisdom Collections*, SAC (Philadelphia: Fortress, 1987), 197–203, rechnet sie zur weisheitlichen Spruchsammlung Q¹. Hingegen weist Schulz, *Q*, 213–28, 419–21, die Spruchgruppe dem „Kerygma der jüngeren Q-Gemeinde Syriens" zu; im Widerspruch zu den weisheitlichen und deuteronomistischen Tendenzen der Schichten in Q stehend ordnet schließlich Arland D. Jacobson, *The First Gospel: An Introduction to Q*, FF (Sonoma, CA: Polebridge, 1992), 151, Q 10,21–22 der spätesten Redaktionsphase zu. Zur Redaktionskritik von Q und der Lokalisierung von Q 10,21–22.23–24 s. a. Christopher M. Tuckett, *Q and the History of Early Christianity: Studies on Q* (Edinburgh: T & T Clark, 1996), 41–82 (56, 59, 61, 63).

[41] Vgl. James M. Robinson, „Jesus' Theology in the Sayings Gospel Q," in *Early Christian Voices: In Texts, Traditions, and Symbols. Essays in Honor of François Bovon*, hg. v. David H. Warren, Ann Graham Brock und David W. Pao, BibInt 66 (Leiden: Brill, 2003), 25–43, hier 39: „To the Q people, nothing was as important as Jesus' revelation of God." Zentrales Beispiel ist Q 10,21a. 22b.

[42] Ein eventuelles (vorredaktionelles) Wachstum (z. B. Bovon, *Evangelium nach Lukas*, 2:69) scheint mir methodisch nicht hinreichend sicher zu begründen zu sein.

[43] Zum Konzept der „Relecture" vgl. den programmatischen Artikel: Jean Zumstein, „Ein gewachsenes Evangelium: Der Relecture-Prozess bei Johannes," in *Das Johannesevangelium –*

schreiben. Der folgende Abschnitt dieses Essays wird zeigen, inwiefern die drei Logien *nunmehr zu einer literarischen Pragmatik verdichtet werden*, was insbesondere für die Fragestellung nach der Funktion des Jesusgebets in Q zu beachten ist. In der redaktionellen Neugestaltung der Jesustradition rahmt der Abschnitt zusammen mit Q 9,57–60(.61–62) die Aussendungsrede Q 10,2–16 und reagiert damit auf die Erfahrung von Widerspruch, Ablehnung und aktiver Ausgrenzung.[44]

C. Q 10,21: Das Dankgebet Jesu zwischen Identitätsstiftung und Selbstvergewisserung der Adressaten

1. Zu Aufbau, Form und Funktion von Q 10,21

Wenden wir uns zunächst einer formalen Analyse von Jesu Gebet über das Verbergen und Enthüllen in seiner rekonstruierten Fassung von Q zu. Es wird durch eine *kurze narrative Einleitung* vorbereitet: „In ‚diesem Augenblick' sagte er (ἐν … εἶπεν[45])." Die Redeeinführung verbindet den Gebetsinhalt mit dem aktuellen Erzählkontext. Das im Gebet bedachte Gotteshandeln ist seine Aktivität in besonders qualifizierter, somit eschatologischer Zeit, wie sie durch Jesu Handeln und sein Aussenden der Jünger[46] gestaltet wird.

Das folgende Gebet selbst ist nach einem a-b-b'-a'-Schema gegliedert:[47]

	Anrede / Exhomologese	
a	ἐξομολογοῦμαί σοι,	Ich preise dich,
	πάτερ,	Vater,
	κύριε τοῦ οὐρανοῦ καὶ τῆς γῆς,	Herr über den Himmel und die Erde,

	Begründung	
b	ὅτι	dass
	ἀπέκρυψας	du verborgen hast
	ταῦτα	dies
	ἀπὸ σοφῶν καὶ συνετῶν	vor den Weisen und Verständigen,
b'	καὶ	aber
	ἀπεκάλυψας	enthüllt hast
	αὐτὰ	es
	νηπίοις·	den Unmündigen.

Mitte oder Rand des Kanons? Neue Standortbestimmungen, hg. v. Thomas Söding, QD 203 (Freiburg i. B.: Herder, 2003), 9–37.

[44] Vgl. Christoph Heil, „Die Missionsinstruktion in Q 10,2–16: Transformation der Jesusüberlieferung im Spruchevangelium Q," in idem, *Das Spruchevangelium Q und der historische Jesus*, SBAB 58 (Stuttgart: Katholisches Bibelwerk, 2014), 119–46, hier 144.
[45] Zum Problem der sprachlichen Rekonstruktion s. o. S. 160–61.
[46] S. a. Schneider, *Evangelium nach Lukas*, 1:243.
[47] Vgl. z. B. Luz, *Evangelium nach Matthäus*, 2:198.

Responsorium	
a′ ναὶ ὁ πατήρ,	Ja, Vater,
ὅτι	denn
οὕτως	so
εὐδοκία ἐγένετο ἔμπροσθέν σου.	war es angemessen vor dir.

Der Aufbau des Gebets besteht aus einer Anrede / Exhomologese (a), einer zweifachen mit ὅτι eingeleiteten Begründung (b und b′) sowie einem die Anrede aufnehmenden, ebenfalls mit ὅτι eingeleiteten – traditionsgeschichtlich möglicherweise späteren – Responsorium.[48]

Die *Exhomologese* gliedert sich in den Dank (ἐξομολογοῦμαί σοι; vgl. Dan 2,23 LXX.Theodotion; Sir 51,1) und eine zweifache Anrede Gottes. Gott wird zunächst als „Vater" vorgestellt, was in alttestamentlicher-jüdischer Tradition eher selten geschieht, aber dem „persönlichen Gebrauch des historischen Jesus" und so seiner Frömmigkeitspraxis entspricht.[49] Damit bestimmt der Beter zunächst seine eigene Nähe zum Dialogpartner seines Gebets; daran wird Q 10,22 anknüpfen. Wichtiger ist, dass durch die Anrede Gott zugleich mit einem verantwortlich handelnden Vater gleichgesetzt wird, der sich seiner unmündigen Kinder[50] annimmt. Folglich wird der Gegensatz zwischen den unmündigen Kindern und den Weisen / Vernünftigen bereits in der Anrede vorbereitet und bestimmt das Verhältnis vom Angeredeten mit den Empfängern seiner Offenbarung als das der Kindschaft (s. u.).[51] Der zweite Teil der Anrede spricht Gott in seiner Beziehung zur Welt als „Herr über den Himmel und die Erde" (vgl. 1QapGen ar XII, 16.21; Tob 7,17) an. Als Herr über die gesamte von ihm erschaffene Welt kann der Vater seine Zuwendung durchsetzen und ist durch ihn allein eine sinnvolle Aufdeckung der aktuellem Wirklichkeit,[52] die seinem Wirken in Jesus entspricht, zu erlangen.

---

[48] Zur formalen Bestimmung vgl. Bovon, *Evangelium nach Lukas*, 2:72.

[49] Bovon, *Evangelium nach Lukas*, 2:69.

[50] Der griechische Begriff νήπιος bezeichnet Kinder „vom Fötus bis hin zur Pubertät": vgl. Peter Müller, *In der Mitte der Gemeinde: Kinder im Neuen Testament* (Neukirchen-Vluyn: Neukirchener, 1992), 226 Anm. 71; Georg Bertram, „νήπιος, νηπιάζω," *TWNT* 4:913–25, hier 913–14; zugleich wird der Begriff für Personen verwendet, deren juristische Stellung (vgl. Bauer[6], ad loc.) oder deren Bildung dem eines Kindes entspricht, ohne dass notwendigerweise an das Kind erinnert wird; dabei wird das Bedeutungsspektrum „unerfahren," „töricht / dumm" bedient: vgl. z. B. LSJ[9], ad loc.; die Bezeichneten stehen somit im Gegensatz zum Weise-Sein (LXX: Spr 1,22.32; 9,4; 26,12 u.ö.). Wer philosophische Bildung nicht annimmt, gilt ebenfalls als νήπιος: Bertram, „νήπιος, νηπιάζω," 915. So scheint νήπιος im „allgemeinen ... negativ" verwendet worden zu sein"; so Simon Legasse, „νήπιος," *EWNT*[2] 2:1142–43, hier 1142. Die Gottesanrede Vater in Q 10,21 öffnet das Bildfeld „Vater – Kind," der Gegensatz zu den Weisen und Verständigen führt darüber hinaus den Bildungsaspekt ein, dessen rhetorischer Zielpunkt noch näher zu bestimmen ist.

[51] Vgl. Ernst, *Evangelium nach Lukas*, 341.

[52] S. a. Hoffmann, *Studien*, 113: „Nicht himmlische Geheimnisse werden ... erschlossen, sondern die Bedeutung des gegenwärtigen Auftretens Jesu."

Identitätsstiftung durch Jesu Gebet 169

An die Anrede schließt sich eine in antithetischem Parallelismus gegebene *Begründung* für den Dank mit ὅτι an, die von einem doppelten Gegensatz zwischen den Weisen / Verständigen (b), denen Gott etwas verhüllt, und den Unmündigen (b'), denen es enthüllt wird, spricht; das Achtergewicht des Gebets gibt das Zentrum des Dankes an: die Enthüllung an diejenigen, die sonst nicht den Zugang zur Offenbarung / Weisheit haben. Mit dem offenen ταῦτα verweist die Enthüllung auf den Kontext, in dem das Gebet gesprochen ist; es ist die von Gott als „Herr über den Himmel und die Erde" aktiv bestimmte Wirklichkeit. Diese Wirklichkeit beinhaltet die Verkündigung Jesu vom kommenden Gottesreich.

Abschließend wird bestätigt, dass solches offenbarendes Handeln Gott als Vater und Herrn über Himmel und Erde angemessen ist: ὅτι οὕτως εὐδοκία ἐγένετο ἔμπροσθέν σου (a').[53] Das Dankgebet zielt auf ein Handeln Gottes, das beide Aktionen, die des Verhüllens und die des Offenbarens zugleich umfasst[54] und zwar als eine Gott gemäße Aktion. Mit der *Abschlusswendung* öffnet sich das Gebet modellhaft für die Antwort der Begünstigten, die sich mit ihrem „Ja" die Enthüllung *responsorisch* zu eigen machen können.

Das Gebet entspricht in seinem Aufbau der Form des jüdischen Dankgebetes / Todah.[55] Eine beachtliche formale und inhaltliche Parallele bietet etwa 1QH XV, 26–27:

(26) [(Leer)] Ich [danke Dir, Herr!] / Denn Du hast mich unterwiesen in Deiner Wahrheit / (27) und in Deinen wunderbaren Mysterien mich belehrt und in Deiner Huld gegenüber einem Mann [....] / in der Fülle Deines Erbarmens für Herzensverkehrte.[56]

Vgl. das Gebet in Dan 2,19–23 als Dank für eine Daniel zuteil gewordene Offenbarung durch Gott:

(20) Der Name des Herrn, des Großen, sei in Ewigkeit gepriesen! Denn sein ist die Weisheit und die Größe, (21) und er ist es, der Zeiten und Zeitspannen verändert, der Könige absetzt und einsetzt, der den Weisen Weisheit gibt und Verstand denen, die Wissen ha-

---

[53] Dass den Weisen sich die Wirklichkeit nicht enthüllt, ist allerdings nach weisheitlichem Verständnis nicht Gott gemäß, da weisheitliche Konzepte Gott gerade dafür loben, dass er sich ihrem Studieren und Verstehen als zugänglich erweist. Insofern stellt sich die Frage, ob das οὕτως εὐδοκία ἐγένετο ἔμπροσθέν σου auf seiner negativen Seite auch ein Element der Polemik beinhaltet, was m. E. weniger auf konkrete Texte (wie Dan 2,19–23 bei Hubert Frankemölle, „Die Offenbarung an die Unmündigen: Pragmatische Impulse aus Mt 11,25f," in idem, *Biblische Handlungsanweisungen: Beispiele pragmatischer Exegese* [Mainz: Matthias Grünewald, 1983], 80–108, hier 91–102), sondern auf eine Interaktion mit textexternen Widersachern der Adressaten verweist.
[54] Vgl. Wolter, *Lukasevangelium*, 388; er paraphrasiert: „... weil du dies nicht den Weisen und Klugen, sondern den Einfältigen offenbart hast."
[55] Vgl. Luz, *Evangelium nach Matthäus*, 2:199; Wolter, *Lukasevangelium*, 387, mit zahlreichen formalen Parallelen.
[56] Übersetzung aus Johann Maier, *Die Qumran-Essener: Die Texte vom Toten Meer. Band 1: Die Texte der Höhlen 1–3 und 5–11*, UTB 1862 (München/Basel: Ernst Reinhardt, 1995), 87.

ben, (22) und der das Tiefe und Dunkle enthüllt und das in der Dunkelheit und (das) im Licht erkennt, und bei ihm (ist) die Wohnung (des Lichts). (23) Dich, Herr meiner Väter, bekenne und lobe ich, denn Weisheit und Klugheit hast du mir gegeben, und nun hast du erklärt, was ich erbat, um dem König offenzulegen (, was) zu dieser Sache (zu sagen ist). (Dan 2,20–23 LXX.D)[57]

Siehe anders im Zusammenhang des abschließenden Dankgebets des nach Weisheit strebenden Jesus Sirach, Sir 51,1.17:

(1) Ich will dich loben, Herr, (du) König, / und ich will dich preisen, Gott, meinen Retter. / Ich lobe deinen Namen .... (17) Erfolg wurde mir in ihr zuteil – / dem, der mir Weisheit gibt, will ich Ehre geben. (Sir 51,1.17 LXX.D)

Anders als in dem inhaltlich nahestehenden Lobpreis für die Gabe von Wahrheit und Weisheit dankt der Beter in Q 10,21 nicht für eine ihm selbst zuteil gewordene Erkenntnis, sondern für das besondere Enthüllungshandeln Gottes. Durch das bereits erfolgte Enthüllen wird den Unmündigen Erkenntnis zugesprochen. Umgekehrt spricht die Enthüllung an die Unmündigen den Weisen und Verständigen ihr gesellschaftlich anerkanntes Verstehen ab. Der Gegensatz und die verwendete Begrifflichkeit zeigen, wie im folgenden Abschnitt entfaltet wird, dass sie in einem ihnen vorgegebenen kognitiven Wahrnehmungsschema verbleiben. Dies Beharren wird als Tat Gottes und somit als ein Akt seines „Verhüllens" gedeutet.

Damit ist die Funktion des Dankgebets seiner Begründung zu entnehmen (b–b′). Der Rückblick auf das Handeln Gottes an einer dritten Gruppe und die öffentliche Proklamation dieses Handelns im Dankgebet sind als identitätsstiftender „Akt des Intellekts im Gewand der kultischen Handlung" zu verstehen, um eine Formulierung von Anja Klein zu variieren,[58] indem der Sprecher im Dialog mit Gott auf seine Adressaten blickt *und deren Identität neu bestimmt*; das Gebet ist Teil von Jesu Verkündigung des Gottesreiches und insofern, wie bereits Martin Dibelius etwas zu pointiert feststellte, „Predigt von den wahren Empfängern der Offenbarung".[59] Die νήπιοι als Gegenfiguren der Weisen / Verständigen werden durch das Gebet zu einer von Gott ausgezeichneten Gruppe. Das Gebet gewährt ihnen eine neue, der Bezeichnung „unmündig" entgegenstehenden Identität. Sie steht für eine andersartige Wirklichkeitsinterpretation, die von der der etablierten Elite abweicht und allein und unmittelbar durch Gottes Zuwendung ermöglicht ist.[60]

---

[57] Übersetzung hier und im Folgenden aus Wolfgang Kraus und Martin Karrer, mit Eberhard Bons (Hg.), *Septuaginta Deutsch: Das griechische Alte Testament in deutscher Übersetzung* (Stuttgart: Deutsche Bibelgesellschaft, 2009).

[58] Anja Klein, *Geschichte und Gebet: Die Rezeption der biblischen Geschichte in den Psalmen des Alten Testaments*, FAT 94 (Tübingen: Mohr Siebeck, 2014), 380.

[59] Dibelius, *Formgeschichte*, 282 (zustimmend Schulz, *Q*, 215); allerdings zielt Vers 20 nicht auf die christologische Pointe in Vers 21, wie die gesamte Komposition nicht mythisch-christologische Unterweisung ist, sondern identitätsstiftende Funktion hat.

[60] Mit unterschiedlicher Begrifflichkeit auch Wolter, *Das Lukasevangelium*, 388.

2. Die Mündigkeit der Unmündigen als Glieder des Gottesreiches

2.1. Der Dank für die Enthüllung des kommenden Gottesreiches an die Nicht-Elite in Israel – zur identitätsstiftenden Funktion des Dankgebetes Jesu (Q 10,21)

Das Dankgebet von Q 10,21 beansprucht, auf Jesus zurückzugehen. Auch wenn für das Gebet kein zweifelsfreier *Sitz im Leben der Verkündigung Jesu* aufzuzeigen ist, so fügt es sich als Teil seiner Zuwendung zu den religiösen und gesellschaftlichen Außenseitern gut in Jesu Predigt vom Gottesreich ein.[61] Die Botschaft des wirkungsvoll genahten Gottesreiches richtet Jesus insbesondere an Menschen aus, die nicht durch ihre wirtschaftliche Potenz, ihre intellektuelle Fähigkeit bzw. durch ihren sozialen Status den Zugang zur Überlieferung und zum Verstehen der religiösen Überlieferung Israels haben, wie es etwa den Weisen und Verständigen möglich ist oder zumindest von ihnen beansprucht wird. Auf diesen Gedanken nimmt der Begriff der νήπιοι Bezug, der im frühchristlichen Gedächtnis, wie die überlieferungsgeschichtlichen Ergänzungen des Gebets zeigen, durchaus interpretationsbedürftig gewesen zu sein scheint; der Gegensatz zwischen Weisen/Verständigen und den Unmündigen entspricht zudem dem radikalen und bisweilen „a-sozialen" Charakter der Jesusverkündigung.[62] Auch das für Jesu Frömmigkeitspraxis grundlegende Verhältnis von Gottesbild und Selbstbild als dem schenkenden Vater und den empfangenden Kind(ern)[63] lässt sich in der historischen Rückführung des Gebets auf die Basileiaverkündigung Jesu gut begründet ansehen.[64] Zunächst soll deshalb das Dankgebet Jesu im Kontext der Gottesreichsverkündigung Jesu analysiert werden,[65] wobei grund-

---

[61] S. a. Hoffmann, *Studien*, 114.

[62] Vgl. kurz Michael Labahn, „Nachfolge, radikaler Verzicht, ‚a-familiäres' Ethos," in: *Jesus-Handbuch*, hg. v. Jens Schröter und Christine Jacobi unter Mitarbeit von Lena Nogossek, Handbücher Theologie (Tübingen: Mohr Siebeck, 2017), 445–54.

[63] Vgl. z. B. Karl-Heinrich Ostmeyer, „Das Beten Jesu, Vater Unser," in Schröter, Jacobi und Nogossek, *Jesus-Handbuch*, 395–402, hier 399–400.

[64] Das Gebet Jesu weisen seiner Reichgottesverkündigung zu: z. B. Christ, *Jesus Sophia*, 92–93; Christoph Heil, „Analphabet oder Rabbi? Zum Bildungsniveau Jesu," in idem, *Das Spruchevangelium Q und der historische Jesus*, 265–91, hier 283; Hoffmann, *Studien*, 111; Paul Hoffmann, „Q^R und der Menschensohn: Eine vorläufige Skizze," in idem, *Tradition und Situation: Studien zur Jesusüberlieferung in der Logienquelle und den synoptischen Evangelien*, NTAbh 28 (Münster: Aschendorff, 1995), 243–78, hier 262; Schneider, „Gott", 11; unentschieden Rudolf Bultmann, *Die Geschichte der synoptischen Tradition*, 9. Aufl., FRLANT 29 (Göttingen: Vandenhoeck & Ruprecht, 1979), 172: „Ich halte es auch hier für möglich, daß es aus einer verlorenen jüdischen Schrift stammt; … Aus dem Rahmen der Jesusworte fällt es heraus; doch liegt andrerseits m. E. kein zwingender Grund vor, es Jesus abzusprechen." Anders z. B. Hahn, *Hoheitstitel*, 322: „palästinische Urgemeinde"; Klein, *Lukasevangelium*, 383; Helmut Merklein, „Zur Entstehung der urchristlichen Aussage vom präexistenten Sohn Gottes," in idem, *Studien zu Jesus und Paulus*, WUNT 43 (Tübingen: Mohr Siebeck, 1987), 247–76, hier 271; Schulz, *Q*, 215.

[65] Die folgenden Überlegungen nehmen den griechischen Text als Basis für den Versuch, Jesu Worte inhaltlich zu verstehen; eine genaue Rekonstruktion möglicher aramäischer *ipsissima verba* Jesu oder einer frühesten griechischen Version der Worte Jesu ist nicht intendiert und durch den Überlieferungsprozess kaum möglich. Den semitischen Charakter des Spruchs

legende inhaltliche Beobachtungen gemacht werden können, die auch für die Rezeption in Q Gültigkeit behalten.

Dankbar lobpreist Jesus den in seiner Schöpfungs- und Geschichtsmacht angesprochenen Vater für sein bereits erfolgtes Handeln, dem Verbergen bzw. Enthüllen an verschiedene Personengruppen, das im doppelten Sinne als subversives Geschehen zu verstehen ist: (a) Das Verb ἀποκαλύπτω bezeichnet die vermittelte Erkenntnis als „Enthüllen"; (b) zugleich lässt sich durch das von Gott gewährte Verstehen die Wirklichkeit im Gegensatz zu einem etablierten Interpretationsansatz, der mit der Gruppe der Weisen und Verständigen verbunden ist, neu erkennen. Gegenstand vom Verbergen bzw. Enthüllen ist das ταῦτα (bzw. αὐτά); mit dem offenen Begriff wird auf Himmel und Erde als Wirkungsstätte des Gottes verwiesen, wo er sein Reich durchsetzt, das im Wirken Jesu bereits partiell präsent ist.[66]

Diese Welt mitsamt Gottes Wirken in ihr zu verstehen, obliegt gewöhnlich den Weisen; den Unverständigen bleibt hingegen ihr Sinn verborgen: z. B. Ijob 28,13–14.21–22; Spr 1,20–25.29–30; 8,36. Diese Figurengruppen repräsentieren abweichende Wirklichkeitsdeutungen. Dabei genießen die Weisen und Verständigen in antiken Kulturen mitsamt ihren Bildungsinstitutionen – religions- und philosophieübergreifend – ein besonderes Ansehen. Weisheit und Wissen stehen für das Verstehen religiöser und philosophischer Verhältnisse und somit für die Befähigung, ein religiös oder philosophisch einwandfreies Leben zu führen. Die subversive Formulierung von der Enthüllung an die Unmündigen, spricht jedoch den Weisen und Verständigen dieses generell anerkannte Verstehen ab; sie verbleiben in einem ihnen vorgegebenen kognitiven Wahrnehmungsschema; ein Beharren, das angesichts des Gotteshandelns in qualifizierter, eschatologischer Zeit negativ zu bewerten ist.

Der Gegensatz von Unmündigen und Weisen/Verständigen selbst trägt einen sarkastischen Beiklang und nimmt als solches wohl das Selbstverständnis der Gegner von Jesu Gottesreichsverkündigung polemisch auf. So gibt der Gegensatz wohl die Ablehnung von Jesu Verkündigung durch die religiöse Elite[67] mit ihrem Deutungsanspruch der Wirklichkeit und der daraus abgeleiteten Pri-

---

werten z. B. Adelbert Denaux, „The Q-Logion Mt 11,27/Lk 10,22 and the Gospel of John," in *John and the Synoptics*, hg. v. Adelbert Denaux, BETL 101 (Leuven: Peeters, 1992), 163–99, hier 172, der „a number of Semitic elements" entdeckt, und Hoffmann, *Studien*, 110–11, positiv – mehr lässt sich sprachanalytisch kaum sagen. Die Worte werden als sprachliche Repräsentationen einer möglichen inhaltlichen Prägung des Jesuswortes verstanden.

[66] Ähnlich Wolter, *Lukasevangelium*, 389. Zum Bezug auf das Gottesreich vgl. Ernst, *Evangelium nach Lukas*, 341.

[67] Vgl. z. B. Hoffmann, „Q^R," 262: „Der hier thematisierte Gegensatz von den in Israel als ‚weise' Geltenden, denen das Mysterium Gottes verborgen bleibt, während es den ‚Kleinen' nach Gottes Willen offenbart wurde, reflektiert ja nur den Gegensatz zwischen denen, die Jesu Botschaft ablehnen, und denen, die sie akzeptieren, theologisch durch die Rückführung auf Gottes Ratschluß."

vilegien wieder (vgl. m. 'Abot 2,7[68]). Den in weisheitlichen, aber auch apokalyptischen Texten artikulierten Anspruch auf Gottes Gabe des Verstehens (vgl. z. B. Dan 2,21[69]) widerspricht Jesu Gebet entschieden. Durch den doppelten Gegensatz werden die anerkannten Bildungs- und Deutungspotenzen unterwandert, indem der beanspruchten Gabe der Weisheit die Verhüllung entgegengesetzt ist.

Als Nutznießer des Handelns Gottes wird eine Gruppe genannt, deren Zugang zu Bildung und Wirklichkeitsdeutung bzw. Offenbarung als begrenzt gilt. Sie ist nunmehr näher zu bestimmen. Das Gebet preist die geschehene Enthüllung an die Unmündigen; dies findet eine Parallele in der Wertschätzung der Kinder in den Glaubenssprüchen der Basileiaverkündigung Jesu. Jesus stellt das Grundvertrauen der unmündigen Kinder vorbildhaft heraus (vgl. Mk 9,37 parr.; 9,42 parr.), das einzig zum Eintritt in das Gottesreich befähigt: ὃς ἂν μὴ δέξηται τὴν βασιλείαν τοῦ θεοῦ ὡς παιδίον, οὐ μὴ εἰσέλθῃ εἰς αὐτήν (Mk 10,15 parr.).[70] Dem unbedingten Gottvertrauen von unmündigen Kindern entspricht die Offenbarung Gottes. Gott wendet sich dem kindlichen Vertrauen so zu, dass er das Verstehen seines Handelns schenkt.[71] Die Enthüllung an die Unmündigen eröffnet eine neue Weltdeutung, die in der Welt die sich durchsetzende Gottesherrschaft erkennt und sich vertrauensvoll an sie hält. Ist das Gottesverhältnis nach dem Vertrauensmuster zwischen Vater und Kinder gestaltet, so zeigt sich hierin eine für Jesus bezeichnende, in der antiken Umwelt ungewöhnliche Aufwertung des Kindes.[72]

---

[68] m. 'Abot 2,7: „Derselbe sprach: Viel Fleisch, viel Würmer; viel Güter, viel Sorge; viel Mägde, viel Unzucht; viel Knechte, viel Raub; viel Frauen, viel Zauberei; viel Tora, viel Leben; viel Weisheit, viel Schüler; viel Almosen, viel Heil. Wer einen guten Namen erworben hat, hat ihn für sich erworben; wer sich Worte der Tora erworben hat, hat sich das Leben der zukünftigen Welt erworben." Übersetzung aus Karl Marti und Georg Beer, 'Abôt (Väter): Text, Übersetzung und Erklärung, Mischna 4/9 (Gießen: Töpelmann, 1927), 45, 47.
[69] Dan 2,21 LXX.D: „und er ist es, der Zeiten und Zeitspannen verändert, der Könige absetzt und einsetzt, der den Weisen Weisheit gibt und Verstand denen, die Wissen haben."
[70] Vgl. z. B. Peter Müller, Mitte der Gemeinde, 78–79, 288–91.
[71] Dabei kann dieser Gedanke sich durchaus weisheitlicher Aussagen bedienen, die Gottes aktive und schenkende Zuwendung zu den νήπιοι herausarbeiten: Ps 18,8 LXX; 114,6 LXX; 118,130 LXX (vgl. die Auflistung bei Frankemölle, „Die Offenbarung an die Unmündigen," 89; Müller, Mitte der Gemeinde, 240–41). Einen grundsätzlichen intellektualitätskritischen Affekt vermag ich demgegenüber nicht zu entdecken; zu Legasse, „νήπιος," 1143. Wie der Reichtum (vgl. z. B. Mk 10,25 parr.) steht der Intellekt des Menschen als Ursache seines Selbstbewusstseins einem kindlichen Vertrauen in Gottes Zuwendung entgegen.
[72] Vgl. die Darstellung von Kindheit in der antiken Welt bei Müller, Mitte der Gemeinde, 81–164, die dieser vor allem durch das „noch nicht" des Erwachsenseins bestimmt (ebd., 162). Kinder gelten nach antikem Verständnis als „ihrem Wesen nach (als; Vf.) un-mündig, un-fertig, un-vollkommen." Dass sie daher „in der uns erhaltenen Literatur überwiegend unter dem Aspekt der Erziehung betrachtet" werden (ebd.), unterstreicht, wie provozierend das im Gebet aufgemachte soziale Bildfeld ist. Nicht allein der weitgehend anerkannte Selbstanspruch der religiös-intellektuellen Elite steht im Fokus, sondern zugleich das antike Verständnis kindlicher Entwicklung. Eine ähnliche Dichotomie liegt in der mt. Einfügung (Müller, Mitte der Gemeinde,

Soziologisch dürfte der Gegensatz des Gebets die gesellschaftlichen Differenzen zwischen Jesus und der religiösen Elite aufnehmen und die wechselseitige Ablehnung verbalisieren. Man kann Jesus dabei durchaus als Exponent einer populären, gering gebildeten religiösen Bewegung in Israel verstehen.[73] Gleichzeitig verdient der prophetische Anspruch (vgl. Jes 29,14), nach dem die Botschaft vom kommenden Gottesreich Menschen ohne religiöse oder intellektuelle Vorbedingungen den Zugang zum Heil des kommenden Gottes ermöglicht, für das Verständnis des Gebets Beachtung, weil sich in der Gegenwart und durch die Verkündigung Jesu die jesajanische Zusage erfüllt.[74] In der Formulierung dieser Umwertung kann der kritische bis polemische Unterton jedoch nicht übersehen werden, der die Würde der gering gebildeten Volksmasse des Am-ha-Arez[75] durch seine Eingliederung unter die Gottesherrschaft neu bestimmt.[76]

Das Gebet spiegelt einerseits die Frömmigkeit Jesu wieder, der Gott besonders als Vater der Unmündigen und Bedürftigen versteht, ist aber nicht als rituelles oder kultisches Handeln zu beschreiben. Das Gebet ist, wie bereits gezeigt, kein primär ‚vertikales' Kommunikationsgeschehen mit Gott, sondern ein ‚horizontales' Kommunikationshandeln, das das Wirklichkeitsverständnis der Hörer/Hörerinnen verändert. Im Dank an Gott bestätigt der Verkündiger des kommenden Gottesreiches die Gültigkeit seiner Enthüllung der Nähe Gottes für die Unmündigen und verändert die Identität der angesprochenen Nicht-Elite so, dass sie als Adressaten der Offenbarung zu einer neuen Elite des anbrechenden Gottesreichs werden.[77] Als Kommunikationsgeschehen reflektiert das Dankgebet den Vollzug dieses Geschehens öffentlich; als Dankgebet, das für den Vollzug dankt, bestätigt es zugleich die gültige Veränderung der Wirklichkeit.

2.2. Die Unmündigen als die wahrhaft Weisen – Q 10,21 im Kontext der Sinnbildung von Q

Die Aufnahme des Gebets Jesu in Q führt den identitätsstiftenden Akt weiter, indem das Gebet mit der Seligpreisung Q 10,23–24 und in Ergänzung der Selbstreflexion 10,22 in den literarischen Kontext eingefügt wird. Das Gebet Jesu passt sich in verschiedene semantische Felder von Q ein (Vater/Sohn, enthüllen/offenbaren/öffentlich machen ↔ verbergen/verhüllen, unmün-

---

225) in die Episode von der Tempelreinigung vor, wo Jesus das Lob der Kinder (Mt 21,15) mit Ps 8,3a LXX (ἐκ στόματος νηπίων καὶ θηλαζόντων κατηρτίσω αἶνον) gegen Priester und Schriftgelehrte (Tempelaristokratie) verteidigt: Mt 21,16.

[73] So vorsichtig erwägend bei Heil, „Analphabet oder Rabbi?," 285.
[74] S. a. Ostmeyer, „Das Beten Jesu," 398.
[75] Vgl. z. B. Frankemölle, „Offenbarung an die Unmündigen," 95.
[76] Mit Bovon, *Evangelium nach Lukas*, 2:71, formuliert: „Jesus gab dem Volk die Theologie Gottes zurück."
[77] Dies entspricht der die Existenz der Adressaten verändernden Qualität durch die Anrede Jesu in seinen Seligpreisungen.

dig/Kinder/Klein[e]) und wird so ein pointierter Bestandteil der narrativen Sinnbildung.[78] Neben dem Gottesbild sind das Themenfeld von Verbergen/Verborgensein und Offenbaren[79] und die marginalisierende Selbstbezeichnung der Anhänger Jesu als kindlich, unmündig und klein von erheblichem Gewicht. Die genannten semantischen Felder von 10,21–24 kulminieren im Gesamtzusammenhang in einem gegen die Außenwelt und ihre religiösen Konzepte gerichteten Selbstbild der Q-Gruppe als von Gott, dem Vater, durch Offenbarung besonders ausgezeichnete eschatologische Elite Israels.[80] Die semantischen Felder haben wesentlichen Anteil an der narrativen Formung einer Gruppenidentität der Q-Gruppe.

Gott wird als Vater und als „Herr über den Himmel und die Erde" angesprochen. Sachlich entspricht der erste Titel dem Vater-Gebet (Q 11,2); der Angerufene ist der verantwortlich handelnde Vater, der sich bestimmt (vgl. Q 11,9–13; s. a. 12,28.30) seinen bittenden Sprechern, den Jüngern, und damit den Adressaten zuwendet; zugleich ist er derjenige, der, bei Zugehörigkeit einer Taufepisode,[81] Jesus als seinen Sohn anspricht (3,[[21–22]]) und vor dem sich Jesus als Sohn bewährt (4,1–13).

Vor dem Hintergrund von Q 11,2–13 zielt die Vateranrede bereits auf die Relation der Adressaten als Empfänger des enthüllenden und den Jesusjüngern zuwendenden Tuns des Vaters.[82] Die Gottesbezeichnung als „Herr über den Himmel und die Erde" bestimmt ihren Lebens- und Orientierungsraum als von Gott beherrschten, der deshalb souverän darüber entscheidet, wem er seine Botschaft enthüllt. Gott als aktiver Weltherr ist zugleich Garant der Gemeinde, die die Verkündigung seines Sohnes fortsetzt. Gott als Herr ist auch Gerichtsherr, der das Gericht der von Jesus ausgesprochenen Weherufe (10,13–15) gegenwärtig oder zukünftig dort aktualisiert, wo der Verkündigung der Jesusjünger Ablehnung zuteil wird (s. a. 10,11–12).

Gott und den von ihm Beschenkten stehen die Weisen und Verständigen gegenüber. Wie bereits gezeigt, ist der Begriff der Weisen eine sarkastische Aufnahme des Selbstanspruchs der religiösen Elite, der die Verkündigung des Beters dennoch verborgen bleibt.[83] Die Weisen und Verständigen repräsentieren eine

---

[78] Zum Verständnis von Q als narrativer Sinnbildung vgl. Labahn, *Der Gekommene*, passim.
[79] Vgl. hierzu auch Labahn, *Der Gekommene*, 446–47.
[80] Zu den νήπιοι als erzählerischer Repräsentanz der Q-Gruppe und ihrer Anhänger z. B. Hoffmann, *Studien*, 114.
[81] Labahn, *Der Gekommene*, 140–45.
[82] Dies wird durch die Seligpreisung in Q 10,23–24 unterstrichen, die die Jesusanhänger als Empfänger der Offenbarung direkt anspricht.
[83] Ronald A. Piper, *Wisdom in the Q-Tradition: The Aphoristic Teaching of Jesus*, SNTSMS 61 (Cambridge: Cambridge University Press, 1989), 171, hat die späte Zuweisung von Q 10,21–22 als isolierter Konzeption verbunden mit dem Hinweis, dass die Vorstellung der göttlichen Enthüllung dem deuteronomistischen Konzept der Verweigerung widerspricht, mit Recht verneint.

gesellschaftlich etablierte und als herausragend anerkannte Wirklichkeitsdeutung von Experten, die sich die Mehrheit in der Gesellschaft zu eigen machen kann; sie repräsentieren ebenso einen religiösen Mainstream, zu dem Q auch die in 11,?39?–44 mit Weherufen kritisierten religiösen Autoritäten der Pharisäer bzw. in 11,46–48 der Gesetzeslehrer rechnet.[84] Dabei dürfte in der Bezeichnung der Weisen und Verständigen durchaus eine sarkastische Bewertung des von dieser Mehrheit artikulierten Selbstanspruches sichtbar werden.[85]

Der semantische Wert ist in Q 10,21 allerdings nicht allein durch den Gegensatz zur herrschenden Deutungselite der Weisen bestimmt, sondern ordnet sich im Dokument Q in ein Wortfeld ein, das die verstehenden Anhänger Jesu als Kleinste (ὁ μικρότερος: 7,28), als Kinder (τεκνία: 7,35) und als Kleine (οἱ μικροί: 17,2) bestimmt.[86] Die Marginalisierung der Jesusanhänger und ihrer Verkündiger[87] spielt offensichtlich mit dem negativen Wert des Wortes,[88] um diese in seinem literarischen Kontext neu und positiv (vgl. Mt 21,15–16) zu bestimmen.[89] Dafür gibt es hinreichend Parallelen im zeitgenössischen Judentum. Der Vergleich gruppenspezifischer Literatur, insbesondere mit Beispielen aus Qum-

---

Die Bezeichnung als „weise" und „verständig" rechnet mit der Möglichkeit des Verstehens, da Weisheit das aktive Bemühen, Gottes Willen zu erfassen und aus dieser Perspektive die Wirklichkeit zu deuten, beinhaltet. Es gehört zum Grundkonzept weisheitlichen Denkens, dass die Weisheit auch in ihrer Verborgenheit (Ijob 28,12–23; Bar 3,1–4,4; Sir 1,4–9) als Gabe Gottes dem Streben des Weisen zugänglich ist. So gesehen deutet die „Verhüllung" diesen Widerspruch im Licht der Enthüllung Gottes an die Unmündigen, worauf das eigentliche rhetorische Gewicht der Tradition wie der literarischen Rezeption liegt.

[84] Für die Polemik innerhalb von Q vgl. z. B. Hoffmann, *Studien*, 117–18, 229. Hoffmann ordnet Q 10,21 somit der Auseinandersetzung mit „dieser Generation" zu, die die Redaktion von Q gestaltet.

[85] So z. B. Arland D. Jacobson, "Wisdom Christology in Q" (Ph.D. diss., Claremont Graduate School, 1978), 155 Anm. 54.

[86] S. a. Heil, „Analphabet oder Rabbi?," 283. Zu ὁ μικρότερος in Q 7,28 s. a. Labahn, *Der Gekommene*, 357–58. Generell sieht Müller die Begriffe des Wortfelds „Kind" in den synoptischen Texten eng verwoben (Müller, *Mitte der Gemeinde*, 381).

[87] Dass das Gebet Jesu in Q 10,21 die „Q-Missionare" im Blick hat, unterstreicht auch Frankemölle, „Die Offenbarung an die Unmündigen," 85; s. a. Schürmann, *Lukasevangelium*, 2/1:106.

[88] Gerade die Komposition von Q, die theologisch und christologisch reflektierte Weiter-Erzählung der aufgenommenen Tradition und die bisweilen hoch interessante schriftgelehrte Interpretation lassen die für die Schriftfassung von Q verantwortliche Gruppe kaum angemessen als ungebildet oder naiv verstehen. Damit ist sie keine Selbstreflexion des eigenen Bildungsstatus; anders etwa Bovon, *Evangelium nach Lukas*, 2:70, nachdem sich in Lk 10,21 das Wissen Jesu und seiner Nachfolger findet, „nicht zur intellektuellen Elite Israels" zu gehören. Die feierliche Form und Sprache von Q 10,21–24 beanspruchen in Konkurrenz zur herrschenden Elite den Status für die Adressaten selbst jenseits der verbreiteten religiösen Erkenntnismodelle.

[89] Risto Uro, *Sheep Among the Wolves: A Study on the Mission Instructions of Q*, AASF.DHL 47 (Helsinki: Suomalainen Tiedeakatemia, 1987), 235, vermag die Unmündigen von 10,21 in einer Linie mit der Rechtfertigung der Kinder der Weisheit von 7,35 zu sehen (s. a. Piper, *Wisdom*, 171); durch Gottes Enthüllung werden die Unmündigen zu den wirklich Weisen (vgl. Hoffmann, *Studien*, 118).

ran,⁹⁰ zeigt, dass „eine Gruppe exklusiv beansprucht, als Einfältige durch Gottes besondere Gnade weise geworden zu sein …, während sie all denen, die sonst in Israel Weisheit beanspruchen, diese absprechen."⁹¹ Die Bezeichnung der Adressaten als „Unmündige" macht sie zu einer Elite, weil sie in diesem scheinbaren Defizit in besonderer Weise durch Gottes Offenbarung ausgezeichnet ist: „10:21–22, 23–24 articulates the community's self-understanding as the privileged recipients of the revelation of the kingdom."⁹² Deshalb sind sie auch die Kleinsten (7,28), Kinder (7,35), Unmündige (10,21) und Kleine (17,2), die Gott ihr Vertrauen schenken und von ihm wie von einem Vater beschenkt werden. Die Bezeichnung als νήπιοι dient der Abgrenzung von vermeintlichen religiösen Eliten, die sich auch sonst im Dokument Q (aber auch der Gottesreichsverkündigung Jesu) findet.⁹³ Sie ist eine elitäre Formel der Selbst-Stigmatisierung, durch die sich die Q-Gruppe von der kritisch beurteilten religiösen Elite der Weisen und Verständigen abgrenzt.⁹⁴ Die Selbst-Stigmatisierung im Gebet von 10,21 als „unmündig" dient der Formierung einer eigenen, sich gegenüber etablierten Gruppen abgrenzenden Identität der Adressaten mit den Mitteln literarischer Darstellung.⁹⁵

Begründet ist diese Neukonstruktion im Enthüllen und Verbergen Gottes im Wirken seines Sohnes Jesus in besonders qualifizierter eschatologischer Zeit. Q 12,2 stellt generalisierend fest, dass die Zeit des gekommenen Jesus die Zeit der universellen Offenlegung allen Verborgenen ist. Daraus ergibt sich für die Jünger Jesu die Folgerung (12,3): „Was ich euch in der Finsternis sage, sagt im Licht, und was ihr ins Ohr verkündigt hört, verkündigt auf den Dächern." Im Blick auf die Überlegungen zur Offenbarung durch den Gekommenen in 12,3–4 wird deutlich, dass das Gebet Jesu in 10,21 mit den „Unmündigen" die Adressaten als aktive Verkündiger der Offenbarung Gottes in den Blick nimmt.

Die literarische Form des Dankgebets Jesu gibt der Identitätsbildung einen retrospektiven Charakter, der auf das erfolgreiche Tun Gottes als zuwendendem Vater und Herrn der Welt und des Himmels im Wirken Jesu zurückblickt. Die

---

⁹⁰ Z. B. 1QpHab XII, 4 (die „Einfältigen Judas": פתאי יהודה); 1QH X, 9; vgl. Heil, „Analphabet oder Rabbi?," 283–84 mit Anm. 78.
⁹¹ Wilckens, *Theologie*, 1/1:116 Anm. 50.
⁹² Kloppenborg, *Formation*, 202.
⁹³ Den polemischen Charakter betont (in seiner Kommentierung für den Matthäusevangelisten) Peter Fiedler, *Das Matthäusevangelium*, ThKNT 1 (Stuttgart: Kohlhammer, 2006), 244.
⁹⁴ Zu der mit Qumran vergleichbaren Aufrichtung von „Abgrenzungen" in der Identitätskonstruktion s. a. Simon J. Joseph, *Jesus, Q, and the Dead Sea Scrolls: A Judaic Approach to Q*, WUNT II 333 (Tübingen: Mohr Siebeck, 2012), 89, dessen Beurteilung als „sectarian orientation" mir allerdings zu weit geht. Zu den Weisen und Verständigen als Negativcharakteren in Q vgl. Labahn, *Der Gekommene*, 450–52.
⁹⁵ Vgl. Wolter, *Lukasevangelium*, 388: die Gruppe postuliert, „dass ihre Welt- und Geschichtsdeutung ihnen im Wege der Offenbarung durch *Gott* vermittelt wurde. Wissenssoziologisch gesagt: es handelt sich um kognitive Außenseiter, die auf diese Weise ihre vom Wirklichkeitsverständnis der Mehrheitsgesellschaft abweichende Daseinsgewissheit legitimieren."

sprachlich gehobene Form des Gebets beansprucht für seine Aussage einen hohen Geltungsanspruch. Die Gebetsform von 10,21 hat somit *eine literarisch-rhetorische Funktion innerhalb des Dokuments*.

3. Gewissheit für die Gemeinde (10,22)

In Q 10,22 beansprucht Jesus, dass ihm „alles" von Gott seinem Vater „übergeben wurde" und, vielleicht noch zentraler, dass niemand Erkenntnis des Sohnes hat außer Gott, dem Vater, und niemand weiß, wer der Vater ist, außer dem Sohn und dem, dem es der Sohn weitergibt. Die in theologisch äußerst dichter Sprache entwickelte Gegenseitigkeit des Verhältnisses von Sprecher und Gott als Vater und Sohn[96] zielt darauf, dass der Vater exklusiv im Sohn zugänglich ist.[97]

Die verwendete Terminologie erinnert, wie erneut Adelbert Denaux sorgsam aufgezeigt hat, an verschiedene johanneische Texte[98] und kann als Vorausschau auf die johanneische Theologie verstanden werden. Es gibt keinen Anlass, einen späteren Einfluss johanneischer Texte auf Q oder die Seitenreferenten anzunehmen. Vielmehr dürfte Q die christologische Reflexion aus seiner Tradition als christologische Fundierung zwischen Gebet und Seligpreisung eingefügt haben. Im vierten Evangelium lebt diese frühe christologische Überlegung in neuartiger Entfaltung fort.[99]

Nach Markus Tiwald wird in Q 10,21–24 das „besondere und exklusive Wissen um Jesus ... in der Tat zur Demarkationslinie, an der sich Erwählte und Verworfene scheiden."[100] Hiervon ausgehend kann gefragt werden, ob in Q 10,22 neben der Vater-Anrede[101] und der Betonung der Autorität des Verkündigers die Aussage der besonderen Nähe des Verkündigers zu Gott nunmehr in neuem und christologisch gefärbtem Sprachgewand an die Gottesreichsverkündigung Jesu erinnert.[102] Die christologische Reflexionstiefe des

---

[96] Betont von Hahn, *Hoheitstitel*, 325: „Das ‚Erkennen' des Sohnes durch den Vater kann nur heißen, daß Gott ihn auserwählt und legitimiert hat, und umgekehrt besagt das ‚Erkennen' des Vaters durch den Sohn, daß der Sohn allein den Vater wahrhaft anerkennt und aus der Gemeinschaft mit dem Vater lebt."

[97] Möglich ist, dass erst durch ein Wachstum der zweite Gedanke aus dem ersten entwickelt wurde, aber solche überlieferungsgeschichtlichen Erwägungen können in diesem Aufsatz nicht weiter verfolgt werden. Für ein Wachstum der Elemente in Vers 22, vgl. z. B. Christ, *Jesus Sophia*, 85, ohne Einzelnachweis und Diskussion.

[98] Denaux, „The Q-Logion Mt 11,27/Lk 10,22," 176–88, der eine literarische Rezeption des Logions in der Form von Mt 11,27 oder Lk 10,22 durch den vierten Evangelisten annimmt (ebd., 188–89).

[99] S. a. Hahn, *Hoheitstitel*, 330.

[100] Tiwald, *Logienquelle*, 95.

[101] Immerhin ist auffällig, dass von acht Vater-Anreden in Q außer der hier diskutierten Q 10,22 sieben der Verkündigung Jesu zugeschrieben werden können; so Schneider, „Gott," 16.

[102] Vgl. z. B. Wilckens, *Theologie*, 1/1:118, der allerdings noch wesentlich weitergeht: „In diesem Wort hat Jesus für seine Jünger zusammengefaßt, was ihm in dem visionären Widerfahrnis am Jordan durch Gottes Stimme zugesprochen worden war: ‚Du bist mein Sohn, der geliebte, an dem ich Wohlgefallen gefunden habe'."

Spruchs zeigt jedoch, dass der Spruch aus einer nachösterlichen Perspektive formuliert ist.[103]

Für die Einarbeitung des Spruchs von der exklusiven Offenbarung Gottes im Sohn als Kommentar zum Jesusgebet hat neben dem Verb ἀποκαλύπτω und der Offenbarungsthematik der Sohnesbegriff geführt.[104] Die Übergabe (παραδίδωμι) von „Allem" (πάντα) durch den Vater an den Sohn hat im Kontext von Q ihren Gegentext in dem Angebot des Satans, Jesus πάσας τὰς βασιλείας τοῦ κόσμου καὶ τὴν δόξαν αὐτῶν (4,5) zu geben (ταῦτά σοι πάντα δώσω; 4,6), wenn er Satan und nicht Gott verehre (ἐὰν προσκυνήσῃς μοι). Q 10,22 scheint die späte explizite Antwort der Q-Schreiber auf die Versuchungsgeschichte Jesu zu sein, in der gezeigt wird, dass Jesus der bewährte Sohn tatsächlich alles von seinem Vater, dem Herrn über den Himmel und die Erde (10,21), bekommen hat, nur um so den Vater den Menschen zu enthüllen.[105]

Im Kontext von Q 10,21–24 zielt die Pragmatik von Jesu Selbstaussage in Vers 22 weniger auf eine christologische Zentrierung, die für die seine Adressaten nicht strittig ist, denn auf die christologische *Fundierung* der Enthüllung Gottes durch Jesus als Grundlage der eigenen Verkündigung der Adressaten.[106] Ihre Botschaft enthüllt die Wirklichkeit, indem sie weitergeben, was Gott seinem Sohn übergeben hat und was sie als Unmündige von Gott zu erkennen bekommen haben. Somit bestätigt die Autorität Jesu zugleich die Autorität der Verkündigung der Adressaten angesichts von Ablehnung und Widerspruch.[107]

4. Die Unmündigen als wahre Elite in Israel (Q 10,21–24)

4.1. Die Seligpreisung der Sehenden (Q 10,23–24)

In Q 10,23–24 liegt eine Seligpreisung der Menschen vor, denen als Augenzeugen das aktuelle Geschehen zu Gute kommt: μακάριοι οἱ ὀφθαλμοὶ οἱ

---

[103] Anders z. B. vorsichtig erwägend Schneider, *Evangelium nach Lukas*, 1:245, da „nicht die Gottessohnschaft als Gegenstand der Offenbarung genannt wird."
[104] S. a. Wanke, *Bezugs- und Kommentarworte*, 50.
[105] Dieser intratextuelle Zusammenhang legt dem πάντα παρεδόθη mehr Gewicht bei als die Offenbarung im Sinne rabbinischer Traditionsweitergabe; Schneider, *Evangelium nach Lukas*, 1:244. Im Wechselverhältnis von Vater und Sohn partizipiert der Sohn an der Macht des Vaters, was die Offenbarung an die Jünger / Gemeinde einschließt (s. a. Denaux, „The Q-Logion Mt 11,27/Lk 10,22," 174).
[106] Vgl. z. B. Wanke, *Bezugs- und Kommentarworte*, 49: „… der Sprecher (schaut; Vf.) auf die (in Jesu Predigt gründende) Verkündigung der Gemeinde(n) …, die in der Gegenwart erfolgt und der eschatologische Qualität zugesprochen wird." S. a. z. B. Hoffmann, *Studien*, 36.
[107] S. a. Dieter Zeller, „Der Zusammenhang der Eschatologie in der Logienquelle," in idem, *Jesus – Logienquelle – Evangelien*, 133–44, hier 139: „Das eschatologische Eingreifen Gottes ist so Inhalt, aber auch Rückhalt der missionarischen Verkündigung, der die Q-Gemeinde ihre Existenz verdankt." In Q liegt die literarische Funktion von Vers 22 nicht die einer „Glaubensregel" (Wanke, *Bezugs- und Kommentarworte*, 50), sondern partizipiert an der Entwicklung der narrativen Identität der Q-Gruppe.

βλέποντες ἃ βλέπετε. Die Gegenwart ist dadurch geprägt, dass die herausragenden und von Gott durch seine Offenbarung und seinen Segen besonders ausgezeichneten Gestalten der Erinnerungsgeschichte Israels[108] – Propheten und Könige – dies Geschehen sehen und hören wollten. Allerdings besagt die Seligpreisung, dass es nicht ihnen gewährt wurde, sondern den Angesprochenen. In diesem Spruch wird nicht ausdrücklich ausgeführt, was die Gegenwart qualifiziert – diese Offenheit macht die Seligpreisung für ihren jeweiligen Kommunikationszusammenhang anschlussfähig –, aber die Seligpreisung ist kontextfähig mit der Verkündigung der Gottesherrschaft durch Jesus,[109] dessen Grunderfahrung sich im Wort wiederspiegelt: „die erlebte Gegenwart" ist „Erfüllung prophetischer Erwartung."[110] Nach Dieter Zeller sind solche Seligpreisungen „Aktualisierungen seines fundamentalen Wissens um die Nähe der Gottesherrschaft."[111]

Wie das Dankgebet Jesu in Q 10,21 erinnert folglich auch die Seligpreisung in Q 10,23-24 an die Reichgottesverkündigung Jesu. Sie bedenkt das besondere eschatologische „Plus der Heilszeit,"[112] in der die mit Jesu Verkündigung im Fragment präsente[113] Gottesherrschaft ihren Adressaten und Adressatinnen neue Identität schafft und ihnen bereits eine neue soteriologische Qualität ihres Gottesverhältnisses zuspricht. Die Seligpreisung ist im Horizont der Heilserwartungen Israels formuliert und sieht sie durch die Wahrnehmung des eschatologisch neuen kommenden Gottesreichs in der Gegenwart des Verkündigers und seiner Zuhörer erfüllt.

Über den sozialen und religiösen Charakter der Sehenden sagt die Tradition soweit ersichtlich nichts aus. Dass wie in den Seligpreisungen von Q 6,20-21.22-23 parr. Mt 5,1-4.6 / Lk 6,20-21 an sozial und religiös Marginalisierte gedacht ist oder an die „Unmündigen" (Q 10,21), ist wahrscheinlich, aber nicht eindeutig zu bestimmen. Die besondere Qualität der Adressaten und Adressatinnen der Seligpreisung ergibt sich aus der Zeit, die durch das gegenwärtige Durchsetzen der Gottesherrschaft qualifiziert ist.

---

[108] S. a. Bovon, *Evangelium nach Lukas*, 2:74.
[109] So schreiben die in Q 10,23-24 aufgenommene Tradition der Gottesreichsverkündigung Jesu zu: z. B. Hoffmann, *Studien*, 210; Dieter Zeller, „Prophetisches Wissen um die Zukunft in synoptischen Jesusworten," in idem, *Jesus – Logienquelle – Evangelien*, 23-40, hier 28.
[110] Hoffmann, *Studien*, 210.
[111] Zeller, „Prophetisches Wissen," 28.
[112] Zeller, „Prophetisches Wissen," 31. Helmut Merklein, „Jesus, Künder des Gottesreiches," in idem, *Studien zu Jesus und Paulus*, 126-56, hier 137, bezieht Q 10,23-24 wie Lk 11,20 par. vor allem auf die Taten Jesu „als eschatologisches Erfüllungsgeschehen," das sich „als schon gegenwärtiges Einbrechen des Heils" erweist: idem, „Basileia und Ekklesia: Jesu Botschaft von der Gottesherrschaft und ihre Konsequenzen für die Kirche," in idem, *Studien zu Jesus und Paulus*, 207-20, hier 210.
[113] Hans Weder, *Gegenwart und Gottesherrschaft: Überlegungen zum Zeitverständnis bei Jesus und im frühen Christentum*, BThSt 20 (Neukirchen-Vluyn: Neukirchener, 1993), 26-34, bes. 33.

4.2. Die Unmündigen als Sehende – die narrative Neukonstruktion der Identität angesichts der Krise der Ablehnung in Q

In der Q vorliegenden Überlieferung war das Gebet Jesu vermutlich bereits Teil eines Spannungsbogens, der bis zur Seligpreisung der Unmündigen als Sehende der heilbringenden Offenbarung Gottes reicht. Dieser Spannungsbogen bleibt um Q 10,22 ergänzt für Q 10,21–24 erhalten. Das Gebet Jesu, das Gott dankt und preist, sagt eine exklusive Begünstigung der als Unmündige bezeichneten Adressaten aus und weist im literarischen Kontext von Q auf die Seligpreisung der Adressaten voraus, die vor den Größen des kulturell-religiösen Gedächtnisses Israels ausgezeichnet sind. Die in der Seligpreisung angesprochene Erfüllung der Heilssehnsucht der Gott nahestehenden Gottesdiener der Geschichte Israels – Propheten und Könige – bestätigt den Anspruch Jesu in Vers 22 wie das Offenbarungshandeln in seinem Gebet von Vers 21. Zugleich bildet es ein Gegengewicht zu Ablehnungserfahrungen, die im Zusammenhang von Q 9,57–11,51 durchscheinen.[114]

Das vermeintliche Stigma mangelnder Weisheit wird mithilfe der Seligpreisung ausdrücklich mit einer von Gott zugesprochenen religiösen Qualität durch Enthüllung und entsprechendes Wahrnehmen des eschatologischen Heils verbunden und damit vom vermeintlichen Stigma zum Elitemerkmal. Die Seligpreisung unterstreicht die im Gebet und in Jesu Selbstanspruch ausgesagte Identität der Gemeinde, „als Offenbarungsempfänger im Ratschluss Gottes und in der Vermittlung des Sohnes" verankert zu sein.[115] Damit ist ihre eigene, gegenwärtig zurückgewiesene Verkündigung (vgl. den Kontext von 10,13–16[116]) in Jesus und in dem sich den „Unmündigen" offenbarenden Gott selbst verankert.[117]

Kann sich Israel, beispielsweise weil es an der Gottesgabe der Weisheit partizipiert (Bar 3,3–4,4), selbst seligpreisen, ὅτι τὰ ἀρεστὰ τῷ θεῷ ἡμῖν γνωστά ἐστιν (Bar 4,4 LXX.D: „Selig sind wir, Israel, denn was Gott gefällt, ist uns bekannt!"), so spricht Q 10,21–24 dem der Verkündigung der Jesusanhänger von Q widersprechenden zeitgenössischen Israel diese Gabe ab. Gleichzeitig stellen sich die Sprecher mit dem eigenen Sehen und Hören des Jesusgeschehens in die Tradition Israels und beanspruchen als Unmündige die Offenbarung Gottes, um vom Sohn und exklusivem Offenbarungsvermittler seliggepriesen zu werden. Die Adressaten stehen in einer zeitlichen Abfolge zu den „Propheten und

---

[114] S. a. Frankemölle, „Die Offenbarung an die Unmündigen," 85–86.
[115] Zeller, „Redaktionsprozesse," 115.
[116] Tuckett, Q, 281: „... the whole preceding section is dominated by the motifs of hostility and rejection."
[117] Nach Uro, Sheep, 230–33, wird die Verweigerungserfahrung nicht mehr durch Polemik gelöst, sondern in Gottes Plan der Verhüllung („Divine concealment"; ebd., 230) aufgelöst. M. E. gehören die theologische Komponente wie das Element der Polemik zu dem in Q erkennbaren Prozess narrativer Identitätsbildung hinzu.

Königen" als vorausgesetzte und positiv bewertete Gestalten der Geschichte Israels. Damit sind sie den Traditionsfiguren Israels durch das Handeln Gottes voraus und ihnen gegenüber ausgezeichnet – anders auch als die Weisen als Repräsentanten der religiösen (und politischen?) Elite, denen das zu Sehende aktiv verhüllt wird.[118] Unbestritten bleibt das gemeinsame Erbe der Vergangenheit Israels, als deren authentische Erfüllung sich die Q-Gruppe sieht, erhalten und wird in die Neu-Konstruktion einer überlegenen Identität integriert.[119]

Die Selbstdarstellung des Beters in Vers 22 charakterisiert die Adressaten als Empfänger der Offenbarung. Zugleich validiert sie die Verkündigung der Q-Gruppe vor allem im Licht der Aussendung in 10,3 wie auch im Auftrag zum Öffentlich-Machen der Offenbarung von 12,2–3; Darstellungen, die allesamt in Jesus als Sohn und Empfänger der Offenbarung von Gott fundiert sind. Im Kontext von Aussendung (10,3–12) und Ablehnung (Q 10,10–12; 10,13–15) dient der Anspruch Jesu als „Trost und Bestärkung aus dem Mund des ‚Sohnes' (Q 10,22) für die meist abgelehnten Q-Boten".[120]

Die narrative Konstruktion der Identität der Adressaten von Q hat dort ihren Sinn, wo die soziale Situation der Angesprochenen, aber wohl auch ihr religiöses Selbstverständnis als von Jesus bestimmte Verkündiger Widerspruch, Ablehnung und wohl auch aktiver Repression ausgesetzt wird. „Angesichts der Zurückweisung, die der Botschaft von den offiziellen Kreisen des Judentums zuteil wird, muß den Außenseitern das Offenbarungsereignis apokalyptisch zugesichert werden."[121]

Zusammenfassend zeigt sich, dass das Gebet Jesu in einen neuen literarisch-pragmatischen Kontext verschmolzen ist und eine identitätsbegründende Funktion erhält, die soziologische Bestimmungen aus ihrem ursprünglichen Sitz im Leben der Verkündigung Jesu aufnimmt und deren Pragmatik wie in Jesu Verkündigung außerhalb der rituellen oder liturgischen Praxis der Gemeinde liegt.

---

[118] Man könnte fast von einem „wunderbaren Wechsel" sprechen, bei dem die Weisen um ihre Weisheit gebracht werden, so dass sie mit den Versen 23–24 weder sehen noch hören, während die Unmündigen als Sehende und Hörende „selig" mit Gott im Frieden sind.

[119] Vgl. Wolter, *Lukasevangelium*, 390: „Neben den Aspekt der Legitimation eines devianten Wirklichkeitsverständnisses (s. bei V. 21) tritt das Postulat einer heilsgeschichtlichen Kontinuität." Insofern wird die Deutung von Q 10,21–24 auf ein „renewal or restoration of Israel" der polemischen Grundstruktur der Spruchgruppe nicht gerecht: so Richard Horsley, „Social Conflict in the Synoptic Sayings Source Q," in *Conflict and Invention: Literary, Rhetorical, and Social Studies on the Sayings Gospel Q*, hg. v. John S. Kloppenborg (Valley Forge, PA: Trinity Press International, 1995), 37–52.

[120] Heil, „Missionsinstruktion," 139, im Anschluss an Kloppenborg, *Formation*, 202.

[121] Zeller, „Redaktionsprozesse," 112.

D. Ergebnis

Die voranstehende Analyse hat erbracht, dass die pragmatische Funktion des Dankgebets Jesu für die Offenbarung Gottes als Akt der Identitätsstiftung der Q-Gruppe zu Ungunsten ihrer Gegner aus der religiösen Elite erfolgt. Somit kommt dem Gebet Q 10,21 im Dokument eine literarisch-rhetorische Funktion zu, die der Ausformung der Identität der Gemeinde dient. Das Gebet Jesu ist Teil einer kleinen Jesusrede geworden, in der die Adressaten als von Gott in besonderer Weise ausgezeichnete neue Elite von der zeitgenössischen Elite Israels abgegrenzt werden. Die christologische Bestätigung des Gebetsinhalts macht das Gebet bleibend zu einem Wort Jesu, das nicht auf kultisch-rituelle Anwendung oder liturgischen Gebrauch zielt. In der Form eines erinnerten Kommunikationsaktes Jesu mit Gott, dem er durch 11,22 als Vater in einer engen Offenbarungsgemeinschaft verbunden ist, stiftet sein Gebet den Adressaten narrativ eine neue Identität. Gegenüber einer Fremdwahrnehmung, aber auch einer marginalisierten Selbstgestaltung als religiös ungebildete Außenseiter macht sie das Gebet Jesu zu den „Kindern der Weisheit" (Q 7,35). Ihr Vorrang ist in Gottes Handeln begründet, das sie als Träger von Gottes endzeitlicher Hoffnung zur wahren religiösen Elite macht; ihnen und nicht den außergemeindlichen Eliten gilt die Offenbarung Gottes durch Jesus, die in der Gemeinde seiner Anhängerinnen und Anhänger zu ihrem soteriologischen Ziel kommt und an denen sich damit zugleich die Heilserwartungen der Geschichte Israels erfüllen (10,23–24).

In dem noch leidlich erkennbaren Wachstum des Dankgebets Jesu bis zu seiner Rezeption durch die Abfassung von Q wird die identitätsstiftende Intention des Gebets aus der Gottesreichsverkündigung Jesu weiter ausgebaut. Die Jesustradition hinter Q 10,21 spiegelt kein Gebetsritual noch eine wiederholte liturgische Praxis Jesu, aber sie ist sehr wohl Ausdruck seiner durch die Basileiabotschaft geprägten Frömmigkeitspraxis in Gott als sich den Bedürftigen und Unmündigen zuwendenden Vater. Jesu Vertrauen in die Durchsetzung der Herrschaft Gottes gerade an den Rändern des zeitgenössischen Israels nutzt die kultisch beheimatete Form des Dankgebets zur Neubestimmung seiner Adressatinnen und Adressaten. Das öffentlich gesprochene Gebet Jesu lässt sich bereits auf der Ebene der Jesustradition als ein Programmwort ansprechen, das sich im Gespräch mit Gott zugleich an die Zuhörer seiner Verkündigung richtet und ihnen neue Identität als Adressaten von Gottes endzeitlicher Offenbarung zuspricht und deren Gültigkeit im rückblickenden Moment des Danks bestätigt. Die Begünstigten werden somit zugleich Teil der Kommunikationsgemeinschaft Jesu mit Gott, die die spätere Erweiterung als Gespräch zwischen Vater und Sohn christologisch interpretiert.

Die frühchristliche Erinnerung bewahrt dieses Gebet Jesu und denkt es weiter als Teil der eigenen Sinn- und Identitätsstiftung, aber nicht als Teil der eigenen Frömmigkeitskultur. Als Jesusgebet ist es weitererzählbar, aber nicht als eigenes Dankgebet rezipierbar. Allerdings kann die weitererzählende Gemeinde auch nicht schweigen, sondern scheint dem Gebet bald eine akklamierende Antwort hinzugefügt zu haben, die ihren Dank in der Gottgefälligkeit des von Jesus bedachten Geschehens formuliert (10,21–24).

Im Überlieferungsprozess bleibt die antielitäre Grundstimmung beibehalten, aber die Autorität des Sprechers wird ebenso hervorgehoben (10,22) wie die Neu-Konstruktion der Begünstigten, die mit der Seligpreisung (10,23–24) sich selbst in der Rolle eschatologischer Erfüllung der Heilserwartungen der Elite der narrativen Traditionen Israels sehen. Damit erschließt die Nacherzählung (*re-narration*) des Dankgebets Jesu die Identitätsstiftung der Q-Gruppe, die auf Ausgrenzungserfahrung antwortet und in der Zustimmung zum Gebet die Selbstbezeichnung als „unmündig" zu einem geradezu subversiven Gegenbegriff gegenüber der religiösen Elite ihrer Umwelt macht. Gerade als „Unmündige" sind die Offenbarungsempfänger Gottes und damit als Verkündiger des Gottessohnes Jesu die wahre Elite.

Praying to God and the Kingdom

Q's Lord's Prayer in Its Rhetorical and Literary Context

Giovanni B. Bazzana

At first sight it might appear that the Sayings Gospel Q contains relatively scanty materials that may be categorized under the label of "prayer." In that perspective, however, the present volume can certainly demonstrate, with its rich collection of exciting contributions, that even a short text such as Q has a lot to say on this crucial aspect of religious life in antiquity. Undoubtedly, the fact that the Sayings Gospel includes such a gem of extraordinary importance as the Lord's Prayer contributes significantly to make of Q an important object of study for scholars interested in the topic.

A primary consequence of such a state of affairs and of the fact that the Lord's Prayer itself has been so influential and beloved throughout the history of Christianity is that the literature on this subject matter is enormous. Thus, it is quite complicated for anyone to find a new way to talk about prayer in Q. That being said, it is important to underscore that the mainstream scholarly opinion on the entire Sayings Gospel has changed its course – often even in quite a radical way – in recent years. A primary example of this "paradigm shift" is certainly the relatively new suggestion (advanced and then argued a few years ago by John Kloppenborg and William Arnal) that the Sayings Gospel might have been composed by Galilean village scribes sometime in the middle of the first century CE.[1] It goes without saying that such a change of perspective can have remarkable consequences on the historical placement of Q at several levels, ranging from our understanding of the socio-political project behind the Gospel to its specific deployment of apocalyptic motives and imagery.[2] I will return to some of these ideological stakes later in this paper, but I would like to begin by tackling the au-

---

[1] John S. Kloppenborg, *Excavating Q: The History and Setting of the Sayings Gospel* (Minneapolis: Fortress, 2000), 166–212, and William E. Arnal, *Jesus and the Village Scribes: Galilean Conflicts and the Setting of Q* (Minneapolis: Fortress, 2001). More recently, see also the discussion in Giovanni B. Bazzana, *Kingdom of Bureaucracy: The Political Theology of Village Scribes in the Sayings Gospel Q*, BETL 274 (Leuven: Peeters, 2015).

[2] See, for instance, the convincing work of Sarah E. Rollens, *Framing Social Criticism in the Jesus Movement: The Ideological Project in the Sayings Gospel Q*, WUNT II 374 (Tübingen: Mohr Siebeck, 2014).

thorship of Q by village scribes and the somewhat narrower theme of prayer in the Gospel from a different angle.

Most certainly, the identification of the first composers and tradents of Q as villages scribes offers a solid socio-cultural placement for the document and illuminates some of the philological as well as historical questions that have often been associated with the Sayings Gospel. However, there are several related issues that are still in need of clarification and that would benefit from further analysis. For instance (and in close relationship with the theme of the present volume), it is worth asking whether Galilean village scribes could have had the linguistic and intellectual resources needed to compose a document of the relative complexity of Q. In several recent studies it has become clear that a good way to answer this crucial question is to have recourse to ancient papyrological materials, which are for the most part of Egyptian provenance and which constitute the richest source of information about the cultural and social habits of the sub-elite individuals whom we can designate as "village scribes."[3] A controlled comparison shows that the Sayings Gospel carries the traces of the quasi-technical language employed in the ancient Hellenistic and later Roman bureaucracies. Moreover, Q presents some of the ideological traits that can be reasonably attributed to such sub-elite intellectuals.

A related question (which acquires some measure of prominence in this context) has to do with the extant evidence for the actual production of writings comparable to Q by the hands of Egyptian village scribes. This is a significant challenge because, while the papyrological record contains several examples of literary or sub-literary papyri carrying collections of sayings that are more or less similar to the Sayings Gospel, it is always difficult to attribute them to the hand of village scribes with a satisfactory degree of certainty. As it is well known, almost all literary pieces preserved on papyrus are entirely anonymous, a situation that creates considerable problems in the attempt of establishing who and when composed and/or copied them. That being said, there are a few papyri that present characteristics (the style of the handwriting, the format, and so on) which – in conjunction with their provenance, when the latter can be ascertained – can confidently be associated with sub-elite village scribes. Elsewhere, I have analyzed a

---

[3] In this discussion I will use the designation "village scribes" to indicate all the sub-elite intellectuals operating at the level of ancient villages (as done by Kloppenborg and Arnal). This category includes not only individuals employed by the royal and imperial administrations, but also those offering their services to the elites (such as real estate managers or teachers). Papyrological literature uses "village scribes" in a more restrictive sense to designate only those bureaucrats whose appointment was specifically as *komogrammateis*: see, for instance, the classic studies of Lucia Criscuolo, "Ricerche sul komogrammateus nell'Egitto tolemaico," *Aegyptus* 58 (1978): 3–101, and Arthur Verhoogt, *Menches, Komogrammateus of Kerkeosiris: The Doings and Dealings of a Village Scribe in the Late Ptolemaic Period (120–110 B. C.)*, PLB 29 (Leiden: Brill, 1997).

couple of examples that would validate the hypothesis according to which village scribes might have been up to the task of composing a text such as Q.[4]

As a starting point for the present contribution, I would like to pose a similar question, but adapted to the specific case of prayers. Is there any evidence that would demonstrate that village scribes, with a socio-cultural profile analogous to those who composed Q, might have also put together prayers similar to those encountered in the Sayings Gospel (in particular, obviously, the Lord's Prayer)?

Before addressing such a question directly, let me just make a preliminary methodological statement that hopefully will prove itself helpful in contextualizing the following remarks. To gesture towards these Egyptian parallels with respect to the prayers preserved in the Sayings Gospel is not and cannot be interpreted as a genealogic or a taxonomic project, but can only be comparative in nature and intent. Several previous studies and even some of the contributions collected in this volume have established without doubt – as far as I am concerned – that whatever prayers one encounters in Q (and *in primis*, obviously, the Lord's Prayer) originated within Jewish circles and were composed by people who had deep knowledge of and were in intense dialogue with the Jewish scriptures understood in a very broad sense. Thus, from a genealogical point of view, that *corpus* and the larger body often called Jewish literature of the Second Temple period are the first places to which one should refer. Elsewhere, I have tried to show that, because of the acquaintance of the village scribes behind Q with the terminology and ideology of Hellenistic administrations, a text such as, for example, the Lord's prayer also shows traces of that influence.[5] However, whatever one makes of that hypothesis, it still stands to reason that the primary referents for the Lord's Prayer should be sought within Jewish texts. As noted before, this implies that the considerations developed here will not be genealogic in nature, but comparative. Thus, the main goal will consist in showing that an examination of Egyptian documents pertaining to prayer and attributable to village scribes may help us in understanding some components of the broader project that stood behind the Sayings Gospel's treatment of the Lord's Prayer and of other attendant materials.

One last preliminary word on the issue of the link between the Lord's Prayer and the historical Jesus. Again, since the present project is comparative in nature, I am not concerned with establishing a historical genealogy for the prayer. A close connection between the historical Jesus and the Lord's Prayer is support-

---

[4] These are PSI I 85 (Pack² 2287; LDAB 5248; Oxyrhynchos, end II – beginning III CE) and 120 (Pack² 1994; LDAB 5633; Oxyrhynchos, end II – beginning I BCE), discussed in Giovanni B. Bazzana, "Galilean Village Scribes as the Authors of the Sayings Gospel Q," in *Q in Context II: Social Setting and Archaeological Background of the Sayings Source*, ed. Markus Tiwald, BBB 173 (Göttingen: Vandenhoeck & Ruprecht, 2015), 133–48, here 143–48.

[5] Bazzana, *Kingdom of Bureaucracy*, chapter 4.

ed by the overwhelming majority of the scholars who have studied it.[6] However, the main focus of the present contribution will be on the way in which the prayer is built into Q, conceived as a writing with at least some measure of textual and theological coherence. In this perspective, questions related to authorship of the Lord's Prayer by the historical Jesus are largely irrelevant. Moreover, even without lingering for too long on this subject matter, the attribution of the prayer to the very mouth of Jesus (albeit surely appealing in many ways) is beset by significant problems. To mention only one of them, the traditional criteria routinely employed in the "quest" for the historical Jesus appear to lead to a negative result when they are applied to a careful analysis of the Lord's Prayer.[7] Moreover (and arguably more importantly), as Melanie Johnson-DeBaufre has argued a few years ago, the exclusive focus on the personality and activity of the individual figure of Jesus unduly reinscribes a romantic view of the singular genius modifying and reshaping the flow of history with his heroic gestures.[8] Such an approach is problematic not only in terms of historical epistemology, but it raises questions of a theological nature as well, at a time when communal efforts towards the establishment of social justice and equality should take a position of preeminence with respect to the often dissatisfying expectations of heroic and intrinsically authoritarian individualism. Thus, in the present analysis the main focus will be on the treatment of the Lord's Prayer and other similar materials by the Q people, without prejudice on the issue whether these texts were initially composed or reshaped in Greek on the basis of a lost Aramaic antecedent by the village scribes who authored the Sayings Gospel.

A. Prayers on Egyptian Papyri

As noted above, it is interesting to inquire whether the composition of prayers similar to the Lord's Prayer is conceivable for local intellectuals who had a sociocultural profile comparable to that of the Q village scribes. Certainly, there is no shortage of prayers, hymns, and other similar compositions extant in the papyrological record. That evidence, in and of itself, would be sufficient to prove the point that village scribes – who were indeed responsible for the production of most of what has survived up to our time – did indeed read quite a lot of prayers

---

[6] See the now slightly dated bibliographical review in James H. Charlesworth, ed., *The Lord's Prayer and Other Prayer Texts from the Greco-Roman Era* (Valley Forge, PA: Trinity Press International, 1994).

[7] See, for instance, the insightful discussion of the applicability of criteria in James G. Crossley, *Jesus and the Chaos of History: Redirecting the Life of the Historical Jesus* (Oxford: Oxford University Press, 2015), chapter 2.

[8] See Melanie Johnson-DeBaufre, *Jesus among Her Children: Q, Eschatology, and the Construction of Christian Origins*, HTS 55 (Cambridge, MA: Harvard University Press, 2005).

even if they did not actually produce them on their own. That being said, it seems that an attentive search of the documents at our disposal can actually attain an even more precise result. There are indeed several papyri, whose formal characteristics enable us to argue with a certain degree of assuredness that they were produced by village scribes.

The first example that could be taken into consideration here is P. Ross.Georg. I 11, a rather long hymn devoted to Dionysus and preserved on the *verso* side of a papyrus that carries on the *recto* a documentary text.[9] Already this initial observation indicates that this writing was in all likelihood the private copy of a village scribe. To utilize the *verso* (the inferior side of a papyrus roll) for writing is a sure indication that this copy was intended for "private" use.[10] The fact that the *recto* (the "good" side) carries an account strengthens the hypothesis that whoever re-employed the papyrus was working in some kind of an administrative context. To these elements one may add the quality of the handwriting that, while displaying an evident effort to achieve clarity and legibility, cannot by any means be classified as a bookhand for the presence of ligatures and several letters whose shapes tend towards cursive forms. Moreover (and this is the most important element to underscore with respect to our interests here), this hymn – whose inscription is datable on paleographic grounds to the second century CE – appears to have been an autograph of the author. There are indeed – interspersed here and there throughout all the extant three columns of writing – corrections and emendations that can be safely identified as interventions of an author working on his or her draft of this prayer.[11]

The hymn itself was probably intended to honor Dionysus, even though we cannot be entirely sure of this, since the very beginning of the poem is lost. Nevertheless, the body of the prayer (which seems to have followed the classic structure of *invocatio – pars epica – preces*) is definitely focused on the god of wine, since it narrates at length the confrontation between him and Lykurgos, ending with the eternal punishment of the latter. The very conclusion of the hymn exhorts the readers (and performers?) to derive moral instruction from the narrative (lines 55–59): "This punishment the mighty thunderer Zeus / decreed for enemies of gods, that punishment / should be their lot, in life as well as death. / Take this to heart! Call to this hymn of god / which is due this day in the seasons' course

---

[9] LDAB 4911; Mertens-Pack 1861: the provenance of the papyrus is in all likelihood the Fayum and it is datable to the second century CE.

[10] On the socio-cultural use of reemployed papyri and the problematic applicability of the notion of "private writing" in antiquity, see Giovanni B. Bazzana, "'You Will Write Two Booklets and Send One to Clement and One to Grapte': Formal Features, Circulation, and Social Function of Ancient Apocalyptic Literature," in *Scribal Practices and Social Structures among Jesus Adherents: Essays in Honour of John S Kloppenborg*, ed. William E. Arnal et al., BETL 285 (Leuven: Peeters, 2016), 261–80.

[11] See the accurate analysis in William D. Furley, "A Lesson to All: Lykurgos' Fate in the Tbilisi Hymn (P. Ross.Georg. I. 11)," *ZPE* 162 (2007): 63–84.

(τῆσδε καλέσαι θεοῦ ἐπ' ἀοιδῆς ἧς κύρει τόδε ἦμαρ ἐπιπλομένων λυκαβάντων)." The very last verse gives precious indications on the probable reason behind the origin of the hymn, since – as it has been suggested by Antonino Zumbo – the prayer was in all likelihood composed for the meeting of a group, possibly a voluntary association, devoted to the worship of Dionysus.[12] Later we will see that the anonymous author of P. Ross.Georg. I 11 was not alone in antiquity in composing prayers and hymns for such purposes.

Another hymn that is in all likelihood an authorial autograph and might very well have been produced by a village scribe has been published by Antonio Carlini as PSI 15 1482.[13] This time the papyrus sheet is much smaller than in the above-mentioned case of the Tbilisi hymn. The *recto* of the papyrus carries only a few verses of a prayer directed to Eirene, while the *verso* has again the same text, copied and improved by what seems to have been the hand of its author.[14] The handwriting is again precise and fluid, datable to the first century CE, but without even an attempt to write in a bookhand for a piece that should be in all likelihood identified as a "private" draft of the author.

In this case as in the preceding one, the amateur poet tries to strike a note of literary sophistication, even though the results are uneven at best, as it happened for the author of the Tbilisi hymn. The prayer begins with a poetic invocation to the Muses and then moves on to the specific celebration of Eirene, first designated as the daughter of Zeus and Themis, the goddess of justice, and then through a description of the state of war, illustrating the negative situation that characterizes the absence of peace. When the poet decided to rewrite these initial fifteen verses in the back of her sheet, she modified the structure adopted in the first draft by adding a longer section devoted to the illustration of the benefits brought to humankind by Eirene, including bolstering monarchical power and assuring the regular management of temples and divine rituals.

Another interesting example of a prayer copied (but in all likelihood this time not composed) by a village scribe is that of P. Gr. 1179 of the Bibliothèque Nationale of Strasbourg, a small sheet of papyrus that carries an account of expenditures on its *recto* and a hymn to Hermes on its *verso*. Again, the handwriting of the piece (an interesting mixture of severe style and chancery script that could be second as well as third century CE) supports the hypothesis that what one has to deal with is the "private" draft redacted by some kind of local administrator.[15]

---

[12] Antonino Zumbo, "P. Ross.Georg. I 11: Hymnus in Dionysum (= fr. LVI Heitsch)," *APF* 3 (1997): 1068–1078.

[13] LDAB 4297; Mertens-Pack 1861.1; the papyrus is of uncertain provenance and dated paleographically to the first century CE.

[14] Antonio Carlini, "Abbozzo di inno ad Εἰρήνη di un poeta dilettante del sec. I d. C.," in *L'antico e la sua eredità. Atti del colloquio internazionale di studi in onore di Antonio Garzya*, ed. Ugo Criscuolo (Naples: D'Auria, 2004), 21–29.

[15] LDAB 5445; Mertens-Pack 1870; the papyrus, whose provenance is Hermoupolis and the

The content of the prayer is one that can be characterized as a straightforward celebration of Hermes in his classic responsibility as guide of the souls after death and as the conveyer of oracles and revelations to humans. Indeed, the entire composition ends on this note with the request that revelation may be granted to the person who prays while he or she will be asleep (lines 22–24): "For I am a human, a pious suppliant, / and your soldier; and so, while I am asleep, / send to me your unerring mantic skill" (ἀνθρώπῳ, ὁσίῳ ἱκέτῃ καὶ σῷ στρατιώτῳ, / καὶ σὴν μαντοσύνην νημερτέα πέμψον ἐν ὕπνῳ). It is important to note that, exactly because of this final request and since similar forms of the same hymn are included in two other "magical" papyri, the text has been included in Preisendanz's collection (PGM 17b) in a form that is a very eclectic recombination of the three variants. But, in this case as in many others that are part of the *Papyri Graecae Magicae*, the labeling reflects more the prejudices of the modern scholars who assembled the collection than the actual evidence of the text. However one wants to define "magic" (a tricky and perhaps impossible task in itself), this text does not appear to have any of the traits that are usually associated with the label.

The last piece that can only be mentioned here very briefly, because the limited space precludes a more detailed discussion, is the famous roll catalogued as P. Oxy. 11 1380 and 1381.[16] With regard to this papyrus (as it used to be the case in several older papyrological editions), the two publication numbers deceptively hide the fact that P. Oxy. 1380 and P. Oxy. 1381 are inscribed on the two sides of the same sheet of papyrus. The *recto* famously contains a long aretalogy of Isis, which is datable on paleographic grounds to the early second century CE. The text designated as 1381 is inscribed on the *verso* and is incorrectly described by Grenfell and Hunt as "analogous" to the aretalogy of the *recto*. In fact, 1381 is a celebration of a deity (in this case Asclepius identified with the Egyptian Imothep), but does not have the generic form of an aretalogy at all. On the contrary, the writing of the *verso* does contain a prayer to Asclepius-Imothep (lines 160–218), but the latter is inserted within a narrative that recounts how the power of the god has forced the reluctant author to translate the divine praises from Egyptian into Greek.

The text on the *recto* is written in "a small semiuncial hand with a tendency to cursive forms" and with the addition of some occasional reading aids (diaereses) and corrections, but not to the point of giving the impression that this papyrus had been prepared as a bookroll. Indeed, Adriano Magnani has convincingly suggested that the papyrus should be understood as a "personal copy," probably produced for the "private use of a believer or an official of the temple" of Isis in

---

dating sometime in the third century CE, is published and its handwriting is described in Otto Plasberg, "Straßburger Anekdota," *APF* 2 (1903): 185–228, here 208–17.

[16] The two texts are catalogued respectively as LDAB 4897; Mertens-Pack 2477, and LDAB 4898; Mertens-Pack 2479.

Oxyrhynchos.[17] This figure would fit quite well the broad definition of "village scribe" that has been advanced at the beginning of this contribution. As far as 1381 is concerned, the very fact that the reemployment of the papyrus resulted in the inscription of a text of similar religious inspiration, if not literary genre, may lead one to hypothesize that the scribe and reader of *recto* and *verso* was the same individual. In any event, whether one agrees with the traditional view that the narrative praising Asclepius-Imothep is indeed the translation of an original Egyptian or is a new creation whose author takes advantage of the popular fiction of translating an authoritative book of the past to bolster his religious message,[18] the socio-cultural context of this piece gives further strength to the comparison with the activities of the village scribes behind Q.

B. Who Wrote Prayers in Antiquity?

In light of what has been seen so far, the conclusion that writing hymns and prayers to various deities was a relatively widely practiced activity even at the sociocultural level of village scribes comparable to those who authored Q should not come as a surprise. Indeed, several analyses of the Sayings Gospel have by now established that the rhetorical flow of the writing was built around *chreiai* and other simple argumentative structures that occur in several ancient manuals of style, such as the well-known *progymnasmata*.[19] The people who composed Q were certainly acquainted with rhetorical forms similar to the *progymnasmata*, since they formed the very basis of Greek education from at least the Hellenistic period through Late Antiquity.

For the purposes of the present discussion, it is important to note that most of the *progymnasmata* or other analogous collections that have survived up to our time also contain basic instructions for the composition of hymns and prayers. Already the first-century textbook of Theon includes a treatment of "hymns" as part of the category of speeches that are called "epideictic" (indicating that they are focused on declamatory and demonstrative rhetoric, to be employed on the occasions in which someone or something has to be praised or blamed). Theon suggests that the designation "hymn" is appropriate for speeches honoring deities, while "encomion" suits the declamations that have human beings as their

---

[17] Adriano Magnani, "Iside, Apuleio e il P. Oxy. XI 1380," *Analecta Papyrologica* 13 (2001): 107–13.

[18] As recently suggested by Franziska Naether and Heinz-Josef Thissen, "Genesis einer Aretalogie: Anmerkungen zu eine Neuedition von P. Oxy. XI 1381," in *Actes du 26e Congrès international de papyrologie*, ed. Paul Schubert, Recherches et Rencontres 30 (Geneva: Droz, 2012), 559–63.

[19] On this point see Kloppenborg, *Excavating Q*, 160–63, and the literature referred to there. For the ancient rhetorical manuals, see Ronald F. Hock and Edward N. O'Neil, eds., *The Chreia in Ancient Rhetoric*, 3 vols. (Atlanta: Scholars Press, 1986–2013).

subjects. But these distinctions are more a matter of theory than actual practice (and one must also note that the Greek distinction between deities and humans was a continuum more than a sharp divide). Theon's theoretical guidelines for the composition of "hymns" are echoed in other authors, such as Quintilian, and are further developed in later manuals of rhetoric. A particularly rich exposition is offered by Menander of Laodicea, who in his third-century textbook discusses several types of prayers and the rules that should direct their composition.[20] On these grounds it appears quite reasonable to hypothesize that Egyptian village scribes may have practiced such a type of rhetorical composition alongside the others attested by their manuals of rhetoric and taught in the classroom in which they learned Greek.

Moreover, it is worth noting, with Matthias Klinghardt, that the ability to write good, or at the very least acceptable, hymns was highly prized in antiquity.[21] Several pieces of evidence witness to the honors that could be conferred on writers of hymns. For instance,[22] in an inscription dated to the end of the third century BCE, the people of Tenos honor with a crown a foreign woman, Alkinoe, for having composed a hymn to Zeus and Poseidon.[23] Again, in a much later inscription (132/3 CE) from the shrine of Apollo at Claros (IGR 4 1587), a certain Nedymianos is mentioned as a "writer of hymns for life (ὑμνογράφος διὰ βίου)." Moreover, as we have seen above with reference to the papyrus carrying a hymn to Dionysus and now in Tbilisi, the concrete use for this type of writing was potentially quite extended and diverse, encompassing not only the more "official" civic cults, but also the rituals of "voluntary" associations of any kind and form. Again, it cannot be surprising to see such a high degree of interest for hymn and prayers, since – as it is insightfully noted by Klinghardt – these crucial components of ancient rituals played a significant role in establishing and reinforcing the communal identity of any type of social group. As we will see later, the same can be argued for the Lord's Prayer in Q, since interestingly the text performs analogous functions both in the Matthean (differentiating the members of the Jesus group from non-Jews) and in the Lukan redactional construction (here differentiating the members of the Jesus group vis-à-vis other Jewish groups, and specifically the followers of John the Baptist).

---

[20] Edgar Krentz, "The Prayer in Menander Rhetor 2.445.25–446.13," in *Prayer from Alexander to Constantine: A Critical Anthology*, ed. Mark Kiley et al. (London: Routledge, 1997), 185–89.

[21] Matthias Klinghardt, "Prayer Formularies for Public Recitation: Their Use and Function in Ancient Religion," *Numen* 46 (1999): 1–52, here 10–11.

[22] Consider also FD 2,78 (230–225 BCE), a Delphic inscription honoring the Athenian Kleochares, author of a paian and a hymn to Apollo, or ID 1497 (165/164 BCE), another decree honoring Agathokles for his hymns for the gods of Delos and his teaching to play the lyre for the youth of the island.

[23] IG XII(5) 812; on other women as itinerant poets and artists in the Hellenistic period, see Pasi Loman, "Travelling Female Entertainers of the Hellenistic Age," *Arctos* 38 (2004): 59–73.

C. Theoretical Interlude: How to Study "Prayers" in Antiquity

Before moving on to a closer examination of the Q materials in light of what has been observed so far, it is worth reviewing a few methodological points that have emerged from the analysis of the documents mentioned in the preceding sections.

First of all, it is worth noting that throughout the present contribution the terms "hymn" and "prayer" have been used as more or less interchangeable. This is because the ancient evidence does not support in any way the existence of a distinction between these two religious practices and literary genres. In particular, the authors of rhetorical manuals that have been mentioned above (such as Theon or Menander) propose some categorizations, which however they are not able to maintain systematically and certainly are not strengthened by the evidence provided by surviving manuscripts and papyri. Recently, Matthew Gordley – in a study devoted primarily to the "hymn" to Christ in Colossians – has reexamined the critical discussion on this point and has reached conclusions similar to those expounded above.[24]

David Furley and Jan Bremer have insisted on a definition of "hymn" that emphasizes the link of the latter with choral performance and dance.[25] While such an approach might have some merit, it is clearly not appropriate for evaluating the materials presented here, since the performative aspect of our texts – despite being something that cannot be excluded in principle in all cases – is impossible to establish with any certainty for the majority of them. Others, such as William Race,[26] have emphasized the differences that would derive from the authorial choice to write in verses or in prose. Again, while this might be an important distinction to observe in literary terms, from a religious-historical point of view it does not help our understanding of these phenomena, particularly when one considers that a large part of the "hymns" datable to the early Roman period are actually in prose (as in the all-important cases of some aretalogies of Isis and of Aelius Aristides's production, to which we will return below).

More subtly problematic than the scholarly opinions reviewed in the preceding paragraphs is the impression that "hymn" and "prayer" are two labels adopted to distinguish materials originating within Jewish and Christian groups from "pagan" cultic texts. Thus, "hymn" would be a suitable designation for formal and highly literary religious expressions that would be ultimately devoid of "true" personal participation, while "prayer" would fit better the passionate and per-

---

[24] Matthew E. Gordley, *The Colossian Hymn in Context: An Exegesis in Light of Jewish and Greco-Roman Hymnic and Epistolary Conventions*, WUNT II 228 (Tübingen: Mohr Siebeck, 2007).
[25] William D. Furley and Jan M. Bremer, *Greek Hymns: Selected Cult Songs from the Archaic to the Hellenistic Period*, 2 vols., STAC 9–10 (Tübingen: Mohr Siebeck, 2001), 1–4.
[26] William H. Race, "Aspects of Rhetoric and Form in Greek Hymns," *GRBS* 23 (1982): 5–14.

sonal engagement of the members of the Christ movement. In this perspective, "hymn" would emerge only later in the history of Christianity, at the time of a liturgical fixation of forms that is often understood as a first step towards "Catholicization" and towards what will become essentially a downward spiral of corruption. Thus, just to give a telling and only relatively surprising example, in the short labels that accompany papyrological pieces in the Leuven Database of Ancient Books almost all the "pagan" materials are designated as "hymns," while almost all the Christian texts are categorized as "prayers."[27] Such a distinction has an obvious theological genealogy that can be traced all the way back to the early Christian anti-pagan polemical attitude that emphasized spontaneity and personal participation over against the coldness and formality that would have characterized the "old" religions.[28] Such a traditional and schematic opposition has persisted in later centuries and has been further strengthened and naturalized since the Reformation with quite evident anti-Jewish and anti-Catholic overtones. The only exception to such a paradigm is constituted by the handful of New Testament passages that are routinely considered and called "hymns" (as in the above-mentioned case of Philippians 2): in these instances the designation is chosen to ennoble them as particularly significant literary products of the earliest Christ-movement. In recent years, however, more studies have shown that non-Christian religious practice involved as much personal engagement as the Christian ones, in particular in prayers and even, for instance, in the imperial cult, which had been previously cast as the paradigmatically negative model of a religious practices entirely formalistic and devoid of personal participation[29] In brief, the distinction between "hymn" and "prayer" (when not understood in purely performative or literary terms) appears to be more of a hindrance than an aid towards a more adequate apprehension of religious-historical phenomena.

Something similar can be said for the other distinction between "private" and "public," which is sometimes employed in talking about ancient prayers. Obviously, the very concept of "private" that is invoked here is a modern European creation and there are good grounds to suspect that it might be inadequate to grasp most of what was really going on in the ancient world. The papyrological record provides powerful evidence to substantiate such a suspect. Indeed, for instance, even though it is rather common to describe some papyri as "private letters," it is evident that these cannot be considered "private" in our modern sense of the term, since most ancient letters needed to be read by a third party to their addressees who were – in the overwhelming majority of the cases – illiterate (and this without examining the process through which "private letters"

---

[27] The Leuven Database of Ancient Books is found at https://www.trismegistos.org/ldab/.

[28] This is obviously visible already in Matthew 6, but more overtly in Tertullian's famous statement that *de pectore oramus* (*Apol.* 30.4), referring to the Christians.

[29] S. R. F. Price, "Gods and Emperors: the Greek Language of the Roman Imperial Cult," *JHS* 104 (1984): 79–95.

were written in the first place). Likewise, it seems quite misleading to conceive of any ancient hymn or prayer that has survived all the way down to us as "private." It does make sense to note that some texts became more widely known because they were inserted in formalized liturgies or in other cultic practices, but, as we have seen for some of the papyrological examples examined above, even some of the texts that have not enjoyed any broad popularity at all were clearly originally composed with a communal use as their goal.

Finally, a third point that needs to be made concerns the fact that prayer formulae are often more fixed and conservative than other literary genres. The principle is undoubtedly true, and Matthias Klinghardt has rightly insisted – in the above-mentioned article – on the fact that Christian prayers were no different in antiquity from the prayers of other religious groups under this respect. Obviously though, it must also be kept in mind that – in light of the relatively high number of new hymns and prayers that one encounters in the papyrological record – these texts could also be reshaped and composed anew all the time. The fact that ancient manuals of rhetoric contained prescriptions for the correct writing of hymns (accompanied by the fact that writers of hymns were often acknowledged and praised in inscriptions) demonstrates that the practice must have been very common. Indeed, one has shown above that prayers were required not just in order to fulfill the need of establishing correct communications with the divine, but also shape and strengthen the communal identity of various types of social groups. In this perspective, it cannot be considered unexpected or aberrant that also the village scribes behind Q included hymnic materials within their Gospel.

D. The Lord's Prayer as a Hymn

The previous observations have tried to build a circumstantial case in support of the hypothesis that the village scribes behind Q had at their disposal the cultural and rhetorical resources needed to compose hymns and prayers. Building further on the strength of this case, it still remains to evaluate whether any of the actual materials included in the Sayings Gospel are arranged in a way that recalls the formal characteristics of a hymn.

Thus, a suitable conclusion for the present contribution might be to explore the possibility that the Lord's Prayer be understood as a "hymn." As a first step one should evaluate whether the structure of the "prayer" follows the rhetorical paradigms that have been exposed before and is analogous to the exemplars encountered in the papyrological record or in other literary remains of the ancient world. Again, it is worth repeating that such a move does not imply that the Lord's Prayer should not be considered a Jewish text, since this examination will focus only on the rhetorical organization of the prayer and thus will be primarily comparative and not genealogical in nature.

It seems that this question is best approached by looking at the threefold structure that ancient textbooks presuppose for hymns (invocation – argument – prayer). However, I would like to suggest that hymnic traits are most conveniently identified not in the Lord's Prayer extrapolated from its Q context, but in the entire section Q 10:21–11:13, which does indeed form a relatively coherent sub-unit also from the point of view of its primary focus on communication with God.[30]

The section opens with an invocation (ἐξομολογοῦμαί σοι, πάτηρ, κύριε τοῦ οὐρανοῦ καὶ τῆς γῆς, "I thank you, father, lord of heaven and earth") that, while obviously steeped in Jewish traditional formulae employed to address God, is patently similar to many other invocations that can be encountered in ancient hymnic materials. Thus, for instance, the above-mentioned aretalogy of Isis preserved in P. Oxy. 1380 contains multiple references to the lordship of the Egyptian deity over the entire cosmos.[31] Moreover, it has been clear for quite some time – mostly thanks to a few pointed contributions of Mary Rose D'Angelo – that the mention of God as "father" in Q reflects and responds to concerns that are at the forefront of the Roman imperial political theological discourse of the time.[32] Finally, with respect to the invocation in Q 10:21 – and to the invocation to the "father" that opens the Lord's Prayer in Q 11:2b – it is often noted that the brevity of this formula contrasts with the fulsome enumeration of divine names and epithets that one encounters in most non-Jewish and non-Christian prayers. However, one should take into due consideration the fact that in our period – mostly under the influence of philosophical reflections on the rational significance of praying – one can detect a tendency not only to group diverse divine designations under henotheistic or even quasi-monotheistic expressions, but also simply to streamline lists that are sometimes perceived as excessively long.[33] In this perspective, a good example is offered by Cleanthes's famous hymn to Zeus, which contains both a reference to the god as "father" (v. 34) and as sovereign of nature (v. 2, Ζεῦ φύσεως ἀρχηγέ).[34]

The continuation in Q 10:21 (with its focus on the hiding of "these things" from the wise and learned and their revelation to "infants") and in v. 24 (with the

---

[30] Eckhard Rau, "Unser Vater im Himmel: eine These zur Metaphorik der Rede von Gott in der Logienquelle," *NovT* 53 (2011): 222–43.

[31] For instance, P. Oxy. 11 1380, col. I, r. 23 (ἄνασσαν); col. II, r. 36 (βασίλεισσαν); col. III, r. 57 (ἄνασσαν); col. VII, r. 142 (κύρια); col. XI, r. 248/249 (σὺ καὶ φωτὸς καὶ φλεγμάτων κύρια).

[32] Mary Rose D'Angelo, "Abba and 'Father': Imperial Theology and the Jesus Tradition," *JBL* 111 (1992): 611–30; eadem, "Theology in Mark and Q: Abba and 'Father' in Context," *HTR* 85 (1992): 149–74.

[33] Reinhard Feldmeier, "'Geheiligt werde dein Name': das Herrengebet im Kontext der paganen Gebetsliteratur," in *Das Vaterunser in seinen antiken Kontexten: zum Gedenken an Eduard Lohse*, ed. Florian Wilk, FRLANT 266 (Göttingen: Vandenhoeck & Ruprecht, 2016), 25–81.

[34] See the Greek text and comment in Johan C. Thom, *Cleanthes' Hymn to Zeus: Text, Translation, and Commentary*, STAC 33 (Tübingen: Mohr Siebeck, 2005), 43–52.

favorable contrast between kings and prophets of the past and the present audience of Jesus) constitutes the "argument" of the hymn, through the identification of the reasons that motivate the praising of God. While other types of arguments are decidedly more common in ancient hymns (in particular, the manuals of rhetoric indicate that one should praise the lineage of a deity or the benefits that the deity has brought to humankind), the revelation of secret knowledge is not altogether absent and anyway fits quite well the Jewish apocalyptic context in which the Q materials arguably originated. That being said, since hymns are often conceived as means through which humans enter into communication with deities, one must also note that putting emphasis on the distance separating divine greatness from human humbleness is a very common rhetorical device, designed to magnify the significance of the present instance of connection between deities and humans. A noteworthy example that leads towards an extreme form of negative theology occurs in Lucius's magnificent thanksgiving prayer to Isis in Apuleius's *Metamorphoses*:[35]

> But I am weak of intelligence to sing your praises and devoid of wealth to perform sacrifices in your honor; neither the eloquence of my voice is sufficient to say what I feel about your majesty nor would a thousand mouths and as many tongues or an eternal sequence of untiring speeches. Therefore I will concern myself with performing only what can be done by a person certainly faithful, but also poor: I will keep forever, hidden in the secret of my breast, the representation of your divine faces and of your most sacred power. (*Metam.* 11.25.5)

Even the brief interlude of Q 10:22 (which establishes the terms of the preferential relationship between God the father and Jesus the son, who is also introduced as the one who actually recites the hymn) is comparable to other ancient hymnic materials. It is indeed very common to encounter – at the beginning of hymns and prayers – relatively articulated rhetorical structures designed to establish the inspired nature of the author's voice. In most cases these rhetorical devices take the form of requests addressed to the Muses (as in the above-mentioned case of PSI 1482). However, some of the most complex mechanisms (and some of the most similar to what happens in Q 10:21–11:13) are deployed by Aelius Aristides in his prose hymns.[36] Quite often Aristides presents his hymns as the renditions in written form of "dreams" that he had previously received from

---

[35] At ego referendis laudibus tuis exilis ingenio et adhibendis sacrificiis tenuis patrimonio; nec mihi vocis ubertas ad dicendas, quae de tua maiestate sentio, sufficit nec ora mille linguaeque totidem vel indefessi sermonis aeterna series. Ergo quod solum potest religiosus quidem, sed pauper alioquin, efficere curabo: divinos tuos vultus numenque sacratissimum intra pectoris mei secreta conditum perpetuo custodiens imaginabor (*Metam.* 11.25.5). Text and translation from Apuleius, *Metamorphoses*, 2 vols., ed. and trans. J. Arthur Hanson, LCL 44, 453 (Cambridge, MA: Harvard University Press, 2014).

[36] These have been analyzed with exquisite insightfulness by Janet Downie, *At the Limits of Art: A Literary Study of Aelius Aristides'* Hieroi Logoi (Oxford: Oxford University Press, 2013), 127–53.

the gods, so that his voice becomes effectively that of the deity and his speeches become oracles (and indeed they are designated as *manteutai* by Menander the Rhetor). For instance, the prose hymn to Athena opens with a statement that also reflects what we have observed above with respect to the combination of "hymn" and "prayer":

> Let the dream be a waking vision for us. And you, o sovereign Athena, grant the other fortune and grace, and touch the present speech, and bring to completion, as they deserve, the visions, as they were shown manifestly at night. So that the visions may indeed be clear and assured, you will have now a speech with a mixture of prayer and hymn. (Aelius Aristides, *Speeches* 37.1)[37]

The function of the actual "prayer" in the hymnic section Q 10:21–11:13 is the easiest one to identify, since the requests contained in the Lord's Prayer (Q 11:2b–4) clearly do perform that function. In truth, there is little need to provide detailed textual examples to show how widespread similar requests for concrete benefits (success of one's own political party, food, and debt relief) are in the ancient literary record pertaining to prayers and hymns.

One last question is worth addressing before bringing this too short treatment to a conclusion. The final verses of the section examined so far (Q 11:9–13) are not certainly part of a hymn, but – as it has been observed by Ronald Piper a few years ago – they contain an argumentative development on the significance and appropriate way of praying.[38] That hymns might be built within larger rhetorical structures is not very common, but not completely unusual either, since after all – as we have seen above – the composition of prayers was presented as part of the general rhetorical training in ancient textbooks. A good example of something similar to what happens in Q is the famous hymn to divine providence that is included in Epictetus's first book of his *Diatribes*. The Stoic philosopher places this prayer at the end of his argument contending that the entire cosmos is ordered in a way that is beneficial for humans and as such their task should be principally and continually that of thanking the divine for such an arrangement:

> If we had reason, what else should we do but to sing hymns to the divine both publicly and privately and praise it and go over its graces? When we dig and when we till and when we eat, should not we sing the hymn to god: 'Great is god, because he provided us with these tools through which we work the fields?' […] But I am a rational being: I must sing hymns

---

[37] Ἔστω τοίνυν ἡμῖν ὕπαρ τὸ ὄναρ· σὺ δ', ὦ δέσποινα Ἀθηνᾶ, τήν τε ἄλλην δίδου τύχην καὶ χάριν καὶ τοῦ παρόντος ἔψαυαι λόγου, τά τε φανθέντα τέλει πρὸς τὴν ἀξίαν, ὡς ἐναργῆ τῆς νυκτὸς ἐδείκνυτο· ὡς δὲ καὶ ἔργῳ συμβῆναι σαφῆ καὶ βέβαια, ὅδε σοὶ λόγος ἔσται μικτὸς εὐχῆς τε καὶ ὕμνου τὰ νῦν (Aelius Aristides, *Speeches* 37.1). Text from Bruno Keil, ed., *Aelii Aristidis Smyrnaei Quae Supersunt Omnia* (Hildesheim: Weidmann, 2000 [1898]); translation my own.

[38] Ronald A. Piper, "Matthew 7:7–11 par. Luke 11:9–13: Evidence of Design and Argument in the Collection of Jesus' Sayings," in *The Shape of Q: Signal Essays on the Sayings Gospel*, ed. John S. Kloppenborg (Minneapolis: Fortress, 1994), 131–37.

to the god. That is my job: I perform it and I will not abandon this post until it will be given to me, and I exhort you to sing the same song. (Epictetus, *Diatr.* 1.16.15–21)[39]

Despite their structural similarities, the two passages have a different organization, since for Epictetus the hymn concludes the argument and contributes *pathos* to the rhetorical construction, while the argument developed in Q 11:9–13 seems to push in a direction that is atypical for prayers, opposing human agency to divine agency.[40] As Niclas Förster has recently demonstrated, Luke will subtly rework the entire passage redactionally in a way that will bring it more in line with the mainstream of ancient philosophical reflection on prayer.[41]

E. Conclusions

The present contribution has examined the possibility that the prayers included in Q might have been composed or reshaped by the village scribes who put together the Sayings Gospel. Egyptian papyri demonstrate that similar texts were normally composed by intellectuals with a socio-cultural profile comparable to that of the Q people. Moreover, writing hymns and prayers was an exercise that was regularly included in ancient basic rhetorical manuals such as the *progymnasmata*. Finally, one can observe that Q 10:21–11:13 is a unit whose rhetorical and argumentative structure recalls the one recommended in textbooks of rhetoric for the composition of hymns and shows indeed significant similarities with the extant hymnic materials dating from the early Roman period.

---

[39] Εἰ γὰρ νοῦν εἴχομεν, ἄλλο τι ἔδει ἡμᾶς ποιεῖν καὶ κοινῇ καὶ ἰδίᾳ ἢ ὑμνεῖν τὸ θεῖον καὶ εὐφημεῖν καὶ ἐπεξέρχεσθαι τὰς χάριτας; οὐκ ἔδει καὶ σκάπτοντας καὶ ἀροῦντας καὶ ἐσθίοντας ᾄδειν τὸν ὕμνον τὸν εἰς τὸν θεόν; 'μέγας ὁ θεός, ὅτι ἡμῖν παρέσχεν ὄργανα ταῦτα δι' ὧν τὴν γῆν ἐργασόμεθα. [...] Νῦν δὲ λογικός εἰμι: ὑμνεῖν με δεῖ τὸν θεόν. τοῦτό μου τὸ ἔργον ἐστίν, ποιῶ αὐτὸ οὐδ' ἐγκαταλείψω τὴν τάξιν ταύτην, ἐφ' ὅσον ἂν διδῶται, καὶ ὑμᾶς ἐπὶ τὴν αὐτὴν ταύτην ᾠδὴν παρακαλῶ (Epictetus, *Diatr.* 1.16.15–21). Text and translation from Epictetus, *The Discourses as Reported by Arrian*, 2 vols., trans. W. A. Oldfather, LCL 131, 218 (Cambridge, MA: Harvard University Press, 2000).

[40] Giovanni B. Bazzana, "Violence and Human Prayer to God in Q 11," *HTS* 70 (2014): 1–8.

[41] Niclas Förster, *Das gemeinschaftliche Gebet in der Sicht des Lukas*, BTS 4 (Leuven: Peeters, 2007), 254–73.

The Lord's Prayer and Debt Recovery

Insights from Graeco-Egyptian Papyri

John S. Kloppenborg

The Lord's Prayer is widely known, more frequently cited in its longer Matthaean form (Matt 6:9–10; Did 8:1–2) than in its more abbreviated but undoubtedly more original Q and Lukan forms (11:2–4).[1] Consistent with the structure of prayers, both Near Eastern and Greek, it begins with an invocation of the deity (πάτερ),[2] followed by statements that claim the deity's attention by displaying the speaker's loyalty (two cohortatives in Q and Luke, three in Matthew), and then the actual petitions (three in Q and Luke, and two pairs of petitions in Matthew).[3]

It has been common to stress the "eschatological" nature of the Lord's prayer, which might more appropriately be termed its "apocalyptic" orientation insofar as, in the words of Raymond Brown, the prayer invokes the "period of the last days, involving the return of Christ, the destruction of the forces of evil, and the

---

[1] The bibliography on the Lord's Prayer is enormous. See James H. Charlesworth, Mark Harding, and Mark Kiley, eds., *The Lord's Prayer and Other Prayer Texts from the Greco-Roman Era* (Valley Forge, PA: Trinity Press International, 1994) and Mark Kiley, ed., *Prayer from Alexander to Constantine: A Critical Anthology* (London: Routledge, 1997).

[2] R. M. Ogilvie, *The Romans and Their Gods in the Age of Augustus*, Ancient Culture and Society (London: Chatto & Windus, 1969), 24 amusingly, but not inaccurately, quips, "Gods, like dogs, will answer only to their names. ... The invocation of a god by name has always been a central feature of prayer and magic." While this is a greater problem in polytheistic systems than in monotheistic systems, since Greek and Roman gods have varying competences, in monotheistic systems it is nonetheless important to attract the deity's attention by employing an epithet that belongs to the deity.

[3] Karl Ausfeld, "De graecorum precationibus quaestiones," *Neue Jahrbücher Supplement* 28 (1903): 502–47, here 515–16: *invocatio, pars epica, precatio*. In contrast to modern (Christian) practices of prayer, which include both private and silent prayer, prayer (εὔχεσθαι) in Greek needed to attract the deity's attention, since it could not be assumed that the deity was omniscient, omnipresent, or omni-attentive. Hence, the prayer typically begins with an address to the deity, followed by statements that either praise the deity (thus indicating the speaker's piety) or remind the deity of the supplicant's piety, or recall prior favourable responses of the deity, all before the requests are made. As H. S. Versnel puts it, "the god had frequently to be persuaded to come nearer so that he could really hear the voice of the supplicant": "Religious Mentality in Ancient Prayer," in *Faith, Hope and Worship: Aspects of Religious Mentality in the Ancient World*, ed. Hendrik S. Versnel, SGRR 2 (Leiden: Brill, 1981), 1–64, here 25.

definite establishment of God's rule."[4] Brown's reading, which focused on the longer Matthaean prayer, of course receives possible support from the second imperative, ἐλθέτω ἡ βασιλεία σου, which could be interpreted in a thoroughly apocalyptic manner. This encouraged Brown to pursue a thoroughly apocalyptic reading for the entire Matthaean version of the prayer. The first petition, τὸν ἄρτον ἡμῶν τὸν ἐπιούσιον δὸς ἡμῖν σήμερον, Brown understood to invoke the eschatological banquet, though he recognized that Luke's version, which uses the present imperative δίδου ("keep giving") and καθ' ἡμέραν ("daily"), are iterative and noneschatological and suggests that for Luke an original apocalyptic outlook gave way to more pressing concerns with daily subsistence.[5] The second petition concerning reciprocal debt relief, according to Brown, takes on an apocalyptic cast especially when seen in the context of the Matthaean (redactional) judgement parables, Matt 18:23–35 (on the "unforgiving slave") and Matt 25:31–46, both of which conclude with dramatic scenes of torture and eternal punishment.[6]

Brown's reading of the final Q petition (and second last Matthaean petition) likewise emphasizes the aorists (μὴ εἰσενέγῃς, ῥῦσαι) which in his view excludes the notion of daily temptations and points instead to a final test such as the apocalyptic θλῖψις of Mark 13:19 or the πειρασμός of Rev 3:10.[7]

Although Brown's reading of the prayer is perhaps plausible as an exegesis of the Matthaean prayer, there are some reasons to doubt his reading as it pertains to Q. Eduard Schweizer, commenting on Matthew rather than Q, gave cause to doubt the thoroughly eschatological reading, at least for the original prayer:

First, Jesus paid attention to earthly needs and their alleviation; second, the next petition, and probably the following one [i. e., Matt 6:12, 13], refer unambiguously to this world, where [people] wrong each other and must find again the path of reconciliation; and third, if the plea [for bread] were eschatological the word "our" would be out of place.

---

[4] Raymond E. Brown, "The *Pater Noster* as an Eschatological Prayer," in idem, *New Testament Essays* (Milwaukee: Bruce, 1965), 217–53, here 217. Brown treats all the imperatives and cohortatives as "petitions," not distinguishing the function of the cohortatives (ἁγιασθήτω, ἐλθέτω, γενηθήτω), which as I have suggested function to attract the deity's attention, from the imperatives (δός, ἄφες, μὴ εἰσενέγκῃς, ῥῦσαι), which are the actual petitions. Hence, I when I enumerate the petitions, I refer only to the imperatives.

[5] Brown, "Pater Noster," 239. In agreement with Brown's "eschatological" interpretation of the first petition, see Donald A. Hagner, *Matthew*, 2 vols., WBC 33A–B (Dallas: Word, 1993–1995), 1:149; W. D. Davies and Dale C. Allison, *A Critical and Exegetical Commentary on Matthew*, 3 vols., ICC (Edinburgh: T & T Clark, 1988–1997), 1:595 (tentatively).

[6] Brown, "Pater Noster," 246–47.

[7] Ibid., 251; similarly, Joachim Jeremias, *The Prayers of Jesus*, SBT 2/6 (Naperville, IL: Allenson, 1967), 105–6: "This word (πειρασμός in Greek) does not mean the little temptations or testings of everyday life, but the great Testing which stands at the door and will extend over the whole earth – the disclosure of the mystery of evil, the revelation of the Antichrist, the abomination of desolation ..., the final persecution and testing of God's saints by pseudo-prophets and false saviours .... The final trial at the end is – apostasy."

Furthermore, wine and fat meat – not bread – are characteristic of the eschatological banquet.[8]

Schweizer's objection appears to presuppose an entirely otherworldly conception of apocalyptic eschatology, as if it refers to a state in which hunger – "earthly needs" as he calls them – and reconciliation are entirely irrelevant, since the imagined state of existence is completely discontinuous with temporal existence. This is hardly the only understanding of the apocalyptic imagination, which might just as well conceive of a state of a renewed temporal existence with material abundance and rectified social relationships. Moreover, on Schweizer's last point, the restoration of manna, and not only wine and meat, was sometimes imagined as a harbinger of the eschatological age, as Davies and Allison note.[9] But Schweizer's objection is nonetheless strong. The appearance of the apparent *hapax*, ἐπιούσιος modifying ἄρτος ἡμῶν, if the adjective means "today's" (i. e., the coming day's bread), orients the petition to the needs of daily subsistence and with that, a strong connection with eschatological expectation disappears.[10]

Giovanni Bazzana has recently offered a way forward in the interpretation of the Q prayer.[11] The connection between the βασιλεία (that is, governance) and debt relief is found in numerous documentary papyri from the Ptolemaic period and articulate the notion that debt remission is part of the ruler's responsibility in establishing and maintaining just rule. Bazzana not only documented instances in which ἀφίημι and the root ὀφειλ- appeared together, referring to release from debts,[12] but, more importantly, several papyri that connect the βασιλεία with fair treatment of taxes and debts or even general amnesty from debts (πάντας τῶν ὀφειλομένων) and crimes (ἁμαρτημ[άτ]ων).[13] These were was not simply amnesties from debts to the Crown, but all debts, employed as a strategy to stabilize society especially in the wake of civil unrest. We can add that

---

[8] Eduard Schweizer, *The Good News According to Matthew*, trans. David E. Green (Atlanta: John Knox, 1975), 154.

[9] Davies and Allison, *Matthew*, 1:609–10.

[10] The unusual nature of ἐπιούσιος was already remarked by Origen (*Or.* 27.7). Some supposed that there was a nearly contemporaneous occurrence in SB 5224.20; the papyrus, once thought to have been lost, has now been identified as P. Yale inv. 19, and the original reading, ιε – επιουσι[ων] C, (i. e., day 15, dr. for the day's expenses) has now been corrected to ιε – ελαίου [[- (-οβολ.)]], "on the 15th: for oil [[cancelled text]]." See M. Nijman and Klaas A. Worp, "ΕΠΙΟΥΣΙΟΣ in a Documentary Papyrus?," in *NovT* 41 (1999): 231–34. This leaves as a plausible conjecture for ἐπιούσιος a derivation from ἐπιέναι "to come to," "to belong to," i. e., "for the following day," "in the sense of 'today'" (Davies and Allison, *Matthew*, 1:609). Davies and Allison recognize that this does not strongly support an eschatological interpretation, but try to rescue an apocalyptic nuance with an equation of ἄρτος = (eschatological) manna. But the ἡμῶν makes this reading far from the obvious one.

[11] Giovanni B. Bazzana, "*Basileia* and Debt Relief: The Forgiveness of Debts in the Lord's Prayer in the Light of Documentary Papyri," in *CBQ* 73 (2011): 511–25.

[12] E. g., P. Köln VII 313, 24–25.

[13] C. Ord.Ptol. 53 and SB 8.9899 and Bazzana, "Basileia and Debt Relief," 516–17.

this strategy is attested not only in Egypt: Suetonius' account of Caesar's actions at the end of the civil war likewise indicate that Caesar returned to Rome there was a general expectation that he would abolish all debts – an expectation that he in fact disappointed, opting instead only to fix the value of the debt at their prewar levels rather than potentially inflated figures.[14] Bazzana observes:

> Egyptian and Hellenistic royal ideologies alike [we might add Roman too] envisage an ideal sovereign figure, for whom providing relief to the people in times of distress is just one aspect of a general policy of attention to the needs of cosmic and civic life.[15]

It is not difficult to see that the second petition of Q's prayer imagines a similar practice that associates the βασιλεία with the release of debts and amnesty for various crimes. Yet Bazzana notes the novelty of Q's evocation of this notion of the sovereign's role in debt forgiveness, since Q frames its request as a response to the initiative that humans take toward debt: ὡς καὶ ἡμεῖς ἀφήκαμεν τοῖς ὀφειλέταις ἡμῶν.

Surprisingly enough, this structure has undergone a significant inversion in the Lord's Prayer: instead of applying the divine standard to human behavior, the text goes in the opposite direction by inviting the members of the community to give an example that God will follow. This formulation might have been particularly effective in unsettling Greco-Roman ideas concerning sovereignty and its ideological justifications.[16]

---

[14] Suetonius, *Jul.* 42.2: *de pecuniis mutuis disiecta nouarum tabularum expectatione, quae crebro mouebatur, decreuit tandem, ut debitores creditoribus satis facerent per aestimationem possessionum, quanti quasque ante ciuile bellum comparassent, deducto summae aeris alieni, si quid usurae nomine numeratum aut perscriptum fuisset; qua condicione quarta pars fere crediti deperibat.* "With respect to debts, he disappointed the expectation which was generally entertained, that they would be totally cancelled; and ordered that the debtors should satisfy their creditors, according to the valuation of their estates, at the rate at which they were purchased before the commencement of the civil war." Similarly, Appian, *Bell. civ.* 2.48: ... αἰτοῦσι δ' αὐτοῖς καὶ χρεῶν ἀποκοπὰς διά τε πολέμους καὶ στάσεις καὶ τὴν ἐκ τῶνδε τοῖς πιπρασκομένοις ἐποῦσαν εὐωνίαν, τὰς μὲν ἀποκοπὰς οὐκ ἔδωκε, τιμητὰς δὲ τῶν ὠνίων ἀπέφηνεν, ὧν ἔδει τοὺς χρήστας τοῖς δανείσασιν ἀντὶ τῶν χρημάτων διδόναι .... "[Returning to Rome], when [Caesar] was asked to decree an abolition of debts, on the ground that the wars and seditions had caused a fall of prices, he refused it, but appointed appraisers of vendible goods which debtors might give to their creditors instead of money." This provision came to be known as the *Lex Iulia de bonis cedendis* (Codex Iustinianus 7.71.4).

[15] Bazzana, "Basileia and Debt Relief," 522. That debt relief was not restricted to Ptolemaic practice is indicated by similar provisions mentioned in Herodotus, *Hist.* 6.59 and 1 Macc 13:36–39. For debt relief in a Roman context, see Tonio Hölscher, "The Concept of Roles and the Malaise of 'Identity': Ancient Rome and the Modern World," in *Role Models in the Roman World: Identity and Assimilation*, ed. Sinclair Bell and Inge Lyse Hansen, MAAR.S 7 (Ann Arbor: University of Michigan Press, 2008), 41–56: the *Anaglypha Traiani* in front of public buildings of the Forum Romanum shows the public burning of the debt records. See also Ann L. Kuttner, *Dynasty and Empire in the Age of Augustus: The Case of the Boscoreale Cups* (Berkeley, CA: University of California Press, 1995), 44–45.

[16] Bazzana, "Basileia and Debt Relief," 524. It might be noted that another such inversion occurs in the measure-for-measure saying (Q 6:36–37), which invokes the common practice of repaying a loan of grain with the same scoop (μέτρον) with which it was initially measured

It could be added that a similar notion of the coordination between human and divine action is attested at Qumran in connection with expectations of the Jubilee:

[Every creditor] who [has] lent something [to] someone, or [who possesses something from his brother] will grant a re[lease (יש[מיט ידו)](#) to his fellow, for [God], your [God had proclaimed the release (תקרא שמטה). You are to demand restitution] from the foreigner, but from your brother you shall not demand restitution, for in that year [God will bless you, forgiving you your iniquities ([לכפר לכם [את עוונ]תיכם]). (1 QDM [1Q22] III, 5–7, quoting Deut 15:1–3)[17]

Bazzana has, I think, established a connection between mention of the kingdom in Q 11:2 and debt forgiveness and other kinds of amnesties in Q 11:4a. The implication of his work goes beyond this, however. Since he has shown that the establishment of a βασιλεία and debt relief was part of the ideology of governance in the Hellenistic period, and not reserved only to futuristic and utopian expectations, the fact that Q's prayer invokes the coming of the kingdom does not necessarily connect it with a Danielic or Enochic kingdom or with Brown's "destruction of the forces of evil, and the definite establishment of God's rule."[18]

This brings us back to the older problem of whether the βασιλεία of Jesus was apocalyptic, or "sich realisierenden Eschatologie" (to use Jeremias' term), or "realized" or some other option. I do not wish to become mired in this question, which probably has no convincing resolution and is implicated in non-historical, theological debates.[19] What concerns me here is the final petition.

A. Μὴ εἰσενέγκῃς εἰς πειρασμόν

The final petition, καὶ μὴ εἰσενέγκῃς ἡμᾶς εἰς πειρασμόν, which Brown and others have interpreted in a strong apocalyptic sense of θλῖψις, has also been subjected to scrutiny. Ulrich Luz, however, objects:

---

out. But the saying is framed from the point of view not of the borrower, but the lender (who "measures out"), and is turned into an injunction to the lender to "show mercy" (Q 6:36) on the calculable outcome that she or he will then receive mercy. See John S. Kloppenborg, "Agrarian Discourse in the Sayings of Jesus," in *Engaging Economics: New Testament Scenarios and Early Christian Interpretation*, ed. Bruce W. Longenecker and Kelly D. Liebengood (Grand Rapids: Eerdmans, 2009), 104–28.

[17] See John S. Kloppenborg, "Discursive Practices in the Sayings Gospel Q and the Quest of the Historical Jesus," in *The Sayings Source Q and the Historical Jesus*, ed. Andreas Lindemann, BETL 158 (Leuven: Peeters, 2001), 149–90, here 177.

[18] Brown, "Pater Noster," 217.

[19] See John S. Kloppenborg, ed., *Apocalypticism, Anti-Semitism, and the Historical Jesus: Subtexts in Criticism*, with John W. Marshall, JSHJ.S/JSNTSup 275 (London: T & T Clark International, 2005).

Almost everything speaks against this view. Neither in Jewish apocalypticism nor in the NT is πειρασμός an apocalyptic technical term. Furthermore, the definite article that one then would expect is missing, and the Jewish parallels lead one to think of the temptations one meets in everyday life.[20]

For Luz and others, the temptations are those "one meets in everyday life."

Most commentators have been preoccupied in this verse by the aorist, μὴ εἰσενέγκῃς, which imputes agency to the deity in the causation of testing or temptation,[21] either opting for a weakened interpretation ("do not let us *succumb* to temptation"[22]) or a permissive interpretation ("do not allow us to be tested"[23])

---

[20] Ulrich Luz, *Matthew 1–7: A Commentary*, Hermeneia (Minneapolis: Fortress, 2007), 322, citing b. Ber. 60b: "On going to bed one says from 'Hear, O Israel' to 'And it shall come to pass if you hearken diligently'. Then one says ... May it be your will, O Lord, my God, to make me lie down in peace, and set my portion in your law and accustom me to the performance of religious duties, but do not accustom me to transgression; and bring me not into sin, or into iniquity, or into temptation (ולא לידי נסיון), or into contempt." See also 11QPs[a] XXIV, 10: "Remember me and forget me not, and lead me not into situations that are too hard for me"; James A. Sanders, ed., *The Psalms Scroll of Qumran Cave 11 (11QPsA)*, DJD 4 (Oxford: Clarendon, 1965), 71.

[21] See the survey of options, including attempts of modern translations to avoid the problem in Joseph A. Fitzmyer, "And Lead Us Not into Temptation," *Bib* 84 (2003): 259–73.

[22] Origen, *Or.* 29.11: χρὴ τοίνυν εὔχεσθαι οὐχ ἵνα μὴ πειρασθῶμεν (τοῦτο γὰρ ἀδύνατον) ἀλλ' ἵνα μὴ ὑπὸ τοῦ πειρασμοῦ περιβληθῶμεν, ὅπερ πάσχουσιν οἱ ἐνεχόμενοι αὐτῷ καὶ νενικημένοι. "We ought therefore to pray, not that we not be tempted – that is impossible – but that we be not encompassed by temptation, which those who are open to it and are overcome experience." See Jeremias, *Prayers*, 95; Robert H. Gundry, *Matthew: A Commentary on His Literary and Theological Art* (Grand Rapids: Eerdmans, 1982), 109. Jeremias later (*Prayers*, 105) argues "thus this reference in the final petition of the Lord's Prayer is indeed not to be preservation *from* temptation but to preservation *in* temptation, corroborated by an ancient extra-canonical saying of Jesus which, according to ancient tradition, Jesus spoke on that last evening, prior to the prayer in Gethsemane: 'No one can obtain the kingdom of heaven who has not passed through temptation,'" citing Tertullian, *Bapt.* 20.2; see Reginald H. Fuller, ed., trans., *Unknown Sayings of Jesus*, 2nd ed. (London: SPCK, 1964), 73–75.

[23] E. g., Tertullian, *Or.* 8.1, who cites the prayer, *ne nos inducas in temptationem*, but then clarifies: *id est, ne nos patiaris induci ab eo utique qui temptat*, "Do not allow us to be led into temptation by him who tempts [i. e., the devil]"; text from Tertullian, *Opera I: Opera catholica; Adversus Marcionem*, ed. E. Dekkers et al., CCSL 1 (Turnhout: Brepols, 1954). See also Didymus the Blind, *Comm. Ps.* 22–26:10, in Michael Gronewald, ed., trans., *Didymos der Blinde, Psalmenkommentar 2: Kommentar zu Psalm 22–26,10*, PTA 4 (Bonn: Habelt, 1968), 246: "μὴ εἰσενέγκῃς ἡμᾶς εἰς πειρασμόν". μὴ γὰρ τοῦτο λέγουσιν· "μὴ ἐάσῃς ἡμᾶς θλιβῆναι". ἐὰν τοῦτο ᾖ{ν}, οὐδέποτε ἠλήθευσαν οἱ ἀπόστολοι λέγοντες· ‹"ἐν παντὶ θλιβόμενοι"›. τὸ μὴ εἰσελθεῖν οὖν εἰς πειρασμὸν τοῦτο λέγομεν τὸ μὴ ἁλῶναι τῷ βουλήματι τοῦ πειράζοντος. "'Do not lead us to temptation.' For they do not say 'do not allow us to suffer tribulation,' for if that were so, the apostles would not be speaking truly when they say 'in every tribulation.' Not entering into temptation therefore is not to be caught by in the will of the tempter." See Marie-Joseph Lagrange, *L'Évangile selon saint Matthieu*, 4th ed., EBib (Paris: Gabalda, 1927), 131. Hagner, *Matthew*, 1:151 and John Nolland, *The Gospel of Matthew: A Commentary on the Greek Text*, NIGTC (Grand Rapids: Eerdmans, 2005), 292 both prefer "test" to "temptation" on the grounds that "God does not lead into temptation" (citing Jas 1:13).

or, with Luz, simply concluding that the Greek translator of the prayer did not worry about whether the verb was causative or permissive.[24]

More than forty years ago, C. F. D. Moule pointed out a more serious problem: "It is intelligible enough to pray, 'Do not let us succumb to temptation when we are brought to the test'; but 'Do not let us even be brought to testing' is harder to explain."[25] Moule rejects the apocalyptic interpretation of πειρασμός, both on the grounds that the definite article is missing and because, apart from Rev 3:10 where the qualifying phrase, τῆς μελλούσης ἔρχεσθαι ἐπὶ τῆς οἰκουμένης ὅλης, makes its apocalyptic sense clear, πειρασμός *simpliciter* does not have an apocalyptic sense at all. Nor does the term mean an enticement to sin.[26] The first instance of πειρασμός with the sense of "temptation" as an interior condition of the ψυχή provoked by emotions is James 1:14, probably at the beginning of the second century CE, and Herm. Mand. 9.1.7, where in both cases πειρασμός stands in parallel with διψυχία and thus points to an interior mental condition.[27] Since Moule supposes that the petition takes for granted that testing, whatever its source and whatever its intended effect, is inevitable, he renews the question, "what is the logic of praying for exemption? Would it not be about as logical as saying 'We know we are at war; but let there be no fighting!'?"[28]

What Moule does not remark is that πειρασμός is oddly undetermined. This means that once one has rejected the apocalyptic nuance of the "test," neither Moule nor any other interpreter offers any characterization of *what kind of test* might be in view. This only compounds the issue to which Moule draws attention: that praying not to be led to testing is even more illogical if one has no inkling of what sort of test there might be.

Πειρασμός in fact is a peculiar term insofar as it does not occur in Greek literature prior to the Septuagint or in papyri and inscriptions prior to the fifth century CE, and in the common era mainly appears in connection with biblical citations. It is found in the Septuagint in several specific contexts where its connotations are determined by juxtaposition with other terms: abuse, war, burning, occasions of fear, humiliation, and betrayal or in allusions to certain events such

---

[24] Luz, *Matthew 1–7*, 323.

[25] C. F. D. Moule, "Unsolved Problem in the Temptation-Clause in the Lord's Prayer," in *RTR* 33 (1974), 66–75, here 66.

[26] Moule, "Unsolved Problem," 66–67.

[27] Jas 1:14: ἕκαστος δὲ πειράζεται ὑπὸ τῆς ἰδίας ἐπιθυμίας ἐξελκόμενος καὶ δελεαζόμενος. This representation of πειρασμοί as interior states of the soul is likely due to Stoic influence. See John S. Kloppenborg, "James 1:2–15 and Hellenistic Psychagogy," in *NovT* 52 (2010): 37–71; Richard Sorabji, *Emotion and Peace of Mind: From Stoic Agitation to Christian Temptation* (Oxford: Oxford University Press, 2000).

[28] Moule, "Unsolved Problem," 71. Moule's own solution is that though illogical, the petition points to a psychological issue: "Is it, then, true humility not to intellectualise, not to be over-logical, but, realizing one's weakness, to pray for escape even from what seems inevitable ('all these things that are going to happen'), while, at the same time, offering one's obedience: Thy will be done'?"

as the sacrifice of Isaac.²⁹ These juxtapositions indicates clearly that πειρασμοί are neither simply daily annoyances nor do they in the first instance refer to interior mental states ("temptations"), even though obviously such circumstances as abuse, war, and betrayal no doubt provoke certain mental states. Moreover, the nature of the events with which πειρασμός is paired puts into question whether πειρασμοί, although they are clearly very adverse circumstances, are imagined to be inevitable. The only text that claims that testing is inevitable is Sirach 2:1, where the author promises that πειρασμοί should be expected in the scribal profession. One suspects that the reason that exegetes such as Moule tend to conclude that πειρασμοί are inevitable is due to a slippage between the notion of πειρασμός as "test" and the later usage that refers to an interior "temptation."

In the few early occurrences of the term outside of Judaean and early Christian literature, its connotations are likewise set by context. Cyranides, a treatise on healing properties of stones, plants and animals attributed to Harpokration of Alexandria (second century CE, but compiled in the fourth century) comments on the hair that is found between the nose and mouth of seals, claiming that it delivers the subject from "every grievous necessity and 'thunderbolt' and hazard and every storm and crisis, of the seas or storms, or πειρασμοί whether on land or sea or from demons or from every disease."³⁰ Ptolemaeus Ascalonius, a first century BCE grammarian, in his list of verbs that have similar meanings, distinguishes σῴζειν (save) from ρῦσαι (deliver): one is saved from diseases and πειρασμοί (but) delivered from captivity and from demons. Ptolemaeus plainly treats πειρασμοί as serious challenges, comparable to disease; but his distinction also aligns πειρασμοί with adverse circumstances that befall a person, in contrast

---

²⁹ At Exod 17:7 (paired with λοιδόρησις, abuse); in Deut 6:16 and Ps 94:8 the allusion is to the "testing" of the deity at Meribah; Deut 4:34 pairs the term with πόλεμος; Deut 7:19 and 29:2, with τὰ σημεῖα καὶ τὰ τέρατα as occasions for fear; 9:22, with ἐμπυρισμός (burning); 1 Macc 2:52 alludes to Abraham's test at the sacrifice of Isaac; in Sir 2:1 it is associated with ἐπαγωγή (distress) and ταπείνωσις (humiliation); 6:7, associated with betrayal of friendship; in 27:5, the testing of speech is compared with testing (δοκιμάζειν) pottery in a kiln; 27:7, testing is through the evaluation of speech; in 33:1 it is associated with κακόν (evil); in 44:20, it is probably an allusion to the sacrifice of Isaac.

³⁰ Cyranides, 1.21: ἀπὸ πάσης ἀνάγκης χαλεπῆς καὶ κεραυνοῦ καὶ κινδύνου καὶ πάσης ζάλης καὶ περιστάσεως θαλασσίων κινδύνων καὶ πειρασμῶν ἔν τε γῇ καὶ θαλάσσῃ καὶ ἀπὸ δαιμόνων καὶ πάσης νόσου; text from Dimitris V. Kaimakes, ed., *Die Kyraniden* (Meisenheim am Glan: Hain, 1976). The sea and its dangers are also invoked in Anon., *in Arist. Rhet.* 103.9 (on Aristotle, *Rhet.* 2.5 1383a. 18): διχῶς οἱ ἄνθρωποι γίνονται ἀπαθεῖς ἤτοι θαρραλέοι, ἢ τῷ μηδέποτε πεπειρᾶσθαι κακοῦ– καὶ διὰ τοῦτο, κἂν πειρασμοῖς ἐμπέσωσι, θαρροῦσιν ἀποφυγεῖν – ἢ ἐν τῷ ἔχειν βοηθείας πολλάς, δι' ὧν ἀποφύγωσι τὰ δεινά· [a29] ὥσπερ εἴ τις ἐν θαλάσσῃ περιπέσῃ κλύδωνι ἄπειρος τοῦ χειμῶνος ἤτοι μὴ ἰδών ποτε κλύδωνα καὶ τὰ ἐκ τούτου κακά, θαρρεῖ περὶ τὸ μέλλον, ὡς οὐ κινδυνεύσει, "In two ways people are impassive or bold, either by never being tested by evil and therefore, even if they fall into adverse circumstances (πειρασμοί), they are courageous enough to escape, or by having much assistance though which they escape whatever it was. For example, is someone who has not experience of winter should fall into the waves of the sea, or not knowing anything of billows and the dangers that these represent, is brave about what will happen, as if it will be no danger."

to instances of active aggression.³¹ It is worth pointing out that Matthew's addition of Matt 6:13b, which, in agreement with Ptolemaeus connects ῥῦσαι with an aggressive agent, ὁ πονηρός, also recontextualizes his use of πειρασμός, aligning it more closely with the world of hostile cosmic forces. Thus Matthew's deployment of πειρασμός moves it closer to the realms of demonic attack (Matt 13:39) and apocalyptic conflicts (Matt 25:41).

From this brief survey one can conclude that the connotations of πειρασμός are potentially broad: on the one hand, the term always denotes serious adverse circumstances rather than trivial daily "temptations," and on the other, the term normally travels in the semantic company of other terms that lend it its specific connotations in any given literary or performative context. Πειρασμός, then, to paraphrase a mediaeval maxim, "hat eine Nase aus Wachs."

B. Πειρασμός and Debt Collection

This immediately raises the question of how to read πειρασμός in Q 11:4, in the absence of the Matthaean context and its parallels between εἰσφέρω and ῥύομαι and between πειρασμός and ὁ πονηρός. Without the Matthaean addition the most obvious context for Q's πειρασμός is set by the semantic domains of hunger (Q 11:3) and debt (11:4a), domains that are also conceptually related and both of which represent adverse circumstances. Q's extended rationale for prayer in 11:9–13 focuses on the issue of hunger – that is, asking for "bread" and "fish." But the most immediate context for πειρασμός is set by the mention of debt in 11:4a.³²

Graeco-Egyptian papyri provide important contextualizations for the issues of debt and debt-forgiveness, as Bazzana has shown; they also provide some insight into the dramas and traumas that were associated with debt-collection, and supply a considerable volume of knowledge about debt, debt instruments, and debt recovery from a period that is contemporaneous with Q. It might be asked

---

³¹ Ptolemaeus Ascalonius (I BCE), *De differentia vocabulorum* Σ146 (= Περὶ διαφορᾶς λέξεων κατὰ στοιχεῖον, e cod. Ambros. E 26 sup.): σῶσον 'τοῦ' ῥῦσαι διαφέρει. σῶσον νόσων καὶ πειρασμῶν, ῥῦσαι αἰχμαλωσίας καὶ τῶν δαιμόνων; text from V. Palmieri, "Ptolemaeus, De differentia vocabulorum," AFALF(N) 24 (1981–1982), 191–225. Less helpful is Dioscurides (I CE), *Materia medica* 5: ὅτι γε μὴν ἀναγκαῖος ὑπάρχει ὁ περὶ φαρμάκων λόγος, παντί που δῆλον, συνεζευγμένος ὅλῃ τῇ τέχνῃ καὶ τὴν ἀφ' ἑαυτοῦ συμμαχίαν ἀήττητον παντὶ μέρει παρεχόμενος, καὶ διότι δύναται αὔξεσθαι κατά τε τὰς σκευασίας καὶ τὰς μείξεις καὶ τοὺς ἐπὶ τῶν παθῶν πειρασμοὺς πλεῖστα συμβαλλομένης τῆς περὶ ἕκαστον τῶν φαρμάκων γνώσεως, "For discourse about medicines is necessary, as is obvious to all, being yoked together with the entire craft and offering the unconquerable alliance in each part; wherefore it can be enhanced as far as preparations and mixtures and the testings of diseases are concerned when knowledge about each of the medicines is collected." The Greek text is from Max Wellmann, *Pedanii Dioscuridis Anazarbei de materia medica libri quinque*, 3 vols. (Berlin: Weidmann, 1906–1914), 1:5.

³² It should also be noted that εἰσφέρω in Q 12:11 (Luke 12:11) means "to bring into court."

how much the debt practice of Hellenistic and early Roman Egypt might tell us about a different political domain, Jewish Palestine. There are only a handful of papyri from Palestine – all found in the ʿArava – to which the hundreds of thousands of Egyptian documentary papyri can be compared. Yet, when we do compare, the similarities are striking. Two debt instruments extant from Jewish Palestine, P. Mur. 18 in Aramaic and P. Mur. 114 in Greek, both from the early second century CE,[33] and the few other extant papyri from Wadi Murabba'at and Naḥal Ḥever contain some loan and lease documents. The Judaean loan documents conform to the morphology of Egyptian debt instruments, with a first-person *homologia* of the borrower declaring the amount borrowed, stipulating the term of the loan, and adding provisions that will come into effect in the case of default and, in the case of P. Mur. 114, adding a *praxis* clause, formulated as a genitive absolute in precisely the same way that the praxis clause is presented in Graeco-Egyptian debt instruments:

τῆ[ς] πράξεώς σοι οὔσης
καὶ ἄλ[λῳ π]αντὶ τῶν διά σου ἢ ὑπέρ σου κυρίως προ-
φερ[όντων τόδε τὸ χ]ειρόγραφον ἐκ τε ἐμοῦ καὶ ἐκ τ-
20 ῶν ὑ[παρχόντων μοι] π[ά]ντων

… the right of execution belonging to you or to anyone else who, (acting) for you and or on your behalf, presents this cheirograph, on me and on all of my possessions ….

Given the striking agreements in morphology, there is little reason to suppose that debt practices in Palestine differed dramatically from those in Ptolemaic and early Imperial Egypt.[34]

This brings me to the question of how the notion of serious "testing" might relate to debt collection, especially in the light of the reference to debt cancellation in the previous petition of the prayer (Q 11:4a). Of course, the petitions are not logically sequential, such that the reception of bread necessarily leads to debt cancellation and alleviation from harsh tests. In what follows, I hope to show that debt and debt collection were complicated matters, at least in Egypt and likely also in Palestine, and fraught with various dangers both for the creditor and the debtor. Douglas Oakman has suggested that the petitions of Q's prayer concern "deliverance from hunger, debt and trials in rigged courts before evil judges," for the latter citing Luke's story of the evil judge (18:2–5) as emblematic of problems that were endemic Roman Palestine, disadvantaging the peasant debtor.[35] There

---

[33] Pierre Benoit, ed., *Les grottes de Murabba'ât*, DJD 2 (Oxford: Clarendon, 1961), 100–104 (P. Mur. 18), 240–43 (P. Mur. 114).

[34] There were, of course, multiple legal practices in effect in Palestine in the early second century and probably earlier. See Jacobine G. Oudshoorn, *The Relationship Between Roman and Local Law in the Babatha and Salome Komaise Archive*, STDJ 69 (Leiden: Brill, 2007).

[35] Douglas E. Oakman, *Jesus and the Peasants*, Matrix: The Bible in Mediterranean Context (Eugene, OR: Cascade, 2008), 236; see also idem, *Jesus, Debt, and the Lord's Prayer: First-Century Debt and Jesus' Intentions* (Eugene, OR: Cascade, 2014), 81–84.

is good reason to think that peasants did not place a great deal of trust in court systems and evidence in Q that the framers of Q reflected some of this concern.[36] Yet I will argue in what follows that it was not only a system of courts that made for πειρασμοί for all but the elite, but the very structure of debt instruments and the mechanisms of debt collection that offered many occasions in which debtors (and also creditors) could find themselves subject to serious hardship.

BGU IV 1148, a papyrus from Alexandria and dated 3 April 13 BCE and addressed to Protarchos, the registrar of legal documents from 30–4 BCE, records a statement made by a certain Apollonia and Taphasies, both now widows. The two acknowledge to the registrar that Taphasies has received payment for two loans that were made to Apollonia and her husband Isidoros by Taphasies' husband Dionysios of 150 drachmae and 872 drachmae. These loans had been made in 27 and 24 BCE and had been repaid. But the document we have is dated eleven years later and mentions a dispute (l. 6, περὶ τῶν διεσταμένων), evidently over whether the debts had actually been repaid or not. We do not have the original debt instrument, but only the agreement that resolved the dispute. The agreement records that Apollonia had indeed repaid the loan to Taphasies. It continues:

(20) Taphasies will not take proceedings against (ἐπελεύσεσθαι) Apollonia, nor shall anyone else acting on her behalf (do so), nor against the belongings that were left by Isidoros [Apollonia's husband], nor concerning any debt (ὀφειλήμα) of Apollonia nor anyone other at all, either demanding back in writing or without writing anything arising from those earlier times until the present day, and that whoever should initiate proceedings against her (Apollonia) in relation to these things (25) in the name of Dionysios' interests shall immediately be held in default at his own expense. The provisions of this agreement are valid, and if she (Taphasies) should violate any of these provisions, she shall be in addition liable for damages and a fine that is established by law.[37]

The complex provisions of this agreement were necessary because debt recovery and compliance with judicial orders could be protracted and did not always bring about resolution to disputes. Several papyri contain complaints of unresolved cases, in which a plaintiff brought a matter to the court but the respondents did not appear, with the result that no resolution was achieved. In 221 BCE a certain Marres petitioned the court in regard to an unresolved dispute over a vineyard, a dispute that was already two or three years old and remained unre-

---

[36] See in general, Roger S. Bagnall, "Official and Private Violence in Roman Egypt," *BASP* 26 (1989): 201–16; and in relation to Q, see Sarah E. Rollens, "'Why Do You not Judge for Yourselves What is Right?': A Consideration of the Synoptic Relationship Between Mt 5,25–26 and Lk 12,57–59," in *ETL* 86 (2010): 449–69.

[37] See also P. Würzb. 6 (Theadelphia, 102 BCE) for a similar declaration of the creditor, to have received repayment of a loan of 12 artabae of wheat (plus the added half of interest), and an undertaking not to pursue any claim against the borrowers. In this case, the certification of repayment is witnessed by six Macedonian landowners, and registered by the συγγραφοφύλαξ, the registrar of contracts in Alexandria.

solved because one of the two parties had failed to appear.[38] Another document, this time from the early Imperial period, records a petition to the *stratēgos* of the Arsinoite nome requesting a summons against a respondent who had illegally occupied a vineyard and who had failed to appear at the first trial.[39] Part of the problem in the resolution of conflicts is that there existed no force of sheriffs that could be deployed reliably to execute the judgments of the court, or even to force persons to comply with summons. Police and soldiers sometimes exercised these roles, but they could not be relied upon to do so with any consistency. In villages and the countryside, enforcement of judicial decisions was quite unreliable.[40]

It is unclear whether, in the case of Apollonia and Taphasies, the creditor Taphasies pursued a case against Apollonia in the courts during the eleven years between the initial loan and the document of 13 BCE. It might be noted that the creditor Taphasies bears an Egyptian name while the debtor has a Greek name, which might imply that Taphasies, though in a financial position to make a loan to Apollonia and her husband Isidoros, was not on par with her socially and hence suffered from a disadvantage in enforcing her claim, whether or not it was justified or not. Whatever the case, the settlement of BGU IV 1148 established that Apollonia had at some point repaid the loan. The provisions enjoining Taphasies as creditor from taking or authorizing any action against Apollonia are standard in such documents. But they point to the vagaries involved in debt collection, complicated no doubt in instances in which both the original lender and the debtor are now deceased and their survivors are now in a dispute concerning whether the debt was collected. These provisions also point to the possibility that even when a loan was repaid or a transaction was legally implemented there was no guarantee that one of the two parties could continued to press for additional payments or act as though there had been no settlement.

The importance of retaining a record of debt repayment is underscored by another papyrus, P. Oxy. XII 1471 (Oxyrhynchus, 81 CE), addressed to the president of a judicial tribunal, and recording a loan of thirty-eight drachmae between a discharged veteran, Marcus Longinus Castresius, and Teteoris, an Egyptian woman acting with her son as guardian. The agreement stipulates that repayment must occur within four months and imposes various penalties in the

---

[38] P. Enteux. 65; John S. Kloppenborg, *The Tenants in the Vineyard: Ideology, Economics, and Agrarian Conflict in Jewish Palestine*, WUNT 195 (Tübingen: Mohr Siebeck, 2006), 450–53 (no. 33). A similar instance of failure to appear in court is recorded in P. Cair.Zen. II 59179 (Philadelphia, 255 BCE).

[39] P. Oxy. XLIX 3564 (Oxyrhynchus, 54–60 CE). The first complaint is dated in the 14th year of Claudius (i. e., 54/55 CE) and the current request for a summons appears to be dated after 55 CE when Ti. Claudius Balbillus became the prefect of Egypt. See Kloppenborg, *Tenants*, 493–96 (no. 43).

[40] See Benjamin Kelly, *Petitions, Litigation, and Social Control in Roman Egypt*, Oxford Studies in Ancient Documents (Oxford: Oxford University Press, 2011), 94–103 (on summons), 108–11 (on enforcing decisions).

case of default or late payment. The papyrus is now struck through, indicating that the loan had been repaid and a record of this repayment was retained in the civic archive. This practice was presumably so that in the case of a further dispute, the cancelled agreement could be retrieved and used by the *achidikastēs* to arbitrate a dispute between Longinus and Teteoris, should that occur. While modern debtors might be inclined to burn their mortgage or car loan papers once the debt was retired, this would have been a remarkably imprudent practice in antiquity, since the creditor or agents acting on his or her behalf might continue to pursue a debtor once the debt was paid.

P. Oxy. XII 1471 points to another potential πειρασμός that might be experienced by a debtor and points to one of the legal responses to the problem of the widespread inability of courts to enforce their judgments. The loan agreement includes the provision in the case of default, Teteoris,

       ἢ εἶναι αὐτὴ[ν ἀγωγί]-
μην καὶ συνέχεσθαι μέχρι τοῦ ἐκτεῖ-
σαι τῷ Μάρκῳ Λογγείνῳ Καστρησίῳ
25 παραχρῆμα τὸ [μ]ὲν δάνειον τὰς τοῦ
ἀργυρίου δραχμὰς τριάκον[τ]α ὀκτὼ
σὺν ἡμιολίᾳ τ[οὺς] δὲ τόκους
καὶ τοῦ ὑπερπεσόντος χρόνου τοὺς [ἴ]-
σους, τῆς πράξεως οὔσης τῷ Μάρκῳ
30 [Λο]γγείνῳ καστρησίῳ παρά τε τῆς Τετεώρι[ος]
[καὶ] ἐκ τῶν [ὑπαρ]χόντων αὐτῇ πάν-
[τ]ων {αὐτῇ [πάντ]ων} καθάπερ ἐγ δίκ[ης.]

is *agōgimē* and can be detained until she pays in full to Marcus Longinus Castresius (25) immediately, both the loan of thirty-eight silver drachmae with an added half and the interest for the extra time at the same rate; the right of execution lies with Marcus (30) Longinus Castresius, upon both Teteoris and all of her property, as if by a legal decision.

Normally creditors were not entitled to seize the person or possessions of debtors in the event of default unless specifically authorized by the loan instrument to do so.[41] Without such an agreement, the creditor risked legal action, as occurred in P. Col.Zen. II 83 (Philadelphia, 245/4 BCE) where a debtor's wife and boy were wrongly imprisoned by a creditor and the debtor petitioned the king to fine the creditor for the imprisoning of a free person.[42] Hence, in our papyrus, Teteoris is specifically designated as ἀγωγιμή (masc. ἀγωγιμός) and the agreement indicates that both her person and "all of her property" could be seized by Longinus in order to recover his loan.

---

[41] Raphael Taubenschlag, *The Law of Greco-Roman Egypt in the Light of the Papyri: 332 B. C.–620 A. D.* (New York: Herald Square, 1944), 407.

[42] See also P. Flor. I 61 (unknown provenance, 85 CE); P. Oxy. VI 902 (Oxyrhynchus, 464 CE).

Earlier Ptolemaic documents often designated a debtor as Πέρσαι τῆς ἐπιγονῆς, "Persian by descent, a legal category of persons who were susceptible to seizure in the case of default."[43] Such persons were also prohibited from resort to a temple as a place of asylum.[44] By the Roman period, both Πέρσαι τῆς ἐπιγονῆς and ἀγωγιμός were commonly used of persons who were susceptible to personal execution in business dealings. Particularly common in loan agreements of this period is the term παραχρῆμα, "immediate," indicating, as it does here, the creditor's right to detail the debtor without resort to a judicial ruling.[45]

P. Oxy. XII 1471 also contains a *praxis*-clause, normally framed as a genitive absolute, τῆς πρά(ξεως) γινομένης ... | τῶι NN ... ἐκ τῶν ὑπαρχόντων αὐτῷ/ αὐτοῖς πάντων (ll. 29–32), and representing a standard execution clause indicating that both the debtor him- or herself was subject to arrest, and all of his or her possessions.[46] Such documents normally stipulate that the recovery of the debt can be καθάπερ ἐγ δίκ[ης, "as if by a legal decision."[47] This in effect constituted an agreement between the creditor and the debtor that in the case of default, the creditor could recover the loan, either by attaching the possessions of the debtor or by imprisoning him or her.[48] In Ptolemaic law the only restriction upon the

---

[43] Fritz Heichelheim, *Die auswärtige Bevölkerung in Ptolemäerreich*, Klio.B 18 (Leipzig: Dieterich, 1925; repr. Aalen: Scientia, 1963), 76–80; Leopold Wenger, "Juristische Literaturübersicht VII," APF 13 (1937): 310–14; Friedrich Zucker, "Πέρσαι," PW 19.1:910–26; Taubenschlag, *Law of Greco-Roman Egypt*, 532; Johannes Herrmann, *Studien zur Bodenpacht im Recht der graeco-ägyptischen Papyri*, MBPF 41 (München: Beck, 1958), 66–67; John F. Oates, "The Status Designation: ΠΕΡΣΗΣ, ΤΗΣ ΕΠΙΓΟΝΗΣ," YCS 18 (1963): 1–126; Victor Tcherikover, Alexander Fuks, and Menahem Stern, eds., *Corpus papyrorum Judaicarum*, 3 vols. (Cambridge, MA: Harvard University Press, 1957–1964), 1:51.

[44] Being subject to arrest (ἀγωγίσμος) excluded the possibility of asylum in a temple. See P. Oxy. XIV 1639.18–20 (73 or 44 BCE): ἀ[γ]ώγιμο‹ὶ› σο[ι δὲ] ἐσόμεθα ἐπί τε τοῦ προωνο|μασμ[έν] ου Σαραπιείου καὶ ἐπὶ παντὸς ἀσύλου καὶ | ἄρχοντ[ο]ς καὶ ὅπου ἂν τῶι καθόλου περιπίπτης ἡμῖν, "we shall be subject to seizure by you both at the aforementioned Sarapeion [in Oxyrhynchus] and at any place of asylum and in whatever place at all you encounter us."

[45] E. g., BGU IV 1122. 24–25 (Alexandria, 13 BCE): εἶναι αὐτοὺς παραχρῆμα ἀγωγίσμους, "subject to immediate arrest." According to Adolf Berger, *Die Strafklauseln in den Papyrusurkunden: Ein Beitrag zum grako-ägyptischen Obligationenrecht* (Leipzig and Berlin: Teubner, 1911; repr. Aalen: Scientia, 1965), 78, the use of παραχρῆμα ("immediate") is particularly common in documents of the Ptolemaic period and in documents of Alexandria in the Augustan period.

[46] E. g., BGU IV 1050.17; 1051.23; 1052.19; 1054.12; 1055.34–35; 1056.19–20; 1057.13, 29; 1099.19; 1101.13; 1115.33; 1116.29; 1117.36; 1118.48; 1121.37; 1122.27; 1127.26; 1131.56; 1133.17; 1134.17; 1136.7; 1143.27; 1144.16; 1145.38; 1146.22; 1147.20; 1150.21; 1156.22; 1161.22; 1175.10; CPapGr I 4.42; 5.127.38; 6.21; 9.19; 10.24; 13.25 (all dated between 30–4 BCE) and mostly addressed to Protarchos. The formula also appears in BGU IV 2044.25 (46 CE); P. Mur. 18.24, 62 (128 CE); P. Oxy. II 270.47 (94 CE); III 496.16 (127 CE); IV 729.21; VIII 1127 (183 CE); XVII 2137.35 (291 CE); LV 3800.34 (219 CE); PSI V 496.21 (334 CE).

[47] Raphael Taubenschlag, "Self-Help in Greco-Roman Egypt," in idem, *Opera Minora*, 2 vols., ed. Vincenzo Arangio Ruiz (Warsaw: Pantsowe Wydawnictwo Naukowe, 1959), 2:135–42, here 140–41.

[48] Ptolemaic law already imagined action both against the possessions of a debtor and against his or her person. P. Hal. 1.115–117: ἐὰν δέ τ[ις γραψάμενος δίκην ....] τ... σ ἢ πληγῶν

creditor was that the surety could not be seized during the night.⁴⁹ Those who fraudulently seized a surety could be brought to court.

The possibility of arrest existed not only between debtors and creditors, but even in the realm of private associations. The members of a guild of salt merchants from Tebtynis in the time of Claudius (P. Mich. V 245, 47 CE) agreed that should any of them fail to pay his share of the club's expenses or pay the public charges or other things owing to the club, the president was entitled to arrest him whether in public or private:

                      τὸν δὲ ἀδωσιδικοῦντα
      [καὶ μ]ὴ [ἀ]γαπλεροῦντά τι τῶν δημοσίων ἢ καὶ τῶν
      [προσε]γκληθησομένων αὐτοῖς ἐξεῖναι τῷ αὐτῷ Ἀπ-
40 [ύνχι ἐνε]χυράζειν αὐτοὺς ἔν τε τῇ πλατείᾳ καὶ ἐν
      [ταῖς οἰκί]αις καὶ ἐν τῷ ἀγρῶι καὶ παραδιδόναι αὐτοὺς

If someone fails to pay his share and does not pay any of the public charges or what is owing (?) to them (the members), Apynchis (40) has the authority to arrest him, whether in the town square or in his house or in the field, and to hand him over as was indicated above.

That such actions occurred from time to time is attested by an earlier complaint on a papyrus from the second century BCE, in which Apollonios, a Macedonian cavalryman, complains to an official of the Ptolemaic government that the president of his guild entered his house to remove an iron lampstand claimed to be worth 3000 drachmae, as a surety against a loan of 150 drachmae.⁵⁰ Apollonios

---

ἡσσηθῆι, προς προσαποτι|νέ[τω][τῶι νικήσαντι τὸ δ]έκατον τοῦ τιμήματος τῆς δίκης καὶ ὁ πράκτωρ ἢ ὁ ὑπηρέτης πρα|ξά[τω καθάπερ ἐκ δίκης ἐκ τ]ῶν ὑπαρχόντων, ἐὰν δὲ μὴ ἐκποιῇι, καὶ ἐκ τοῦ σώματος, "If anyone [after bring suit for outrage] or blows is defeated, he shall pay to [the winner] an additional tenth of the value of the suit, and the *praktor* or his assistant shall exact it from the property [in accordance with a court decision. If he does not completely do this, from his person also." Authorizing action by the creditor was also codified in Roman law, although it did not extend to action against the person of the debtor: Justinian, codex 8.13.3: *Imperatores Severus, Antoninus. creditores, qui non reddita sibi pecunia conventionis legem ingressi possessionem adipisci debent. PP. k. Mai Antonino A. II et Geta II Conss*; "Emperors Severus and Antoninus. Creditors, who have made an agreement with their debtors that if the money due is not paid to them at the designated time they may take possession of their property, are not considered to have used violence if they do so, but they should, nevertheless, obtain possession by authority of the Governor. Published on the Kalends of May, during the second Consulate of Antoninus and Geta, [206]."

⁴⁹ P. Hal. 1.238–241 (Antinoopolis, 259 BCE but recording the laws of Alexandria): [ἐ]ὰν δέ τις ἐ[νεχυράσηι, ἀναγρα]|φέτωσαν οἱ θεσμοφύλακ[ες] τὴ[ν] ἐνεχυρασί[αν. ὡς δὲ ἂν ἥλιος]|| δύηι, μηδὲ εἷς ἐνεχυραζ[έ]τω μηδὲ πρὶν ἥ[λιον ἀνατέλλειν,] | ἢ [ὑ]πόδικοι ἔστωσαν οἱ η[....] ες τῆς ψευδε[νεχυρασίας], "If someone exacts a pledge, let the magistrates record the pledge. Whenever the sun has (240) set, no one can exact a pledge, or before the sun rises, and those take pledges falsely will be liable to put on trial."

⁵⁰ P. Würzb. 4 (Philadelphia?, after 142 BCE) = Ulrich Wilcken, *Mitteilungen aus der Würzburger Papyrussammlung*, Abhandlungen der preussischen Akademie der Wissenschaften, Jhrg. 1933, 6 (Berlin: Akademie der Wissenschaften, 1934), 37–41 (no. 4).

insists that the loan he owed had already been repaid and alleges that the president had acted in this manner because he was under the obligation to supply an offering (πρόθεσις), presumably a cultic obligation in the association. The cavalryman therefore requests a judgment that would lead to the return of the lampstand. The story is rather muddy: although Apollonios alleges that the president had removed the lampstand in order to fulfil an obligation to provide an offering, there is no indication that the lampstand was sold, since Apollonios expects its return. Whether Apollonios had not in fact repaid the debt or the president trying to collect twice remains unclear. What this papyrus does indicate, however, is that the association's νόμος provided extra-judicial powers to the president to recoup debts owed to the guild.

Another petitioner in the early imperial period, Marsisouchos, claims to the royal scribe that as a state farmer and irrigator, he had the responsibility to care for public land (P. Col. VIII 209, Theadelphia, 3 CE). For reasons that he does not supply, Soterichos the scribe of the *komogrammateus* sent the bailiff (*praktor*) and the guard to arrested him "even though I owed absolutely (ὀφείλοντος) nothing." Although Marsisouchos was eventually released, it was not until he had provided a surety. The *komogrammateus* also took (ἀπηνέγκατο) his cloak, six years of Marsisouchos' receipts for the poll tax, and later was alleged to have harassed Marsisouchos' field work, which, he threatens, would result in a loss of revenues to the state.

This complaint is just as puzzling as that of Apollonios the cavalryman: Soterichos' confiscation of receipts for the poll tax raises the possibility that Marsisouchos was in fact in arrears for the collection of the poll tax, though he claims to have owed nothing. Moreover, since in his petition he asks that Soterichos be required to produce the receipts, he evidently believes that the receipts will show that he owes no tax. It seems likely that his reference to the potential loss of state revenues is a diversion from what is the real issue, which remains clouded to us.

Although the *praxis* clause permitted seizure of property, it also permitted the seizure of the person of the debtor. An example of this is found in a much later petition, P. Oxy. XII 902 (Oxyrhynchus, 464 CE) in which a cultivator, Aurelius Makarios, claims that after the death of his former patron and employer, the deceased's brother assumed management of the estate and "like a tyrant seized eight fine animals from my herd" and imprisoned the cultivator, so that the remainder of his herd starved to death. Makarios states that he had been willing to pay a debt, "provided that written proof of any debt could be produced" (ὅσα ἐποφείλω αὐτῷ ἐγγράφως), perhaps an indication that the debtor knew that no such proof was available. The petitioner asks that his herd be restored to him and that he be released from prison. If one assumes that the creditor in fact did not have a copy of the debt instrument (and therefore any record of a praxis-clause with a καθάπερ ἐγ δίκης provision, we should have to suppose that the creditor acted extra-judicially and in fact in violation of prevailing laws.

The analysis of these papyri illustrates several problems associated with debt recovery. First, given the vagaries of judicial practices and the lack of a police force that could compel litigants to appear in court and to enforce judicial decisions thereafter, it could not be taken for granted the debts that were owed could be recovered at all. Second, the agreement between Apollonia and Taphasies in BGU IV 1148 indicates that even when a debt had been repaid, there was no guarantee that the creditor might continue to seek payment or otherwise harass the debtor. And third, the use of *praxis*-clauses that authorized execution on the property and persons of debtors and the extra-judicial mechanism of seizure καθάπερ ἐγ δίκης meant that the entire process of debt recovery was laced with physical confrontations and the possibility of financial ruin, when sureties were seized that were worth much more than the original debt, or even when creditors seized the person of the debtor, thereby putting the financial position of the debtor at risk.

That mechanisms similar to those in effect in Egypt were also practiced in Palestine is suggested by Q 12:58–59, the advice to settle quickly with an accuser, lest the plaintiff – in this case no doubt a creditor – "hand you over to the judge, and the judge to the assistant (ὑπηρέτης; Luke uses the official title, ὁ πράκτωρ) and the assistant will cast you into prison,"[51] punctuating this advice with the warning, "I tell you, you will not get out from there until you repay the final *quadrans*." As Sugranyes de Franch has observed, Q here has in mind a formal judicial procedure, initiated by a judge (κρίτης) and reflecting the ordinary Ptolemaic legal procedures.[52] But as I have suggested above, extra-judicial actions in the case of debt recovery were also quite "ordinary" in Ptolemaic and early Roman Egypt and there is little reason to suppose that these procedures were not current also in Roman Palestine.

Conclusion

I have argued in this paper several theses: first, at least until the early second century CE, πειρασμοί denoted serious and adverse circumstances rather than more trivial "daily" temptations. Moreover, contrary to widespread views, πειρασμοί were not depicted as inevitable until they became interiorized and treated as ordinary conditions of the human ψυχή that was subject to the vicissitudes of life due to the instability of the emotions. Second, πειρασμός, as a term denoting "testing," does not appear in Greek literature prior to the Septuagint and only rarely outside of Jewish and Christian literature; it was used of a broad range of

---

[51] Q 12:58: μήποτέ σε παραδῷ ⟦ὁ ἀντίδικος⟧ τῷ κριτῇ καὶ ὁ κριτὴς τῷ ὑπηρέτῃ καὶ ⟦ὁ 'ὑπηρέτης' σε⟧ β⟦α⟧λ⟦εῖ εἰς φυλακήν⟧.

[52] Ramon Sugranyes de Franch, *Études sur le droit palestinien à l'époque évangélique: la contrainte par corps*, AJSUF 1 (Fribourg: Librairie de l' Université, 1946), 134–35.

adverse circumstances affecting human life. Hence its nuance in any particular literary or performative setting was determined by its immediate context.

Third, although Matthew's performative context, which associates πειρασμός ultimately with vistas of apocalyptic judgment (Matt 18:23–35; 25:31–46) and more immediately with the verb ῥύομαι and the agency of ὁ πονηρός, moves the nuance of "testing" in the direction of an apocalyptic test, the performative context of Q associates πειρασμός not with apocalyptic scenarios but rather with debt and the expectation of debt relief as a result of the coming of the kingdom. That debt and debt recovery could be characterized as πειρασμοί becomes clear once the practices and vagaries surrounding debt recovery are known, as they are from an examination of Graeco-Egyptian papyri. In contrast to the regularized, bureaucratized, and relatively efficient mechanisms of the registration and retirement of debts in North Atlantic contexts, debt and debt recovery were fraught in the ancient world with multiple uncertainties. Not only was there a good possibility that creditors would attempt to collect on debts that were already paid would, but that the mechanisms for debt recovery often involved seizure of the possessions and even the person of the debtor, imprisonment and possible financial ruin. A petition not to be led into such a πειρασμός makes perfect sense in the context of a prayer that petitions the deity for subsistence and freedom from debt.

Lukas 11,5–8

Freundschaft, Gastfreundschaft und ἀναίδεια

Thomas Klampfl

A. Einleitung

In diesem Beitrag soll es um die für das Verständnis des Gleichnisses vom bittenden Freund (Lk 11,5–8) zentrale Frage nach der Bedeutung des Begriffs ἀναίδεια (11,8) gehen. Der gegebene Text bringt mehrere Verstehensschwierigkeiten mit sich: Ist die Antwort des gebetenen Freundes in Vers 7 als real gesprochen anzunehmen, oder als hypothetisch, als zur Frage Jesu gehörend, anzusehen? Was bedeutet ἀναίδεια, und auf wen bezieht sich das diesem Wort beigestellte αὐτός (11,8), also wem wird „Schamlosigkeit" zugesprochen? Letztere Frage ist verbunden mit der Einschätzung der sozialen Gegebenheiten von Freundschaft und Gastfreundschaft in der damaligen Gesellschaft: Wenn Freunde einander weitgehend beistehen, wenn einander in der Struktur des Dorfes geholfen wurde, und schließlich der Gastfreundschaft in der antiken Welt ein hoher Stellenwert zukommt, kann dann die Bitte des Freundes als unverschämt charakterisiert werden? Stellt der Text eine literarische Einheit dar, oder ist Vers 8 sekundär? War dieser Text Teil des Spruchevangeliums Q? Und schließlich, spricht dieser Text vom Gebet, und wenn ja, was sagt er über dieses aus?

Nicht alle dieser Fragen werden im Folgenden gleich umfangreich thematisiert, vielmehr steht die Klärung der Bedeutung des Wortes ἀναίδεια im Mittelpunkt. Zunächst wird kurz die Forschungsgeschichte der Auslegung des Gleichnisses dargestellt (Abschnitt 3), dann die Bedeutung des Wortes αἰδώς bestimmt (Abschnitt 4). Im 5. Abschnitt wird nach der Semantik von ἀναίδεια gefragt. In Kapitel 6 werden die Vorkommen dieses Wortes in den dokumentarischen Papyri besprochen. In den letzten drei Kapiteln geht es um die Traditionsgeschichte von Lk 11,5–8 und um das Verständnis dieses Textes in seiner traditionellen Gestalt und im Lukasevangelium.

B. Text und Übersetzung

Lk 11,5–8:

5a Καὶ εἶπεν πρὸς αὐτούς·
 b τίς ἐξ ὑμῶν ἕξει φίλον
 c καὶ πορεύσεται πρὸς αὐτὸν μεσονυκτίου
 d καὶ εἴπῃ αὐτῷ·
 e φίλε, χρῆσόν μοι τρεῖς ἄρτους,
6a ἐπειδὴ φίλος μου παρεγένετο ἐξ ὁδοῦ πρός με
 b καὶ οὐκ ἔχω ὃ παραθήσω αὐτῷ·
7a κἀκεῖνος ἔσωθεν ἀποκριθεὶς εἴπῃ·
 b μή μοι κόπους πάρεχε·
 c ἤδη ἡ θύρα κέκλεισται
 d καὶ τὰ παιδία μου μετ' ἐμοῦ εἰς τὴν κοίτην εἰσίν·
 e οὐ δύναμαι ἀναστὰς δοῦναί σοι.
8a λέγω ὑμῖν,
 b εἰ καὶ οὐ δώσει αὐτῷ ἀναστὰς διὰ τὸ εἶναι φίλον αὐτοῦ,
 c διά γε τὴν ἀναίδειαν αὐτοῦ ἐγερθεὶς δώσει αὐτῷ ὅσων χρῄζει.

5a Und er sprach zu ihnen:
 b Wenn jemand unter euch einen Freund hat
 c und ginge zu ihm um Mitternacht
 d und spräche zu ihm:
 e Lieber Freund, leih mir drei Brote;
6a denn mein Freund ist zu mir gekommen auf der Reise,
 b und ich habe nichts, was ich ihm vorsetzen kann,
7a und der drinnen würde antworten und sprechen:
 b Mach mir keine Mühe.
 c Die Tür ist schon zugeschlossen,
 d und meine Kinder und ich liegen schon zu Bett;
 e ich kann nicht aufstehen und dir etwas geben.
8a Ich sage euch:
 b Und wenn er schon nicht aufsteht und ihm etwas gibt, weil er sein Freund ist,
 c dann wird er doch wegen seiner Schamlosigkeit aufstehen und ihm geben, soviel er bedarf.

C. Positionen der Forschung

1. Adolf Jülicher

Das Moment, aus welchem sich das Nicht-Geben des gebetenen Freundes in ein Geben verwandelt, sieht Adolf Jülicher in der Beharrlichkeit des Bittenden.[1] Zwar weiß er, daß ἀναίδεια Unverschämtheit bedeutet, meint aber, daß der Sinn

---

[1] Adolf Jülicher, *Die Gleichnisreden Jesu*, 2. Teil: *Auslegung der Gleichnisreden der drei ersten Evangelien*, 2. Aufl. (Tübingen: Mohr Siebeck, 1910), 272–73.

von Beharrlichkeit hier unentbehrlich ist.² Im Rahmen der Unterweisung über das Gebet, der schon bei Jesus gegeben war, erfolgt die Übertragung in das religiöse Gebiet, mittels des Schlusses vom Kleineren auf das Größere, durch den Hörer wie von selbst: Gott erhört ein Gebet, sofern es nur anhaltend und unermüdlich vorgebracht wird.³ Der Hauptpunkt der Geschichte liegt in der Erhörung nach anfänglicher Abweisung, als Folge der Erneuerung der Bitte.⁴

2. Anton Fridrichsen

Anton Fridrichsen wendet sich gegen die weitverbreitete Deutung, daß das Gleichnis die Macht der beharrlichen Bitte lehren will.⁵ Diese Deutung nimmt die ablehnenden Worte in Vers 7 als tatsächlich gesprochen an, und liest aus Vers 8 die Wiederholung der Bitte heraus.⁶ Demgegenüber meint Fridrichsen, daß der gebetene Freund im Inneren des Hauses die Bitte nicht ablehnt; Vers 7 ist nicht wirklich ausgesprochen worden, sondern zeigt nur an, welchen Widerstand der Gebetene zu überwinden hat. Er überwindet diesen aber und gibt dem Bittenden.⁷ Dem entspricht, daß im Milieu des Dorfes eine „tief eingewurzelte Hilfsbereitschaft" herrscht, gegen die der Gebetene, sollte er nicht geben, verstoßen würde.⁸ Dies sagen auch die Worte διά γε τὴν ἀναίδειαν αὐτοῦ. Diese sind so zu verstehen, daß der Gebetene gibt wegen seiner eigenen Schamlosigkeit, die sich zeigen würde, wenn er nicht gibt. Schamlosigkeit würde bedeuten, der gebotenen Pflicht zu widersprechen.⁹ Das hier angenommene Verständnis von διά im Sinn von „um zu verhüten" finde sich auch in Joh 12,42: διὰ τοὺς Φαρισαίους οὐχ ὡμολόγουν – „um der Pharisäer willen bekannten sie es nicht," und 1 Kor 7,2: διὰ δὲ τὰς πορνείας ἕκαστος τὴν ἑαυτοῦ γυναῖκα ἐχέτω – „Aber um Unzucht zu vermeiden, soll jeder seine eigene Frau haben."¹⁰

3. Joachim Jeremias

Joachim Jeremias sind einige grundlegende Feststellungen hinsichtlich dieses Gleichnisses zu verdanken: Zunächst die Beobachtung, daß τίς ἐξ ὑμῶν Gleichnisse auf eine entschiedene positive bzw. negative Antwort abzielen: „Unmög-

---

[2] Ebd., 2:273.
[3] Ebd., 2:274.
[4] Ebd., 2:275.
[5] Anton Fridrichsen, „Exegetisches zum Neuen Testament," SO 13 (1934): 38–46, hier 40–41.
[6] Ebd., 41.
[7] Ebd.
[8] Ebd.
[9] Ebd., 42.
[10] Ebd., 43.

lich! Niemand!' oder ‚Selbstverständlich! Jeder!'"[11] Weiters die Position, daß die Frage des Gleichniserzählers von Vers 5 bis 7 geht, also eine lange zusammenhängende rhetorische Frage bildet.[12]

Jeremias meint, daß das Gleichnis nicht im Kontext von Lk 11,1–13, einem Abschnitt über das Gebet, verstanden werden darf; deshalb steht nicht der bittende Freund im Mittelpunkt wie im Lukas-Zusammenhang, sondern der gebetene Freund. Die Schamlosigkeit sei auf den gebetenen Freund zu beziehen: Um nicht als schamlos dazustehen, wird er seinem Freund geben.[13] Es geht nicht um die Beharrlichkeit des Bittenden, sondern um die Gewißheit, daß Gott die Bitten, die an ihn gerichtet werden, erfüllt.[14]

4. Alan F. Johnson

Nachdem Alan Johnson ausgeschlossen hat, daß ἀναίδεια Ausdauer („persistence") bedeutet, bezieht er ebenso wie Jeremias die Schamlosigkeit auf den Freund im Haus, der handelt und das gebetene Brot gibt, um Scham und Beschämung zu vermeiden.[15]

5. Joseph Fitzmyer

Joseph Fitzmyer versteht die Schamlosigkeit als Aufdringlichkeit des Bittenden bzw. als Belästigung des Gebetenen („importunity") durch das Bitten, auch aufgrund der späten Stunde,[16] und interpretiert sie als Ausdauer („persistence").[17]

6. Heinz Schürmann

Die Irrealität der Frage in den Versen 5 bis 7 wird nach Heinz Schürmann durch die Futura ἕξει und πορεύσεται und dem Konjunktiv εἴπῃ signalisiert.[18] Das Bitten versteht er als „mutig-dreistes," nicht als unablässiges; im Zentrum der Parabel steht aber der gebetene Freund, der sich hilfsbereit zeigt, wie Gott, der von der vorgetragenen Not berührt wird. Es gehe nicht um hartnäckiges Bitten.[19]

---

[11] Joachim Jeremias, *Die Gleichnisse Jesu*, 11. Aufl. (Göttingen: Vandenhoeck & Ruprecht, 1998), 158.
[12] Ebd.
[13] Ebd., 157, 158.
[14] Ebd., 159.'
[15] Alan F. Johnson, „Assurance for Man: The Fallacy of Translating ANAIDEIA by ‚Persistence' in Luke 11:5–8," *JETS* 22 (1979): 123–31, hier 131.
[16] Joseph A. Fitzmyer, *The Gospel according to Luke X–XXIV: Introduction, Translation and Notes*, AB 28A (New York: Doubleday, 1985), 912.
[17] Ebd., 910.
[18] Heinz Schürmann, *Das Lukasevangelium*, 2. Teil, 1. Folge: *Kommentar zu Kapitel 9,51–11,54*, HThKNT 3/2.1 (Freiburg i. B.: Herder, 1993), 208.
[19] Ebd., 210–11.

7. William R. Herzog

William R. Herzog beginnt seine Auslegung mit einer Bestimmung der Verpflichtungen, die sich aus dem nächtlichen Besuch ergeben: Der Gastgeber ist verpflichtet, dem Ankommenden eine Mahlzeit vorzusetzen; diese Obligation betrifft aber nicht nur den Gastgeber allein, sondern das ganze Dorf, sodaß er auf dessen Ressourcen zurückgreifen kann. Sowohl für den Gastgeber als auch für das Dorf handelt es sich dabei um eine Frage der Ehre; und es ist eine Ehre für alle Beteiligten, dem Gastfreund ein Mahl zu bereiten.[20] Die Antwort des um Brot Gebetenen (V. 7), ist nicht als wirklich gesprochen anzusehen, sondern gehört zur rhetorischen Frage.[21]

Herzog beschreibt das Leben im Dorf als vom Streben, die Subsistenz zu sichern, bestimmt. Daraus ergibt sich, daß das Verhältnis zu den Eliten, den Landeignern, den Geldverleihern und dem Staat gesehen wurde unter der Perspektive, inwieweit durch diese die Subsistenz im Krisenfall gesichert wurde; auch wenn damit Ausbeutung verbunden war. Weiters folgt aus diesem Streben, daß im Dorf reziproke Solidarität geübt wurde, also wenn jemand um Hilfe bat, diesem geholfen wurde, weil die umgekehrte Situation ebenso möglich war.[22] Im ersten Jahrhundert litten die kleinen Landeigentümer unter zunehmender Belastung durch die römische Kolonisation, die Herodianische Herrschaft und die Steuerbedürfnisse der Tempelhierarchie. Diese Situation belastet auch die Institution der Gastfreundschaft.[23]

Jesus hat ein neues, fiktives Verwandtschaftsnetzwerk etabliert, um dem ökonomischen Druck zu begegnen, das sowohl Heimatlose als auch Niedergelassene umfaßt.[24]

Herzog sieht zwei konkurrierende Konzepte von Freundschaft bzw. Gastfreundschaft: In der Torah wird die positive Haltung gegenüber dem Fremden damit motiviert, daß Israel fremd war in Ägypten (Lev 19,34; Ex 22,22–24). Weiters konnte Gastfreundschaft verstanden werden als im Modell Abraham exemplifiziert, der im Gegensatz zu Sodom gastfreundlich handelt (Gen 18,1–21; 19,1–14). Andererseits war die Freundschaft in Patron-Klient-Verhältnissen eine Mystifikation von Macht- und Abhängigkeitsverhältnissen.[25]

Die Bedeutung von ἀναίδεια wird einerseits gesehen als Gier, andererseits als ein Verhalten, das sozial konstruierte Grenzen und Konventionen nicht respektiert. Diese Grenzen wurden zur Zeit Jesu von den Jerusalemer Eliten als

---

[20] William R. Herzog II, *Parables as Subversive Speech: Jesus as Pedagogue of the Oppressed* (Louisville, KY: Westminster John Knox Press, 1994), 200–201.
[21] Ebd., 202.
[22] Ebd., 204–5.
[23] Ebd., 206–7.
[24] Ebd., 208–9.
[25] Ebd., 210–11.

Reinheitsvorschriften definiert. Aus der Perspektive dieser Eliten war die Gastfreundschaft der Dorfbewohner schamlos. Jesus wendet das dominante negative Werturteil in eine Affirmation der Gastfreundschaft. Diese Gastfreundschaft im Sinne der fremdenfreundlichen Aussagen der Torah und der Abrahamstradition war grenzüberschreitend.[26]

8. François Bovon

François Bovon spricht von zwei Rätseln, die diese Parabel beinhaltet: Einerseits was der Gebetene schließlich tut, andererseits was sein Beweggrund dafür ist.[27] Er sieht zwei mögliche Antworten durch die Hörerin: Nach der ersten geht es um Gott, der bei allen Bedenken, die er haben mag, sich um seine Freunde kümmert. Nach der zweiten geht es um die Ermutigung zum Anklopfen. Die dem Lukas vorausgehende Tradition habe die erste Möglichkeit im Blick gehabt, Lukas, wie er durch die Anfügung von Vers 9 und des Kommentars zur Parabel von der Witwe und dem Richter in Lk 18,1 zu erkennen gibt, die zweite.[28] Bovon notiert, daß ἀναίδεια Unverschämtheit bedeutet, und die Unsicherheit auf wen diese sich bezieht. Würde man die Unverschämtheit auf den Gebetenen beziehen, würde man ein anderes Wort erwarten und ein reflexives ἑαυτοῦ. Weiters bemerkt der Autor, daß der Begriff nicht als eine positive Haltung verstanden werden darf, also als Mut oder Hartnäckigkeit.[29]

9. Klyne Snodgrass

Gegen Interpretationen, die dem Wort ἀναίδεια einen positiven Sinn abzugewinnen versuchen, z. B. im Sinne von „Vermeidung von Scham," wendet sich Klyne Snodgrass. Das Wort hat durchwegs negative Bedeutung und das viermalige αὐτός verweist auf den Bittenden und nicht auf den Schlafenden.[30] Der Autor betont weiters, daß von ausdauerndem Bitten keine Rede sein kann: Der Bittende wiederholt seine Bitte nicht, und die Aussage des Gebetenen in Vers 7 ist hypothetisch und irreal.[31] Die Parabel sei eine solche des Kontrasts: Gott zögert nicht, sondern ist bereit zu geben, wenn er gebeten wird.[32]

---

[26] Ebd., 212–14.
[27] François Bovon, *Das Evangelium nach Lukas, 2. Teilband: Lk 9,51–14,35* (Zürich: Benziger Verlag; Neukirchen-Vluyn: Neukirchener Verlag, 1996), 151.
[28] Ebd.
[29] Ebd., 2:150–51.
[30] Klyne Snodgrass, „*Anaideia* and the Friend at Midnight (Luke 11:8)," *JBL* 116 (1997): 505–13, hier 510.
[31] Ebd., 511.
[32] Ebd., 512–13.

10. Herman C. Waetjen

Ebenfalls auf den Bittenden bezieht Herman C. Waetjen die Schamlosigkeit von Vers 8; diese wird aber als positiv angesehen: Um seine Ehre zu retten, indem er dem von der Reise Gekommenen etwas zu essen vorsetzen kann, muß der Bittende ehrlos handeln.³³ Er zeige ein rüdes und aggressives Verhalten³⁴ und unterläuft so die von den Werten Ehre und Scham bestimmten kulturellen Verhaltensnormen.³⁵

11. Hans Klein

Hans Klein interpretiert ohne detaillierte Diskussion ἀναίδεια als Zudringlichkeit. Der gebetene Freund handelt, damit er seine Ruhe hat.³⁶

12. Michael Wolter

Wie Joachim Jeremias betont Michael Wolter, daß die Antwort auf die rhetorische Frage in den Versen 5 bis 6 negativ ist: Niemand hat einen Freund, der wie in Vers 7 beschrieben reagieren würde.³⁷ Von den zwei möglichen Ausgängen der Erzählung in den Versen 7 und 8 ist nur der in letzterem geschilderte denkbar. Es gehe in dem Gleichnis um die „Erfolgsaussichten" des Handelns. Wolter versteht ἀναίδεια als ein Verhalten von Menschen, „die ihre Interessen rücksichtslos durchzusetzen suchen und dabei auch einen Verstoß gegen die gesellschaftlichen Konventionen in Kauf nehmen." Entscheidend sei aber, daß so oder so das Bitten Erfolg hat.³⁸

13. Martin Ebner

Martin Ebner versteht Lk 11,5–8 nicht als Parabel, sondern als Beispielerzählung, also als Erzählung, die vorbildliches Verhalten schildert, die erst sekundär auf das Gebet appliziert wurde.³⁹ Er versteht unter ἀναίδεια ein Verhalten, das ge-

---

³³ Herman C. Waetjen, „The Subversion of ‚World' by the Parable of the Friend at Midnight," *JBL* 120 (2001): 703–21, hier 713.
³⁴ Ebd., 715.
³⁵ Ebd., 717.
³⁶ Hans Klein, *Das Lukasevangelium*, KEK I/3 (Göttingen: Vandenhoeck & Ruprecht, 2006), 408.
³⁷ Michael Wolter, *Das Lukasevangelium*, HNT 5 (Tübingen: Mohr Siebeck, 2008), 410, 411.
³⁸ Ebd., 412.
³⁹ Martin Ebner, „Face to face – Widerstand im Sinne der Gottesherrschaft: Jesu Wahrnehmung seines sozialen Umfeldes im Spiegel seiner Beispielgeschichten," *Early Christianity* 1 (2010): 406–40, hier 417, 432–34.

sellschaftlichen Konventionen zuwiderläuft. Ein solches sei durch das hellenistische Freundschaftsideal gedeckt (Cicero, *Amic.* 16.57).[40] Ebner fragt, ob es sich beim Bittenden um einen Sozialbanditen handelt, der aufgrund der ökonomischen Entwicklung sein Dorf, oder um einen Jesusjünger, der Haus und Hof, Eltern und Kinder verlassen hat.[41] Die Erzählung versichert, daß auf die alten Sozialbande Verlaß ist.[42]

14. Giovanni B. Bazzana

Giovanni Bazzana sieht in Q das Werk von Dorfschreibern in Galiläa; diese verwenden die terminologischen und imaginativen Ressourcen, die sich aus ihrer beruflichen Tätigkeit ergeben.[43] Dazu gehört auch eine Sprache der Gewalt im Zusammenhang der Charakterisierung der Gegner der Q-Leute, zur Beschreibung des Handelns Gottes bzw. des Reiches Gottes, sowie zur Erfassung des Verhältnisses der Menschen zu Gott. Dieser letzte Punkt wird festgemacht einerseits am Wort κρούω (Q 11,9), das ein aggressives Anklopfen an eine Tür bezeichnet[44], andererseits am mit ἀναίδεια gekennzeichnetem Verhalten des an die Tür seines Freundes Klopfenden in Lk 11,5–8. Bazzana versteht unter ἀναίδεια *Schamlosigkeit* und sieht eine Verbindung der Bedeutung des Wortes mit illegalen und kriminellen Handlungen.[45] Er nennt als Belege dafür drei dokumentarische Papyri (*SB* 6, 9458; 6, 9105; 6, 9421) und kommt zu dem Schluß, daß das Gleichnis vom bittenden Freund die an Gott gerichtete Bitten mit aggressiven und illegalen Akten vergleicht.[46]

---

[40] Ebd., 432. Vgl. Cicero, *Amic.* 16.57: Quam multa enim quae nostra causa numquam faceremus, facimus causa amicorum! precari ab indigno, supplicare, tum acerbius in aliquem invehi insectarique vehementius, quae in nostris rebus non satis honeste, in amicorum fiunt honestissime; multaeque res sunt, in quibus de suis commodis viri boni multa detrahunt detrahique patiuntur, ut iis amici potius quam ipsi fruantur. – „Wie vieles tun wir doch den Freunden zuliebe, was wir für uns niemals tun würden: einen Unwürdigen bitten, ihn demütig anflehen, dann wieder einen scharf anfahren und ihm recht heftig zusetzen, Dinge, die in eigener Sache uns nicht gerade zur Ehre gereichen würden, für Freunde aber höchst ehrenvoll sind. Und so gibt es viele Lebenslagen, in denen gutgesinnte Menschen ihren eigenen Vorteil vielfach zurückstellen und Nachteile hinnehmen, damit die Vorteile lieber ihren Freunden als ihnen selbst zugutekommen." Zitiert nach: Marcus Tullius Cicero, *Laelius de amicitia – Laelius über die Freundschaft: Lateinisch Deutsch*, hg. und übers. v. Marion Giebel, Universal-Bibliothek 19293 (Stuttgart: Reclam, 2015).
[41] Ebner, „Face to face," 435.
[42] Ebd.
[43] Giovanni B. Bazzana, „Violence and Human Prayer to God in Q 11," *HTS Teologiese Studies / Theological Studies* 70 (2014), 8 pages, http://dx.doi.org/10.4102/hts.v70i1.2733, hier 1.
[44] Ebd., 3–5.
[45] Ebd., 7.
[46] Ebd., 7–8.

15. Ernest van Eck

Ernest van Eck wendet sich gegen ein Verständnis des Gleichnisses im Rahmen seines jetzigen Kontextes im Lukasevangelium, wo es um das Gebet geht.[47] Die Parabel hat nichts mit dem Gebet zu tun. Vielmehr wird gezeigt, daß dann, wenn Nachbarn sich nicht als Nachbarn verhalten, auch das Reich Gottes nicht sichtbar ist.[48] Van Eck versucht das Gleichnis im Rahmen des kulturellen und historischen Kontexts des historischen Jesus zu verstehen: Es werden im Gleichnis eine Reihe von kulturellen Werten aufgerufen: nicht nur Ehre und Scham, Gastfreundschaft, Freundschaft und Dorfleben, sondern auch Reziprozität und Patron-Klientel-Verhältnisse.[49]

Freundschaft ist eine freiwillige Angelegenheit mit dem Inhalt, die Ehre des jeweils anderen zu schützen und zu fördern. Zentrales Element der Freundschaft ist es, das Wohl des anderen zu fördern, insbesondere wenn dieser sich in Not befindet.[50]

Van Eck unterscheidet generalisierte, ausgeglichene und negative Reziprozität. Generalisierte Reziprozität bedeutet zu geben, ohne etwas zurückzubekommen; sie ist vorrangig in der Familie oder im Clan beheimatet. Ausgeglichene Reziprozität dient wechselseitigem Interesse; Es wird gegeben, und dafür erhält man auch wieder etwas zurück. Die gesellschaftlichen Relationen der ausgeglichenen Reziprozität sind z.B. nachbarschaftliche Hilfe, Freundschaft oder Patron-Klient-Verhältnisse. Negative Reziprozität bedeutet, den anderen zu Gunsten seiner selbst auszunützen.[51]

Die Situation in Galiläa im ersten Jahrhundert wird vom Autor so gesehen, daß die urbanen Eliten die ländliche Bevölkerung ausbeuteten. Dies führte dazu, daß diese ländliche Bevölkerung am oder unter dem Existenzminimum leben mußte.[52] Als Folge davon beginnt sich die Solidarität innerhalb der lokalen Dorfgemeinschaft aufzulösen.[53]

Entgegen den Werten von Freundschaft zwischen zwei Personen und Gastfreundschaft zwischen einem Besucher und einem Haushalt bzw. dem ganzen Dorf lehnt der gebetene Freund die Bitte um Hilfe ab und wechselt in ein anderes Register sozialer Interaktion, indem er dem Bittenden anbietet, sein Klient zu werden. Dieses Verhalten wird mit Schamlosigkeit bezeichnet, die bedeutet

---

[47] Ernest van Eck, *The Parables of Jesus the Galilean: Stories of a Social Prophet*, Matrix: The Bible in Mediterranean Context 9 (Eugene, OR: Cascade, 2016), 227.
[48] Ebd.
[49] Ebd., 235.
[50] Ebd., 236–37.
[51] Ebd., 237.
[52] Ebd., 239, 246.
[53] Ebd., 246–47.

soziale Konventionen bzw. soziale und religiös sanktionierte Grenzen zu mißachten.[54]

Die Absicht, die Jesus mit diesem Gleichnis verfolgt, besteht darin, daß ein Gegenbild zum Reich Gottes gezeichnet wird, für das generalisierte Reziprozität charakteristisch sein soll. Wenn Nachbarn als Nachbarn handeln würden, würde das Reich Gottes sichtbar werden.[55]

D. Die Bedeutung von αἰδώς

Mit dem Wort αἰδώς wird eine Emotion bezeichnet, die als solche einen physiologischen und einen kognitiven Aspekt hat. Eine einfache Übersetzung ins Deutsche ist nicht möglich, da ein äquivalentes Wort fehlt.[56] Die Bedeutung kann wiedergegeben werden mit den Begriffen: Beschämung, Scham, Verlegenheit, Hemmung, Respekt, Sinn für Ehre, Schamgefühl, Anstand. An dieser Bedeutungsvielfalt ist ersichtlich, daß im Deutschen die korrelierenden Gefühle sich nicht zu einer konzeptuellen Einheit bündeln, die mit einem Wort repräsentiert wird. Von zentraler Bedeutung für das Verständnis ist die Verknüpfung dieser Emotion mit der Wahrnehmung von Ehre und Dignität (τιμή) von Menschen (und Göttern) in ihrer agonalen wie kooperativen Bezogenheit. In sozialer Interaktion treffen zwei oder mehrere Trägerinnen von Ehre aufeinander; dazu kommt noch das Publikum, sei es real, imaginiert oder internalisiert.[57]

In den Homerischen Epen begegnet das Verb αἰδέομαι in Form von zwei Konstruktionen: Einerseits gefolgt von einem Infinitiv, der die Handlung ausdrückt, deren Ausführung, durch das Empfinden von αἰδώς verhindert wird.[58] So wird die Reaktion der Achaier auf die Aufforderung des Hektor zur Auswahl eines von ihnen zum Zweikampf geschildert: „Sie empfanden Scham (αἰδέομαι) abzulehnen, aber Furcht zuzustimmen" (Homer, *Il.* 7.93).[59] Andererseits regierend einen Akkusativ, der immer ein personales Objekt ist, mit den Bedeutungen: „Ich fühle Scham vor," oder: „Ich habe Respekt vor."[60] So zum Beispiel in der Aussage des Hektor: „Jetzt, nachdem ich verderbte das Volk durch meine Betörung, scheue ich (αἰδέομαι) Trojas Männer und saumnachschleppende Frau-

---

[54] Ebd., 250–51; die Definition von ἀναίδεια übernimmt van Eck von Herzog, *Parables as Subversive Speech*, 213.
[55] van Eck, *Parables of Jesus*, 251–53.
[56] Douglas L. Cairns, *Aidōs: The Psychology and Ethics of Honour and Shame in Ancient Greek Literature* (Oxford: Clarendon, 1993), 5–7.
[57] Ebd., 13–18.
[58] Ebd., 48–49.
[59] Αἴδεσθεν μὲν ἀνήνασθαι, δεῖσαν δ᾽ ὑποδέχθαι (Homer, *Il.* 7.93). Zitiert hier und im Folgenden nach: Homer, *Ilias: Mit Urtext, Anhang und Registern*, übers. v. Hans Rupé, 8. Aufl., Sammlung Tusculum (Zürich; München: Artemis, 1983).
[60] Cairns, *Aidōs*, 49–50.

en, daß nicht einst mir sage ein Schlechterer: ‚Hektor verderbte das Volk, auf eigene Stärke vertrauend'" (*Il.* 22.104–107).[61] Ein entscheidender Faktor für das Empfinden von Scham bzw. Respekt ist die Rücksichtnahme auf das, was die Menschen sagen, also auf die öffentliche Meinung.[62] Z. B.: „Fühlt auch ihr Empörung, und fühlt ihr Scham vor denen, die eure Nachbarn sind" (Homer, *Od.* 2.64–66).[63] Dieser Aspekt ist auch von Bedeutung für die einfachste Verwendung des Wortes αἰδώς, nämlich als Ausruf im Rahmen von Kriegshandlungen, um Fahnenflucht zu vermeiden: „Schande, Argos Volk, ihr Verworfenen, trefflich in der Erscheinung" (Homer, *Il.* 5.787).[64] Drei Aspekte spielen hier zusammen: Feigheit oder Niederlage gehen zu Lasten der Ehre jedes Einzelnen wie auch zu Lasten der ganzen Gruppierung, und ein jeder ist Zeuge eines jeden im Falle des Versagens.[65] Der Einzelne ist Inhaber von Ehre im Rahmen einer Gemeinschaft von Trägern von Ehre, die von den jeweils anderen anerkannt wird.

Αἰδώς hat seinen Sitz in den Augen: αἰδὼς ἐν ὀφθαλμοῖσι γίγνεται, τέκνον (Euripides, Frag. 457),[66] und: τὸ ἐν ὀφθαλμοῖς εἶναι αἰδῶ (Aristoteles, *Rhet.* 1384a 18).[67] Aristoteles bezieht dies auf das Gesehenwerden durch andere. Wenn Herakles, nachdem ihm seine Tat der Auslöschung seiner Familie bewußt geworden ist, sein Haupt vor seinem Freund Theseus verbirgt, geht es vielleicht auch um die Scham für das eigene Sehen: „Sich schämen für sein Auge, für die verwandtschaftliche Freundschaft, für das Blut getöteter Kinder" (Euripides, *Herc. fur.* 1199–1201).[68]

1. Bettler, Fremde und αἰδώς

Neben sozialer Interaktion im Allgemeinen können spezifische Kontexte benannt werden, in denen αἰδώς eine bedeutende Rolle spielt: Freundschaft, der

---

[61] Νῦν δ' ἐπεὶ ὤλεσα λαὸν ἀτασθαλίῃσιν ἐμῇσιν, Αἰδέομαι Τρῶας καὶ Τρῳάδας ἑλκεσιπέπλους, Μήποτέ τις εἴπῃσι κακώτερος ἄλλος ἐμεῖο· Ἕκτωρ ἧφι βίηφι πιθήσας ὤλεσε λαόν (Homer, *Il.* 22.104–107).

[62] Cairns, *Aidōs*, 50–54.

[63] Νεμεσσήθητε καὶ αὐτοί, ἄλλους τ' αἰδέσθητε περικτίονας ἀνθρώπους, οἳ περιναιετάουσι (Homer, *Od.* 2.64–66). Zitiert hier und im Folgenden nach: Homer, *Odyssee, Griechisch/Deutsch: Übersetzung, Nachwort und Register*, hg. v. Roland Hampe, Reclams Universal Bibliothek 18640 (Stuttgart: Philipp Reclam, 2010).

[64] Αἰδώς, Ἀργεῖοι, κάκ' ἐλέγχεα, εἶδος ἀγητοί (Homer, *Il.* 5.787).

[65] Cairns, *Aidōs*, 68–69.

[66] Text aus: August Nauck, *Tragicorum Graecorum Fragmenta*, 2. Aufl. (Leipzig: Teubner, 1889), 501.

[67] Zitiert hier und im Folgenden nach: Aristotle, *The Art of Rhetoric: With an English Translation*, übers. v. John Henry Freese, LCL (London: Heinemann, 1926).

[68] αἰδόμενος τὸ σὸν ὄμμα καὶ φιλίαν ὁμόφυλον αἷμά τε παιδοφόνον (Euripides, *Herc. fur.* 1199–1201). Text und Übersetzung aus: Euripides, *Die bittflehenden Mütter; Der Wahnsinn des Herakles; Die Troerinnen; Elektra*, hg. v. Gustav Adolf Seek, übers. v. Ernst Buschor, Sämtliche Tragödien und Fragmente, Griechisch-Deutsch 3 (München: Heimeran, 1972).

Umgang mit Bettlern, die Begegnung mit Fremden, Sexualität und Bittstellen (Supplikation). Fremde treffen von außen auf eine Gemeinschaft und haben so eine unbestimmte Stellung hinsichtlich ihrer Ehre, auf die mit αἰδώς reagiert werden könnte; diese wird ihnen aber von Zeus, deren Beschützer, geliehen.[69] Zeus verschafft dem Fremden Ehre, die nach Respekt verlangt: „doch wir, hier angelangt, nahen uns deinen Knieen, ob du ein Gastgeschenk uns bringst oder sonstwie uns eine Gabe gewährst, wie es Brauch ist gegen den Gastfreund. Scheue denn, Bester, die Götter, denn Schutz Erflehende sind wir. Ist doch Zeus der Rächer für Schutz erflehende Fremde. Zeus, der Gastliche, der den zu achtenden Fremden Geleit gibt" (Homer, *Od.* 9.266–271).[70] Hinsichtlich des Erweises von Gastfreundschaft kommen mehrere Motive zusammen: Zunächst das weitverbreitete der Theoxenie: „Unrecht war's, Antinoos, daß du den elenden Bettler trafst, Unseliger; wenn es nun einer der Himmlischen wäre! Denn oft gleichen die Götter von fernher kommenden Fremden und durchstreifen die Städte in mannigfachen Gestalten, um nach der Menschen Frevel zu sehn oder rechtem Verhalten" (*Od.* 17.483–487). Weiters das Motiv der Achtung vor dem Menschen selbst: „Auch du, Alter, Leidbeladener, da dich ein Dämon zu mir führte, lull mich nicht ein mit gefälligen Lügen; denn nicht darum will ich dich achten und dich bewirten, sondern aus Furcht vor dem gastlichen Zeus und aus eigenem Mitleid" (*Od.* 14.386–389).[71] Einen Fremden schlecht behandelt zu haben, kann in der Gemeinschaft bekannt werden und durch üble Nachrede die eigene Ehre schmälern: „Alter, da fehlte wirklich nicht viel und es hätten die Hunde dich zerrissen im Nu, und du hättest mit Schimpf mich beladen" (*Od.* 14.37–38). Schließlich verbreiten Fremde den Ruhm ihres Gastgebers: „Wer jedoch Edles tut und ist von edler Gesinnung, dessen Ruhm verbreiten die fremden Gäste zu allen Menschen über die Erde; und viele nennen ihn edel" (*Od.* 19.332–334).[72] Bettler sind von der Verpflichtung αἰδώς zu zeigen ausgenommen: „Denn die Scham steht nicht gut an einem darbenden Manne" (*Od.* 17.347).[73] Sie dürfen andere Menschen direkt angehen ohne Rücksicht auf die Etikette.[74] Auf seiner Rückreise nach Ithaka kommt Odysseus als Bettler zu Antinoos, welcher ihm aber nicht hilft, sondern ihn mißhandelt und zu ihm sagt: „Was bist du für ein dreister und unverfrorener Bettler?" (*Od.* 17.449).[75]

---

[69] Cairns, *Aidōs*, 105.
[70] ἡμεῖς δ' αὖτε κιχανόμενοι τὰ σὰ γοῦνα ἱκόμεθ', εἴ τι πόροις ξεινήϊον ἠὲ καὶ ἄλλως δοίης δωτίνην, ἥ τε ξείνων θέμις ἐστίν. ἀλλ' αἰδεῖο, φέριστε, θεούς· ἱκέται δέ τοί εἰμεν. Ζεὺς δ' ἐπιτιμήτωρ ἱκετάων τε ξείνων τε, ξείνιος, ὅς ξείνοισιν ἅμ' αἰδοίοισιν ὀπηδεῖ (*Od.* 270–71).
[71] καὶ σύ, γέρον πολυπενθές, ἐπεί σέ μοι ἤγαγε δαίμων, μήτε τί μοι ψεύδεσσι χαρίζεο μήτε τι θέλγε· οὐ γὰρ τοὔνεκ' ἐγώ σ' αἰδέσσομαι οὐδὲ φιλήσω, ἀλλὰ Δία ξένιον δείσας αὐτόν τ' ἐλεαίρων (*Od.* 14.386–389).
[72] Cairns, *Aidōs*, 108–112.
[73] αἰδὼς δ' οὐκ ἀγαθὴ κεχρημένῳ ἀνδρὶ παρεῖναι (*Od.* 17.347).
[74] Cairns, *Aidōs*, 106.
[75] ὥς τις θαρσαλέος καὶ ἀναιδής ἐσσι προΐκτης (*Od.* 17.449).

Aber selbst die Untergebenen des Antinoos finden dieses Verhalten unangemessen (*Od.* 17.483–87).

2. Freundschaft und Scham

Freundschaft ist von großer Bedeutung in der antiken griechischen Kultur[76] und wurde dementsprechend breit thematisiert.[77] Bei Homer sind freundschaftliche Verhältnisse stets auch von αἰδώς mitgeprägt. Kinder zeigen Scham/Respekt gegenüber ihren Eltern (z. B.: Homer, *Il.* 3.172), und Freunde (im engeren Sinn) reagieren wechselseitig mit αἰδώς auf die Ehre des jeweils anderen (z. B. *Il.* 9.640).[78]

In seinen Ausführungen über Freundschaft in der *Rhetorik* kommt Aristoteles auch auf die Verbindung von Freundschaft und Scham zu sprechen (*Rhet.* 2.4). Es handelt sich um eine Aufzählung derer, die wir lieben bzw. denen wir freundschaftlich begegnen: „weiterhin Leute, zu denen wir so ein Verhältnis haben, daß wir uns, was unseren Ruf betrifft, nicht schämen (αἰσχύνομαι), ohne sie aber zu verachten; und auch diejenigen, vor denen wir Scham empfinden (αἰσχύνομαι), was die Wahrheit betrifft" (2. 4. 22–23).[79] Es dürfte damit ein Vorbehalt zum Ausdruck kommen der öffentlichen Meinung gegenüber. Vor Freunden schämt man sich nicht dessen, wie die Menge etwas einschätzt, sondern man schämt sich dessen, was in Wahrheit schamvoll ist.[80] Diese Unterscheidung gibt vermutlich das Freundschaftsideal des Aristoteles wieder und ist nicht als Beschreibung von realen Freundschaftsverhältnissen zu verstehen.

In den *Erinnerungen an Sokrates* thematisiert Xenophon anhand eines Streites zwischen zwei Brüdern das Problem des „ersten Schrittes" (*Mem.* 2.3). Einen feindlich gesinnten Hund versucht man mit Futter freundlich zu stimmen (*Mem.* 2.3.9). Um zu einem Mahl geladen zu werden, lädt man zuvor selbst ein (*Mem.* 11). Damit ein Freund sich während der eigenen Abwesenheit um die Güter kümmert, kümmert man sich zuvor selbst um die Angelegenheiten des

---

[76] Zur Einführung (mit weiterer Literatur) vgl.: Barbara von Reibnitz, „Freundschaft (Antike)," *DNP* 4:669–73; K. Treu, „Freundschaft," *RAC* 8:418–434; Gustav Stählin, „φιλέω κτλ," *TWNT* 9:112–168; David Konstan, *Friendship in the Classical World*, KTAH (Cambridge: Cambridge University Press, 1997); Mary Whitlock Blundell, *Helping Friends and Harming Enemies: A Study in Sophocles and Greek Ethics* (Cambridge: Cambridge University Press, 1989).

[77] Hier sind vorrangig zu nennen: Lucian, *Toxaris*; Cicero, *De Amicitia*; Plutarch, „Wie man den Schmeichler vom Freund unterscheiden kann" (*Mor.* 48E–74E); Plutarch, *Amic. mult.*; Isokrates, *Demon.* (*Or.* 1), 24–26; Aristoteles, *Eth. nic.* 8.1–9.12; Xenophon, *Mem.* 2.4–6; Epiktet, *Diatr.* 2.22; Gellius, *Noctes Atticae* 1.3; 17.5; Valerius Maximus, *Facta et dicta* 4.7; weiters noch die Dialoge Platons: *Symposium*, *Phaedrus* und *Lysis*.

[78] Cairns, *Aidōs*, 89–95.

[79] καὶ πρὸς οὓς οὕτως ἔχουσιν ὥστε μὴ αἰσχύνεσθαι τὰ πρὸς δόξαν, μὴ καταφρονοῦντες. καὶ πρὸς οὓς αἰσχύνονται τὰ πρὸς ἀλήθειαν (*Rhet.* 2. 4. 22–23).

[80] Marlene K. Sokolon, „The Shameless Truth: Shame and Friendship in Aristotle," *European Journal of Political Theory* 12 (2013) 447–465, 454.

Freundes (*Mem.* 12). Um von einem Gastfreund Unterkunft zu erhalten, nimmt man zuerst diesen auf. Die Schlußfolgerung, die Sokrates zieht, lautet schließlich: „Zögerst du nun etwa, den Anfang zu machen, aus Furcht, du könntest in Schande dastehen (μὴ αἰσχρὸς φανῇς), wenn du zuerst deinem Bruder eine Wohltat erweist? Sonst scheint doch wahrlich ein Mann des höchsten Ruhmes würdig, wenn er zuvorkommt, den Feinden Schlechtes zuzufügen und den Freunden Gutes" (*Mem.* 14).[81] Dieser Satz geht mit dem Hinweis auf ein Scham verursachendes Handeln (wie auch auf den Ruhm) über das utilitaristische Schema der voranstehenden Beispiele hinaus. Sei es, daß im Geben eine Hoffnung auf eine gelingende Beziehung oder auf Erwiederung steckt, sei es, daß in der Erwiederung zugleich Anerkennung des anderen impliziert ist – hier können nur Vermutungen angestellt werden –, festzustellen bleibt, daß behauptet wird, dass ein Geschenk ohne Erfolg zu Scham führt.

Die Rede des Isokrates an Demonikos will eine Unterweisung zu richtigem Lebenswandel sein. Das Thema Freundschaft kommt darin öfters vor; hinsichtlich der Verbindung dieser mit Scham finden sich folgende zusammenfassende Sätze: „Empfinde Scheu vor den Göttern, halte deine Eltern in Ehren, deinen Freunden gegenüber zeige Respekt (τοὺς δὲ φίλους αἰσχύνου), den Gesetzen erweise Gehorsam" (Isokrates, *Demon.* 1.16).[82] Das Wort αἰσχύνω mit dem Akkusativ einer Person bedeutet präzise: „Scham fühlen vor."[83]

Im Alten Testament spielt Freundschaft im Vergleich zur griechischen Welt eine geringere Rolle.[84] Im Buch Jesus Sirach finden sich aber einige Abschnitte zum Thema Freundschaft, die für unsere Frage nach dem Zusammenhang von Freundschaft und Scham von Bedeutung sind.[85] Sir 6,1 lautet: „Und gegenüber dem Freund werde nicht zum Feind, ein böser Name nämlich wird Schande (αἰσχύνη) und Schmach erben. So (geht es) dem doppelzüngigen Sünder."[86] Dieser Satz steht in einem Abschnitt, in dem es um die rechte Art des

---

[81] Text aus: Xenophon, *Memorabilia; Oeconomicus; Symposium; Apology*, übers. v. Edgar C. Marchant und Otis J. Todd, LCL (Cambridge, MA: Harvard University Press, 1923): Übersetzung aus: Xenophon, *Erinnerungen an Sokrates*, übers. v. Rudolf Preiswerk, Reclams Universal Bibliothek 1855 (Stuttgart: Reclam, 2010).

[82] Text aus: Isocrates, *Works Volume 1*, übers. v. George Norlin, LCL 209 (Cambridge, MA: Harvard University Press, 1928). Übersetzung aus: Isokrates, *Sämtliche Werke, 1: Reden I–VIII*, übers. v. Christine Ley-Hutton, Bibliothek der Griechischen Literatur 36 (Stuttgart: Anton Hiersemann, 1993).

[83] *An Intermediate Greek-English Lexicon: Founded Upon the Seventh Edition of Liddell and Scott's Greek-English Lexicon* (Oxford: University Press, 1889), ad loc.

[84] Zur Freundschaft im Alten Testament: Jan Dietrich, „Von der Freundschaft im Alten Testament und Alten Orient," WO 44 (2014): 37–56.

[85] Dazu siehe: Friedrich V. Reiterer (Hg.), *Freundschaft bei Ben Sira: Beiträge des Symposions zu Ben Sira Salzburg 1995*, BZAW 244 (Berlin: de Gruyter, 1996).

[86] Zitiert hier und im Folgenden nach: Wolfgang Kraus und Martin Karrer (Hgg.)., *Septuaginta Deutsch: Das griechische Alte Testament in deutscher Übersetzung* (Stuttgart: Deutsche Bibelgesellschaft, 2009); Text aus: Alfred Rahlfs, Robert Hanhart, et al. (Hgg.), *Septuaginta: Id*

Redens geht. Etwas zu sagen, was den Freund schädigt, bedeutet Scham für einen selbst, vermutlich weil man seinen eigenen Ruf schädigt, indem man sich als Verleumder und unzuverlässiger Freund erweist, und sich vor den anderen schämen muß.[87] Der zweite Text ist für den Zusammenhang von Freundschaft und Geben von größerer Bedeutung: „Es gibt den, der um der Scham (αἰσχύνη) willen (seinem) Freund (etwas) verspricht, und (schon) hat er ihn sich zum Feind erworben, ohne Grund" (Sir 20,23). Dadurch, daß ein Versprechen einem Freund gegenüber nicht eingehalten wird, wird dieser einem zum Feind. Warum das Versprechen um der Scham willen erfolgt, ist schwer zu sagen. Es könnte sein, daß der, der das Versprechen macht, nicht als mittellos dastehen will; nach dem bisher Beobachteten ist es wahrscheinlicher, daß es eine der Freundschaftsbeziehung immanente Scham gibt, die dazu verpflichtet, dem Freund zu geben.

E. ἀναίδεια

Walter Bauer nennt im Wörterbuch zum Neuen Testament als Bedeutung von ἀναίδεια „Unverschämtheit" und „Zudringlichkeit."[88] Im Liddell-Scott findet sich die Bedeutungsangabe „shamelessness."[89] Franco Montanari übersetzt „impudence," „lack of sense of proportion or consideration," „intemperance."[90] Im Greek-English Lexicon of the New Testament von Danker werden als Übersetzungen genannt: „lack of sensitivity to what is proper," „carelessness about the good opinion of others," „shamelessness," „impertinence," „impudence," „ignoring of convention."[91] Diese Bedeutungsangaben sind sicher nicht falsch, was aber fehlt ist ein Hinweis auf die eigentliche Bedeutung des Wortes, nämlich Mangel an Anerkennung der Ehre eines anderen oder seiner selbst.

Der für den Plot der Ilias zentrale Konflikt zwischen Agamemnon, dem Oberbefehlshaber der Griechen, und Achilleus, dem Anführer eines Teilverbandes, besteht darin, daß Chryses zu den Achaiern kommt, um seine Tochter freizukaufen; dies wird ihm von Agamemnon verweigert, worauf Apollon die Pest sendet. Nachdem ein Seher über den Grund der Seuche befragt wurde, wird die Tochter des Chryses nach Troia zurückgesandt; zugleich fordert Agamemnon von Achilleus, auch die Tochter des Brises freizugeben. Dieser ist darüber

---

est Vetus Testamentum graece iuxta LXX interpretes, editio altera (Stuttgart: Deutsche Bibelgesellschaft, 2006).

[87] Ingrid Krammer, „Scham im Zusammenhang mit Freundschaft," in Reiterer, *Freundschaft bei Ben Sira*, 171–201, hier 187.

[88] Bauer, ad loc.

[89] LSJ, ad loc.

[90] Franco Montanari, *The Brill Dictionary of Ancient Greek*, ed. Madeleine Goh and Chad Schroeder (Leiden: Brill, 2015), ad loc.

[91] BDAG, ad loc.

entzürnt und beschwert sich über seinen Gegner in ἀναίδεια gekleidet zu sein (Homer, *Il.* 1.149; 9.372; 1.158), weil er seine Ehre nicht achtet.[92]

Bei Hesiod wird der Reichtum, der durch Diebstahl zustande kommt, als schamlos bezeichnet (Hesiod, *Op.* 324), vermutlich deshalb, weil nicht der Konsequenzen für die eigene Ehre gedacht wird, falls man entdeckt wird, und aufgrund der mangelnden Sorge für die Ehre der beraubten Person.[93] Weitere Beispiele für ἀναίδεια werden im folgenden genannt: Mißhandlung von Fremden, Unzucht mit der Gattin des Bruders oder den greisen Vater zu beschimpfen (*Op.* 326–334).

Ein interessanter Text, da er Geben und Nehmen im nachbarschaftlichen Milieu thematisiert, ist der folgende aus *Werke und Tage* von Hesiod (351–362):

Suche nicht schlechten Gewinn, schlechter Gewinn ist so viel wie Verderben. Freund sei dem Freund und besuche den, der dich besucht. Gib dem, der dir gibt, und gib dem nicht, der nicht gibt. Dem Geber gibt jeder gern, dem Nichtgeber niemand. Geben ist gut, Nehmen ist schlecht und bringt Tod. Schenkt nämlich ein Mann bereitwillig, und wäre es ein Großes, freut ihn die eigene Gabe, und er spendet fröhlichen Herzens. Wer aber der Schamlosigkeit Raum gibt und etwas für sich nimmt, auch wenn es nur um Geringes geht, erkaltet sein Herz. Denn legst du nämlich zu Kleinem auch nur ein Kleines hinzu und tust du es häufig, wird bald ein Großes daraus. Er aber, der zum Vorrat hinzulegt, der wehrt dem brennenden Hunger.[94]

Dieser Abschnitt stellt das Unbehagen des Mannes, der nimmt, dem Wohlergehen dessen gegenüber, der gibt. Derjenige, der etwas annimmt, gerät in die Position des Unterlegenen, und der Gebende wird zum Überlegenen. Auch kleine Gaben addieren sich zu einer großen Verpflichtung auf.[95] Der letzte Satz spricht von Hesiods Ideal der Selbstgenügsamkeit, dem man nachkommt, wenn man durch harte Arbeit sich Ersparnisse schafft. Geben ist nicht nur eine Sache der Freude, sondern auch der Ehre.[96] Der, der nimmt, verfehlt seine eigene Ehre und handelt deshalb schamlos.

In dem Homerischen Hymnus an Hermes stiehlt Hermes die Herde des Apollo. Aufgrund dieses Diebstahls wird er von seiner Mutter als schamlos bezeichnet (*Hymni Hom.* 156). Der Grund für diese Bezeichnung ist dieselbe wie bei der zuvor genannten Hesiodstelle, nur wird die Schamlosigkeit als Charakteristikum einer trickster-Gestalt positiv gesehen. Hermes läßt es zugunsten seiner eigenen Ehre an Respekt vor der Ehre anderer vermissen (*Hymni Hom.* 172–73, 381–

---

[92] Cairns, *Aidōs*, 99–100.
[93] Cairns, *Aidōs*, 159.
[94] Eigene Übersetzung in Anlehnung an: Hesiod, *Werke und Tage: Griechisch/Deutsch*, hg. und *übers.* v. Otto Schönberger, Universal-Bibliothek 9445 (Stuttgart: Reclam, 2004), und Paul Millett, *Lending and Borrowing in Ancient Athens* (Cambridge: Cambridge University Press, 1991), 33.
[95] Millett, *Lending and Borrowing*, 33–34.
[96] Hendrik Bolkestein, *Wohltätigkeit und Armenpflege im vorchristlichen Altertum: Ein Beitrag zum Problem „Moral und Gesellschaft"* (Utrecht: A. Oosthoek, 1939), 150–56.

82).⁹⁷ Es ist anzumerken, daß ἀναίδεια hier positiv gesehen wird. Vielleicht besteht ein Traditionskontinuum – etwa über die griechische Komödie vermittelt – hin zur kynischen Tugend der Schamlosigkeit.

In der Tragödie *Alkestis* des Euripides stirbt Alkestis anstelle ihres Ehemannes Admetus. Zwischen diesem und seinem Vater Pheres kommt es zu einer Auseinandersetzung darüber, wem nun Schamlosigkeit zu eigen ist. Admetus bezeichnet seinen Vater als schamlos, weil er keine Rücksicht nimmt auf die öffentliche Meinung und keinen Respekt zeigt für die Verpflichtungen sich selbst gegenüber (Euripides, *Alc.* 727). Hinzu kommt, daß der Vater die Gunst (χάρις), die ihm sein Sohn erwiesen hat, nicht respektiert (658–661).⁹⁸ Der Vater gibt die Vorwürfe gleichlautend zurück (694). Alkestis war nicht schamlos, da ihr αἰδώς gegenüber ihrem Ehemann zu eigen war und sie um die öffentliche Meinung Sorge trug (728).⁹⁹ Den Status eines anderen anzuerkennen, bedeutet den eigenen Platz zu kennen, und den eigenen Platz zu kennen, bedeutet seinen Platz in der Gruppe einzunehmen.¹⁰⁰

Ein in das selbe Feld von Begriffen rund um Ehre und Scham gehörender Ausdruck ist ὕβρις: Mutwille, Böswilligkeit, Überheblichkeit. Definieren läßt sich dieses Wort als freiwilliger Angriff auf die Ehre eines anderen verbunden mit einem Vergnügen daran, Überlegenheit zum Ausdruck zu bringen.¹⁰¹ In der Beschreibung des Pausanias des Areopags in Athen findet sich folgendes Zitat: τοὺς δὲ ἀργοὺς λίθους, ἐφ' ὧν ἑστᾶσιν ὅσοι δίκας ὑπέχουσι καὶ οἱ διώκοντες, τὸν μὲν Ὕβρεως τὸν δὲ Ἀναιδείας αὐτῶν ὀνομάζουσι. – „Von den beiden rohen Steinen, auf denen Angeklagte und Ankläger stehen, nennen sie den einen den Stein des Frevels, den anderen den der Schamlosigkeit" (Pausanias, *Descr.* 1.28.5).¹⁰² Dies kann dahingehend verstanden werden, daß der Angeklagte am Stein der ὕβρις stand, der die kriminelle Intention des Täters repräsentierte, während der Ankläger am Stein der ἀναίδεια stand, der repräsentierte, daß der Geschädigte nicht bereit war Vergebung zu gewähren, nicht bereit war in einen Status des αἰδώς mit diesem zurückzukehren, und so auf seiner Vergeltung be-

---

⁹⁷ Cairns, *Aidōs*, 159.
⁹⁸ Text aus: Euripides, *Fabulae, vol. 1: Cyclops, Alcestis, Medea, Heraclidae, Hippolytus, Andromacha, Hecuba*, ed. James Diggle, Scriptorum classicorum bibliotheca Oxoniensis (Oxford: Oxford University Press, 1984).
⁹⁹ Cairns, *Aidōs*, 268.
¹⁰⁰ Ebd., 269.
¹⁰¹ N. R. E. Fisher, *Hybris: A Study in the Values of Honour and Shame in Ancient Greece* (Warminster: Aris & Phillips, 1992), 1.
¹⁰² Pausanias, *Description of Greece: Books I–II*, trans. W. H. S. Jones, LCL 93 (Cambridge, MA: Harvard University Press, 1918), 148–49: „The unhewn stones on which stand the defendants and the prosecutors, they call the stone of Outrage and the stone of Ruthlessness." Vgl. Pausanias, *Reisen in Griechenland: Gesamtausgabe in drei Bänden*, 3 Bde., hg. v. Felix Eckstein, übers. v. Ernst Meyer, Bibliothek der Alten Welt: Griechische Reihe (Zürich; München: Artemis, 1986), 1:128–29: „Von den beiden rohen Felsblöcken, auf denen Angeklagte und Ankläger stehen, nennen sie den einen den Stein des Frevels, den anderen den des Nichtverzeihens."

stand.¹⁰³ Dieser Stein ermöglichte das weitverbreitete Mißverständnis, es sei in Athen ein Gott der Schamlosigkeit verehrt worden. Z. B. heißt es in einem Fragment des Menander: „O thou who now art chief amongst the gods, O Effrontery (ἀναίδεια), if it is right to name thee god – and it is right, for now-a-days the thing that sways is deemed a god – to what lengths thou dost go and what a goal, methinks, thou'lt reach!" (257 K).¹⁰⁴

F. ἀναίδεια in dokumentarischen Papyri

Beschwerdebrief eines Römers an einen εἰρηνοφύλαξ wegen rechtswidriger Steuereintreibung eines Beamten von einem Krüppel; Fayum, Ende 2. Jhd. n.Chr. (SB 6, 9105).

To Philip, chosen *eirenophylax* of Theadelphia out of 3 *euschemones*, from Ulpia Herois with the guardian granted me according to Roman usage, Gaius Lucretius Papirianus.
You are not aware of the shameless enterprises connected with Ababikis, whom you have at other times chastised for shameless extortion: now this same man has elected to give an exhibition of his tyranny; for he has demanded a sum of money from the man who is being cared for in my orchard, a diseased cripple, who had been exempted from all liability for poll-tax according to the rule of the prefect; this on the pretext that he was deferring to the elders. Since therefore such conduct demands severe punishment, or certainly (?) the man must be delivered from extortion, I tender this petition, that you may take him under guard to the metropolis together with the cripple; for he further alleges that he has given the copies to the public officials in charge of the storehouse; and I have produced witnesses to this.
I, Gaius Lucretius Papirianus, append my signature, being guardian of Ulpia Herois.¹⁰⁵

Eingabe an den πραιπόσιτος des 5. πάγος von Arsinoites; Karanis, 24. Okt. 316 n. Chr. (SB 6, 9184).

To Aurelius Gerontius, preaepositus of the 5th pagus, from Aurelius Isidorus, son of Ptolemaeus, of the village of Karanis.
Although I possess a great deal of land and am occupied with its cultivation, and I am not involved with any persons in the village but keep to myself, somehow or other, on the day before yesterday, during the middle of the day, while I was in the field, Kalas the son of Onnophris, Seuthes the son of Timotheus, Eras the son of Seuthes, Paesis the son of Apolinarius, Sotas the son of Achillas and Serenis the son of Ariston, of the same village, without any grievance against me, but because they were heavily intoxicated with wine and emboldened by their wealth, appeared before our house equipped with farm tools and broke down the door; and having gained entrance they smashed all the utensils that

---

¹⁰³ Fisher, *Hybris*, 199.
¹⁰⁴ Übersetzung aus: Menander, *The Principal Fragments*, übers. v. Francis G. Allinson, LCL (Cambridge, MA: Harvard University Press, 1951), 366–67.
¹⁰⁵ SB 6, 9105; John Barns, „Three Fayum Papyri," *CdE* 45 (1949): 295–305, hier 303.

we had for household service and they carried off whatever else they found in the place. If our people, who were women, had not raised an outcry, these men from the village would have made an onslaught on the place itself. Probably they were plotting even more grievous harm against me.

Wherefore, since their gross shamelessness demands the punishment prescribed by the laws, and the doors as well as the shattered utensils are there to see, I am constrained to submit this report with the request that they be brought before you, so that the consequences provided by the laws can be exacted, whereby I shall have peace with respect to them. Farewell.

In the consultship of Sabinus and Rufinus, the most illustrious. Phaophi 27.[106]

Anzeige bei der Polizei (dem ὁ ἐπὶ τῆς εἰρήνης) wegen einer tätlichen Beleidigung; Oxyrhynchus, 3. Jhd. n.Chr. (SB 6, 9421).

To Aurelius Alexander, of the police magistrates, from Aurelius A[-] alias Aphynchis, former exhibitor of games in the city of Oxyrhynchites.

Yesterday evening a certain Didyme, the wife of Agathos Daimon, the cook, passing my house and finding me standing there with our family, treated us with insolence, using speakable and unspeakable expressions – a woman abundantly furnished with the utmost shamelessness and effrontery. Thereupon, when I stopped her, advising her to keep off from us, she advanced to such a degree of madness that, taking advantage of the obscurity of the hour, she leapt upon me, and, being distracted in her senses, even stretched out her hands and smote me, and railed furiously at some of my daughter's sons, whom I called to witness, and not only at them, but even at one of the officials of our city who was present. Having suffered so much, I, the victim of the assault, deliver to you this petition, asking you to give orders that she shall be brought before you, so that I may experience your beneficence toward all men. Farewell.[107]

Beschwerde wegen überhöhter Frachsätze; Tebtynis, 2. Hälfte des 2. Jhd. n.Chr. (SB 6, 9458).

From Kronion, son of Pakebkis and grandson of Harpokration, exempt priest of the notable temple of the village of Tebtunis and deputy prophet of the same temple, who has suffered no ordinary insolence from Kronios, a certain reckless man. The situation is this. Now he incited himself to demand freight charges (naula) for the wheat brought down from the village to the harbor, and in stead of the freight paid by him, namely 19 obols each sakkos, he is demanding a total of 30 obols with his (customary) recklessness and shamelessness. And I, according, paid him the total of what he himself spent for the grain which I had delivered to him, but wishing to make a profit out of me, he came in my absence to my house and displayed the extreme of insolence, to the point that he stripped my maidservants of their clothing in the midst of the street – not satisfied with what else he had done, but he even made a profit out of them. And when I came and spoke to him about these things, paying no heed, he tried to employ the same recklessness upon me. There-

---

[106] SB 6, 9184; A. E. R. Boak and H. C. Youtie, „Two Petitions from Karanis," Aeg 31 (1951): 317–26, hier 320.

[107] SB 6, 9421; S. Eitrem and Leiv Amundsen, „Complaint of an Assault, with Petition to the Police," JEA 40 (1954): 30–33, hier 31.

fore, of necessity, I report this, and ask you to take measures against his surly actions; and so I shall be succored. Farewell.[108]

Der erste Papyrustext (*SB* 6, 9105) ist ein Beschwerdebrief an einen εἰρηνοφύλαξ. Darin beklagt sich der Beschwerdeführer, daß ein Beamter namens Ababikis von einem Krüppel gegen das Recht Steuern eintrieb. Dieser Beamte war schon einmal durch schamlose Unternehmungen aufgefallen, und zwar wegen schamloser Erpressung bzw. Wucher.

Der zweite Text (*SB* 6, 9184) ist eine Anzeige durch Aurelius Isidorus von sechs Männern, die die Tür seines Hauses aufgebrochen und den Hausrat zerstört bzw. gestohlen haben. Er fürchtet den Plan, daß sie noch mehr Unheil gegen ihn aushecken. Deren Absichten werden als schamlos bezeichnet.

Im dritten Text (*SB* 6, 9421) zeigt ein Mann namens Aphynchis eine Frau namens Didyme bei der Polizei an, weil sie ihn und seine Familie beschimpft und tätlich angegriffen hat. Dieser Frau sei große Schamlosigkeit zu eigen.

Der letzte Text (*SB* 6, 9458) schließlich ist eine Beschwerde des Priesters Kronion über einen Frächter namens Kronios, der überhöhte Gebühren kassiert und sich an der Familie des Priesters vergangen hat. Dieses Verhalten wird als schamlos bezeichnet.

Giovanni Bazzana sieht – wie gesagt – die Bedeutung, die ἀναίδεια in diesen Texten zukommt, in der Aggressivität und Gewalthaftigkeit des beschriebenen Handelns.[109] Demgegenüber könnte man vermuten, daß es der Mangel an Respekt ist, der den jeweils anderen entgegengebracht wird, der zu der Bezeichnung „Schamlosigkeit" Anlaß gegeben hat. Einmal wird das Innere des Hauses bzw. die Schwelle nicht respektiert (*SB* 6, 9184), zweimal handelt es sich um einen tätlichen Angriff (*SB* 6, 9421, *SB* 6, 9458).

Es ist natürlich möglich, daß die Bedeutung von ἀναίδεια sich im Lauf der Jahrhunderte seit Homer und Hesiod verändert bzw. verengt hat. Es dürfte aber den Belegen aus der Zeit um das Neue Testament nichts Eindeutiges dahingehend zu entnehmen sein, etwa bei Josephus (*B. J.* 1.224; 1.276; 1.616) oder in den Oracula Sibyllina (Sib 1.175; 2.33; 8.184).

G. ἀναίδεια in Lk 11,5–8

Mein Vorschlag, die Bedeutung von ἀναίδεια zu bestimmen, besteht darin, diese als relationalen Begriff zu verstehen. Schamlos ist ein Verhalten, wenn es die Ehre eines anderen bzw. einer anderen nicht anerkennt oder respektiert. Weiters ist eine Haltung oder Handlung schamlos, die nicht auf die Ehre seiner selbst

---

[108] *SB* 6, 9458; C. Bradford Welles, „Complaint From a Priest of Tebtunis Concerning Grain Transportation Charges, of the Late Second Century," *EPap* 8 (1957): 103–11, hier 104–5.

[109] Bazzana, „Violence and Human Prayer," 7.

achtet und schließlich nicht darauf Rücksicht nimmt, welche Meinung andere von einem haben. Ausgehend davon bestehen zwei Möglichkeiten: Die Schamlosigkeit könnte dem gebetenen Freund zukommen, da es ihm an Selbstachtung fehlt bzw. weil er nicht um die Meinung des Dorfes besorgt ist. Dagegen spricht, daß in Vers 8 das reflexive Pronomen αὐτός dreimal sich auf den bittenden Freund bezieht, weshalb auch das vierte Vorkommen in diesem Sinn anzunehmen wahrscheinlich ist. Dies bedeutet dann, daß der gebetene Freund die Schamlosigkeit des Bittenden vermeiden will, also vermeiden will, von diesem nicht mehr respektiert zu werden. Der Gebetene fürchtet kurz gesagt, sein Gesicht zu verlieren.

H. War dieser Text Teil des Spruchevangeliums Q?

Alle Positionen, die im Laufe der Forschungsgeschichte vertreten wurden, finden sich gesammelt im *Documenta Q*-Band zu Q 11,5–13.[110] Es wird allgemein anerkannt, daß sich in Lk 11,5–8 sowohl traditionelle, als auch redaktionelle Elemente, also Vokabeln und Stileigentümlichkeiten finden.[111] Für gewöhnlich wird deshalb damit gerechnet, daß hier Tradition vorliegt, die von Lukas überarbeitet worden ist. Nur Harry T. Fleddermann meint, daß es für lukanische Redaktion charakteristisch sei, Q-Features zu imitieren, weshalb, nach diesem Autor, der ganze Text Lk 11,5–8 von Lukas stammt.[112]

Vergleicht man die „Wer unter euch"-Gleichnisse miteinander, zeigt sich folgendes Bild: Lk 11,5–8 ist dadurch bestimmt, daß auf die Frage (V. 5–7) eine Antwort durch den Sprecher folgt (V. 8), die auf der Bildebene verbleibt, zugleich das Bild, in dem es um Freundschaft geht, überboten wird, durch den Hinweis auf die Schamlosigkeit. Denn das Argument besteht darin, daß die Sorge um die

---

[110] Thomas Klampfl (Hg.), *Q 11:5–8: The Friend at Midnight; Q 11:9–13: The Certainty of the Answer to Prayer*, in Zusammenarbeit mit Paul Hoffmann et al., Documenta Q (Leuven: Peeters, in Vorbereitung für 2019).

[111] Redaktionell: πορεύεσθαι, Partizip ἀναστάς, ἐπειδή, lokales εἰς statt ἐν, πρός mit Akkusativ nach Verba dicendi, παραγίνομαι, διὰ τὸ εἶναι, εἰ καὶ οὐ … διά γε. Traditionell: τίς ἐξ ὑμῶν mit ἔχειν, Fragesatz statt konditionalem Vordersatz, in rhetorischen Fragen, Häufung von satzverbindendem καί, Nebenordnung von Sätzen bei logischer Unterordnung. Vgl. Joachim Jeremias, *Die Sprache des Lukasevangeliums: Redaktion und Tradition im Nicht-Markusstoff des dritten Evangeliums*, KEK Sonderband (Göttingen: Vandenhoeck & Ruprecht, 1980), 196–98; Reinhard von Bendemann, *Zwischen ΔΟΞΑ und ΣΤΑΥΡΟΣ: Eine exegetische Untersuchung der Texte des sogenannten Reiseberichts im Lukasevangelium*, BZNW 101 (Berlin: de Gruyter, 2001), 441–42.

[112] Harry T. Fleddermann, „Three Friends at Midnight (Luke 11,5–8)," in *Luke and His Readers: Festschrift A. Denaux*, hg. v. Reimund Bieringer, Gilbert Van Belle und Joseph Verheyden, BETL 182 (Leuven: Peeters, 2005), 265–82, hier 269–71; idem, *Q: A Reconstruction and Commentary*, BTS 1 (Leuven: Peeters, 2005), 460; idem, „Mid-Level Techniques in Luke's Redaction of Q," *ETL* 79 (2003): 53–71.

Ehre stärker ist, als der Verpflichtungscharakter, der sich aus dem Freundschaftsverhältnis ergibt. Eine selbstgegebene Antwort findet sich nur noch in Lk 22,27: Der bei Tisch Sitzende ist größer als der Bedienende. In Lk 11,13 findet sich die Auswertung des Gleichnisses in der Form eines Übergangs von der Bildebene auf die Sachebene mittels des Schlußes vom Kleineren auf das Größere: Wenn schon irdische Eltern geben, um wieviel mehr Gott. Sonst bleiben die Gleichnisfragen ohne Antwort (Lk 14,5: Herausziehen von Sohn oder Ochsen aus dem Brunnen) bzw. folgt eine Auswertung auf der Sachebene (12,25–26: Sachebene ist mit der Bildebene identisch mit dem Thema „Sorgen"; 14,28.31.33: Bildebene: Turmbau und Kriegszug – Sachebene: Nachfolge; 15,4–6.7: Bildebene: verlorenes Schaf – Sachebene: Freude über umkehrenden Sünder; 17,7–9.10: Bildebene ist mit der Sachebene identisch: Sklavendienst). Die Absicht hinter diesem Vergleich ist die Frage, ob es möglich ist, anzunehmen, daß die Gleichnisfrage, also Verse 5–7, allein tradierbar war. Lk 14,5 zeigt, daß dies möglich ist. Weiters hat sich gezeigt, daß das Phänomen einer selbstgegebenen Antwort, die nicht bei einer einfach abschlägigen bleibt („Niemand hat so einen Freund!"), sondern die im Bildfeld sich ausspielende Argumentationsstrategie noch einmal überbietet („sondern aufgrund seiner Schamlosigkeit wird er geben"),[113] nur hier in 11,5–8 vorkommt. Dieses, zusammen mit dem Argument, daß sich in Vers 8 die Lukanismen häufen, legt die Vermutung nahe, daß dieser Vers redaktionell eingefügt wurde. Die Frage, ob 11,5–7 Teil von Q war, muß bis auf weiteres offen bleiben; die Argumente für und wider eine Zugehörigkeit zu Q finden sich wieder in den Evaluationen im zugehörigen *Documenta Q*-Band.

I. Lk 11,5–8 und das Gebet

Hans Dieter Betz hat den im Lukasevangelium folgenden Text, der aus dem Spruchevangelium Q stammt, die Sprüche vom *Suchen und Finden* (Q 11,9–10), aufgrund ihrer Generalität und des Mangels eines Objekts dahingehend interpretiert, daß damit Vertrauen in das Leben generell vermittelt werden soll. Vertrauen in das Leben ist gerechtfertigt aufgrund unserer alltäglichen Erfahrung und aufgrund Gottes Vorsorge dafür.[114] In dieser Richtung ist möglicherweise auch das Gleichnis vom bittenden Freund, Lk 11,5–7 zu verstehen, das vermitteln will, daß es verläßliche kulturelle Einrichtungen gibt. Die soziale Situation, in die hinein dieses Wort spricht, könnte man sich so vorstellen, daß es um die Interaktion von besitzlosen Jesusanhängerinnen und -anhängern mit besitzenden

---

[113] Zwei unterschiedliche kommunikative Strategien konstatiert am ausführlichsten: Alan Kirk, „Evaluation to Q 11:5–8 (1995)," in Klampfl, *Q 11:5–8; Q 11:9–13* (mit weiteren Referenzen).

[114] Hans Dieter Betz, *The Sermon on the Mount: A Commentary on the Sermon on the Mount including the Sermon on the Plain*, hg. v. Adela Yarbro Collins, Hermeneia (Minneapolis: Fortress, 1995), 504, 507.

Haushalten, im speziellen mit seßhaften Sympatisantinnen und Sympatisanten geht.

Um das Gleichnis vom Richter und der Witwe (Lk 18,1–8) zu einer Aussage über das beständige Gebet zu machen, unternimmt Lukas einiges an redaktionellem Aufwand (18,1.6–8). Das Gleichnis vom bittenden Freund (Lk 11,5–8) in der Interpretation, die ihm hier gegeben wurde, fügt sich leichter in den redaktionellen Kontext (Lk 11,9–13), der von Zuversicht hinsichtlich der Erfüllung von Bitten durch Gott spricht. Der gebetene Freund gibt selbstverständlich, wenn auch nicht aus Freundschaft, so doch, um einen Ehrverlust im Blick des Bittenden zu vermeiden. Lukas scheint der Institution der Freundschaft einerseits weniger getraut zu haben, wenn es um die Zuverlässigkeit gegenseitiger Hilfe geht, andererseits mehr, wenn es um die Motivation durch Ehre und deren drohenden Verlust geht.

Hinsichtlich der Rezeption dieses Textes, die die Schamlosigkeit zu einer positiven Tugend der Beständigkeit uminterpretiert hat, ist zu bemerken, daß ein Mißverständnis von ἀναίδεια im Sinne von Unverschämtheit, die in der anstandslosen Verhaltensweise des Bittstellers, der keine Rücksicht auf die Konvention nimmt, besteht, leicht möglich ist, gemäß der oben zitierten Odysseestelle (Homer, *Od.* 17.449).

Die lukanische Rezeption der Gebetstexte in Q im Kontext des frühen Judentums und Christentums

Niclas Förster

Die lukanische Rezeption der das Gebet betreffenden Passagen der Q-Quelle wurde trotz der schon zahlreichen und noch immer anwachsenden Forschungsliteratur zum Gebet im lukanischen Doppelwerk – soweit ich sehe – noch nicht zum Thema einer speziellen Untersuchung gemacht. In wichtigen einschlägigen Monographien wie in den Studien von Wilhelm Ott,[1] Ludger Feldkämper[2] oder David Crump[3] wird die Thematik nur gestreift, aber nicht in den Focus der Erörterung genommen. Ich nehme davon mein Buch zum gemeinschaftlichen Gebet in der Sicht des Lukas keineswegs aus.[4] Dies mag verwundern, gehören doch zu den aus Q adaptierten Passagen Stellen wie Lk 10,21–22, die z. B. für François Bovon zum „Kern des Evangeliums" schlechthin zählen.[5] Eine mögliche Erklärung für die Zurückhaltung in der Forschung könnte vielleicht darin zu suchen sein, dass sich die lukanische Rezeption der einschlägigen Q-Passagen, zu denen auch für mich vornehmlich die Stelle Lk 4,8; 6,28; 10,2 bzw. 21 und Lk 11,2b–4 bzw. 9–13 zählen, sich kaum in wenigen klar umrissenen theologischen Leitlinien oder Themenstellungen zusammenfassen lässt. Dazu ist der Adaptionsprozess zu komplex, vielschichtig und thematisch divergent.

Ein wichtiges Interesse des Lukas lässt sich m. E. jedoch feststellen. Es betrifft seine Absicht, die ich bewusst vorsichtig und offen formuliere, einer spezifischen Selbstvergewisserung der Rezipienten seines Evangeliums zu dienen. Ich knüpfe hierbei an Tendenzen der neueren Gebetsforschung an, die die identitätsbildende Wirkung des Gebets in den Mittelpunkt des Forschungsinteresses gerückt hat. Dafür seien beispielhaft der aus einer im Jahr 2001 im Rahmen des Sonder-

---

[1] Wilhelm Ott, *Gebet und Heil: Die Bedeutung der Gebetsparänese in der lukanischen Theologie*, SANT 12 (München: Kösel, 1965).

[2] Ludger Feldkämper, *Der betende Jesus als Heilsmittler nach Lukas*, VMStA 29 (St. Augustin: Steyler, 1978).

[3] David M. Crump, *Jesus the Intercessor: Prayer and Christology in Luke-Acts*, WUNT II 49 (Tübingen: Mohr Siebeck, 1992).

[4] Niclas Förster, *Das gemeinschaftliche Gebet in der Sicht des Lukas*, BTS 4 (Leuven: Peeters, 2007).

[5] François Bovon, *Das Evangelium nach Lukas*, 2. Teilband: *Lk 9,51–14,35*, EKK 3/2 (Zürich: Benziger; Neukirchen-Vluyn: Neukirchener, 1996), 66.

forschungsbereichs 534 „Juden und Christen" an der Rheinischen Friedrich-Wilhelms-Universität Bonn veranstalteten Tagung hervorgegangene Aufsatzband „Identität durch Gebet,"[6] herausgegeben von Albert Gerhards, Andrea Doeker und Peter Ebenbauer, und das Projekt „Early Christian Prayer and Identity Formation" am Department of New Testament Studies der Norwegian School of Theology (MF) in Oslo erwähnt, in dessen Rahmen 2011 und 2012 Workshops durchgeführt wurden, deren Beiträge – herausgegeben von Reider Hvalvik und Karl Olav Sandnes – mittlerweile publiziert sind.[7] Ich bin mir bewusst, dass die Kategorie der Identität ebenso modisch wie heuristisch schwer fruchtbar zu machen ist. Daher beschränke ich mich in einer mir geboten erscheinenden Vorsicht auf Strategien der Selbstvergewisserung, die Lukas in seiner Rezeption des das Gebet betreffenden Q-Materials den Rezipienten seines Textes anbietet. Diese sind im Rahmen seiner Redaktionsarbeit oft nur aspekthaft nachzuweisen. Dennoch eignet sich das Gebet – auch auf der Ebene des erzählten lukanischen Textes – in besonderem Maße, um Divergenzen zu markieren und diese über den erzählten Text hinaus auf dessen Rezipienten hin transparent werden zu lassen.

Ich analysiere die betreffenden Stellen des Lukasevangeliums aus praktischen Erwägungen, ohne damit eine bestimmte Deutung schon implizieren zu wollen, in der Reihenfolge ihres Vorkommens und beginne mit der Versuchungsgeschichte, die wahrscheinlich schon am Anfang der Q-Quelle zu finden war.

A. Die Versuchung Jesu

In der Versuchungsgeschichte, die von Lukas aus Q-Material gestaltet wurde, wird das Beten im Rahmen der zweiten Versuchung Jesu – in der lukanischen Reihenfolge – erwähnt. Die engen Parallelen im Matthäusevangelium sind dabei kaum zu bestreiten. Gerade in den wenigen Abweichungen zeigt sich aber die Intention des Lukas.

Die Grundzüge der Versuchungsgeschichte stimmen nämlich zwischen dem ersten und dritten Evangelisten überein und sind der gemeinsamen Vorlage entlehnt. Es sind die Folgenden:

- Der Satan zeigt Jesus alle Reiche der Welt (Mt 4,8/Lk 4,5).
- Er verspricht, Jesus die Herrschaft über diese Reiche zu übergeben (Mt 4,9/Lk 4,6).
- Dafür muss Jesus als Vorbedingung den Teufel anbeten und vor ihm niederfallen (Mt 4,9/Lk 4,7).

---

[6] Albert Gerhards, Andrea Doeker und Peter Ebenbauer (Hg.), *Identität durch Gebet: Zur gemeinschaftsbildenden Funktion institutionalisierten Betens in Judentum und Christentum*, Studien zu Judentum und Christentum (Paderborn: Schöningh, 2003).
[7] Reidar Hvalvik und Karl Olav Sandnes (Hg.), *Early Christian Prayer and Identity Formation*, WUNT 336 (Tübingen: Mohr Siebeck, 2014).

- Jesus verweigert sich dieser Versuchung und zitiert dafür Dtr 6,13 bzw. 10,20 als Weisung der Tora.[8]

Die Differenzen sind ebenso leicht festzustellen:

- Matthäus setzt ein Raumwunder voraus, bei dem der Teufel Jesus auf einen hohen Berg bringt, während Lukas den Ort des Totalblicks auf alle Reiche nicht näher spezifiziert. Dafür betont er, dass alles in einem „einzigen Augenblick" geschah (Lk 4,5).
- Die Reiche nennt er anders als Matthäus τὰς βασιλείας τῆς οἰκουμένης, wobei οἰκουμένη wie auch an anderen Stellen seines Doppelwerks höchstwahrscheinlich auf das römische Reich anspielt.[9]
- Lukas führt den Begriff ἐξουσία ein, der die Jesus versprochene Macht bezeichnet und wie an anderen Stellen seines Werkes[10] politisch konnotiert ist.
- Der Teufel hat dabei für Lukas keine eigenständige Machtvollkommenheit, sondern auch ihm ist seine Machtstellung lediglich übergeben, wobei das Passiv παραδέδοται andeutet, dass er in Gottes Auftrag die politischen Reiche in seiner Gewalt hat.
- Schließlich finden sich bei Lukas keine räumlichen Bezüge der verlangten Proskynese, während Matthäus diese durch das Partizip πεσών genauer als fußfälliges Niederwerfen auf den Boden spezifiziert.

Überblickt man die lukanischen redaktionellen Eingriffe, wobei auch ich davon ausgehe, dass Matthäus den Textbestand der Q-Quelle besser als Lukas bewahrt hat, so zeigt sich eine besondere Sensibilität für die politischen Implikationen der Versuchung, denn in einem solchen Zusammenhang taucht bei ihm die Verehrungsgeste des Fußfalls auf. Der Satan offeriert nach Lukas Jesus nämlich nichts weniger als die Weltherrschaft, wobei der Begriff οἰκουμένη diese auf das römische Reich hin zuspitzt (vgl. Lk 2,1) und zugleich deutlich macht, dass der Teufel provozieren wollte, dass Jesus in Konkurrenz zum römischen Kaiser tritt. Die Proskynese ist dabei die vom Satan gestellte Vorbedingung, die die Anerkennung seiner Autorität impliziert und durch die anschließende Machtübergabe belohnt wird. Dieses zweigliedrige Ritual aus Niederwerfen und Einsetzung in ein Herrscheramt knüpft an Vorbilder orientalischer Großreiche an,[11] die aber auch im römischen Reich bekannt waren und mitunter sogar, wenn es politisch opportun erschien, von römischer Seite praktiziert wurden. Bei der Übertragung der Regierungsgewalt an einen Unterkönig markierte eine solche Zeremonie nämlich den Akt der Einsetzung in dessen neue Stellung und den Beginn einer Art von Lehensverhältnis zu seinem Oberherrn. Im römischen Reich

---

[8] Das Verb προσκυνεῖν begegnet in Dtr 5,9 als Verbot der Verehrung von Fremdgöttern.

[9] Lk 2,1; Apg 11,28; 17,6; 19,27; 24,5; dazu Robert Morgenthaler, „Roma-Sedes Satanae (Röm. 13,1 ff. im Lichte von Luk 4,5–8)," TZ 12 (1956): 289–304, hier 291–92; Günther Baumbach, Das Verständnis des Bösen in den synoptischen Evangelien, ThA 19 (Berlin: Evangelische Verlagsanstalt, 1963), 170–72; Petr Pokorný, Theologie der lukanischen Schriften, FRLANT 174 (Göttingen: Vandenhoeck & Ruprecht, 1998), 105–6.

[10] Lk 12,11; 19,27; 20,20; 23,7.

[11] Zur Rolle der Proskynese in den Krönungsritualen orientalischer Großreiche s. meine Nachweise in Förster, Das gemeinschaftliche Gebet, 87–88.

erregte insbesondere der Fall des Arsakidenprinzen[12] Tiridates Aufsehen, der im Jahr 66 n.Chr. in Rom von Kaiser Nero zum König von Armenien ernannt wurde.[13] Während dieses Ereignisses warf sich Tiridates nach dem Bericht des Cassius Dio in aller Öffentlichkeit mitten auf dem *forum Romanum* vor dem römischen *Imperator* nieder und verkündete laut, er komme als „Sklave" zu Nero „als meinem Gott"[14]. Die Proskynese dokumentierte dabei für die versammelte Menschenmenge die Anerkennung des Kaisers als Gottheit. Tiridates setzte darum laut dem Historiker Cassius Dio ausdrücklich in seiner Ansprache hinzu, er habe dem Kaiser gehuldigt und habe sich vor ihm wie sonst vor seinem Gott Mithras auf den Boden geworfen. Durch diese Proskynese wurde Nero also zu seinen Lebzeiten entsprechend der Gepflogenheit der parthischen Heimat des Tiridates als Gottheit geehrt und zugleich öffentlichkeitswirksam als römischer Oberherr des künftigen armenischen Klientelkönigs[15] akzeptiert. Der allgemein bekannte Ablauf eines solchen aus der politischen Sphäre herrührenden Einsetzungsritus mit seinen spezifischen Anbetungsgesten lag wohl auch dem Angebot des Satans zugrunde, wie es Lukas schilderte. Die Deuteronomiumstellen (Dtr 6,13 bzw. 10,20)[16], die Jesus ausdrücklich zitiert, weist jedoch genau diese vom Teufel offerierte Machtübertragung mit all ihren religiösen Implikationen zu-

---

[12] Er war schon zuvor armenischer König, war aber von den Römern besiegt worden und wollte nun das Diadem von Neros Hand erhalten, dazu: Hans Volkmann, „Tiridates," *KlPauly* 5:860–61, hier 861.

[13] Zu den politischen Umständen und Gründen der Reise des Tiridates s. Fritz Geyer, „Tiridates," PW 6.A.2:1437–45, hier 1443; Marie-Louise Chaumont, „L'Arménie entre Rome et l'Iran I: De l'avènement d'Auguste a l'avènement de Diocletien," *ANRW* II 9.1:71–194, hier 116–21; Matthäus Heil, *Die orientalische Außenpolitik des Kaisers Nero*, Quellen und Forschungen zur Antiken Welt 26 (München: Herbert Utz, 1997), 131–34.

[14] Cass. Dio 62.5.2: „ἦλθον τε πρὸς σὲ τὸν ἐμὸν θεόν."

[15] Die historische Grundvoraussetzung für das Vasallenverhältnis des Tiridates zum römischen Kaiser war die feudale Struktur des Partherreichs, dessen Verwaltung in den Händen von Unterkönigen lag. Die ihm durch den parthischen Feudalismus vertraute Stellung des Lehnsmanns wurde von Tiridates auf Kaiser Nero übertragen, s. dazu Werner Schur, „Parthia IIB," PW 18.4:1987–2029, hier 1987–88; Ferdinand Lehmann-Haupt, „Satrap," PW II 2A.1:82–188, hier 176–77; sowie Geo Widengren, „Iran, der große Gegner Roms: Königsgewalt, Feudalismus, Militärwesen,"*ANRW* II 9.1:219–306, hier 265–66.

[16] Die Septuagintahandschriften überliefern jedoch mit Ausnahme des Codex Alexandrinus einen anderen Text als die Zitate bei Matthäus und Lukas. In ihnen findet sich φοβηθήσῃ anstatt προσκυνήσεις. Es fehlt ferner das erläuternde μόνῳ, das wahrscheinlich unterstreichen sollte, dass die Verehrung allein Gott zukomme. Der Codex Alexandrinus könnte dabei u. U. dem Evangelientext angeglichen worden sein, s. David Flusser „Die Versuchung Jesus und ihr jüdischer Hintergrund," in *Entdeckungen im Neuen Testament*, Bd. 2: *Jesus – Qumran – Urchristentum*, hg. v. Martin Majer (Neukirchen-Vluyn: Neukirchener, 1998), 193–211, hier 194 Anm. 4; Nachdr. v. *Judaica* 45 (1989): 110–28; Morgenthaler, „Roma-Sedes Satanae," 257 vermutet hingegen eine Beeinflussung des Lukas durch einen Septuagintatext, wie er im Codex Alexandrinus überliefert ist, s. auch Jacques Dupont, *Die Versuchungen Jesu in der Wüste*, SBS 37 (Stuttgart: Katholisches Bibelwerk, 1969), 56; Hermann Mahnke, *Die Versuchungsgeschichte im Rahmen der synoptischen Evangelien: Ein Beitrag zur frühen Christologie*, BBET 9 (Frankfurt a. M.: Peter Lang, 1978), 131–32.

rück. Sie macht zudem – ganz in jüdischer Tradition – die Exklusivität der Verehrung des einen Gottes deutlich.

Das Wesen der uns hier interessierenden zweiten Versuchung Jesu im Lukasevangelium besteht demnach darin, dass Jesus sich mittels der Teufelsanbetung gegen den Kaiser und dessen Herrschaftsanspruch stellen sollte. Implizit ist dabei die Möglichkeit in den Blick genommen, dass man den Zweck von Jesu Auftreten als eine politische Rebellion auffassen könnte. Lukas war für diese gefährliche Option sicherlich sensibilisiert und er lässt sie nicht zufällig als eine vorgeschobene Anklage der Gegner Jesu in der Gerichtsszene vor Pilatus in Lk 23,2 viel deutlicher als die Seitenreferenten anklingen. Dieselbe Tendenz lässt sich in der Apostelgeschichte nachweisen: In Apg 17,6 werfen Juden in Thessaloniki den ersten Christen vor, sie würden „τὴν οἰκουμένην" in Unruhe versetzen, was hier als Stichwort eindeutig auf das römische Reich bezogen ist. Danach setzen sie noch die politisch höchst brisante Anklage hinzu, dass die Christen gegen die Vorschriften des Kaisers Jesus als „einen anderen König" verkünden würden (Apg 17,7).[17] Eine ähnliche Anschuldigung wird von jüdischen Anklägern vor dem Statthalter Felix gegen Paulus erhoben, der angeblich Unruhen (στάσεις; Apg 24,5) unter allen Juden der οἰκουμένη geschürt habe, was entsprechend römischer Rechtauffassung eine *seditio*, d. h. eine geplante Rebellion mit dem Ziel eines Coup d'Etat, implizierte.[18] Ein solches einseitiges und zudem strafbares, irdisch-politisches Verständnis[19] seines Wirkens hat Jesus nach Lukas jedoch schon im Rahmen der Versuchungsgeschichte unumwunden zurückgewiesen. Irdische Macht, die einen politischen Umsturz nach sich ziehen würde, wollte er gerade nicht erringen. Die Rezipienten des Lukasevangeliums konnten ähnliche Anklagen gegen Christen, wie sie in Apg 17,7 und 24,5 deutlich vorausgesetzt werden, als eine schon von Jesus selbst, sogar noch vor seinem ersten öffentlichen Auftreten in Galiläa,[20] das erst ab Lk 4,14 geschildert wird, abgelehntes Ansinnen, das satanischen Ursprungs ist, einordnen und von sich weisen.[21]

---

[17] Dass sich beide Stellen ergänzen und die Vorwürfe entsprechen, hebt Gerhard Schneider, *Die Apostelgeschichte*, 2. Teil: *Kommentar zu Kap. 9,1–28,31*, HThKNT 5 (Freiburg i. B.: Herder, 1982), 225 hervor.
[18] Dies stellt Schneider, *Die Apostelgeschichte*, 2:346 heraus.
[19] Joachim Jeremias legt diese Stelle auf Jesu „Auftreten als politischer Führer" hin aus, idem, *Neutestamentliche Theologie, Erster Teil: Die Verkündigung Jesu*, 3. Aufl. (Gütersloh: Gütersloher Verlagshaus Mohn, 1979), 76.
[20] Julius Wellhausen, *Das Evangelium Lucae* (Berlin: Reimer, 1904; Nachdr. Evangelienkommentare, Berlin: de Gruyter, 1987), 8.
[21] Zur Ablehnung eines politischen Verständnisses des Auftretens Jesu s. Henry A. Kelly, „The Devil in the Desert," *CBQ* 26 (1964): 190–220, hier 213; Paul Hoffmann, „Die Versuchungsgeschichte in der Logienquelle: Zur Auseinandersetzung der Judenchristen mit dem politischen Messianismus," *BZ* 13 (1969): 207–23, hier 214; Mahnke, *Die Versuchungsgeschichte*, 139–44; Dieter Zeller, „Die Versuchungen Jesu in der Logienquelle," *TTZ* 89 (1980): 61–73, hier 66 sowie Förster, *Das gemeinschaftliche Gebet*, 84.

Gleichzeitig enthält Lk 4,6b höchstwahrscheinlich einen etwas versteckten Seitenhieb gegen das römische Reich, das wie alle Herrschaftsgebiete der Welt dem Einflussbereich des Teufels angehört, der dort die Macht nach seinem Gutdünken verteilen kann. Dies verleiht der römischen οἰκουμένη ein dunkles und durchaus negativ gemeintes Gepräge, was Lukas allerdings nur vorsichtig andeutet. Er setzt dabei in Lk 4,6b voraus, wie das Verb παραδέδοται, das doch wohl als ein *passivum divinum* auf Gott zu beziehen ist, andeutet, dass Gott dem Teufel die von ihm für sich reklamierte Fähigkeit tatsächlich verliehen habe,[22] alle Königreiche an jeden zu übergeben, den er dafür ausersehen hat. Zum gegenwärtigen Zeitpunkt ist der Bereich politischer Machtausübung damit ihm unterstellt, wie der Vers implizit insinuiert, allerdings ohne dies gleich plakativ in den Mittelpunkt zu stellen, und gehört damit zum satanischen Einflussbereich. Dass hier für Jesus und seine Anhänger – von Statthaltern wie Pilatus oder von Seiten der Kaiser wie Nero – nichts Gutes zu erwarten ist, liegt damit nahe, selbst wenn es natürlich nicht explizit von Lukas gesagt ist.

Die zurückgewiesene Geste der Proskynese passt zur angedeuteten negativen Sicht römischer Machtausübung. Sie war für die Zeitgenossen des Lukas sicherlich auf den Herrscherkult, und zwar in einer durchaus auch für die heidnische Reichselite abzulehnenden Ausprägung hin transparent. Das Niederwerfen vor dem Kaiser wurde nämlich nicht nur von Nero in der erwähnten Tiridates-Episode erwartet und akzeptiert, sondern auch von anderen Kaisern wie z. B. Caligula bei offiziellen Anlässen verlangt. Allerdings bewertete dies die römische Oberschicht wegen der in ihr noch lebendigen Tradition eines republikanischen Freiheitsverständnisses durchweg negativ. Nicht zufällig wurde Caligula ermordet, und beging Nero als vom Senat geächteter Staatsfeind Selbstmord. Beide waren Beispiel für in der römischen Öffentlichkeit gemeinhin negativ bewertete historische Herrschergestalten, die nach ihrem Tod der *damnatio memoriae* verfielen. Die Ablehnung der Proskynese durch Jesus in einem in der Versuchungsgeschichte durchaus politisch konnotierten Umfeld erhält vor diesem Hintergrund ein zusätzliches Profil, war diese Geste doch auch in einer nichtchristlichen Umgebung – wenn auch aus ganz und gar anderen Gründen – eher verpönt. Es stellt demnach eine besondere Pointe dar, dass Jesus in diesem Punkt mit der reservierten Haltung weiter Kreise der römischen Machtelite gegen diese Verehrungsgeste konvergierte.

---

[22] Diese Stelle bildet höchstwahrscheinlich einen lukanischen Zusatz, s. Albert Fuchs, „Versuchung Jesu," *SNTSU* 9 (1984): 95–159, hier 136–37; Fritz Neugebauer, *Jesu Versuchung: Wegentscheidung am Anfang* (Tübingen: Mohr Siebeck, 1986), 77, 82.

B. Feindesliebe und Gebet

Kommen wir zu einer weiteren von Lukas aus der Q-Quelle übernommenen Passage, d. h. dem Gebot Jesu, für seine Gegner zu beten, das sich in Lk 6,28 im Rahmen der an die Jünger gerichteten Feldrede findet. Das Gebot der Feindesliebe ist ausdrücklich an die Gruppe der Jünger adressiert, wie das betont vorangestellte ὑμῖν in Lk 6,27 andeutet. Dies scheint auf eine besondere Situation der Jesusjünger hinzudeuten.[23] In dieser haben sie gemeinsam bestimmte „Feinde," die ihnen mit Hass entgegentreten. Auf diese Feindschaft sollen sie mit Liebe, auf Hass mit guten Taten, auf Fluch mit Segen und auf alle diejenigen, die sie bedrohen, mit Gebet reagieren. Lukas ersetzt an dieser Stelle das Verb „verfolgen" (διώκειν) als Bezeichnung der Angriffe derer, denen die Fürbitte gilt, durch das allgemeiner gemeinte „bedrohen" bzw. „misshandeln" (ἐπηρεάζειν), das „ein breites Band von Erfahrungen"[24] abdeckt. Der Sinn aber dürfte klar sein: Die Rezipienten dieses Textes befinden sich in einer Lage, die von Ablehnung und Verfolgung, wozu neben verbalen Attacken gewalttätige Übergriffe[25] gehören, gekennzeichnet ist, sollen sich aber keineswegs zu ebensolchen Gegenangriffen hinreißen lassen. Eine angemessene Reaktion ist vielmehr u. a. das fürbittende Gebet.

C. Die Gebetsbitte der ausgesandten Jünger in Lk 10,2

Eine weitere Stelle im Lukasevangelium, an der sich der Umgang des dritten Evangelisten mit seiner Q-Vorlage im Hinblick auf das Gebet studieren lässt, steht in der Erzählung von der Aussendung der 70 bzw. 72 Jünger. Die Anzahl dieser Jünger ist in der handschriftlichen Tradition uneinheitlich überliefert und die ursprüngliche Lesart nur schwer zu eruieren,[26] was für unsere Untersuchung aber keine wesentliche Rolle spielt. Wichtig ist, dass die Aussendungserzählung des dritten Evangelisten sich im Rahmen des in Lk 9,51 beginnenden Berichts

---

[23] Gerhard Schneider, *Das Evangelium nach Lukas Kapitel 1–10*, 3. Aufl., ÖTK 3/1 (Gütersloh: Gütersloher Verlagshaus Mohn; Würzburg: Echter, 1992), 155.

[24] Eduard Schweizer, *Das Evangelium nach Lukas*, NTD 3 (Göttingen: Vandenhoeck & Ruprecht, 1982), 80. Es ist wohl kein sich nur in Worten äußerndes, ablehnendes Verhalten gemeint; anders: Heinz Schürmann, *Das Lukasevangelium, 1. Teil: Kommentar zu Kapitel 1,1–9,50*, HThKNT 3/1 (Freiburg i. B.: Herder, 1981), 344 Anm. 11.

[25] Urs von Arx, „Fürbittendes Gebet im Neuen Testament," in *Das Gebet im Neuen Testament: Vierte europäische orthodox-westliche Exegetenkonferenz in Sâmbăta de Sus, 4.–8. August 2007*, hg. v. Hans Klein et al., WUNT 249 (Tübingen: Mohr Siebeck, 2009), 25–75, hier 56.

[26] 72 Jünger werden z. B. in den Papyri wie etwa in P75 erwähnt; vgl. dazu Theodor Zahn, *Das Evangelium des Lucas*, 3. u. 4. Aufl., KNT 3 (Leipzig: Deichert, 1920), 407–8 mit Anm. 58, und Joseph A. Fitzmyer, *The Gospel according to Luke X–XXIV: Introduction, Translation and Notes*, AB 28A (New York: Doubleday, 1985), 845. Auf der Grundlage der handschriftlichen Überlieferung ist die ursprüngliche Zahl der Jünger wohl letztlich kaum noch mit hinreichender Sicherheit zu eruieren.

über Jesu letzte Reise nach Jerusalem findet. Schon in Lk 9,52 hatte Lukas mitgeteilt, dass Jesus Boten in die Dörfer der Samaritaner vorausgeschickt hatte.[27] Nun sollen nach diesen ersten Sendboten die 70 bzw. 72 Jünger in diejenigen Städte und Orte vorausreisen, die Jesus später selbst noch aufsuchen wollte.[28] Ihr Dienst dient also der Vorbereitung von Jesu Kommen, hat aber auch andere, darüber hinausgehende Aufgaben. Insbesondere die Symbolzahl der 70 bzw. 72 Ausgesandten könnte an dieser Stelle über den Erzählzusammenhang hinausweisen und auf die Missionierung der Heidenwelt und deren entsprechende Völkerzahl anspielen,[29] denn Lukas versteht die zweite Jüngeraussendung anscheinend als Vorstufe dieses noch viel größeren, künftigen Vorhabens, zu dem noch wesentlich mehr Boten als die 70 bzw. 72 Jünger benötigt werden. Daher hat er mit Bedacht in Lk 10,2 das Logion: „Die Ernte ist groß, die Zahl der Arbeiter aber gering; bittet daher den Herrn der Ernte, dass er Arbeiter in seine Ernte aussende!" aus seiner Q-Vorlage an den Anfang einer längeren Jesus-Rede platziert. Die weiteren Verse dieser Rede stammen ebenfalls aus der Q-Quelle, wobei Lukas seine Vorlage anders als die Parallelen bei Matthäus in der ursprünglichen Form bewahrt haben dürfte.[30] In ihnen folgen weitere Anweisungen, die wohl als eine Art von Missionsinstruktionen bezeichnet werden können. Das einleitende Logion in Lk 10,2 hat jedoch eine besondere Funktion: In ihm werden die Ausgesandten mit kurzfristig angeworbenen Lohnarbeitern verglichen, die im Dienst des „Herrn der Ernte" stehen, worunter höchstwahrscheinlich Gott zu verstehen ist, denn das Wort κύριος ist zweifellos als eine Gottesbezeichnung zu entschlüsseln.[31] Auf der Bildebene ist dabei gemeint, dass die Unterstützung zusätzlicher Saisonarbeiter in der Erntezeit unabdingbar war, da sonst der größere Arbeitsaufwand z. B. bei der Getreideernte gar nicht bewältigt werden konnte. Auf der Sachebene ist dies auf Gott zu beziehen, der weitere Helfer zur Missionsarbeit bereitstellt.

Die durch das Logion Angesprochenen, womit im Kontext der lukanischen Erzählung die 70 bzw. 72 ausgeschickten Jünger gemeint sind, sollen durch ihre Gebetsbitte[32] die benötigte weitere Hilfe von Gott mobilisieren, denn es sind

---

[27] Hier besteht ein Zusammenhang, den Fitzmyer, *Luke X–XXIV*, 842–43 hervorhebt.

[28] I. Howard Marshall, *The Gospel of Luke: A Commentary on the Greek Text*, NIGTC (Grand Rapids: Eerdmans, 1978), 416.

[29] Oft wird auf Gen 10,2–31 und die Zahl der dort erwähnten Völker hingewiesen, wo im masoretischen Text 70 Völker als Nachkommen von Sem, Ham und Jafet erwähnt sind; s. Christopher Francis Evans, *Saint Luke*, TPINTC (London: SCM, 1990), 445; Fitzmyer, *Luke X–XXIV*, 846; Marshall, *Luke*, 415. In der Septuagintaübersetzung der betreffenden Verse beträgt die Anzahl der Völker, die aus den Nachkommen hervorgehen, dann 72. Vgl. Ruben Zimmermann, „Folgenreiche Bitte! (Arbeiter für die Ernte): Q 10,2," in *Kompendium der Gleichnisse Jesu*, hg. v. Ruben Zimmermann et al. (Gütersloh: Gütersloher Verlagshaus, 2007), 111–18, hier 117.

[30] Matthäus hat die Logion auf 9,37–38; 10,7–16 bzw. 11,24 verteilt.

[31] Zimmermann, „Folgenreiche Bitte," 117.

[32] Eine Bitte an Gott wie in Apg 8,22 ist hier gemeint, Marshall, *Luke*, 416.

im Hinblick auf die ins Auge gefasste Gesamtaufgabe viel zu wenige Erntehelfer, d. h. Glaubensboten, im Einsatz.[33] Durch die Kombination dieses aus Q entlehnten Logions mit seiner redaktionell gestalteten Einleitung in Lk 10,1 weist Lukas also seine Rezipienten recht geschickt auf das weitere, viel größere Unterfangen hin, das aus der Erzählperspektive künftig noch anstehen wird, in der Zeit des Erzählers aber schon mitten im Gang ist.[34] Damit ist wahrscheinlich auf die weltweite Heidenmission angespielt, deren Anfänge dann in der Apostelgeschichte geschildert werden. Für sie sollen die 70 bzw. 72 Jünger – so ist implizit vorausgesetzt – sowie alle weiteren Jünger, die in Jesu Namen ausziehen, um Gottes Beistand bitten, der ihre Anzahl den großen missionarischen Anforderungen entsprechend vermehren möge.

D. Die Freude der Jünger und Jesu Jubelruf in Lk 10,21

Ein weiterer wichtiger Gesichtspunkt der lukanischen Redaktion tritt hervor, wenn der Evangelist in Lk 10,17 von der freudigen Hochstimmung berichtet, in der die Ausgeschickten nach einiger Zeit „mit Freude" zu Jesus zurückkehrten. Dieser Vers dürfte wie auch die nachfolgende Rede Jesu in Lk 10,18–20 vom Evangelisten redaktionell mittels Material, das nicht aus Q stammt, gestaltet sein. Der darin vorausgesetzte, beeindruckende Erfolg ist keinesfalls das Resultat des in 10,2 angeregten Bittgebets, wie gelegentlich in der Forschung vermutet wurde, denn das Gebet war auf dieses Ziel ja gar nicht ausgerichtet, sondern intendierte lediglich die künftige göttliche Vermehrung der geschickten Boten.[35] Der Stimmungsumschwung ist vielmehr durch die Entmachtung der Dämonen ausgelöst, was mit der Jesus-Rede in Lk 10,18–20 insofern korrespondiert, als in ihr u. a. der Fall Satans vom Himmel erwähnt wird. Die erfolgreichen Exorzismen[36] im Namen Jesu, die mit den in Lk 10,9 erwähnten Krankenheilungen einhergingen, riefen also die Begeisterung der Rückkehrer (Lk 10,17) hervor und belegen gleichzeitig die Entmachtung des Teufels und seines dämonischen Gefolges.[37]

---

[33] Marshall, *Luke*, 416.

[34] Die große Zahl der ausgeschickten Jünger will keineswegs das Gebet als schon erfüllt kennzeichnen, denn warum wären diese Jünger noch von Jesus zu einer ausdrücklichen Bitte an Gott aufgefordert worden, wenn diese Gebetsbitte bereits durch die vergleichsweise hohe Zahl der Mitglieder ihrer Gruppe als eingelöst zu betrachten wäre? Anders argumentiert Zimmermann, „Folgenreiche Bitte," 117.

[35] Sonst hätten die Boten berichten müssen, dass andere sich ihnen angeschlossen haben und ihre Zahl schon vermehrt haben, wovon aber gerade nicht die Rede ist; anders: Zimmermann, „Folgenreiche Bitte," 117.

[36] Gelungene Krankenheilungen, die – wie man voraussetzen kann – Dämonen vertreiben, werden in Lk 10,9 erwähnt. Dass die Missionare erfolgreiche Exorzisten im Name Jesu waren, setzt Apg 19,13 voraus.

[37] David E. Garland, *Luke*, Zondervan Exegetical Commentary on the New Testament 3 (Grand Rapids: Zondervan, 2012), 429.

Mit dem „Feind", über den die Jünger nach Lk 10,19 Macht erhalten haben, dürfte der satanische Anführer der Krankheitsdämonen gemeint sein. Damit geht es in diesem Vers also um die Macht über den Satan und die übrige Geisterwelt, die Jesus vergibt. Dieses Motiv hat auch an anderen Stellen des lukanischen Doppelwerks Spuren hinterlassen: Entsprechende Schilderungen der Vertreibung der bösen Geister im Namen Jesu finden sich ebenfalls im Rahmen der Missionserzählungen der Apostelgeschichte, wie z. B. im Hinblick auf Paulus in Philippi bzw. in Ephesos (Apg 16,18; 19,11–12.15). Doch kehren wir zum Lukasevangelium zurück: Dort hat es mit der Schilderung der ein Hochgefühl auslösenden ersten Erfolge der 70 bzw. 72 Jünger bei Lukas gerade nicht sein Bewenden. In einer bemerkenswerten Wendung im Text korrigiert nämlich Jesus in Lk 10,21 das Verhalten der Jünger und weist sie auf den richtigen Grund ihrer freudigen Reaktion hin, denn der sollte eigentlich darin bestehen, dass die Namen der Jünger im Himmel, wo Satan nach seinem Fall seinen Platz verlassen musste, aufgeschrieben stehen.[38] Ihre Erwählung durch Gott, die das Bild des himmlischen Lebensbuches umschreibt,[39] und nicht ihre beeindruckenden Dämonenaustreibungen ist demnach das wirklich Entscheidende. In dieser Präferenz spiegelt sich eine gewisse Reserve gegenüber Exorzismen. Worin diese ihre Wurzeln hatte, lässt sich nur vermuten. Könnte dabei hereingespielt haben, dass Außenstehende das Christentum gern mit verbotener Magie gleichsetzten? Vielleicht ist in diesem Zusammenhang an den römischen Historiker Sueton zu erinnern, der die neronischen Verfolgungsmaßnahmen gegen die Christen bekanntlich damit rechtfertigte, dass es sich bei ihnen um Leute handle, die einem „neuen und gefährlichen Aberglauben" (*superstitionis novae ac maleficae*)[40] anhingen. Bei dem Begriff „*superstitio*" schwingt für römische Ohren stets eine Nähe zu Magie, Astrologie und Wahrsagerei mit.[41] Davon mussten sich Christen tunlichst abgrenzen, und Lukas könnte dies stets im Blick gehabt haben. Man wird in diesem Punkt jedoch über Mutmaßungen wohl schwerlich hinausgelangen: Wollte Lukas möglicherweise unterstreichen, dass Christen mehr als eine Gruppe von herumziehenden Teufelsaustreibern und Exorzisten waren? Ihr Stolz und ihre Freude sollte nicht in solchen Machttaten, die von Lukas an und für sich gar nicht in Abrede gestellt werden, sondern in ihrer einzigartigen Stellung vor Gott liegen, aus der sie ihre innere Zuversicht ableiten können. Daher ordnete er das ihm bekannte Logienmaterial so an, dass die Mahnung Jesu in Vers 20

---

[38] Gemeint ist das Buch des Lebens, in dem ihre Namen verzeichnet sind, s. Marshall, *Luke*, 430. Der Kontrast, dass ihre Namen aufgeschrieben stehen, wo zuvor der Teufel weichen musste, ist sicherlich bewusst gewählt, s. Fitzmyer, *Luke X–XXIV*, 860.

[39] Die Vorstellung rekurriert auf Stelle wie Ex 32,32; Ps 69,29; 139,16; Dan 12,1. Dass Namen im Himmel aufgeschrieben sind, setzt auch Hebr 12,23 voraus, vgl. ferner Phil 4,3 und Apk 3,5; 13,8; 20,15.

[40] Suetonius, *Nero* 16.2.

[41] vgl. z. B. Cicero, *Div.* 2.149.

am Ende zu stehen kommt. Diesen Gedanken scheint auch der folgende Vers 21 noch einmal aufzunehmen und unter anderen Gesichtspunkten herauszuarbeiten. Auch Lk 10,21 bestimmt nämlich in auffälliger Betonung die Freude, in der nun Jesus selbst von Jubel erfüllt ein Gebet spricht, das lautet: „Ich preise dich, Vater, Herr des Himmels und der Erde, dass du dies vor Weisen und Einsichtsvollen verborgen und es Unmündigen offenbart hast. Ja, Vater, denn so ist es wohlgefällig gewesen vor dir". Diese Worte müssen sich nach Lukas schon wegen ihrer Einordnung im Text auf Jesu unmittelbar zuvor gegenüber den 70 bzw. 72 Ausgesendeten geäußerte Zusage beziehen, „dass Eure Namen im Himmel geschrieben stehen." Allein darüber sollten sich die Jünger freuen, wie Jesus ihnen eingeschärft hatte, und in eben diese Freude stimmt nun auch er selbst mit ein. Allerdings betet Jesus – anders als die freudigen Berichte der Ausgesandten – erfüllt vom heiligen Geist, wie Lukas ausdrücklich festhält. Sein „pneumatisches Jubeln"[42] ist damit von jeder allgemein menschlichen Begeisterung deutlich unterschieden. Dabei bleibt das Wirken des Geistes an dieser Stelle des Lukasevangeliums auf Jesus beschränkt. Über seine Jünger wird der heilige Geist – anders als ihre bereits erfolgreiche Zurüstung im Kampf gegen Dämonen – erst nach der Jesuszeit ausgeschüttet werden.[43]

Nun noch einige Bemerkungen zum Inhalt des Gebets: Sein Text ist von Lukas bis auf die überleitenden Worte in Vers 21a ohne gravierende textliche Veränderungen[44] aus der Q-Vorlage adaptiert worden, in der ihm die Verse 21–24 wahrscheinlich bereits als eine Einheit verbunden vorlagen. Wie Lukas das Gebet verstanden haben wollte, wird – wie schon dargelegt – m. E. durch seine Position im Fortgang der Erzählung und seine Einleitung erhellt, denn es bezieht sich auf die an die Jünger zuvor ergangene Offenbarung. Mit dem Demonstrativpronomen ταῦτα (bzw. mit αὐτά), womit dasjenige bezeichnet ist, das ver- bzw. enthüllt wird, ist die Erwählung aller Jünger, deren Namen im Himmel aufgezeichnet sind, gemeint.[45] Sie, die als νηπίοι zu den Ungebildeten und Verachteten gehören, erfahren die Gnade einer speziellen Offenbarung, die ihnen durch Jesus vermittelt wird, was die zweite eindringliche Anrede an Gott, den Vater, in Vers 21b noch einmal unterstreicht.

Den folgenden Vers 22, der schon in der Q-Quelle an das Gebet angeschlossen war, verstehe ich nicht mehr als Teil des Gebets. Er wechselt das Thema und handelt von der Übergabe von Wissen und Macht durch den Vater. Je-

---

[42] Josef Ernst, *Das Evangelium nach Lukas*, 6. Aufl., RNT (Regensburg: Pustet, 1993), 257.

[43] Vgl. den Hinweis bei Hans Conzelmann, *Die Mitte der Zeit. Studien zur Theologie des Lukas*, 6. Aufl., BHT 17 (Tübingen: Mohr Siebeck, 1977), 99 Anm. 3. Dass in etlichen Textzeugen τῷ ἁγίῳ fehlt, spielt im Hinblick auf die Aussageabsicht keine wesentliche Rolle; s. Bovon, *Lukas*, 2:67 Anm. 3.

[44] Lukas formuliert in 10,21 ἀπέκρυψας in Angleichung an ἀπεκάλυψας. Matthäus bietet mit ἔκρυψας den ursprünglichen Text; Fitzmyer, *Luke X–XXIV*, 867.

[45] Ernst, *Lukas*, 257.

sus spricht hier als der Sohn, der den Vater vertritt und dessen Stellvertretung übernimmt.

E. Das Vaterunser

Kommen wir nun zum lukanischen Vaterunsertext, der ebenfalls eine Übernahme aus der Q-Quelle darstellt. Er steht am Beginn einer größeren Einheit, die sich mit dem Bitten beschäftigt, worauf ich noch zurückkommen werde. Das lukanische Verständnis des Vaterunsers wird für uns in erster Linie wieder einmal in der Einleitung des Textabschnitts fassbar, die darlegt, wie und warum Jesus seinen Jünger dieses Gebet gegeben hat: „Und es geschah, als er an einem Ort betete, da sagte, als er geendet hatte, einer von seinen Jüngern zu ihm: Herr lehre uns beten, wie auch Johannes seine Jünger gelehrt hat. Er aber sprach zu ihnen: Wenn ihr betet, dann sprecht …".

Analysiert man diese einleitende Schilderung, so lässt sich aus ihr das lukanische Vaterunserverständnis in mehrfacher Hinsicht ableiten. Mit diesem einleitenden Vers werde ich mich daher eingehend beschäftigen. Ich beginne mit dem möglichen Konnex des Vaterunsers zu Jesu eigener Gebetspraxis: Es fällt nämlich m. E. auf, dass die Gebetsanweisung Jesu durch eine Jüngerfrage ausgelöst wird, nachdem er mit seinem eigenen Gebet aufgehört hatte. Sie hat gar nichts mit dem Inhalt dieses von Jesus soeben beendeten Betens zu tun, dessen Inhalt den Jüngern auch nicht mitgeteilt wird. Es ist darum sicherlich kein Zufall, dass Jesus, wie Lukas herausstellt, zuerst ganz für sich allein an einem abgeschiedenen Ort (ἐν τόπῳ τινι; Lk 11,1a) betete. Seine später erfolgende Jüngerbelehrung ist davon deutlich getrennt.[46] Sein persönliches Beten macht Jesus also im Vaterunser keinesfalls öffentlich.[47] Bekanntlich spricht Jesus das Vaterunser auch niemals gemeinsam mit seinen Jüngern.[48] Es ist ganz allein das ihnen für

---

[46] Es steht im Hinblick auf die Gebetsbelehrung der Jünger eben nicht im Text, „dass Jesus gerade auch das Vaterunser gebetet hat, das er sie nachher lehrt," s. Hans Klein, „Das Vaterunser: Seine Geschichte und sein Verständnis bei Jesus und im frühen Christentum,"in Klein et al., *Das Gebet im Neuen Testament*, 77–114, hier 102 und idem, *Das Lukasevangelium*, KEK I/3 (Göttingen: Vandenhoeck & Ruprecht, 2006), 404. Hinter dieser Vermutung Kleins steht der Wunsch, mittels des Vaterunsers mehr über Jesus persönliches Gebetsleben zu erfahren und dieses dann gleichsam selbst im eigenen Beten nachvollziehen zu können, s. z. B. auch Joseph Ratzinger (Benedikt XVI), *Jesus von Nazareth*, 1. Teil: *Von der Taufe im Jordan bis zur Verklärung* (Freiburg i. B.: Herder, 2007), 166. So verständlich dieser Wunsch ist, so wenig hat Lukas ihn uns erfüllt.

[47] Anders: Wolfgang Wiefel, *Das Evangelium nach Lukas*, THKNT 3 (Berlin: Evangelische Verlagsanstalt, 1988), 214. Man kann aus der Einleitung m. E. auch nicht herauslesen, dass für Lukas das Vaterunser Jesu ureigenes Gebetsleben gleichsam im Kern verkörperte, s. z. B. N. T. Wright, „The Lord's Prayer as a Paradigm of Christian Prayer," in *Into God's Presence: Prayer in the New Testament*, hg. v. Richard N. Longenecker (Grand Rapids: Eerdmans, 2001), 132–54, hier 133–34.

[48] Günther Bornkamm, *Jesus von Nazareth*, 12. Aufl. (Stuttgart: Kohlhammer, 1980), 125.

ihre eigene Gebetspraxis vermittelte Gebet, aber keineswegs das Band einer Gebetsgemeinschaft mit Jesus, was Lukas wichtig zu sein scheint. Dies heißt natürlich nicht, dass die Sitte des regelmäßigen Betens von Jesus erst begründet oder den Jüngern verpflichtend auferlegt wurde. Hier bewegten sich die Anhänger Jesu anscheinend in lange üblichen Bahnen, was auch in der lukanischen Vaterunsereinleitung als gegeben angenommen wird. Das Vaterunser ist vielmehr ein Gebetstext, der sich für die schon allgemein als selbstverständlich akzeptierte Wiederholung[49] durch eine Gruppe eignet. Dem korrespondiert, dass das Vaterunser expressis verbis für die Gemeinschaft (δίδαξον ἡμᾶς) der Jünger, nicht für den einzelnen Fragesteller erbeten wird. Damit rücken im Hinblick auf den Gebetsinhalt gerade die Wir-Bitten des Vaterunsers für Lukas in den Mittelpunkt. Er interpretiert meiner Meinung nach das Vaterunser also als Merkmal einer auf Jesus zurückgehenden, sozialen Gruppe,[50] die sich als solche im Gebetsvollzug zusammenschließt. Dies bleibt auch nach Jesu Tod als Möglichkeit bestehen, und so können sich Christen, wenn sie das Vaterunser sprechen, als in Kontinuität mit Jesu ersten Jüngern begreifen.

Damit legt sich die Frage nahe, ob dies für Lukas die einzige Aufgabe des Vaterunsers ist: Gibt es etwa in lukanischer Perspektive auch eine bewusst abgrenzende Funktion des Vaterunsers? Es ist wohl kaum zu bestreiten, dass Lukas, wenn es um das Vaterunser geht, Jesus und Johannes der Täufer eng zusammenrückt, wobei Johannes keineswegs nur als negativ gezeichnete Figur im Text vorkommt. Nach Lukas ist – so verstehe ich Lk 11,1 – der Ursprung der Idee, dass religiöse Gruppen sich mittels eines gemeinsamen Gebets konstituieren,[51] nicht etwa bei Jesus bzw. Jesu Anhänger zu suchen. Er verweist hierfür durch die einleitende Jüngerfrage ausdrücklich auf Johannes den Täufer[52]. In diesem Zusammenhang ist zudem wohl nicht ganz zufällig von einer Lehre des Täufers für seine Jünger die Rede (ἐδίδαξεν τοὺς μαθητὰς αὐτοῦ). Ich verstehe dies als Fingerzeig auf eine textlich feststehende Gebetsformel, nicht etwa nur auf von Johannes unbestimmt fixierte Gebetsthemen oder -anliegen, die dann von den Täuferjüngern in ihrem Beten frei variiert wurden. Den Wortlaut dieses Täufergebets erfahren wir leider nicht. Fest scheint mir nur zu stehen, dass mit dem

---

[49] Es ist wahrscheinlich gemeint, dass das Gebet durch Wiederholen fester Bestandteil des Lebens der Gruppe werden sollte, s. Joel B. Green, *The Gospel of Luke*, NICNT (Grand Rapids: Eerdmans, 1997), 440.

[50] Karl Heinrich Rengstorf, *Das Evangelium nach Lukas*, NTD 3 (Göttingen: Vandenhoeck & Ruprecht, 1969), 143.

[51] Marc Philonenko, *Das Vaterunser: Vom Gebet Jesu zum Gebet der Jünger*, UTB 2312 (Tübingen: Mohr Siebeck, 2002), 11, formuliert treffend: „die Bitte der Jünger Jesu zeigt ihren Willen, durch ein eigenes Gebet eine unabhängige Gemeinschaft zu werden." Er greift dabei Joachim Jeremias Hinweis auf, der das den Jüngern vermittelte Gebet als „wesentliches Kennzeichen ihrer Gemeinschaft" bezeichnete: idem, *Neutestamentliche Theologie*, 167.

[52] „Die Johannesjünger haben die Priorität," wie Julius Wellhausen richtig bemerkte und sie besitzen nach Lukas schon ein „Mustergebet" ihres Meisters Johannes des Täufers: Wellhausen, *Das Evangelium Lucae*, 55.

Wort καθώς keineswegs auf ein dem Vaterunser in Inhalt und Aufbau genau entsprechendes Gebet abgehoben ist, das sich aus dem Vaterunser möglicherweise sogar noch rekonstruieren ließe.[53] Es bleibt nur festzuhalten, dass Lukas voraussetzt, Johannes habe als maßgebliche Autorität der auf ihn zurückgehenden Gruppe hinter deren Gebeten gestanden und diese für seine Anhänger formuliert und legitimiert. Damit ist das Vaterunser in lukanischer Perspektive sicherlich etwas Ähnliches wie die Lehrergebete, die in der späteren rabbinischen Literatur mitunter auftauchen[54] und mit berühmten rabbinischen Autoritäten als deren Urheber assoziiert sind.[55]

Gehen wir dem Bezug des Vaterunsers auf Johannes den Täufer noch etwas genauer nach: Selbst wenn man der bisher vorgetragenen Deutung zustimmt, so ist dennoch zu konzedieren, dass das Vaterunser bei Lukas aufs Ganze gesehen in einem merkwürdig schwebenden Verhältnis zu dem von dem fragenden Jünger erwähnten Johannesgebet bleibt. Unbestreitbar ist allein: Einen harsch abgrenzenden oder die Johannesgruppe gar explizit verwerfenden[56] Gegensatz kann ich aus dem Text beim besten Willen nicht herauslesen. Dieses Problem ist bekanntlich in der Forschung immer wieder erörtert worden. Jesus- und Johannesanhänger sind m. E. in Lk 11,1 vielmehr in deutlicher Parallelität gezeichnet worden, wobei sich Jesus im Hinblick auf das Vaterunser an den Täufer als sein Vorbild anlehnt, dessen Gebet aber nicht nur einfach entlehnt und Johannes zugleich keineswegs rundweg ablehnt[57]. Die lukanische Vaterunsereinleitung könnte daher – in Aufnahme einer von Manuel Vogel vorgeschlagenen Deutung des Verhältnisses von Täuferbewegung und frühen Christentum – als „auf irenische Weise vereinnahmend" bezeichnet werden und als „Ausbildung einer Gruppenidentität, die der Fremdgruppe eine relative Geltung zuerkennt."[58]

---

[53] Vgl. meine Erwägungen in Förster, *Das gemeinschaftliche Gebet*, 220. Angebliche Täufergebete in späterer patristischer Tradition sind ohne historischen Wert, s. Zahn, *Lukas*, 442 Anm. 6. Über das Gebet des Johannes des Täufers wissen wir nichts, Philonenko, *Das Vaterunser*, 11.

[54] Beispielsweise b. Ber. 29b; dazu: Clemens Leonhard, „Vaterunser II: Judentum," TRE 34:512–15, hier 513.

[55] Dass diese Lehrer ihre Gebete mehrfach mit Abweichungen übermittelten, was die Differenzen zwischen der matthäischen und lukanischen Überlieferung des Vaterunsers erklären würde, s. Joseph Heinemann, *Prayer in the Talmud: Forms and Patterns*, SJ 9 (Berlin: de Gruyter, 1977), 43, scheint mir wenig überzeugend. Hier ist doch eher mit Abweichungen wegen einer langen mündlichen Tradition zu rechnen, zumal die Gebete nicht als in ihrem Wortlaut feststehende Texte galten.

[56] Peter Böhlemann, *Jesus und der Täufer: Schlüssel zur Theologie und Ethik des Lukas*, SNTSMS 99 (Cambridge: University Press, 1997), 91.

[57] Dies meint aber keineswegs eine Kontinuität, die mir Geir Otto Holmås, „Prayer, Othering and the Construction of Early Christian Identity in the Gospel of Matthew and Luke," in Hvalvik und Sandnes, *Early Christian Prayer and Identity Formation*, 91–113, hier 103 unterstellt.

[58] Manuel Vogel, „Jesusgemeinden und Täufergruppen zwischen Abgrenzung und Wertschätzung – eine Skizze," in *Juden und Christen unter römischer Herrschaft: Selbstwahrnehmung*

Man könnte vielleicht sogar cum grano salis von einer freundlichen Überbietung ohne explizite Verneinung sprechen. Hierin könnte ein besonderes Merkmal des lukanischen Vaterunserverständnisses zu suchen sein.

Diese Besonderheit sticht umso mehr ins Auge, wenn man auf die Parallele im Matthäusevangelium oder auf die urchristliche Entwicklung im Allgemeinen blickt. Die lukanische Form der Auseinandersetzung mit der Johannesgruppe, wenn es um das Vaterunser geht, unterscheidet sich nämlich signifikant vom polemischen Grundton, mit dem sich Matthäus im Kontext seiner Version des Vaterunsers in Mt 6,5 gegen die Heuchler (ὑποκριταί) wendet, was auf Juden an sich bezogen ist, ohne die Täufergruppe davon auszunehmen. Dasselbe gilt mutatis mutandis für die matthäische Kritik am Plappern der Heiden in Mt 6,7. Auch die spätere Gemeindeordnung der Didache übernimmt zwar zustimmend die jüdische Sitte, dreimal am Tag zu beten, lehnt aber die jüdischen „ὑποκριταί" explizit ab und ersetzt ihre Gebete durch das Vaterunser, so dass die *oratio dominica* die Christen von ihrem jüdischen Gegenüber unterscheidet.[59] In der späteren Kirche setzte sich diese Entwicklung fort, und das Vaterunser wurde bekanntlich den Neugetauften erst nach dem Taufakt feierlich vermittelt, so dass es von ihnen dann als erstes Gebet der Wiedergeborenen gesprochen werden konnte. Damit wurde es liturgisch zum Merkmal ihrer neuen christlichen Existenz.[60] Von dem Modell einer solchen Gebetsdifferenz zum jüdischen bzw. paganen Umfeld, die die eigene Gruppenidentität über gezielte Abgrenzung befestigt und in der späteren Entwicklung mit der Taufe eng verknüpft ist, findet sich m. E. bei Lukas noch keine Spur. Über die Gründe lässt sich wohl nur spekulieren: Zeigt sich hierin eine besondere irenische Tendenz des Lukas?

Ich schließe noch einige nur skizzenhafte Bemerkungen zum Text des Vaterunsers an: Bekanntlich sind Abweichungen zwischen der Fassung des Matthäus und der des Lukas unverkennbar gegeben, wobei auch ich davon ausgehe, dass Lukas mit dem überlieferten Text insgesamt konservativer umgegangen ist[61]. Ich kann hier aber keine umfassende Auslegung dieses Gebets vorlegen. Sie würde weit über den Rahmen dieser Studie hinausführen. Daher begnüge ich mich mit dem kurzen Hinweis auf das besondere Interesse des Lukas an den Wir-Bitten des Vaterunsers, das mir redaktionelle Änderungen im Text nahezulegen scheinen: In der Brotbitte geht die Zeitangabe τὸ καθ' ἡμέραν wahrscheinlich auf Lukas zurück. Auch der Imperativ δίδου in derselben Bitte dürfte redaktionell sein. In der Vergebungsbitte hat wahrscheinlich erst Lukas τὰς ἁμαρτίας eingefügt.

---

und Fremdwahrnehmung in den ersten beiden Jahrhunderten n.Chr., hg. v. Niclas Förster und Jacobus Cornelis de Vos, SIJD 10 (Göttingen: Vandenhoeck & Ruprecht, 2015), 74–84, hier 82.

[59] Kurt Niederwimmer, *Die Didache*, KAV 1 (Göttingen: Vandenhoeck & Ruprecht, 1989), 168 bzw. 173.

[60] Vgl. dazu zusammenfassend Ulrich Luz, „Vaterunser I: Neues Testament," *TRE* 34:504–12, hier 506.

[61] Ebd., 505.

Die Wendung παντὶ ὀφείλοντι dürfte von ihm erweitert sein.[62] Dieses Interesse an den Bitten und deren Erfüllung prägt dann auch den weiteren lukanischen Textverlauf, auf den ich genauer eingehen werde. Unmittelbar nach dem Vaterunser hat Lukas das Gleichnis vom bittenden Freund positioniert. Es lässt sich m. E. kaum bestreiten, dass es ihm dabei um den Bittcharakter des Vaterunsers ging. Zudem ist die Brotbitte des Vaterunsers thematisch eng mit dem Gleichnis verbunden und bildet durch das gemeinsame Stichwort eine Art Überleitung.[63] Das Gleichnis vom bittenden Freund gehört allerdings zum Sondergut des Lukas. Dass es aus der Q-Vorlage des Lukas übernommen wurde, ist m. E. nicht sicher beweisbar. Ich werde daher dieses Gleichnis hier nicht genauer erörtern.[64] Anders verhält es sich mit dem unmittelbar folgenden Abschnitt in Lk 11,9–13, der eine Parallele in Mt 7,7–11 hat und aus der Q-Quelle stammen wird. Auf diese Verse werde ich daher ausführlicher eingehen.

F. Das Bittgebet in Lk 11,9–13

In den Versen Lk 11,9–13 kommt Lukas noch einmal auf die Thematik des Bittens zurück. Besonderes Augenmerk muss in diesem Zusammenhang dem Schlussvers Lk 11,13 zukommen, auf den die ganze Perikope zuläuft. Der ganze Abschnitt lässt sich nämlich in drei Teile gliedern:
- Den Anfang bilden die Verse 9 und 10 mit den drei Imperativen: αἰτεῖτε, ζητεῖτε, und κρούετε.
- In den Versen 11 und 12 ist vom gebenden Vater und bittenden Sohn die Rede. Das Geben illustrieren die Gegensatzpaare Fisch und Schlange bzw. Skorpion und Ei.
- Vers 13 spitzt die Erfüllung der Bitten auf den heiligen Geist zu, den Gott den Bittenden vermitteln wird.

Die ersten beiden Verse mit den drei Imperativen könnten sich auf den Erfahrungshorizont der Bettler beziehen[65] und fordern zu einem unverzagten und zuversichtlichen Bitten auf. Lk 11,10 betont mit dem vorangestellten πᾶς die Gewissheit des Erfolgs des Bittens, was auch für Gott und die an ihn gerichteten Gebete gilt.

Die folgenden zwei Verse vertiefen dasselbe Thema und dürften an dieser Stelle schon in der Logienquelle gestanden haben, wie die Parallele in Mt 7,7–11 anzeigt. Sie vergleichen Gott mit einem Vater, der seinem Kind dessen Wünsche erfüllen wird. Dabei rekurriert Jesus auf die Grundannahme, dass der Vater sei-

---

[62] Klein, „Das Vaterunser," 88.
[63] Bovon, *Lukas*, 2:148.
[64] Für eine Auslegung s. Förster, *Das gemeinschaftliche Gebet*, 258–62.
[65] Ott, *Gebet und Heil*, 104.

nem Kind absichtlich nichts Schlechtes oder sogar Gefährliches geben wird, was mit dem Gegensatzpaar von Fisch und Schlange bzw. Ei und Skorpion illustriert wird. Hier geht es offenbar darum, alle Zweifel daran auszuräumen, dass Gott die Wünsche der Menschen erfüllen werde oder ihnen sogar etwas Schlechtes anstatt dessen, was sie so sehr wünschen, widerfahren lassen werde.

Besonders deutlich macht sich die lukanische Redaktion aber in Lk 11,13 bemerkbar. Dieser Vers ist für die Sicht des Evangelisten sicherlich zentral, denn in ihm hat Lukas die Vorlage an einer entscheidenden Stelle abgeändert[66] und den heiligen Geist – in einer Formulierung von Heinrich Holtzmann – „als die höchste und beste aller Gottesgaben"[67] eingefügt. Ihn wird der Vater aus dem Himmel denjenigen nicht verweigern, die ihn im Gebet darum ersuchen. Damit sind in der Erzählperspektive zunächst die Jünger Jesu gemeint, die ab Lk 11,1 als Hörer vorausgesetzt sind und mit ὑμεῖς direkt angesprochen werden. Der Ton liegt in Lk 11,13 damit ganz auf dem πνεῦμα ἅγιον, womit Lukas von seiner Q-Vorlage abweichen dürfte. In ihr wurde wie der Paralleltext des Matthäus nahelegt, allgemein von guten Dingen (ἀγαθά) gehandelt, die Jesus den Bittenden verspricht. Durch seine redaktionelle Änderung wollte Lukas möglicherweise dem Problem ausweichen, dass Jesus hier allerlei irdische Güter in Aussicht gestellt haben könnte und zudem der irrigen Annahme entgegenwirken, dass Gott alle an ihn gerichteten Gebetswünsche unterschiedslos erfüllen werde. Das Gut bleibt ja letztlich relativ und ist vom jeweiligen Blickwinkel des Bittenden abhängig[68]. Lukas könnte allerdings noch ein weiteres Motiv für seinen redaktionellen Eingriff gehabt haben. Er wollte darauf anspielen, dass die Jünger mit „allen" anderen Christen beim Pfingstfest nach Jesu Tod und Auferstehung den heiligen Geist erhalten werden (Apg 2,1–21).[69] Zu diesem in der Erzählperspektive noch ausstehenden künftigen Ereignis könnte auch das Futur δώσει gut passen.[70] Auf diese Weise verbindet Lukas also die Zeit Jesu proleptisch mit der Zeit der frühen Kirche.[71] Dazu kommt das Motiv des Wirkens des heiligen Geistes, das in seinen beiden Werken immer wieder begegnet. Zum Beleg sei hierfür auf die lukanische Schilderung vom Kommen des Geistes nach dem Gebet der verfolgten Gemeinde in Apg 4,24–30 hingewiesen. Nach Apg 4,31 erfüllt „τὸ ἅγιον πνεῦμα" die versammelte Urgemeinde, was ihr dann die Verkündigung in Frei-

---

[66] Dass sich hier lukanische Redaktion zeigt, wird von vielen Exegeten angenommen, s. den Überblick bei Heinz Schürmann, *Das Lukasevangelium*, 2. Teil: *Kommentar zu Kapitel 9,51–11,54*, HThKNT 3/2 (Freiburg i. B.: Herder, 1994), 219 Anm. 332.

[67] Heinrich J. Holtzmann, *Hand-Commentar zum Neuen Testament*, 1. Band: *Die Synoptiker – Die Apostelgeschichte*, 2. Aufl. (Freiburg: Mohr, 1892), 125.

[68] Ott, *Gebet und Heil*, 108.

[69] Gerhard Schneider, *Das Evangelium nach Lukas: Kapitel 11–24*, 2. Aufl., ÖTK 3/2 (Gütersloh: Gütersloher Verlagshaus Mohn; Würzburg: Echter, 1984), 261, und Schürmann, *Lukasevangelium*, 2:219.

[70] Bovon, *Lukas*, 2:156; vgl. auch Förster, *Das gemeinschaftliche Gebet*, 265.

[71] Schürmann, *Lukasevangelium*, 2:219.

mut (παρρησία),⁷² die die Voraussetzung missionarischen Erfolgs und auch Zeichen und Wunder,⁷³ die diese Missionspredigt begleiten⁷⁴, möglich macht. Auch diese Erzählung, in der die Gabe des Geistes zudem mit dem vorherigen Beten eng verknüpft ist, nimmt Lk 11,13 in gewisser Weise auf und beschreibt die Erfüllung der Zusage Jesu. Aus der Sicht der Rezipienten des lukanischen Doppelwerks blieb das Kommen des Geistes damit eine Gebetshoffnung, die sich schon einmal in der Vergangenheit erfüllt hatte, und sie konnten versichert sein, dass dasselbe Kommen weiterhin auf ihr Gebet hin eintreten werde. Lukas selbst hat dieses daher in seiner Apostelgeschichte, wie man annehmen kann, nicht ohne Bedacht an den genannten Stellen ausführlich beschrieben.

Zusammenfassung

Überblickt man die lukanische Rezeption des Q-Materials in den gebetsrelevanten Passagen seines Evangeliums, so lässt sich die Redaktionstätigkeit des Lukas sicherlich nicht, wie bereits eingangs dargelegt, auf wenige Grundsätze reduzieren, wohl aber lassen sich einige Grundtendenzen ausmachen. Sie sollen abschließend noch einmal skizzenhaft umrissen werden: Lukas versucht m. E. den von ihm intendierten Rezipienten seines Doppelwerks zu vermitteln, dass ihr Gebet in ihrer schweren Lage, in der die οἰκουμένη – hier als römisches Reich verstanden – zwar das Ziel ihrer Mission nicht aber einer politischen Rebellion, welche ihnen allerdings von der paganen Gegenseite unterstellt wurde, ist, Gott allein gelten muss. Jedes Versprechen irdischer Machtausübung ist und bleibt satanischen Ursprungs und war schon von Jesus selbst eindeutig abgewiesen worden. Ferner sind die Christen und ihre Gebete von jeder Form von Magie geschieden, selbst wenn die Dämonen ihnen selbstverständlich untertan sind und exorzistische Erfolge ihre missionarische Tätigkeit und erfolgreiche Ausbreitung begleiten. Gott wird zudem die Bitten der Seinen, deren Namen im Himmel geschrieben sind, erhören, ihre Zahl wie die der Arbeiter im Ernteeinsatz vermehren und sie immer wieder aufs Neue mit seinem heiligen Geist, wenn sie ihn bitten, ausrüsten.

---

⁷² Nicht zufällig setzt Lukas diesen Begriff in Apg 28,31 betont an das Ende der Apostelgeschichte, wo er über Paulus freimütige und ungehinderte Verkündigungstätigkeit in Rom berichtet. Dies wird zuvor auch schon Petrus durch das πνεῦμα ermöglicht; vgl. Apg 4,8 und Lukas Notiz über Apollos' Synagogenpredigt in 18,25–26; dazu Heinrich Schlier, „παρρησία, παρρησιάζομαι," TWNT 5:869–84, hier 880.

⁷³ Um diese erfolgreichen Wundertaten hatte die Gemeinde in Apg 4,30 ausdrücklich gebetet.

⁷⁴ Wilfried Eckey, Die Apostelgeschichte: Der Weg des Evangeliums von Jerusalem nach Rom, Tbd. 1: Apg 1,1–15,35 (Neukirchen-Vluyn: Neukirchener, 2000), 123; sowie Förster, Das gemeinschaftliche Gebet, 394.

The Influence of Q's Prayer Texts in Matthew

Daniel A. Smith

A. Introduction

The original working title of this paper was "The Matthean Reception of the Prayer Texts in Q," but upon reflection, that terminology seemed inadequate for describing Matthew's use of Q. The present title was inspired by the work of Ulrich Luz who, in his magisterial commentary on the Gospel of Matthew (EKKNT/Hermeneia), attended to matters not only of the historical setting, sources, composition, meaning, and theology of Matthew, but also of Matthew's *Wirkungsgeschichte*, somewhat inelegantly rendered in English as "effective history" or sometimes "history of influence."[1] He borrows the term from Gadamer, whose original meaning is somewhat different (and which need not concern us at present).[2] For Luz, *Wirkungsgeschichte* refers to how the text – here, Matthew – is "received and actualized in media other than commentaries," in verbal and nonverbal media and indeed in the activity and history of the church.[3] Luz writes that he prefers *Wirkungsgeschichte* to *Rezeptionsgeschichte* because while the latter "connotes for me primarily the people who receive the text," the former "suggests for me the effective power of the texts themselves."[4]

This opening detour from the topic at hand is meant to signal that the focus of this paper is the influence that Q exerts on the composition of the Gospel of Matthew. In this regard, Q is not simply "received" or integrated into the new composition as inert content, but rather has, in its reception, a discernible effect on the shape of that composition. Ironically perhaps, Luz himself, who has also written on the topic of Matthew's use of Q, seems not to think along these lines. "For Matthew, Q did not have its own literary dignity as a compositional unity

---

[1] Ulrich Luz, *Matthew 1–7: A Commentary*, Hermeneia (Minneapolis: Fortress, 2007), 61–66; see also Luz, "Hermeneutics of Effective History and the Church," in idem, *Studies in Matthew* (Grand Rapids: Eerdmans, 2005), 349–69.

[2] Hans Georg Gadamer, *Truth and Method*, 2nd ed. (London: Bloomsbury, 2013 [1975²]), 311–18.

[3] Luz, *Matthew 1–7*, 61. Luz therefore distinguishes *Wirkungsgeschichte* from *Auslegungsgeschichte*, which for him refers to the history of the text's interpretation specifically in commentaries.

[4] Ibid.

[as did Mark]; the Sayings Source was a mere collection of materials he freely excerpted."[5] Luz sees Q as "sub-literary," a "minor religious text" in contrast with the Gospel of Mark. "[Matthew] does not use Q as a second Jesus narrative but as a collection of material from which he adds the 'gospel of the kingdom' to the Markan narrative which transmits it in only rudimentary form."[6] In other words, in Luz's view Q was not a "structuring hypotext," and it therefore has a correspondingly low theological significance for the author of Matthew.[7]

In his major study of *Q in Matthew*, Alan Kirk reaches the opposite conclusion.[8] He argues that the author of Matthew held Q in the same regard as Mark, that is, as a normative, authoritative memory artifact, particularly because, as Kirk explains it, Matthew used Q and Mark in the same way.[9] In his view, the failure of proponents of the Two-Document Hypothesis to account convincingly for Matthew's utilization of Q results first from a devaluation of Q as "subliterary," and secondly from an inadequate appreciation of Matthew's "*trained, expert memory competence in both sources.*"[10] Kirk writes:

Matthew coordinates Mark and Q such that the Markan and Q configurations of the tradition continue to structure, in their combination, his new composition. Matthew is intent on building the essential structures and programmatic concerns of his primary sources right into his new gospel artifact. This points to the normativity of Mark and Q in the Matthean community.[11]

For Kirk, the fact that Mark and Q "function alongside each other as normative artifacts" in both Matthean and Lukan circles can only mean that these two texts have a shared origin in a "common matrix of tradition"; therefore, Kirk suggests, "it is hard to reconcile Q's manifest normativity for Matthew with the notion that it represents a radically distinctive formation in early Christianity."[12] Clearly there is more at stake in these questions than only whether Matthew's composi-

---

[5] Ulrich Luz, "Intertexts in the Gospel of Matthew," *HTR* 97 (2004): 119–37, here 127.

[6] Luz, "Matthew and Q," in idem, *Studies in Matthew*, 39–53, here 51.

[7] Luz, "Intertexts," 127. See also Luz, "Matthew and Q," 50–52.

[8] Alan Kirk, *Q in Matthew: Ancient Media, Memory, and Early Scribal Transmission of the Jesus Tradition*, LNTS 564 (London: Bloomsbury T & T Clark, 2016).

[9] Ibid., 294–96.

[10] See Kirk, *Q in Matthew*, 151–61 (to the first point); 146–47, 298–99 (to the second); 299 (citation, emphasis original).

[11] Ibid., 231.

[12] Ibid., 302. Cf. Daniel A. Smith, "What Difference Does Difference Make? Assessing Q's Place in Christian Origins," in *Scribal Practices and Social Structures among Jesus Adherents: Essays in Honour of John S. Kloppenborg*, ed. William E. Arnal et al., BETL 285 (Leuven: Peeters, 2016), 183–211. Kirk has clarified to me (in personal correspondence, 21 March 2017) that he thinks "Q and Mark do in fact arise out of different theological and Christological contexts," but the real question is "how sharply the differences should be drawn." Kirk acknowledges that what he calls a "common matrix of tradition" was actually "multi-centered theologically and Christologically, not theologically uniform by any means."

tional techniques are comprehensible, given what can be known about human memory, ancient media, and source utilization.

The question addressed in this essay is how the Q prayer texts have exerted an influence in Matthew's composition. The two passages examined are Q 10:21–22, Jesus' prayer of thanksgiving for divine revelation, and Q 11:2b–4, 9–13, the Lord's Prayer and the adjacent cluster on asking, seeking, and knocking. Q 10:21–22 is found in Matt 11:25–27, and follows a transposition of Q's John the Baptist material (Q 7:18–35 in Matt 11:1–19), after which Matthew returns to material from the end of Q's Mission Speech (Q 10:13–15, 21–22 in Matt 11:20–27).[13] The Lord's Prayer in Matthew's Sermon on the Mount (Matt 6:9–13) is situated in the second piece of a three-part section on piety (covering almsgiving, prayer, and fasting, Matt 6:1–18). The Q cluster on asking, seeking, and knocking, however, is found much later in the Matthean Sermon (Matt 7:7–11), with a considerable amount of Q material in between. The examination of Matthew's use of these two texts from Q will demonstrate first of all that Q was a literary text whose own compositional integrity contributed to Matthew's compositional plan (as Kirk argues). Secondly, however, Q also seems to have been a kind of rhetorical resource which Matthew emulated (as John Kloppenborg has argued about James), and this has contributed to the composition of new material in the new Matthean contexts of these two Q texts on prayer.[14]

It is not difficult to find instances in which Matthew has both used a Q text and emulated it elsewhere in a new composition. One may be seen in Matthew's rewriting of the Markan controversy on plucking grain on the Sabbath (Mark 2:23–28 par. Matt 12:1–8). In reworking this story, Matthew is faced with the problem that Mark's Jesus justifies the activity of the disciples by invoking a scriptural warrant that has nothing to do with Sabbath observance (Mark 2:25–26 par. Matt 12:3–4; 1 Sam 21:1–6). For Mark's reader, the story really illustrates Jesus' authority to make determinations on proper observance, as the Son of David, one assumes. Matthew retains the reference to 1 Samuel but also adds a new saying: "Or have you not read in the law that on the Sabbath priests in the temple profane the Sabbath and yet are blameless? But I tell you that something greater than the temple is here" (12:5–6). Matthew has adapted the phrasing τοῦ ἱεροῦ μεῖζόν ἐστιν ὧδε from Q 11:31–32, a passage he uses later in the chapter (12:41–42).[15] Here, Matthew's Jesus speaks with the same authority as the Jesus

---

[13] Q 10:23–24 is used later by Matthew in his parables discourse (Matt 13:16–17, after Mark's material on the reason for parables: Mark 4:10–12 par. Matt 13:10–15).

[14] John S. Kloppenborg, "The Emulation of the Jesus Tradition in the Letter of James," in *Reading James with New Eyes: Methodological Reassessments of the Book of James*, ed. Robert L. Webb and John S. Kloppenborg, LNTS 342 (London: T & T Clark, 2007), 121–50; see especially the summary, ibid., 149–50.

[15] So also Luz, *Matthew 8–20: A Commentary*, Hermeneia (Minneapolis: Fortress, 2001), 180. Q 11:31–32 reads καὶ ἰδοὺ πλεῖον X ὧδε (bis), so Matthew has adapted the wording somewhat freely.

of Matthew's Q material, despite being one step removed from the authoritative artifact (to use Kirk's language). As John Kloppenborg explains it, the purpose of emulation is to create a new composition "that is apt to the argument at hand, 'beautiful' in its deployment, and at the same time subtly calls on the authority of the predecessor."[16] This is just what we have here, although from another perspective we might refer to this as midrashic composition, particularly because the addition to the controversy story is a legal interpretation based on Scripture (Hos 6:6 explicitly; Num 28:9–10 implicitly).[17] However, it is not clear whether in this case the success of the new saying depends on the reader/hearer discerning Q behind it, as was typical in rhetorical emulation; more importantly, the author seems to think it coheres with the voice of the Jesus of Q. The new saying carries "his" authority because it sounds like him. As W. D. Davies and Dale Allison wrote, "Matthew found it did not suffice to be simply a channel for tradition; he had to become a source."[18]

B. Q 10:21–22 in Matthew 11

The reconstruction of Q 10:21–22 is relatively unproblematic: the IQP noted only eight points of variation between Matthew and Luke in these verses.[19] Matthew's version of the saying differs from the IQP reconstruction in only one minor point (ἐπιγινώσκει for γινώσκει twice in Matt 11:27). Although the first verse is addressed to the "Father, Lord of heaven and earth," and elaborates on the restriction of revelation to the "infants" instead of the "wise and intelligent," the second verse is more a declaration of the speaker's unique position as sole mediator of this revelation. This has suggested to many scholars that Q 10:21–22 is composite.[20] Nevertheless, the two sayings clearly work together, with v. 22 explaining the means of revelation for which Jesus praises God in v. 21; the sequel verse seems to be a commentary addition.

---

[16] Kloppenborg, "Emulation," 150. See also Kirk, *Q in Matthew*, 182: "A gauge of a work's cultural authority was its capacity to generate further texts, from its own augmentation in the course of its transmission all the way to its transformation into another work."

[17] For the allusions, see Luz, *Matthew 8–20*, 181; W. D. Davies and Dale C. Allison Jr., *A Critical and Exegetical Commentary on the Gospel According to Saint Matthew*, 3 vols., ICC (Edinburgh: T & T Clark, 1988–1997), 2:314. For vv. 5–6 as "a halachic argument" composed by Matthew, see Robert H. Gundry, *Matthew: A Commentary on His Handbook for a Mixed Church under Persecution*, 2nd ed. (Grand Rapids: Eerdmans, 1994), 223.

[18] Davies and Allison, *Matthew*, 1:96.

[19] James M. Robinson, Paul Hoffmann, and John S. Kloppenborg, eds., *The Critical Edition of Q*, Hermeneia Supplements (Minneapolis: Fortress; Leuven: Peeters, 2000), 190–93.

[20] See John S. Kloppenborg, *The Formation of Q: Trajectories in Ancient Wisdom Collections*, SAC (Philadelphia: Fortress, 1987), 198–99 and n. 121 for literature; cf. Harry T. Fleddermann, *Q: A Reconstruction and Commentary*, BTS 1 (Leuven: Peeters, 2005), 451: "the same hand composed the prayer and the comment."

As is well known, Q 10:22 is sometimes referred to as the "Johannine Logion" or the "Johannine Thunderbolt" because of the themes it shares in common with the Fourth Gospel.[21] Adelbert Denaux noted the following features: "the 'giving' of all things to the Son, the mutual, exclusive knowledge of the Father and the Son, the position of the Son as the only revealer of God."[22] Together the two verses represent, arguably, the Christological pinnacle of Q, in which Jesus as speaker is (implicitly) identified with Wisdom and speaks in her voice (as he also does in Q 11:49–51; 13:34–35).[23] For this and for other reasons, Q 10:21–22 is normally connected with the Q redaction by those who view Q's composition as occurring in successive stages.[24] James Robinson even argued that "Christology as such really only emerges at this secondary level" of Q's composition; what emerges from the primary stratum of Q, which Robinson identified as an instance of the genre "sayings of the wise," was a Sophia Christology.[25] Paul Hoffmann, on the other hand, caught in these verses a glimpse of the original Christological insight that led to the compilation of Q.[26] In addition, some scholars have proposed an influence of this verse, in either its Matthean or Lukan form, on the Christology of the Fourth Gospel.[27]

There are several questions that arise concerning the use of this double logion by Matthew, and it is impossible to address them without also attending to matters of the broader compositional activities of the evangelist. First, it is curious that Matthew has separated Q 10:21–22 (and Q 10:13–15, the woes against the Galilean towns) from the end of the Q Mission material. In composing

---

[21] The expression originated with Karl von Hase, *Geschichte Jesu: Nach akademischen Vorlesungen* (Leipzig: Breitkopf und Härtel, 1876), 421–23 ("wie ein Aerolith aus dem johanneischen Himmel gefallen"); cited by Adelbert Denaux, "The Q-Logion Mt 11,27 / Lk 10,22 and the Gospel of John," in *John and the Synoptics*, ed. Adelbert Denaux, BETL 101 (Leuven: Peeters, 1992), 163–99, here 163.

[22] Denaux, "Q-Logion," 163.

[23] See James M. Robinson, "Jesus as Sophos and Sophia: Wisdom Tradition and the Gospels," in Robinson, *The Sayings Gospel Q: Collected Essays*, ed. Christoph Heil and Joseph Verheyden, BETL 189 (Leuven: Peeters, 2005 [1975]), 119–30; John S. Kloppenborg, "'Easter Faith' and the Sayings Gospel Q," in *The Apocryphal Jesus and Christian Origins*, ed. Ron Cameron, Semeia 49 (Atlanta: Scholars Press, 1990), 71–99, here 90–92; cf. John S. Kloppenborg, "Wisdom Christology in Q," *LTP* 34 (1978): 129–47, here 147.

[24] See for example Kloppenborg, *Formation of Q*, 202–3; Arland D. Jacobson, *The First Gospel: An Introduction to Q*, FF (Sonoma, CA: Polebridge, 1992), 44, 149–51, who situates Q 10:21–22 in the intermediate redaction. Cf. Alan Kirk, *The Composition of the Sayings Source: Genre, Synchrony, and Wisdom Redaction in Q*, NovTSup 91 (Leiden: Brill 1998), 339–42, and Fleddermann, *Q: Reconstruction and Commentary*, 447–54, who both see Q 10:21–22 as part of larger macro-compositions within a single act of composition for Q.

[25] James M. Robinson, "The Q Trajectory: Between John and Matthew via Jesus," in *The Sayings Gospel Q* [1991] 285–307, here 301–2; see the brief explanation in John S. Kloppenborg, *Excavating Q: The History and Setting of the Sayings Gospel* (Edinburgh: T & T Clark, 2000), 348.

[26] Paul Hoffmann, *Studien zur Theologie der Logienquelle*, 3. Aufl., NTAbh 8 (Münster: Aschendorff, 1982), 141–42.

[27] See for example Denaux, "Q-Logion," 176–87; summary, 187–88.

Matthew 10, the author has significantly reordered the Q 10 material, combining it with Markan material and other material from elsewhere in Q and Mark. Secondly, the author also transposes the material about John the Baptist from Q 7:18–35 to here after the Mission Speech. This is usually explained in connection with the major reorientation of Markan material in Matthew 8–9.[28] This insertion does not just interrupt the conclusion of the Mission Speech, for Matthew has written his own conclusion (Matt 11:1); Q 10:13–15 and 10:21–22, two of the last three elements of the Q Mission Speech not yet used by Matthew, now are connected instead to the John material. This new context will mean our Q prayer text may read differently in Matthew than it did in Q. Thirdly, and this is more easily solved, Matthew separates Q 10:23–24 from its original context in Q and uses it in an expanded version of Mark's explanation for teaching in parables (Matt 13:16–17). As Kirk explains, "the βλέποντες ... ἀκούοντες thematic of Mark 4:12 is the reason Matthew waits to adjoin Q 10:23–24 ... to the Markan narrative [there]."[29] In Kirk's view, Matthew knew both his sources well enough to know where these verses would neatly fit into Mark. Finally, there is the question of the origin and significance of the sayings that conclude this section of Matthew (Matt 11:28–30), after which Matthew's composition aligns carefully with the Markan order (Mark 2:23–28 par. Matt 12:1–8).

The first question – why Matthew extracted Q 10:13–15 and 10:21–22 from the Q Mission Speech – is best answered in light of the second question, why Matthew delayed using Q 7:18–35. In their original context, Q 10:13–15 (with v. 12) answered the problem of the rejection of the message of the basileia (or the emissaries) with woes against those who rejected it. These verses seem to intrude in the context because they are directed against outsiders, not adherents.[30] Further, vv. 12–15 disrupt a nice parallelism between vv. 10 and 16 which share the theme of reception; in fact, this may have prompted Matthew to transfer these verses to the following chapter.[31] Some scholars see Q 10:16 as the conclusion to the Mission Speech, with 10:21–22 (or 10:21–24) following or attached to it; others see Q 10:21–22 as the conclusion of the Mission Speech, particularly because the contrast between acceptance and non-acceptance of revelation coheres thematically with the material on acceptance and rejection just before (Q 10:5–9, 10–16).[32] Ja-

---

[28] See for example James M. Robinson, "The Matthean Trajectory from Q to Mark," in *The Sayings Gospel Q* [1998], 599–627, here 617–19; Kirk, *Q in Matthew*, 273–74.

[29] Kirk, *Q in Matthew*, 276.

[30] Dieter Lührmann, *Die Redaktion der Logienquelle*, WMANT 33 (Neukirchen-Vluyn, Neukirchener Verlag, 1969), 62–63, with v. 12 as redactional seam; Kloppenborg, *Formation*, 195.

[31] Kloppenborg, *Excavating Q*, 147, 149.

[32] For Q 10:16 as the conclusion to the "Q Mission Discourse," see Hoffmann, *Studien*, 288–89; Risto Uro, *Sheep Among the Wolves: A Study on the Mission Instructions of Q*, AASF.DHL 47 (Helsinki: Academia Scientiarum Fennicae, 1987), 95–96, 162 (with vv. 21–22, 23–24 following as part of a major section on discipleship); Jacobson, *First Gospel*, 149–50 (with vv. 21–22 "attached to the Mission Charge"); Fleddermann, *Q: Reconstruction and Commentary*, 114, 437, and else-

cobson argued that this represents a late reinterpretation of the failure of the mission, "the expression of a radically sectarian group whose alienation from their own people exceeds anything found anywhere else in Q."[33]

Matthew, however, decided to exploit the theme of rejection found in these verses, situating them after the transposed section on John the Baptist, while saving Q 10:23–24 for the Parables Discourse, as noted above (Matt 13:16–17). By situating Q 7:18–35 after the composite Mission Speech, the author achieved several effects. As is often noted, this transposition is in keeping with the reordering of Markan material after the Sermon on the Mount, which moves around various miracle stories in Matthew 8–9 in preparation for the question of John from prison: "Are you the Coming One, or are we to expect another?" (Q 7:19; Matt 11:3).[34] Jesus' response in Matthew – in contrast with Q – is now supported with a full narrative account. This section begins with Q's healing in Capernaum, which looks ahead to the woe against Capernaum, now after Matthew's Mission Speech (Q 7:1–10; Matt 8:5–13; cf. Matt 8:1–4). Matthew also transposes into this section three Markan controversy stories to prepare for the accusation that Jesus was "a glutton and a drunkard, a friend of tax-collectors and sinners" (Q 7:34; Matt 11:19; cf. Mark 2:1–12, 13–17, 18–22 par. Matt 9:1–8, 9–13, 14–17).[35] Finally, delaying Jesus' exchange with John until after the Mission Speech, the declaration that "the poor are evangelized" (Q 7:22; Matt 11:5) has now been prepared for both by the Sermon on the Mount and by the mission of the Twelve (Matt 10:1–4, 5). Gerd Häfner has suggested that situating the exchange with John (and adjacent Q material) after the mission of the Twelve explains how John comes to hear of Jesus' activities, both miraculous and controversial.[36] For what reaches John's ears according to Matthew are not the exploits of the Twelve, but τὰ ἔργα τοῦ Χριστοῦ (Matt 11:2; cf. v. 1).

---

where; for 10:22 as the conclusion, see Kirk, *Composition*, 336–40; for 10:24 as the conclusion, the result of the Q² redactional addition of 10:21–24 to 10:2–16, see Kloppenborg, *Formation*, 202–3.

[33] Jacobson, *First Gospel*, 149.

[34] On the transpositions of Markan material in Matthew 8–9, see Heinz Joachim Held, "Matthew as Interpreter of the Miracle Stories," in Günther Bornkamm, Gerhard Barth, and Heinz Joachim Held, *Tradition and Interpretation in Matthew* (Philadelphia: Westminster, 1963), 165–299; see also Robinson, "Matthean Trajectory," 602, arguing (mainly against Luz) that "Matthew 3–11 is not primarily oriented to editing Mark, but rather to editing Q," so that "Mark is … only a subordinate factor in Matthew 3–11, just as Q is only a subordinate factor in Matthew 12–28." The latter point is arguable: for the importance of Q to the composition of Matthew 24–25, see Daniel A. Smith, "Matthew and Q: The Matthean Deployment of Q and Mark in the Apocalyptic Discourse," *ETL* 85 (2009): 99–116.

[35] Kirk, *Q in Matthew*, 267–68, following Linden E. Youngquist, "Matthew and Q" (Ph.D. diss., Claremont Graduate School, 2003), 120.

[36] Gerd Häfner, "Das Matthäusevangelium und seine Quellen," in *The Gospel of Matthew at the Crossroads of Early Christianity*, ed. Donald P. Senior, BETL 243 (Leuven: Peeters, 2011), 25–71, here 66; cited by Kirk, *Q in Matthew*, 255.

According to Davies and Allison, Matthew 11 becomes a turning point in the Gospel. After the Sermon ("Jesus' revelatory words") and chs. 8–9 ("Jesus' marvellous and salvific acts"), "the apostles are commanded to do what Jesus has done and preach what Jesus has preached" (ch. 10). With John's question, "the issue now becomes response to Jesus. ... Matthew 1–10 records the offer, Matthew 11–27 the refusal."[37] Or as Kirk has put it: "Chapter 11 is the fulcrum upon which the principal redactional development of the Gospel turns: ἀρθήσεται ἀφ' ὑμῶν ἡ βασιλεία τοῦ θεοῦ καὶ δοθήσεται ἔθνει ποιοῦντι τοὺς καρποὺς αὐτῆς," as Matthew's Jesus declares in an addition to the Tenants parable (Matt 21:43).[38] Considering this large-scale plan, it becomes clear why Matthew delayed using Q 10:13–15 and Q 10:21–22. For Matthew, Q 10:13–15 has a more generalizing effect in this new context than it did in Q, where it announced judgment on those towns who rejected the emissaries. In Matthew, this rejection is heightened in the Mission Discourse: the disciples will be persecuted in "all the cities of Israel until the Son of Humankind comes" (Matt 10:23); they will be maligned and rejected just as their Master (vv. 24–25). However, the woes against these cities are saved until after the parable about the rejection of John and Jesus by "this generation" (Q 7:31–35; Matt 11:16–19). They are thereby connected more explicitly with the rejection of Jesus' powerful acts, τὰ ἔργα τοῦ Χριστοῦ (Matt 11:2): these are seen by Matthew as the deeds by which Wisdom is vindicated, in the concluding statement of the parable of the children in the agoras (Matt 11:19 diff. Q 7:35).[39] Luz (and many others) observe here, correctly in my view, an indirect identification of Jesus with divine Wisdom, in which Matthew without much reflection on the consequences "simply presupposes their identity."[40]

With all this in view, Matthew's repositioning of Q 10:21–22 in chapter 11 makes perfect sense. "Their contribution is to distinguish those who reject [revelation] (ironically, the σοφοί καὶ συνετοί) sharply from those who receive it (νήπιοι)."[41] Again, the rejection of the revelation that comes from the "Father, the Lord of heaven and earth" is in this new context directly connected with the works of Jesus, which encompass all his activity up to this point in the Gospel. In its original context in Q, "these things (ταῦτα)" in v. 21 might have referred to the preaching of the basileia message; in Luke, there might be a reference to Jesus' vision of the fall of Satan from heaven, or to the success of the disciples'

---

[37] Davies and Allison, *Matthew*, 2:294–95.
[38] Kirk, *Q in Matthew*, 275–76, with further literature referenced, 275 n. 167.
[39] Q 7:35 (IQP) reads, καὶ ἐδικαιώθη ἡ σοφία ἀπὸ τῶν τέκνων αὐτῆς. For Matthew's purposes, this seems to equate John too closely with Jesus; he makes the minor modification to ἀπὸ τῶν ἔργων αὐτῆς (cf. Matt 11:12–14, where John is identified with Elijah).
[40] Luz, *Matthew 8–20*, 149; so also Davies and Allison, *Matthew*, 2:264–65: "so it is Jesus who is vindicated by his works." See similarly Matthias Konradt, *Das Evangelium nach Matthäus*, NTD 1 (Göttingen: Vandenhoeck & Ruprecht, 2015), 184.
[41] Kirk, *Q in Matthew*, 274.

mission (Luke 10:17–20); but the situation is different in Matthew.[42] The immediate antecedent for ταῦτα (Matt 11:25), the condemnation of the Galilean towns (vv. 20–24), can be excluded as the probable referent. Instead, Matthew seems to have in view τὰ ἔργα τοῦ Χριστοῦ, the deeds by which Wisdom is vindicated (11:2, 19).[43] Despite the public character of all these acts – the preaching of Jesus, the healings and miracles, the controversies with his opponents – they were still hidden by God from the wise and intelligent, and revealed only to children, who for Matthew are probably members of the ἐκκλησία. Q 10:22, about the mutual revelation of the Father and the Son, is no longer such a bolt from the blue, for Matthew has prepared the hearer for this by already forming a connection between Jesus and Wisdom.

The prayer of these two verses is curiously introduced in Matthew as a "reply" or "response" of Jesus (ἀποκριθεὶς ὁ Ἰησοῦς εἶπεν, 11:25), despite the fact that his speech so far has not been interrupted by any of its hearers ("the crowds," v. 7). This connecting device might simply "[add] a touch of solemnity" by imitating the style of the Hebrew Bible; Luke takes a different approach to a similar end by adding ἠγαλλιάσατο ἐν τῷ πνεύματι τῷ ἁγίῳ καὶ εἶπεν (Luke 10:21).[44] The prayer itself begins with a common Septuagintal turn of phrase, ἐξομολογέω with σοι.[45] Luz also notes the strong affinities with Qumranic songs of praise, especially 1QH XV, 26–33: "I give you [thanks, Lord], because you have taught me your truth, you have made me know your wonderful mysteries …."[46] The shift in Matthew between the two parts of this short sayings cluster is just as obvious as it was in Q: in Matt 11:27 (Q 10:22) the speech shifts from first-person self-reference to third person discussion of the Son after the start of the verse; on the other hand, the second part has some obvious catchword connections (πατήρ, ἀποκαλύπτω) with the first, and so probably it originated as a commentary on the prayer in the first part of the cluster.[47] In this last verse, the only significant alteration made by Matthew to the Q wording is to change γινώσκω to ἐπιγινώσκω. It is unclear whether a distinction such as that between "knowledge" and "recognition" is intended.[48] However, it is difficult to see how, in the context of Matthew (or even of

---

[42] Kloppenborg, *Excavating Q*, 128.
[43] Konradt, *Matthäus*, 187.
[44] Davies and Allison, *Matthew*, 2:273.
[45] Ibid.
[46] Luz, *Matthew 8–20*, 157 n. 10; translation from Florentino García Martínez, *The Dead Sea Scrolls Translated: The Qumran Texts in English*, 2nd ed. (Leiden: Brill; Grand Rapids: Eerdmans, 1996).
[47] Davies and Allison, *Matthew*, 2:270; Luz, *Matthew 8–20*, 158. Luz notes that "verses 25 and 26 are usually and justifiably attributed to Jesus," but this question lies beyond the interest of the present author.
[48] Davies and Allison say this small difference "[does] not change the sense" (*Matthew*, 2:280–81); so also Gundry, *Matthew*, 217.

Q), it can legitimately be said that "no one knows the Son except the Father." As noted above, were not all the deeds of the Messiah openly visible? It is likely, as many commentators have noted, that an identification with Wisdom is approximated here: "Only the Father knows the Son, just as only God knows Wisdom (Job 28:12–27; Sir 1:6–9; Bar 3:32). Only the Son knows the Father, just as only Wisdom knows God (Wisd 8:4; 9:1–18)."[49] It may also be that the Father not only knows but also reveals the Son, even though only the opposite is stated explicitly. Here we tread closely to a Matthean dilemma between claims about human responsibility or culpability on the one hand and divine will and restricted revelation on the other (see further Matt 13:10–17).

In Matthew's presentation, then, the seriousness of the rejection of Jesus is heightened by this piece of Q material. First, and obviously, to reject Jesus even though the deeds of the Messiah testify to him is to reject the only source for knowledge of God, the only mediator of divine knowledge (surpassing, in the end, even the still-valid Torah).[50] However, the Son is also the one to whom "all things have been handed over" (11:27a). To reject the only one thus authorized is therefore also to reject the Father. The language and form here are reminiscent of Daniel 7. Although Davies and Allison do not think the verse alludes to Dan 7:14 LXX (and looks ahead to Matt 28:18), this is because they see Matt 11:27a as about "eschatological revelation" rather than "authority and power."[51] Such a fine distinction is not justified. The one who uniquely gives insight into the character and will of God must be authorized by God; in addition, the idea that the Son reveals the Father to whomever he wishes (βούληται), that is, at his own discretion, parallels the idea in the previous verses that the Father reveals "these things" to infants because that is his good pleasure (Matt 11:26; Q 10:21b). In both Q 10:22 and Matt 11:27 Jesus is functionally identified with Sophia. How can this not be a matter of authority, even if an allusion to Dan 7:14 is to be excluded, and even if all authority is not granted to the Son until he is exalted (see Matt 28:18)?[52] It is possible to see this verse – in keeping with the fulcrum function of this chapter, as described by Kirk – as a middle point between the Temptation story, in which the devil offers Jesus "all these" (ταῦτα ... πάντα), that is, all the kingdoms of the world (Matt 4:8–9; Q 4:5–6), and the final resurrection appearance and commis-

---

[49] Davies and Allison, *Matthew*, 2:272; see also, with more detail and parallels, Kloppenborg, "Wisdom Christology," 143–44.

[50] Regarding the Antitheses in Matthew 5, see Kari Syreeni, "Matthew, Luke, and the Law: A Study in Hermeneutical Exegesis," in *The Law in the Bible and Its Environment*, ed. Timo Veijola, SESJ 51 (Helsinki: Finnish Exegetical Society; Göttingen: Vandenhoeck & Ruprecht, 1990), 125–55, here 141; cited in Heikki Räisänen, *The Rise of Christian Beliefs: The Thought World of Early Christians* (Minneapolis: Fortress, 2010), 266.

[51] Davies and Allison, *Matthew*, 2:279; see also Gundry, *Matthew*, 216: "the idea approaches that of handing on tradition."

[52] See similarly Konradt, *Matthäus*, 188.

sioning scene, in which Jesus declares that "all authority has been given to me, in heaven and on earth."⁵³

In the concluding scene, Matthew has emulated this prayer text from Q and developed it into a new saying, this time for the risen Jesus, and more explicitly referencing Daniel 7. However, an influence of Q 10:21–22 on the new saying can also be seen.⁵⁴

ἐδόθη μοι πᾶσα ἐξουσία ἐν οὐρανῷ καὶ ἐπὶ γῆς. (Matt 28:18)

καὶ ἐδόθη αὐτῷ ἐξουσία, καὶ πάντα τὰ ἔθνη τῆς γῆς κατὰ γένη καὶ πᾶσα δόξα αὐτῷ λατρεύουσα. (Dan 7:14a Theodotion⁵⁵)

ἐξομολογοῦμαί σοι, πάτερ, κύριε τοῦ οὐρανοῦ καὶ τῆς γῆς … (Q 10:21a).

πάντα μοι παρεδόθη ὑπὸ τοῦ πατρός μου … (Q 10:22a).

Dan 7:14a seems to exert a significant influence in Matthew's composition of Matt 28:18, particularly in the structure ἐδόθη + dative indirect object + ἐξουσία. Daniel's πάντα τὰ ἔθνη is also reproduced in verse 19.⁵⁶ However, there are also arguably some traces of an influence of Q 10:21–22 in Matt 28:18. Luz concludes, in his discussion of Matthew 11, that "Matthew presumably has formed [28:18b] redactionally by taking up the traditional logion of 11:27 and consciously expanding it," although in his discussion of Matthew 28 he does not mention Matt 11:27 at all.⁵⁷ As already noted, some scholars are reluctant to see too close a connection between Matt 11:27 and Matt 28:18b because the former is about revelation, while the latter is about universal authority; but this is to draw too fine a distinction between these ideas and to ignore two verbal similarities between Matthew and the Q prayer text.⁵⁸ First, in Q 10:22, πάντα is the direct object of the verb, and this is reflected in Matthew's new formulation, based on both Q and Daniel, ἐδόθη μοι πᾶσα ἐξουσία (v. 18b). Second, in Q 10:21 (Matt 11:25) the lordship of the Father encompasses both heaven and earth; this precise formulation has no parallel in Dan 7:13–14, so Matthew has imitated the language of Q in order to strengthen the connection between the two passages. As a result, there is an

---

⁵³ Gundry (*Matthew*, 595) supposes that the author of Matthew drew upon "the tradition behind Luke 4:6b," which reads σοὶ δώσω τὴν ἐξουσίαν ταύτην ἅπασαν. The IQP saw this, however, as a Lukan expansion of the original text of Q 4:6b: ταῦτά σοι πάντα δώσω. See Robinson et al., *Critical Edition of Q*, 36–37.

⁵⁴ Luz says that Matt 28:18b–20 is "a 'logion of the Lord' that Matthew composed": Luz, *Matthew 21–28: A Commentary*, Hermeneia (Minneapolis: Fortress, 2005), 620.

⁵⁵ The Old Greek differs considerably.

⁵⁶ Davies and Allison, *Matthew*, 3:682–83; Luz, *Matthew 21–28*, 619; Konradt, *Matthäus*, 461.

⁵⁷ Citation from Luz, *Matthew 8–20*, 166; cf. Luz, *Matthew 21–28*, 616–20 on "sources and motifs" in Matt 28:16–20. Davies and Allison (*Matthew*, 3:682) and Konradt (*Matthäus*, 461) draw attention to Matt 11:27 as a parallel (Konradt: "Vorwegnahme") in their discussions of Matthew 28.

⁵⁸ For an older discussion, see John P. Meier, "Two Disputed Questions in Matt 28:16–20," *JBL* 96 (1977): 407–24, here 413: "this is not exactly the same motif as is found in 28:18b."

interesting shift between the two claims of Matt 11:27 and 28:18: the first leads directly to an invitation to come and learn, with a promise of rest (11:28–29), while the other to a command to go and disciple and teach, with a promise of Jesus' enduring presence (28:19–20).[59]

To draw some of these threads together: given the heightened theme of rejection in the new Matthean context of Q 10:21–22, especially when read with Matthew's version of the Tenants parable, it is justified to see the new mission to disciple πάντα τὰ ἔθνη (Matt 28:19–20) as a mission to add to the number of νηπίοι to whom "these things" will been revealed by the Father (Matt 11:25; Q 10:21). The content of "these things" in the Q prayer has now been identified more precisely as "all that I have commanded you" (πάντα ὅσα ἐνετειλάμην ὑμῖν, Matt 28:20), that is, the teachings of Jesus contained in Matthew's Gospel. As I have recently argued elsewhere, the "divine imperium" Jesus receives after his resurrection is in fact the authority, delegated to the Eleven, by which Jesus will conquer and civilize the nations. Matthew thus imitates Roman imperialism but substitutes Christ for Caesar and the teachings of Jesus for the assimilating influence of Greek culture and Roman customs and cults.[60]

Although not an instance of emulation, the insertion (or creation?) of the new Wisdom saying in Matt 11:28–30 seems also to have been inspired by the implicit identification of Jesus with Wisdom in Q 10:21–22. In these verses, Jesus is not like the sage who exhorts others to take Wisdom's yoke; here he speaks as Wisdom herself would. This is characteristic of Matthew elsewhere: for example, he alters the introduction to Q 11:49–51 so that Jesus, and not Wisdom, sends prophets, sages, and scribes (Matt 23:34). Both the origins and primary influences and/or allusions of Matt 11:28–30 have long been in dispute. The literature is well known and often discussed, so a brief report will suffice here.[61] Most commentators agree that Sirach 51 (compare v. 1 with Q 10:21a), which stands out among all the Wisdom parallels as being particularly close to the invitation of Jesus in Matt 11:28–30, is the likely source or reference here.[62] Kirk acknowledges the significant parallel material from the Wisdom tradition but

---

[59] Graham Stanton, "Matthew 11:28–30: Comfortable Words?," *ExpTim* 94 (1982): 3–9, here 8.

[60] See Daniel A. Smith, "Excursion, Incursion, Conquest: A Spatial Approach to Mission in the Synoptics," in *The Gospels and Their Stories in Anthropological Perspective*, ed. Joseph Verheyden and John S. Kloppenborg, WUNT 409 (Tübingen: Mohr Siebeck, 2018), 191–214; for "divine imperium" applied to the risen Jesus of Matthew, see Wendy Cotter, "Greco-Roman Apotheosis Traditions and the Resurrection Appearances in the Gospel of Matthew," in *The Gospel of Matthew in Current Study: Studies in Memory of William G. Thompson, S. J.*, ed. David E. Aune (Grand Rapids: Eerdmans, 2001), 127–53, here 151.

[61] For a recent discussion, see Patricia Sharbaugh, "The New Moses and the Wisdom of God: A Convergence of Themes in Matthew 11:25–30," *Hor* 40 (2013): 199–217.

[62] See for example (in addition to the standard commentaries on Matthew) M. Jack Suggs, *Wisdom, Christology, and Law in Matthew's Gospel* (Cambridge, MA: Harvard University Press, 1970), 77–97; Celia M. Deutsch, *Hidden Wisdom and the Easy Yoke: Wisdom, Torah, and Dis-*

instead, focussing on the compositional and structural dynamics of this section, sees shepherd/sheep imagery as more prominent: this imagery, he argues, connects Matt 11:28–30 with 9:36 as an inclusio bracketing the Mission and John material in chapters 10–11.[63] However, Davies and Allison see some strong similarities with Exodus 33 and propose that not Wisdom but Mosaic themes dominate throughout Matt 11:25–30.[64] Davies and Allison therefore think that Matt 11:25–30 came from a Matthean recension of Q: "A tradent of Q^{mt}, recognizing the dependence of Matt 11:27 upon Exod 33:12–13, composed 11:28–30 in order to further the Exodus allusion and the comparison/contrast between Jesus and Moses and their two revelations."[65] Luz sees vv. 28–30 as a pre-Matthean saying into which the author has inserted some redactional lines.[66] Robert Gundry, on the other hand, believes the whole saying is a Matthean creation, for it "exhibits his characteristic attention to parallelism, diction typical of him, and his habit of conforming phraseology to the OT."[67] Regardless of how these exegetical problems are solved, it seems clear that the Q saying inspired Matthew to make this addition here. Matthew's hinge chapter, with its focus on rejection, therefore ends with an invitation to accept Jesus' yoke and burden, which are easy and light in contrast with the burdens imposed by the Pharisees (see Matt 23:4).

C. Q 11:2b–4, 9–13 in Matthew 6–7

The reconstruction of the Lord's Prayer in Q is generally unproblematic, because of the evidently secondary aspects in Matthew's version of the prayer: the additional descriptors for the vocative πάτερ, which are clearly Matthean; Matthew's third petition about the will of the Father; and the final petition for rescue from

---

cipleship in Matthew 11:25–30, JSNTSup 18 (Sheffield: JSOT Press, 1987); Deutsch, *Lady Wisdom, Jesus, and the Sages: Metaphor and Social Context in Matthew's Gospel* (Valley Forge, PA: Trinity Press International, 1996).

[63] Kirk, *Q in Matthew*, 275.

[64] Davies and Allison, *Matthew*, 2:283–86, evidently at pains to disprove any "Hellenistic" or "syncretistic" influence in these lines (ibid., 283, 287), against Eduard Norden, *Agnostos Theos: Untersuchungen zur Formengeschichte religiöser Rede* (Leipzig: Teubner, 1913), 277–308; see also Dale C. Allison, *The New Moses: A Matthean Typology* (Minneapolis: Fortress, 1993), 218–33. Sharbaugh, "Moses and Wisdom" attempts to read these two themes together; she refers to Deutsch and (Davies and) Allison as representative proponents of the Wisdom and Mosaic themes (respectively).

[65] Davies and Allison, *Matthew*, 2:238.

[66] Luz, *Matthew 8–20*, 157; so also many others, e. g. Huub van de Sandt, "Matthew 11:28–30: Compassionate Law Interpretation in Wisdom Language," in Senior, *The Gospel of Matthew at the Crossroads*, 313–37, here 326–29.

[67] Gundry, *Matthew*, 218.

evil (or the evil one).⁶⁸ Although apparently secondary to Q, the additional petitions are disputed as to their origin. Some commentators resist the possibility that they are Matthean creations because they cannot see how the author could alter a prayer that so clearly, in their view, was an established part of the liturgical practice of the Matthean community.⁶⁹ Current scholarship questions the now-traditional idea of "communities" behind the Gospels, but it is not at all implausible that an expanded version of the prayer was already in liturgical use before Matthew wrote.⁷⁰ In addition, the intense polemics we find in the immediate context of the prayer (both in Matthew and in the Didache) suggest a kind of communal perspective on Pharisaic Judaism.⁷¹ For Q 11:9–13, the IQP generally reconstructed Q following Matthew's wording; Luke's alterations cluster in the things hypothetically given to the child asking for food (Matt 7:9; Luke 11:12). The only other difference from Q is, again, Matthew's characteristic "your Father who is in the heavens" (Matt 7:11; see Matt 6:9).

As with Q 10:21–22, the main concern in the following discussion will be to examine the influence that these two adjacent Q clusters had on Matthew's composition. Four main issues present themselves upon consideration. First, why did Matthew insert the Lord's Prayer here, bringing it forward from its original place in Q (between Q's Mission Speech and the Beelzebub controversy)? Second, what effect did the Lord's Prayer have on the composition of Matthew 6? Third, to what end did Matthew separate from the Lord's Prayer its Q sequel, the instruction on asking, seeking, and knocking, and how does Q 11:9–13 function in its new Matthean context? Fourth, did either of these Q units provide resources for Matthew to emulate in new compositions, either in the Sermon on the Mount or elsewhere in the Gospel?

As Kirk has recently explained, proponents of the Two-Document Hypothesis have sometimes resorted to modifications that propose a pre-Matthean

---

⁶⁸ For surveys of scholarship, discussions, and evaluations, see Shawn Carruth and Albrecht Garsky, *Q 11:2b–4*, ed. Stanley D. Anderson, Documenta Q (Leuven: Peeters, 1996), 75–127, 178–94.

⁶⁹ See the discussion in Luz, *Matthew 1–7*, 309–10, in conversation with Joachim Jeremias, "The Lord's Prayer in Modern Research," *ExpTim* 71.5 (1960): 141–46; see also Warren Carter, "Recalling the Lord's Prayer: The Authorial Audience and Matthew's Prayer as Familiar Liturgical Experience," *CBQ* 57 (1995): 514–30, here 516–18. For the significance of Aramaic parallels to the distinctively Matthean parts of the Lord's Prayer, see the essay by Ursula Schattner-Rieser in this volume.

⁷⁰ Luz, *Matthew 1–7*, 310, but he also notices the problem of the obviously Matthean language of the prayer, which suggests to Luz that "at important points Matthew's redactional language is rooted in worship" (ibid., 43). For the idea of "community" in the study of Christian origins, see Stanley Stowers, "The Concept of 'Community' and the History of Early Christianity," *MTSR* 23 (2011): 238–56.

⁷¹ Peter Tomson, "The Lord's Prayer (Didache 8) at the Faultline of Judaism and Christianity," in *The Didache: A Missing Piece of the Puzzle in Early Christianity*, ed. Jonathan A. Draper and Clayton N. Jefford, SBLECL 14 (Atlanta: SBL, 2015), 165–87, summary 186–87.

Q version of the Sermon, or to approaches that devalue or diminish the literary integrity of the Sayings Gospel, in order to account for the similarities and differences between Matthew's Sermon on the Mount and Luke's Sermon on the Plain (which according to the IQP was much closer to the Q Sermon). The first main problem is that although the sermons of Matthew and Luke "have a common macro-sequence" which derives from Q, it is in these materials that their wordings tend to differ the most.[72] The second main problem is how to explain how and why Matthew excerpted additional material from later in Q and used it in the Sermon.[73] Instead of proposals that imagine Matthew redacting an amorphous Q (e. g. Günther Bornkamm, "Spruchgut"), or utilizing a pre-Matthean Sermon (e. g. Hans Dieter Betz), Kirk advocates an approach that integrates both source-utilization factors and redaction-critical factors.[74] To put it simply, Kirk argues that Matthew takes over from Q the "common macro-sequence" just mentioned, that is, "the *topoi* sequence of the Q Sermon, and makes it foundational for his Sermon while augmenting it with *topoi* of his own." The Matthean *topoi* prompt a "memory-based retrieval" of relevant Q material for which Matthew knows there is no appropriate location later in the Markan sequence. Generally, according to Kirk, the Q material excerpted is retained in its Q order. "In short, Matthew's collocation of double tradition into his Sermon is part of a comprehensive strategy for solving the technical problem of combining two sources coherently into a new work."[75] Kirk's approach is an economical solution that not only accounts for Matthew's composition but also the author's relatively high regard for the Sayings Gospel as a source.

The prayer unit in Matthew's Sermon (Matt 6:5–15) is, as already noted, the second part of a three-part section on traditional Judean practices of piety (almsgiving, prayer, and fasting: Matt 6:1–18). Except for Q's Lord's Prayer and Mark's instruction on forgiveness, the section has no Synoptic parallel; it follows the second major Q section in Matthew's Sermon, on retaliation and love of neighbour (Matt 5:38–42; Q 6:27–36). Some scholars have argued that in this section Matthew used another source text, called by Betz the "cultic didache." According to this view, the "cultic didache" source originally consisted of three short instructions on not imitating the hypocrites in their performance of piety (Matt 6:2–4, 5–6, 16–18), into which the author of Matthew inserted the material on prayer from Q and Mark (vv. 9–13 Q, vv. 14–15 Mk; vv. 7–8 MtS).[76] Luz, for example, ap-

---

[72] Kirk, *Q in Matthew*, 184. The common macro sequence is: (1) the beatitudes; (2) instruction on love of enemy; (3) instruction on judging; (4) sayings about trees and fruit; (5) the concluding parable about two houses.
[73] Ibid.
[74] See Kirk, *Q in Matthew*, 184–89 for a brief overview of approaches; he cites (among others) Günther Bornkamm, "Der Aufbau der Bergpredigt," *NTS* 24 (1978): 419–32; Hans Dieter Betz, *The Sermon on the Mount: A Commentary*, Hermeneia (Minneapolis: Fortress, 1995).
[75] Kirk, *Q in Matthew*, 189–90.
[76] See Hans Dieter Betz, "A Jewish-Christian Cult Didache in Matt 6:1–18," in idem, *Essays*

proves of this theory, although he notes – as he also did with the Lord's Prayer itself – that the clear Matthean linguistic traits indicate that "in his language and theology the evangelist is rooted in his community," and the thematic similarity to its context indicates that "the source was connected to the source for the primary antitheses" (i. e. on murder, adultery, and oaths).[77]

It is true that Matt 6:7–15 does look like an insertion that interrupts a tidy three-part structure. However, the "cultic didache" theory is not compelling because it proposes a source text that is virtually indistinguishable from Matthew's own redactional hand, both linguistically and thematically; obviously, the simpler solution is to see Matthew himself as the composer throughout. According to Kirk, the instruction on almsgiving fits here because it picks up the Q themes of unconditional giving and unrestricted love in the preview section (Matt 5:38–42; Q 6:27–36, reordered by Matthew).[78] However, the instructions on almsgiving, prayer, and fasting unfold "in an outer/inner contrastive pattern" in which the practices of "the hypocrites" are "counter-posed [by] the acceptable cultic practice that actualizes a truly reciprocal relationship with God."[79]

> This is a simple permutation of the Antithesis pattern, the distinction being that the Antitheses center on Torah dicta pertaining to human relationships, these on the principal cult practices which, accordingly, are introduced by ὅταν κτλ. The "Cult Didache" is no source: its units are formed on the same redactional pattern as the Antitheses.[80]

The *Sondergut* in this section, according to Kirk, derives from traditional ideas and motifs about ritual piety, but also from the "deliberative concerns of [Matthew's] Sermon."[81] The prayer unit is based on the same antithetical pattern, contrasting appropriate prayer with the prayers of the hypocrites (vv. 5–6: not in public for show, but in private in the divine presence) and of the non-Israelites (vv. 7–8: not in ritual repetition, but in the words of the Lord's prayer).[82] This means that the same structure found in the supposed "cultic didache" is also found in material thought not to belong to it. This could support either the Matthean origin of the whole section, or, by supposing that the author imitated

---

on the Sermon on the Mount, trans. L. L. Welborn (Philadelphia: Fortress, 1985), 55–69; Betz, *Sermon on the Mount*, 330 and throughout; so also Davies and Allison, *Matthew*, 1:573–75. Luz maintains "cultic" language is inappropriate (he rightly suggests "ritual" would be better), but otherwise also approves of the idea (*Matthew 1–7*, 296–98). Konradt says only that "Das Grundgerüst des Abschnitts bildet eine zum mt Sondergut gehörende dreistrophige Mahnung" (*Matthäus*, 100).

[77] Luz, *Matthew 1–7*, 297; on the origin of the antitheses, see ibid., 227–28.
[78] Kirk, *Q in Matthew*, 202.
[79] Ibid., 203.
[80] Ibid.
[81] Ibid., 202.
[82] On suggestions about divine presence in this section, see Daniel A. Smith, "'Pray to Your Father [Who Is] in Secret' (Matt 6:6): Considerations about Divine Presence and Sacred Space," in Senior, *The Gospel of Matthew at the Crossroads*, 653–63.

the style of the source text, the originality of the cultic didache.[83] Kirk identifies in the *Sondergut* in this section other aspects that show dependence on Q material used later in the Sermon (e. g. Matt 6:7–8 with v. 32, from Q 12:30).[84] Interestingly, material that seems to show the influence of Q is found both outside (vv. 7–8) and within the tight structure noted by Betz and other proponents of the "cultic didache" source theory. For example, "pray/prayer" and "Father" occur repeatedly in vv. 5–6, and Kirk sees this as influenced by the Q Prayer; proponents of the "cultic didache" theory could see these as linguistic catchwords that prompted the insertion of the Q Prayer here. In the end, certainty on this question is elusive, although the theory of Matthean composition throughout has much to commend it; either way, Kirk makes the important observation that the Q material on unconditional giving provided the thematic prompt for the change of topic to almsgiving, and thus to practices of ritual piety, in this part of the Sermon.

As for the Q sequel to the Lord's Prayer (Q 11:9–13), it may be that this Q cluster has also left its mark on the prayer section of Matthew's Sermon, because the idea that "your Father knows what you need before you ask him" (6:8) reflects both the repeated use of αἰτέω and the extended illustration about fathers knowing what to give in Q 11:9–13.[85] Robinson argues that this shows that Matthew was aware that this interpretation belonged to the Prayer.[86] However, the Ask-Seek-Knock passage does not appear until much later in Matthew's Sermon. Curiously, Matthew did not align it with the Q speech on anxiety about food and clothing (Matt 6:25–34; Q 12:22–31), but positioned the Q 12 passage midway between the Prayer section and Ask-Seek-Knock. As is well known, this section of the Sermon has proven difficult to explain in terms of its structure and rationale.[87] Why Matthew has separated Q 11:9–13 from the Lord's Prayer (Matt 7:7–11) is only part of the problem: even if the general structure makes sense, some of the details – that is, why certain bits of Q and *Sondergut* are found in this section, in the order and arrangement in which they appear – are difficult to explain.

According to Kirk, who follows Robinson on this point, Matthew uses Q 11:9–13 to conclude his "second course of *topoi*" (Matt 6:1–7:11) in this part of the Sermon; the Q Prayer initiates the sequence (integrated into its context with *Sondergut*), the Ask-Seek-Knock unit concludes it, and the speech on anxiety stands in the middle.[88] To quote Kirk again:

---

[83] Davies and Allison, *Matthew*, 1:592: "an attempt has been made – by Matthew? – to maintain the traditional arrangement of the received 'cult-didache'."
[84] Kirk, *Q in Matthew*, 203; Luz, *Matthew 1–7*, 305 thinks this is an independent logion, but seems not to see the parallels with Matt 6:32.
[85] Kirk, *Q in Matthew*, 203–4, mentioning αἰτῆσαι but not the fathers' knowledge.
[86] Robinson, "Matthean Trajectory," 614.
[87] See Robinson, "Matthean Trajectory," 609, referencing Bornkamm, "Aufbau."
[88] Kirk, *Q in Matthew*, 204–5, referencing Robinson, "Matthean Trajectory," 139–40.

In effect … Matthew has conceived the second *topoi* sequence as an expansion of the Q 11:9–13 commentary on the Q 11:2–4 prayer. He breaks open the Q prayer topos, in the middle as it were, to frame sequences of material from Q 12, Q 11, Q 16, Q 6, and Mark 11, bringing each into connection with the prayer.[89]

To step back, Kirk suggests that following the Beatitudes, Matthew used the Q text on "the Law and the Prophets" – which are fulfilled in the double command to love God and one's neighbour (see Matt 22:34–40; Mark 12:28–34) – to initiate two long sequences of *topoi*, the first on one's relationship to others, in the Antitheses, and the second on one's relationship to God, in the long stretch Matt 6:1–7:11, whose "controlling motif is prayer and the profound trust that is to define this relationship."[90] On this reading – leaving aside the details of the second section identified by Kirk – the original sequence Q 11:2–4 and 11:9–13 exerted a significant amount of influence on Matthew's composition in this part of the Sermon. Apart from the question of the details, which demands a closer examination than is possible in this paper, the other remaining question is why, if Matthew was concerned to preserve the "macro-sequence" of the original Q Sermon, he seemingly imposed his own second *topoi* sequence in such a way that it straddles original units of the Q Sermon. On the other hand, by preserving the original order of the two major sections (Q 6:27–36 followed by Q 6:37–41; Matt 5:38–42, 7:1–5), Matthew evidently prioritizes the Q macro-sequence over his own compositional interests, because the section on judging seems to fit better in his first *topoi* sequence than in his second.

It remains only to ask whether Matthew has emulated the prayer material from Q 11 in composing new sayings. One instance has already been mentioned in the previous discussion, namely, Matt 6:8: in contrast with the ἐθνικοί (cf. Q 12:30; Matt 6:32), the followers of Jesus are to pray with confidence because "your Father who is in the heavens knows what you need before you ask." This verse appears to have been composed on the basis of Q 12:30 as well as Q 11:11–13, which argues from the lesser principle that human fathers know to give their children what they need, to the greater principle about the Father giving good gifts. There is some unusual vocabulary in the previous verse, about not imitating the behaviour of non-Judeans in their prayers. The adjective ἐθνικός could arguably be seen as Matthean (Matt 5:47 (Q?); 6:8; 18:17), but three other words are hapaxes (βατταλογέω, πολυλογία, εἰσακούω); this, however, need not pose any real difficulty for the view that Matthew composed these lines.

Aside from this verse, the candidates are few and seem to depend on Matthew's distinctive version of the Lord's Prayer. A second possible example is found in Matt 18:19–20. The connection is perhaps a bit tenuous, but in these verses, Jesus promises that for any two who agree on earth in what they ask, "it

---

[89] Kirk, *Q in Matthew*, 214, referencing Bornkamm, "Aufbau," 430.
[90] Kirk, *Q in Matthew*, 202.

will come to pass for them with my Father who is in the heavens" (γενήσεται αὐτοῖς παρὰ τοῦ πατρός μου τοῦ ἐν οὐρανοῖς, v. 19). Asking, of course, features strongly in the Q prayer material and in the context created for it by Matthew; but the rest of the verse is reminiscent of the prayer to the Father, in the Matthean version's third petition: γενηθήτω τὸ θέλημά σου, ὡς ἐν οὐρανῷ καὶ ἐπὶ γῆς (Matt 6:10b). This is not from Q, but from Matthew's prayer.[91] Interestingly, however, Jesus' promise that he would be in the midst of two or three gathered in his name (ἐκεῖ εἰμι ἐν μέσῳ αὐτῶν, v. 20) is also reminiscent of the idea of praying in the divine presence, in the immediate context of the Lord's Prayer in Matthew 6. There, it is possible that the expression "your Father who is in secret" (τῷ πατρί σου τῷ ἐν τῷ κρυπτῷ, Matt 6:6, 18) is not an ellipsis for "your Father who sees in secret" (vv. 4, 6, 18), but actually refers to the divine presence invoked when one prays alone in a private space. There is a rich tradition in rabbinic literature of locating the divine presence with those who study Torah, even alone.[92] Here in chapter 18, prayer to the Father (6:5–13) is replaced with prayer in Jesus' name (18:19–20).[93] In any case, this takes us somewhat further from Q, but it seems evident that in these verses Matthew intentionally evokes language and ideas from his prayer *topos* in ch. 6, where Q was so influential.

The third example is found in Matthew's Gethsemane scene. In Mark, Jesus instructs the three disciples to "watch and pray lest you come into temptation," but Matthew's Jesus more closely echoes the wording of the Q Prayer's fifth petition (ἵνα μὴ εἰσέλθητε εἰς πειρασμόν, Matt 26:41; cf. Mark 14:38, ἔλθητε; cf. Q 11:4, μὴ εἰσενέγκῃς ἡμᾶς εἰς πειρασμόν).[94] Prompted by this, Matthew has Jesus echo the words of Matthew's Prayer: he addresses God as "Father," rather than "Abba Father" (Matt 26:39, 42 diff. Mark 14:36; see Matt 6:9; Q 11:2); and he prays "your will come to pass" (γενηθήτω τὸ θέλημά σου, Matt 26:42 diff. Mark 14:39; Matt 6:10b diff. Q 11:2). The close parallel to the petition about testing makes it likely that the author of Mark knew the Lord's Prayer in one of its forms (see also Mark 11:25).[95] More importantly, however, Matthew's Jesus "prays as

---

[91] Luz lists the Mattheanisms here but is reluctant to attribute these verses in their entirety to Matthew. He does note γενήσεται "instead of γενηθήτω" but does not draw any connection to the Lord's Prayer (*Matthew 8–20*, 449 and n. 15). Gundry sees vv. 19–20 as Matthean composition but also does not mention the Lord's Prayer (*Matthew*, 369–70). Davies and Allison see vv. 19–20 as M material which (in this case) they think Matthew knew as oral tradition; they likewise do not mention the Lord's Prayer (*Matthew*, 3:781, 788).

[92] Smith, "Pray to Your Father," 659–62: see, for example, m. ʾAbot 3.2.

[93] Gundry (*Matthew*, 370) wonders whether "Jesus' name has taken the place of the Torah, and Jesus himself the place of the Shekinah" in v. 20, but in the end decides against this interpretation; Davies and Allison (*Matthew*, 2:790), however, call this "a Christified bit of rabbinism."

[94] So Gundry, *Matthew*, 534; Luz, *Matthew 21–28*, 394; Davies and Allison, *Matthew*, 3:499–500.

[95] Joel Marcus, *Mark 8–16: A New Translation with Introduction and Commentary*, AYB 27A (New Haven, CT: Yale University Press, 2009), 985; Adela Yarbro Collins, *Mark: A Commentary*, Hermeneia (Minneapolis: Fortress, 2007), 681.

an example, just as he has taught his disciples."[96] As noted, in these last two examples, the connection to Q 11:2–4; 11–13 as used by Matthew is either tenuous (Matt 18:19–20) or is partly indirect owing to Matthew's use of his own version of the Lord's Prayer (Matt 26:39–42, in part at least); and the commentators disagree as to whether Matthew created these *Sondergut* verses himself. Perhaps with these Q passages on prayer, their influence on Matthew is to be seen more in the composition and arrangement of Matthew's Sermon, than in the creation of new material.

D. Conclusion

This study has examined the influence of the prayer texts of Q in Matthew with respect to two issues, namely, Matthew's arrangement of material as he integrated his two sources into his new story of Jesus, and his composition of new material as part of that process. Limiting the investigation to only two texts from Q, the prayer texts Q 10:21–22 and Q 11:2–4, 9–13, has meant that it has been impossible to study this double influence throughout Matthew. Nevertheless, these two texts seem to have been pivotal for Matthew as he composed both the Sermon on the Mount and the so-called "hinge" Chapter 11. Even beyond these passages, the Q Prayer texts have left their influence, for example in the way Jesus prays the Lord's Prayer in Gethsemane, or in Danielic declaration of authority at the conclusion of the Gospel. Further, on this basis it seems clear that Matthew regarded Q not only as a source whose contents he wished to include in his new composition, but also as a literary text – or, to use Kirk's expression, "memory artifact" – whose rhetorical strategies he integrated structurally as he sought to combine Q with Mark so as to preserve their own authority as texts and thus to instill his own composition with that authority. Kirk has analyzed this second aspect in great detail. A third aspect of Q's influence in Matthew, however, has yet to receive a programmatic study, and that is the extent to which Q served as a rhetorical resource for the composition of new sayings. To some extent, this has not been necessary as long as scholars have imagined stores of M tradition (whether oral or written), distinctive pre-Matthean compositions such as Betz's "cultic didache," or indeed scribes from Matthew's ecclesial context who contributed material, for example prophecies about Jesus discovered in the Scriptures. The source of Matthew's *Sondergut*, however, might not always have been his community "store-room," out of which he brought new things and old to compose his Gospel (Matt 13:52). In any case, this is a topic for further exploration elsewhere.

Kirk's solution to the long-standing question of Matthew's use of Q and Mark has many things to commend it, especially the emphasis on Q as a literary text of

---

[96] Luz, *Matthew 21–28*, 397.

its own rather than as simply a sayings "source," and the detailed examinations of how the rhetorical structures in Q's speeches have given shape to Matthew's composition, notably in the difficult passages examined here (the Sermon and chapters 10–11 with the strange transposition of the Q 7 material on John). Kirk evades the difficulties posed by a strictly media-based source utilization solution by appealing instead to memory. Certain text-based approaches have either tended to downgrade the literary character of Q, or else to prove unfeasible given recent studies of ancient media. Kirk's memory-based solution requires that Matthew regarded both Mark and Q as "normative" memory-artifacts which he had committed to memory, although Kirk does believe Matthew was also handling the written artifacts. The authority that Q had for Matthew is evident in its importance to different aspects of his composition, as this paper has attempted to show. Exactly what "the influence of Q" on Matthew means for how we assess Q's place in Christian origins, however, also remains a matter for further study and reflection.

List of Contributors

Irmtraud Fischer, Institut für Alttestamentliche Bibelwissenschaft, Karl-Franzens-Universität Graz, Austria

Ursula Schattner-Rieser, Martin-Buber-Institut für Judaistik, Universität zu Köln, Germany

Simon J. Joseph, University of California at Los Angeles, USA

Karl-Heinrich Ostmeyer, Institut für Evangelische Theologie, Technische Universität Dortmund, Germany

Catherine Hezser, SOAS University of London, England

Hildegard Scherer, Theologische Hochschule Chur, Switzerland

Markus Tiwald, Institut für Katholische Theologie, Universität Duisburg-Essen, Germany

Michael Labahn, Theologische Fakultät, Martin-Luther-Universität Halle-Wittenberg, Germany

Giovanni B. Bazzana, Harvard Divinity School, Cambridge, MA, USA

John S. Kloppenborg, University of Toronto, Canada

Thomas Klampfl, Rohrbach a. d. Lafnitz, Austria

Niclas Förster, Evangelisch-Theologische Fakultät, Universität Münster, Germany

Daniel A. Smith, Huron University College, London, Canada

Index of Ancient Sources

Hebrew Bible/Old Testament

Genesis		3	13
1:28	13	5:13 LXX	42
3:16	16	7–12	96
3:29	60	8:4–9	131
5:24	66	8:24–27	131
5:28–15:4	95	9:27–33	131
10:2–31	250	10:16–19	131
12	97	10:17	43
12:1	94	12:29	98
12:2	94	12:35	99
12:4	94	15–17	50
12:10–20	4, 92–93, 95	15:9	125
12:10	94	15:18	37
12:13	92	15:25	45
12:16	99	16	40
12:17	93–96, 98	16:4–5	3, 41–42, 50
12:19	93	16:4–5 LXX	42
15	13	16:4	33, 50
18:1–21	223	16:4 LXX	39, 42
19:1–14	223	16:5	39
19:38	42	16:5 LXX	42
20	4, 93	16:15 LXX	39
20:6–7	93	16:25 LXX	40
20:6	93, 98–99	17:7	44–45, 208
20:7	92–93, 100	17:7 LXX	44
20:14	93	20:7	150
20:15	93	22:22–24	223
20:16	93	23:4–5	92
20:17–18	93	32:32	252
20:17	4, 93, 100, 131	33	273
24:12–14	17	33:12–13	273
25	95	34:7 LXX	43
26:6–11	92	34:9 LXX	43
32:10–13	17		
47:15 LXX	39, 42	*Leviticus*	
47:15	33, 42	7:34	149
50:17	43	19	124
		19:2	18
Exodus		19:34	223
1:7	13	22:24 LXX	39

22:32	150	*2 Kings*	
23:37 LXX	42	2	13
26:7–8	125	2:9	66
		6:18–23	91–92
Numbers		6:18–20	100
4:16 LXX	42	6:18	62, 91–92, 101
14:19 LXX	43	6:20	92, 131
16:28–35	100	6:23	92
28:3	42	14:25	13
28:9–10	264		
		1 Chronicles	
Deuteronomy		16:35 LXX	36
2	14	17:14	38
2:6	14	29	50
2:28	14	29:11	38
4:34	208		
4:39 LXX	38	*2 Chronicles*	
5:9	245	24:20–21	12
6:4–9	106, 109	24:22	138
6:4	106, 108, 115		
6:7	107, 109	*Ezra*	24
6:13	20, 245–46	7:18	38
6:16	20, 44, 208		
6:16 LXX	44	*Nehemiah*	
7:19	208	8–9	24
8:3	20–21, 42	12:47 LXX	42
8:10	120		
9:22	208	*Esther*	13
10:20	20, 245–46		
11:13–21	106, 109	*Job*	
15:1–3	205	Prologue	20
28:35	20	2:7	20
29:2	208	28:12–27	270
32:51	150	28:12–23	176
		28:13–14	172
Judges		28:21–22	172
10:15 LXX	45		
		Psalms	
1 Samuel		1:1	83
13:14 LXX	37	6:9	21
17:47–51	13	8:3 LXX	174
20:31 LXX	37	18:8 LXX	173
21:1–6	263	22	16
		22:4–6	12, 16
1 Kings		22(21):2	43
8:23 LXX	34	24:17	116
11	14	25(24):18 LXX	43
		32:1–2	83

34:1	130	*Proverbs*	61
34:13 LXX	130	1:7	18
35	131	1:20–25	172
35:12–15	130	1:22 LXX	168
36:7	117	1:24	18
39:3	99	1:28	18
39(40):9 LXX	38	1:29–30	172
39:10	99	1:32 LXX	168
40:9	39	8:22–26	79
41:1	83	8:36	172
50:5	24	9:4 LXX	168
50:13–14	24	22:17–24:22	69
50:23	149	23:25	111
51:1–2	17	25:11	100
51:17–19	24	25:21–22	62, 92
58:7–11	100	26:12 LXX	168
69:29	252		
69:30–31	24	*Ecclesiastes*	
83:10–18	100	5:1 LXX	34
88:27 LXX	34		
89	50	*Isaiah*	
91:11–12	20, 143	1:11–13	24
92:13	97–98	1:17	24
94:8	208	4:1 LXX	39
103:19	38	6:3	150
103:22	38	6:9–10	160
104:14	60	7:12	44
104:35	101	25:4 LXX	45
108:4 LXX	130	29:14	174
109:4–5	130	29:23	149
109:6–20	100	48:14 LXX	38
112:1	83	53:13	131
113:11(115:3) LXX	33–34	55–66	24
114:6 LXX	173	55:1–3	13
118:130 LXX	173	55:1–2	14
119:1–2	83	55:6	18
128:1–2	83	63	50
134(135):6 LXX	38	63:11–15	36
137:8–9	83	63:16 MT	19, 52, 59
139:16	252	63:16 LXX	34
142(143):10 LXX	38	64:7 MT	36, 52
143:10	39	64:7 LXX	33
144(145):1 LXX	36	64:8	59
144(145):13 LXX	37	65:1–2	18
145	37		
145:1–2	38	*Jeremiah*	
145:13	38	7:22	24
145:15–19	60	14:11	131

15:21 LXX	45	5:26 LXX	37
18:20	131	6:11	24
18:21–22	131	6:28 LXX	38
29:7	131	7	71–72, 80, 270–71
52:34 LXX	42	7:13–14	271
		7:13	74, 76, 79
Ezekiel		7:14 LXX	270–71
36:22–23	149	7:27	37–38
36:23 LXX	36	9:1–6	24
38:23	149	9:3–23	24
39:7	149	12:1	252
44:30	149		
		Hosea	24
Daniel	26	3:4	24
2:19–23	169	6:6	264
2:20–21 LXX	169–70	14:3	24
2:21	173		
2:23 LXX (Theodotion)	168	*Jonah*	13
3:26 LXX	36	1:2	14
3:33	37–38	2	13, 17
3:52 LXX	36	2:2	17
4:13	76	3	13
4:17	76		
4:17 LXX	38	*Malachi*	
4:23	76	3:23	13
4:34	37–38		

Deuterocanonical Books

Baruch		4:9	125
3:1–4:4	176	4:15	125
3:3–4:4	181	13:36–39	204
3:32	270	14:14 LXX	45
4:4	181		
6:40–41	100	*2 Maccabees*	91, 138
		3:18–22	62, 91, 101
Prayer of Azariah		3:29	99–100
1:29 LXX	36	3:31	91
		3:32	91
Judith	13		
13:4–10	13	*Sirach*	
		1:4–9	176
1 Maccabees		1:6–9	270
1:1–9	117	2:1	44, 208
2:52	208	6:1	232
3:5	125	6:7	208

14:1–2	83	*Tobit*	26, 39
20:23	233	3:6	28
23:3 LXX	33	3:11	53
23:4	33	3:11 LXX	36–37
23:4 LXX	33	5:17 LXX	34
24	81	7:17	168
25:8–9	83	13:4	34, 59
27:5	208	13:9	34
27:7	208	13:13	34
33:1	208	13:14	83
44–49	12		
44:20	208	*Wisdom*	
50:16–21	121	8:4	270
51:1–30	160	9:1–18	270
51:1–2	143	14:3	33
51:1	168, 170, 272	16:20–28	42
51:17	170		

New Testament

Q		6:27–49	86
3–7	163	6:27–36	275–76, 278
3:5	144	6:27–35	59, 62
3:7–8	80	6:27–28	4–5, 61, 84, 91, 101,
3:8	19, 84		104, 116, 129, 136,
3:9	63		143, 145, 151
3:17	63, 165	6:27	5, 61, 89–90, 135, 145
3:21–22	175	6:28–29	127
4:1–13	2, 82, 165, 175	6:28	1, 4–5, 8, 18, 58, 61–
4:1–3	20		62, 85, 90, 101, 103,
4:4–8	103		123–39, 145
4:4	21, 143	6:29–30	5, 136
4:5–8	1, 84, 114, 116	6:29	127, 129, 135, 145
4:5–7	8	6:31	61
4:5–6	153, 270	6:32–34	61, 84
4:5	164, 179	6:32	85
4:6	179, 271	6:35	61, 116, 145, 151
4:8	4, 103, 114–15, 143	6:36–37	204
4:9–12	20	6:36	61, 205
4:11–12	143	6:37–41	278
6:20–23	4, 84	6:37–39	61
6:20–21	180	6:40	82
6:20	61	6:49	18, 63
6:22–23	82–86, 135–36, 180	7	281
6:22	71, 82	7:1–10	267
6:23	84–85	7:9	84

7:18–38	81	11:2	61, 114, 175, 197, 205, 279
7:18–35	263, 266–67		
7:19	267	11:3	4, 109, 119–20, 151, 209
7:22	61, 64, 84, 267		
7:28	176–77	11:4	2, 4, 7, 59, 109, 118, 135, 151, 205, 209–10, 279
7:31–35	268		
7:34	81–82, 267		
7:35	81–82, 176–77, 183, 268	11:5–13	239
		11:9–13	1, 7–9, 59, 61, 103–04, 143, 146, 175, 199–200, 209, 263, 273–80
9:57–11:51	6, 157, 162–63, 181		
9:57–60	162, 165, 167		
9:57–58	81		
9:58	71, 81–82, 85	11:9–12	135
9:61–62	162, 167	11:9–10	60, 113, 240
10	266	11:9	109, 144, 226
10:2–16	162, 167, 267	11:10	60
10:2	1, 2, 4, 8, 19, 103–04, 109, 117, 136, 143	11:11–13	113
		11:11–12	4, 120
10:3–12	182	11:11	61, 119
10:3	135, 182	11:12	119
10:5–9	266	11:13	59
10:5–6	145	11:14–52	163
10:7	151	11:14–20	144, 153
10:10–16	266	11:16	13–14
10:10–12	63, 182	11:18	144, 153
10:11–12	135, 175	11:20	148
10:12–15	266	11:21–22	144
10:13–24	163	11:21	153
10:13–15	8, 89, 100, 181	11:23–24	160
10:13	163	11:23	63
10:16	163, 266	11:29–35	13–14
10:21–11:13	7, 197–200	11:31–32	14–15, 263
10:21–24	6–7, 145, 148–49, 157–84, 266–67	11:39–44	163, 176
		11:46–48	163, 176
10:21–22	2, 8–9, 59, 263–74, 280	11:49–51	84, 135, 265, 272
		11:51	12, 63
10:21	1, 8, 19, 59, 103, 105, 112–13, 135, 143, 146, 154, 167–82, 197	12	277
		12:2–22:30	163
		12:2–3	84, 163, 182
10:22	178–79, 198	12:2	177
10:23–24	179–80, 263, 266–67	12:3–4	177
10:23	143	12:3	177
11	278	12:4	135
11:2–13	175	12:8–9	79–80
11:2–4	1–3, 7–9, 58, 61, 103–04, 109, 135, 143, 199, 201, 263, 273–80	12:8	71
		12:10	71, 90
		12:11	209
		12:12	135, 161

12:22–31	59–60, 156, 277	4:8	244
12:22	120	4:9	244
12:24	120	5	270
12:28	175	5:1–4	180
12:29–31	145–46	5:6	180
12:29–30	151	5:9	63
12:30	175, 277–78	5:10–12	125
12:39–40	79	5:10	136
12:40	71, 80	5:14	161
12:51	145	5:38–42	63, 275–76, 278
12:53	145	5:39–41	137
12:57–59	135	5:39	127, 136–37
12:58–59	217	5:43–44	4
12:58	217	5:43	89
13:18–19	84	5:44	18, 91, 101, 123–24, 129
13:20–21	84		
13:21	142, 153	5:47	278
13:24	63	5:48	18
13:27	21	6–7	8, 273–80
13:30	84	6	195
13:34–35	65, 81, 84, 135, 149, 153, 265	6:1–7:11	277–78
		6:1–18	263, 275
14:11	84	6:1–5	17–18
14:16–18	61, 84	6:2–4	275
14:21	61	6:4	279
14:23	61	6:5–15	275
14:26	84	6:5–13	279
14:27	82	6:5–6	110, 136, 275–77
15:4–5	61	6:5	257
15:7	61	6:6	17, 279
15:8–10	61	6:7–15	276
16:18	84	6:7–8	136, 276–77
17:2	90, 100, 176–77	6:7	17, 257
17:3–4	61, 135	6:8	9, 17, 277–78
17:6	144	6:9–13	3, 17, 23, 30, 32–33, 58, 110, 263
17:20–21	144		
17:22–30	79		201
17:23	71	6:9–10	33, 36, 110, 274, 279
17:26–27	80	6:9	29, 37–38, 136, 152, 279
17:30	80	6:10	
17:33	84, 135		
17:34–35	63	6:11	40–41
22–31	146	6:12	18, 42, 44, 202
22:28–30	145	6:13	7, 44–46, 136, 202, 209
		6:16–18	18, 275
Matthew		6:18	279
4:1–11	153	6:25–34	277
4:8–9	270	6:32	277–78

7:1–5	278	12:3–4	263
7:7–11	258, 263, 277	12:5–6	263
7:9	274	12:40	14
7:11	274	12:41–42	15, 263
7:12	12	13:10–17	270
8–9	266–68	13:10–15	263
8:1–4	267	13:13–15	161–62
8:5–13	267	13:16–17	159, 263, 266–67
9:1–8	267	13:16	161
9:9–13	267	13:17	162
9:14–17	267	13:25–26	161
9:36	273	13:27	161
9:37–38	117–18, 250	13:35	161
10–11	273, 281	13:39	209
10	266	13:44	161
10:1–4	267	13:52	280
10:5	267	14:1	161
10:7–16	250	16:14	13
10:23	125, 268	16:21	86
10:24–25	268	16:27	67
10:25	136	17:10–12	13
10:32	86	18:6	90, 100
11	8–9, 264–73, 280	18:17	278
11:1–19	263	18:19–20	9, 278–80
11:1	266–67	18:23–35	202, 218
11:2	267–69	19:28	67
11:3	267	21:12–13	136
11:5	267	21:13	107
11:7	269	21:15–16	176
11:12–14	268	21:15	174
11:13	12	21:16	174
11:14	13	21:19	136
11:16–19	268	21:43	268
11:19	267–69	22:34–40	278
11:20–27	263	23	135
11:20–24	89, 100, 160, 269	23:4	273
11:24	250	23:13–36	89, 100
11:25–30	160, 273	23:14	108
11:25–27	159, 263	23:34	125, 272
11:25–26	1	23:53	136
11:25	19, 269, 271–72	24–25	267
11:26	270	25:18	161
11:27	178, 264, 269–73	25:25	161
11:28–30	9, 159–60, 266, 272–73	25:31–46	202, 218
		25:31	67
11:28–29	272	25:41	209
12:1–8	263, 266	26:28	126
12:1	161	26:39–42	9, 280

26:39	279	13:12–13	134
26:41	279	13:18	134
26:42	137, 279	13:19	202
26:52	136	14:22	134
26:55	42	14:24	126
26:67–68	137	14:26	134
27:46	43	14:35–36	134
28	271	14:35	134
28:16–20	271	14:36	36, 279
28:18–20	9, 271	14:38	134, 279
28:18	270–72	14:39	134, 279
28:19–20	272	14:49	42
28:19	271	14:58	153
28:20	272	15:34	43, 134
Mark		*Luke*	
1:12–13	153	1:10	107, 137
1:35	134	1:13	137
2:1–12	267	1:20–22	100
2:13–17	267	1:32–35	77
2:18–22	267	1:33	37
2:23–28	263, 266	1:47–55	137
2:25–26	263	1:64	137
3:2	134	1:68–78	137
3:5	134	1:74	137
4:10–12	160, 263	2:1	245
4:12	266	2:28–32	137
4:17	134	2:37	137
5:41	35	2:38	137, 161
6:41	134	3:21	137
6:46	134	4:1–3	153
8:6	134	4:5–7	8
8:35	134	4:5	244–45
9:29	134	4:6	244, 248
9:37	173	4:7	244
9:42	90, 100, 173	4:8	243
10:15	173	4:14	247
10:25	173	4:29–30	137
11:15–19	153	6:12	137
11:17	107, 134	6:20–21	180
11:24	134	6:24–26	89, 100
11:25	134–135, 279	6:27–32	63
12:1–9	134	6:27–28	18, 123–24
12:28–34	278	6:27	90, 249
12:40	108, 134	6:28	8, 123, 125, 138, 243, 249
13:8	145		
13:9	134	6:47	19
13:11	134	6:49	19

9:23	42	17:10	240
9:35	78	18:1–8	113, 241
9:51	249	18:1–7	137
9:52	250	18:1	224, 241
10:1	251	18:2–5	210
10:2	8, 117, 243, 249–51	18:6–8	241
10:9	251	18:10	107, 137
10:17–20	269	18:11–13	137
10:17	251	18:25–26	260
10:18–20	251	19:27	245
10:19	252	19:46	107
10:20	252	19:47	42
10:21–24	159, 253	20:19	161
10:21–22	243	20:20	245
10:21	1, 8, 161, 176, 243, 251–54, 269	21:22–23	90, 100
		22:20	126
10:22	161, 178, 253	22:27	240
10:23	161	22:36	137
10:24	162	22:51	137
11:1–13	222	22:53	42
11:1–2	18	23:2	247
11:1	254–56, 259	23:7	245
11:2–4	3, 8, 18, 23, 30, 32–33, 58, 110, 201, 243	23:24	133
		23:33–34	137
11:2	33, 36, 110, 143	23:34	92, 101, 131, 133
11:3	39, 41–42	23:35	78
11:4	7, 42, 44, 119	23:46	137
11:5–13	18	24:30	137
11:5–8	2, 7, 8, 113, 219–41		
11:8	7–8	*John*	
11:9–13	8, 241, 243, 258–60	1:34	78
11:12	274	2:19	153
11:13	240	4:20–24	154
11:20	180	12:31	144
11:50–51	138	12:42	221
12:11	209, 245	16:11	144
12:12	161		
12:25–26	240	*Acts*	139
13:21	161	2:1–21	259
14:5	240	2:46	42
14:28	240	2:47	42
14:31	137, 240	3:1	107
14:33	240	3:2	42
15:4–6	240	4:8	260
15:7	240	4:24–30	259
16:16	12	4:30	260
16:19	42	4:31	259
17:7–9	240	7:60	92, 133

8:22	250	12:22	41
9:11	99	15:51	154
9:17	99, 101	16:22	87
9:18	99		
10:30	107	*Galatians*	
11:28	245	4:6	36
16:5	42	4:21–31	15
16:18	161, 252		
17:6	245, 247	*Philippians*	
17:7	247	2	195
17:11	42	3:5	47
19:9	42	4:3	252
19:11–12	252		
19:13	251	*1 Thessalonians*	
19:15	252	5:12–22	126
19:27	245		
21–22	47	*Hebrews*	
21:37	47	12:23	252
21:40	47	13:15	149
22:2	47		
22:13	161	*James*	
24:5	245, 247	1:13	206
26:14	47	1:14	207
28:8	99		
28:31	260	*1 Peter*	138
		3	126–27, 129
Romans		3:8–19	5, 126
8:15	36	3:9	126–28
11:25	154	3:14	84
12	126–27, 129	3:16	125, 127
12:9–21	5, 126	4:13–14	84
12:14	127		
12:17	126, 128	*Revelation*	
12:20	62, 127–28	3:5	252
		3:10	7, 202, 207
1 Corinthians		8:3	149
2:7	154	13:8	252
4:12	127	20:15	252
7:2	221	21:22	153

Old Testament Pseudepigrapha

2 Baruch		*1 Enoch*	26, 69, 72, 78
29:3–8	42	1–36	76, 79
70:2	144	1:1	69
		10:6–7	83

10:7	76	53:7	75
10:9	76	54:1–2	80
12:2–3	76	55:4	79
13:10	76	56:5–7	74
14:1	76	58:4	75
37–71	3, 57–87	60:10	75
37:2	80	61:5	65
38:1–2	81	61:8	67, 79
38:3	81	61:12–13	150
39:12–13	150	61:12	150
39:12	150	61:13	151
41:1	81	62	75
42	69, 81	62:2	67, 79
42:1–2	81	62:3	65, 79
45:3–4	65	62:5	75, 79–80
45:3	67, 79	62:7	75, 79
46:1	79	62:9	75, 79
46:2–4	75	62:11	75
46:2	79	62:13–15	82
46:3	75	62:13	65
46:4	75, 79	62:14	75, 79
46:8	82	62:15	82
47:1–2	75	63:1	65
47:1	74	63:11	75, 79
47:2	82	65:1–67:3	80
47:4	82	67:4–13	74
48:1	81	68:1	78
48:2–6	79	69:26–27	75
48:2	75, 79	69:26	75, 79
48:3	79	69:27	67, 75, 79
48:4	82	69:29	75, 79
48:6	79, 81	70:1	75, 79
48:7	79, 81–82	71:14	75, 79
48:8	65	71:17	75, 79
48:10	79	83–90	76, 79
49	78	90	74
49:1–4	79	96:1	67
49:3	81	106:2	78
50:1–5	82	106:10	78
50:22	67	108:12	67
51:1–3	79		
51:1	65	2 Enoch	
51:3–4	65	42:6–14	83
51:3	79, 81	52:1–5	83
51:5	65		
52:4	79	4 Ezra	72
52:7	65	4:28–29	144
53:2	79	9:17	144

Jubilees

13:11	95
23:19	145
50:9	147

Letter of Aristeas

227	130

3 Maccabees

2:19 LXX	43
6:3 LXX	33
6:8 LXX	33

4 Maccabees

	138

Odes

14:43	38

Psalms of Solomon

5:10	60

Sibylline Oracles

1.175	238
2.33	238
8.184	238

Testaments of the Twelve Patriarchs

	129, 132, 139

Testament of Benjamin

3:6	5, 132–33
3:8	132
4:2–3	132
5:5	132

Testament of Joseph

3–9	133
3:3	133
3:7	133
4:8	133
7:4	133
8:1	133
10:1	133
11–16	133
17–18	133
17	132
18:2–4	133
18:2	5, 90, 100, 132–33

Testament of Levi

2:3 [19]	99

Dead Sea Scrolls and Related Texts

1Q20 [1QapGen ar XX]	4, 94	1QapGen ar XIX, 23	95
1Q20 XX, 12–16	62, 93	1QapGen ar XX, 5	40
1Q20 XX, 23	39	1QapGen ar XX, 12–29	93
1Q20 XX, 30	40	1QapGen ar XX, 12–16	4, 94–99, 101
1Q26	154	1QapGen ar XX, 16–17	95
1QapGen	39	1QapGen ar XX, 18	96
1QapGen ar	26, 49	1QapGen ar XX, 21–22	100–101
1QapGen ar II, 14	34	1QapGen ar XX, 28–29	4, 99–101, 131
1QapGen ar II, 24	35	1QapGen ar XX, 29	99
1QapGen ar VII, 7	34	1QapGen ar XX, 30	40
1QapGen ar XI, 12–14	26	1QapGen ar XX, 32	99
1QapGen ar XI, 12–13	53	1QapGen ar XX, 33–XXI, 4	95
1QapGen ar XI, 28–29	26	1QapGen ar XXI, 23–24	94
1QapGen ar XII, 16.21	168	1QapGen ar XXII, 11	46
1QapGen ar XII, 17 34,	53	1QapGen ar XXII, 19	40
1QapGen ar XIX, 7–10	95	1QDM [1Q22] III, 5–7	205
1QapGen ar XIX, 10–XX, 32	95	1QH IV, 15	73
1QapGen ar XIX, 14–23	97	1QH X, 9	177

1QH XV, 26–33	269	4Q423	154
1QH XV, 26–27	169	4Q504 3 II, 6	37
1QM XII, 7–8	147	4Q504 VII, 4–5	73
1QpHab XII, 4	177	4Q525	85
1QS I, 9–10	89	4Q534–36	77
1QS I, 10	61	4Q534	77–79
1QS III, 4	37	4Q534 I, 7–9	78
1QS IV, 22–23	73	4Q542 1 I, 3	39
1QS IX, 5	25	4Q545 4, 18	39
1QS X, 17–21	61	4QEnGiants^b ar 2 II + 6–12(?), 16	34
4Q171	73	4QInstruction	154
4Q174	73	4QMess Ar = 4QNoah	77
4Q174 III, 6–7	149	4QpapLXXLev^b (4Q120)	34
4Q196 [papTob^a ar] 18, 11 = Tob 13:3	53	4QTestament of Qahat	26, 28
4Q196 [papTob^a ar] 6, 7 = QA Tob 3:11	36, 53	4QTobit	26
		4QTobit^b ar 4 I, 17	35
4Q196, 18, 11 = QA Tob 13:3	36	4QTobit^b ar 5, 10	37
4Q198 [Tob^c ar] I, 5	38–39	4QVisions of Amram	26
4Q213a	99	11Q5	151
4Q242 1 III, 4	43	11Q5 XXIV, 10–11	151
4Q243–245	76	11Q5 XXVI, 9–16	150
4Q246	37, 76–77, 79	11Q5 XXVI, 9–15	151
4Q258 2 II, 5	25	11Q13 II, 1–6 [11QMelch]	59
4Q400–407	146	11Q19 XLVI, 15	152
4Q400–405	147	11QapGen ar XII, 11	45
4Q400 2 VII	149	11QPs^a XXIV, 10	206
4Q400 2,1–2	148	11QTgJob	49
4Q401 14 I,7	148	11QTgJob XIV, 6	45–46
4Q403	154	11QTgJob XVI, 1	46
4Q403 1 I, 30–39	148	11QTgJob XXIII 1	46
4Q403 1 II, 26	149	11QTgJob XXXVIII, 3	43
4Q403 1 II, 27	154	CD III, 20	73
4Q404	154	Book of Giants (4Q530)	76
4Q404 3+4+5	148	Genesis-Apokryphon	90, 93–94, 97–98
4Q405	154		
4Q405 23 II, 12	149	Rule of the Community (1/4QS)	61
4Q405 XI, 9	154	War Scroll (1QM)	61
4Q415–418	154		

Philo

Philo	109, 122	121–124	108
Against Flaccus		121	116
47.52	125	*Embassy to Gaius*	
52	125	213	125

Life of Abraham		Life of Moses	
95	95	2.199	125
96–98	95	Questions on Exodus	
Life of Joseph		2.11	61
71	125		

Josephus

Josephus	108–09, 122	1.224	238
Jewish Antiquities		1.276	238
1.210	93, 101	1.616	238
4.212	107	2.135	61
4.40–50	100	2.139–140	61
9.56–57	101	2.147–149	152
14.22	111	2.152–153	61
14.24	101	2.174	61
16.27	125	2.197	61
17.6.5	74	2.427	118
Jewish War		2.567	61
1.13	125	4.307	129
1.33.5.657–58	74	Life	
		290–295	108

Mishnah, Talmud, and Related Literature

Babylonian Talmud	112	m. 'Abot 2:16	118
b. 'Arak. 10b	101	m. 'Abot 3:2	279
b. Ber. 10a	101	m. Ber. 1:1–2	107
b. Ber. 12a	28, 49	m. Ber. 4:1	107
b. Ber. 29b	256	m. Ber. 4:4	121
b. Ber. 40b	28–29, 49	m. Ber. 6:1	120
b. Ber. 46a	28, 49	m. Ber. 6:3	120
b. Ber. 49a	28	m. Ber. 6:4–5	120
b. Ber. 60b	45, 206	m. Ma'as. 2:7	117
b. Šabb. 12b	27	m. Roš. Haš. 3:8	111
b. Sanh. 39b	101	m. Soṭah 7:1	27, 47
b. Soṭah 32b–33a	27	m. Soṭah 9:15	59, 111–12, 114
b. Soṭah 33a	27	m. Ta'an. 3:8	4, 110–12
b. Ta'an. 23a	113	m. Yoma 8:9	59, 111
b. Ta'an. 25b	112	t. Ber. 1:8	115
m. 'Abot	118	t. Pe'ah 4:8	119
m. 'Abot 2:7	173	Talmud Yerushalmi	116–17
m. 'Abot 2:15	118	y. B. Meṣ. 2:5, 8c	115–17

Targumic Texts

Tg. Gen 22:1	45	Tg. Jer 15:21	55
Tg. Gen 32:12	55	Tg. Ezek 36:23	36
Tg. Gen 47:15	39–40	Tg. Micah 4:8	38
Tg. Gen 49:10	38	Tg. Sir 2:1	44
Tg. Exod 16:4	39, 45, 54	Tg. Sir 23:1	33
Tg. Exod 16:15	39	Tg. Sir 23:4	33
Tg. Exod 16:25	39	Tg. Onq. Gen 47:15	40, 54
Tg. Exod 17:7	54	Tg. Onq. Gen 49:10	37, 53
Tg. Exod 32:32	43	Tg. Onq. Exod 16:29	40
Tg. Exod 34:9	43, 54	Tg. Onq. Exod 16:4–5	40–41
Tg. Lev 5:26	43, 54	Tg. Onq. Exod 16:4	51, 54
Tg. Lev 8:34	39	Tg. Onq. Exod 16:15	54
Tg. Lev 20:7	36	Tg. Onq. Exod 16:25	54
Tg. Lev 22:32	53	Tg. Onq. Exod 17:7	44
Tg. Lev 24:19–20	39	Tg. Onq. Exod 20:20	45
Tg. Lev 29:23	36	Tg. Onq. Exod 32:32	44
Tg. Num 14:19	43	Tg. Onq. Exod 34:9	43, 54
Tg. Deut 6:16	54	Tg. Onq. Num 14:19	44, 51, 54
Tg. Judg 10:15	55	Tg. Onq. Deut 6:16	54
Tg. Ruth 1:1	38	Tg. Neof. Gen 22:1	44–45
Tg. 1 Sam 12:10	55	Tg. Neof. Gen 30:33	40
Tg. 1 Sam 13:14	39	Tg. Neof. Gen 47:15	54
Tg. 1 Kings 8:34	54	Tg. Neof. Gen 49:10	38, 53
Tg. 2 Kings 18:12	39	Tg. Neof. Exod 16:4–5	41
Tg. 2 Chron 6:26	36, 43, 54	Tg. Neof. Exod 16:15	54
Tg. Job 34:36	33	Tg. Neof. Exod 16:25	54
Tg. Ps 40:9	38, 53	Tg. Neof. Exod 16:4	40–41, 51, 54
Tg. Ps 66:10	44, 45, 54	Tg. Neof. Exod 16:5	41
Tg. Ps 81:8	55	Tg. Neof. Exod 5:13	41
Tg. Ps 89:27	33, 52	Tg. Neof. Exod 5:19	41
Tg. Ps 95:9	43	Tg. Neof. Lev 22:32	53
Tg. Ps 110:9	36	Tg. Neof. Lev 23:37	41
Tg. Ps 119:153	45, 55	Tg. Neof. Num 14:19	51, 54
Tg. Ps 119[118]:153	55	Tg. Neof. Num 20:13	53
Tg. Ps 135:6	38–39, 53	Tg. Neof. Deut 33:8	45
Tg. Ps 143:10	38, 53	Tg. Ps.-J. Exod 16:4–5	41
Tg. Ps 145:13	38	Tg. Ps.-J. Exod 16:13	40
Tg. Qoh 7:24	38	Tg. Ps.-J. Num 14:19	51
Tg. Song 7:19	45	Tg. Ps.-J. Jer 2:27	52
Tg. Isa 48:14	38–39, 53	Tg. Esth. II 1:2	53
Tg. Isa 53:5	54	Tg. Esth. II 3:3	34
Tg. Isa 53:5	43	Tg. Esth. II 3:8	39, 53–54
Tg. Isa 53:12	43	Tg. Esth. II 3:18	40
Tg. Isa 63:16	34	Tg. Esth. II 5:1	45
Tg. Isa 64:7	34	Cairo Tg. Exod 16:4	41

Cairo Tg. Exod 16:5	41		Cairo Tg. Exod 5:19	41
Cairo Tg. Exod 5:13	41		Cairo Tg. Lev 23:37	41

Other Rabbinic Works

Amoraic Midrashim	116		Lev. Rab. 27:1	116
Genesis (Bereschit) Rabbah	98		Mekhilta to Exod 15:2	39
Gen. Rab. 33:1	116		Midrasch Sifre Devarim 306	150
Gen. Rab. 41 to Gen 12:17	95, 98		Midrasch Tanchuma, Lekh 5	96
Gen. Rab. 45 to Gen 16:1	99		Mishna Berurah 101	27
Gen. Rab. 52 to Gen 20:17	93		Pirqe R. El. 26	98

Apostolic Fathers

Didache	38, 110, 274		10:6	87
8:1–2	201			
8:2	23		*Shepherd of Hermas*	
8:3	144		Mandate 9.1.7	207

New Testament Apocrypha and Pseudepigrapha

Gospel of Thomas	69		69	84
68:1	85		86	69, 81, 84

Classical and Ancient Christian Writings

Acts of Crispina			Aristoteles	
1.3–4	115		*Eth. nic.* 8.1–9.12	231
2.1	115		*Rhet.* 2. 4. 22–23	231
2.4	115		*Rhet.* 2.5 1383a18	208
			Rhet. 2.5 1383a29	208
Aelius Aristides	194, 198		*Rhet.* 1384a 18	229
Speeches 37.1	199			
			In Arist. Rhet.	
Appian			103.9	208
Bell. civ. 2.48	204			
			Augustine	
Apuleius			*Civ.* 4.4	117
Metam. 11.25.5	198			
			Cassius Dio	
			62.5.2	246

Cicero
De Amicitia 231
Amic. 16.57 226
Div. 2.149 252

Cleanthes
Hymn to Zeus 197

Codex Iustinianus
7.71.4 204
8.13.3 215

Curtius Rufus
Hist. Alex. Magn. 9.8.12–30 117

Didymus the Blind
Comm. Ps. 22–26:10 206

Dioscurides
Materia medica 5 209

Epictetus
Diatr. 1.16.15–21 199–200
Diatr. 2.22 231

Euripides
Alc. 658–661 235
Alc. 694 235
Alc. 727 235
Alc. 728 235
Frag. 457 229
Herc. fur. 1199–1201 229

Gellius
Noctes Atticae 1.3; 17.5 231

Harpokration of Alexandria
Cyranides 1.21 208

Herodotus
Hist. 6.59 204

Hesiod
Works and Days
324 234
326–334 234
351–362 234

Homer
Iliad
1.149 234
1.158 234
3.172 231
5.787 229
7.93 228
9.372 234
9.640 231
22.104–107 229

Odyssey
2.64–66 229
9.266–71 230
14.37–38 230
14.386–89 230
17.347 230
17.449 230, 241
17.483–87 230–31
19.332–34 230

Hymni Hom.
156 234
172–73, 381–82 234–35

Isokrates
Demon. 1.16 232
Demon. (*Or.* 1), 24–26 231

Lucian
Toxaris 231

Marcus Aurelius
8.51.2 129

Menander of Laodicea 193, 194, 199
Fragment 257 K 236

Origen
Or. 27.7 203
Or. 29.11 206

Pausanias
Descr. 1.28.5 235

Plato
Lysis 231
Phaedrus 231

Symposium	231		*Nero* 16.2	252	
Plutarchus			Tertullian		
Alc. 3,1	125		*Apol.* 30.4	195	
Amic. mult.	231		*Bapt.* 20.2	206	
Flam. 18	125		*Or.* 8.1	206	
Mor. 48E–74E	231				
Quest. Conv. 1,4	125		Theon	192–93, 194	
Ptolemaeus Ascalonius	208		Valerius Maximus		
De differentia voca-			*Facta et dicta* 4.7	231	
bulorum Σ146	209				
			Xenophon		
Quintillian	193		*Mem.* 2.3	231	
			Mem. 2.3.9	231	
Sentences of Sextus			*Mem.* 2.4–6	231	
213	129		*Mem.* 11	231	
			Mem. 12	232	
Suetonius			*Mem.* 14	232	
Jul. 42.2	204				

Papyri and Inscriptions

BGU IV 1050.17	214		BGU IV 1145.38	214
BGU IV 1051.23	214		BGU IV 1146.22	214
BGU IV 1052.19	214		BGU IV 1147.20	214
BGU IV 1054.12	214		BGU IV 1148	211–12, 217
BGU IV 1055.34–35	214		BGU IV 1150.21	214
BGU IV 1056.19–20	214		BGU IV 1156.22	214
BGU IV 1057.13, 29	214		BGU IV 1161.22	214
BGU IV 1099.19	214		BGU IV 1175.10	214
BGU IV 1101.13	214		BGU IV 2044.25	214
BGU IV 1115.33	214		C. Ord.Ptol. 53	203
BGU IV 1116.29	214		CPapGr I 10.24	214
BGU IV 1117.36	214		CPapGr I 4.42	214
BGU IV 1118.48	214		CPapGr I 5.127.38	214
BGU IV 1121.37	214		CPapGr I 6.21	214
BGU IV 1122.24–25	214		CPapGr I 9.19	214
BGU IV 1122.27	214		CPapGr I 13.25	214
BGU IV 1127.26	214		FD 2,78	193
BGU IV 1131.56	214		ID 1497	193
BGU IV 1133.17	214		IG XII(5) 812	193
BGU IV 1134.17	214		IGR 4 1587	193
BGU IV 1136.7	214		P75	249
BGU IV 1143.27	214		P. Cair.Zen. II 59179	212
BGU IV 1144.16	214		P. Col. VIII 209	216

P. Col.Zen. II 83	213	P. Oxy. XIV	
P. Enteux. 65	212	1639.18–20	214
P. Flor. I 61	213	P. Oxy. XVII 2137.35	214
P. Gr. 1179	190	P. Oxy. XLIX 3564	212
P. Hal. 1.115–117	214	P. Oxy. LV 3800.34	214
P. Hal. 1.238–241	215	P. Ross.Georg. I 11	189–90
P. Köln VII 313, 24–25	203	P. Würzb. 4	215
P. Mich. V 245, 47	215	P. Würzb. 6	211
P. Mur. 18	210	P. Yale inv. 19	203
P. Mur. 18.24, 62	214	PGM 17b	191
P. Mur. 114	210	PSI 1482	198
P. Oxy. 11 1380	191, 197	PSI 15 1482	190
P. Oxy. 11 1381	191–92	PSI I 120	187
P. Oxy. II 270.47	214	PSI I 85	187
P. Oxy. III 496.16	214	PSI V 496.21	214
P. Oxy. IV 729.21	214	SB 6, 9105	226, 236, 238
P. Oxy. VI 902	213	SB 6, 9184	236–38
P. Oxy. VIII 1127	214	SB 6, 9421	226–38
P. Oxy. X 1224, 2.1	130	SB 6, 9458	226–38
P. Oxy. XII 902	216	SB 8, 9899	203
P. Oxy. XII 1471	212–14	SB 5224.20	203

Index of Authors

Abegg, M. 78
Adair-Toteff, C. 114
Ådna, J. 149
Albrecht, F. 35
Allinson, F. G. 236
Allison, D. C. 202
Allison, D. C., Jr. 58–59, 73, 84, 111, 129–31, 203, 264, 268–71, 273, 276–77, 279
Almer, F. 9
Amundsen, L. 237
Anderson, S. D. 274
Andrejevs, O. 59, 65, 81
Arangio Ruiz, V. 214
Arnal, W. E. 6, 57, 60, 63, 84–85, 87, 185–86, 189, 262
Arx, U. von 249
Asgeirsson, J. M. 20, 59, 61, 124, 157
Assmann, A. 158
Aune, D. E. 106, 272
Ausfeld, K. 201
Austin, M. M. 117
Avemarie, F. 152
Avery-Peck, A. J. 110
Ayo, N. 119

Baasten M. F. J. 51
Bagnall, R. S. 211
Balz, H. 124, 126
Barns, J. 236
Barth, G. 267
Bauckham, R. 70, 108
Bauer, W. 62, 168, 233
Baumbach, G. 245
Bautsch, R. J. 106
Bazzana, G. B. 6, 57, 59, 103, 185, 187, 189, 200, 203–05, 226, 238
Beard, M. 115
Becker, A. H. 118
Becker, J. 62, 73, 90, 132
Beer, G. 173
Beilby, J. K. 73

Bell, S. 204
Bendemann, R. von 239
Benoit, P. 210
Berger, A. 214
Berger, K. 95, 145
Bergmann, R. 9
Berthelot, K. 26, 77
Bertram, G. 168
Betz, H. D. 89, 240, 275–77, 280
Beyer, K. 96–97, 99
Bieringer, R. 111, 152, 239
Bilde, P. 63
Billerbeck, P. 89, 92
Black, M. 46, 70, 78
Boak, A. E. R. 237
Boccaccini, G. 65–66, 74–76, 79, 82
Bock, D. L. 74
Böhlemann, P 256
Bokser, B. M. 113
Bolkestein, H. 234
Bons, E. 77, 170
Bork, A. 5, 142, 155
Bornkamm, G. 160, 254, 267, 275, 277–78
Børresen, K. E. 16
Bovon, F. 125, 128–29, 132–33, 161–62, 165–66, 168, 174, 176, 180, 224, 243, 253, 258–59
Boyarin, D. 75
Brandon, S. G. F. 118
Bremer, J. M. 194
Brock, A. G. 166
Brooke, G. J. 74
Brown, R. E. 58, 202, 205
Bruner, F. D. 118
Bultmann, R. 64, 66–67, 70–71, 89, 171
Bunge, M. J. 111
Burkett, D. 79, 104
Buschor, E. 229
Busse, U. 20, 153
Butting, K. 13

Cairns, D. L. 228–31, 234–35
Cameron, R. 67, 265
Camponovo, O. 147
Cancik, H. 48
Caquot, A. 74
Carlini, A. 190
Carlson, S. C. 104
Carmignac, J. 42, 77
Carruth, S. 274
Carter, W. 274
Casey, P. M. 70
Catchpole, D. R. 58–59, 73, 84–86
Charlesworth, J. H. 74, 149, 188, 201
Chaumont, M.-L. 246
Chazon, E. G. 25, 28, 49–50, 58, 78
Chester, A. 77
Christ, F. 160, 171, 178
Clements, R. 25
Collins, J. J. 65, 73, 76–77, 79
Colpe, C. 70, 79
Conzelmann, H. 70–71, 253
Cook, E. 78
Cordoni, C. 13
Cotter, W. 272
Criscuolo, L. 186
Criscuolo, U. 190
Cromhout, M. 57
Crossan, J. D. 111
Crossley, J. G. 188
Crump, D. M. 133, 137–38, 243

Dalby, A. 119
Dalman, G. 39, 45, 49
D'Angelo, M. R. 197
Danker 233
David, N. 28
Davies, W. D. 58, 129–31, 202–03, 264, 268–71, 273, 276–77, 279
de Boer, M. C. 76
de Certeau, M. 11
Deißmann, A. 100
de Jonge, M. 99, 132
Dekkers, E. 206
Denaux, A. 172, 178–79, 265
Dennert, B. C. 104
DeSilva, D. A. 132
De Troyer, K. 20, 28, 34, 59, 61, 124, 157
Deutsch, C. M. 272–73

de Vos, J. C. 257
Dibelius, M. 160, 170
Dietrich, J. 232
Diggle, J. 235
Dimant, D. 74
Dinkler, E. 57
Doeker, A. 58, 244
Doering, L. 35
Dormeyer, D. 162
Douglas, R. C. 62
Downie, J. 198
Draper, J. A. 104, 274
Dunn, J. D. G. 73, 76
Dupont, J. 246
Dupont-Sommer, A. 77

Ebenbauer, P. 58, 244
Ebner, M. 61, 124, 127–28, 137, 225–26
Eckey, W. 128, 132, 137–38, 260
Eckstein, F. 235
Eddy, P. R. 73
Egger-Wenzel, R. 23
Ehrlich, U. 115
Eisele, W. 129–30
Eitrem, S. 237
Elbogen, I. 121
Ernst, J. 160, 168, 172, 253
Euler, A. 128
Evans, C. A. 76–78, 113
Evans, C. F. 250

Falk, D. K. 108
Feldkämper, L. 243
Feldmeier, R. 35, 197
Fiedler, P. 90, 91, 128, 177
Fischer, I. 2, 11–13, 15, 19–20, 92
Fisher, N. R. E. 235–36
Fitzmyer, J. A. 29, 77–78, 206, 222, 249–50, 252–53
Fleddermann, H. T. 84, 160–64, 239, 264–66
Fleischer, E. 106
Flint, P. W. 76
Flusser, D. 77, 246
Förster, N. 8, 200, 243, 245, 247, 256–60
Folmer, M. L. 52
Foster, P. 12, 14, 19

Frankemölle, H. 62, 125, 169, 173–74, 176, 181
Freese, J. H. 229
Frenschkowski, M. 59, 157
Fretheim, T. E. 111
Frey, J. 11, 23, 48, 158
Fridrichsen, A. 221
Friese, H. 158
Fuchs, A. 248
Fuks, A. 214
Fuller, R. H. 70, 206
Furley, W. D. 189, 194

Gadamer, H. G. 261
Gärtner, B. 73
García Martínez, F. 77–79, 269
Garland, D. E. 251
Garsky, A. 274
Gass, E. 13
Genova, C. 121
Gerhards, A. 58, 244
Geyer, F. 246
Giebel, M. 226
Giordan, G. 114, 121
Gnilka, J. 160–62
Goergen, D. J. 70
Goff, M. 64
Goh, M. 233
Goldsmith, D. 59
Goodblatt, D. M. 106
Gordley, M. E. 194
Gorges-Braunwarth, S. 18
Graf, F. 128
Green, J. B. 255
Greeven, H. 60
Grelot, P. 29–30, 45, 48, 50, 52, 77
Groh, D. E. 70
Gronewald, M. 206
Grundmann, W. 89, 91–92
Guenther, H. O. 48
Gundry, R. H. 206, 264, 269–71, 273, 279
Gutekunst, K. 9
Gzella, H. 52

Hadas-Lebel, M. 30, 74
Häfner, G. 267
Hagner, D. A. 202, 206
Hahn, F. 160, 171, 178

Hallikainen, O. 58, 63
Hammer, R. 112
Hampe, R. 229
Hampel, V. 73
Handl-Prutsch, E. 9
Hanhart, R. 232
Hannah, D. D. 79
Hansen, I. L. 204
Hanson, J. A. 198
Harb, G. 158
Harding, M. 201
Hare, D. R. A. 72
Harl, M. 51
Hartin, P. J. 57
Hase, K. von 265
Heckel, U. 48
Heichelheim, F. 214
Heil, C. 1, 11, 15, 20–21, 23, 57, 142, 157–59, 161, 167, 171, 174, 176–77, 182, 265
Heil, M. 246
Heinemann, J. 28–29, 49, 256
Held, H. J. 267
Hengel, M. 29, 48, 78, 87, 147
Herrmann, J. 214
Herzog, W. R. 223–24, 228
Hezser, C. 4–5, 103, 109, 116
Hieke, T. 19–20
Hochholzer, M. 124, 128, 136
Hock, R. F. 192
Hölscher, T. 204
Hoffman, L. A. 105
Hoffmann, P. 1, 15, 61, 68–69, 81, 85, 103, 142, 144, 159, 161, 163, 165, 168, 171–72, 175–76, 179–80, 239, 247, 264–66
Hollander, H. W. 132
Holmås, G. O. 256
Holmén, T. 63, 73
Holtzmann, H. J. 259
Homolka, W. 150
Horsley, R. A. 104, 182
Hossfeld, F.-L. 130
Howes, L. 64, 72
Hurtado, L. W. 72, 79
Hvalvik, R. 58, 244, 256

Instone-Brewer, D. 107

Jackson-McCabe, M. 57

Jacobi, C. 126–29, 171
Jacobson, A. D. 58, 81, 85, 166, 176, 265–67
Janowski, B. 26
Jaritz, I. M. 9
Jassen, A. P. 61
Jastrow, M. 41
Jefford, C. N. 274
Jeremias, J. 35, 43, 45, 49, 58, 202, 205–06, 221–22, 225, 239, 247, 255, 274,
Jewett, R. 70
Johnson, A. F. 222
Johnson-DeBaufre, M. 188
Jones, W. H. S. 235
Joosten, J. 32, 51–52
Joseph, S. J. 3, 47, 57, 59, 75, 78, 83, 103–04, 177
Jousse, M. 30, 48
Jülicher, A. 220–21
Justnes, Å 77
Juusola, H. 61

Kaimakes, D. V. 208
Kalimi, I. 12
Karrer, M. 170, 232
Katz, S. T. 105
Kearns, R. 70
Keil, B. 199
Kelly, B. 212
Kelly, H. A. 247
Kertelge, K. 62, 125
Kiley, M. 106, 193, 201
Kim, S. 76
Kimelman, R. 106
Kirk, A. 9, 58–59, 71, 86, 240, 262–68, 270, 272–78, 280–81
Klaiber, W. 89, 92
Klampfl, T. 7–9, 219, 239–40
Klassen, W. 62, 83
Klein, A. 170
Klein, H. 125, 161, 165, 171, 225, 249, 254, 258
Klinghardt, M. 193
Kloppenborg, J. S. 1, 6–7, 48, 57–60, 62–64, 67–72, 81, 83–86, 103–04, 157, 166, 177, 182, 185–86, 192, 199, 201, 205, 207, 212, 263–67, 269–70, 272
Knibb, M. A. 72, 74–75, 79
Koester, H. 69–71

Konradt, M. 89, 91, 125, 128, 132, 137, 149–50, 268–71, 276
Konstan, D. 231
Krammer, I. 233
Kratz, R. G. 13
Kraus, H.-J. 17
Kraus, T. J. 130
Kraus, W. 158, 170, 232
Krentz, E. 193
Kreplin, M. 73
Krieger, K.-S. 157
Krüger, T. 13
Kuhn, H.-W. 62, 125, 130, 132
Kuhn, K. G. 45, 49
Kuttner, A. L. 204
Kvanvig, H. S. 65, 80

Laato, A. 76
Labahn, M. 5–6, 8, 129, 142, 157–58, 162, 164, 166, 171, 175–77
Lachs, S. T. 119
Lagrange, M.-J. 206
Lang, M. 129
Lange, A. 94–95, 154
Langer, G. 13
Lapide, P. 131
Laronde, A. 30
Laulainen, J. 61
Leclan, J. 30
Legasse, S. 168, 173
Legrand, T. 52
Lehmann-Haupt, F. 246
Lehnardt, A. 150
Leonhard, C. 256
Leonhardt, J. 108
Leuenberger, M. 16
Levine, A.-J. 111
Levine, L. I. 106
Levinson, B. M. 12
Levy, J. 41
Ley-Hutton, C. 232
Liber, M. 24
Liddell-Scott 233
Liebengood, K. D. 205
Liess, K. 26
Lindars, B. 70
Lindemann, A. 58, 60, 64, 72, 103–04, 205
Lohmeyer, E. 58, 90–91

Index of Authors

Loman, P. 193
Longenecker, B. W. 205
Longenecker, R. N. 254
Lührmann, D. 62–63, 67, 86, 160, 266
Luomanen, P. 103
Luz, U. 17, 121, 128, 135–37, 144, 160–61, 167, 169, 205–07, 257, 261–64, 267–69, 271, 273–77, 279–80

MacDonald, N. 119
Magnani, A. 191–92
Magness, J. 152–53
Mahnke, H. 246–47
Maier, C. M. 15
Maier, J. 94, 146–47, 149, 169
Majer, M. 246
Marchant, E. C. 232
Marcus, J. 279
Markschies, C. 29, 130
Marshall, I. H. 76, 250–52
Marshall, J. W. 205
Marti, K. 173
Mason, S. 107
Matthews, S. 131, 133, 137–38
Mauss, M. 110
McNamara, M. 111
Mealand, D. L. 60
Mearns, C. L. 70
Meier, J. P. 58, 271
Merklein, H. 141, 171, 180
Merz, A. 63, 86, 152
Meßner, R. 149
Meuter, N. 158
Meyer, E. 235
Meyer, M. W. 59, 61, 124, 157
Meyers, E. M. 106
Meyers, M. W. 20
Michel, A. 20
Milik, J. T. 76
Millett, P. 234
Minear, P. S. 59
Montanari, F. 233
Montefiore, C. G. 60
Morano Rodríguez, C. 16
Morgenthaler, R. 245–46
Morray-Jones, C. R. A. 64–65
Moule, C. F. D. 207
Mournet, T. C. 104

Müller, M. 72
Müller, P. 168, 173, 176
Müller, U. 79
Muraoka, T. 51
Myllykoski, M. 68

Naether, F. 192
Nauck, A. 229
Neubauer, J. 9
Neugebauer, F. 248
Newman, J. H. 25, 58, 100
Nickelsburg, G. W. E. 65, 75, 79–81
Nicklas, T. 12, 121
Niederwimmer, K. 257
Niehr, H. 19
Nijman, M. 203
Nissen, A. 63
Nixon, C. E. V. 115
Nogossek, L. 171
Nolland, J. 60, 206
Norden, E. 160–61, 273
Norlin, G. 232

Oakman, D. E. 104, 110, 118, 210
Oates, J. F. 214
Ofner, T. 9
Ogilvie, R. M. 201
Oldfather, W. A. 200
O'Neil, E. N. 192
Osten-Sacken, P. von der 110
Ostmeyer, K.-H. 4, 62, 89, 130–31, 133, 171, 174
Ott, W. 243, 258–59
Oudshoorn, J. G. 210
Owen, P. L. 72, 79

Palmieri, V. 209
Palva, H. 61
Pao, D. W. 166
Pearson, B. A. 64, 73
Penner, J. 106–07
Perrin, N. 71
Pesch, R. 68
Peterson, J. 104
Peyrer, C.-K. 9
Philonenko, M. 38, 255–56
Pickering, W. S. F. 110
Pinnik, A. 25

Piper, J. 62, 116
Piper, R. A. 57–60, 62, 68, 71, 81, 86, 175–76, 199
Plasberg, O. 191
Poirier, J. C. 104
Pokorny, P. 245
Popkes, E. E. 23
Porter, S. E. 63, 73, 76
Powell, M. A. 110
Preiswerk, R. 232
Price, S. R. F. 195
Prinzivalli, E. 16
Puech, É. 77

Race, W. H. 194
Radday, Y. T. 93
Radl, W. 125, 130, 132
Räisänen, H. 113, 270
Rahlfs, A. 232
Rakel, C. 13
Ratzinger, J. 254
Rau, E. 197
Reibnitz, B. von 231
Reichardt, M. 20, 153
Reif, S. C. 23, 106
Reinmuth, E. 158
Reiser, M. 86
Reiterer, F. V. 232–33
Rengstorf, K. H. 255
Renn, J. 158
Riaud, J. 74
Riches, J. 60
Ricoeur, P. 158
Roberts Gaventa, B. 111
Robinson, J. M. 1, 57, 59, 64, 69–71, 83–84, 103, 166, 264–67, 271, 277
Rösel, M. 34
Rollens, S. E. 185, 211
Rosenblum, J. D. 119
Roth, D. T. 162
Rowland, C. 64–65
Rubenstein, J. L. 111, 113
Rüger, H. P. 48
Rupé, H. 228

Safrai, S. 120
Safrai, Z. 119–20
Sanders, J. A. 206

Sandnes, K. O. 58, 244, 256
Sarason, R. S. 25
Saß, G. 152
Sato, M. 84, 157
Saylor Rodgers, B. 115
Schattner-Rieser, U. 2–3, 23, 25–27, 29–31, 33–36, 44, 48–49, 57, 97, 274
Schelbert, G. 35
Scherer, H. 5, 123, 129
Schiffman, L. H. 76–77, 149, 152
Schlegel, J. 158
Schlier, H. 260
Schmauch, W. 90
Schmid, K. 12–13
Schmidt, T. E. 76
Schnackenburg, R. 68
Schneemelcher, W. 67
Schneider, G. 160–61, 165, 167, 171, 178–79, 247, 249, 259
Schnelle, U. 129, 157–58
Schönberger, O. 234
Schreiber, S. 79
Schroeder, C. 233
Schröter, J. 73, 130, 171
Schubert, P. 192
Schürmann, H. 68, 85–86, 164, 176, 222, 249, 259
Schulz, S. 161–62, 166, 170–71
Schur, W. 246
Schwartz, G. 72
Schweizer, E. 91, 202–03, 249
Schwemer, A. M. 147–48, 152–54
Schwertner, S. M. 9
Schwiderski, D. 31, 34
Seek, G. A. 229
Seeley, D. 85
Seitz, O. J. F. 62
Senior, D. P. 267, 273, 276
Sevenster J. N. 29
Sharbaugh, P. 272–73
Shinan, A. 105
Sienaert, E. 30
Silva, M. 76
Smith, D. A. 1, 8–9, 23, 57, 65–66, 82, 87, 158, 261–62, 267, 272, 276, 279
Smith, M. H. 73
Snodgrass, K. 224
Snyder, G. F. 83

Söding, T. 167
Sokoloff, M. 41
Sokolon, M. K. 231
Sollama, R. 61
Sorabji, R. 207
Spicq, C. 124
Stählin, G. 231
Stanton, G. 272
Starcky, J. 77
Steck, O. H. 84
Stegemann, E. W. 110
Stegemann, H. 94
Stegemann, W. 110
Stemberger, G. 96, 98
Stern, M. 214
Stökl Ben Ezra, D. 26, 77, 79, 147
Stone, M. E. 78, 132
Stoneman, R. 115
Stowers, S. 274
Straub, J. 158
Strawn, B. A. 111
Strotmann, A. 19, 35
Stuckenbruck, L. T. 65–66, 75–76, 78
Suggs, M. J. 272
Sugranyes de Franch, R. 217
Swartley, W. M. 62
Syreeni, K. 270

Tabory, J. 120
Tätweiler, S. 23
Talmon, S. 58
Taubenschlag, R. 213–14
Tcherikover, V. 214
Telford, W. R. 60
Thaler, R. J. 9
Theisohn, J. 66, 79
Theissen, G. 63, 86, 152, 163
Theobald, M. 20, 153
Thissen, H.-J. 192
Thom, J. C. 197
Thornton, C.-J. 87
Tiwald, M. 5, 57, 59, 142, 146, 152–53, 157, 163, 178, 187
Todd, O. J. 232
Tödt, H. E. 67–68, 71, 86
Tomson, P. 274
Tov, E. 152
Treu, K. 231

Tropper, A. 118
Tuckett, C. M. 12, 57, 60, 69, 71–72, 81, 83–84, 86, 166, 181
Tukasi, E. O. 58
Tzoref, S. 28

Uhlig, S. 150
Uro, R. 68, 176, 181, 266

Vaage, L. E. 48, 64, 72, 85
Van Belle, G. 239
VanderKam, J. C. 65, 75, 78–81, 152
van de Sandt, H. 273
van der Horst, P. W. 100, 108, 116
van Eck, E. 227–28
van Henten, J. W. 91
Vanoni, G. 19
van Peursen, W. Th. 51
Van Segbroeck, F. 68
van Unnik, W. C. 62
Veijola, T. 270
Verheyden, J. 57, 239, 265, 272
Verhoogt, A. 186
Vermes, G. 70, 110
Versnel, H. S. 201
Vielhauer, P. 67–71
Vogel, M. 256
Volkmann, H. 246
Vonach, A. 149

Waddell, J. A 73
Waetjen, H. C. 225
Walcher, J. 9
Walck, L. W. 66, 75, 80–83
Wanke, J. 165, 179
Warren, D. H. 166
Webb, R. L. 263
Weber, M. 114, 122
Weder, H. 180
Wehnert, J. 110
Weiss, J. 58
Weissensteiner, L. 9
Welles, C. B. 238
Wellhausen, J. 247, 255
Wellmann, M. 209
Wenger, L. 214
Wengst, K. 152
Werman, C. 78

Westermann, C. 92
Whitlock Blundell, M. 231
Widengren, G. 246
Wiefel, W. 89, 254
Wilcken, U. 215
Wilckens, U. 69, 161, 165, 177–78
Wilk, F. 11, 104, 110, 197
Wilke, A. F. 131
Wise, M. O. 74, 78
Witherington, B. 113
Wolter, M. 125–26, 131, 133, 137, 161, 165, 169–70, 172, 177, 182, 225
Woodhead, L. 114, 121
Worp, K. A. 203
Worth, R. H., Jr. 131
Wright, N. T. 254
Wünsche, A. 93, 98

Xeravits, G. 12

Yarbro Collins, A. 73, 240, 279
Yoshiko Reed, A. 118
Youngquist, L. E. 267
Youtie, H. C. 237

Zahn, T. 249, 256
Zamfir, K. 121
Zeitlin, S. 106
Zeller, D. 57, 66, 123, 125, 128, 132, 165, 179–82, 247
Zenger, E. 130
Zgoll, A. 26
Zimmermann, C. 35
Zimmermann, R. 163, 250–51
Zucker, F. 214
Zumbo, A. 190
Zumstein, J. 166

Subject Index

Abba – *see also* God, as father 28, 33, 35–36, 49–50, 52, 279
Abraham 4, 17, 19, 26, 45, 92–101, 131, 208, 223
ἀγαπάω; *see also* love 124, 130
almsgiving 17, 173, 263, 275–76, 278
Amidah 28, 105–06, 108–09, 112, 115, 121–22
αἰδώς – *see also* shame 7, 219, 228–31, 235
ἀναίδεια – *see also* shamelessness 2, 7–8, 219–41
apocalypticism
– expectation, imminent (*Naherwartung*) 5, 31, 46, 65–71, 73, 76, 79–80, 85–87, 89, 144–45, 164, 173, 182, 206
– in the Lord's Prayer 201–03, 205
– in Q 3–5, 64, 82, 141–42, 145, 147–49, 155, 185, 198
– and testing 207, 209, 218
Apollo 193, 233–34, 260
Aramaic (language) 2–3, 23–55, 70, 73–74, 77, 94, 96, 104, 150, 171, 188, 210, 274
– retroversion into 3, 31–32, 43, 45–46, 49–52
Asclepius 191–92
associations, voluntary or private 190, 193, 215, 216
Athena 199
assumption 11, 13, 65, 66

βασιλεία – *see also* kingdom of God 5, 32, 37, 135, 141–42, 144–46, 149, 153, 164, 171, 173, 179, 183, 202–05, 245, 266, 268
beatitudes 4, 6, 62, 83–85, 136, 160–61, 164, 166, 174–75, 178–81, 184, 275, 278
Bᵉrakhot (blessing formulae) 28–29, 49, 106
bread, request for 8, 30, 32–33, 36, 39–40, 42, 50, 52–54, 110, 119–21, 135, 151, 202, 209, 223, 257–58
borrowing – *see also* lending/loan 7, 205, 210–11

bureaucracy, ancient 185

children – *see also* revelation, to children
– attitude in prayer 145–46, 151, 156, 171, 173
– Jesus' followers as 5, 175–76
– parent/child metaphor – *see also* God, as father 105, 111–13, 120–22, 145–46, 151, 155, 167–68, 171, 173, 258–59, 278
– of Wisdom 176, 183
courts 7, 209–13, 215, 217

debt – *see also* forgiveness, of debt
– default on 7, 210–11, 213–14
– instruments (contracts) 7, 118, 204, 209–13, 216
– relief, or release from 4, 7, 49, 59, 109–10, 118–19, 121, 151, 199, 202–05, 210, 218
– recovery, or repayment 7, 118, 201–18
devil – *see also* Satan 1, 8, 20, 103, 114, 116, 121, 143, 164, 206, 244–48, 251–52, 270
Dionysus 189–90, 193

Egypt/Egyptian 2, 4, 6–7, 33, 40, 43–44, 51, 53–54, 92–98, 108, 186–88, 191–93, 197, 200–01, 204, 209–10
Elijah 13, 66, 268
Elisha 91–92, 101, 131
emulation 264, 272
enemies
– blessing of 99, 127–28, 139
– hatred for 61, 89–90
– love of 4–5, 18, 61–62, 89–92, 101, 104–05, 116, 123–30, 132, 135–39, 145, 249, 275
– prayer for 1, 4–5, 61–62, 89–101, 123, 129–35, 139, 143, 145, 249
Enoch/Enochic 3, 26, 35, 57, 65–70, 73, 75–76, 78–80, 95, 205
ἐπιούσιος 41–42, 50–51, 203
exile, Babylonian 14, 24, 131
Ezra 24, 34

fasting 18, 130, 263, 275–76
forgiveness
- of debt 30, 39, 42–44, 52, 119, 135, 204–05, 209
- of guilt 43–44, 54
- of sins 30, 42–44, 51, 54, 59, 121, 135, 146, 151, 153, 275
friends, friendship 7–8, 18, 208, 219–41, 258

Galilee/Galilean 6, 48–49, 59, 89, 103, 119, 121, 153, 161, 163, 185–86, 226–27, 247, 265, 269
God – *see also* judgment, God/Jesus as judge
- as father – *see also* Abba 1, 3–5, 19, 30–31, 33–36, 50, 52–53, 59–61, 63, 86, 105, 111–14, 121–22, 145–46, 151, 153, 156, 164–75, 177–79, 183, 197–98, 253–54, 258–59, 264–65, 268–74, 277–79
- holiness of 5, 35, 37, 135, 149–53
- kingdom of – *see* kingdom of God
- name of – *see* name, divine
- as sovereign 28–29, 37–39, 59, 95, 112, 141–42, 144–47, 164, 169, 173–75, 177, 180, 204
Gentiles 29, 47, 80, 82, 103, 145, 151, 248, 250–51, 257, 278
Grace After Meals 28, 119–20
Greek (language) 3, 23, 26, 29–34, 36–37, 39, 42–48, 51, 103–04, 119, 123, 150, 161, 168, 171, 188, 191, 201, 207, 210, 217, 271
guilds 215–16

halakha/halachic 18, 28, 115, 137, 264
heaven/heavenly 16, 19, 23, 27, 29–31, 33, 35–42, 45, 49–50, 52–54, 66–67, 69, 73, 75–76, 79, 81, 83–85, 87, 111, 112–14, 143, 145–48, 150–52, 154, 162, 164–65, 167–69, 172, 175, 177, 179, 197, 206, 230, 251–53, 259, 260, 264, 268, 271, 274, 278–79
Hebrew (language) 3, 26–27, 29–51, 150
Hermes 190–91, 234
Honi the circle-drawer 4, 110–14, 121–22
honour – *see also* shame 8, 125, 223, 225–35, 238, 240–41
hospitality 7, 219–41

hymns 6–7, 27, 108, 116, 146, 151, 188–200, 234
- distinction from prayers 6, 192–200
hypocrites 257, 275, 276
θλῖψις 202, 205

identity construction 6, 8, 157–84, 243–44
International Q Project (IQP) 103, 264, 268, 271, 274–75
Isis 191, 194, 197–98
Israel/Israelites 6, 12, 16, 20, 24–25, 53–54, 82, 92, 96, 98, 111, 129, 142, 148–49, 162, 166, 171, 174–75, 177, 179–84, 223, 268
- land of 47, 92, 105, 120
- twelve tribes of 145

Jerusalem 24–25, 38, 47–48, 75, 91, 103, 109, 118, 120, 147, 149, 154, 223, 250
Jesus – *see also* judgment, God/Jesus as judge
- crucifixion/death of 78, 87, 138–39, 255, 259
- historical 31, 36, 47, 62–64, 68, 72–73, 86, 168, 187–88, 227
- instruction of 2, 4, 5, 7, 18, 31–32, 61–62, 89, 91, 104, 110, 112–14, 116, 136, 146, 249, 254, 272, 279
- and prayer – *see also* Lord's Prayer 1, 6, 8, 18–19, 23, 27–28, 31–32, 35–36, 45–47, 50, 52, 58, 103–05, 109–10, 113–14, 120, 122, 133–34, 137–38, 141–44, 157–84, 253–56, 258–59, 263, 279
- as Son 19, 77, 111, 113, 121–22, 162, 164–65, 174–75, 177–79, 182, 198, 254, 258–59
- as Son of Man/Son of Humankind 3–4, 64–76, 78–83, 85–87, 268
- temptation of 2, 8, 19–20, 114–16, 143–44, 163–65, 179, 244–48, 270
John the Baptist 64, 80, 193, 255, 263, 266–67
Jonah 13–15
Joseph 13, 40, 54, 132–33
Jubilee 145, 205
Judea/Judean 2, 7, 24, 29–30, 74, 103, 208, 210, 275
judgment
- in court 210, 212–13, 216–17

- God/Jesus as judge 3, 61, 63–65, 71–72, 75, 79–87, 95, 127, 135, 144, 175, 202, 218, 268

kingdom of God – *see also* βασιλεία 5, 30–31, 34, 37–38, 52–53, 59–60, 68, 80, 90–91, 114, 141–56, 169–74, 177–178, 180, 183, 205, 218, 226–27

law – *see also* Torah
- Ptolemaic 214, 217
- Roman 214, 217
lending/loan – *see also* borrowing 7, 205, 210–18, 223
Lord's Prayer – *see also* Jesus, and prayer 1–3, 5–8, 11, 17–18, 23–55, 58–59, 104, 109–10, 114, 118–20, 122, 135–36, 143–44, 146, 148–52, 185–218, 254–58, 263, 273–80
love – *see* enemies, love of; neighbours, love of; *see also* ἀγαπάω

magic 8, 191, 201, 252, 260
mission/missionaries 8, 82, 87, 103, 109, 118, 142, 144–45, 151, 162–63, 165, 167, 182, 249–52, 260, 263, 265–69, 272–74
Moses 40, 45, 54, 100, 107, 273

name, divine – *see also* Tetragrammaton 19, 28–29, 31, 34–35, 37, 49, 53, 135, 149–51, 153, 197, 201
neighbours
- love of 63, 89, 124, 275, 278
Noah 26, 66, 77–78, 80, 95
nonviolence – *see also* violence 61–62, 128

parables 2–3, 7, 57–87, 113, 117–18, 134, 141–42, 160, 202, 219, 221–22, 225–28, 239–41, 258, 263, 266–68, 272, 275
paraenesis 5, 123, 126–29, 134–37
patronage 216, 223, 227
Paul 47, 73–74, 99, 103, 127–29, 138–39, 247, 252, 260
πειρασμός, *see also* temptation/testing 2, 7, 33, 44, 202, 205–18, 279
persecution 5, 18, 61, 82, 84–87, 90, 92, 99, 116–17, 125, 134, 136, 143, 145, 151, 178, 202, 249, 252, 259, 268

Pharaoh 4, 93–99, 101, 131
Pharisees 47, 89, 107–08, 112, 122, 163, 176, 221, 273–74
πονηρός 33, 45, 132, 209, 218
Poseidon 193
prayer
- communal 18, 23–27, 105, 109, 255
- composition of 6, 28, 30, 32, 49, 163–69, 178, 188–93, 195, 197, 199–201, 263, 273–77
- for enemies, *see* enemies, prayer for
- formulae 2–3, 23, 25–29, 31, 35, 38, 46–47, 49–50, 105–07, 109–10, 119, 122, 196–97, 255
- as genre – *see also* hymns 6, 26, 30, 58, 191, 194–96
- individual (personal) 3–4, 16, 18, 24–29, 36, 47–50, 105–06, 109–10, 114, 202
- intercession 25, 90–91, 93, 99, 130–31, 133–34, 139, 249
- invocation 7, 28, 190, 197, 201
- languages 23, 27, 29, 31–32, 45–51, 122
- at meals – *see also* Grace After Meals 28, 119–20, 134
- petitions 3, 7, 19, 23, 27, 30–33, 36–40, 42–43, 45–46, 48, 48–51, 58–59, 121, 126, 128, 134–38, 201–05, 204, 207, 210, 218, 221–22, 224–27, 241, 249–51, 255, 257–60, 273, 274, 279
- praise 19, 26, 31, 58, 95, 99, 108, 116, 120, 134–35, 137, 148–50, 253
- supplication 18, 21, 30, 59, 94–95, 121, 134–35, 251, 257
- thanksgiving 1, 6, 26, 58–59, 121, 134, 158, 165, 167–71, 174, 177, 180, 183–84, 198, 263
- times of 105, 107–09, 122
progymnasmata 192, 200
proseuchē (place of prayer) 107–08
προσεύχομαι 58, 61, 124, 130
προσκυνέω/προσκύνησις 8, 179, 245–46
prostration 4, 114–15, 245–46, 248
purity 5, 94, 152–53, 224

Q community 4, 67, 70–71, 85, 104, 122, 142–43, 145, 157, 163, 179
Qaddish 28, 38, 47, 150–51
Qumran community 24–25, 76, 90, 147

reciprocity 18, 174, 178, 202, 223, 227–28, 241, 276
redaction
- Lukan 137, 193, 200, 239–41, 244–45, 251, 257, 259–60
- Matthean 127, 136, 138, 203, 268, 271, 273–75
- of Q 3, 6, 63, 68–70, 72, 84–86, 139, 163, 166–67, 176, 265–68
resurrection 65–66, 259, 270, 272
revelation 1, 6, 8, 87, 157–84, 191, 198, 253, 263–64, 266, 268–71, 273
- to children 6, 145–46, 154, 157–84, 164, 168, 173–75, 177, 197, 253, 264, 268–69
ritual 4, 105–06, 109, 115, 122, 152, 156, 158, 183, 190, 193, 245, 276–77

Sabbath 5, 38, 112, 119, 141–56, 263
sacrifice 5, 23–25, 27, 107–09, 115, 122, 149, 198
Sarah 4, 15, 92–99
Satan – *see also* devil 20, 80, 143–44, 153, 164, 179, 244–46, 251–52, 260, 268
scribes 19, 24, 75, 80, 103, 108–09, 112, 122, 174, 216, 272, 280
- village 6–7, 103, 185–90, 192–93, 196, 200, 226
shame – *see also* αἰδώς; honour 7, 8, 127, 222, 224–25, 227–33
shamelessness – *see also* ἀναίδεια 2, 7, 219–22, 224–27, 233–41
Shema Yisrael 20, 105–09, 115, 122
Shemoneh Esreh 28, 105
sins, forgiveness of – *see* forgiveness, of sins

Solomon 15
Son of Man/Son of Humankind – *see* Jesus, as Son of Man
Sondergut (special material)
- Lukan 137, 258
- Matthean 136, 276–77, 280
synagogues 24, 29, 47, 108, 110, 125, 135
taxes, taxation 59, 203, 216, 236

Tefillah 28, 105, 107
Temple (Jerusalem) 24–25, 27, 74, 103, 106, 109, 147, 149, 153–54
temptation/testing – *see also* πειρασμός 2, 36, 44–45, 49–52, 54, 134–35, 151, 202, 206–10, 217–18, 279
Temptation of Jesus, *see* Jesus, Temptation of
Tetragrammaton (divine name); *see also* name, divine 28–29, 34
Torah 12, 18–20, 24, 45, 64, 81, 109, 112, 118, 137, 223–24, 245, 270, 276, 279

violence – *see also* nonviolence 7, 15, 55, 61, 63, 92, 95, 97, 125, 135–37, 226, 238, 245, 249

Wisdom/Sophia, personification of 9, 64–65, 69, 75, 79–81, 83, 265, 268–70, 272–73
woes 4, 89, 100, 135, 159, 162–63, 165, 175–76, 265–68
worship 1, 23–24, 27, 33, 115, 121, 190, 246, 274

Zeus 189, 190, 193, 197, 230

Wissenschaftliche Untersuchungen zum Neuen Testament

Edited by Jörg Frey (Zürich)

Associate Editors:
Markus Bockmuehl (Oxford) · James A. Kelhoffer (Uppsala)
Tobias Nicklas (Regensburg) · Janet Spittler (Charlottesville, VA)
J. Ross Wagner (Durham, NC)

WUNT I is an international series dealing with the entire field of early Christianity and its Jewish and Graeco-Roman environment. Its historical-philological profile and interdisciplinary outlook, which its long-term editor Martin Hengel was instrumental in establishing, is maintained by an international team of editors representing a wide range of the traditions and themes of New Testament scholarship. The sole criteria for acceptance to the series are the scholarly quality and lasting merit of the work being submitted. Apart from the specialist monographs of experienced researchers, some of which may be habilitations, *WUNT I* features collections of essays by renowned scholars, source material collections and editions as well as conference proceedings in the form of a handbook on themes central to the discipline.

WUNT II complements the first series by offering a publishing platform in paperback for outstanding writing by up-and-coming young researchers. Dissertations and monographs are presented alongside innovative conference volumes on fundamental themes of New Testament research. Like Series I, it is marked by a historical-philological character and an international orientation that transcends exegetical schools and subject boundaries. The academic quality of Series II is overseen by the same team of editors.

WUNT I:
ISSN: 0512-1604
Suggested citation: WUNT I
All available volumes can be found at *www.mohrsiebeck.com/wunt1*

WUNT II:
ISSN: 0340-9570
Suggested citation: WUNT II
All available volumes can be found at *www.mohrsiebeck.com/wunt2*

Mohr Siebeck
www.mohrsiebeck.com